FUNDAMENTALS
OF ALGORITHMICS

FUNDAMENTALS OF ALGORITHMICS

Gilles Brassard and Paul Bratley

Département d'informatique et de recherche opérationelle
Université de Montréal

PRENTICE HALL
Englewood Cliffs, New Jersey 07632

Library of Congress Cataloging-in-Publication Data

BRASSARD, GILLES
    Fundamentals of Algorithmics / Gilles Brassard and Paul Bratley.
       p.   cm.
    Includes bibliographical references and index.
    ISBN 0-13-335068-1
    1. Algorithms. I. Bratley, Paul. II. Title
QA9.58.B73   1996   95-45581
511'.8--dc20   CIP

Acquisitions editor: *Alan Apt*
Production editor: *Irwin Zucker*
Copy Editor: *Brenda Melissaratos*
Buyer: *Donna Sullivan*
Cover design: *Bruce Kenselaar*
Editorial Assistant: *Shirley McGuire*
Composition: *PreTₑX, Inc.*

© 1996 by Prentice-Hall, Inc.
A Simon & Schuster Company
Englewood Cliffs, New Jersey 07632

The author and publisher of this book have used their best efforts in preparing this book. These efforts include the development, research, and testing of the theories and formulas to determine their effectiveness. The author and publisher shall not be liable in any event for incidental or consequential damages in connection with, or arising out of, the furnishing, performance, or use of these formulas.

Printed in the United States of America

10 9 8 7 6 5 4 3

ISBN   0-13-335068-1

Prentice-Hall International (UK) Limited, *London*
Prentice-Hall of Australia Pty. Limited, *Sydney*
Prentice-Hall Canada Inc., *Toronto*
Prentice-Hall Hispanoamericana, S.A., *Mexico*
Prentice-Hall of India Private Limited, *New Delhi*
Prentice-Hall of Japan, Inc., *Tokyo*
Simon & Schuster Asia Pte. Ltd., *Singapore*
Editora Prentice-Hall do Brasil, Ltda., *Rio de Janeiro*

À nos parents

Contents

PREFACE   **xv**

▶   **1   PRELIMINARIES**   **1**

1.1   Introduction   1

1.2   What is an algorithm?   1

1.3   Notation for programs   6

1.4   Mathematical notation   7
       1.4.1   Propositional calculus   7
       1.4.2   Set theory   8
       1.4.3   Integers, reals and intervals   8
       1.4.4   Functions and relations   9
       1.4.5   Quantifiers   10
       1.4.6   Sums and products   11
       1.4.7   Miscellaneous   12

1.5   Proof technique 1 — Contradiction   13

1.6   Proof technique 2 — Mathematical induction   16
       1.6.1   The principle of mathematical induction   18
       1.6.2   A horse of a different colour   23
       1.6.3   Generalized mathematical induction   24
       1.6.4   Constructive induction   27

1.7   Some reminders   31
       1.7.1   Limits   31
       1.7.2   Simple series   34
       1.7.3   Basic combinatorics   38
       1.7.4   Elementary probability   41

1.8   Problems   48
1.9   References and further reading   55

▶   2   ELEMENTARY ALGORITHMICS   57

2.1   Introduction   57
√ 2.2   Problems and instances   58
√2.3   The efficiency of algorithms   59
√2.4   Average and worst-case analyses   61
√2.5   What is an elementary operation?   64
2.6   Why look for efficiency?   66
2.7   Some examples   67
       2.7.1   Calculating determinants   68
       2.7.2   Sorting   68
       2.7.3   Multiplication of large integers   70
       2.7.4   Calculating the greatest common divisor   71
       2.7.5   Calculating the Fibonacci sequence   72
       2.7.6   Fourier transforms   73
2.8   When is an algorithm specified?   74
2.9   Problems   74
2.10   References and further reading   78

▶   3   ASYMPTOTIC NOTATION   79

3.1   Introduction   79
√ 3.2   A notation for "the order of"   79
√3.3   Other asymptotic notation   85
√3.4   Conditional asymptotic notation   88
√3.5   Asymptotic notation with several parameters   91
√3.6   Operations on asymptotic notation   91
3.7   Problems   92
3.8   References and further reading   97

▶   4   ANALYSIS OF ALGORITHMS   98

4.1   Introduction   98
√4.2   Analysing control structures   98
       4.2.1   Sequencing   98
       √4.2.2   "For" loops   99
       √ 4.2.3   Recursive calls   101
       √4.2.4   "While" and "repeat" loops   102

4.3   Using a barometer   104

4.4   Supplementary examples   106

√ 4.5   Average-case analysis   111

√ 4.6   Amortized analysis   112

√ 4.7   Solving recurrences   116
         4.7.1   Intelligent guesswork   116
         4.7.2   Homogeneous recurrences   118
         4.7.3   Inhomogeneous recurrences   123
         4.7.4   Change of variable   130
         4.7.5   Range transformations   136
         4.7.6   Asymptotic recurrences   137

4.8   Problems   139

4.9   References and further reading   146

▶   5   SOME DATA STRUCTURES   147

√ 5.1   Arrays, stacks and queues   147

√ 5.2   Records and pointers   150

√ 5.3   Lists   151

√ 5.4   Graphs   152

√ 5.5   Trees   154

√ 5.6   Associative tables   159

√ 5.7   Heaps   162

√ 5.8   Binomial heaps   170

√ 5.9   Disjoint set structures   175

5.10   Problems   181

5.11   References and further reading   186

▶   √ 6   GREEDY ALGORITHMS   187

6.1   Making change (1)   187

6.2   General characteristics of greedy algorithms   188

6.3   Graphs: Minimum spanning trees   190
         6.3.1   Kruskal's algorithm   193
         6.3.2   Prim's algorithm   196

6.4   Graphs: Shortest paths   198

6.5   The knapsack problem (1)   202

6.6   Scheduling   205
         6.6.1   Minimizing time in the system   205
         6.6.2   Scheduling with deadlines   207

6.7   Problems   214

6.8   References and further reading   217

▶   √ 7   DIVIDE-AND-CONQUER   219

7.1   Introduction: Multiplying large integers   219

7.2   The general template   223

7.3   Binary search   226

7.4   Sorting   228
        7.4.1   Sorting by merging   228
        7.4.2   Quicksort   231

7.5   Finding the median   237

7.6   Matrix multiplication   242

7.7   Exponentiation   243

7.8   Putting it all together: Introduction to cryptography   247

7.9   Problems   250

7.10   References and further reading   257

▶   √ 8   DYNAMIC PROGRAMMING   259

8.1   Two simple examples   260
        8.1.1   Calculating the binomial coefficient   260
        8.1.2   The World Series   261

8.2   Making change (2)   263

8.3   The principle of optimality   265

8.4   The knapsack problem (2)   266

8.5   Shortest paths   268

8.6   Chained matrix multiplication   271

8.7   Approaches using recursion   274

8.8   Memory functions   276

8.9   Problems   278

8.10   References and further reading   283

▶   9   EXPLORING GRAPHS   285

9.1   Graphs and games: An introduction   285

9.2   Traversing trees   291
        9.2.1   Preconditioning   292

√ 9.3   Depth-first search: Undirected graphs   294
        9.3.1   Articulation points   296

√ 9.4   Depth-first search: Directed graphs   298
        9.4.1   Acyclic graphs: Topological sorting   300

✓ 9.5   Breadth-first search   302
✓ 9.6   Backtracking   305
         9.6.1   The knapsack problem (3)   306
         9.6.2   The eight queens problem   308
         9.6.3   The general template   311
✓ 9.7   Branch-and-bound   312
         9.7.1   The assignment problem   312
         9.7.2   The knapsack problem (4)   315
         9.7.3   General considerations   316
✓ 9.8   The minimax principle   317
  9.9   Problems   319
  9.10   References and further reading   326

▶   10   PROBABILISTIC ALGORITHMS   328

  10.1   Introduction   328
  10.2   Probabilistic does not imply uncertain   329
✓ 10.3   Expected versus average time   331
✓ 10.4   Pseudorandom generation   331
  10.5   Numerical probabilistic algorithms   333
          10.5.1   Buffon's needle   333
          10.5.2   Numerical integration   336
          10.5.3   Probabilistic counting   338
  10.6   Monte Carlo algorithms   341
          10.6.1   Verifying matrix multiplication   341
          10.6.2   Primality testing   343
          10.6.3   Can a number be probably prime?   348
          10.6.4   Amplification of stochastic advantage   350
  10.7   Las Vegas algorithms   353
          10.7.1   The eight queens problem revisited   355
          10.7.2   Probabilistic selection and sorting   358
          10.7.3   Universal hashing   360
          10.7.4   Factorizing large integers   362
  10.8   Problems   366
  10.9   References and further reading   373

▶   11   PARALLEL ALGORITHMS   376

✓ 11.1   A model for parallel computation   376
  11.2   Some basic techniques   379
          11.2.1   Computing with a complete binary tree   379
          11.2.2   Pointer doubling   380
  11.3   Work and efficiency   383
  11.4   Two examples from graph theory   386
          11.4.1   Shortest paths   386
          11.4.2   Connected components   387

11.5   Parallel evaluation of expressions   392

11.6   Parallel sorting networks   397
         11.6.1   The zero-one principle   399
         11.6.2   Parallel merging networks   400
         11.6.3   Improved sorting networks   402

11.7   Parallel sorting   402
         11.7.1   Preliminaries   403
         11.7.2   The key idea   404
         11.7.3   The algorithm   405
         11.7.4   A sketch of the details   406

11.8   Some remarks on EREW and CRCW p-rams   406

11.9   Distributed computation   408

11.10   Problems   409

11.11   References and further reading   412

▶   12   COMPUTATIONAL COMPLEXITY   413

12.1   Introduction: A simple example   414

✓12.2   Information-theoretic arguments   414
         12.2.1   The complexity of sorting   418
         12.2.2   Complexity to the rescue of algorithmics   421

✓12.3   Adversary arguments   423
         12.3.1   Finding the maximum of an array   424
         12.3.2   Testing graph connectivity   425
         12.3.3   The median revisited   426

12.4   Linear reductions   427
         12.4.1   Formal definitions   430
         12.4.2   Reductions among matrix problems   433
         12.4.3   Reductions among shortest path problems   438

✓12.5   Introduction to $\mathcal{NP}$–completeness   441
         12.5.1   The classes $\mathcal{P}$ and $\mathcal{NP}$ 441
         12.5.2   Polynomial reductions   445
         12.5.3 $\mathcal{NP}$–complete problems   450
         12.5.4   A few $\mathcal{NP}$–completeness proofs   453
         12.5.5 $\mathcal{NP}$–hard problems   457
         12.5.6   Nondeterministic algorithms   458

12.6   A menagerie of complexity classes   460

12.7   Problems   464

12.8   References and further reading   471

▶   13   HEURISTIC AND APPROXIMATE ALGORITHMS   474

✓13.1   Heuristic algorithms   475
         13.1.1   Colouring a graph   475
         13.1.2   The travelling salesperson   477

√13.2   Approximate algorithms   478
        13.2.1   The metric travelling salesperson   478
        13.2.2   The knapsack problem (5)   480
        13.2.3   Bin packing   482

13.3 $\mathcal{NP}$–hard approximation problems   484
        13.3.1   Hard absolute approximation problems   486
        13.3.2   Hard relative approximation problems   487

13.4   The same, only different   489

13.5   Approximation schemes   492
        13.5.1   Bin packing revisited   493
        13.5.2   The knapsack problem (6)   493

13.6   Problems   496

13.7   References and further reading   500

REFERENCES   501

INDEX   517

Preface

> *As soon as an Analytical Engine exists, it will necessarily guide the future course of the science. Whenever any result is sought by its aid, the question will then arise—By what course of calculation can these results be arrived at by the machine in the shortest time?*
> — Charles Babbage, 1864

In August 1977, *Scientific American* challenged its readers to decipher a secret message and win one hundred dollars. This sounded safe: it was estimated at the time that the fastest existing computer using the most efficient known algorithm could not earn the award until it had run without interruption for millions of times the age of the Universe. Nevertheless, eight months of computation started sixteen years later sufficed for the task. What happened? The increase in raw computing power during those years cannot be discounted, but far more significant was the discovery of better algorithms to solve the problem—see Sections 7.8, 7.10 and 10.7.4 for details. Additional examples of how the development of efficient algorithms have extended the frontiers of feasible computation are given in Section 2.7 and throughout this book.

The importance of efficient algorithms was realized well before the era of electronic computers. The best-known ancient example of a nontrivial algorithm is Euclid's algorithm for the calculation of greatest common divisors; but mankind has also witnessed the almost universal development of pencil-and-paper algorithms for performing arithmetic operations such as multiplication. Many mathematicians —Gauss for example—have investigated efficient algorithms for a variety of tasks throughout history. Perhaps none was more prophetic than Charles Babbage, whose 19th century analytical engine would have been the first (mechanical) computer had he only succeeded in building it. His strikingly modern thought, quoted at the beginning of this preface, is nowadays more valid than ever, because the faster your computing equipment, the more you stand to gain from efficient algorithms.

Our book is not a programming manual. Still less is it a "cookbook" containing a long catalogue of programs ready to be used directly on a machine to solve certain specific problems, but giving at best a vague idea of the principles involved in their design. On the contrary, it deals with *algorithmics*: the systematic study of the design and analysis of algorithms. The aim of our book is to give readers some basic tools needed to develop their own algorithms, in whatever field of application they may be required.

We concentrate on the fundamental techniques used to design and analyse efficient algorithms. These techniques include greedy algorithms, divide-and-conquer, dynamic programming, graph techniques, probabilistic algorithms and parallel algorithms. Each technique is first presented in full generality. Thereafter it is illustrated by concrete examples of algorithms taken from such different applications as optimization, linear algebra, cryptography, computational number theory, graph theory, operations research, artificial intelligence, and so on. We pay special attention to integrating the design of algorithms with the analysis of their efficiency. Although our approach is rigorous, we do not neglect the needs of practitioners: besides illustrating the design techniques employed, most of the algorithms presented also have real-life applications.

To profit fully from this book, you should have some previous programming experience. However, we use no particular programming language, nor are the examples for any particular machine. This and the general, fundamental treatment of the material ensure that the ideas presented here will not lose their relevance. On the other hand, you should not expect to be able to use directly the algorithms we give: you will always be obliged to make the necessary effort to transcribe them into some appropriate programming language. The use of Pascal or a similarly structured language will help reduce this effort to the minimum necessary.

Our book is intended as a textbook for an undergraduate course in algorithmics. Some 500 problems are provided to help the teacher find homework assignments. The first chapter includes most of the required mathematical preliminaries. In particular, it features a detailed discussion of mathematical induction, a basic skill too often neglected in undergraduate computer science education. From time to time a passage requires more advanced mathematical knowledge, but such passages can be skipped on the first reading with no loss of continuity. Our book can also be used for independent study: anyone who needs to write better, more efficient algorithms can benefit from it.

To capture the students' attention from the outset, it is particularly effective to begin the first lecture with a discussion of several algorithms for a familiar task such as integer multiplication. James A. Foster, who used preliminary versions of this book at the University of Idaho, described his experience in the following terms: "My first lecture began with a discussion of 'how do you multiply two numbers'. This led to what constitutes the size of the input, and to an analysis of the classical algorithm. I then showed multiplication *à la russe*, with which they were soon taken. We then discussed the divide-and-conquer algorithm (Section 7.1). All of this was done informally, but at the end of the class (a single lecture, mind you) they understood the fundamentals of creating and analysing algorithms. [...] This is the approach of this text: *It works!"*

It is unrealistic to hope to cover all the material in this book in an undergraduate course with 45 hours or so of classes. In making a choice of subjects, the teacher should bear in mind that the first chapter can probably be assigned as independent reading, with Section 1.7.4 being optional. Most of Chapter 2 can be assigned as independent reading as well, although a one or two hour summary in class would be useful to cover notions such as problems versus instances and average versus worst-case analysis, and to motivate the importance of efficient algorithms. Chapter 3, on asymptotic notation, is short but crucial; its first three sections must be understood if any benefit is to be gained from this book, and the original material on conditional asymptotic notation from Section 3.4 is often called upon. We avoid "one-sided equalities" by using a more logical set notation. The first five sections of Chapter 4, which give the basic ideas behind the analysis of algorithms, are important but rather straightforward. Section 4.6 defines the notion of amortized analysis, which is more subtle but may be skimmed on first reading. Section 4.7 gives techniques for solving recurrences; though long, it is indispensable for the analysis of many algorithms. Chapter 5 ends the preliminary material; it describes basic data structures essential for the design of efficient algorithms. The first five sections cover notions such as arrays, lists and graphs: this material should be well-known already, and it can probably be assigned as independent reading. The remainder of Chapter 5 describes more sophisticated data structures such as associative tables (hashing), ordinary and binomial heaps, and disjoint set structures. Ordinary heaps (Section 5.7) and disjoint set structures (Section 5.9) are used several times in the following chapters, whereas associative tables (Section 5.6) and binomial heaps (Section 5.8) are only occasionally necessary.

The other chapters are to a great extent independent of one another. Each one (with the exception of Chapter 12) presents a basic technique for the design of efficient algorithms. An elementary course should certainly cover Chapters 6 (greedy algorithms), 7 (divide-and-conquer) and 8 (dynamic programming). It is not necessary to go over each and every example given there of how the techniques can be applied; the choice depends on the teacher's preferences and inclinations. Many students find Section 7.8 particularly appealing: it illustrates how the notions introduced so far can be used to produce secret messages. Chapter 9 describes basic techniques for searching graphs; this includes searching implicit graphs with the help of techniques such as backtracking and branch-and-bound. Sections 9.7 and 9.8 should probably be skipped in an introductory course.

The last four chapters are more advanced and it is not possible to cover them in detail in a first undergraduate algorithmics class. Nevertheless, it would be a pity not to include some material from each of them. The teacher may find it interesting to discuss these topics briefly in an undergraduate class, perhaps to lay the ground for a subsequent graduate class. Chapter 10 deals with probabilistic algorithms; Sections 10.6.2 and 10.7.1 provide the most striking examples of how useful randomness can be for computational purposes. Chapter 11 gives an introduction to the increasingly important topic of parallel algorithms. Chapter 12 introduces computational complexity. $\mathcal{NP}$–completeness, the topic of Section 12.5, must be covered in any self-respecting undergraduate computer science programme, but not necessarily in an algorithmics course; the notion of reductions is introduced independently of $\mathcal{NP}$–completeness. Finally, Chapter 13 tells you what you can do and what you should not even dream about when you are faced with an intractable problem that you must nevertheless solve.

Each chapter ends with suggestions for further reading. The references from each chapter are combined at the end of the book in an extensive bibliography including well over 300 items. Although we give the origin of a number of algorithms and ideas, our primary aim is not historical. You should therefore not be surprised if information of this kind is sometimes missing. Our goal is to suggest supplementary reading that can help you deepen your understanding of the ideas we introduce. In addition, pointers to the solution of many of the more challenging problems are given there.

Readers familiar with our 1988 graduate-level text *Algorithmics: Theory and Practice* will notice similarities between both books. In particular, our strong conviction that algorithmics should be taught according to design techniques rather than application domains pervades them both, which explains why the tables of contents are similar. Furthermore, some material was lifted almost verbatim from the former text. Nevertheless, no effort was spared to make this new book easier, both for the undergraduate student and the teacher. We benefited greatly from feedback from some of the professors who taught from our former text in well over 100 universities in the United States alone. In particular, problems are now collected at the end of each chapter, and the first chapter on mathematical preliminaries is entirely new. Chapter 4 provides more background material on the analysis of algorithms, and introduces the notion of amortized analysis. The review of simple data structures in Chapter 5 is more extensive than before. Each chapter on design techniques was revised to present easier, more relevant and more interesting algorithms. Chapter 10 on probabilistic algorithms, already one of the strong points of the previous text, was made crisper. Most importantly, an entire new chapter was added to cover the increasingly popular topic of parallel algorithms, whose omission from our earlier text was the most frequent source of criticism. Chapter 12 on computational complexity has new sections on adversary arguments and on complexity classes more exotic than $\mathcal{P}$ and $\mathcal{NP}$. Chapter 13 is new: it covers heuristic and approximate algorithms. Finally, the bibliography was updated and significantly expanded, and the problem set was completely revised.

Writing this book would have been impossible without the help of many people. Our thanks go first to the students who have followed our courses in algorithmics over more than 15 years at the Université de Montréal, the University of California in Berkeley, the École polytechnique fédérale in Lausanne, and on the occasion of several international short courses. The experience we gained from writing our previous 1988 text, as well as its 1987 predecessor *Algorithmique: conception et analyse* (in French), was invaluable in improving this book; our gratitude extends therefore to all those people acknowledged in our earlier works. Our main source of encouragement and of constructive suggestions was friends and colleagues such as Manuel Blum, who used one of our earlier texts. Equally important were the comments provided on a regular basis by reviewers sponsored by Prentice-Hall: these included Michael Atkinson, James A. Foster, Richard Newman–Wolfe, Clifford Shaffer, Doug Tygar and Steve Hoover. Our colleagues Pierre L'Écuyer, Christian Léger and Pierre McKenzie helped us straighten up some of the chapters. The material on adversary arguments in Chapter 12 was inspired by course notes written by Faith Fich.

We are also grateful to those who made it possible for us to work intensively on our book during long periods spent away from Montréal. Parts of this book were written while Paul Bratley was on sabbatical at the Universities of Strasbourg, Fribourg and Nice, and while Gilles Brassard was on sabbatical at the Ecole normale supérieure in Paris and the University of Wollongong in Australia. We particularly wish to thank Jean–François Dufourd, Jürg Kohlas, Olivier Lecarme, Jacques Stern and Jennifer Seberry for their kindness and hospitality. Earlier parts of this book were written while Gilles Brassard was enjoying the freedom offered by his E. W. R. Steacie Memorial Fellowship, for which he is grateful to the Natural Sciences and Engineering Research Council of Canada. He also thanks Lise DuPlessis who made her country house available; its sylvan serenity provided once again the setting and the inspiration for writing many a chapter.

We thank the team at Prentice-Hall for their support and enthusiasm. It was Tom McElwee, then Editor for computer science, who first suggested that we should follow up our earlier text with an easier one targeted specifically toward undergraduate students. Once launched, our project of course took longer than expected—longer, in fact, than writing the first book. It was overseen by several computer science editors; we are grateful to Bill Zobrist and Irwin Zucker for their continued support. Continuity was assured by Phyllis Morgan. The final typesetting was taken care of by Paul Mailhot, working from our original LATEX files. The head of the laboratories at the Université de Montréal's Département d'informatique et de recherche opérationnelle, Robert Gérin–Lajoie, and his team of technicians and analysts, provided unstinting support throughout the project.

Last but not least, we owe a considerable debt of gratitude to our wives, Isabelle and Pat, for their encouragement, understanding, and exemplary patience—in short, for putting up with us—while we were working together on another book. Gilles Brassard is also grateful for the patience of his wonderful daughters Alice and Léonore who were not even born on the previous occasion. Paul Bratley is just grateful that his cats are elegant, sensual, and utterly indifferent to algorithmics.

Gilles Brassard, Fairy Meadow
Paul Bratley, Pointe-Claire

Chapter 1

Preliminaries

1.1 Introduction

In this book we shall be talking about algorithms and about algorithmics. This introductory chapter begins by defining what we mean by these two words. We illustrate this informal discussion by showing several ways to do a straightforward multiplication. Even such an everyday task has hidden depths! We also take the opportunity to explain why we think that the study of algorithms is both useful and interesting.

Next we explain the notation we shall use throughout the book for describing algorithms. The rest of the chapter consists essentially of reminders of things we expect the reader to have seen already elsewhere. After a brief review of some standard mathematical notation, we recall two useful proof techniques: proof by contradiction and proof by mathematical induction. Next we list some results concerning limits, the sums of series, elementary combinatorics and probability.

A reader familiar with these topics should read Sections 1.2 and 1.3, then simply glance through the rest of the chapter, skipping material that is already known. Special attention should be paid to Section 1.6.4. Those whose basic maths and computer science are rusty should at least read through the main results we present to refresh their memories. Our presentation is succinct and informal, and is not intended to take the place of courses on elementary analysis, calculus or programming. Most of the results we give are needed later in the book; conversely, we try in later chapters not to use results that go beyond the basics catalogued in this chapter.

1.2 What is an algorithm?

An algorithm, named for the ninth-century Persian mathematician al-Khowârizmî, is simply a set of rules for carrying out some calculation, either by hand or, more usually, on a machine. In this book we are mainly concerned with algorithms for use on a computer. However, other systematic methods for calculating a result could be included. The methods we learn at school for adding, multiplying and dividing numbers are algorithms, for instance. Many an English choirboy, bored by a dull sermon, has whiled away the time by calculating the date of Easter using the algorithm explained in the Book of Common Prayer. The most famous algorithm in history dates from well before the time of the ancient Greeks: this is Euclid's algorithm for calculating the greatest common divisor of two integers.

The execution of an algorithm must not normally involve any subjective decisions, nor must it call for the use of intuition or creativity. Hence a cooking recipe can be considered to be an algorithm if it describes precisely how to make a certain dish, giving exact quantities to use and detailed instructions for how long to cook it. On the other hand, if it includes such vague notions as "add salt to taste" or "cook until tender" then we would no longer call it an algorithm.

One apparent exception to this rule is that we shall accept as algorithms some procedures that make random choices about what to do in a given situation. Chapter 10 in particular deals with these *probabilistic algorithms*. The important point here is that "random" does not mean arbitrary; on the contrary, we use values chosen in such a way that the probability of choosing each value is known and controlled. An instruction such as "choose a number between 1 and 6", with no further details given, is not acceptable in an algorithm. However it would be acceptable to say "choose a number between 1 and 6 in such a way that each value has the same probability of being chosen". In this case, when executing the algorithm by hand, we might perhaps decide to obey this instruction by throwing a fair dice; on a computer, we could implement it using a pseudorandom number generator.

When we use an algorithm to calculate the answer to a particular problem, we usually assume that the rules will, if applied correctly, indeed give us the correct answer. A set of rules that calculate that 23 times 51 is 1170 is not generally useful in practice. However in some circumstances such *approximate algorithms* can be useful. If we want to calculate the square root of 2, for instance, no algorithm can give us an exact answer in decimal notation, since the representation of $\sqrt{2}$ is infinitely long and nonrepeating. In this case, we shall be content if an algorithm can give us an answer that is as precise as we choose: 4 figures accuracy, or 10 figures, or whatever we want.

More importantly, we shall see in Chapter 12 that there are problems for which no practical algorithms are known. For such problems, using one of the available algorithms to find the exact answer will in most cases take far too long: several centuries, for instance. When this happens, we are obliged, if we must have some kind of solution to the problem, to look for a set of rules that we believe give us a good approximation to the correct answer, and that we can execute in a reasonable time. If we can prove that the answer computed by this set of rules is not too badly in error, so much the better. Sometimes even this is not possible, and we can rely only on good luck. This kind of procedure, based largely on optimism and often with minimal theoretical support, is called a *heuristic algorithm*, or simply a *heuristic*. Notice one crucial difference between approximate algorithms and heuristics: with the former we can specify the error we are willing to accept; with the latter, we cannot control the error, but we may be able to estimate how large it is.

In the first twelve chapters of this book, unless the context clearly indicates the contrary, we assume that an algorithm is a set of rules for calculating the *correct* answer to some problem. Chapter 13, on the other hand, deals entirely with approximate algorithms and heuristics.

Algorithmics can now be defined simply as the study of algorithms. When we set out to solve a problem, there may be a choice of algorithms available. In this case it is important to decide which one to use. Depending on our priorities and on the limits of the equipment available to us, we may want to choose the algorithm that takes the least time, or that uses least storage, or that is easiest to program, and so on. The answer can depend on many factors, such as the numbers involved, the way the problem is presented, or the speed and storage capacity of the available computing equipment. It may be that none of the available algorithms is entirely suitable so that we have to design a new algorithm of our own. Algorithmics is the science that lets us evaluate the effect of these various external factors on the available algorithms so that we can choose the one that best suits our particular circumstances; it is also the science that tells us how to design a new algorithm for a particular task.

Take elementary arithmetic as an example. Suppose you have to multiply two positive integers using only pencil and paper. If you were raised in North America, the chances are that you will multiply the multiplicand successively by each figure of the multiplier taken from right to left, that you will write these intermediate results one beneath the other shifting each line one place left, and that finally you will add all these rows to obtain your answer. Thus to multiply 981 by 1234 you would produce an arrangement like that of Figure 1.1(a). If, on the other hand, you went to school in England, you would be more likely to work from left to right, producing the arrangement shown in Figure 1.1(b).

$$
\begin{array}{r}
981 \\
\underline{1234} \\
3924 \\
2943 \\
1962 \\
\underline{981} \\
1210554
\end{array}
\qquad
\begin{array}{r}
981 \\
\underline{1234} \\
981 \\
1962 \\
2943 \\
\underline{3924} \\
1210554
\end{array}
$$

(a)   (b)

Figure 1.1. Multiplication (a) American (b) English

These two algorithms for multiplication are very similar: so similar, in fact, that we shall refer to them as the "classic" multiplication algorithm, without worrying precisely which one we mean. A third, different algorithm for doing the same thing is illustrated in Figure 1.2.

Write the multiplicand and the multiplier side by side. Make two columns, one under each operand, by repeating the following rule until the number in the left-hand column is 1: divide the number in the left-hand column by 2, ignoring

981	1234	1234
490	2468	
245	4936	4936
122	9872	
61	19744	19744
30	39488	
15	78976	78976
7	157952	157952
3	315904	315904
1	631808	631808
		1210554

Figure 1.2. Multiplication *à la russe*

any fractions, and double the number in the right-hand column by adding it to itself. Next cross out each row where the number in the left-hand column is even, and finally add up the numbers that remain in the right-hand column. The figure illustrates how to multiply 981 by 1234. The answer obtained is

$$1234 + 4936 + 19744 + 78976 + \cdots + 631808 = 1210554.$$

This algorithm, sometimes called multiplication *à la russe*, resembles the one used in the hardware of a binary computer. It has the advantage that there is no need to memorize any multiplication tables. All we need to know is how to add up, and how to divide a number by 2. Although it is not the algorithm usually taught in school, it certainly offers an alternative paper-and-pencil method for multiplying two positive integers.

Still another algorithm for multiplying two positive integers is illustrated in Figures 1.3 and 1.4. Again we illustrate the method by multiplying 981 by 1234. For this algorithm, however, we require that both the multiplicand and the multiplier have the same number of figures, and furthermore that this number be a power of 2, such as 1, 2, 4, 8, 16, etc. This is easily fixed by adding zeros on the left if necessary: in our example, we add just one 0 on the left of the multiplicand, making it into 0981, so that both operands have four figures.

	Multiply		Shift	Result
i)	09	12	4	108····
ii)	09	34	2	306··
iii)	81	12	2	972··
iv)	81	34	0	2754
				1210554

Figure 1.3. Multiplying 0981 by 1234 by divide-and-conquer

Now to multiply 0981 by 1234 we first multiply the left half of the multiplicand (09) by the left half of the multiplier (12), and write the result (108) shifted left as many places as there are figures in the multiplier: four, in our example. Next we multiply the left half of the multiplicand (09) by the right half of the multiplier (34), and write the result (306) shifted left by half as many places as there are figures in the multiplier: two, in this case. Thirdly we multiply the right half of the multiplicand (81) by the left half of the multiplier (12), and write the result (972) also shifted left by half as many places as there are figures in the multiplier; and fourthly we multiply the right half of the multiplicand (81) by the right half of the multiplier (34) and write the result (2754), not shifted at all. Finally we add up the four intermediate results as shown in Figure 1.3 to obtain the answer 1210554.

	Multiply		Shift	Result
i)	0	1	2	0··
ii)	0	2	1	0·
iii)	9	1	1	9·
iv)	9	2	0	18
				108

Figure 1.4. Multiplying 09 by 12 by divide-and-conquer

If you have followed the working of the algorithm so far, you will have seen that we have reduced the multiplication of two four-figure numbers to four multiplications of two-figure numbers (09×12, 09×34, 81×12 and 81×34) together with a certain number of shifts and a final addition. The trick is to observe that each of these multiplications of two-figure numbers can be carried out in exactly the same way, except that each multiplication of two-figure numbers requires four multiplications of one-figure numbers, some shifts, and an addition. For instance, Figure 1.4 shows how to multiply 09 by 12. We calculate $0 \times 1 = 0$, shifted left two places; $0 \times 2 = 0$, shifted left one place; $9 \times 1 = 9$, shifted left one place; and $9 \times 2 = 18$, not shifted. Finally we add these intermediate results to obtain the answer 108. Using these ideas the whole of our calculation can be carried out in such a way that the multiplications involve only one-figure operands. (Although we described Figure 1.3 before Figure 1.4, this was only to simplify the presentation. Of course we have to do the four multiplications of two-figure numbers first, since we use the values thus calculated when we do the multiplication of the four-figure numbers.)

This unusual algorithm is an example of the technique called "divide-and-conquer", which we shall study in Chapter 7. If you think it unlikely that it could outperform the classic algorithm, you are perfectly right. However we shall see in Chapter 7 that it is possible to reduce the multiplication of two large numbers to *three*, and not four, multiplications of numbers roughly half the size, together with a certain number of shifts and additions. (If you are stimulated by challenges, try to figure out how to do this!) With this improvement, the divide-and-conquer multiplication algorithm runs faster on a computer than any of the preceding methods, provided the numbers to be multiplied are sufficiently large. (Still faster methods are known for *very* large operands.) It is not absolutely necessary for the length of the operands to be a power of two, nor that they have the same length. Problem 1.6 shows one case where the algorithm can be useful in practice, even when the operands are relatively small, and even when we use four submultiplications instead of three.

The point of all these examples is that, even in an area as simple as elementary arithmetic, there may be several algorithms available to us for carrying out the necessary operations. One may appeal by its familiarity, a second because of the elementary nature of the intermediate calculations involved, or a third by its speed on a machine. It is by making a more formal study of the properties of the algorithms—by using algorithmics, in other words—that we can make a wise choice of the technique to use in any given situation. As we shall see, a good choice can save both money and time; in some cases, it can make all the difference between success and failure when solving a large, hard problem. The aim of our book is to teach you how to make such choices.

1.3 Notation for programs

It is important to decide how we are going to *describe* our algorithms. If we try to explain them in English, we rapidly discover that natural languages are not at all suited to this kind of thing. To avoid confusion, we shall in future specify our algorithms by giving a corresponding *program*. We assume that the reader is familiar with at least one well-structured programming language such as Pascal. However, we shall not confine ourselves strictly to any particular programming language: in this way, the essential points of an algorithm will not be obscured by relatively unimportant programming details, and it does not really matter which well-structured language the reader prefers.

A few aspects of our notation for programs deserve special attention. We use phrases in English in our programs whenever this makes for simplicity and clarity. Similarly, we use mathematical language, such as that of algebra and set theory, whenever appropriate—including symbols such as $\div$ and $\lfloor \ \rfloor$ introduced in Section 1.4.7. As a consequence, a single "instruction" in our programs may have to be translated into several instructions—perhaps a **while** loop—if the algorithm is to be implemented in a conventional programming language. Therefore, you should not expect to be able to run the algorithms we give directly: you will always be obliged to make the necessary effort to transcribe them into a "real" programming language. Nevertheless, this approach best serves our primary purpose, to present as clearly as possible the basic concepts underlying our algorithms.

To simplify our programs further, we usually omit declarations of scalar quantities (integer, real, or Boolean). In cases where it matters—as in recursive **functions** and **procedures**—all variables used are implicitly understood to be *local* variables, unless the context makes it clear otherwise. In the same spirit of simplification, proliferation of **begin** and **end** statements, that plague programs written in Pascal, is avoided: the range of statements such as **if**, **while**, or **for**, as well as that of declarations such as **procedure**, **function**, or **record**, is shown by indenting the statements affected. The statement **return** marks the dynamic end of a **procedure** or a **function**, and in the latter case it also supplies the value of the **function**.

We do not declare the type of parameters in **procedures** and **functions**, nor the type of the result returned by a **function**, unless such declarations make the algorithm easier to understand. Scalar parameters are passed by value, which means they are treated as local variables within the **procedure** or **function**, unless they are declared to be **var** parameters, in which case they can be used to return a value to the calling program. In contrast, **array** parameters are passed by reference, which means that any modifications made within the **procedure** or **function** are reflected in the array actually passed in the calling statement.

Finally, we assume that the reader is familiar with the concepts of recursion, **record**, and pointer. The last two are denoted exactly as in `Pascal`, except for the omission of **begin** and **end** in **record**s. In particular, pointers are denoted by the symbol "↑".

To wrap up this section, here is a program for multiplication *à la russe*. Here ÷ denotes integer division: any fraction in the answer is discarded. Compare this program to the informal English description of the same algorithm in Section 1.2. Which do you prefer?

> **function** *russe*(m, n)
>   *result* ← 0
>   **repeat**
>   **if** m is odd **then** *result* ← *result* + n
> $m ← m ÷ 2$
> $n ← n + n$
>   **until** $m = 1$
>   **return** *result*

1.4 Mathematical notation

This section reviews some mathematical notation that we shall use throughout the book. Our review is succinct, as we expect the reader to be familiar with most of it. Nevertheless, you are encouraged to read it at least summarily because we introduce most of the symbols that will be used, and some of them (such as $[i..j]$, $\overset{\infty}{\forall}$, $\overset{\infty}{\exists}$, lg, $\lfloor x \rfloor$, ÷, and $\mathbb{R}^{\geq 0}$) are not universally accepted.

1.4.1 Propositional calculus

There are two *truth values*, "true" and "false". A *Boolean* (or *propositional*) *variable* may only take one of these two values. If p is a Boolean variable, we write "p is *true*", or simply "p", to mean "$p = true$". This generalizes to arbitrary truth-valued expressions. Let p and q be two Boolean variables. Their *conjunction* $p \wedge q$, or "p and q", is *true* if and only if both p and q are *true*. Their *disjunction* $p \vee q$, or "p or q", is *true* if and only if at least one of p or q is *true*. (In particular the disjunction of p and q is *true* when both p and q are *true*.) The *negation* of p, denoted by $\neg p$ or "not p", is *true* if and only if p is *false*. If the truth of p implies that of q, we write "$p \Rightarrow q$", pronounced "if p then q". If the truth of p is *equivalent* to that of q, which means that they are either both *true* or both *false*, we write "$p \Longleftrightarrow q$". We can build up Boolean *formulas* from Boolean variables, constants (*true* and *false*), connectives ($\wedge, \vee, \neg, \Rightarrow, \Longleftrightarrow$) and parentheses in the obvious way.

1.4.2 Set theory

Although we review here the main symbols used in set theory, we assume that the reader is already familiar with the notion of a set. Therefore, no formal definition is provided below. For all practical purposes, it is enough to think of a set as an *unordered collection* of *distinct* elements. A set is *finite* if it contains a finite number of elements; otherwise, the set is *infinite*. If X is a finite set, $|X|$, the *cardinality* of X, denotes the number of elements in X. If X is an infinite set, we may write $|X| = \infty$. The *empty set*, denoted $\varnothing$, is the unique set whose cardinality is 0.

The simplest way to denote a set is to surround the enumeration of its elements with braces. For instance, $\{2, 3, 5, 7\}$ denotes the set of single-figure prime numbers. When no ambiguity can arise, the use of ellipses is allowed, as in "$\mathbb{N} = \{0, 1, 2, 3, \ldots\}$ is the set of natural numbers".

If X is a set, $x \in X$ means that x *belongs* to X. We write $x \notin X$ when x does *not belong* to X. The vertical bar " $|$ " is read "such that" and it is used to define a set by describing the property that its members share. For instance, $\{n \mid n \in \mathbb{N}$ and n is odd$\}$ denotes the set of all odd natural numbers. Alternative simpler notations for the same set are $\{n \in \mathbb{N} \mid n$ is odd$\}$ or even $\{2n + 1 \mid n \in \mathbb{N}\}$.

If X and Y are two sets, $X \subseteq Y$ means that each element of X also belongs to Y; it is read "X is a *subset* of Y". The notation $X \subset Y$ means that $X \subseteq Y$ and moreover that there is at least one element in Y that does not belong to X; it is read "X is a *proper* subset of Y". Be aware that some authors use "$\subset$" to mean what we denote by "$\subseteq$". The sets X and Y are *equal*, written $X = Y$, if and only if they contain precisely the same elements. This is equivalent to saying $X \subseteq Y$ and $Y \subseteq X$.

If X and Y are two sets, we denote their *union* by $X \cup Y = \{z \mid z \in X$ or $z \in Y\}$, their *intersection* by $X \cap Y = \{z \mid z \in X$ and $z \in Y\}$, and their *difference* by $X \setminus Y = \{z \mid z \in X$ but $z \notin Y\}$. Note in particular that $z \in X \cup Y$ when z belongs to both X and Y.

We denote by (x, y) the *ordered pair* that consists of the elements x and y in that order. The *Cartesian product* of X and Y is the set of ordered pairs whose first component is an element of X and whose second component is an element of Y; that is, $X \times Y = \{(x, y) \mid x \in X$ and $y \in Y\}$. Ordered n-tuples for $n > 2$ and the Cartesian product of more than two sets are defined similarly. We denote $X \times X$ by X^2 and similarly for X^i, $i \geq 3$.

1.4.3 Integers, reals and intervals

We denote the set of *integers* by $\mathbb{Z} = \{\ldots, -2, -1, 0, 1, 2, \ldots\}$, the set of *natural numbers* by $\mathbb{N} = \{0, 1, 2, \ldots\}$, and the set of *positive integers* by $\mathbb{N}^+ = \{1, 2, 3, \ldots\}$. We sometimes emphasize that 0 is not included in $\mathbb{N}^+$ by referring explicitly to the set of *strictly* positive integers. We shall sometimes refer to the natural numbers as the *nonnegative integers*.

We denote the set of *real numbers* by $\mathbb{R}$, and the set of *positive* real numbers by

$$\mathbb{R}^+ = \{x \in \mathbb{R} \mid x > 0\}.$$

We sometimes emphasize that 0 is not included in $\mathbb{R}^+$ by referring explicitly to the set of *strictly* positive real numbers. The set of *nonnegative* real numbers is denoted by $\mathbb{R}^{\geq 0} = \{x \in \mathbb{R} \mid x \geq 0\}$.

An *interval* is a set of real numbers lying between two bounds. Let a and b be two real numbers such that $a \le b$. The *open* interval (a, b) denotes

$$\{x \in \mathbb{R} \mid a < x < b\}.$$

This interval is empty if $a = b$. The *closed* interval $[a, b]$ denotes

$$\{x \in \mathbb{R} \mid a \le x \le b\}.$$

There are also *semi-open* intervals

$$(a, b] = \{x \in \mathbb{R} \mid a < x \le b\}$$

and

$$[a, b) = \{x \in \mathbb{R} \mid a \le x < b\}.$$

Moreover, $a = -\infty$ and $b = +\infty$ are allowed with their obvious meaning provided they fall on the open side of an interval.

An *integer interval* is a set of integers lying between two bounds. Let i and j be two integers such that $i \le j + 1$. The integer interval $[i..j]$ denotes

$$\{n \in \mathbb{Z} \mid i \le n \le j\}.$$

This interval is empty if $i = j + 1$. Note that $|[i..j]| = j - i + 1$.

1.4.4 Functions and relations

Let X and Y be two sets. Any subset ρ of their Cartesian product $X \times Y$ is a *relation*. When $x \in X$ and $y \in Y$, we say that x is in relation with y according to ρ, denoted $x \rho y$, if and only if $(x, y) \in \rho$. For instance, one may think of the relation "$\le$" over the integers as the set of pairs of integers such that the first component of the pair is less than or equal to the second.

Consider any relation f between X and Y. The relation is called a *function* if, for each $x \in X$, there exists one and only one $y \in Y$ such that $(x, y) \in f$. This is denoted $f : X \to Y$, which is read "f is a function from X to Y". Given $x \in X$, the unique $y \in Y$ such that $(x, y) \in f$ is denoted $f(x)$. The set X is called the *domain* of the function, Y is its *image*, and the set $f[X] = \{f(x) \mid x \in X\}$ is its *range*. In general, $f[Z]$ denotes $\{f(x) \mid x \in Z\}$ provided that $Z \subseteq X$.

A function $f : X \to Y$ is *injective* (or *one-to-one*) if there do not exist two distinct $x_1, x_2 \in X$ such that $f(x_1) = f(x_2)$. It is *surjective* (or *onto*) if for each $y \in Y$ there exists at least one $x \in X$ such that $f(x) = y$. In other words, it is surjective if its range is the same as its image. It is *bijective* if it is both injective and surjective. If f is bijective, we denote by f^{-1}, pronounced "f *inverse*" the function from Y to X defined by $f(f^{-1}(y)) = y$ for all $y \in Y$.

Given any set X, a function $P : X \to \{true, false\}$ is called a *predicate* on X. There is a natural equivalence between predicates on X and subsets of X: the subset corresponding to P is $\{x \in X \mid P(x)\}$. When P is a predicate on X, we sometimes say that P is a *property* of X. For instance, *oddness* is a property of the integers, which is *true* of the odd integers and *false* of the even integers. There is also a natural interpretation of Boolean formulas in terms of predicates. For instance, one can define a predicate $P : \{true, false\}^3 \rightarrow \{true, false\}$ by

$$P(p, q, r) = (p \wedge q) \vee (\neg q \wedge r),$$

in which case $P(true, false, true) = true$.

1.4.5 Quantifiers

The symbols $\forall$ and $\exists$ are pronounced "for all" and "there exists", respectively. To illustrate this, consider an arbitrary set X and a property P on X. We write $(\forall x \in X)\,[P(x)]$ to mean "every x in X has property P". Similarly,

$$(\exists x \in X)\,[P(x)]$$

means "there exists at least one x in X that has property P". Finally, we write $(\exists! x \in X)\,[P(x)]$ to mean "there exists exactly one x in X that has property P". If X is the empty set, $(\forall x \in X)\,[P(x)]$ is always vacuously true—try to find a counterexample if you disagree!—whereas $(\exists x \in X)\,[P(x)]$ is always trivially false. Consider the following three concrete examples.

$$(\forall n \in \mathbb{N}) \left[\sum_{i=1}^{n} i = \frac{n(n+1)}{2} \right]$$

$$(\exists! n \in \mathbb{N}^+) \left[\sum_{i=1}^{n} i = n^2 \right]$$

$$(\exists m, n \in \mathbb{N})\,[m > 1, n > 1 \text{ and } mn = 12573]$$

These examples state that the well-known formula for the sum of the first n integers is always valid (see Section 1.7.2), that this sum is also equal to n^2 for exactly one positive value of n, and that 12573 is a composite integer, respectively.

An *alternation* of quantifiers may be used in a single expression. For instance,

$$(\forall n \in \mathbb{N})\,(\exists m \in \mathbb{N})\,[m > n]$$

says that for every natural number, there exists another natural number larger still. When using alternation of quantifiers, the order in which the quantifiers are presented is important. For instance, the statement $(\exists m \in \mathbb{N})\,(\forall n \in \mathbb{N})\,[m > n]$ is obviously false: it would mean that there is an integer m that is larger than every natural number (including m itself!).

Provided the set X is infinite, it is sometimes useful to say that not only is there an $x \in X$ such that property $P(x)$ holds, but that there are infinitely many of them. The appropriate quantifier in this case is $\overset{\infty}{\exists}$. For instance, $(\overset{\infty}{\exists} n \in \mathbb{N})$ $[n \text{ is prime}]$. Note that $\overset{\infty}{\exists}$ is stronger than $\exists$ but weaker than $\forall$. Another useful quantifier, stronger than $\overset{\infty}{\exists}$ but still weaker than $\forall$, is $\overset{\infty}{\forall}$, which is used when a property holds in all cases except possibly for a finite number of exceptions. For instance, $(\overset{\infty}{\forall}\, n \in \mathbb{N})$ [if n is prime, then n is odd] means that prime numbers are always odd, except possibly for a finite number of exceptions (in this case there is exactly one exception: 2 is both prime and even).

When we are interested in properties of the natural numbers, there is an equivalent definition for these quantifiers, and it is often better to think of them accordingly. A property P of the natural numbers holds infinitely often if, no matter how large m is, there is an $n \geq m$ such that $P(n)$ holds. Similarly, property P holds on all natural numbers except possibly for a finite number of exceptions if there is an integer m such that $P(n)$ holds for all integers $n \geq m$. In the latter case, we say that "property P holds *for all sufficiently large* integers". Formally,

$$(\overset{\infty}{\exists}\, n \in \mathbb{N})\, [P(n)] \text{ is equivalent to } (\forall\, m \in \mathbb{N})\, (\exists\, n \geq m)\, [P(n)],$$

whereas

$$(\overset{\infty}{\forall}\, n \in \mathbb{N})\, [P(n)] \text{ is equivalent to } (\exists\, m \in \mathbb{N})\, (\forall\, n \geq m)\, [P(n)].$$

The *duality principle* for quantifiers says that "it is not the case that property P holds for all $x \in X$ if and only if there exists at least one $x \in X$ for which property P does not hold". In other words,

$$\neg(\forall\, x \in X)\, [P(x)] \text{ is equivalent to } (\exists\, x \in X)\, [\neg P(x)].$$

Similarly,

$$\neg(\exists\, x \in X)\, [P(x)] \text{ is equivalent to } (\forall\, x \in X)\, [\neg P(x)].$$

The duality principle also holds between $\overset{\infty}{\forall}$ and $\overset{\infty}{\exists}$.

1.4.6 Sums and products

Consider a function $f : \mathbb{N} \to \mathbb{R}$ and an integer $n \geq 0$. (This includes $f : \mathbb{N} \to \mathbb{N}$ as a special case.) The sum of the values taken by f on the first n positive integers is denoted by

$$\sum_{i=1}^{n} f(i) = f(1) + f(2) + \cdots + f(n),$$

pronounced "the sum of $f(i)$ as i goes from 1 to n".

In the case $n = 0$, the sum is defined to be 0. This is generalized in the obvious way to denote a sum as i goes from m to n whenever $m \leq n + 1$. It is sometimes useful to consider *conditional* sums. If P is a property of the integers,

$$\sum_{P(i)} f(i)$$

denotes the sum of $f(i)$ for all the integers i such that $P(i)$ holds. This sum may not be well-defined if it involves an infinite number of integers. We may also use a mixed notation, such as

$$\sum_{\substack{i=1 \\ P(i)}}^{n} f(i),$$

which denotes the sum of the values taken by f on those integers between 1 and n for which property P holds. If there are no such integers, the sum is 0. For example,

$$\sum_{\substack{i=1 \\ i \text{ odd}}}^{10} i = 1 + 3 + 5 + 7 + 9 = 25.$$

More on sums can be found in Section 1.7.2.

The product of the values taken by f on the first n positive integers is denoted by

$$\prod_{i=1}^{n} f(i) \;=\; f(1) \times f(2) \times \cdots \times f(n),$$

pronounced "the product of $f(i)$ as i goes from 1 to n". In the case $n = 0$, the product is defined to be 1. This notation is generalized in the same way as the sum notation.

1.4.7 Miscellaneous

If $b \neq 1$ and x are strictly positive real numbers, then $\log_b x$, pronounced "the *logarithm* of x in base b", is defined as the unique real number y such that $b^y = x$. For instance, $\log_{10} 1000 = 3$. Note that although b and x must be positive, there is no such restriction on y. For instance, $\log_{10} 0.001 = -3$. When the base b is not specified, we take it to be $e = 2.7182818\ldots$, the base of the so-called *natural* logarithm. (Some authors take the base to be 10 when it is not specified and denote the natural logarithm by "ln".) In algorithmics, the base most often used for logarithms is 2, which deserves a notation of its own: $\lg x$ is short for $\log_2 x$. Although we assume that the reader is familiar with logarithms, let us recall the most important logarithmic identities:

$$\log_a(xy) = \log_a x + \log_a y,$$
$$\log_a x^y = y \log_a x,$$
$$\log_a x = \frac{\log_b x}{\log_b a},$$
$$\text{and } x^{\log_b y} = y^{\log_b x}.$$

Remember too that $\log \log n$ is the logarithm of the logarithm of n, but $\log^2 n$ is the square of the logarithm of n.

If x is a real number, $\lfloor x \rfloor$ denotes the largest integer that is not larger than x, called the *floor* of x. For instance, $\lfloor 3^{1}/_{2} \rfloor = 3$. When x is positive, $\lfloor x \rfloor$ is the integer you obtain by discarding the fractional part of x if there is one. When x is negative and not itself an integer, however, $\lfloor x \rfloor$ is smaller than this by 1. For instance, $\lfloor -3^1/_2 \rfloor = -4$. Similarly, we define the *ceiling* of x, denoted by $\lceil x \rceil$, as the smallest integer that is not smaller than x. Note that $x - 1 < \lfloor x \rfloor \leq x \leq \lceil x \rceil < x + 1$ for all x.

If $m \geq 0$ and $n > 0$ are integers, m/n denotes as always the result of dividing m by n, which is not necessarily an integer. For instance, $7/2 = 3^1/_2$. We denote the *quotient* by the symbol "$\div$", so that $7 \div 2 = 3$. Formally, $m \div n = \lfloor m/n \rfloor$. We also use mod to denote the "modulo" operator defined by

$$m \bmod n = m - n \times (m \div n).$$

In other words, $m \bmod n$ is the remainder when m is divided by n.

If m is a positive integer, we denote the product of the first m positive integers by $m!$, which is read *"m factorial"*. It is natural to define $0! = 1$. Now $n! = n \times (n - 1)!$ for each positive integer n. A useful approximation to the factorial function is given by *Stirling's formula*: $n! \approx \sqrt{2\pi n}\ (n/e)^n$, where e is the base of the natural logarithm. If n and r are integers such that $0 \leq r \leq n$, we denote by $\binom{n}{r}$ the number of ways of choosing r elements from a set of cardinality n, without regard to the order in which we make our choices; see Section 1.7.3.

1.5 Proof technique 1 — Contradiction

We have seen that there may be a choice of algorithms available when we set out to solve a problem. To decide which is best suited to our specific application, it is crucial to establish mathematical properties of the different algorithms, such as their running time as a function of the size of the instance to be solved. This may involve demonstrating these properties by way of a mathematical proof. This section and the next review two proof techniques that are often useful in algorithmics: proof by contradiction and proof by mathematical induction.

Proof by contradiction, also known as *indirect proof*, consists of demonstrating the truth of a statement by proving that its negation yields a contradiction. In other words, assume you wish to prove statement S. For example, S could be "there are infinitely many prime numbers". To give an indirect proof of S, you start by assuming that S is false (or, equivalently, by assuming that "not S" is true). What can you conclude if, from that assumption, mathematical reasoning establishes the truth of an obviously false statement? Naturally, it could be that the reasoning in question was flawed. However, if the reasoning is correct, the only remaining explanation is that the original assumption was false. Indeed, only from a false hypothesis is it possible to mathematically "prove" the truth of another falsehood.

We illustrate this principle with two examples, the second being a striking illustration that indirect proof sometimes leaves a bitter aftertaste. Our first example is the one already mentioned, which was known to the ancient Greeks (Proposition 20 of Book IX of Euclid's *Elements*).

> Theorem 1.5.1 (Euclid)   *There are infinitely many prime numbers.*

Proof   Let P denote the set of all prime numbers. Assume *for a contradiction* that P is a finite set. The set P is not empty since it contains at least the integer 2. Since P is finite and nonempty, it makes sense to multiply all its elements. Let x denote that product, and let y denote $x + 1$. Consider the smallest integer d that is larger than 1 and that is a divisor of y. Such an integer certainly exists since y is larger than 1 and we do not require that d be different from y. First note that d itself is prime, for otherwise any proper divisor of d would also divide y and be smaller than d, which would contradict the definition of d. (Did you notice that the previous sentence is itself a proof by contradiction, nested in the larger scheme of things?) Therefore, according to our assumption that P contains each and every prime, d belongs to P. This shows that d is also a divisor of x since x is the product of a collection of integers including d. We have reached the conclusion that d exactly divides both x and y. But recall that $y = x + 1$. Therefore, we have obtained an integer d larger than 1 that divides two consecutive integers x and y. This is clearly impossible: if indeed d divides x, then the division of y by d will necessarily leave 1 as remainder. The inescapable conclusion is that the original assumption was equally impossible. But the original assumption was that the set P of all primes is finite, and therefore its impossibility establishes that the set P is in fact infinite. ∎

For the constructively-minded reader (which every algorithmicist should be at heart!), this proof of Euclid's can be turned into an *algorithm*—albeit not a very efficient one—capable of finding a new prime given any finite set of primes.

> **function** *Newprime*(P **:** set of integers)
>   {The argument P should be a nonempty finite set of primes}
> $x \leftarrow$ product of the elements in P
> $y \leftarrow x + 1$
> $d \leftarrow 1$
>   **repeat** $d \leftarrow d + 1$ **until** d divides y
>   **return** d

Euclid's proof establishes that the value returned by *Newprime*(P) is a prime number that does not belong to P. But who needs Euclid when writing an algorithm for this task? What about the following, much simpler algorithm?

> **function** *DumpEuclid*(P **:** set of integers)
>   {The argument P should be a nonempty finite set of primes}
> $x \leftarrow$ the largest element in P
>   **repeat** $x \leftarrow x + 1$ **until** x is prime
>   **return** x

It is obvious that this second algorithm returns as its result a prime that does not belong to P, isn't it? The answer is yes, *provided the algorithm terminates at all*. The trouble is that *DumpEuclid* would loop forever if P happened to contain the largest prime. Naturally, this situation cannot occur because there is no such thing as "the largest prime", but Euclid's proof is needed to establish this. In sum, *DumpEuclid* does work, but the proof of its termination is not immediate. In contrast, the fact that *Newprime* always terminates is obvious (in the worst case it will terminate when d reaches the value y), but the fact that it returns a new prime requires proof.

We have just seen that it is sometimes possible to turn a mathematical proof into an algorithm. Unfortunately, this is not always the case when the proof is by contradiction. We illustrate this with an elegant example.

Theorem 1.5.2   *There exist two irrational numbers x and y such that x^y is rational.*

Proof   Assume *for a contradiction* that x^y is necessarily irrational whenever both x and y are irrational. It is well known that $\sqrt{2}$ is irrational (this was known in the days of Pythagoras, who lived even earlier than Euclid). Let z stand for $\sqrt{2}^{\sqrt{2}}$. By our assumption, z is irrational since it is the result of raising an irrational ($\sqrt{2}$) to an irrational power (again $\sqrt{2}$). Now let w stand for $z^{\sqrt{2}}$. Again, we have that w is irrational by our assumption since this is so for both z and $\sqrt{2}$. But

$$w = z^{\sqrt{2}} = (\sqrt{2}^{\sqrt{2}})^{\sqrt{2}} = (\sqrt{2})^{(\sqrt{2} \times \sqrt{2})} = (\sqrt{2})^2 = 2.$$

We have arrived at the conclusion that 2 is irrational, which is clearly false. We must therefore conclude that our assumption was false: it must be possible to obtain a rational number when raising an irrational to an irrational power.   ∎

Now, how would *you* turn this proof into an algorithm? Clearly, the algorithm's purpose should be to exhibit two irrationals x and y such that x^y is rational. At first, you may be tempted to say that the algorithm should simply output $x = z$ (as defined in the proof) and $y = \sqrt{2}$ since it was proven above that z is irrational and that $z^{\sqrt{2}} = 2$. But beware! The "proof" that z is irrational depends on the false assumption that we started with, and therefore this proof is not valid. (It is only the *proof* that is not valid. It is in fact true that z is irrational, but this is difficult to establish.) We must always be careful not to use later an intermediate result "proved" in the middle of a proof by contradiction.

There is no direct way to extract the required pair (x, y) from the proof of the theorem. The best you can do is to extract *two* pairs and claim with confidence that one of them does the trick—but you will not know which. Such a proof is called *nonconstructive* and is not unusual among indirect proofs. Although some mathematicians do not accept nonconstructive proofs, most see them as perfectly valid. In any case, we shall as much as possible refrain from using them in the context of algorithmics.

1.6 Proof technique 2 — Mathematical induction

Of the basic mathematical tools useful in algorithmics, perhaps none is more important than *mathematical induction*. Not only does it allow us to prove interesting statements about the correctness and efficiency of algorithms, but we shall see in Section 1.6.4 that it can even be used to *determine* the actual statements that need to be proved.

Before the technique is discussed, a digression on the nature of scientific discovery is in order. There are two contrasting fundamental approaches in science: *induction* and *deduction*. According to the *Concise Oxford Dictionary*, induction consists of "inferring of general law from particular instances", whereas a deduction is an "inference from general to particular". We shall see that even though induction can yield false conclusions, it is not to be sneezed at. Deduction, on the other hand, is always valid provided it is applied properly.

We cannot in general trust the outcome of inductive reasoning. As long as there are cases that have not been considered, it remains possible that the general rule induced is wrong. For instance, everyday experience may have convinced you inductively that "it is always possible to cram one more person into a trolley". But a moment's thought shows that this rule is absurd. As a more mathematical example, consider the polynomial $p(n) = n^2 + n + 41$. If you compute $p(0)$, $p(1)$, $p(2), \dots, p(10)$, you find 41, 43, 47, 53, 61, 71, 83, 97, 113, 131 and 151. It is straightforward to verify that all these integers are prime numbers. Therefore, it is natural to infer *by induction* that $p(n)$ is prime for all integer values of n. But in fact $p(40) = 1681 = 41^2$ is composite. For a beautiful geometric example of induction gone wrong, we encourage you to work Problem 1.19.

A more striking example of misleading induction is given by a conjecture of Euler's, which he formulated in 1769. Is it possible for the sum of three fourth powers to be a fourth power? Formally, can you find four positive integers A, B, C and D such that

$$A^4 + B^4 + C^4 = D^4?$$

After failing to come up with even a single example of this behaviour, Euler conjectured that this equation can never be satisfied. (This conjecture is related to Fermat's Last Theorem.) More than two centuries elapsed before Elkies in 1987 discovered the first counterexample, which involved seven and eight-figure numbers. It has since been shown by Frye, using hundreds of hours of computing time on various Connection Machines, that the *only* counterexample with D less than one million is

$$95800^4 + 217519^4 + 414560^4 = 422481^4$$

(not counting the solution obtained by multiplying each of these numbers by 2). Note that 422481^4 is a 23-figure number.

Pell's equation provides an even more extreme case of compelling but incorrect inductive reasoning. Consider the polynomial $p(n) = 991n^2 + 1$. The question is whether there is a positive integer n such that $p(n)$ is a perfect square. If you try various values for n, you will find it increasingly tempting to assume inductively that the answer is negative. But in fact a perfect square can be obtained with this polynomial: the *smallest* solution is obtained when

$$n = 12\,055\,735\,790\,331\,359\,447\,442\,538\,767.$$

In contrast, deductive reasoning is not subject to errors of this kind. Provided that the rule invoked is correct and that it applies to the situation under discussion, the conclusion reached is necessarily correct. Mathematically, if it is true that some statement $P(x)$ holds for each x in some set X, and if indeed y belongs to X, then the fact that $P(y)$ holds can be roundly asserted. This is not to say that we cannot infer something false using deductive reasoning. From a false premise, we can deductively derive a false conclusion; this is the principle underlying indirect proofs. For instance, if it is correct that $P(x)$ is true for all x in X, but we are careless in applying this rule to some y that does not belong to X, we may erroneously believe that $P(y)$ holds. Similarly, if our belief that $P(x)$ is true for all x in X is based on careless inductive reasoning, then $P(y)$ may be false even if indeed y belongs to X. In conclusion, deductive reasoning can yield a wrong result, but *only* if the rules that are followed are incorrect or if they are not followed properly.

As a computer science example, consider again multiplication *à la russe*, described in Section 1.2. If you try this algorithm on several pairs of positive integers, you will find that it gives the correct answer each time. By induction, you may formulate the conjecture that the algorithm is always correct. In this case, the conjecture reached inductively happens to be right: we shall prove rigorously (by deductive reasoning) the correctness of this algorithm with Theorem 1.6.4. Once correctness has been established, if you use the algorithm to multiply 981 by 1234 and obtain 1210554, you may conclude that

$$981 \times 1234 = 1210554.$$

Here, the correctness of this specific instance of integer multiplication is a special case of the correctness of the algorithm in general. Therefore the conclusion that $981 \times 1234 = 1210554$ is based on deductive reasoning. However, the proof of correctness of the algorithm says nothing about its behaviour on negative and fractional numbers, and therefore you cannot deduce anything about the result given by the algorithm if run on -12 and 83.7.

You may well wonder at this point why anyone would use error-prone induction rather than fool-proof deduction. There are two basic reasons for using induction in the process of scientific discovery. If you are a physicist whose goal is to determine the fundamental laws that govern the Universe, you *must* use an inductive approach: the rules you infer should reflect actual data obtained from experiments. Even if you are a theoretical physicist—such as Einstein—you still need actual experiments carried out by others. For instance, it was by inductive reasoning that Halley predicted the return of his eponymous comet and that Mendeleev predicted not only the existence of yet undiscovered chemical elements, but their chemical properties as well.

But surely, only deduction is legitimate in mathematics and rigorous computer science? After all, mathematical statements such as the fact that there are infinitely many prime numbers (Theorem 1.5.1) and that multiplication *à la russe* is a correct algorithm (Theorem 1.6.4) can be proved in a rigorous deductive manner, without any need for experimental data. Inductive reasonings are to be banned from mathematics. Right? Wrong! In reality, mathematics is often very much an experimental science. It is not unusual that a mathematician will discover a mathematical truth by considering several special cases and inferring from them *by induction* a general rule that seems plausible. For instance, if I notice that

$$
\begin{array}{rcccc}
1^3 & = & 1 & = & 1^2 \\
1^3 + 2^3 & = & 9 & = & 3^2 \\
1^3 + 2^3 + 3^3 & = & 36 & = & 6^2 \\
1^3 + 2^3 + 3^3 + 4^3 & = & 100 & = & 10^2 \\
1^3 + 2^3 + 3^3 + 4^3 + 5^3 & = & 225 & = & 15^2,
\end{array}
$$

I may begin to suspect that the sum of the cubes of the first n positive integers is always a perfect square. It turns out in this case that inductive reasoning yields a correct law. If I am even more perceptive, I may realize that this sum of cubes is precisely the square of the sum of the first n positive integers; see Problem 1.21.

However, no matter how compelling the evidence becomes when more and more values of n are tried, a general rule of this sort cannot be asserted on the basis of inductive evidence only. The difference between mathematics and the inherently experimental sciences is that once a general mathematical law has been discovered by induction, we may hope to prove it rigorously by applying the deductive approach. Nevertheless, induction has its place in the mathematical process. Otherwise, how could you hope to prove rigorously a theorem whose statement has not even been formulated? To sum up, induction is necessary for formulating conjectures and deduction is equally necessary for proving them or sometimes disproving them. Neither technique can take the place of the other. Deduction alone is sufficient for "dead" or frozen mathematics, such as Euclid's *Elements* (perhaps history's highest monument to deductive mathematics, although much of its material was no doubt discovered by inductive reasoning). But induction is required to keep mathematics alive. As Pólya once said, "mathematics presented with rigor is a systematic deductive science but mathematics in the making is an experimental inductive science".

Finally, the punch line of this digression: one of the most useful *deductive* techniques available in mathematics has the misfortune to be called *mathematical induction*. This terminology is confusing, but we must live with it.

1.6.1 The principle of mathematical induction

Consider the following algorithm.

```
function sq(n)
    if n = 0 then return 0
    else return 2n + sq(n − 1)−1
```

If you try it on a few small inputs, you find that

$$sq(0) = 0, \quad sq(1) = 1, \quad sq(2) = 4, \quad sq(3) = 9, \quad sq(4) = 16.$$

By induction, it seems obvious that $sq(n) = n^2$ for all $n \geq 0$, but how could this be proved rigorously? Is it even true? Let us say that the algorithm *succeeds* on integer n whenever $sq(n) = n^2$, and that it *fails* otherwise.

Consider any integer $n \geq 1$ and assume for the moment that the algorithm succeeds on $n - 1$. By definition of the algorithm, $sq(n) = 2n + sq(n-1) - 1$. By our assumption $sq(n-1) = (n-1)^2$. Therefore

$$sq(n) = 2n + (n-1)^2 - 1 = 2n + (n^2 - 2n + 1) - 1 = n^2.$$

What have we achieved? We have proved that the algorithm must succeed on n whenever it succeeds on $n - 1$, provided $n \geq 1$. In addition, it clearly succeeds on $n = 0$.

The *principle of mathematical induction*, described below, allows us to infer from the above that the algorithm succeeds on all $n \geq 0$. There are two ways of understanding why this conclusion follows: constructively and by contradiction. Consider any positive integer m on which you wish to prove that the algorithm succeeds. For the sake of argument, assume that $m \geq 9$ (smaller values can be proved easily). We know already that the algorithm succeeds on 4. From the general rule that it must succeed on n whenever it succeeds on $n - 1$ for $n \geq 1$, we infer that it also succeeds on 5. Applying this rule again shows that the algorithm succeeds on 6 as well. Since it succeeds on 6, it must also succeed on 7, and so on. This reasoning continues as many times as necessary to arrive at the conclusion that the algorithm succeeds on $m - 1$. Finally, since it succeeds on $m - 1$, it must succeed on m as well. It is clear that we could carry out this reasoning explicitly—with no need for "and so on"—for any fixed positive value of m.

If we prefer a single proof that works for all $n \geq 0$ and that does not contain and-so-on's, we must accept the *axiom of the least integer*, which says that every nonempty set of positive integers contains a smallest element; see Problem 1.24. The axiom allows us to use this smallest number as a foundation from which to prove theorems.

Now, to prove the correctness of the algorithm, assume *for a contradiction* that there exists at least one positive integer on which the algorithm fails. Let n stand for the smallest such integer, which exists by the axiom of the least integer. Firstly, n must be greater than or equal to 5 since we have already verified that $sq(i) = i^2$ when $i = 1, 2, 3$ or 4. Secondly, the algorithm must succeed on $n - 1$ for otherwise n would not be the smallest positive integer on which it fails. But this implies by our general rule that the algorithm also succeeds on n, which contradicts our assumption about the choice of n. Therefore such an n cannot exist, which means that the algorithm succeeds on every positive integer. Since we also know that the algorithm succeeds on 0, we conclude that $sq(n) = n^2$ for all integers $n \geq 0$.

We now spell out a simple version of the principle of mathematical induction, which is sufficient in many cases. A more powerful version of the principle is given in Section 1.6.3. Consider any property P of the integers. For instance, $P(n)$ could be "$sq(n) = n^2$", or "the sum of the cubes of the first n integers is equal to the square of the sum of those integers", or "$n^3 < 2^n$". The first two properties hold for every $n \geq 0$, whereas the third holds provided $n \geq 10$. Consider also an integer a, known as the *basis*. If

1. $P(a)$ holds and
2. $P(n)$ must hold whenever $P(n-1)$ holds, for each integer $n > a$,

then property $P(n)$ holds for all integers $n \geq a$. Using this principle, we could assert that $sq(n) = n^2$ for all $n \geq 0$, immediately after showing that $sq(0) = 0 = 0^2$ and that $sq(n) = n^2$ whenever $sq(n-1) = (n-1)^2$ and $n \geq 1$.

Our first example of mathematical induction showed how it can be used to prove rigorously the correctness of an algorithm. As a second example, let us see how proofs by mathematical induction can sometimes be *turned into* algorithms. This example is also instructive as it makes explicit the proper way to write a proof by mathematical induction. The discussion that follows stresses the important points common to all such proofs.

Consider the following tiling problem. You are given a board divided into equal squares. There are m squares in each row and m squares in each column, where m is a power of 2. One arbitrary square of the board is distinguished as *special*; see Figure 1.5(a).

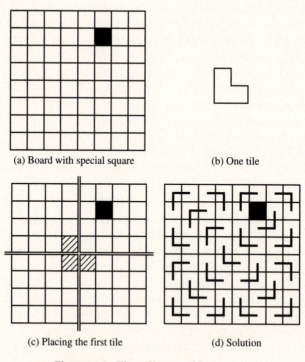

(a) Board with special square   (b) One tile

(c) Placing the first tile   (d) Solution

Figure 1.5. The tiling problem

You are also given a supply of tiles, each of which looks like a 2×2 board with one square removed, as illustrated in Figure 1.5(b). Your puzzle is to cover the board with these tiles so that each square is covered exactly once, with the exception of the special square, which is not covered at all. Such a covering is called a *tiling*. Figure 1.5(d) gives a solution to the instance given in Figure 1.5(a).

Theorem 1.6.1   *The tiling problem can always be solved.*

Proof
The proof is by mathematical induction on the integer n such that $m = 2^n$.

◊ *Basis*: The case $n = 0$ is trivially satisfied. Here $m = 1$, and the 1×1 "board" is a single square, which is necessarily special. Such a board is tiled by doing nothing! (If you do not like this argument, check the next simplest case: if $n = 1$, then $m = 2$ and any 2×2 board from which you remove one square looks exactly like a tile by definition.)

◊ *Induction step*: Consider any $n \geq 1$. Let $m = 2^n$. Assume the *induction hypothesis* that the theorem is true for $2^{n-1} \times 2^{n-1}$ boards. Consider an $m \times m$ board, containing one arbitrarily placed special square. Divide the board into 4 equal sub-boards by halving it horizontally and vertically. The original special square now belongs to exactly one of the sub-boards. Place one tile in the middle of the original board so as to cover exactly one square of each of the other three sub-boards; see Figure 1.5(c). Call each of the three squares thus covered "special" for the corresponding sub-board. We are left with four $2^{n-1} \times 2^{n-1}$ sub-boards, each containing one special square. By our induction hypothesis, each of these sub-boards can be tiled. The final solution is obtained by combining the tilings of the sub-boards together with the tile placed in the middle of the original board.

Since the theorem is true when $m = 2^0$, and since its truth for $m = 2^n$ follows from its assumed truth for $m = 2^{n-1}$ for all $n \geq 1$, it follows from the principle of mathematical induction that the theorem is true for all m provided m is a power of 2. ∎

The reader should have no difficulty in transforming this proof of a mathematical theorem into an algorithm for performing the actual tiling (perhaps not a computer algorithm, but at least an algorithm suitable for "hand processing"). This tiling algorithm follows the general template known as divide-and-conquer, which we encountered in Section 1.2, and which we study at length in Chapter 7. This situation is not unusual when a theorem is proved constructively by mathematical induction.

Let us now look in detail at all the aspects of a well-formed proof by mathematical induction, such as the one above. Consider again an abstract property P of the integers, an integer a, and assume you wish to prove that $P(n)$ holds for all $n \geq a$. You must begin your proof with the *basis step*, which consists of proving that $P(a)$ holds. This basis step is usually easy, sometimes even trivial, but it is crucial that it be carried out properly; otherwise, the whole "proof" is literally without foundation.

The basis step is followed by the *induction step*, which is usually more substantial. This should start with "consider any $n > a$" (or equivalently "consider any $n \geq a + 1$"). It should continue with an explicit statement of the *induction hypothesis*, which essentially states that we assume $P(n-1)$ to hold. At that point, it remains to prove that we can infer that $P(n)$ holds assuming the induction hypothesis. Finally, an additional sentence such as the one at the end of the proof of Theorem 1.6.1 can be inserted to conclude the reasoning, but this is generally unnecessary.

Concerning the induction hypothesis, it is important to understand that we assume that $P(n-1)$ holds on a *provisional* basis; we do not really know that it holds until the theorem has been proved. In other words, the point of the induction step is to prove that the truth of $P(n)$ would follow logically from that of $P(n-1)$, regardless of whether or not $P(n-1)$ actually holds. If in fact $P(n-1)$ does *not* hold, the induction step does not allow us to conclude anything about the truth of $P(n)$.

For instance, consider the statement "$n^3 < 2^n$", which we shall denote $P(n)$. For positive integer n, it is easy to show that $n^3 < 2 \times (n-1)^3$ if and only if $n \geq 5$. Consider any $n \geq 5$ and provisionally assume that $P(n-1)$ holds. Now

$$
\begin{aligned}
n^3 \quad &< \quad 2 \times (n-1)^3 \quad &&\text{because } n \geq 5 \\
&< \quad 2 \times 2^{n-1} \quad &&\text{by the assumption that } P(n-1) \text{ holds} \\
&= \quad 2^n.
\end{aligned}
$$

Thus we see that $P(n)$ follows logically from $P(n-1)$ whenever $n \geq 5$. Nevertheless $P(4)$ does *not* hold (it would say $4^3 < 2^4$, which is $64 < 16$) and therefore nothing can be inferred concerning the truth of $P(5)$. By trial and error, we find however that $P(10)$ does hold ($10^3 = 1000 < 2^{10} = 1024$). Therefore, it *is* legitimate to infer that $P(11)$ holds as well, and from the truth of $P(11)$ it follows that $P(12)$ holds also, and so on. By the principle of mathematical induction, since $P(10)$ holds and since $P(n)$ follows from $P(n-1)$ whenever $n \geq 5$, we conclude that $n^3 < 2^n$ is true for all $n \geq 10$. It is instructive to note that $P(n)$ holds also for $n = 0$ and $n = 1$, but that we cannot use these points as the basis of the mathematical induction because the induction step does not apply for such small values of n.

It may happen that the property to be proved is not concerned with the set of all integers not smaller than a given basis. Our tiling puzzle, for instance, concerns only the set of integers that are powers of 2. Sometimes, the property does not concern integers at all. For instance, it is not unusual in algorithmics to wish to prove a property of graphs. (It could even be said that our tiling problem is not *really* concerned with integers, but rather with boards and tiles, but that would be hairsplitting.) In such cases, if simple mathematical induction is to be used, the property to be proved should first be transformed into a property of the set of all integers not smaller than some basis point. (An alternative approach is given in Section 1.6.3.) In our tiling example, we proved that $P(m)$ holds for all powers of 2 by proving that $Q(n)$ holds for all $n \geq 0$, where $Q(n)$ is equivalent to $P(2^n)$. When this transformation is necessary, it is customary to begin the proof (as we did) with the words "The proof is by mathematical induction *on such-and-such a parameter*". Thus we find proofs on the number of nodes in a graph, on the length of a character string, on the depth of a tree, and so on.

There is one aspect of proofs by mathematical induction that most beginners find puzzling, if not downright paradoxical: *it is sometimes easier to prove a stronger statement than a weaker one!* We illustrate this with an example that we have already encountered. We saw that it is easy to conjecture by induction (not *mathematical* induction) that the sum of the cubes of the first n integers is always a perfect square. Proving this by mathematical induction is not easy. The difficulty is that an induction hypothesis like "the sum of the cubes of the first $n - 1$ integers is a square" is not much help in proving that this is also the case for the first n integers because it does not say *which* square: in general, there is no reason to believe that a square is obtained when n^3 is added to another square. In contrast, it is easier to prove the stronger theorem that our sum of cubes is precisely the square of the sum of the first n integers: the induction hypothesis is now much more meaningful; see Problem 1.21.

1.6.2 A horse of a different colour

The most common pitfall in the design of proofs by mathematical induction deserves a subsection of its own. Consider the following absurd "theorem".

Theorem 1.6.2   *All horses are the same colour.*

Proof   We shall prove that any set of horses contains only horses of a single colour. In particular, this will be true of the set of all horses. Let $\mathcal{H}$ be an arbitrary set of horses. Let us prove by mathematical induction on the number n of horses in $\mathcal{H}$ that they are all the same colour.

⋄ *Basis*: The case $n = 0$ is trivially true: if there are no horses in $\mathcal{H}$, then surely they are all the same colour! (If you do not like this argument, check the next simplest case: if $n = 1$, then there is only one horse in $\mathcal{H}$, and again it is vacuously clear that "they" are "all" the same colour.)

⋄ *Induction step*: Consider any number n of horses in $\mathcal{H}$. Call these horses $h_1, h_2, \ldots, h_n$. Assume the induction hypothesis that any set of $n - 1$ horses contains only horses of a single colour (but of course the horses in one set could a priori be a different colour from the horses in another). Let $\mathcal{H}_1$ be the set obtained by removing horse h_1 from $\mathcal{H}$, and let $\mathcal{H}_2$ be defined similarly; see Figure 1.6.

$$\mathcal{H}_1: \qquad h_2 \quad h_3 \quad h_4 \quad h_5$$
$$\mathcal{H}_2: \quad h_1 \qquad\quad h_3 \quad h_4 \quad h_5$$

Figure 1.6. Horses of the same colour ($n = 5$)

There are $n - 1$ horses in each of these two new sets. Therefore, the induction hypothesis applies to them. In particular, all the horses in $\mathcal{H}_1$ are of a single colour, say c_1, and all the horses in $\mathcal{H}_2$ are also of a single (possibly different) colour, say c_2. But is it really possible for colour c_1 to be different from colour c_2? Surely not, since horse h_n belongs to both sets and therefore both c_1 and c_2 must be the colour of that horse! Since all the horses in $\mathcal{H}$ belong to either $\mathcal{H}_1$ or $\mathcal{H}_2$ (or both), we conclude that they are all the same colour $c = c_1 = c_2$. This completes the induction step and the proof by mathematical induction. ∎

Before you continue, figure out the fallacy in the above "proof". If you think the problem is that our induction hypothesis ("any set of $n-1$ horses must contain only horses of a single colour") was absurd, think again!

Solution: The problem is that "h_n belongs to both sets" is *not* true for $n = 2$ since h_2 does *not* belong to $\mathcal{H}_2$! Our reasoning was impeccable for the basis cases $n = 0$ and $n = 1$. Moreover, it is true that our theorem follows for sets of n horses assuming that it is true for $n - 1$, *but only when* $n \geq 3$. We can go from 2 to 3, from 3 to 4, and so on, but *not* from 1 to 2. Since the basis cases contain only 0 and 1, and since we are not allowed to go from 1 to 2, the induction step cannot get started. This small missing link in the proof is enough to invalidate it completely. We encountered a similar situation when we proved that $n^3 < 2^n$: the induction step did not apply for $n < 5$, and thus the fact that the statement is true for $n = 0$ and $n = 1$ was irrelevant. The important difference was that $n^3 < 2^n$ is true for $n = 10$, and therefore also for all larger values of n.

1.6.3 Generalized mathematical induction

The principle of mathematical induction described so far is appropriate for proving many interesting statements. There are cases, however, when a slightly more powerful principle is preferable. This is known as *generalized* mathematical induction. The situation is illustrated by the following example.

Suppose you wish to prove that every composite integer can be expressed as a product of prime numbers. (The *fundamental theorem of arithmetic* tells us that this decomposition is unique; this is *not* what we are trying to prove here.) Let us not worry about the basis of the mathematical induction yet, but rather let us jump right into the induction step. When trying to prove that n can be expressed as a product of prime numbers (assuming that it is composite), the "natural" induction hypothesis would be that $n - 1$ can be so decomposed. However, we challenge the reader to find anything in the prime decomposition of $n - 1$ that can be useful or even relevant to the prime decomposition of n. What we really need is the stronger induction hypothesis that *every* composite integer smaller than n can be decomposed into a product of prime numbers. The correct proof of our theorem is given below as Theorem 1.6.3, after we state formally the generalized principle of mathematical induction.

Another useful generalization concerns the basis. It is sometimes necessary to prove an *extended* basis, that is to prove the basis on more than one point. Note that we proved extended bases for the correctness of the *sq* algorithm and for the tiling problem, but it was a luxury: the induction step could really have been applied to prove the case $n = 1$ from the basis $n = 0$. Such is not always the case: sometimes we must prove independently the validity of several basis points before the induction step can take off. We shall encounter examples of this behaviour later in this book; see Problems 1.27 and 1.28 for instance.

We are now ready to formulate a more general principle of mathematical induction. Consider any property P of the integers, and two integers a and b such that $a \le b$. If

1. $P(n)$ holds for all $a \le n < b$ and

2. for any integer $n \ge b$, the fact that $P(n)$ holds follows from the assumption that $P(m)$ holds for all m such that $a \le m < n$,

then property $P(n)$ holds for all integers $n \ge a$.

Yet a further generalization of the principle of mathematical induction is convenient when we are not interested in proving a statement about *every* integer not smaller than the basis. It is often the case that we wish to prove that some property P holds, but only for those integers for which some other property Q holds as well. We have seen two examples of this situation already: the tiling problem applies only when m is a power of 2, and our statement about prime decomposition applies only to composite numbers (although we could extend it in a natural way to prime numbers). When this occurs, it suffices to mention Q explicitly in the statement of the theorem to be proved, to prove the (possibly extended) basis only for points on which Q applies, and to prove the induction step also only on those points. Of course, the induction hypothesis will be similarly weakened. Consider any n beyond the basis such that $Q(n)$ holds. To prove that $P(n)$ holds, you are only entitled to assume that $P(m)$ holds when $a \le m < n$ and when $Q(m)$ holds as well. In our tiling example, we are allowed to use the induction hypothesis to tile 4×4 boards when proving that an 8×8 board can be tiled, but we are *not* allowed to assume that a 5×5 board can be tiled.

Before we illustrate this principle, note that it allows the basis to be empty. This happens when $a = b$ because in that case there are no integers n such that $a \le n < b$. It can also happen when $a < b$ if $Q(n)$ never holds when $a \le n < b$. This does not invalidate the proof because in such a case the validity of $P(n)$ for the smallest n on which the induction step applies is proved under an empty induction hypothesis, which is to say that it is proved without any assumptions at all. Our first example illustrates this. The second shows how to prove the correctness of an algorithm by generalized mathematical induction.

Theorem 1.6.3   *Every positive composite integer can be expressed as a product of prime numbers.*

Proof   The proof is by generalized mathematical induction. In this case, there is no need for a basis.

⋄ *Induction step*: Consider any composite integer $n \ge 4$. (Note that 4 is the smallest positive composite integer, hence it would make no sense to consider smaller values of n.) Assume the induction hypothesis that any positive composite integer smaller than n can be expressed as a product of prime numbers. (In the smallest case $n = 4$, this induction hypothesis is vacuous.) Consider the smallest integer d that is larger than 1 and that is a divisor of n. As argued in the proof of Theorem 1.5.1, d is necessarily prime. Let $m = n/d$. Note that $1 < m < n$ because n is composite and $d > 1$. There are two cases.

- If m is prime, we have decomposed n as the product of two primes: $n = d \times m$.
- If m is composite, it is positive and smaller than n, and therefore the induction hypothesis applies: m can be expressed as a product of prime numbers, say $m = p_1 p_2 \cdots p_k$. Therefore $n = d \times m$ can be expressed as $n = d p_1 p_2 \cdots p_k$, also a product of prime numbers.

In either case, this completes the proof of the induction step and thus of the theorem.   ■

Until now, the induction hypothesis was always concerned with a finite set of instances (exactly one for simple mathematical induction, usually many but sometimes none for generalized mathematical induction). In our final example of proof by generalized mathematical induction, the induction hypothesis covers an infinity of cases even when proving the induction step on a finite instance! This time, we shall prove that multiplication *à la russe* correctly multiplies any pair of positive integers. The key observation is that the tableau produced when multiplying 490 by 2468 is almost identical to Figure 1.2, which was used to multiply 981 by 1234. The only differences are that the first line is missing when multiplying 490 by 2468 and that consequently the term 1234 found in that first line is not added into the final result; see Figure 1.7. What is the relationship between instances (981 1234) and (490 2468)? Of course, it is that $490 = 981 \div 2$ and $2468 = 2 \times 1234$.

981	1234	1234			
490	2468		490	2468	
245	4936	4936	245	4936	4936
122	9872		122	9872	
61	19744	19744	61	19744	19744
30	39488		30	39488	
15	78976	78976	15	78976	78976
7	157952	157952	7	157952	157952
3	315904	315904	3	315904	315904
1	631808	631808	1	631808	631808
		1210554			1209320

Figure 1.7. Proving multiplication *à la russe*

Theorem 1.6.4   *Multiplication à la russe correctly multiplies any pair of positive integers.*

Proof   Suppose we wish to multiply m by n. The proof is by mathematical induction on the value of m.

◇ *Basis*: The case $m = 1$ is easy: we have only one row consisting of 1 in the left-hand column and n in the right-hand column. That row is not crossed out since 1 is not even. When we "add up" the only number that "remains" in the right-hand column, we obviously get n, which is the correct result of multiplying 1 by n.

◇ *Induction step*: Consider any $m \geq 2$ and any positive integer n. Assume the induction hypothesis that multiplication *à la russe* correctly multiplies s by t for any positive integer s smaller than m and for any positive integer t. (Note that we do *not* require t to be smaller than n.) There are two cases to consider.

– If m is even, the second row in the tableau obtained when multiplying m by n contains $m/2$ in the left-hand column and $2n$ in the right-hand column. This is identical to the first row obtained when multiplying $m/2$ by $2n$. Because any noninitial row in these tableaux depends only on the previous row, the tableau obtained when multiplying m by n is therefore identical to the tableau obtained when multiplying $m/2$ by $2n$, except for its additional first row, which contains m in the left-hand column and n in the right-hand column. Since m is even, this additional row will be crossed out before the final addition. Therefore, the final result obtained when multiplying m by n *à la russe* is the same as when multiplying $m/2$ by $2n$. But $m/2$ is positive and smaller than m. Thus, the induction hypothesis applies: the result obtained when multiplying $m/2$ by $2n$ *à la russe* is $(m/2) \times (2n)$ as it should be. Therefore, the result obtained when multiplying m by n *à la russe* is also equal to $(m/2) \times (2n) = mn$ as it should be.

– The case when m is odd is similar, except that $m/2$ must be replaced throughout by $(m - 1)/2$ and the first row when multiplying m by n is not crossed out. Therefore the final result of multiplying m by n *à la russe* is equal to n plus the result of multiplying $(m - 1)/2$ by $2n$ *à la russe*. By the induction hypothesis, the latter is correctly computed as $((m - 1)/2) \times 2n$, and thus the former is computed as $n + ((m - 1)/2) \times 2n$, which is mn as it should be.

This completes the proof of the induction step and thus of the theorem.   ■

1.6.4 Constructive induction

Mathematical induction is used primarily as a proof technique. Too often, it is employed to prove assertions that seem to have been produced from nowhere like a rabbit out of a hat. While the truth of these assertions is thus established, their origin remains mysterious. However, mathematical induction is a tool sufficiently powerful to allow us to discover not merely the truth of a theorem, but also its precise statement. By applying the technique of *constructive* induction described in this section, we can simultaneously prove the truth of a partially specified assertion and discover the missing specifications thanks to which the assertion is correct. We illustrate this technique with two examples featuring the *Fibonacci sequence*, defined below. The second example shows how the technique can be useful in the analysis of algorithms.

The sequence named for Fibonacci, an Italian mathematician of the twelfth century, is traditionally introduced in terms of rabbits (although this time not out of a hat). This is how Fibonacci himself introduced it in his *Liberabaci*, published in 1202. Suppose that every month a breeding pair of rabbits produce a pair of offspring. The offspring will in their turn start breeding two months later, and so on. Thus if you buy a pair of baby rabbits in month 1, you will still have just one pair in month 2. In month 3 they will start breeding, so you now have two pairs; in month 4 they will produce a second pair of offspring, so you now have three pairs; in month 5 both they and their first pair of offspring will produce baby rabbits, so you now have five pairs; and so on. If no rabbits ever die, the number of pairs you have each month will be given by the terms of the Fibonacci sequence, defined more formally by the following recurrence:

$$\begin{cases} f_0 = 0; f_1 = 1 & \text{and} \\ f_n = f_{n-1} + f_{n-2} & \text{for } n \geq 2. \end{cases}$$

The sequence begins $0, 1, 1, 2, 3, 5, 8, 13, 21, 34 \ldots$ It has numerous applications in computer science, in mathematics, and in the theory of games. De Moivre obtained the following formula, which is easy to prove by mathematical induction (see Problem 1.27):

$$f_n = \frac{1}{\sqrt{5}}[\phi^n - (-\phi)^{-n}],$$

where $\phi = (1 + \sqrt{5})/2$ is the *golden ratio*. Since $0 < \phi^{-1} < 1$, the term $(-\phi)^{-n}$ can be neglected when n is large. Hence the value of f_n is roughly $\phi^n/\sqrt{5}$, which is exponential in n.

But where does de Moivre's formula come from? In Section 4.7 we shall see a general technique for solving Fibonacci-like recurrences. In the meantime, assume you do not know any such techniques, nor do you know de Moivre's formula, yet you would like to have an idea of the behaviour of the Fibonacci sequence. If you compute the sequence for a while, you soon discover that it grows quite rapidly (f_{100} is a 21-figure number). Thus, the conjecture "the Fibonacci sequence grows exponentially fast" is reasonable. How would you prove it? The difficulty is that this conjecture is too vague to be proved directly by mathematical induction: remember that it is often easier to prove a stronger theorem than a weaker one. Let us therefore guess that there exists a real number $x > 1$ such that $f_n \geq x^n$ for each sufficiently large integer n. (This statement could not possibly be true for *every* positive integer n since it obviously fails on $n \leq 2$.) In symbols,

Conjecture: $(\exists x > 1) (\overset{\infty}{\forall} n \in \mathbb{N}) [f_n \geq x^n].$

There are two unknowns in the theorem we wish to prove: the value of x and the precise meaning of "for each sufficiently large". Let us not worry about the latter for the time being. Let $P_x(n)$ stand for "$f_n \geq x^n$". Consider any sufficiently large integer n. The approach by constructive induction consists of asking ourselves for which values of x $P_x(n)$ follows from the *partially specified induction hypothesis* that

$P_x(m)$ holds for each integer m that is less than n but that is still sufficiently large. Using the definition of the Fibonacci sequence and this hypothesis, and provided $n-1$ and $n-2$ are also "sufficiently large",

$$f_n = f_{n-1} + f_{n-2} \geq x^{n-1} + x^{n-2} = (x^{-1} + x^{-2})x^n.$$

To conclude that $f_n \geq x^n$, we need $x^{-1} + x^{-2} \geq 1$, or equivalently $x^2 - x - 1 \leq 0$. By elementary algebra, since we are only interested in the case $x > 1$, solving this quadratic equation implies that $1 < x \leq \phi = (1 + \sqrt{5})/2$.

We have established that $P_x(n)$ follows from $P_x(n-1)$ and $P_x(n-2)$ provided $1 < x \leq \phi$. This corresponds to proving the induction step in a proof by mathematical induction. To apply the principle of mathematical induction and conclude that the Fibonacci sequence grows exponentially fast, we must also take care of the basis. In this case, because the truth of $P_x(n)$ depends only on that of $P_x(n-1)$ and $P_x(n-2)$, it is sufficient to verify that property P_x holds on two consecutive positive integers to assert that it holds from that point on.

It turns out that there are no integers n such that $f_n \geq \phi^n$. However, finding two consecutive integers on which property P holds is easy for any x strictly smaller than ϕ. For instance, both $P_x(11)$ and $P_x(12)$ hold when $x = 3/2$. Therefore, $f_n \geq (\frac{3}{2})^n$ for all $n \geq 11$. This completes the proof that the Fibonacci sequence grows *at least* exponentially. The same process can be used to prove that it grows *no faster* than exponentially: $f_n \leq y^n$ for every positive integer n provided $y \geq \phi$. Here again, the condition on y is not God-given: it is obtained by constructive induction when trying to find constraints on y that make the induction step go through. Putting those observations together, we conclude that f_n grows exponentially; more precisely, it grows like a power of a number close to ϕ. The remarkable thing is that we can reach this conclusion with no need for an explicit formula such as de Moivre's.

Our second example of constructive induction concerns the analysis of the obvious algorithm for computing the Fibonacci sequence.

> **function** *Fibonacci*(n)
>   **if** $n < 2$ **then return** n
>   **else return** *Fibonacci*($n-1$)+*Fibonacci*($n-2$) $(\star)$

Let $g(n)$ stand for the number of times instruction $(\star)$ is performed when *Fibonacci*(n) is called (counting the instructions performed in recursive calls). This function is interesting because $g(n)$ gives a bound on the time required by a call on *Fibonacci*(n).

Clearly, $g(0) = g(1) = 0$. When $n \geq 2$, instruction $(\star)$ is executed once at the top level, and $g(n-1)$ and $g(n-2)$ times by the first and second recursive calls, respectively. Therefore,

$$\begin{cases} g(0) = g(1) = 0 & \text{and} \\ g(n) = g(n-1) + g(n-2) + 1 & \text{for } n \geq 2. \end{cases}$$

This formula is similar to the recurrence that defines the Fibonacci sequence itself. It is therefore reasonable to conjecture the existence of positive real constants

a and b such that $a f_n \le g(n) \le b f_n$ for each sufficiently large integer n. Using constructive induction, it is straightforward to find that $a f_n \le g(n)$ holds for each sufficiently large n provided it holds on two consecutive integers, regardless of the value of a. For instance, taking $a = 1$, $f_n \le g(n)$ holds for all $n \ge 2$.

However when we try to prove the other part of our conjecture, namely that there exists a b such that $g(n) \le b f_n$ for each sufficiently large n, we run into trouble. To see what happens, let $P_b(n)$ stand for "$g(n) \le b f_n$", and consider any sufficiently large integer n (to be made precise later). We wish to determine conditions on the value of b that make $P_b(n)$ follow from the hypothesis that $P_b(m)$ holds for each sufficiently large $m < n$. Using the definition of the Fibonacci sequence and this partially specified induction hypothesis, and provided $n - 1$ and $n - 2$ are also sufficiently large,

$$g(n) = g(n-1) + g(n-2) + 1 \le b f_{n-1} + b f_{n-2} + 1 = b f_n + 1,$$

where the last equality comes from $f_n = f_{n-1} + f_{n-2}$. Thus, we infer that $g(n) \le b f_n + 1$, but not that $g(n) \le b f_n$. Regardless of the value of b, we cannot make the induction step work!

Does this mean the original conjecture was false, or merely that constructive induction is powerless to prove it? The answer is: neither. The trick is to use constructive induction to prove there exist positive real constants b and c such that $g(n) \le b f_n - c$ for each sufficiently large n. This may seem odd, since $g(n) \le b f_n - c$ is a stronger statement than $g(n) \le b f_n$, which we were unable to prove. We may hope for success, however, on the ground that if the statement to be proved is stronger, then so too is the induction hypothesis it allows us to use; see the end of Section 1.6.1.

Consider any sufficiently large integer n. We must determine for which values of b and c the truth of $g(n) \le b f_n - c$ follows from the partially specified induction hypothesis that $g(m) \le b f_m - c$ for each sufficiently large $m < n$. Using the definition of the Fibonacci sequence and this hypothesis, and provided $n - 1$ and $n - 2$ are also sufficiently large,

$$g(n) = g(n-1) + g(n-2) + 1$$
$$\le b f_{n-1} - c + b f_{n-2} - c + 1 = b f_n - 2c + 1.$$

To conclude that $g(n) \le b f_n - c$, it suffices that $-2c + 1 \le -c$, or equivalently that $c \ge 1$. We have thus established that the truth of our conjecture on any given integer n follows from its assumed truth on the two previous integers provided $c \ge 1$, regardless of the value of b. Before we can claim the desired theorem, we still need to determine values of b and c that make it work on two consecutive integers. For instance, $b = 2$ and $c = 1$ make it work on $n = 1$ and $n = 2$, and therefore $g(n) \le 2 f_n - 1$ for all $n \ge 1$.

The key idea of strengthening the incompletely specified statement to be proved when constructive induction fails may again appear to be produced like a rabbit out of a hat. Nevertheless, this idea comes very naturally with experience. To gain such experience, work Problems 1.31 and 1.33. Unlike the Fibonacci examples, which could have been handled easily by the techniques of Section 4.7, the cases tackled in these problems are best handled by constructive induction.

1.7 Some reminders

In this section we remind the reader of some elementary results concerning limits, the sums of some simple series, combinatorics, and probability. Later chapters will use the propositions presented here. Our presentation is succinct, and most proofs are omitted, since we expect most readers to have covered all this material already.

1.7.1 Limits

Let $f(n)$ be any function of n. We say that $f(n)$ tends to a limit a as n tends to infinity if $f(n)$ is nearly equal to a when n is large. The following formal definition makes this notion more precise.

> **Definition 1.7.1**   *The function $f(n)$ is said to tend to the limit a as n tends to infinity if for any positive real number δ, no matter how small, $f(n)$ differs from a by less than δ for all sufficiently large values of n.*

In other words, however small the positive number δ, we can find a threshold $n_0(\delta)$ corresponding to δ, such that $f(n)$ differs from a by less than δ for all values of n greater than or equal to $n_0(\delta)$. When $f(n)$ tends to a limit a as n tends to infinity, we write

$$\lim_{n \to \infty} f(n) = a$$

Many functions, of course, do not tend to a limit as n tends to infinity. The function n^2, for example, can be made as large as we please by choosing a sufficiently large value of n. Such a function is said to tend to infinity as n tends to infinity. Here is the formal definition.

> **Definition 1.7.2**   *The function $f(n)$ is said to tend to $+\infty$ if for any number Δ, no matter how large, $f(n)$ is greater than Δ for all sufficiently large values of n.*

Once again this means that we can find a threshold $n_0(\Delta)$ corresponding to Δ, such that $f(n)$ is greater than Δ for all values of n greater than or equal to $n_0(\Delta)$. We write

$$\lim_{n \to \infty} f(n) = +\infty.$$

A similar definition takes care of functions such as $-n^2$ that take increasingly large negative values as n tends to infinity. Such functions are said to tend to minus infinity.

Finally, when $f(n)$ does not tend to a limit, nor to $+\infty$ nor to $-\infty$, we say that $f(n)$ *oscillates* as n tends to infinity. If it is possible to find a positive constant K such that $-K < f(n) < K$ for all values of n, then we say that $f(n)$ oscillates *finitely*; otherwise $f(n)$ oscillates *infinitely*. For example, the function $(-1)^n$ oscillates finitely; the function $(-1)^n n$ oscillates infinitely.

The following propositions state some general properties of limits.

Proposition 1.7.3 *If two functions $f(n)$ and $g(n)$ tend to limits a and b respectively as n tends to infinity, then $f(n)+g(n)$ tends to the limit $a + b$.*

Proposition 1.7.4 *If two functions $f(n)$ and $g(n)$ tend to limits a and b respectively as n tends to infinity, then $f(n)g(n)$ tends to the limit ab.*

Both these propositions may be extended to the sum or product of any finite number of functions of n. An important particular case of Proposition 1.7.4 is when $g(n)$ is constant. The proposition then states that if the limit of $f(n)$ is a, then the limit of $cf(n)$ is ca, where c is any constant. It is perfectly possible for either $f(n)+g(n)$ or $f(n)g(n)$ to tend to a limit even though neither $f(n)$ nor $g(n)$ does so; see Problem 1.34. Finally the following proposition deals with division.

Proposition 1.7.5 *If two functions $f(n)$ and $g(n)$ tend to limits a and b respectively as n tends to infinity, and b is not zero, then $f(n)/g(n)$ tends to the limit a/b.*

These propositions, although simple, are surprisingly powerful. For instance, suppose we want to know the behaviour as n tends to infinity of the most general rational function of n, namely

$$S(n)= \frac{a_0 n^p + a_1 n^{p-1} + \cdots + a_p}{b_0 n^q + b_1 n^{q-1} + \cdots + b_q},$$

where neither a_0 nor b_0 is zero. Writing $S(n)$ in the form

$$S(n)= n^{p-q}\left\{\left(a_0 + \frac{a_1}{n} + \cdots + \frac{a_p}{n^p}\right)\middle/\left(b_0 + \frac{b_1}{n} + \cdots + \frac{b_q}{n^q}\right)\right\},$$

and applying the above propositions, it is easy to see that the function in braces tends to the limit a_0/b_0 as n tends to infinity. Furthermore n^{p-q} tends to the limit 0 if $p < q$; $n^{p-q} = 1$ and therefore n^{p-q} tends to the limit 1 if $p = q$; and n^{p-q} tends to infinity if $p > q$. Hence

$$\lim_{n\to\infty} S(n)= 0 \text{ when } p < q,$$

$$\lim_{n\to\infty} S(n)= a_0/b_0 \text{ when } p = q,$$

and $S(n)$ tends to plus or minus infinity when $p > q$, depending on the sign of a_0/b_0.

Proposition 1.7.6 *If $\lim_{n\to\infty}(f(n + 1)/f(n))= a$, $-1 < a < 1$, then $\lim_{n\to\infty} f(n)= 0$. If $f(n)$ is positive and $\lim_{n\to\infty}(f(n + 1)/f(n))= a > 1$, then $f(n)$ tends to infinity.*

This proposition can be used to determine the behaviour as n tends to infinity of $f(n) = n^r x^n$, where r is any positive integer. If $x = 0$ then $f(n) = 0$ for all values of n. Otherwise

$$\frac{f(n+1)}{f(n)} = \left(\frac{n+1}{n}\right)^r x$$

which tends to x as n tends to infinity. (Use the propositions above.) Hence if $-1 < x < 1$ then $f(n)$ tends to 0, and if $x > 1$ then $f(n)$ tends to infinity. If $x = 1$ then $f(n) = n^r$, which clearly tends to infinity. Finally it is easy to see that if $x \le -1$ then $f(n)$ oscillates infinitely. Problem 1.35 shows that the behaviour of $n^{-r} x^n$ is the same, except that $f(n)$ tends to 0 when $x = 1$ or $x = -1$.

De l'Hôpital's rule can sometimes be used when it is impossible to apply Proposition 1.7.5. One simple form of this rule is the following.

Proposition 1.7.7 (De l'Hôpital)   *Suppose that*

$$\lim_{n \to \infty} f(n) = \lim_{n \to \infty} g(n) = 0,$$

or alternatively that both these limits are infinite. Suppose further that the domains of f and g can be extended to some real interval $[n_0, +\infty)$ in such a way that (a) the corresponding new functions $\hat{f}$ and $\hat{g}$ are differentiable on this interval, and also that (b) $\hat{g}'(x)$, the derivative of $\hat{g}(x)$, is never zero for $x \in [n_0, +\infty)$, then

$$\lim_{n \to \infty} f(n)/g(n) = \lim_{x \to \infty} \hat{f}'(x)/\hat{g}'(x).$$

For a simple example, suppose $f(n) = \log n$ and $g(n) = n^a$, where $a > 0$ is an arbitrary positive constant. Now both $f(n)$ and $g(n)$ tend to infinity as n tends to infinity, so we cannot use Proposition 1.7.5. However if we extend $f(n)$ to $\hat{f}(x) = \log x$ and $g(n)$ to $\hat{g}(x) = x^a$, de l'Hôpital's rule allows us to conclude that

$$\lim_{n \to \infty} \log n / n^a = \lim_{x \to \infty} (1/x)/(ax^{a-1}) = \lim_{x \to \infty} 1/(ax^a) = 0$$

whatever the positive value of a.

Finally, the following proposition is sometimes useful even though it is very easy to prove.

Proposition 1.7.8   *If two functions $f(n)$ and $g(n)$ tend to limits a and b respectively as n tends to infinity, and if $f(n) \le g(n)$ for all sufficiently large n, then $a \le b$.*

1.7.2 Simple series

Suppose that $u(n)$ is any function of n defined for all values of n. If we add the values of $u(i)$ for $i = 1, 2, \ldots, n$, we obtain another function of n, namely

$$s(n) = u(1) + u(2) + \cdots + u(n).$$

It is often convenient to change the notation slightly, and to write this equation in the form

$$s_n = u_1 + u_2 + \cdots + u_n,$$

or simply

$$s_n = \sum_{i=1}^{n} u_i,$$

which we read as "the sum of u_i as i goes from 1 to n". Now if s_n tends to a limit s when n tends to infinity, we have

$$s = \lim_{n \to \infty} \sum_{i=1}^{n} u_i,$$

which is usually written either as

$$s = \sum_{i=1}^{\infty} u_i$$

or as

$$s = u_1 + u_2 + \cdots$$

where the dots show that the series is continued indefinitely. In this case we say that the series is *convergent*, and we call s the *sum* of the series.

If on the other hand s_n does not tend to a limit, but s_n tends to $+\infty$ or to $-\infty$, then we say that the series *diverges*, to $+\infty$ or $-\infty$ as the case may be. Finally if s_n does not tend to a limit, nor to $+\infty$ or $-\infty$, then we say that the series oscillates (finitely or infinitely, as the case may be). It is evident that a series with no negative terms must either converge, or else diverge to $+\infty$: it cannot oscillate.

Two particularly simple kinds of series are *arithmetic series* and *geometric series*. In an arithmetic series the difference between successive terms is constant, so we may represent the first n terms of the series as

$$a, a + d, a + 2d, \ldots, a + (n-1)d,$$

where a, the first term, and d, the difference between successive terms, are suitable constants. In a geometric series, the ratio of successive terms is constant, so that here the first n terms of the series may be represented as

$$a, ar, ar^2, \ldots, ar^{n-1}.$$

The following propositions give the sums of these series.

Proposition 1.7.9 (Arithmetic series)   *Let s_n be the sum of the first n terms of the arithmetic series $a, a + d, a + 2d, \ldots$ Then $s_n = an + n(n-1)d/2$.*

The series diverges unless $a = d = 0$, in which case $s_n = 0$ for all n. The proposition is easily proved. First write the sum as

$$s_n = a + (a + d) + \cdots + (a + (n-2)d) + (a + (n-1)d),$$

and then write it again as

$$s_n = (a + (n-1)d) + (a + (n-2)d) + \cdots + (a + d) + a.$$

Adding corresponding terms from these two equations, we get

$$2s_n = (2a + (n-1)d) + (2a + (n-1)d) + \cdots + (2a + (n-1)d) + (2a + (n-1)d),$$

where there are n equal terms on the right. The result follows immediately.

Proposition 1.7.10 (Geometric series)   *Let s_n be the sum of the first n terms of the geometric series $a, ar, ar^2, \ldots$ Then $s_n = a(1 - r^n)/(1 - r)$, except in the special case in which $r = 1$, when $s_n = an$.*

To see this, write
$$s_n = a(1 + r + r^2 + \cdots + r^{n-1}),$$
so that
$$r s_n = a(r + r^2 + r^3 + \cdots + r^n).$$

Subtracting the second equation from the first, we obtain immediately

$$(1 - r)s_n = a(1 - r^n).$$

In the general case (that is, when $r \neq 1$) the sum s_n of a geometric series tends to a limit if and only if r^n does so. This gives us the following proposition.

Proposition 1.7.11 (Infinite geometric series)   *The infinite geometric series $a + ar + ar^2 + \cdots$ is convergent and has the sum $a/(1 - r)$ if and only if $-1 < r < 1$.*

A similar technique can be used to obtain a useful result concerning yet another series. If we write

$$s_n = r + 2r^2 + 3r^3 + \cdots + (n-1)r^{n-1}$$

we have that

$$r s_n = r^2 + 2r^3 + 3r^4 + \cdots (n-1)r^n.$$

Subtracting the second equation from the first, we obtain

$$(1-r)s_n = r + r^2 + r^3 + \cdots + r^{n-1} - (n-1)r^n$$
$$= r(1 + r + r^2 + \cdots + r^{n-1}) - nr^n$$
$$= r(1 - r^n)/(1 - r) - nr^n$$

by virtue of Proposition 1.7.10. Hence

$$r + 2r^2 + \cdots + (n-1)r^{n-1} = \frac{r(1 - r^n)}{(1-r)^2} - \frac{nr^n}{(1-r)}.$$

The right-hand side tends to a limit as n tends to infinity if $-1 < r < 1$ (use Proposition 1.7.6), giving us the following result.

Proposition 1.7.12 *The infinite series $r + 2r^2 + 3r^3 + \cdots$ converges when $-1 < r < 1$, and in this case its sum is $r/(1-r)^2$.*

Next we turn to series of the form $1^r, 2^r, 3^r, \ldots$, where r is a positive integer. When $r = 0$ the series is simply $1, 1, 1, \ldots$, and we have the trivial result $\sum_{i=1}^{n} 1 = n$. The following proposition gives us a general way of handling the cases when $r > 0$.

Proposition 1.7.13 *For any integer $k \geq 0$ we have*

$$\sum_{i=1}^{n} i(i+1)\ldots(i+k) = n(n+1)\ldots(n+k+1)/(k+2).$$

The proposition is easily proved by mathematical induction on n. Notice that we do *not* need to use induction on k, which is merely a parameter in the formula.

Using Proposition 1.7.13, it is easy to obtain the sums of various series of interest.

Proposition 1.7.14 $\displaystyle\sum_{i=1}^{n} i = n(n+1)/2.$

This is simply Proposition 1.7.13 with $k = 0$.

Proposition 1.7.15 $\displaystyle\sum_{i=1}^{n} i^2 = n(n+1)(2n+1)/6.$

To see this, take

$$\sum_{i=1}^{n} i^2 = \sum_{i=1}^{n} (i(i+1)-i)$$

$$= \sum_{i=1}^{n} i(i+1) - \sum_{i=1}^{n} i$$

$$= n(n+1)(n+2)/3 - n(n+1)/2$$

$$= n(n+1)(2n+1)/6$$

where we have used Proposition 1.7.13 twice to evaluate the two sums.

A similar line of attack may be used to evaluate any other series of this type. In fact, as we sketch below, it is easy to prove the following general proposition.

Proposition 1.7.16 *Let r be any positive integer. Then*

$$\sum_{i=1}^{n} i^r = n^{r+1}/(r+1) + p_r(n),$$

where $p_r(n)$ is a polynomial of degree at most r.

The outline of the argument is as follows:

$$\sum_{i=1}^{n} i^r = \sum_{i=1}^{n} i(i+1)\dots(i+r-1) + \sum_{i=1}^{n} p(i)$$

$$= n(n+1)\dots(n+r)/(r+1) + p'(n)$$

$$= n^{r+1}/(r+1) + p''(n)$$

where $p(i)$ is a polynomial of degree not more than $r-1$, and $p'(n)$ and $p''(n)$ are polynomials of degree not more than r. We leave the reader to fill in the details of the argument.

Finally we consider briefly series of the form $1^{-r}, 2^{-r}, \dots$ where r is a positive integer. When $r = 1$ we obtain the series $1, 1/2, 1/3, \dots$ known as the *harmonic series*. It is easy to show that this series diverges. The following proposition gives us a better idea of its behaviour.

Proposition 1.7.17 (Harmonic series)   *Let H_n be the sum of the first n terms of the harmonic series $1, 1/2, 1/3, \dots$ Then $\log(n+1) < H_n \le 1 + \log n$.*

To see this, consider Figure 1.8. The area under the "staircase" gives the sum of the harmonic series; the area under the lower curve, $y = 1/(x+1)$, is less than this sum, while the area under the upper curve, which is $y = 1$ for $x < 1$ and $y = 1/x$ thereafter, is greater than or equal to the sum. Hence

$$\int_0^n \frac{dx}{x+1} < H_n \leq 1 + \int_1^n \frac{dx}{x}$$

from which the proposition follows immediately. A more precise estimate of H_n for large n can be obtained from

$$\lim_{n \to \infty} \left(1 + \frac{1}{2} + \frac{1}{3} + \cdots + \frac{1}{n} - \log n\right) = \gamma,$$

where $\gamma \approx 0.57721\ldots$ is *Euler's constant,* but the proof of this is beyond the scope of our book.

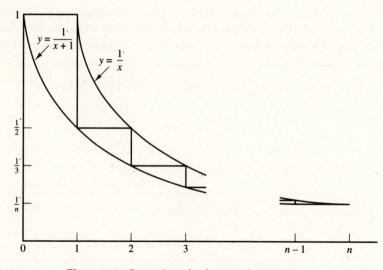

Figure 1.8. Summing the harmonic series

It is easy to show that series of the form $1, 1/2^r, 1/3^r, \ldots$ with $r > 1$ are all convergent, and that the sum of such a series is less than $r/(r-1)$; see Problem 1.39. For example

$$\lim_{n \to \infty} \left(1 + \frac{1}{2^2} + \frac{1}{3^2} + \cdots + \frac{1}{n^2}\right) = \frac{\pi^2}{6} \approx 1.64493\ldots$$

However it is not easy to calculate the exact values of such sums.

1.7.3 Basic combinatorics

Suppose we have n objects that are sufficiently unlike that we can tell which one is which: we say the objects are *distinguishable.* To make it easy to talk about them, suppose they are labelled a, b, and so on, with each object having a distinct label. From now on we shall simply refer to a, for example, when we mean "the object labelled a".

Our first definition concerns the number of ways we can arrange these n objects in order.

Definition 1.7.18   *A permutation of n objects is an ordered arrangement of the objects.*

For example, if we have four objects a, b, c and d, we can arrange them in order in 24 different ways:

$$
\begin{array}{cccccc}
abcd & abdc & acbd & acdb & adbc & adcb \\
bacd & badc & bcad & bcda & bdac & bdca \\
cabd & cadb & cbad & cbda & cdab & cdba \\
dabc & dacb & dbac & dbca & dcab & dcba
\end{array}
$$

The first object in the permutation may be chosen in n ways; once the first object has been chosen, the second may be chosen in $n - 1$ different ways; once the first and second have been chosen, the third may be chosen in $n - 2$ different ways, and so on. There are two possibilities when we choose last but one object, and there is only one way of choosing the last object. The total number of permutations of n objects is therefore

$$n(n - 1)(n - 2) \cdots 2 \cdot 1 = n!$$

Next we consider the number of ways of choosing a certain number of these objects, without regard to the order in which we make our choices.

Definition 1.7.19   *A combination of r objects from n objects is a selection of r objects without regard to order.*

For example, if we have five objects a, b, c, d and e, we can choose three of them in 10 different ways if order is not taken into account:

$$
\begin{array}{ccccc}
abc & abd & abe & acd & ace \\
ade & bcd & bce & bde & cde
\end{array}
$$

A choice such as *eba* does not appear in this list, since it is the same as *abe* when the order of the objects is disregarded.

When we make our choice of r objects from among n, there are n ways of making the first choice. When the first object has been chosen, there remain $n - 1$ ways of choosing the second, and so on. When we choose the last of the r objects we want, there remain $n - r + 1$ possibilities. Hence there are

$$n(n - 1)(n - 2) \cdots (n - r + 1)$$

ways of choosing r objects from n *when order is taken into account*. However when we do *not* take order into account, we can permute the r chosen objects any way we like, and it still counts as the same combination. In the example above, for instance, the six ordered choices abc, acb, bac, bca, cab and cba all count as the same combination. Since there are $r!$ ways of permuting r objects, the number of ways of choosing r objects from n when order is not taken into account is

$$\binom{n}{r} = \frac{n(n-1)(n-2)\cdots(n-r+1)}{r!}. \tag{1.1}$$

Several alternative notations are used for the number of combinations of n objects taken r at a time: among others, you may encounter $_nC_r$ and C_r^n. This accounts for the common, but illogical, habit of writing $\binom{n}{r}$ but reading this symbol aloud as "$n\ C\ r$".

When $r > n$, Equation 1.1 gives $\binom{n}{r} = 0$, which is sensible: there are no ways of choosing more than n objects from n. It is convenient to take $\binom{n}{0} = 1$ (there is just one way of not choosing any objects), and when $r < 0$, which has no combinatorial meaning, we define $\binom{n}{r} = 0$. When $0 \le r \le n$, Equation 1.1 can conveniently be written in the form

$$\binom{n}{r} = \frac{n!}{r!(n-r)!}$$

A simple argument allows us to obtain an important relation. Pick any one of the n objects, and say that this object is "special". Now when we choose r objects from the n available, we can distinguish those choices that include the special object, and those that do not. For instance, if we are to choose three objects among a, b, c, d and e, and the special object is b, then the choices that include the special object are abc, abd, abe, bcd, bce and bcd, while those that do not include the special object are acd, ace, ade and cde. To make a selection of the first kind, we can first choose the special object (since the order of our choices is not important), and then complete our selection by picking $r - 1$ objects among the $n - 1$ that are left; this can be done in $\binom{n-1}{r-1}$ ways. To make a selection of the second kind, we must choose our r objects among the $n - 1$ that are not special; this can be done in $\binom{n-1}{r}$ ways. Since every selection of r objects from among the n available is of one kind or the other, we must have

$$\binom{n}{r} = \binom{n-1}{r-1} + \binom{n-1}{r}, \ 1 \le r \le n.$$

This formula can also be proved using Equation 1.1.

The formula gives us a simple way of tabulating the values of $\binom{n}{r}$, as illustrated in Figure 1.9.
Here each row of the table can be calculated easily from the elements of the preceding row. A table of this type displaying the values of $\binom{n}{r}$ is often called *Pascal's triangle*.

The values $\binom{n}{r}$ are also known as the *binomial coefficients* because of the role they play in the following theorem. The theorem, which we shall not attempt to prove, is usually ascribed to Newton, although it seems to have been known to Omar Khayyam some 600 years earlier.

$n \backslash r$	0	1	2	3	4	5
0	1					
1	1	1				
2	1	2	1			
3	1	3	3	1		
4	1	4	6	4	1	
5	1	5	10	10	5	1

Figure 1.9. Combinations of n objects taken r at a time

Theorem 1.7.20 (Newton)   *Let n be a positive integer. Then*

$$(1 + x)^n = 1 + \binom{n}{1}x + \binom{n}{2}x^2 + \cdots + \binom{n}{n-1}x^{n-1} + x^n.$$

Using this theorem it is easy to obtain interesting results concerning the binomial coefficients. For example, on setting $x = 1$ we obtain immediately

$$\sum_{r=0}^{n} \binom{n}{r} = 2^n.$$

In combinatorial terms, the sum on the left is the number of ways of choosing an arbitrary number of objects (including 0 objects) from n when order is not taken into account. Since there are 2 possibilities for each of the n objects—we can take it or leave it—there are 2^n ways this can be done. Similarly, on setting $x = -1$ in Theorem 1.7.20 we find

$$\sum_{\substack{r=0 \\ r \text{ odd}}}^{n} \binom{n}{r} = \sum_{\substack{r=0 \\ r \text{ even}}}^{n} \binom{n}{r}.$$

1.7.4 Elementary probability

Probability theory is concerned with the study of random phenomena, that is, of phenomena whose future is not predictable with certainty. To apply probability theory, we view the phenomenon of interest as a *random experiment* whose result is not certain in advance. Such an experiment might consist, for instance, of throwing a dice and noting which face shows on top, or of counting how many cars pass a particular point in a given period of time, or of measuring the response time of a computer system. The result of such an experiment is called its *outcome*.

The set of all possible outcomes of a random experiment is called the *sample space* of the experiment. In the following paragraphs we denote this sample space by S. The individual outcomes are called *sample points* or *elementary events*. For example, when we throw an ordinary dice, there are six possible outcomes, namely the values from 1 to 6. For this experiment, then, the sample space is $S = \{1, 2, 3, 4, 5, 6\}$. For the random experiment that consists of counting the cars passing a given point, the sample space is $S = \{0, 1, 2, \ldots\}$. For the random experiment that consists of measuring the response time of a computer system, the sample space is $S = \{t \mid t > 0\}$.

A sample space can be finite or infinite, and it can be discrete or continuous. A sample space is said to be discrete if the number of sample points is finite, or if they can be labelled 1, 2, 3, and so on using the positive integers; otherwise the sample space is continuous. In the examples above, S is finite and therefore discrete for the random experiment of throwing a dice; S is infinite but discrete for the experiment of counting cars, for the possible outcomes can be made to correspond to the positive integers; and S is continuous for the experiment of measuring a response time. In this book we shall be concerned almost entirely with random experiments whose sample space is finite, and therefore discrete.

An *event* is now defined as a collection of sample points, that is, as a subset of the sample space. An event A is said to *occur* if the random experiment is performed and the observed outcome is an element of the set A. For example, when we throw a dice, the event described by the statement "The number shown on the dice is odd" corresponds to the subset $A = \{1, 3, 5\}$ of the sample space. When we count cars, the event described by "The observed number of cars is less than 20" corresponds to the subset $A = \{0, 1, 2, \ldots, 18, 19\}$, and so on. Informally, we use the word "event" to refer either to the statement describing it, or to the corresponding subset of the sample space. In particular, the entire sample space S is an event called the *universal event*, and the empty set $\varnothing$ is an event called the *impossible event*.

Since a sample space S is a set and an event A is a subset of S, we can form new events by the usual operations of set theory. Thus to any event A there corresponds an event $\bar{A}$ consisting of all the sample points of S that are not in A. Clearly $\bar{A}$ is the event "A does not occur". Similarly the event $A \cup B$ corresponds to the statement "Either A or B occurs", while the event $A \cap B$ corresponds to "Both A and B occur". Two events are said to be *mutually exclusive* if $A \cap B = \varnothing$.

Finally a *probability measure* is a function that assigns a numerical value $\Pr[A]$ to every event A of the sample space. Obviously the probability of an event is supposed to measure in some sense the relative likelihood that the event will occur if the underlying random experiment is performed. The philosophical bases of the notion of probability are controversial (What *precisely* does it mean to say that the probability of rain tomorrow is 0.25?), but there is agreement that any sensible probability measure must satisfy the following three axioms:

1. For any event A, $\Pr[A] \geq 0$.

2. $\Pr[S] = 1$.

3. If the events A and B are mutually exclusive, that is, if $A \cap B = \varnothing$, then $\Pr[A \cup B] = \Pr[A] + \Pr[B]$.

It follows by mathematical induction from axiom 3 that

$$\Pr[A_1 \cup A_2 \cup \cdots \cup A_n] = \Pr[A_1] + \Pr[A_2] + \cdots + \Pr[A_n]$$

for any finite collection $A_1, A_2, \ldots, A_n$ of mutually exclusive events. (A modified form of axiom 3 is necessary if the sample space is infinite, but that need not concern us here.) The axioms lead to a number of consequences, among which are

4. $\Pr[\bar{A}] = 1 - \Pr[A]$ for any event A; and

5. $\Pr[A \cup B] = \Pr[A] + \Pr[B] - \Pr[A \cap B]$ for any events A and B.

The basic procedure for solving problems in probability can now be outlined: first, identify the sample space S; second, assign probabilities to the elements in S; third, identify the events of interest; and finally, compute the desired probabilities. For instance, suppose we want to know the probability that a random number generator will produce a value that is prime. We have first to identify the sample space. Suppose we know that the generator can produce any integer value between 0 and 9999 inclusive. The sample space (that is, the set of possible outcomes) is therefore $\{0, 1, 2, \ldots, 9999\}$. Next, we must assign probabilities to the elements of S. If the generator produces each possible elementary event with equal probability, it follows that $\Pr[0] = \Pr[1] = \cdots = \Pr[9999] = 1/10000$. Third, the interesting event is "the generator produces a prime", which corresponds to the subset $A = \{2, 3, 5, \ldots, 9967, 9973\}$. Finally the interesting probability is $\Pr[A]$, which can be computed as $\sum_{e \in A} \Pr[e]$, where the sum is over the elementary events that compose A. Since the probability of each elementary event is $1/10000$, and there are 1229 elementary events in A, we find $\Pr[A] = 0.1229$.

So far we have assumed that all we know about the outcome of some random experiment is that it must correspond to some sample point in the sample space S. However it is often useful to calculate the probability that an event A occurs when it is known that the outcome of the experiment is contained in some subset B of the sample space. For example, we might wish to calculate the probability that the random number generator of the previous paragraph has produced a prime when we know that it has produced an odd number. The symbol for this probability is $\Pr[A|B]$, called *the conditional probability of A given B*. Obviously this conditional probability is only interesting when $\Pr[B] \neq 0$.

In essence, the extra information tells us that the outcome of the experiment lies in a new sample space, namely B. Since the sum of the probabilities of the elementary events in the sample space must be 1, we scale up the original values to fulfill this condition. Furthermore we are only interested now in that part of A that lies in B, namely $A \cap B$. Thus the conditional probability is given by

$$\Pr[A|B] = \frac{\Pr[A \cap B]}{\Pr[B]}.$$

For our example, A is the event "the generator produces a prime" and B is the event "the generator produces an odd number". Now B includes 5000 elementary events, so $\Pr[B] = 0.5$. There are 1228 odd primes less than 10000 (only the even prime 2 drops out), so $\Pr[A \cap B] = 0.1228$. Hence the probability that the generator has produced a prime, given that it has produced an odd number, is

$$\Pr[A|B] = 0.1228/0.5 = 0.2456.$$

Two events A and B are said to be *independent* if

$$\Pr[A \cap B] = \Pr[A]\Pr[B].$$

In this case, providing $\Pr[B] \neq 0$, we have that

$$\Pr[A|B] = \frac{\Pr[A \cap B]}{\Pr[B]} = \frac{\Pr[A]\Pr[B]}{\Pr[B]} = \Pr[A],$$

and hence the knowledge that event B has occurred does not change the probability that event A will occur. In fact this condition can be used as an alternative definition of independence.

In Chapter 10 we shall be looking at probabilistic algorithms for determining whether or not a given integer is prime. In this context the following approximations are useful. Suppose the sample space S contains a large number n of consecutive integers, and that the probability of each of these outcomes is the same, namely $1/n$. For example, S might be the set $\{1, 2, \ldots, n\}$. Let D_i be the event "the outcome is divisible by i". Since the number of outcomes in S that are divisible by i is approximately n/i, we have that $\Pr[D_i] \approx (n/i) \times (1/n) = 1/i$. Furthermore, if p and q are two different primes, the events D_p and D_q are approximately independent, so that

$$\Pr[D_p \cap D_q] \approx \Pr[D_p]\Pr[D_q] \approx 1/pq.$$

Of course this may not be true if either p or q is not prime: clearly the events D_2 and D_4 are not independent; also when S contains only a small number of elements, the approximations do not work very well, as Problem 1.46 illustrates. Now the Prime Number Theorem (whose proof is well beyond the scope of this book) tells us that the number of primes less than n is approximately $n/\log n$, so that if S is indeed $\{1, 2, \ldots, n\}$, with equal probability for each outcome, and A is the event "the outcome is prime", we have that $\Pr[A] \approx 1/\log n$.

Consider for instance the following problem. A random number generator produces the value 12262409. We would like to know whether this number is prime, but we don't have the computing power to compute the answer in a deterministic way. (Of course this is unrealistic for such a small example.) So what can we say with the help of a little probability theory?

The first thing to note is that a question such as "What is the probability that 12262409 is prime?" is meaningless. No random experiment is involved here, so we have no sample space to talk about, and we cannot even begin to assign probabilities to outcomes. On the other hand, a question such as "What is the probability that our random number generator has produced a prime?" *is* meaningful and can be answered quite easily.

As before, the first step is to identify our sample space, and the second to assign probabilities to the elements of S. Suppose we know that the generator produces each of the values from 0 to 99999999 with equal probability: then $S = \{0, 1, \ldots, 99999999\}$, and the probability of each elementary event in S is $1/10^8$. The Prime Number Theorem tells us that approximately $10^8 / \log 10^8 \approx 5.43 \times 10^6$

elements of S are prime. (The correct value is actually 5761455, but the approximation is good enough for our purposes.) So if A is the event "our generator produces a prime", we have that $\Pr[A] \approx 0.0543$.

Now let the event D_p be "our generator produces a number that is divisible by the prime p". Since $\Pr[D_p] \approx 1/p$, the probability of the complementary event "our generator produces a number that is *not* divisible by the prime p" is $\Pr[\bar{D}_p] \approx 1 - 1/p$. Suppose we test 12262409 by trying to divide it by 2. The attempt fails, but now we have some additional information, and we can ask "What is the probability that our generator produces a prime, given that it produces a number not divisible by 2?" In symbols,

$$\Pr[A|\bar{D}_2] = \Pr[A \cap \bar{D}_2]/\Pr[\bar{D}_2]$$
$$\approx 2\Pr[A] \approx 0.109.$$

Here $\Pr[A \cap \bar{D}_2]$ is essentially the same as $\Pr[A]$ because all the primes save one are not divisible by 2. If we next try dividing 12262409 by 3, the attempt again fails, so now we can ask "What is the probability that our generator produces a prime, given that it produces a number divisible neither by 2 nor by 3?" This probability is

$$\Pr[A|\bar{D}_2 \cap \bar{D}_3] = \frac{\Pr[A \cap \bar{D}_2 \cap \bar{D}_3]}{\Pr[\bar{D}_2 \cap \bar{D}_3]}$$
$$\approx \Pr[A]/\Pr[\bar{D}_2]\Pr[\bar{D}_3]$$
$$\approx 3\Pr[A] = 0.163.$$

Continuing in this way, each successive failure to divide 12262409 by a new prime allows us to ask a more precise question, and to be a little more confident that our generator has indeed produced a prime. Suppose, however, that at some stage we try to divide 12262409 by 3121. Now the trial division succeeds, so our next question would be "What is the probability that our generator has produced a prime, given that it has produced a number divisible by none of 2, 3, …, but divisible by 3121?" The answer is of course 0: once we have found a divisor of the number produced by the generator, we are sure it is not prime. Symbolically, this answer is obtained because

$$\Pr[A \cap \bar{D}_2 \cap \cdots \cap D_{3121}] = 0.$$

Notice that we cannot start this process of calculating a new probability after each trial division if we are unable to estimate $\Pr[A]$, the unconditional probability that our generator has produced a prime. In the example we did this using the Prime Number Theorem plus our knowledge that the generator produces each value from 0 to 99999999 with equal probability. Suppose on the other hand we are presented with the number 12262409 and simply told that it has been selected for the purposes of the example. Then the first question to ask is "What is the probability that a number selected in some unspecified way for the purposes of an example is prime?" Clearly this is impossible to answer. The sample space of the random experiment consisting of choosing a number to serve as an example is unknown, as are the probabilities associated with the elementary events in this sample space. We can therefore make *no* meaningful statement about the probabilities associated with a number selected in this way.

In many random experiments we are interested less in the outcome itself, than in some number associated with this outcome. In a horse-race, for instance, we may be less interested in the name of the winning horse than in the amount we win or lose on the race. This idea is captured by the notion of a *random variable*. Formally, a random variable is a function (and not a variable at all, despite its name) that assigns a real number to each sample point of some sample space S.

If X is a random variable defined on a sample space S, and x is a real number, we define the event A_x to be the subset of S consisting of all the sample points to which the random variable X assigns the value x. Thus

$$A_x = \{s \in S \,|\, X(s) = x\}.$$

The notation $X = x$ is a convenient way to denote the event A_x. Hence we can write

$$\Pr[X = x] = \Pr[A_x] = \sum_{\substack{s \in S \\ X(s)=x}} \Pr[s].$$

If we define $p(x)$ by

$$p(x) = \Pr[X = x]$$

then $p(x)$ is a new function associated with the random variable X, called the *probability mass function* of X. We define the *expectation* $E[X]$ of X (also called the *mean* or the *average*) by

$$E[X] = \sum_{s \in S} X(s)\Pr[s] = \sum_x x\, p(x).$$

The expectation $E[X]$ is also commonly denoted by μ_X.

To pull these ideas together, consider the following example. The random experiment concerned is a horse-race with five runners. The outcome of the experiment is the name of the winner. The sample space S is the set of all possible outcomes, so we might have, for instance

$$S = \{\text{Ariel, Bonbon, Coffee, Demon, Eggcup}\}.$$

We have to assign a probability measure to each possible outcome. Although the accuracy with which we do this may make a great deal of difference to our financial situation, probability theory gives no help about how to proceed. Suppose that in the light of experience we assign the values shown in Figure 1.10.

Outcome	Probability	Winnings
Ariel	0.10	50
Bonbon	0.05	100
Coffee	0.25	−30
Demon	0.50	−30
Eggcup	0.10	15

Figure 1.10. Probability of each outcome

(Remember that the probabilities must sum to 1.) We have made a number of wagers on the race so that, depending on the outcome, we will win or lose some money. The amount we win or lose is also shown in Figure 1.10. This amount is a function of the outcome, that is, a random variable. Call this random variable W; then the table shows that $W(\text{Ariel}) = 50$, $W(\text{Bonbon}) = 100$, and so on. The random variable W can take the values $-30, 15, 50,$ or 100, and for instance

$$p(-30) = \Pr[W = -30]$$

$$= \sum_{\substack{s \in S \\ W(s)=-30}} \Pr[s]$$

$$= \Pr[\text{Coffee}] + \Pr[\text{Demon}] = 0.25 + 0.50 = 0.75.$$

Similarly $p(15) = \Pr[W = 15] = 0.10$, $p(50) = \Pr[W = 50] = 0.10$ and $p(100) = \Pr[W = 100] = 0.05$. Our expected winnings can be calculated as

$$E[W] = \sum_x x p(x)$$

$$= -30p(-30) + 15p(15) + 50p(50) + 100p(100)$$

$$= -11.$$

Once we have obtained $E[X]$, we can calculate a second useful measure called the *variance* of X, denoted by $\text{Var}[X]$ or σ_X^2. This is defined by

$$\text{Var}[X] = E[(X - E[X])^2] = \sum_x p(x)(x - E[X])^2.$$

In words, it is the expected value of the square of the difference between X and its expectation $E[X]$. The *standard deviation* of X, denoted by σ_X, is the square root of the variance. For the horse-race example above, we have

$$\text{Var}[W] = \sum_x p(x)(x - E[X])^2$$

$$= p(-30) \times 19^2 + p(15) \times 26^2 + p(50) \times 61^2 + p(100) \times 111^2$$

$$= 1326.5,$$

and $\sigma_W = \sqrt{1326.5} \approx 36.42$.

Why are the expected value and the variance of X useful? Suppose the underlying random experiment can be repeated many times. The i–th repetition of the experiment will have some particular outcome o_i, to which the function X assigns a value x_i. Suppose we repeat the experiment n times in all. If n is large, it is almost always reasonable to expect that the average observed value of x_i, namely $\sum_{i=1}^n x_i/n$, will be close to the expected value of X, namely $E[X]$. Only in rare circumstances is this likely not to be true. Thus $E[X]$ allows us to predict the average observed value of x_i.

The variance serves to quantify how good this prediction is likely to be. There exists a famous probability distribution called the *normal* distribution. Under very general conditions, the *Central Limit Theorem* suggests that when n is large, the average observed value of x_i will have a distribution that is approximately normal with mean $E[X]$ and variance $\mathrm{Var}[X]/n$. To take advantage of this, all we need is a table of the normal distribution. These are widely available. Such a table tells us, among other things, that a normal deviate lies between plus or minus 1.960 standard deviations of its mean 95% of the time; 99% of the time it lies within plus or minus 2.576 standard deviations of its mean.

For example, suppose that by some magic the horse-race described above could be run 50 times under identical conditions. Suppose we win w_i on the i-th repetition, and let our average winnings be $\bar{w} = \sum_{i=1}^{50} w_i/50$. Then we can expect that $\bar{w}$ will be approximately $E[W] = -11$. The variance of $\bar{w}$ will be $\mathrm{Var}[W]/50 = 1326.5/50 = 26.53$, and its standard deviation will be the square root of this, or 5.15, while the Central Limit Theorem tells us that the distribution of $\bar{w}$ will be approximately normal. Therefore 95% of the time we can expect our average winnings $\bar{w}$ to lie between $-11 - 1.960 \times 5.15$ and $-11 + 1.960 \times 5.15$, that is between -21.1 and -0.9. A similar calculation shows that 99% of the time $\bar{w}$ will lie between -24.3 and $+2.3$; see Problem 1.47.

It is usually safe to use the Central Limit Theorem when n is greater than about 25 or so.

1.8 Problems

Problem 1.1. The word "algebra" is also connected with the mathematician al-Khowârizmî, who gave his name to algorithms. What is the connection?

Problem 1.2. Easter Sunday is in principle the first Sunday after the first full moon after the spring equinox. Is this rule sufficiently precise to be called an algorithm? Justify your answer.

Problem 1.3. While executing an algorithm by hand, you have to make a random choice. To help you, you have a fair coin, which gives the values *heads* and *tails* with equal probability, and a fair dice, which gives each of the values 1 to 6 with equal probability. You are required to choose each of the values *red*, *yellow* and *blue* with equal probability. Give at least three different ways of doing this.
Repeat the problem with five colours instead of three.

Problem 1.4. Is it possible that there exists an algorithm for playing a perfect game of billiards? Justify your answer.

Problem 1.5. Use multiplication *à la russe* to multiply (a) 63 by 123, and (b) 64 by 123.

Problem 1.6. Find a pocket calculator accurate to at least eight figures, that is, which can multiply a four-figure number by a four-figure number and get the correct eight-figure answer. You are required to multiply 31415975 by 8182818. Show how the divide-and-conquer multiplication algorithm of Section 1.2 can be used to reduce the problem to a small number of calculations that you can do on your calculator, followed by a simple paper-and-pencil addition. Carry out the calculation. *Hint*: Don't do it recursively!

Problem 1.7.   You are required to multiply two numbers given in Roman figures. For instance, XIX times XXXIV is DCXLVI. You may *not* use a method that involves translating the numbers into Arabic notation, multiplying them, and then translating them back again. Devise an algorithm for this problem.

Hint: Find ways to translate back and forth between true Roman notation and something similar that does not involve any subtractions. For instance, XIX might become XVIIII in this "pseudo-Roman" notation. Next find easy ways to double, halve and add figures in pseudo-Roman notation. Finally adapt multiplication *à la russe* to complete the problem.

Problem 1.8.   As in Problem 1.6, suppose you have available a pocket calculator that can multiply a four-figure number by a four-figure number and get the correct eight-figure answer. Devise an algorithm for multiplying two large numbers based on the classic algorithm, but using blocks of four figures at a time instead of just one. (If you like, think of it as doing your calculation in base 10000 arithmetic.) For instance, when multiplying 1234567 by 9876543, you might obtain the arrangement shown in Figure 1.11.

			0123	4567
			0987	6543
		0080	7777	1881
	0012	1851	7629	
	0012	1932	5406	1881

Figure 1.11. Multiplication in base 10000

Here the first line of the calculation is obtained, from right to left, as

$$4567 \times 6543 = 29881881$$

(that is, a result of 1881 and a carry of 2988), followed by $0123 \times 6543 + 2988 = 807777$ (that is, a result of 7777 and a carry of 0080). The second line of the calculation is obtained similarly, and the final result is found by adding the columns. All the necessary arithmetic can be done with your calculator.

Use your algorithm to multiply 31415975 by 8182818. Check that your answer is the same as the one you found in Problem 1.6.

Problem 1.9.   Figure 1.12 shows yet another method of multiplying two positive integers, sometimes called Arabic multiplication.

In the figure, as before, 981 is multiplied by 1234. To use this method, draw a rectangle with as many columns as there are figures in the multiplicand (here 3) and as many rows as there are figures in the multiplier (here 4). Write the multiplicand above the columns, and the multiplier down the right-hand side of the rectangle. Draw diagonal lines as shown. Next fill in each cell of the rectangle with the product of the figure at the top of the column and the figure at the right-hand end of the row. The tens figure of the result (which may be 0) goes above the diagonal line,

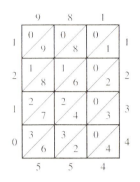

Figure 1.12. Multiplication using a rectangle

and the units figure below it. Finally add the diagonals of the rectangle starting at the bottom right. Here the first diagonal gives 4; the second gives $2 + 0 + 3 = 5$; the third gives $6 + 3 + 4 + 0 + 2 = 15$, so write down 5 and carry 1; and so on. Now the result 1210554 can be read off down the left-hand side and along the bottom of the rectangle.

Once again, use this algorithm to multiply 31415975 by 8182818, checking your result against the answers to previous problems.

Problem 1.10.   Are the two sets $X = \{1, 2, 3\}$ and $Y = \{2, 1, 3\}$ equal?

Problem 1.11.   Which of the following sets are finite: $\varnothing$, $\{\varnothing\}$, $\mathbb{N}$, $\{\mathbb{N}\}$? What is the cardinality of those among the above sets that are finite?

Problem 1.12.   For which values of Boolean variables p, q and r is the Boolean formula $(p \wedge q) \vee (\neg q \wedge r)$ true?

Problem 1.13.   Prove that
  $\neg (\forall x \in X) [P(x)]$ is equivalent to $(\exists x \in X) [\neg P(x)]$ and
  $\neg (\exists x \in X) [P(x)]$ is equivalent to $(\forall x \in X) [\neg P(x)]$.

Problem 1.14.   Prove that
  $\neg (\overset{\infty}{\forall} x \in X) [P(x)]$ is equivalent to $(\overset{\infty}{\exists} x \in X) [\neg P(x)]$ and
  $\neg (\overset{\infty}{\exists} x \in X) [P(x)]$ is equivalent to $(\overset{\infty}{\forall} x \in X) [\neg P(x)]$.

Problem 1.15.   Prove that
  $\log_a (xy) = \log_a x + \log_a y$,
  $\log_a x^y = y \log_a x$,
  $\log_a x = \frac{\log_b x}{\log_b a}$,
  and $x^{\log_b y} = y^{\log_b x}$.

Problem 1.16.   Prove that $x - 1 < \lfloor x \rfloor \le x \le \lceil x \rceil < x + 1$ for every real number x.

Problem 1.17.   An alternative proof of Theorem 1.5.1, to the effect that there are infinitely many primes, begins as follows. Assume for a contradiction that the set of prime numbers is finite. Let p be the largest prime. Consider $x = p!$ and $y = x + 1$. Your problem is to complete the proof from here and to distill from your proof an algorithm *Biggerprime*(p) that finds a prime larger than p. The proof of termination for your algorithm must be obvious, as well as the fact that it returns a value larger than p.

Problem 1.18.   Modify the proof of Theorem 1.5.1 to prove that there are infinitely many primes of the form $4k - 1$, where k is an integer.

Hint: Define x as in the proof of Theorem 1.5.1, but then set $y = 4x - 1$ rather than $y = x + 1$. Even though y itself may not be prime and the smallest integer d larger than 1 that divides y may not be of the form $4k - 1$, prove *by contradiction* that y has at least one prime divisor of the required form.

It is also true that there are infinitely many primes of the form $4k + 1$, but this is more involved to prove. Where does your reasoning for the case $4k - 1$ break down in trying to use the same idea to prove the case $4k + 1$?

Problem 1.19.   Let n be a positive integer. Draw a circle and mark n points regularly spaced around the circumference. Now, draw a chord inside the circle between each pair of these points. In the case $n = 1$, there are no pairs of points and thus no chords are drawn; see Figure 1.13.

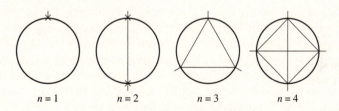

$n = 1$　　　$n = 2$　　　$n = 3$　　　$n = 4$

Figure 1.13. Carving out a circle

Finally, denote by $c(n)$ the number of sections thus carved inside the circle. You should find that $c(1) = 1$, $c(2) = 2$, $c(3) = 4$ and $c(4) = 8$. By induction, what do you think the general formula for $c(n)$ is? Determine $c(5)$ by drawing and counting. Was your inductively found formula correct? Try again with $c(6)$. What if you allow the points to be spaced irregularly? (Optional and much harder: determine the correct formula for $c(n)$, and prove that it is correct.)

Problem 1.20.   Why do you think that mathematical induction received this name even though it really is a deductive technique?

Problem 1.21.   Prove by mathematical induction that the sum of the cubes of the first n positive integers is equal to the square of the sum of these integers.

Problem 1.22. Following Problem 1.21, prove that the sum of the cubes of the first n positive integers is equal to the square of the sum of these integers, but now use Proposition 1.7.13 rather than mathematical induction. (Of course, Proposition 1.7.13 was proved by mathematical induction, too!)

Problem 1.23. Determine by induction all the positive integer values of n for which $n^3 > 2^n$. Prove your claim by mathematical induction.

Problem 1.24. The *axiom of the least integer* says that every nonempty set of positive integers contains a smallest element. (This is *not* true in general for sets of positive *real* numbers—consider for instance the set of all reals strictly between 0 and 1.) Using this axiom, give a rigorous proof by contradiction that the simple principle of mathematical induction is valid. More precisely, consider any integer a and any property P of the integers such that $P(a)$ holds, and such that $P(n)$ holds whenever $P(n-1)$ holds for any integer $n > a$. Assume furthermore that it is *not* the case that $P(n)$ holds for all $n \geq a$. Use the axiom of the least integer to derive a contradiction.

Problem 1.25. Problem 1.24 asked you to prove the validity of the principle of mathematical induction from the axiom of the least integer. In fact the principle and the axiom are equivalent: prove the axiom of the least integer by mathematical induction!
Hint: As a first step, prove that any nonempty *finite* set of positive integers contains a smallest element by mathematical induction on the number of elements in the set. Note that your proof would hold just as well for any finite set of real numbers, which shows clearly that it does not apply directly to infinite sets. To generalize the result to infinite sets of positive integers, consider any such set X. Let m be any element in X (we do not need an axiom for this: any infinite set contains at least one element by definition). Let Y be the set of elements of X that are not larger than m. Show that Y is a nonempty finite set of positive integers, and therefore your proof by mathematical induction applies to conclude that Y contains a smallest element, say n. Finish the proof by arguing that n is also the smallest element in X.

Problem 1.26. Give a rigorous proof that the *generalized* principle of mathematical induction is valid.
Hint: Prove it by simple mathematical induction.

Problem 1.27. Recall that the *Fibonacci sequence* is defined as
$$\begin{cases} f_0 = 0; f_1 = 1 & \text{and} \\ f_n = f_{n-1} + f_{n-2} & \text{for } n \geq 2. \end{cases}$$
Prove by generalized mathematical induction that
$$f_n = \frac{1}{\sqrt{5}} [\phi^n - (-\phi)^{-n}],$$
where
$$\phi = \frac{1 + \sqrt{5}}{2}$$
is the *golden ratio*. (This is known as de Moivre's formula.)

Problem 1.28.   Following Problem 1.27, prove by mathematical induction that $f_n > (\frac{3}{2})^n$ for all sufficiently large integer n. How large does n have to be? Do *not* use de Moivre's formula.

Problem 1.29.   Following Problem 1.27, prove that $\sum_{i=0}^k \binom{k}{i} f_{n+i} = f_{n+2k}$.

Problem 1.30.   Following Problem 1.27, prove by generalized mathematical induction that $f_{2n+1} = f_n^2 + f_{n+1}^2$ for all integers $n \geq 0$.
Hint: Prove the stronger theorem that $f_{2n} = 2f_n f_{n+1} - f_n^2$ as well.

Problem 1.31.   Consider arbitrary positive real constants a and b.   Define $t : \mathbb{N}^+ \to \mathbb{R}^+$ by the recurrence

$$\begin{cases} t(1) = a & \text{and} \\ t(n) = bn + nt(n-1) & \text{for } n \geq 2. \end{cases}$$

This function is sufficiently similar to the recurrence $n! = n \times (n-1)!$ that characterizes the factorial that it is natural to conjecture the existence of two positive real constants u and v such that $un! \leq t(n) \leq vn!$ for each sufficiently large integer n. Prove this conjecture by constructive induction.
Hint: Prove the stronger statement that there exist three positive real constants u, v and w such that $un! \leq t(n) \leq vn! - wn$ for each sufficiently large integer n.
Note: This problem shows that the time taken by direct use of the recursive definition to compute the determinant of an $n \times n$ matrix is proportional to $n!$, which is much worse than if the time were merely exponential. Of course, the determinant can be computed more efficiently by Gauss–Jordan elimination. See Section 2.7.1 for more detail.

Problem 1.32.   Work Problem 1.31 again, but now define $t(n) = bn^k + nt(n-1)$ for $n \geq 2$, where k is an arbitrary positive integer constant.

Problem 1.33.   Consider an arbitrary positive real constant d and a function $t : \mathbb{N} \to \mathbb{R}^+$ such that

$$t(n) \leq dn + \frac{2}{n} \sum_{k=0}^{n-1} t(k)$$

for each positive integer n.   Using constructive induction, prove the existence of a real positive constant c such that $t(n) \leq cn \log n$ for each sufficiently large integer n.

Problem 1.34.   Give two functions $f(n)$ and $g(n)$ such that neither $f(n)$ nor $g(n)$ tends to a limit as n tends to infinity, but both $f(n)+g(n)$ and $f(n)/g(n)$ do tend to a limit.

Problem 1.35.   Determine the behaviour as n tends to infinity of $f(n) = n^{-r}x^n$, where r is any positive integer.

Problem 1.36.   Use de l'Hôpital's rule to find the limit as n tends to infinity of $(\log \log n)^a / \log n$, where $a > 0$ is an arbitrary positive constant.

Problem 1.37. Prove Proposition 1.7.8.

Problem 1.38. Give a simple proof, not using integrals, that the harmonic series diverges.

Problem 1.39. Use a technique similar to the one illustrated in Figure 1.8 to show that for $r > 1$ the sum

$$s_n = 1 + \frac{1}{2^r} + \frac{1}{3^r} + \ldots + \frac{1}{n^r},$$

converges to a limit less than $r/(r-1)$.

Problem 1.40. (**Alternating series**) Let $f(n)$ be a positive, strictly decreasing function of n that tends to 0 as n tends to infinity. Show that the series $f(1) - f(2) + f(3) - f(4) + \cdots$ is convergent, and that its sum lies between $f(1)$ and $f(1) - f(2)$. For example,

$$1 - \frac{1}{2} + \frac{1}{3} - \frac{1}{4} + \ldots = \log 2 \approx 0.69314\ldots$$

Show further that the error we make if we approximate the sum of the whole series by the sum of the first n terms is less than $f(n+1)$.

Problem 1.41. Show that $\binom{n}{r} \leq 2^{n-1}$ for $n > 0$ and $0 \leq r \leq n$.

Problem 1.42. Prove that

$$\binom{2n}{n} \geq 4^n/(2n+1).$$

Problem 1.43. Show that $\sum_{r=1}^{n} r\binom{n}{r} = n2^{n-1}$ for $n > 0$.
Hint: Differentiate both sides of Theorem 1.7.20.

Problem 1.44. Show that $\dfrac{1}{(1+x)^2} = 1 - 2x + 3x^2 - 4x^3 + 5x^4 + \cdots$ for $-1 < x < 1$.
Hint: Use Proposition 1.7.12.

Problem 1.45. Show that two mutually exclusive events are *not* independent except in the trivial case that at least one of them has probability zero.

Problem 1.46. Consider a random experiment whose sample space S is $\{1, 2, 3, 4, 5\}$. Let A and B be the events "the outcome is divisible by 2" and "the outcome is divisible by 3", respectively. What are $\Pr[A]$, $\Pr[B]$ and $\Pr[A \cap B]$? Are the events A and B independent?

Problem 1.47. Show that for the horse-race of Section 1.7.4, 99% of the time our expected winnings $\bar{w}$ averaged over 50 races lie between -24.3 and $+2.3$.

1.9 References and further reading

We distinguish three kinds of books on the design and analysis of algorithms. *Specific* books cover algorithms that are useful in a particular application area: sorting and searching, graph theory, computational geometry, and so on. *General* books cover several application areas: they give algorithms useful in each area. Finally, books on *algorithmics* concentrate on the techniques of algorithm design and analysis: they illustrate each technique by examples of algorithms taken from various applications areas. The distinction between these three types of books is necessarily fuzzy at times. Harel (1987) takes a broader view at algorithmics and considers it as no less than "the spirit of computing".

The most ambitious collection of algorithms ever attempted is no doubt due to Knuth (1968, 1969, 1973), originally intended to consist of seven volumes. Several chapters of the *Handbook of Theoretical Computer Science*, edited by van Leeuwen (1990), are of great interest to the study of algorithms. Many other general books are worth mentioning: in chronological order Aho, Hopcroft and Ullman (1974), Baase (1978), Dromey (1982), Sedgewick (1983), Gonnet and Baeza-Yates (1984), Melhorn (1984a, 1984b, 1984c), Manber (1989), Cormen, Leiserson and Rivest (1990), Kingston (1990), Lewis and Denenberg (1991), Kozen (1992) and Nievergelt and Hinrichs (1993).

Specific books will be referred to in the following chapters whenever they are relevant to our discussion; we may mention, however, Nilsson (1971), Brigham (1974), Borodin and Munro (1975), Christofides (1975), Lawler (1976), Reingold, Nievergelt and Deo (1977), Gondran and Minoux (1979), Even (1980), Papadimitriou and Steiglitz (1982), Tarjan (1983), Akl (1989), Lakshmivarahan and Dhall (1990), Ja'Ja' (1992) and Leighton (1992).

Besides our own books—this one and Brassard and Bratley (1988)—and Harel's, we are aware of three more works on algorithmics: Horowitz and Sahni (1978), Stinson (1985) and Moret and Shapiro (1991). For a more popular account of algorithms, see Knuth (1977) and Lewis and Papadimitriou (1978).

Multiplication *à la russe* is described in Warusfel (1961), a remarkable little French book of popular mathematics, but the basic idea was known to the ancient Egyptians, perhaps as early as 3500 B.C.; see Ahmes (1700bc) and Kline (1972). Divide-and-conquer multiplication is attributed to Karatsuba and Ofman (1962), while Arabic multiplication is described in Eves (1983). For a discussion of constructive mathematics and nonconstructive proofs such as that we gave for Theorem 1.5.2, consult Bishop (1972). The principle of mathematical discovery is discussed by Pólya (1945, 1954). The first counterexample to Euler's conjecture to the effect that it is not possible for the sum of three positive fourth powers to be a fourth power was given by Elkies (1988).

Although we do not use any specific programming language in the present book, we suggest that a reader unfamiliar with `Pascal` would do well to look at one of the numerous books on this language, such as Jensen and Wirth (1985) or Lecarme and Nebut (1985).

Rosen (1991) is a comprehensive and simple introduction to such topics as the propositional calculus, sets, probability, mathematical reasoning and graphs.

Leonardo Pisano (c. 1170–c. 1240), or Leonardo Fibonacci, was the first great western mathematician of the Middle Ages. There is a brief account of his life and an excerpt from *Liberabaci* in Calinger (1982). The proof that

$$\lim_{n \to \infty} \left(1 + \frac{1}{2^2} + \frac{1}{3^2} + \cdots + \frac{1}{n^2} \right) = \frac{\pi^2}{6}$$

is due to Euler; see Eves (1983) or Scharlau and Opolka (1985). These references also give the history of the binomial theorem.

Chapter 2

Elementary Algorithmics

2.1 Introduction

In this chapter we begin our detailed study of algorithms. First we define some terms: we shall see that a *problem*, such as multiplying two positive integers, will normally have many—usually infinitely many—*instances*, such as multiplying the particular integers 981 and 1234. An algorithm must work correctly on *every* instance of the problem it claims to solve.

Next we explain what we mean by the *efficiency* of an algorithm, and discuss different ways for choosing the most efficient algorithm to solve a problem when several competing techniques are available. We shall see that it is crucial to know how the efficiency of an algorithm changes as the problem instances get bigger and therefore (usually) harder to solve. We also distinguish between the average efficiency of an algorithm when it is used on many instances of a problem and its efficiency in the worst possible case. The pessimistic, worst-case estimate is often appropriate when we have to be sure of solving a problem in a limited amount of time, for instance.

Once we have defined what we mean by efficiency, we can begin to investigate the methods used to analyse algorithms. Our line of attack is to try to count the number of elementary operations, such as additions and multiplications, that an algorithm performs. However we shall see that even such commonplace operations as these are not straightforward: both addition and multiplication get slower as the size of their operands increases. We also try to convey some notion of the practical difference between a good and a bad algorithm in terms of computing time.

One topic we shall *not* cover, either in this chapter or elsewhere, is how to prove rigorously that the programs we use to represent algorithms are correct. Such an approach requires a formal definition of programming language semantics well beyond what we consider necessary; an adequate treatment of this subject would deserve a book to itself. For our purposes we shall be content to rely on informal proofs using common-sense arguments.

The chapter concludes with a number of examples of algorithms from different areas, some good and some poor, to show how the principles we put forward apply in practice.

2.2 Problems and instances

In Section 1.1 we presented several different ways of multiplying two positive integers, taking as an example the multiplication of 981 by 1234. However the algorithms outlined there do not simply provide a way of multiplying these two particular numbers. In fact, they give a general solution to the *problem* of multiplying two positive integers. We say that (981, 1234) is an *instance* of this problem. Multiplying 789 by 9742, which we can express as (789, 9742), is another instance of the same problem. However multiplying −12 by 83.7 is not, for two reasons: −12 is not positive, and 83.7 is not an integer. (Of course, (−12, 83.7) *is* an instance of another, more general multiplication problem.) Most interesting problems have an infinite collection of instances. However, there are exceptions. Strictly speaking, the problem of playing a perfect game of chess has only one instance, since a unique starting position is given. Moreover there are only a finite number of subinstances (the legal intermediate positions). Yet this does not mean the problem is devoid of algorithmic interest.

An algorithm must work correctly on every instance of the problem it claims to solve. To show that an algorithm is incorrect, we need only find one instance of the problem for which it is unable to find a correct answer. Just as a proposed theorem can be disproved by a single counterexample, so an algorithm can be rejected on the basis of a single wrong result. On the other hand, just as it may be difficult to prove a theorem, it is usually difficult to prove the correctness of an algorithm. (However, see Section 1.6.3 for one simple case.) To make this possible at all, when we specify a problem, it is important to define its *domain of definition*, that is, the set of instances to be considered. The multiplication algorithms given in Chapter 1 will not work for negative or fractional operands, at least not without some modification. However this does not mean that the algorithms are invalid: instances of multiplication involving negative numbers or fractions are not in the domain of definition we chose at the outset.

Any real computing device has a limit on the size of the instances it can handle, either because the numbers involved get too big or because we run out of storage. However this limit cannot be attributed to the algorithm we choose to use. Different machines have different limits, and even different programs implementing the same algorithm on the same machine may impose different constraints. In this book we shall almost always be content to prove that our algorithms are correct in the abstract, ignoring the practical limitations present in any particular program for implementing them.

2.3 The efficiency of algorithms

When we have a problem to solve, there may be several suitable algorithms available. We would obviously like to choose the best. This raises the question of how to decide which of several algorithms is preferable. If we have only one or two small instances of a rather simple problem to solve, we may not care too much which algorithm we use: in this case we might simply choose the one that is easiest to program, or one for which a program already exists, without worrying about their theoretical properties. However if we have lots of instances to solve, or if the problem is hard, we may have to choose more carefully.

The *empirical* (or *a posteriori*) approach to choosing an algorithm consists of programming the competing techniques and trying them on different instances with the help of a computer. The *theoretical* (or *a priori*) approach, which we favour in this book, consists of determining mathematically the quantity of resources needed by each algorithm *as a function of the size of the instances considered*. The resources of most interest are computing time and storage space, with the former usually being the more critical. Throughout the book, therefore, we shall usually compare algorithms on the basis of their execution times, and when we speak of the *efficiency* of an algorithm, we shall simply mean how fast it runs. Only occasionally will we also be interested by an algorithm's storage requirements, or by its need for other resources. (Examples of other resources are the number of processors required by a parallel algorithm, and also some artificial yet meaningful combinations: we might be interested in minimizing the product of storage space used by the time for which it is occupied, if that is how our bills are calculated.)

The *size* of an instance corresponds formally to the number of bits needed to represent the instance on a computer, using some precisely defined and reasonably compact coding scheme. However, to make our analyses clearer, we shall usually be less formal than this, and use the word "size" to mean any integer that in some way measures the number of components in an instance. For example, when we talk about sorting, we shall usually measure the size of an instance by the number of items to be sorted, ignoring the fact that each of these items would take more than one bit to represent on a computer. Similarly, when we talk about graphs, we usually measure the size of an instance by the number of nodes or edges (or both) involved. Departing a little from this general rule, however, when we talk about problems involving integers, we shall sometimes give the efficiency of our algorithms in terms of the *value* of the instance being considered, rather than its size (which would be the number of bits needed to represent this value in binary).

The advantage of the theoretical approach is that it depends on neither the computer being used, nor the programming language, nor even the skill of the programmer. It saves both the time that would have been spent needlessly programming an inefficient algorithm and the machine time that would have been wasted testing it. More significantly, it allows us to study the efficiency of an algorithm when used on instances of any size. This is often not the case with the empirical approach, where practical considerations may force us to test our algorithms only on a small number of arbitrarily chosen instances of moderate size. Since it is often the case that a newly discovered algorithm begins to perform better than its predecessor only when they are both used on large instances, this last point is particularly important.

It is also possible to analyse algorithms using a *hybrid* approach, where the form of the function describing the algorithm's efficiency is determined theoretically, and then any required numerical parameters are determined empirically for a particular program and machine, usually by some kind of regression. Using this approach we can predict the time an actual implementation will take to solve an instance much larger than those used in the tests. Beware however of making such an extrapolation solely on the basis of a small number of empirical tests, ignoring all theoretical considerations. Predictions made without theoretical support are likely to be very imprecise, if not plain wrong.

If we want to measure the amount of storage an algorithm uses as a function of the size of the instances, there is a natural unit available to us, namely the bit. Regardless of the machine being used, the notion of one bit of storage is well defined. If on the other hand, as is more often the case, we want to measure the efficiency of an algorithm in terms of the time it takes to arrive at an answer, there is no such obvious choice. Clearly there can be no question of expressing this efficiency in seconds, say, since we do not have a standard computer to which all measurements might refer.

An answer to this problem is given by the *principle of invariance*, which states that two different implementations of the same algorithm will not differ in efficiency by more than some multiplicative constant. If this constant happens to be 5, for example, then we know that, if the first implementation takes 1 second to solve instances of a particular size, then the second implementation (maybe on a different machine, or written in a different programming language) will not take longer than 5 seconds to solve the same instances. More precisely, if two implementations of the same algorithm take $t_1(n)$ and $t_2(n)$ seconds, respectively, to solve an instance of size n, then there always exist positive constants c and d such that $t_1(n) \le ct_2(n)$ and $t_2(n) \le dt_1(n)$ whenever n is sufficiently large. In other words, the running time of either implementation is bounded by a constant multiple of the running time of the other; the choice of which implementation we call the first, and which we call the second, is irrelevant. The condition that n be sufficiently large is not really necessary: see the "threshold rule" in Section 3.2. However by including it we can often find smaller constants c and d than would otherwise be the case. This is useful if we are trying to calculate good bounds on the running time of one implementation when we know the running time of the other.

This principle is not something we can prove: it simply states a fact that can be confirmed by observation. Moreover it has very wide application. The principle remains true whatever the computer used to implement an algorithm (provided it is of conventional design), regardless of the programming language and the compiler employed, and regardless even of the skill of the programmer (provided he or she does not actually modify the algorithm!). Thus a change of machine may allow us to solve a problem 10 times or 100 times faster, giving an increase in speed by a constant factor. A change of algorithm, on the other hand—and only a change of algorithm—may give us an improvement that gets more and more marked as the size of the instances increases.

Returning to the question of the unit to be used to express the theoretical efficiency of an algorithm, the principle of invariance allows us to decide that there will be no such unit. Instead, we only express the time taken by an algorithm to within a multiplicative constant. We say that an algorithm for some problem takes a time *in the order of* $t(n)$, for a given function t, if there exist a positive constant c and an implementation of the algorithm capable of solving every instance of size n in not more than $ct(n)$ seconds. (For numerical problems, as we remarked earlier, n may sometimes be the value rather than the size of the instance.)

The use of seconds in this definition is obviously arbitrary: we only need to change the constant to bound the time by $at(n)$ years or $bt(n)$ microseconds. By the principle of invariance, if any one implementation of the algorithm has the required property, then so do all the others, although the multiplicative constant may change from one implementation to another. In the following chapter we give a more rigorous treatment of this important concept known as the *asymptotic notation*. It will be clear from the formal definition why we say *"in the order of"* rather than the more usual *"of the order of."*

Certain orders occur so frequently that it is worth giving them a name. For example, suppose the time taken by an algorithm to solve an instance of size n is never more than cn seconds, where c is some suitable constant. Then we say that the algorithm takes a time in the order of n, or more simply that it takes *linear* time. In this case we also talk about a *linear algorithm*. If an algorithm never takes more than cn^2 seconds to solve an instance of size n, then we say it takes time in the order of n^2, or *quadratic* time, and we call it a *quadratic algorithm*. Similarly an algorithm is *cubic, polynomial* or *exponential* if it takes a time in the order of n^3, n^k or c^n, respectively, where k and c are appropriate constants. Section 2.6 illustrates the important differences between these orders of magnitude.

Do not fall into the trap of completely forgetting the *hidden constants*, as the multiplicative constants used in these definitions are often called. We commonly ignore the exact values of these constants and assume that they are all of about the same order of magnitude. This lets us say, for instance, that a linear algorithm is faster than a quadratic one without worrying whether our statement is true in every case. Nevertheless it is sometimes necessary to be more careful.

Consider, for example, two algorithms whose implementations on a given machine take respectively n^2 days and n^3 seconds to solve an instance of size n. It is only on instances requiring more than 20 million years to solve that the quadratic algorithm outperforms the cubic algorithm! (See Problem 2.7.) From a theoretical point of view, the former is *asymptotically* better than the latter; that is, its performance is better on all sufficiently large instances. From a practical point of view, however, we will certainly prefer the cubic algorithm. Although the quadratic algorithm may be asymptotically better, its hidden constant is so large as to rule it out of consideration for normal-sized instances.

2.4 Average and worst-case analyses

The time taken by an algorithm, or the storage it uses, can vary considerably between two different instances of the same size. To illustrate this, consider two elementary sorting algorithms: sorting by *insertion*, and sorting by *selection*.

```
procedure insert(T[1 .. n])
    for i ← 2 to n do
        x ← T[i]; j ← i – 1
        while j > 0 and x < T[j] do T[j + 1]← T[j]
                                        j ← j – 1
        T[j + 1]← x

procedure select(T[1 .. n])
    for i ← 1 to n – 1 do
        minj ← i; minx ← T[i]
        for j ← i + 1 to n do
            if T[j]< minx then = minj ← j
                                 minx ← T[j]
        T[minj]← T[i]
        T[i]← minx
```

Simulate the operation of these two algorithms on a few small arrays to make sure you understand how they work. The main loop in insertion sorting looks successively at each element of the array from the second to the n–th, and inserts it in the appropriate place among its predecessors in the array. Selection sorting works by picking out the smallest element in the array and bringing it to the beginning; then it picks out the next smallest, and puts it in the second position in the array; and so on.

Let U and V be two arrays of n elements, such that U is already sorted in ascending order, whereas V is sorted in descending order. Problem 2.9 shows that both these algorithms take more time on V than on U. In fact, array V represents the worst possible case for these two algorithms: no array of n elements requires more work. Nonetheless, the time required by the selection sort algorithm is not very sensitive to the original order of the array to be sorted: the test "**if** $T[j]< minx$" is executed exactly the same number of times in every case. The variation in execution time is only due to the number of times the assignments in the **then** part of this test are executed. When we programmed this algorithm and tested it on a machine, we found that the time required to sort a given number of elements did not vary by more than 15% whatever the initial order of the elements to be sorted. As we will show in Section 4.4, the time required by $select(T)$ is quadratic, regardless of the initial order of the elements.

The situation is different if we compare the times taken by the insertion sort algorithm on the same two arrays. Because the condition controlling the **while** loop is always false at the outset, $insert(U)$ is very fast, taking linear time. On the other hand, $insert(V)$ takes quadratic time because the **while** loop is executed $i – 1$ times for each value of i; see Section 4.4 again. The variation in time between these two instances is therefore considerable. Moreover, this variation increases with the number of elements to be sorted. When we implemented the insertion sort algorithm, we found that it took less than one-fifth of a second to sort an array of 5000 elements already in ascending order, whereas it took three and a half minutes—that is, a thousand times longer—to sort an array with the same number of elements, this time initially in descending order.

If such large variations can occur, how can we talk about the time taken by a algorithm solely in terms of the size of the instance to be solved? We usually consider the *worst case* of the algorithm, that is, for each size of instance we only consider those on which the algorithm requires the most time. This is why we said in the preceding section that an algorithm must be able to solve *every* instance of size n in not more than $ct(n)$ seconds, for an appropriate constant c that depends on the implementation, if it is to run in a time in the order of $t(n)$: we implicitly had the worst case in mind.

Worst-case analysis is appropriate for an algorithm whose response time is critical. For example, if it is a question of controlling a nuclear power plant, it is crucial to know an upper limit on the system's response time, regardless of the particular instance to be solved. On the other hand, if an algorithm is to be used many times on many different instances, it may be more important to know the *average* execution time on instances of size n. We saw that the time taken by the insertion sort algorithm varies between the order of n and the order of n^2. If we can calculate the average time taken by the algorithm on the $n!$ different ways of initially ordering n distinct elements, we shall have an idea of the likely time taken to sort an array initially in random order. We shall see in Section 4.5 that if the $n!$ initial permutations are equally likely, then this average time is also in the order of n^2. Insertion sorting thus takes quadratic time both on the average and in the worst case, although for some instances it can be much faster. In Section 7.4.2 we shall see another sorting algorithm that also takes quadratic time in the worst case, but that requires only a time in the order of $n \log n$ on the average. Even though this algorithm has a bad worst case—quadratic performance is slow for a sorting algorithm—it is probably the fastest algorithm known on the average for an in-place sorting method, that is, one that does not require additional storage.

It is usually harder to analyse the average behaviour of an algorithm than to analyse its behaviour in the worst case. Furthermore, such an analysis of average ✓ behaviour can be misleading if in fact the instances to be solved are not chosen randomly when the algorithm is used in practice. For example, we stated above that insertion sorting takes quadratic time on the average when all the $n!$ possible initial arrangements of the elements are equally probable. However in many applications this condition may be unrealistic. If a sorting program is used to update a file, for instance, it might mostly be asked to sort arrays whose elements are already nearly in order, with just a few new elements out of place. In this case its average behaviour on randomly chosen instances will be a poor guide to its real performance.

A useful analysis of the average behaviour of an algorithm therefore requires some a priori knowledge of the distribution of the instances to be solved. This is normally an unrealistic requirement. Especially when an algorithm is used as an internal procedure in some more complex algorithm, it may be impractical to estimate which instances it is most likely to encounter, and which will only occur rarely. In Section 10.7, however, we shall see how this difficulty can be circumvented for certain algorithms, and their behaviour made independent of the specific instances to be solved.

In what follows we shall only be concerned with worst-case analyses unless stated otherwise.

2.5 What is an elementary operation?

An *elementary operation* is one whose execution time can be bounded above by a constant depending only on the particular implementation used—the machine, the programming language, and so on. Thus the constant does *not* depend on either the size or the other parameters of the instance being considered. Because we are concerned with execution times of algorithms defined to within a multiplicative constant, it is only the number of elementary operations executed that matters in the analysis, not the exact time required by each of them.

For example, suppose that when we analyse some algorithm, we find that to solve an instance of a certain size we need to carry out a additions, m multiplications, and s assignment instructions. Suppose we also know that an addition never takes longer than t_a microseconds, a multiplication never more than t_m microseconds, and an assignment never more than t_s microseconds, where t_a, t_m and t_s are constants depending on the machine used. Addition, multiplication and assignment can therefore all be considered as elementary operations. The total time t required by our algorithm can by bounded by

$$t \leq at_a + mt_m + st_s$$
$$\leq \max(t_a, t_m, t_s) \times (a + m + s),$$

that is, t is bounded by a constant multiple of the number of elementary operations to be executed.

Since the exact time required by each elementary operation is unimportant, we simplify by saying that elementary operations can be executed *at unit cost.*

In the description of an algorithm, a single line of program may correspond to a variable number of elementary operations. For example, if T is an array of n elements ($n > 0$), the time required to compute

$$x \leftarrow \min \{T[i] \mid 1 \leq i \leq n\}$$

increases with n, since this is an abbreviation for

```
x ← T[1]
for i ← 2 to n do
    if T[i] < x then x ← T[i].
```

Similarly, some mathematical operations are too complex to be considered elementary. If we allowed ourselves to count the evaluation of a factorial and a test for divisibility at unit cost, regardless of the size of the operands, Wilson's theorem (which states that the integer n divides $(n-1)! + 1$ if and only if n is prime for all $n > 1$) would let us test an integer for primality with astonishing efficiency:

```
function Wilson(n)
    {Returns true if and only if n is prime, n > 1}
    if n divides (n − 1)! + 1 exactly then return true
    else return false
```

The example at the beginning of this section suggested that we can consider addition and multiplication to be unit cost operations, since it assumed that the time required for these operations could be bounded by a constant. In theory, however, these operations are not elementary since the time needed to execute them increases with the length of the operands. In practice, on the other hand, it may be sensible to consider them as elementary operations so long as the operands concerned are of a reasonable size in the instances we expect to encounter. Two examples will illustrate what we mean.

function *Sum(n)*
    {Calculates the sum of the integers from 1 to n}
    sum $\leftarrow$ 0
    for $i \leftarrow 1$ **to** n **do** *sum* $\leftarrow$ *sum* + *i*
    return *sum*

function *Fibonacci(n)*
    {Calculates the n–th term of the Fibonacci sequence;
      see Section 1.6.4}
    $i \leftarrow 1; j \leftarrow 1$
    for $k \leftarrow 1$ **to** n **do** $j \leftarrow i + j$
                        $i \leftarrow j - i$
    return *j*

In the algorithm called *Sum* the value of *sum* stays reasonable for all the instances that the algorithm can realistically be expected to meet in practice. If we are using a machine with 32-bit words, all the additions can be executed directly provided n is no greater than 65 535. In theory, however, the algorithm should work for *all* possible values of n. No real machine can in fact execute these additions at unit cost if n is chosen sufficiently large. The analysis of the algorithm must therefore depend on its intended domain of application.

The situation is different in the case of *Fibonnaci*. Here it suffices to take $n = 47$ to have the last addition "$j \leftarrow i + j$" cause arithmetic overflow on a 32-bit machine. To hold the result corresponding to $n = 65\,535$ we would need 45 496 bits, or more than 1420 computer words. It is therefore not realistic, as a practical matter, to consider that these additions can be carried out at unit cost. Rather, we must attribute to them a cost proportional to the length of the operands concerned. In Section 4.2.2 this algorithm is shown to take quadratic time, even though at first glance its execution time appears to be linear.

In the case of multiplication it may still be reasonable to consider this an elementary operation for sufficiently small operands. However it is easier to produce large operands by repeated multiplication than by addition, so it is even more important to ensure that arithmetic operations do not overflow. Furthermore, when the operands do start to get large, the time required to perform an addition grows linearly with the size of the operands, but the time required to perform a multiplication is believed to grow faster than this.

A similar problem can arise when we analyse algorithms involving real numbers if the required precision increases with the size of the instances to be solved.

One typical example of this phenomenon is the use of de Moivre's formula (see Problem 1.27) to calculate values in the Fibonacci sequence. This formula tells us that f_n, the n–th term in the sequence, is approximately equal to $\phi^n / \sqrt{5}$, where $\phi = (1 + \sqrt{5})/2$ is the *golden ratio*. The approximation is good enough that we can in principle obtain the exact value of f_n by simply taking the nearest integer; see Problem 2.23. However we saw above that 45 496 bits are required to represent f_{65535} accurately. This means that we would have to calculate the approximation with the same degree of accuracy to obtain the exact answer. Ordinary single or double precision floating-point arithmetic, using one or two computer words, would certainly not be accurate enough. In most practical situations, however, the use of single or double precision floating-point arithmetic proves satisfactory, despite the inevitable loss of precision. When this is so, it is reasonable to count such arithmetic operations at unit cost.

To sum up, even deciding whether an instruction as apparently innocuous as "$j \leftarrow i + j$" can be considered as elementary or not calls for the use of judgement. In what follows, we shall consider additions, subtractions, multiplications, divisions, modulo operations, Boolean operations, comparisons and assignments to be elementary operations that can be executed at unit cost unless we explicitly state otherwise.

2.6 Why look for efficiency?

As computing equipment gets faster and faster, it may hardly seem worthwhile to spend our time trying to design more efficient algorithms. Would it not be easier simply to wait for the next generation of computers? The principles established in the preceding sections show that this is not true. Suppose, to illustrate the argument, that to solve a particular problem you have available an exponential algorithm and a computer that can run this algorithm on instances of size n in $10^{-4} \times 2^n$ seconds. Your program can thus solve an instance of size 10 in $10^{-4} \times 2^{10}$ seconds, or about one-tenth of a second. Solving an instance of size 20 will take about a thousand times as long, or nearly two minutes. To solve an instance of size 30 would take a thousand times as long again, so that even a whole day's computing would not be sufficient. Supposing you were able to run your computer without interruption, and without errors, for a year, you would only just be able to solve an instance of size 38; see Problem 2.15.

Suppose you need to solve bigger instances than this, and that with the money available you can afford to buy a new computer one hundred times faster than the first. With the same algorithm you can now solve an instance of size n in only $10^{-6} \times 2^n$ seconds. You may feel you have wasted your money, however, when you figure out that now, when you run your new machine for a whole year, you cannot even solve an instance of size 45. In general, if you were previously able to solve an instance of size n in some given time, your new machine will solve instances of size at best $n + \lg 100$, or about $n + 7$, in the same time.

Suppose you decide instead to invest in algorithmics, and that, having spent the same amount of money, you have managed to find a cubic algorithm to solve your problem. Imagine, for example, that using the original machine and the new algorithm you can solve an instance of size n in $10^{-2} \times n^3$ seconds. Thus to solve an instance of size 10 will take you 10 seconds, and an instance of size 20 will still require between one and two minutes. But now an instance of size 30 can be solved in four and a half minutes, and in one day you can solve instances whose size is greater than 200; with one year's computation you can almost reach size 1500. This is illustrated by Figure 2.1.

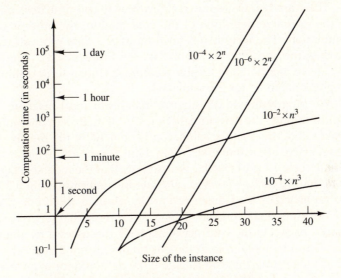

Figure 2.1. Algorithmics versus hardware

Not only does the new algorithm offer a much greater improvement than the purchase of new hardware, it will also, supposing you are able to afford both, make such a purchase much more profitable. If you can use both your new algorithm and a machine one hundred times faster than the old one, then you will be able to solve instances four or five times bigger than with the new algorithm alone, in the same length of time—the exact factor is $\sqrt[3]{100}$. Compare this to the situation with the old algorithm, where you could *add* 7 to the size of the instance; here you can *multiply* the size of the instance by four or five. Nevertheless the new algorithm should not be used uncritically on all instances of the problem, in particular on rather small ones. We saw above that on the original machine the new algorithm takes 10 seconds to solve an instance of size 10, which is one hundred times *slower* than the old algorithm. The new algorithm is faster only for instances of size 20 or greater. Naturally, it is possible to combine the two algorithms into a third one that looks at the size of the instance to be solved before deciding which method to use.

2.7 Some examples

Maybe you are wondering whether it is really possible in practice to speed up an algorithm to the extent suggested in the previous section. In fact, there have been cases where even more spectacular improvements have been made, even for well-established algorithms.

2.7.1 Calculating determinants

Determinants are important in linear algebra, and we need to know how to calculate them efficiently. In our context, they provide the best example of the difference that a good algorithm can make, when compared to another *classic* algorithm. (You do not have to know what a determinant is to enjoy this section.)

There are two well-known algorithms to compute determinants. One is based on the recursive definition of the determinant; the other is called Gauss–Jordan elimination. The recursive algorithm takes a time proportional to $n!$ to compute the determinant of an $n \times n$ matrix; see Problem 1.31. This is even worse than taking exponential time. In sharp contrast, Gauss–Jordan elimination takes a time proportional to n^3 for the same task.

We programmed both algorithms on our local machine. The Gauss–Jordan algorithm finds the determinant of a 10×10 matrix in one-hundredth of a second; it takes about five and a half seconds on a 100×100 matrix. On the other hand, the recursive algorithm takes more than 20 seconds on a mere 5×5 matrix and 10 minutes on a 10×10 matrix. We estimate that the recursive algorithm would need more than 10 million *years* to calculate the determinant of a 20×20 matrix, a task accomplished by the Gauss–Jordan algorithm in about one-twentieth of a second!

You should *not* conclude from this example that recursive algorithms are necessarily bad. On the contrary, Chapter 7 discusses a technique where recursion plays a fundamental role in the design of efficient algorithms. In particular, a recursive algorithm that can calculate the determinant of an $n \times n$ matrix in a time proportional to $n^{\lg 7}$, or about $n^{2.81}$, follows from Strassen's work, thus proving that Gauss–Jordan elimination is not optimal.

2.7.2 Sorting

The sorting problem is of major importance in computer science, and in particular in algorithmics. We are required to arrange in order a collection of n objects on which a *total ordering* is defined. By this we mean that when we compare any two objects in the collection, we know which should come first. For many kinds of objects, this requirement is trivial: obviously 123 comes before 456 in numerical order, and 1 August 1991 comes before 25 December 1995 in calendar order, so that both integers and dates are totally ordered. For other, equally common objects, though, defining a total order may not be so easy. For example, how do you order two complex numbers? Does "general" come before or after "General" in alphabetical order, or are they the same word (see Problem 2.16)? Neither of these questions has an obvious answer, but until an answer is found the corresponding objects cannot be sorted.

Sorting problems are often found inside more complex algorithms. We have already seen two standard sorting algorithms in Section 2.4: insertion sorting and selection sorting. Both these algorithms, as we saw, take quadratic time both in the worst case and on the average. Although they are excellent when n is small, other sorting algorithms are more efficient when n is large. Among others, we might use Williams's *heapsort* algorithm (see Section 5.7), *mergesort* (see Section 7.4.1), or Hoare's *quicksort* algorithm (see Section 7.4.2). All these algorithms take a time in the order of $n \log n$ on the average; the first two take a time in the same order even in the worst case.

To have a clearer idea of the practical difference between a time in the order of n^2 and a time in the order of $n \log n$, we programmed the insertion sort algorithm and *quicksort* on our local machine. The difference in efficiency between the two algorithms is marginal when the number of elements to be sorted is small. *Quicksort* is already almost twice as fast as insertion when sorting 50 elements, and three times as fast when sorting 100 elements. To sort 1000 elements, insertion takes more than three seconds, whereas *quicksort* requires less than one-fifth of a second. When we have 5000 elements to sort, the inefficiency of insertion sorting becomes still more pronounced: one and a half minutes are needed on average, compared to little more than one second for *quicksort*. In 30 seconds, *quicksort* can handle 100 000 elements; we estimate it would take nine and a half hours to do the same job using insertion sorting.

We shall see in Chapter 12 that no sorting algorithm that proceeds by comparing the elements to be sorted can be faster than the order of $n \log n$, so that in this sense *heapsort*, *mergesort* and *quicksort* are as fast as an algorithm can be (although *quicksort* has a bad worst case). Of course their actual running times depend on the hidden multiplicative constants in the definition of "the order of." Other, faster sorting algorithms can be found in special cases, however. Suppose for instance that the elements to be sorted are integers known to lie between 1 and 10 000. Then the following algorithm can be used.

```
procedure pigeonhole(T[1 .. n])
    {Sorts integers between 1 and 10000}
    array U[1 .. 10000]
    for k ← 1 to 10000 do U[k] ← 0
    for i ← 1 to n do
        k ← T[i]
        U[k] ← U[k]+1
    i ← 0
    for k ← 1 to 10000 do
        while U[k] ≠ 0 do
            i ← i + 1
            T[i] ← k
            U[k] ← U[k]-1
```

Here U is an array of "pigeon-holes" for the elements to be sorted. There must be a separate pigeon-hole for every possible element that might be found in T. The first loop clears the pigeon-holes, the second puts each element of T into the appropriate place, and the third pulls them out again in ascending order. It is easy to show (see Problem 2.17) that this algorithm and its variants take a time in the order of n. (The hidden multiplicative constant depends on the bound on the value of the elements to be sorted, here 10 000.) When they are applicable they therefore beat any algorithm that works by comparing elements; on the other hand, the requirement that we should be able to use one pigeon-hole for every possible key means that they are applicable far less often than the general sorting methods.

Parallel sorting methods, which use many processors to carry out several comparisons simultaneously, allow us to go faster still. An example of a parallel sorting algorithm is outlined in Chapter 11.

2.7.3 Multiplication of large integers

When a calculation requires very large integers to be manipulated, it can happen that the operands become too long to be held in a single word of the computer in use. Such operations thereupon cease to be elementary. When this occurs, we can use a representation such as Fortran's "double precision", or, more generally, multiple-precision arithmetic. Most object-oriented programming languages, such as C++ or Smalltalk, have predefined classes that make this easy. Now, however, we must ask ourselves how the time necessary to add, subtract, multiply or divide two large integers increases with the size of the operands. We can measure this size by either the number of computer words needed to represent the operands on a machine or the length of their representation in decimal or binary. Since these measures differ only by a multiplicative constant, this choice does not alter our analysis of the order of efficiency of the algorithms in question (but see Problem 2.18).

In this section we shall consider only the multiplication operation. Analysis of addition and subtraction is much simpler, and is left as Problem 2.19. Suppose then that two large integers of sizes m and n respectively are to be multiplied. (Do not confuse the size of the integers with their value!) The classic algorithm of Section 1.1 can easily be adapted to this context. We see that it multiplies each digit of one of the operands by each digit of the other, and that it executes approximately one elementary addition for each of these multiplications. (There are a few more, in fact, because of the carries that are generated.) On a machine we multiply each word of one of the operands by each word of the other, and then do about one double-length addition for each of these multiplications, but the principle is exactly the same. The time required is therefore in the order of mn. Multiplication *à la russe* also takes a time in the order of mn, provided we put the smaller operand in the left-hand column and the larger on the right; see Problem 2.20. Thus there is no reason for preferring it to the classic algorithm, particularly as the hidden constant is likely to be larger.

More efficient algorithms exist to solve the problem of multiplying two large integers. Divide-and-conquer, which we encountered in Section 1.2, and which we shall study further in Section 7.1, takes a time in the order of $nm^{\lg(3/2)}$, or approximately $nm^{0.59}$, where n is the size of the larger operand and m is the size of the smaller. If both operands are of size n, the algorithm thus takes a time in the order of $n^{1.59}$, which is preferable to the quadratic time taken by both the classic algorithm and multiplication *à la russe*.

The difference between the order of n^2 and the order of $n^{1.59}$ is less spectacular than that between the order of n^2 and the order of $n \log n$, which we saw in the case of sorting algorithms. To verify this, we programmed the classic algorithm and the divide-and-conquer algorithm, and tested them on operands of different sizes. The theoretically better divide-and-conquer algorithm gives little real improvement on 600–figure numbers: it takes about 300 milliseconds, whereas the classic algorithm takes about 400 milliseconds. For operands ten times this length, however, the fast algorithm is some three times more efficient than the classic algorithm: they take about 15 seconds and 40 seconds, respectively. The gain in efficiency continues to increase as the size of the operands goes up.

More sophisticated algorithms exist, the fastest at present taking a time in the order of $n \log n \log \log n$ to multiply two integers of size n. However these more sophisticated algorithms are largely of theoretical interest; the hidden constants involved are such that they only become competitive for *much* larger operands. For "small" instances involving operands with only a few thousand decimal digits, they are considerably slower than the algorithms mentioned above.

2.7.4 Calculating the greatest common divisor

Let m and n be two positive integers. The greatest common divisor of m and n, denoted by $\gcd(m, n)$, is the largest integer that divides both m and n exactly. When $\gcd(m, n) = 1$, we say that m and n are *coprime*. For example, $\gcd(10, 21) = 1$ and $\gcd(6, 15) = 3$, so 10 and 21 are coprime, but 6 and 15 are not. The obvious algorithm for calculating $\gcd(m, n)$ is obtained directly from the definition.

> **function** $\gcd(m, n)$
> $\quad i \leftarrow \min(m, n) + 1$
> $\quad$ **repeat** $i \leftarrow i - 1$ **until** i divides both m and n exactly
> $\quad$ **return** i

The time taken by this algorithm is in the order of the difference between the smaller of the two arguments and their greatest common divisor. When m and n are of similar size and coprime, it therefore takes a time in the order of n. (Notice that this is the *value* of the operand, not its size.)

A classic algorithm for calculating $\gcd(m, n)$ consists of first factorizing m and n, and then taking the product of the prime factors common to m and n, each prime factor being raised to the lower of its powers in the two arguments. For example, to calculate $\gcd(120, 700)$ we first factorize $120 = 2^3 \times 3 \times 5$ and $700 = 2^2 \times 5^2 \times 7$. The common factors of 120 and 700 are therefore 2 and 5, and their lower powers are 2 and 1, respectively. The greatest common divisor of 120 and 700 is therefore $2^2 \times 5 = 20$.

Even though this algorithm is better than the one given previously, it requires us to factorize m and n, an operation nobody knows how to do efficiently when m and n are large; see Section 10.7.4. In fact there exists a much more efficient algorithm for calculating greatest common divisors, known as Euclid's algorithm, even though it can be traced back well before the time of the ancient Greeks.

> **function** *Euclid*(m, n)
> $\quad$ **while** $m > 0$ **do**
> $\quad\quad t \leftarrow m$
> $\quad\quad m \leftarrow n \bmod m$
> $\quad\quad n \leftarrow t$
> $\quad$ **return** n

If we consider the arithmetic operations involved to have unit cost, this algorithm takes a time in the order of the logarithm of its arguments—that is, in the order of their size—even in the worst case; see Section 4.4. To be historically exact, Euclid's original algorithm works using successive subtractions rather than by calculating a modulo. In this form it is more than 3500 years old.

2.7.5 Calculating the Fibonacci sequence

The Fibonacci sequence was introduced in Section 1.6.4. We remind the reader that the terms of this sequence are defined by the following recurrence:

$$\begin{cases} f_0 = 0; \; f_1 = 1 & \text{and} \\ f_n = f_{n-1} + f_{n-2} & \text{for } n \geq 2. \end{cases}$$

As we saw, the sequence begins 0, 1, 1, 2, 3, 5, 8, 13, 21, 34 ... We also saw de Moivre's formula

$$f_n = \frac{1}{\sqrt{5}} [\phi^n - (-\phi)^{-n}],$$

where $\phi = (1 + \sqrt{5})/2$ is the *golden ratio*, and we pointed out that the term $(-\phi)^{-n}$ can be neglected when n is large. Hence the value of f_n is in the order of ϕ^n, and therefore the size of f_n is in the order of n. However, de Moivre's formula is of little immediate help in calculating f_n exactly, since the larger n becomes, the greater is the degree of precision required in the values of $\sqrt{5}$ and ϕ; see Section 2.5. On our local machine, a single-precision computation produces an error for the first time when calculating f_{66}.

The recursive algorithm obtained directly from the definition of the Fibonacci sequence was given in Section 1.6.4 under the name *Fibonacci*.

> **function** *Fibrec*(n)
>   **if** $n < 2$ **then return** n
>   **else return** *Fibrec*($n - 1$)+*Fibrec*($n - 2$)

This algorithm is very inefficient because it recalculates the same values many times. For instance, to calculate *Fibrec*(5) we need the values of *Fibrec*(4) and *Fibrec*(3); but *Fibrec*(4) also calls for the calculation of *Fibrec*(3). It is simple to check that *Fibrec*(3) will be calculated twice, *Fibrec*(2) three times, *Fibrec*(1) five times, and *Fibrec*(0) three times. (The number of calls of *Fibrec*(5), *Fibrec*(4), ..., *Fibrec*(1), are thus 1, 1, 2, 3 and 5 respectively. It is no coincidence that this is the beginning of the Fibonacci sequence; see Problem 2.24.)

In fact, the time required to calculate f_n using this algorithm is in the order of the value of f_n itself, that is, in the order of ϕ^n. To see this, note that the recursive calls only stop when *Fibrec* returns a value 0 or 1. Adding these intermediate results to obtain the final result f_n must take at least f_n operations, and hence the complete algorithm certainly takes a number of elementary operations at least in the order of f_n. This was proven formally by constructive induction in Section 1.6.4, together with a proof that the number of operations required is not more than the order of f_n provided the additions are counted at unit cost. The case when additions are not counted at unit cost yields the same conclusion, as the more precise analysis given in Section 4.2.3 shows.

To avoid wastefully calculating the same values over and over, it is natural to proceed as in Section 2.5, where a different algorithm *Fibonacci* was introduced, which we rename *Fibiter* for comparison with *Fibrec*.

> **function** *Fibiter*(n)
> $i \leftarrow 1;\ j \leftarrow 0$
>   **for** $k \leftarrow 1$ **to** n **do** $j \leftarrow i + j$
> $i \leftarrow j - i$
> **return** j

This second algorithm takes a time in the order of n, assuming we count each addition as an elementary operation. Figure 2.2, which shows some computation times we observed in practice, illustrates the difference. To avoid the problems caused by ever-longer operands, the computations reported in this figure were carried out modulo 10^7, which is to say that we only computed the seven least significant figures of the answer. The times for *Fibrec* when $n \geq 50$ were estimated using the hybrid approach.

n	10	20	30	50	100
Fibrec	8 msec	1 sec	2 min	21 days	10^9 years
Fibiter	$\frac{1}{6}$ msec	$\frac{1}{3}$ msec	$\frac{1}{2}$ msec	$\frac{3}{4}$ msec	$1\frac{1}{2}$ msec

Figure 2.2. Comparison of modulo 10^7 Fibonacci algorithms

If we do not make the assumption that addition is an elementary operation, *Fibiter* takes a time in the order of n^2, which is still much faster than the exponential-time *Fibrec*. Surprisingly, there exists a third algorithm that gives as great an improvement over *Fibiter* as *Fibiter* does over *Fibrec*. This third algorithm takes a time in the order of the logarithm of n, provided we count arithmetic operations at unit cost. Otherwise the new algorithm is still faster than *Fibiter*, but less spectacularly so; see Problem 7.33.

2.7.6 Fourier transforms

The *Fast Fourier Transform* algorithm is perhaps the one algorithmic discovery that has had the greatest practical impact in history. Fourier transforms are of fundamental importance in such disparate applications as optics, acoustics, quantum physics, telecommunications, systems theory and signal processing including speech recognition. For years, progress in these areas was limited by the fact that the known algorithms for calculating Fourier transforms all took far too long.

The "discovery" by Cooley and Tukey in 1965 of a fast algorithm revolutionized the situation: problems previously considered infeasible could now at last be tackled. In one early test of the "new" algorithm, the Fourier transform was used to analyse data from an earthquake that had taken place in Alaska in 1964. While the classic algorithm took more than 26 minutes of computation, the "new" algorithm was able to perform the same task in less than two and a half seconds.

Ironically it turned out that an efficient algorithm had already been published in 1942 by Danielson and Lanczos, and all the necessary theoretical groundwork for Danielson and Lanczos's algorithm had been published by Runge and König in 1924. And if *that* were not sufficient, Gauss describes a similar algorithm in a paper written around 1805 and published posthumously in 1866!

2.8 When is an algorithm specified?

At the beginning of the book we said that execution of an algorithm must not normally involve any subjective decisions, nor must it call for the use of intuition or creativity; later on, we said that we should almost always be content to prove that our algorithms are correct in the abstract, ignoring practical limitations; and later still, we proposed to consider most arithmetic operations to be elementary unless we explicitly stated otherwise.

This is all very well, but what should we do if practical considerations force us to abandon this convenient position, and to take account of the limitations of the available machinery? For instance, any algorithm that is to compute the exact value of f_{100} will be forced to consider that certain arithmetic operations—certainly addition, and possibly multiplication as well (see Problem 7.33)—are not elementary (recall that f_{100} is a number with 21 decimal digits). Most probably this will be taken into account by using a program package that allows arithmetic operations on very large integers. If we do not specify exactly how the package should implement multiple-precision arithmetic, then the choice of a method to use can be considered to be a subjective decision, and the proposed algorithm will be incompletely specified. Does this matter?

The answer is that yes, in certain cases it does. Later in the book we shall come across algorithms whose performance does indeed depend on the method they use to multiply large integers. For such algorithms (and formally speaking, for *any* algorithm) it is not sufficient simply to write an instruction like $x \leftarrow y \times z$, leaving the reader to choose any technique that comes to hand to implement this multiplication. To completely specify the algorithm, we must also specify how the necessary arithmetic operations are to be implemented.

To make life simpler, however, we shall continue to use the word *algorithm* for certain incomplete descriptions of this kind. The details will be filled in later should our analyses require them.

2.9 Problems

Problem 2.1.   Find a more practical algorithm for calculating the date of Easter than the one given in Problem 1.2. What will be the date of Easter in the year 2000? What is the domain of definition of your algorithm?

Problem 2.2.   In the game of chess, your opponent's pieces and moves are all visible. We say that chess is a game with *complete information*. In games such as bridge or poker, however, you do not know how the cards have been dealt. Does this make it impossible to define an algorithm for playing good bridge or poker? Would such an algorithm necessarily be probabilistic?

What about backgammon? Here you can see your opponent's pieces and moves, but you cannot predict how the dice will fall on future throws. Does this alter the situation?

Problem 2.3.   It is sometimes claimed that nowadays hardware is so cheap and manpower ("liveware") so expensive that it is never worth wasting a programmer's time to shave a few seconds off the running time of a program. Does this mean that algorithmics is fated to be a theoretical pursuit of formal interest only, with no practical applications? Justify your answer.

Problem 2.4.   Using the technique called "virtual memory", it is possible to free a programmer from most worries about the actual size of the storage available on his machine. Does this mean that the quantity of storage used by an algorithm is never of interest in practice? Justify your answer.

Problem 2.5.   Suppose you measure the performance of a program, perhaps using some kind of run-time trace, and then you optimize the heavily-used parts of the code. However, you are careful not to change the underlying algorithm. Would you expect to obtain (a) a gain in efficiency by a constant factor, whatever the problem being solved, or (b) a gain in efficiency that gets proportionally greater as the problem size increases? Justify your answer.

Problem 2.6.   A sorting algorithm takes 1 second to sort 1000 items on your local machine. How long would you expect it to take to sort 10 000 items (a) if you believe that the algorithm takes a time roughly proportional to n^2, and (b) if you believe that the algorithm takes a time roughly proportional to $n \log n$?

Problem 2.7.   Two algorithms take n^2 days and n^3 seconds respectively to solve an instance of size n. Show that it is only on instances requiring more than 20 million years to solve that the quadratic algorithm outperforms the cubic algorithm.

Problem 2.8.   Two algorithms take n^2 days and 2^n seconds respectively to solve an instance of size n. What is the size of the smallest instance on which the former algorithm outperforms the latter? Approximately how long does such an instance take to solve?

Problem 2.9.   Simulate both the insertion sort and the selection sort algorithms of Section 2.4 on the following two arrays: $U = [1, 2, 3, 4, 5, 6]$ and $V = [6, 5, 4, 3, 2, 1]$. Does insertion sorting run faster on the array U or the array V? And selection sorting? Justify your answers.

Problem 2.10.   Suppose you try to "sort" an array $W = [1, 1, 1, 1, 1, 1]$ all of whose elements are equal, using (a) insertion sorting and (b) selection sorting. How does this compare to sorting the arrays U and V of the previous problem?

Problem 2.11.   You are required to sort a file containing integers between 0 and 999 999. You cannot afford to use one million pigeon-holes, so you decide instead to use one thousand pigeon-holes numbered from 0 to 999. You begin the sort by putting each integer into the pigeon-hole corresponding to its first three figures. Next you use insertion sorting one thousand times to sort the contents of each pigeon-hole separately, and finally you empty the pigeon-holes in order to obtain a completely sorted sequence.

Would you expect this technique to be faster, slower or the same as simply using insertion sorting on the whole sequence (a) on the average, and (b) in the worst case? Justify your answers.

Problem 2.12.   Is it reasonable, as a practical matter, to consider division as an elementary operation (a) always, (b) sometimes, or (c) never? Justify your answer. If you think it necessary, you may treat the division of integers and the division of real numbers separately.

Problem 2.13.   Suppose n is an integer variable in a program you are writing. Consider the instruction $x \leftarrow \sin(n)$, where n may be supposed to be in radians. As a practical matter, would you regard the execution of this instruction as an elementary operation (a) always, (b) sometimes, or (c) never? Justify your answer. What about the instruction $x \leftarrow \sin(n\pi)$?

Problem 2.14.   In Section 2.5, we saw that Wilson's theorem could be used to test any number for primality in constant time if factorials and tests for integer divisibility were counted at unit cost, regardless of the size of the numbers involved. Clearly this would be unreasonable.

Use Wilson's theorem together with Newton's binomial theorem to design an algorithm capable of deciding in a time in the order of $\log n$ whether or not an integer n is prime, provided additions, multiplications and tests for integer divisibility are counted at unit cost, but factorials and exponentials are not. The point of this exercise is *not* to provide a useful algorithm, but to demonstrate that it is unreasonable to consider multiplications as elementary operations in general.

Problem 2.15.   A certain algorithm takes $10^{-4} \times 2^n$ seconds to solve an instance of size n. Show that in a year it could just solve an instance of size 38. What size of instance could be solved in a year on a machine one hundred times as fast?

A second algorithm takes $10^{-2} \times n^3$ seconds to solve an instance of size n. What size instance can it solve in a year? What size instance could be solved in a year on a machine one hundred times as fast?

Show that the second algorithm is nevertheless slower than the first for instances of size less than 20.

Problem 2.16.   Suppose for the moment that a word is defined as a string of letters with no intervening spaces or punctuation, so that "can't" is considered as two words, and "jack-in-a-box" as four. You want to sort a file of such words. Devise an algorithm which, given any two strings of letters, decides whether or not they represent the same word, and if not, which should come first. What would your algorithm do with (a) "MacKay" and "Mackay," and (b) "anchorage" and

"Anchorage"? A self-respecting algorithm should certainly *not* put "Mackay" and "Anchorage" before "aardvark" or after "zymurgy."

For a much harder problem, devise an algorithm for comparing entries in the telephone book. This must deal with all kinds of odd strings, including punctuation ("E-Z Cleaners"), numbers ("A–1 Pharmacy"), accents and other diacritics ("Adèle Nuñez"), and abbreviations ("St Catherine St. Tavern"). How does the telephone company do it?

Problem 2.17.   Show that pigeon-hole sorting takes a time in the order of n to sort n elements that are within bounds.

Problem 2.18.   In Section 2.7.3 we said that the analysis of algorithms for large integers is not affected by the choice of a measure for the size of the operands: the number of computer words needed, or the length of their representation in decimal or binary will do equally well. Show that this remark would in fact be false were we considering exponential-time algorithms.

Problem 2.19.   How much time is required to add or subtract two large integers of size m and n respectively? Sketch the appropriate algorithm.

Problem 2.20.   How much time is required to multiply two large integers of size m and n, respectively, using multiplication *à la russe* (a) if the smaller operand is in the left-hand column, and (b) if the larger operand is in the left-hand column? Of course you should *not* take addition, doubling and halving to be elementary operations in this problem.

Problem 2.21.   How much time is required to multiply two large integers of size m and n, respectively, using multiplication round a rectangle (see Problem 1.9).

Problem 2.22.   Calculate gcd(606, 979) (a) by factorizing 606 and 979, and picking out the common factors to the appropriate power, and (b) using Euclid's algorithm.

Problem 2.23.   Use de Moivre's formula for f_n to show that f_n is the nearest integer to $\phi^n/\sqrt{5}$ for all $n \geq 1$.

Problem 2.24.   Show that when calculating f_n using *Fibrec* from Section 2.7.5, there are in all f_{n+1-i} calls of *Fibrec*(i) for $i = 1, 2, \ldots, n$, and f_{n-1} calls of *Fibrec*(0).

Problem 2.25.   Let $g(n)$ be the number of ways to write a string of n zeros and ones so that there are never two successive zeros. For example, when $n = 1$ the possible strings are 0 and 1, so $g(1) = 2$; when $n = 2$ the possible strings are 01, 11 and 10, so $g(2) = 3$; when $n = 3$ the possible strings are 010, 011, 101, 110 and 111, so $g(3) = 5$. Show that $g(n) = f_{n+2}$.

2.10 References and further reading

To reinforce our remarks on the importance of designing efficient algorithms, we encourage the reader to look at Bentley (1984), which offers experimental proof that intelligent use of algorithmics may allow a TRS–80 to run rings round a CRAY–1!

An algorithm capable of calculating the determinant of an $n \times n$ matrix in a time in the order of $n^{2.81}$ follows from the work of Strassen (1969) and Bunch and Hopcroft (1974). Several sorting algorithms are discussed in this book; Knuth (1973) is much more thorough on this topic. The divide-and-conquer algorithm that can multiply n-figure numbers in a time in the order of $n^{1.59}$ is attributed to Karatsuba and Ofman (1962); it is described in detail in Chapter 7. A faster large integer multiplication algorithm, due to Schönhage and Strassen (1971), runs in a time in the order of $n \log n \log \log n$; see Brassard, Monet and Zuffellato (1986) for more details. Euclid's algorithm can be found in Book VII of Euclid's *Elements*: see Heath (1926). The fast algorithm for calculating the Fibonacci sequence alluded to at the end of Section 2.7.5 is explained in Gries and Levin (1980) and Urbanek (1980); see also Brassard and Bratley (1988) for a race between this fast algorithm and those given in Section 2.7.5.

The first published algorithm for calculating discrete Fourier transforms efficiently is by Danielson and Lanczos (1942). These authors mention that the source of their method goes back to Runge and König (1924). In view of the great practical importance of Fourier transforms, it is astonishing that the existence of a fast algorithm remained almost entirely unknown until its rediscovery nearly a quarter of a century later by Cooley and Tukey (1965). For a more complete account of the history of the fast Fourier transform, read Cooley, Lewis and Welch (1967). More details and applications to fast integer multiplication and symbolic polynomial arithmetic are provided in Brassard and Bratley (1988).

A solution to Problem 2.1 attributed to Gauss can be found in either Larousse (1968) or Kirkerud (1989); see also the *Book of Common Prayer*, available in any Anglican church. The solution to Problem 2.14 is given by Shamir (1979).

Chapter 3

Asymptotic Notation

3.1 Introduction

An important aspect of this book concerns determining the efficiency of algorithms. In Section 2.3, we saw that this may, for instance, help us choose among several competing algorithms. Recall that we wish to determine mathematically the quantity of resources needed by an algorithm as a function of the size (or occasionally of the value) of the instances considered. Because there is no standard computer to which all measurements of *computing time* might refer, we saw also in Section 2.3 that we shall be content to express the time taken by an algorithm to within a multiplicative constant. To this end, we now introduce formally the *asymptotic notation* used throughout the book. In addition, this notation permits substantial simplifications even when we are interested in measuring something more tangible than computing time, such as the number of times a given instruction in a program is executed.

This notation is called "asymptotic" because it deals with the behaviour of functions in the limit, that is for sufficiently large values of its parameter. Accordingly, arguments based on asymptotic notation may fail to have practical value when the parameter takes "real-life" values. Nevertheless, the teachings of asymptotic notation are usually of significant relevance. This is because, as a rule of thumb, an asymptotically superior algorithm is very often (albeit not always) preferable even on instances of moderate size.

3.2 A notation for "the order of"

Let $t : \mathbb{N} \to \mathbb{R}^{\geq 0}$ be an arbitrary function from the natural numbers to the nonnegative reals, such as $t(n) = 27n^2 + \frac{355}{113}n + 12$. You may think of n as representing the size of the instance on which a given algorithm is required to perform, and of

$t(n)$ as representing the quantity of a given resource spent on that instance by a particular implementation of this algorithm. For example, it could be that the implementation spends $t(n)$ microseconds in the worst case on an instance of size n, or perhaps $t(n)$ represents the amount of storage. As we have seen, the function $t(n)$ may well depend on the implementation rather than uniquely on the algorithm. Recall however the principle of invariance, which says that the *ratio* of the running times of two different implementations of the same algorithm is always bounded above and below by fixed constants. (The constants may depend on the implementations but not on the size of the instance.)

Now, consider another function $f : \mathbb{N} \rightarrow \mathbb{R}^{\geq 0}$ such as $f(n) = n^2$. We say that $t(n)$ is *in the order of* $f(n)$ if $t(n)$ is bounded above by a positive real multiple of $f(n)$ for all sufficiently large n. Mathematically, this means that there exist a positive real constant c and an integer *threshold* n_0 such that $t(n) \leq c f(n)$ whenever $n \geq n_0$.

For instance, consider the functions $f(n)$ and $t(n)$ defined above. It is clear that both $n \leq n^2$ and $1 \leq n^2$ whenever $n \geq 1$. Therefore, provided $n \geq 1$,

$$
\begin{aligned}
t(n) &= 27n^2 + \frac{355}{113} n + 12 \\
&\leq 27n^2 + \frac{355}{113} n^2 + 12n^2 \\
&= 42\frac{16}{113} n^2 = 42\frac{16}{113} f(n).
\end{aligned}
$$

Taking $c = 42\frac{16}{113}$ (or anything larger) and $n_0 = 1$, we therefore conclude that $t(n)$ is in the order of $f(n)$ since $t(n) \leq c f(n)$ whenever $n \geq n_0$. It is easy to see that we could just as well have chosen $c = 28$ and $n_0 = 6$. Such a tradeoff between the smallest possible value for n_0 and that for c is common.

Thus, if an implementation of an algorithm takes in the worst case $27n^2 + \frac{355}{113} n + 12$ microseconds to solve an instance of size n, we may simplify by saying that the time is in the order of n^2. Naturally, there is no point stating that we are talking about the order of n^2 *microseconds* since this differs only by a constant factor from, say, n^2 years. More importantly, "the order of n^2" characterizes not only the time required by a particular implementation of the algorithm, but the time taken by *any* implementation (by the principle of invariance). Therefore, we are entitled to assert that *the algorithm itself* takes a time in the order of n^2 or, more simply, that it takes *quadratic time*.

It is convenient to have a mathematical symbol to denote *the order of*. Again, let $f : \mathbb{N} \rightarrow \mathbb{R}^{\geq 0}$ be an arbitrary function from the natural numbers to the nonnegative reals. We denote by $O(f(n))$—pronounced "big Oh of $f(n)$"—the *set* of all functions $t : \mathbb{N} \rightarrow \mathbb{R}^{\geq 0}$ such that $t(n) \leq c f(n)$ for all $n \geq n_0$ for some positive real constant c and integer threshold n_0. In other words,

$$
O(f(n)) = \{t : \mathbb{N} \rightarrow \mathbb{R}^{\geq 0} \mid (\exists c \in \mathbb{R}^+)(\overset{\infty}{\forall} n \in \mathbb{N})[t(n) \leq c f(n)]\}.
$$

Even though it is natural to use the set-theoretic symbol " $\in$ " to denote the fact that n^2 is in the order of n^3 as in " $n^2 \in O(n^3)$ ", be warned that the traditional notation for this is $n^2 = O(n^3)$. Therefore, do not be surprised if you find these so-called "one-way equalities" (for one would never write $O(n^3) = n^2$) in other books or scientific papers. Those using one-way equalities say that n^2 is *of* (or sometimes *on*) the order of n^3, or simply n^2 *is* $O(n^3)$. Another significant difference you may encounter in the definition of the O notation is that some writers allow $O(f(n))$ to include functions from the natural numbers to the entire set of reals—including negative reals—and define a function to be in $O(f(n))$ if its *absolute value* is in what we call $O(f(n))$.

For convenience, we allow ourselves to misuse the notation from time to time (as well as other notation introduced later in this chapter). For instance, we may say that $t(n)$ is in the order of $f(n)$ even if $t(n)$ is negative or undefined for a finite number of values of n. Similarly, we may talk about the order of $f(n)$ even if $f(n)$ is negative or undefined for a finite number of values of n. We shall say that $t(n) \in O(f(n))$ if there is a positive real constant c and integer threshold n_0 such that both $t(n)$ and $f(n)$ are well-defined and $0 \le t(n) \le cf(n)$ whenever $n \ge n_0$, regardless of what happens to these functions when $n < n_0$. For example, it is allowable to talk about the order of $n/\log n$, even though this function is not defined when $n = 0$ or $n = 1$, and it is correct to write $n^3 - 3n^2 - n - 8 \in O(n^3)$ even though $n^3 - 3n^2 - n - 8 < 0$ when $n \le 3$.

The threshold n_0 is often useful to simplify arguments, but it is never necessary when we consider *strictly* positive functions. Let $f, t : \mathbb{N} \to \mathbb{R}^+$ be two functions from the natural numbers to the strictly positive reals. The **threshold rule** states that $t(n) \in O(f(n))$ if and only if there exists a positive real constant c such that $t(n) \le cf(n)$ for *each* natural number n. One direction of the rule is obvious since any property that is true for each natural number is also true for each sufficiently large integer (simply take $n_0 = 0$ as the threshold). Assume for the other direction that $t(n) \in O(f(n))$. Let c and n_0 be the relevant constants such that $t(n) \le cf(n)$ whenever $n \ge n_0$. Assume $n_0 > 0$ since otherwise there is nothing to prove. Let $b = \max\{t(n)/f(n) \mid 0 \le n < n_0\}$ be the largest value taken by the ratio of t and f on natural numbers smaller than n_0 (this definition makes sense precisely because $f(n)$ cannot be zero and $n_0 > 0$). By definition of the maximum, $b \ge t(n)/f(n)$, and therefore $t(n) \le bf(n)$, whenever $0 \le n < n_0$. We already know that $t(n) \le cf(n)$ whenever $n \ge n_0$. Therefore $t(n) \le af(n)$ for each natural number n, as we had to prove, provided we choose a at least as large as both b and c, such as $a = \max(b, c)$. The threshold rule can be generalized to say that if $t(n) \in O(f(n))$ and if $f(n)$ is strictly positive for all $n \ge n_0$ for some n_0, then this n_0 can be used as the threshold for the O notation: there exists a positive real constant c such that $t(n) \le cf(n)$ for all $n \ge n_0$.

A useful tool for proving that one function is in the order of another is the **maximum rule**. Let $f, g : \mathbb{N} \to \mathbb{R}^{\ge 0}$ be two arbitrary functions from the natural numbers to the nonnegative reals. The maximum rule says that $O(f(n) + g(n)) = O(\max(f(n), g(n)))$. More specifically, let $p, q : \mathbb{N} \to \mathbb{R}^{\ge 0}$ be defined for each natural number n by $p(n) = f(n) + g(n)$ and $q(n) = \max(f(n), g(n))$, and consider an arbitrary function $t : \mathbb{N} \to \mathbb{R}^{\geq 0}$. The maximum rule says that $t(n) \in O(p(n))$ if and only if $t(n) \in O(q(n))$. This rule generalizes to any finite constant number of functions. Before proving it, we illustrate a natural interpretation of this rule. Consider an algorithm that proceeds in three steps: initialization, processing and finalization. Assume for the sake of argument that these steps take time in $O(n^2)$, $O(n^3)$ and $O(n \log n)$, respectively. It is therefore clear (see Section 4.2) that the complete algorithm takes a time in $O(n^2 + n^3 + n \log n)$. Although it would not be hard to prove directly that this is the same as $O(n^3)$, it is immediate from the maximum rule.

$$O(n^2 + n^3 + n \log n) = O(\max(n^2, n^3, n \log n))$$
$$= O(n^3)$$

In other words, even though the time taken by an algorithm is logically the sum of the times taken by its disjoint parts, it is in the order of the time taken by its most time-consuming part, provided the number of parts is a constant, independent of input size.

We now prove the maximum rule for the case of two functions. The general case of any fixed number of functions is left as an exercise. Observe that

$$f(n) + g(n) = \min(f(n), g(n)) + \max(f(n), g(n))$$

and

$$0 \leq \min(f(n), g(n)) \leq \max(f(n), g(n)).$$

It follows that

$$\max(f(n), g(n)) \leq f(n) + g(n) \leq 2 \max(f(n), g(n)). \tag{3.1}$$

Now consider any $t(n) \in O(f(n) + g(n))$. Let c be an appropriate constant such that $t(n) \leq c(f(n) + g(n))$ for all sufficiently large n. By Equation 3.1, it follows that $t(n) \leq 2c \max(f(n), g(n))$. Therefore, $t(n)$ is bounded above by a positive real multiple—namely $2c$—of $\max(f(n), g(n))$ for all sufficiently large n, which proves that $t(n) \in O(\max(f(n), g(n)))$. For the other direction, consider any $t(n) \in O(\max(f(n), g(n)))$. Let $\hat{c}$ be an appropriate new constant such that $t(n) \leq \hat{c} \max(f(n), g(n))$ for all sufficiently large n. By Equation 3.1 again, it follows that $t(n) \leq \hat{c}(f(n) + g(n))$. By definition of the O notation, this implies directly that $t(n) \in O(f(n) + g(n))$, which completes the proof of the maximum rule. In accordance with our allowed occasional misuse of the notation, we are entitled to invoke the maximum rule even if the functions concerned are negative or undefined on a finite set of values. Be careful however not to use the rule if some of the functions are negative infinitely often; otherwise you risk reasoning as follows:

$$O(n) = O(n + n^2 - n^2) = O(\max(n, n^2, -n^2)) = O(n^2),$$

where the middle equality is obtained by incorrect use of the maximum rule.

The maximum rule tells us that if $t(n)$ is a complicated function such as $t(n) = 12n^3 \log n - 5n^2 + \log^2 n + 36$ and if $f(n)$ is the most significant term of $t(n)$ with its coefficient discarded, here $f(n) = n^3 \log n$, then $O(t(n)) = O(f(n))$, which allows for dramatic yet automatic simplifications in asymptotic notation. In other words, lower-order terms can be ignored because they are negligible compared to the higher-order term for n sufficiently large. Note in this case that one should *not* prove $O(t(n)) = O(f(n))$ by reasoning along the lines of

$$O(t(n)) = O(\max(12n^3 \log n, -5n^2, \log^2 n, 36))$$
$$= O(12n^3 \log n) = O(n^3 \log n)$$

where the second line is obtained from the maximum rule. This does not use the maximum rule properly since the function $-5n^2$ is negative. Nevertheless, the following reasoning is correct:

$$O(t(n)) = O(11n^3 \log n + n^3 \log n - 5n^2 + \log^2 n + 36)$$
$$= O(\max(11n^3 \log n, n^3 \log n - 5n^2, \log^2 n, 36))$$
$$= O(11n^3 \log n) = O(n^3 \log n).$$

Even though $n^3 \log n - 5n^2$ is negative and 36 is larger than $11n^3 \log n$ for small values of n, all is well since this does not occur whenever n is sufficiently large.

Another useful observation is that it is usually unnecessary to specify the base of a logarithm inside an asymptotic notation. This is because $\log_a n = \log_a b \times \log_b n$ for all positive reals a, b and n such that neither a nor b is equal to 1. The point is that $\log_a b$ is a positive constant when a and b are constants larger than 1. Therefore $\log_a n$ and $\log_b n$ differ only by a constant multiplicative factor. From this, it is elementary to prove that $O(\log_a n) = O(\log_b n)$, which we usually simplify as $O(\log n)$. This observation also applies to more complicated functions, such as positive polynomials involving n and $\log n$, and ratios of such polynomials. For instance, $O(n \lg n)$ is the same as the more usual $O(n \log n)$, and $O(n^2 / (\log_3 n \sqrt{n \lg n}))$ is the same as $O((n/\log n)^{1.5})$. However, the base of the logarithm cannot be ignored when it is smaller than 1, when it is not a constant, as in $O(\log_{\sqrt{n}} n) \neq O(\log n)$, or when the logarithm is in the exponent, as in $O(2^{\lg n}) \neq O(2^{\log n})$.

It is easy to prove that the notation "$\in O$" is <u>reflexive</u> and <u>transitive.</u> In other words, $f(n) \in O(f(n))$ for any function $f : \mathbb{N} \to \mathbb{R}^{\geq 0}$, and it follows from $f(n) \in O(g(n))$ and $g(n) \in O(h(n))$ that $f(n) \in O(h(n))$ for any functions $f, g, h : \mathbb{N} \to \mathbb{R}^{\geq 0}$; see Problems 3.9 and 3.10. As a result, this notation provides a way to define a partial order on functions and consequently on the relative efficiency of different algorithms to solve a given problem; see Problem 3.21. However, the induced order is not total as there exist functions $f, g : \mathbb{N} \to \mathbb{R}^{\geq 0}$ such that neither $f(n) \in O(g(n))$ nor $g(n) \in O(f(n))$; see Problem 3.11.

We have seen several examples of functions $t(n)$ and $f(n)$ for which it is easy to prove that $t(n) \in O(f(n))$. For this, it suffices to exhibit the appropriate constants c and n_0 and show that the desired relation holds. How could we go about proving that a given function $t(n)$ is *not* in the order of another function $f(n)$? The simplest way is to use a proof by contradiction. The following example makes the case. Let $t(n) = \frac{1}{1000} n^3$ and $f(n) = 1000n^2$. If you try several values of n smaller than one million, you find that $t(n) < f(n)$, which may lead you to believe by induction that $t(n) \in O(f(n))$, taking 1 as the multiplicative constant. If you attempt to prove this, however, you are likely to end up with the following proof by contradiction that it is false. To prove that $t(n) \notin O(f(n))$, assume for a contradiction that $t(n) \in O(f(n))$. Using the generalized threshold rule, this implies the existence of a positive real constant c such that $t(n) \leq cf(n)$ for all $n \geq 1$. But $t(n) \leq cf(n)$ means $\frac{1}{1000} n^3 \leq 1000cn^2$, which implies that $n \leq 10^6 c$. In other words, assuming $t(n) \in O(f(n))$ implies that every positive integer n is smaller than some fixed constant, which is clearly false.

The most powerful and versatile tool both to prove that some functions are in the order of others and to prove the opposite is the **limit rule**, which states that, given arbitrary functions f and $g : \mathbb{N} \to \mathbb{R}^{\geq 0}$,

1. if $\lim\limits_{n \to \infty} \dfrac{f(n)}{g(n)} \in \mathbb{R}^+$ then $f(n) \in O(g(n))$ and $g(n) \in O(f(n))$,

2. if $\lim\limits_{n \to \infty} \dfrac{f(n)}{g(n)} = 0$ then $f(n) \in O(g(n))$ but $g(n) \notin O(f(n))$, and

3. if $\lim\limits_{n \to \infty} \dfrac{f(n)}{g(n)} = +\infty$ then $f(n) \notin O(g(n))$ but $g(n) \in O(f(n))$.

We illustrate the use of this rule before proving it. Consider the two functions $f(n) = \log n$ and $g(n) = \sqrt{n}$. We wish to determine the relative order of these functions. Since both $f(n)$ and $g(n)$ tend to infinity as n tends to infinity, we use de l'Hôpital's rule to compute

$$\lim_{n \to \infty} \frac{f(n)}{g(n)} = \lim_{n \to \infty} \frac{\log n}{\sqrt{n}} = \lim_{n \to \infty} \frac{1/n}{1/(2\sqrt{n})}$$
$$= \lim_{n \to \infty} 2/\sqrt{n} = 0.$$

Now the limit rule immediately shows that $\log n \in O(\sqrt{n})$ whereas $\sqrt{n} \notin O(\log n)$. In other words, $\sqrt{n}$ grows asymptotically faster than $\log n$. We now prove the limit rule.

1. Assume $\lim_{n \to \infty} f(n)/g(n) = \ell \in \mathbb{R}^+$. Let $\delta = \ell$ and $c = 2\ell$. By definition of the limit, the difference in absolute value between $f(n)/g(n)$ and ℓ is no more than δ for all sufficiently large n. But this means that $f(n)/g(n) \leq \ell + \delta = c$. We have thus exhibited a positive real constant c such that $f(n) \leq cg(n)$ for all sufficiently large n, which proves that $f(n) \in O(g(n))$. The fact that $g(n) \in O(f(n))$ is automatic since $\lim_n {}_{\to\infty} f(n)/g(n) = \ell \in \mathbb{R}^+$ implies that $\lim_{n \to \infty} g(n)/f(n) = 1/\ell \in \mathbb{R}^+$ and thus the above reasoning applies *mutatis mutandis* with $f(n)$ and $g(n)$ interchanged.

2. Assume $\lim_{n \to \infty} f(n)/g(n) = 0$. Arbitrarily fix $\delta = 1$. By definition of the limit, the absolute value of $f(n)/g(n)$ is no more than δ for all sufficiently large n. Therefore $f(n)/g(n) \le \delta$, which implies that $f(n) \le g(n)$ since $\delta = 1$, still for all sufficiently large n. This proves that $f(n) \in O(g(n))$. To prove that $g(n) \notin O(f(n))$, assume for a contradiction that $g(n) \in O(f(n))$. This assumption implies the existence of a positive real constant c such that

$$g(n) \le cf(n),$$

and therefore $1/c \le f(n)/g(n)$, for all sufficiently large n. Since

$$\lim_{n \to \infty} f(n)/g(n)$$

exists by assumption that it equals 0 and $\lim_{n \to \infty} 1/c = 1/c$ exists as well, Proposition 1.7.8 applies to conclude that $1/c \le \lim_{n \to \infty} f(n)/g(n) = 0$, which is a contradiction since $c > 0$. We have contradicted the assumption that $g(n) \in O(f(n))$ and therefore established as required that $g(n) \notin O(f(n))$.

3. Assume $\lim_{n \to \infty} f(n)/g(n) = +\infty$. This implies that

$$\lim_{n \to \infty} g(n)/f(n) = 0$$

and therefore the previous case applies *mutatis mutandis* with $f(n)$ and $g(n)$ interchanged.

The converse of the limit rule does not necessarily apply: it is not always the case that $\lim_{n \to \infty} f(n)/g(n) \in \mathbb{R}^+$ when $f(n) \in O(g(n))$ and $g(n) \in O(f(n))$. Although it does follow that the limit is strictly positive if it exists, the problem is that it may not exist. Consider for instance $f(n) = n$ and $g(n) = 2^{\lfloor \lg n \rfloor}$. It is easy to see that $g(n) \le f(n) \le 2g(n)$ for all $n \ge 1$, and thus $f(n)$ and $g(n)$ are each in the order of the other. However, it is equally easy to see that $f(n)/g(n)$ oscillates between 1 and 2, and thus the limit of that ratio does not exist.

3.3 Other asymptotic notation

The Omega notation

Consider the sorting problem discussed in Section 2.7.2. We saw that most obvious algorithms such as insertion sorting and selection sorting take a time in $O(n^2)$, whereas more sophisticated algorithms such as *heapsort* are more efficient since they make do in a time in $O(n \log n)$. But it is easy to show that $n \log n \in O(n^2)$. As a result, *it is correct* to say that *heapsort* takes a time in $O(n^2)$, or even in $O(n^3)$ for that matter! This is confusing at first, but it is the unavoidable consequence of the fact that the O notation is designed solely to give *upper bounds* on the amount of resources required. Clearly, we need a dual notation for *lower* bounds. This is the Ω notation.

Consider again two functions $f, t : \mathbb{N} \to \mathbb{R}^{\geq 0}$ from the natural numbers to the nonnegative reals. We say that $t(n)$ is in Omega of $f(n)$, denoted $t(n) \in \Omega(f(n))$, if $t(n)$ is bounded *below* by a positive real multiple of $f(n)$ for all sufficiently large n. Mathematically, this means that there exist a positive real constant d and an integer threshold n_0 such that $t(n) \geq df(n)$ whenever $n \geq n_0$:

$$\Omega(f(n)) = \{t : \mathbb{N} \to \mathbb{R}^{\geq 0} \mid (\exists d \in \mathbb{R}^+)(\overset{\infty}{\forall} n \in \mathbb{N})[t(n) \geq df(n)]\}.$$

It is easy to see the **duality rule**: $t(n) \in \Omega(f(n))$ if and only if $f(n) \in O(t(n))$ because $t(n) \geq df(n)$ if and only if $f(n) \leq \frac{1}{d} t(n)$. You may therefore question the usefulness of introducing a notation for Ω when the O notation seems to have the same expressive power. The reason is that it is more natural to say that a given algorithm takes a time in $\Omega(n^2)$ than to say the mathematically equivalent but clumsy "n^2 is in O of the time taken by the algorithm".

Thanks to the duality rule, we know from the previous section that $\sqrt{n} \in \Omega(\log n)$ whereas $\log n \notin \Omega(\sqrt{n})$, among many examples. More importantly, the duality rule can be used in the obvious way to turn the limit rule, the maximum rule and the threshold rule into rules about the Ω notation.

Despite strong similarity between the O and the Ω notation, there is one aspect in which their duality fails. Recall that we are most often interested in the *worst-case* performance of algorithms. Therefore, when we say that an implementation of an algorithm takes $t(n)$ microseconds, we mean that $t(n)$ is the maximum time taken by the implementation on all instances of size n. Let $f(n)$ be such that $t(n) \in O(f(n))$. This means that there exists a real positive constant c such that $t(n) \leq cf(n)$ for all sufficiently large n. Because no instance of size n can take more time than the maximum time taken by instances of that size, it follows that the implementation takes a time bounded by $cf(n)$ microseconds on all sufficiently large instances. Assuming only a finite number of instances of each size exist, there can thus be only a finite number of instances, all of size less than the threshold, on which the implementation takes a time greater than $cf(n)$ microseconds. Assuming $f(n)$ is never zero, these can all be taken care of by using a bigger multiplicative constant, as in the proof of the threshold rule.

In contrast, let us also assume $t(n) \in \Omega(f(n))$. Again, this means that there exists a real positive constant d such that $t(n) \geq df(n)$ for all sufficiently large n. But because $t(n)$ denotes the worst-case behaviour of the implementation, we may infer only that, for each sufficiently large n, there exists *at least one* instance of size n such that the implementation takes at least $df(n)$ microseconds on that instance. This does not rule out the possibility of much faster behaviour on other instances of the same size. Thus, there may exist infinitely many instances on which the implementation takes less than $df(n)$ microseconds. Insertion sort provides a typical example of this behaviour. We saw in Section 2.4 that it takes quadratic time in the worst case, yet there are infinitely many instances on which it runs in linear time. We are therefore entitled to claim that its worst-case running time is both in $O(n^2)$ and in $\Omega(n^2)$. Yet the first claim says that every sufficiently large instance can be sorted in quadratic time, whereas the second merely says that at least one instance of each sufficiently large size genuinely requires quadratic time: the algorithm may be much faster on other instances of the same size.

Some authors define the Ω notation in a way that is subtly but importantly different. They say that $t(n) \in \Omega(f(n))$ if there exists a real positive constant d such that $t(n) \geq df(n)$ for *an infinite number* of values of n, whereas we require the relation to hold for all but finitely many values of n. With this definition, an algorithm that takes a time in $\Omega(f(n))$ in the worst case is such that there are infinitely many instances on which it takes at least $df(n)$ microseconds for the appropriate real positive constant d. This corresponds more closely to our intuitive idea of what a lower bound on the performance of an algorithm should look like. It is more natural than what *we* mean by "taking a time in $\Omega(f(n))$". Nevertheless, we prefer our definition because it is easier to work with. In particular, the modified definition of Ω is not transitive and the duality rule breaks down.

In this book, we use the Ω notation mainly to give lower bounds on the running time (or other resources) of algorithms. However, this notation is often used to give lower bounds on the intrinsic difficulty of solving problems. For instance, we shall see in Section 12.2.1 that *any* algorithm that successfully sorts n elements must take a time in $\Omega(n \log n)$, provided the only operation carried out on the elements to be sorted is to compare them pairwise to determine whether they are equal and, if not, which is the greater. As a result, we say that the problem of sorting by comparisons has running time *complexity* in $\Omega(n \log n)$. It is in general much harder to determine the complexity of a problem than to determine a lower bound on the running time of a given algorithm that solves it. We elaborate on this topic in Chapter 12.

The Theta notation

When we analyse the behaviour of an algorithm, we are happiest if its execution time is bounded simultaneously both above and below by possibly different positive real multiples of the same function. For this reason, we introduce the Θ notation. We say that $t(n)$ is in Theta of $f(n)$, or equivalently that $t(n)$ is in the *exact order* of $f(n)$, denoted $t(n) \in \Theta(f(n))$, if $t(n)$ belongs to both $O(f(n))$ and $\Omega(f(n))$. The formal definition of Θ is

$$\Theta(f(n)) = O(f(n)) \cap \Omega(f(n)).$$

This is equivalent to saying that $\Theta(f(n))$ is

$$\{t : \mathbb{N} \to \mathbb{R}^{\geq 0} \mid (\exists c, d \in \mathbb{R}^+) (\overset{\infty}{\forall} n \in \mathbb{N}) [df(n) \leq t(n) \leq cf(n)]\}.$$

The threshold rule and the maximum rule, which we formulated in the context of the O notation, apply *mutatis mutandis* to the Θ notation. More interestingly, for the Θ notation the limit rule is reformulated as follows. Consider arbitrary functions f and $g : \mathbb{N} \to \mathbb{R}^{\geq 0}$.

1. if $\lim\limits_{n \to \infty} \dfrac{f(n)}{g(n)} \in \mathbb{R}^+$ then $f(n) \in \Theta(g(n))$,

2. if $\lim\limits_{n \to \infty} \dfrac{f(n)}{g(n)} = 0$ then $f(n) \in O(g(n))$ but $f(n) \notin \Theta(g(n))$, and

3. if $\lim\limits_{n \to \infty} \dfrac{f(n)}{g(n)} = +\infty$ then $f(n) \in \Omega(g(n))$ but $f(n) \notin \Theta(g(n))$.

As an exercise in manipulating asymptotic notation, let us now prove a useful fact:

$$\sum_{i=1}^{n} i^k \in \Theta(n^{k+1}),$$

for any fixed integer $k \geq 0$, where the left-hand side summation is considered as a function of n. Of course, this is immediate from Proposition 1.7.16, but it is instructive to prove it directly.

The "O" direction is easy to prove. For this, simply notice that $i^k \leq n^k$ whenever $1 \leq i \leq n$. Therefore $\sum_{i=1}^{n} i^k \leq \sum_{i=1}^{n} n^k = n^{k+1}$ for all $n \geq 1$, which proves $\sum_{i=1}^{n} i^k \in O(n^{k+1})$ using 1 as the multiplicative constant.

To prove the "Ω" direction, notice that $i^k \geq (n/2)^k$ whenever $i \geq \lceil n/2 \rceil$ and that the number of integers between $\lceil n/2 \rceil$ and n inclusive is greater than $n/2$. Therefore, provided $n \geq 1$ (which implies that $\lceil n/2 \rceil \geq 1$),

$$\sum_{i=1}^{n} i^k \geq \sum_{i=\lceil \frac{n}{2} \rceil}^{n} i^k \geq \sum_{i=\lceil \frac{n}{2} \rceil}^{n} \left(\frac{n}{2}\right)^k \geq \frac{n}{2} \times \left(\frac{n}{2}\right)^k = \frac{n^{k+1}}{2^{k+1}}.$$

This proves $\sum_{i=1}^{n} i^k \in \Omega(n^{k+1})$ using $1/2^{k+1}$ as the multiplicative constant. A tighter constant is obtained in Problem 3.23.

3.4 Conditional asymptotic notation

Many algorithms are easier to analyse if initially we restrict our attention to instances whose size satisfies a certain condition, such as being a power of 2. Consider for example the "divide-and-conquer" algorithm for multiplying large integers that we saw in Section 1.2. Let n be the size of the integers to be multiplied. (We assumed them to be of the same size.) The algorithm proceeds directly if $n = 1$, which requires a microseconds for an appropriate constant a. If $n > 1$, the algorithm proceeds by multiplying four pairs of integers of size $\lceil n/2 \rceil$ (or three pairs in the better algorithm that we shall study in Chapter 7). Moreover, it takes a linear amount of time to carry out additional tasks. For simplicity, let us say that the additional work takes bn microseconds for an appropriate constant b. (To be precise, it would take a time between $b_1 n$ and $b_2 n$ microseconds for appropriate constants b_1 and b_2—more on this in Section 4.7.6.)

The time taken by this algorithm is therefore given by the function $t : \mathbb{N} \to \mathbb{R}^{\geq 0}$ recursively defined by

$$t(n) = \begin{cases} a & \text{if } n = 1 \\ 4t(\lceil n/2 \rceil) + bn & \text{otherwise.} \end{cases} \tag{3.2}$$

We study techniques for solving recurrences in Section 4.7, but unfortunately Equation 3.2 cannot be handled directly by those techniques because the ceiling function $\lceil n/2 \rceil$ is troublesome. Nevertheless, our recurrence is easy to solve provided we consider only the case when n is a power of 2: in this case $\lceil n/2 \rceil = n/2$ and the ceiling vanishes. The techniques of Section 4.7 yield

$$t(n) = (a + b)n^2 - bn$$

provided n is a power of 2. Since the lower-order term "$-bn$" can be neglected, it follows that $t(n)$ is in the exact order of n^2, still provided n is a power of 2. This is denoted by $t(n) \in \Theta(n^2 \mid n \text{ is a power of 2})$.

   More generally, let $f, t : \mathbb{N} \to \mathbb{R}^{\geq 0}$ be two functions from the natural numbers to the nonnegative reals, and let $P : \mathbb{N} \to \{true, false\}$ be a property of the integers. We say that $t(n)$ is in $O(f(n) \mid P(n))$ if $t(n)$ is bounded above by a positive real multiple of $f(n)$ for all sufficiently large n such that $P(n)$ holds. Formally, $O(f(n) \mid P(n))$ is defined as

$$\{ t : \mathbb{N} \to \mathbb{R}^{\geq 0} \mid (\exists c \in \mathbb{R}^+)(\overset{\infty}{\forall} n \in \mathbb{N})[P(n) \Rightarrow t(n) \leq cf(n)] \}.$$

The sets $\Omega(f(n) \mid P(n))$ and $\Theta(f(n) \mid P(n))$ are defined similarly. Abusing notation in a familiar way, we write $t(n) \in O(f(n) \mid P(n))$ even if $t(n)$ and $f(n)$ are negative or undefined on an arbitrary—perhaps infinite—number of values of n on which $P(n)$ does not hold.

   Conditional asymptotic notation is more than a mere notational convenience: its main interest is that it can generally be eliminated once it has been used to facilitate the analysis of an algorithm. For this, we need a few definitions. A function $f : \mathbb{N} \to \mathbb{R}^{\geq 0}$ is *eventually nondecreasing* if there exists an integer threshold n_0 such that $f(n) \leq f(n + 1)$ for all $n \geq n_0$. This implies by mathematical induction that $f(n) \leq f(m)$ whenever $m \geq n \geq n_0$. Let $b \geq 2$ be any integer. Function f is *b–smooth* if, in addition to being eventually nondecreasing, it satisfies the condition $f(bn) \in O(f(n))$. In other words, there must exist a constant c (depending on b) such that $f(bn) \leq cf(n)$ for all $n \geq n_0$. (There is no loss of generality in using the same threshold n_0 for both purposes.) A function is *smooth* if it is b–smooth for every integer $b \geq 2$.

   Most functions you are likely to encounter in the analysis of algorithms are smooth, such as $\log n$, $n \log n$, n^2, or any polynomial whose leading coefficient is positive. However, functions that grow too fast, such as $n^{\lg n}$, 2^n or $n!$, are not smooth because the ratio $f(2n)/f(n)$ is unbounded. For example,

$$(2n)^{\lg(2n)} = 2n^2 \, n^{\lg n},$$

which shows that $(2n)^{\lg(2n)} \notin O(n^{\lg n})$ because $2n^2$ cannot be bounded above by a constant. Functions that are bounded above by some polynomial, on the other hand, are usually smooth provided they are eventually nondecreasing; and even if they are not eventually nondecreasing there is a good chance that they are in the exact order of some other function that is smooth. For instance, let $b(n)$ denote the number of bits equal to 1 in the binary expansion of n—such as $b(13) = 3$ because 13 is written 1101 in binary—and consider $f(n) = b(n) + \lg n$. It is easy to see that $f(n)$ is not eventually nondecreasing—and therefore it is not smooth—because $b(2^k - 1) = k$ whereas $b(2^k) = 1$ for all k; nevertheless, $f(n) \in \Theta(\log n)$, a smooth function. (This example is not as artificial as it may seem; see Section 7.8.) Seldom will you encounter slow-growing functions that are not in the exact order of a smooth function.

A useful property of smoothness is that if f is b–smooth for any specific integer $b \geq 2$, then it is in fact smooth. To prove this, consider any two integers a and b not smaller than 2. Assume f is b–smooth. We must show that f is a–smooth as well. Let c and n_0 be constants such that $f(bn) \leq cf(n)$ and $f(n) \leq f(n + 1)$ for all $n \geq n_0$. Let $i = \lceil \log_b a \rceil$. By definition of the logarithm, $a = b^{\log_b a} \leq b^{\lceil \log_b a \rceil} = b^i$. Consider any $n \geq n_0$. It is easy to show by mathematical induction from b–smoothness of f that $f(b^i n) \leq c^i f(n)$. But $f(an) \leq f(b^i n)$ because f is eventually nondecreasing and $b^i n \geq an \geq n_0$. It follows that $f(an) \leq \hat{c} f(n)$ for $\hat{c} = c^i$, and thus f is a–smooth.

Smooth functions are interesting because of the **smoothness rule**. Let $f : \mathbb{N} \to \mathbb{R}^{\geq 0}$ be a smooth function and let $t : \mathbb{N} \to \mathbb{R}^{\geq 0}$ be an eventually nondecreasing function. Consider any integer $b \geq 2$. The smoothness rule asserts that $t(n) \in \Theta(f(n))$ whenever $t(n) \in \Theta(f(n) \mid n$ is a power of $b)$. The rule applies equally to O and Ω notation. Before proving the rule, we illustrate it with the example used at the beginning of this section.

We saw that it is easy to obtain the conditional asymptotic formula

$$t(n) \in \Theta(n^2 \mid n \text{ is a power of } 2) \tag{3.3}$$

from Equation 3.2, whereas it is harder to carry out the analysis of $t(n)$ when n is not a power of 2. The smoothness rule allows us to infer directly from Equation 3.3 that $t(n) \in \Theta(n^2)$, provided we verify that n^2 is a smooth function and $t(n)$ is eventually nondecreasing. The first condition is immediate since n^2 is obviously nondecreasing and $(2n)^2 = 4n^2$. The second is easily demonstrated by mathematical induction from Equation 3.2; see Problem 3.28. Thus the use of conditional asymptotic notation as a stepping stone yields the final result that $t(n) \in \Theta(n^2)$ unconditionally.

We now prove the smoothness rule. Let $f(n)$ be a smooth function and let $t(n)$ be an eventually nondecreasing function such that $t(n) \in \Theta(f(n) \mid n$ is a power of $b)$ for some integer $b \geq 2$. Let n_0 be the largest of the thresholds implied by the above conditions: $f(m) \leq f(m + 1)$, $t(m) \leq t(m + 1)$ and $f(bm) \leq cf(m)$ whenever $m \geq n_0$, and $df(m) \leq t(m) \leq af(m)$ whenever $m \geq n_0$ is a power of b, for appropriate constants a, c and d. For any positive integer n, let $\underline{n}$ denote the largest power of b not larger than n (formally, $\underline{n} = b^{\lfloor \log_b n \rfloor}$) and let $\overline{n} = b\underline{n}$. By definition, $n/b < \underline{n} \leq n < \overline{n}$ and $\overline{n}$ is a power of b. Consider any $n \geq \max(1, bn_0)$.

$$t(n) \leq t(\overline{n}) \leq af(\overline{n}) = af(b\underline{n}) \leq acf(\underline{n}) \leq acf(n)$$

This equation uses successively the facts that t is eventually nondecreasing (and $\overline{n} > n \geq n_0$), $t(m)$ is in the order of $f(m)$ when m is a power of b (and $\overline{n}$ is a power of b no smaller than n_0), $\overline{n} = b\underline{n}$, f is b–smooth (and $\underline{n} > n/b \geq n_0$), and f is eventually nondecreasing (and $n \geq \underline{n} > n_0$). This proves that $t(n) \leq acf(n)$ for *all* values of $n \geq \max(1, bn_0)$, and therefore $t(n) \in O(f(n))$. The proof that $t(n) \in \Omega(f(n))$ is similar.

3.5 Asymptotic notation with several parameters

It may happen when we analyse an algorithm that its execution time depends simultaneously on more than one parameter of the instance in question. This situation is typical of certain algorithms for problems involving graphs, for example, where the time depends on both the number of vertices and the number of edges. In such cases the notion of "size of the instance" that we have used so far may lose much of its meaning. For this reason the asymptotic notation is generalized in a natural way to functions of several variables.

Let $f : \mathbb{N} \times \mathbb{N} \to \mathbb{R}^{\geq 0}$ be a function from pairs of natural numbers to the nonnegative reals, such as $f(m, n) = m \log n$. Let $t : \mathbb{N} \times \mathbb{N} \to \mathbb{R}^{\geq 0}$ be another such function. We say that $t(m, n)$ is in the order of $f(m, n)$, denoted $t(m, n) \in O(f(m, n))$, if $t(m, n)$ is bounded above by a positive multiple of $f(m, n)$ whenever both m and n are sufficiently large. Formally, $O(f(m, n))$ is defined as

$$\{t : \mathbb{N} \times \mathbb{N} \to \mathbb{R}^{\geq 0} \mid (\exists c \in \mathbb{R}^+)\, (\overset{\infty}{\forall}\, m, n \in \mathbb{N})\, [t(m, n) \leq cf(m, n)]\}.$$

(There is no need for two distinct thresholds for m and n in $\overset{\infty}{\forall}\, m, n \in \mathbb{N}$.) Generalization to more than two parameters, of the conditional asymptotic notation and of the Ω and Θ notation, is done in the same spirit.

Asymptotic notation with several parameters is similar to what we have seen so far, except for one essential difference: the threshold rule is no longer valid. Indeed, the threshold is sometimes indispensable. This is explained by the fact that while there are never more than a finite number of nonnegative integers smaller than any given threshold, there are in general an infinite number of pairs $\langle m, n \rangle$ of nonnegative integers such that at least one of m or n is below the threshold; see Problem 3.32. For this reason, $O(f(m, n))$ may make sense even if $f(m, n)$ is negative or undefined on an infinite set of points, provided all these points can be ruled out by an appropriate choice of threshold.

3.6 Operations on asymptotic notation

To simplify some calculations, we can manipulate the asymptotic notation using arithmetic operators. For instance, $O(f(n)) + O(g(n))$ represents the set of functions obtained by adding pointwise any function in $O(f(n))$ to any function in $O(g(n))$. Intuitively this represents the order of the time taken by an algorithm composed of a first stage taking a time in the order of $f(n)$ followed by a second stage taking a time in the order of $g(n)$. Strictly speaking, the hidden constants that multiply $f(n)$ and $g(n)$ may well be different, but this is of no consequence because it is easy to prove that $O(f(n)) + O(g(n))$ is identical to $O(f(n) + g(n))$. By the maximum rule, we know that this is also the same as $O(\max(f(n), g(n)))$ and, if you prefer, $\max(O(f(n)), O(g(n)))$.

More formally, if **op** is any binary operator and if X and Y are sets of functions from $\mathbb{N}$ into $\mathbb{R}^{\geq 0}$, in particular sets described by asymptotic notation, then "X **op** Y" denotes the set of functions that can be obtained by choosing one function from X and one function from Y, and by "**op**ing" them together pointwise. In keeping with the spirit of asymptotic notation, we only require the resulting function to be the correct **op**ed value beyond some threshold. Formally, X **op** Y denotes

$$\{t : \mathbb{N} \to \mathbb{R}^{\geq 0} \mid (\exists f \in X)\,(\exists g \in Y)\,(\overset{\infty}{\forall} n \in \mathbb{N})\,[t(n) = f(n)\ \mathbf{op}\ g(n)]\}.$$

If g is a function from $\mathbb{N}$ into $\mathbb{R}^{\geq 0}$, we stretch the notation by writing g **op** X to denote $\{g\}$ **op** X, the set of functions that can be obtained by **op**ing function g with one function from X. Furthermore, if $a \in \mathbb{R}^{\geq 0}$, we use a **op** X to denote cst_a **op** X, where cst_a denotes the constant function $cst_a(n) = a$ for every integer n. In other words, a **op** X denotes the set of functions that can be obtained by **op**ing a to the value of a function from X. We also use the symmetrical notation X **op** g and X **op** a, and all this theory of operations on sets is extended in the obvious way to operators other than binary and to functions.

As an example, consider the meaning of $n^{O(1)}$. Here, "n" and "1" denote the identity function $Id(n) = n$ and the constant function $cst_1(n) = 1$, respectively. Thus a function $t(n)$ belongs to $n^{O(1)}$ if there exists a function $f(n)$ bounded above by a constant c such that $t(n) = n^{f(n)}$ for all $n \geq n_0$, for some n_0. In particular, this implies that $t(n) \leq k + n^k$ for all $n \geq 0$, provided $k \geq c$ and $k \geq t(n)$ for all $n < n_0$. Therefore, every function in $n^{O(1)}$ is bounded above by a polynomial. Conversely, consider any polynomial $p(n)$ whose leading coefficient is positive and any function $t(n)$ such that $1 \leq t(n) \leq p(n)$ for all sufficiently large n. Let k be the degree of $p(n)$. It is easy to show that $p(n) \leq n^{k+1}$ for all sufficiently large n. Let $g(n) = \log_n t(n)$, and thus $t(n) = n^{g(n)}$. Since $1 \leq t(n) \leq n^{k+1}$, it follows that $0 \leq g(n) \leq k + 1$ for all sufficiently large n. Therefore, $g(n) \in O(1)$, which shows that $t(n) \in n^{O(1)}$. The conclusion is that $n^{O(1)}$ denotes the set of all functions bounded above by some polynomial, provided the function is bounded below by the constant 1 for all sufficiently large n.

3.7 Problems

Problem 3.1.   Consider an implementation of an algorithm that takes a time that is bounded above by the unlikely function

$$t(n) = 3 \text{ seconds } - 18n \text{ milliseconds } + 27n^2 \text{ microseconds}$$

to solve an instance of size n. Find the simplest possible function $f : \mathbb{N} \to \mathbb{R}^{\geq 0}$ such that the algorithm takes a time in the order of $f(n)$.

Problem 3.2.   Consider two algorithms A and B that take time in $\Theta(n^2)$ and $\Theta(n^3)$, respectively, to solve the same problem. If other resources such as storage and programming time are of no concern, is it necessarily the case that algorithm A is *always* preferable to algorithm B? Justify your answer.

Problem 3.3.   Consider two algorithms A and B that take time in $O(n^2)$ and $O(n^3)$, respectively. Could there exist an implementation of algorithm B that would be more efficient (in terms of computing time) than an implementation of algorithm A on *all* instances? Justify your answer.

Problem 3.4.   What does $O(1)$ mean? $\Theta(1)$?

Problem 3.5.   Which of the following statements are true? Prove your answers.

1. $n^2 \in O(n^3)$ T
2. $n^2 \in \Omega(n^3)$ F
3. $2^n \in \Theta(2^{n+1})$ T
4. $n! \in \Theta((n+1)!)$

Problem 3.6.   Prove that if $f(n) \in O(n)$ then $[f(n)]^2 \in O(n^2)$.

Problem 3.7.   In contrast with Problem 3.6, prove that $2^{f(n)} \in O(2^n)$ does not necessarily follow from $f(n) \in O(n)$.

Problem 3.8.   Consider an algorithm that takes a time in $\Theta(n^{\lg 3})$ to solve instances of size n. Is it correct to say that it takes a time in $O(n^{1.59})$? In $\Omega(n^{1.59})$? In $\Theta(n^{1.59})$? Justify your answers. (Note: $\lg 3 \approx 1.58496\ldots$)

Problem 3.9.   Prove that the O notation is reflexive: $f(n) \in O(f(n))$ for any function $f : \mathbb{N} \to \mathbb{R}^{\geq 0}$.

Problem 3.10.   Prove that the O notation is transitive: it follows from

$$f(n) \in O(g(n)) \text{ and } g(n) \in O(h(n))$$

that $f(n) \in O(h(n))$ for any functions $f, g, h : \mathbb{N} \to \mathbb{R}^{\geq 0}$.

Problem 3.11.   Prove that the ordering on functions induced by the O notation is not total: give explicitly two functions $f, g : \mathbb{N} \to \mathbb{R}^{\geq 0}$ such that $f(n) \notin O(g(n))$ and $g(n) \notin O(f(n))$. Prove your answer. $f = \sin x$ $g = \cos x$

Problem 3.12.   Prove that the Ω notation is reflexive and transitive: for any functions $f, g, h : \mathbb{N} \to \mathbb{R}^{\geq 0}$,

1. $f(n) \in \Omega(f(n))$
2. if $f(n) \in \Omega(g(n))$ and $g(n) \in \Omega(h(n))$ then $f(n) \in \Omega(h(n))$.

Rather than proving this directly (which would be easier!), use the duality rule and the results of Problems 3.9 and 3.10.

Problem 3.13. As we explained, some authors give a different definition for the Ω notation. For the purpose of this problem, let us say that $t(n) \in \tilde{\Omega}(f(n))$ if there exists a real positive constant d such that $t(n) \geq df(n)$ for *an infinite number* of values of n. Formally,

$$\tilde{\Omega}(f(n)) = \{t : \mathbb{N} \to \mathbb{R}^{\geq 0} \mid (\exists d \in \mathbb{R}^+) (\overset{\infty}{\exists} n \in \mathbb{N}) [t(n) \geq df(n)]\}.$$

Prove that this notation is *not* transitive. Specifically, give an explicit example of three functions $f, g, h : \mathbb{N} \to \mathbb{R}^+$ such that $f(n) \in \tilde{\Omega}(g(n))$ and $g(n) \in \tilde{\Omega}(h(n))$, yet $f(n) \notin \tilde{\Omega}(h(n))$.

Problem 3.14. Let $f(n) = n^2$. Find the error in the following "proof" by mathematical induction that $f(n) \in O(n)$.

  ⋄ *Basis:* The case $n = 1$ is trivially satisfied since $f(1) = 1 \leq cn$, where $c = 1$.
  ⋄ *Induction step:* Consider any $n > 1$. Assume by the induction hypothesis the existence of a positive constant c such that $f(n-1) \leq c(n-1)$.

$$f(n) = n^2 = (n-1)^2 + 2n - 1 = f(n-1) + 2n - 1$$
$$\leq c(n-1) + 2n - 1 = (c+2)n - c - 1 < (c+2)n$$

Thus we have shown as required the existence of a constant $\hat{c} = c + 2$ such that $f(n) \leq \hat{c}n$. It follows by the principle of mathematical induction that $f(n)$ is bounded above by a constant times n for all $n \geq 1$ and therefore that $f(n) \in O(n)$ by definition of the O notation.

Problem 3.15. Find the error in the following "proof" that $O(n) = O(n^2)$. Let $f(n) = n^2$, $g(n) = n$ and $h(n) = g(n) - f(n)$. It is clear that $h(n) \leq g(n) \leq f(n)$ for all $n \geq 0$. Therefore, $f(n) = \max(f(n), h(n))$. Using the maximum rule, we conclude

$$O(g(n)) = O(f(n) + h(n)) = O(\max(f(n), h(n))) = O(f(n)).$$

Problem 3.16. Prove by mathematical induction that the maximum rule can be applied to more than two functions. More precisely, let k be an integer and let $f_1, f_2, \ldots, f_k$ be functions from $\mathbb{N}$ to $\mathbb{R}^{\geq 0}$. Define $g(n) = \max(f_1(n), f_2(n), \ldots, f_k(n))$ and $h(n) = f_1(n) + f_2(n) + \cdots + f_k(n)$ for all $n \geq 0$. Prove that $O(g(n)) = O(h(n))$.

Problem 3.17. Find the error in the following proof that $O(n) = O(n^2)$.

$$O(n) = O(\max(\underbrace{n, n, \ldots, n}_{n \text{ times}})) = O(\underbrace{n + n + \cdots + n}_{n \text{ times}}) = O(n^2),$$

where the middle equality comes from the generalized maximum rule that you proved in Problem 3.16.

Problem 3.18.   Prove that the Θ notation is reflexive, symmetric and transitive: for any functions $f, g, h : \mathbb{N} \to \mathbb{R}^{\geq 0}$,

1. $f(n) \in \Theta(f(n))$
2. if $f(n) \in \Theta(g(n))$ then $g(n) \in \Theta(f(n))$
3. if $f(n) \in \Theta(g(n))$ and $g(n) \in \Theta(h(n))$ then $f(n) \in \Theta(h(n))$.

Problem 3.19.   For any functions $f, g : \mathbb{N} \to \mathbb{R}^{\geq 0}$, prove that

$$O(f(n)) = O(g(n)) \text{ if and only if } f(n) \in \Theta(g(n))$$
$$\text{if and only if } \Theta(f(n)) = \Theta(g(n)).$$

Problem 3.20.   For any functions $f, g : \mathbb{N} \to \mathbb{R}^{\geq 0}$, prove that

$$O(f(n)) \subset O(g(n)) \quad \text{if and only if} \quad f(n) \in O(g(n)) \quad \text{but} \quad f(n) \notin \Omega(g(n)).$$

Recall that "$\subset$" denotes *strict* set inclusion.

Problem 3.21.   To illustrate how the asymptotic notation can be used to rank the efficiency of algorithms, use the relations "$\subset$" and "$=$" to put the orders of the following functions into a sequence, where ε is an arbitrary real constant, $0 < \varepsilon < 1$.

$$n \log n \qquad n^8 \qquad n^{1+\varepsilon} \qquad (1 + \varepsilon)^n \qquad n^2 / \log n \qquad (n^2 - n + 1)^4$$

Do *not* use the symbol "$\subseteq$". Prove your answers.

Problem 3.22.   Repeat Problem 3.21 but this time with functions

$$n! \qquad (n + 1)! \qquad 2^n \qquad 2^{n+1} \qquad 2^{2n} \qquad n^n \qquad n^{\sqrt{n}} \qquad n^{\log n}.$$

Problem 3.23.   We saw at the end of Section 3.3 that $\sum_{i=1}^{n} i^k \in \Omega(n^{k+1})$ for any fixed integer $k \geq 0$ because $\sum_{i=1}^{n} i^k \geq n^{k+1}/2^{k+1}$ for all n. Use the idea behind Figure 1.8 in Section 1.7.2 to derive a tighter constant for the inequality: find a constant d (depending on k) much larger than $1/2^{k+1}$ such that $\sum_{i=1}^{n} i^k \geq dn^{k+1}$ holds for all n. Do *not* use Proposition 1.7.16.

Problem 3.24.   Prove that $\log(n!) \in \Theta(n \log n)$. Do *not* use Stirling's formula. *Hint*: Mimic the proof that $\sum_{i=1}^{n} i^k \in \Omega(n^{k+1})$ given at the end of Section 3.3. Resist the temptation to improve your reasoning along the lines of Problem 3.23.

Problem 3.25.   Recall that a function $f : \mathbb{N} \to \mathbb{R}^{\geq 0}$ is eventually nondecreasing if there exists an integer threshold n_0 such that $f(n) \leq f(n + 1)$ for all $n \geq n_0$. Prove by mathematical induction that this implies that $f(n) \leq f(m)$ whenever $m \geq n \geq n_0$.

Problem 3.26.   Give a function $t : \mathbb{N} \to \mathbb{R}^+$ such that $t(n) \notin \Theta(f(n))$ whenever $f(n)$ is an eventually nondecreasing function. Give a *natural* example of an algorithm whose running time is in $\Theta(t(n))$. You may consider numerical algorithms for which n is the value of the instance rather than its size.

Problem 3.27.   Consider any b–smooth function $f : \mathbb{N} \to \mathbb{R}^{\geq 0}$. Let c and n_0 be constants such that $f(bn) \leq cf(n)$ for all $n \geq n_0$. Consider any positive integer i. Prove by mathematical induction that $f(b^i n) \leq c^i f(n)$ for all $n \geq n_0$.

Problem 3.28.   Consider the function $t : \mathbb{N} \to \mathbb{R}^{\geq 0}$ recursively defined by

$$t(n) = \begin{cases} a & \text{if } n = 1 \\ 4t(\lceil n/2 \rceil) + bn & \text{otherwise} \end{cases}$$

in which a and b are arbitrary positive constants (this was Equation 3.2 in Section 3.4). Prove by mathematical induction that $t(n)$ is eventually nondecreasing.

Problem 3.29.   Complete the proof of the smoothness rule (end of Section 3.4) by providing details of the proof that $t(n) \in \Omega(f(n))$ whenever $f(n)$ is a smooth function and $t(n)$ is an eventually nondecreasing function such that $t(n) \in \Theta(f(n) \mid n$ is a power of $b)$.

Note that the smoothness rule applies equally well if we replace Θ by O or by Ω in its statement. This is because your proof that $t(n) \in \Omega(f(n))$ does not use the fact that $t(n) \in O(f(n) \mid n$ is a power of $b)$, just as the proof we gave in Section 3.4 that $t(n) \in O(f(n))$ did not use the fact that $t(n) \in \Omega(f(n) \mid n$ is a power of $b)$. *Hint*: This is very similar to the proof that $t(n) \in O(f(n))$ under the same conditions. Use the fact that if $f(bm) \leq cf(m)$ then $f(m) \geq c^{-1}f(bm)$.

Problem 3.30.   Show by explicit examples that all the preconditions to apply the smoothness rule are necessary. Specifically, we are interested in functions $f, t : \mathbb{N} \to \mathbb{R}^{\geq 0}$ such that $t(n) \in \Theta(f(n) \mid n$ is a power of $b)$ for some integer $b \geq 2$, yet $t(n) \notin \Theta(f(n))$. You have to give three such pairs of functions, subject to the following additional constraints:

1. $f(n)$ is smooth but $t(n)$ is not eventually nondecreasing;
2. $f(n)$ and $t(n)$ are both eventually nondecreasing but $f(bn) \notin O(f(n))$;
3. $f(bn) \in O(f(n))$ and $t(n)$ is eventually nondecreasing but $f(n)$ is not eventually nondecreasing.

Problem 3.31.   Show by an explicit example that being eventually nondecreasing and bounded above by a polynomial is not a guarantee of smoothness. In other words, give two functions $f, p : \mathbb{N} \to \mathbb{R}^{\geq 0}$ such that $f(n)$ is eventually nondecreasing, $p(n)$ is a polynomial and $f(n) \leq p(n)$ for all n, yet $f(n)$ is not smooth.

Problem 3.32.   Show that the threshold rule does not apply to functions of several parameters. Specifically, give an explicit example of two functions $f, g : \mathbb{N} \times \mathbb{N} \to \mathbb{R}^+$ such that $f(m, n) \in O(g(m, n))$, yet there does not exist a constant c such that $f(m, n) \leq cg(m, n)$ for every $m, n \in \mathbb{N}$.

Problem 3.33.   Consider any two functions $f, g : \mathbb{N} \to \mathbb{R}^{\geq 0}$. Prove that

$$O(f(n)) + O(g(n)) = O(f(n) + g(n))$$

$$= O\big(\max(f(n), g(n))\big) = \max\big(O(f(n)), O(g(n))\big).$$

Note: We already know that $O(f(n) + g(n)) = O(\max(f(n), g(n)))$ by the maximum rule.

Problem 3.34.   Prove that $\Theta(n-1)+\Theta(n)=\Theta(n)$. Does it follow that

$$\Theta(n)=\Theta(n)-\Theta(n-1)?$$

Justify your answer.

Problem 3.35.   Find a function $f : \mathbb{N} \rightarrow \mathbb{R}^{\geq 0}$ that is bounded above by some polynomial, yet $f(n) \notin n^{O(1)}$.

3.8 References and further reading

The asymptotic notation O has existed for some while in mathematics: see Bachmann (1894) and de Bruijn (1961). However, the notation Θ and Ω is more recent: it was invented for analysing algorithms and for the theory of computational complexity. Knuth (1976) gives an account of the history of asymptotic notation and proposes a standard form for it. Conditional asymptotic notation and the notion of smoothness were introduced by Brassard (1985), who also suggested that "one-way equalities" should be abandoned in favour of a notation based on sets.

Chapter 4

Analysis of Algorithms

4.1 Introduction

The primary purpose of this book is to teach you how to design your own efficient algorithms. However, if you are faced with several different algorithms to solve the same problem, you have to decide which one is best suited for your application. An essential tool for this purpose is the *analysis of algorithms*. Only after you have determined the efficiency of the various algorithms will you be able to make a well-informed decision. But there is no magic formula for analysing the efficiency of algorithms. It is largely a matter of judgement, intuition and experience. Nevertheless, there are some basic techniques that are often useful, such as knowing how to deal with control structures and recurrence equations. This chapter covers the most commonly used techniques and illustrates them with examples. More examples are found throughout the book.

4.2 Analysing control structures

The analysis of algorithms usually proceeds from the inside out. First, we determine the time required by individual instructions (this time is often bounded by a constant); then we combine these times according to the control structures that combine the instructions in the program. Some control structures such as sequencing—putting one instruction after another—are easy to analyse whereas others such as **while** loops are more subtle. In this section, we give general principles that are useful in analyses involving the most frequently encountered control structures, as well as examples of the application of these principles.

4.2.1 Sequencing

Let P_1 and P_2 be two fragments of an algorithm. They may be single instructions or complicated subalgorithms. Let t_1 and t_2 be the times taken by P_1 and P_2, respectively. These times may depend on various parameters, such as the instance size. The **sequencing rule** says that the time required to compute "$P_1; P_2$", that is first P_1 and then P_2, is simply $t_1 + t_2$. By the maximum rule, this time is in $\Theta(\max(t_1, t_2))$.

Despite its simplicity, applying this rule is sometimes less obvious than it may appear. For example, it could happen that one of the parameters that control t_2 depends on the result of the computation performed by P_1. Thus, the analysis of "$P_1; P_2$" cannot always be performed by considering P_1 and P_2 independently.

4.2.2 "For" loops

For loops are the easiest loops to analyse. Consider the following loop.

> **for** $i \leftarrow 1$ **to** m **do** $P(i)$

Here and throughout the book, we adopt the convention that when $m = 0$ this is not an error; it simply means that the controlled statement $P(i)$ is not executed at all. Suppose this loop is part of a larger algorithm, working on an instance of size n. (Be careful not to confuse m and n.) The easiest case is when the time taken by $P(i)$ does not actually depend on i, although it could depend on the instance size or, more generally, on the instance itself. Let t denote the time required to compute $P(i)$. In this case, the obvious analysis of the loop is that $P(i)$ is performed m times, each time at a cost of t, and thus the total time required by the loop is simply $\ell = mt$. Although this approach is usually adequate, there is a potential pitfall: we did not take account of the time needed for *loop control*. After all, our **for** loop is shorthand for something like the following **while** loop.

> $i \leftarrow 1$
> **while** $i \leq m$ **do**
> $\quad P(i)$
> $\quad i \leftarrow i + 1$

In most situations, it is reasonable to count at unit cost the test $i \leq m$, the instructions $i \leftarrow 1$ and $i \leftarrow i + 1$, and the sequencing operations (**go to**) implicit in the **while** loop. Let c be an upper bound on the time required by each of these operations. The time ℓ taken by the loop is thus bounded above by

$$
\begin{aligned}
\ell \quad \leq \quad & c & & \text{for } i \leftarrow 1 \\
+ \quad & (m+1)c & & \text{for the tests } i \leq m \\
+ \quad & mt & & \text{for the executions of } P(i) \\
+ \quad & mc & & \text{for the executions of } i \leftarrow i + 1 \\
+ \quad & mc & & \text{for the sequencing operations} \\
\leq \quad & (t + 3c)m + 2c.
\end{aligned}
$$

Moreover this time is clearly bounded below by mt. If c is negligible compared to t, our previous estimate that ℓ is roughly equal to mt was therefore justified, except for one crucial case: $\ell \approx mt$ is completely wrong when $m = 0$ (it is even worse if m is negative!). We shall see in Section 4.3 that neglecting the time required for loop control can lead to serious errors in such circumstances.

Resist the temptation to say that the time taken by the loop is in $\Theta(mt)$ on the pretext that the Θ notation is only asked to be effective beyond some threshold such as $m \geq 1$. The problem with this argument is that if we are in fact analysing the entire algorithm rather than simply the **for** loop, the threshold implied by the Θ notation concerns n, the instance size, rather than m, the number of times we go round the loop, and $m = 0$ could happen for arbitrarily large values of n. On the other hand, provided t is bounded *below* by some constant (which is always the case in practice), and provided there exists a threshold n_0 such that $m \geq 1$ whenever $n \geq n_0$, Problem 4.3 asks you to show that ℓ is indeed in $\Theta(mt)$ when ℓ, m and t are considered as functions of n.

The analysis of **for** loops is more interesting when the time $t(i)$ required for $P(i)$ varies as a function of i. (In general, the time required for $P(i)$ could depend not only on i but also on the instance size n or even on the instance itself.) If we neglect the time taken by the loop control, which is usually adequate provided $m \geq 1$, the same **for** loop

    for $i \leftarrow 1$ **to** m **do** $P(i)$

takes a time given not by a multiplication but rather by a sum: it is $\sum_{i=1}^{m} t(i)$. The techniques of Section 1.7.2 are often useful to transform such sums into simpler asymptotic notation.

We illustrate the analysis of **for** loops with a simple algorithm for computing the Fibonacci sequence that we evaluated empirically in Section 2.7.5. We repeat the algorithm below.

    function *Fibiter*(n)
        $i \leftarrow 1;\ j \leftarrow 0$
        for $k \leftarrow 1$ **to** n **do** $j \leftarrow i + j$
                          $i \leftarrow j - i$
        return j

If we count all arithmetic operations at unit cost, the instructions inside the **for** loop take constant time. Let the time taken by these instructions be bounded above by some constant c. Not taking loop control into account, the time taken by the **for** loop is bounded above by n times this constant: nc. Since the instructions before and after the loop take negligible time, we conclude that the algorithm takes a time in $O(n)$. Similar reasoning yields that this time is also in $\Omega(n)$, hence it is in $\Theta(n)$.

We saw however in Section 2.5 that it is not reasonable to count the additions involved in the computation of the Fibonacci sequence at unit cost unless n is very small. Therefore, we should take account of the fact that an instruction as simple as "$j \leftarrow i + j$" is increasingly expensive each time round the loop. It is easy to program long-integer additions and subtractions so that the time needed to add or subtract two integers is in the exact order of the number of figures in the larger operand. To determine the time taken by the k–th trip round the loop, we need to know the length of the integers involved. Problem 4.4 asks you to prove by mathematical induction that the values of i and j at the end of the k–th iteration are f_{k-1} and f_k, respectively. This is precisely why the algorithm works: it returns the value of j at the end of the n–th iteration, which is therefore f_n as required. Moreover, we saw in Section 2.7.5 that de Moivre's formula tells us that the size of f_k is in $\Theta(k)$. Therefore, the k–th iteration takes a time $\Theta(k-1)+\Theta(k)$, which is the same as $\Theta(k)$; see Problem 3.34. Let c be a constant such that this time is bounded above by ck for all $k \geq 1$. If we neglect the time required for the loop control and for the instructions before and after the loop, we conclude that the time taken by the algorithm is bounded above by

$$\sum_{k=1}^{n} ck = c \sum_{k=1}^{n} k = c \frac{n(n+1)}{2} \in O(n^2).$$

Similar reasoning yields that this time is in $\Omega(n^2)$, and therefore it is in $\Theta(n^2)$. Thus it makes a crucial difference in the analysis of *Fibrec* whether or not we count arithmetic operations at unit cost.

The analysis of **for** loops that start at a value other than 1 or proceed by larger steps should be obvious at this point. Consider the following loop for example.

for $i \leftarrow 5$ **to** m **step** 2 **do** $P(i)$

Here, $P(i)$ is executed $((m-5) \div 2)+1$ times provided $m \geq 3$. (For a **for** loop to make sense, the endpoint should always be at least as large as the starting point *minus* the step).

4.2.3 Recursive calls

The analysis of recursive algorithms is usually straightforward, at least up to a point. Simple inspection of the algorithm often gives rise to a recurrence equation that "mimics" the flow of control in the algorithm. Once the recurrence equation has been obtained, general techniques covered in Section 4.7 can be applied to transform the equation into simpler nonrecursive asymptotic notation.

As an example, consider again the problem of computing the Fibonacci sequence, but this time with the recursive algorithm *Fibrec*, which we compared to *Fibiter* in Section 2.7.5.

function *Fibrec*(n)
    if $n < 2$ **then return** n
    else return *Fibrec*($n-1$)+*Fibrec*($n-2$)

Let $T(n)$ be the time taken by a call on *Fibrec*(n). If $n < 2$, the algorithm simply returns n, which takes some constant time a. Otherwise, most of the work is spent in the two recursive calls, which take time $T(n-1)$ and $T(n-2)$, respectively. Moreover, one addition involving f_{n-1} and f_{n-2} (which are the values returned by the recursive calls) must be performed, as well as the control of the recursion and the test "**if** $n < 2$". Let $h(n)$ stand for the work involved in this addition and control, that is the time required by a call on *Fibrec*(n) ignoring the time spent inside the two recursive calls. By definition of $T(n)$ and $h(n)$ we obtain the following recurrence.

$$T(n) = \begin{cases} a & \text{if } n = 0 \text{ or } n = 1 \\ T(n-1) + T(n-2) + h(n) & \text{otherwise} \end{cases} \qquad (4.1)$$

If we count the additions at unit cost, $h(n)$ is bounded by a constant and the recurrence equation for $T(n)$ is very similar to that already encountered for $g(n)$ in Section 1.6.4. Constructive induction applies equally well to reach the same conclusion: $T(n) \in O(f_n)$. However, it is easier in this case to apply the techniques of Section 4.7 to solve recurrence 4.1. Similar reasoning shows that $T(n) \in \Omega(f_n)$, hence $T(n) \in \Theta(f_n)$. Using de Moivre's formula, we conclude that *Fibrec*(n) takes a time exponential in n. This is *double* exponential in the size of the instance since the *value* of n is exponential in the *size* of n.

If we do not count the additions at unit cost, $h(n)$ is no longer bounded by a constant. Instead $h(n)$ is dominated by the time required for the addition of f_{n-1} and f_{n-2} for sufficiently large n. We have already seen that this addition takes a time in the exact order of n. Therefore $h(n) \in \Theta(n)$. The techniques of Section 4.7 apply again to solve recurrence 4.1. Surprisingly, the result is the same regardless of whether $h(n)$ is constant or linear: it is still the case that $T(n) \in \Theta(f_n)$. In conclusion, *Fibrec*(n) takes a time exponential in n whether or not we count additions at unit cost! The only difference lies in the multiplicative constant hidden in the Θ notation.

4.2.4 "While" and "repeat" loops

While and **repeat** loops are usually harder to analyse than **for** loops because there is no obvious a priori way to know how many times we shall have to go round the loop. The standard technique for analysing these loops is to find a function of the variables involved whose value decreases each time around. To conclude that the loop will eventually terminate, it suffices to show that this value must be a positive integer. (You cannot keep decreasing an integer indefinitely.) To determine how many times the loop is repeated, however, we need to understand better how the value of this function decreases. An alternative approach to the analysis of **while** loops consists of treating them like recursive algorithms. We illustrate both techniques with the same example. The analysis of **repeat** loops is carried out similarly; we do not give examples in this section.

We shall study *binary search* in detail in Section 7.3. Nevertheless, we use it now because it illustrates perfectly the analysis of **while** loops. The purpose of binary search is to find an element x in an array $T[1 .. n]$ that is in nondecreasing order. Assume for simplicity that x is guaranteed to appear at least once in T. (The general case is handled in Section 7.3.) We require to find an integer i such that $1 \leq i \leq n$ and $T[i] = x$. The basic idea behind binary search is to compare x with the element y in the middle of T. The search is over if $x = y$; it can be confined to the upper half of the array if $x > y$; otherwise, it is sufficient to search the lower half. We obtain the following algorithm. (A slightly better algorithm is given in Section 7.3; see Problem 7.11.)

> **function** *Binary_Search*$(T[1..n], x)$
>   {This algorithm assumes that x appears in T}
> $i \leftarrow 1; \; j \leftarrow n$
>   **while** $i < j$ **do**
> $\{\, T[i] \le x \le T[j] \,\}$
> $k \leftarrow (i + j) \div 2$
>   **case** $x < T[k]: j \leftarrow k - 1$
> $x = T[k]: i, j \leftarrow k$ {**return** k}
> $x > T[k]: i \leftarrow k + 1$
>   **return** i

Recall that to analyse the running time of a **while** loop, we must find a function of the variables involved whose value decreases each time round the loop. In this case, it is natural to consider $j - i + 1$, which we shall call d. Thus d represents the number of elements of T still under consideration. Initially, $d = n$. The loop terminates when $i \ge j$, which is equivalent to $d \le 1$. (In fact, d can never be smaller than 1, but we do not use this.) Each time round the loop, there are three possibilities: either j is set to $k - 1$, i is set to $k + 1$, or both i and j are set to k. Let d and $\hat{d}$ stand respectively for the value of $j - i + 1$ before and after the iteration under consideration. We use i, j, $\hat{\imath}$ and $\hat{\jmath}$ similarly. If $x < T[k]$, the instruction "$j \leftarrow k - 1$" is executed and thus $\hat{\imath} = i$ and $\hat{\jmath} = [(i + j) \div 2] - 1$. Therefore,

$$\hat{d} = \hat{\jmath} - \hat{\imath} + 1 = (i + j) \div 2 - i \le (i + j)/2 - i < (j - i + 1)/2 = d/2.$$

Similarly, if $x > T[k]$, the instruction "$i \leftarrow k + 1$" is executed and thus

$$\hat{\imath} = [(i + j) \div 2] + 1 \text{ and } \hat{\jmath} = j.$$

Therefore,

$$\hat{d} = \hat{\jmath} - \hat{\imath} + 1 = j - (i + j) \div 2 \le j - (i + j - 1)/2 = (j - i + 1)/2 = d/2.$$

Finally, if $x = T[k]$, then i and j are set to the same value and thus $\hat{d} = 1$; but d was at least 2 since otherwise the loop would not have been reentered. We conclude that $\hat{d} \le d/2$ whichever case happens, which means that the value of d is at least halved each time round the loop. Since we stop when $d \le 1$, the process must eventually stop, but how much time does it take?

To determine an upper bound on the running time of binary search, let d_ℓ denote the value of $j - i + 1$ at the end of the ℓ-th trip round the loop for $\ell \ge 1$ and let $d_0 = n$. Since $d_{\ell-1}$ is the value of $j - i + 1$ *before* starting the ℓ-th iteration, we have proved that $d_\ell \le d_{\ell-1}/2$ for all $\ell \ge 1$. It follows immediately by mathematical induction that $d_\ell \le n/2^\ell$. But the loop terminates when $d \le 1$, which happens at the latest when $\ell = \lceil \lg n \rceil$. We conclude that the loop is entered at most $\lceil \lg n \rceil$ times. Since each trip round the loop takes constant time, binary search takes a time in $O(\log n)$. Similar reasoning yields a matching lower bound of $\Omega(\log n)$ in the worst case, and thus binary search takes a time in $\Theta(\log n)$. This is true even though our algorithm can go much faster in the best case, when x is situated precisely in the middle of the array; see Problem 7.11.

The alternative approach to analysing the running time of binary search begins much the same way. The idea is to think of the **while** loop as if it were implemented recursively instead of iteratively. Each time round the loop, we reduce the range of possible locations for x in the array. Let $t(d)$ denote the maximum time needed to terminate the **while** loop when $j - i + 1 \leq d$, that is when there are at most d elements still under consideration. We have seen already that the value of $j - i + 1$ is at least halved each time round the loop. In recursive terms, this means that $t(d)$ is at most the constant time b required to go round the loop once, plus the time $t(d \div 2)$ sufficient to finish the loop from there. Since it takes constant time c to determine that the loop is finished when $d = 1$, we obtain the following recurrence.

$$t(d) \leq \begin{cases} c & \text{if } d = 1 \\ b + t(d \div 2) & \text{otherwise} \end{cases} \qquad (4.2)$$

The techniques of Section 4.7 apply easily to conclude that $t(n) \in O(\log n)$.

4.3 Using a barometer

The analysis of many algorithms is significantly simplified when one instruction— or one test—can be singled out as *barometer*. A barometer instruction is one that is executed at least as often as any other instruction in the algorithm. (There is no harm if some instructions are executed up to a constant number of times more often than the barometer since their contribution is absorbed in the asymptotic notation). Provided the time taken by each instruction is bounded by a constant, the time taken by the entire algorithm is in the exact order of the number of times that the barometer instruction is executed.

This is useful because it allows us to neglect the exact times taken by each instruction. In particular, it avoids the need to introduce constants such as those bounding the time taken by various elementary operations, which are meaningless since they depend on the implementation, and they are discarded when the final result is expressed in terms of asymptotic notation. For example, consider the analysis of *Fibiter* in Section 4.2.2 when we count all arithmetic operations at unit cost. We saw that the algorithm takes a time bounded above by cn for some meaningless constant c, and therefore that it takes a time in $\Theta(n)$. It would have been simpler to say that the instruction $j \leftarrow i + j$ can be taken as barometer, that this instruction is obviously executed exactly n times, and therefore the algorithm takes a time in $\Theta(n)$. Selection sorting will provide a more convincing example of the usefulness of barometer instructions in the next section.

When an algorithm involves several nested loops, any instruction of the innermost loop can usually be used as barometer. However, this should be done carefully because there are cases where it is necessary to take account of the implicit loop control. This happens typically when some of the loops are executed zero times, because such loops do take time even though they entail no executions of the barometer instruction. If this happens too often, the number of times the barometer instruction is executed can be dwarfed by the number of times empty loops are entered—and therefore it was an error to consider it as a barometer. Consider for instance pigeon-hole sorting (Section 2.7.2). Here we generalize the algorithm to handle the case where the elements to be sorted are integers known to lie between 1 and s rather than between 1 and 10 000. Recall that $T[1 .. n]$ is the array to be sorted and $U[1 .. s]$ is an array constructed so that $U[k]$ gives the number of times integer k appears in T. The final phase of the algorithm rebuilds T in nondecreasing order as follows from the information available in U.

$$i \leftarrow 0$$
$$\textbf{for } k \leftarrow 1 \textbf{ to s do}$$
$$\textbf{while } U[k] \neq 0 \textbf{ do}$$
$$i \leftarrow i + 1$$
$$T[i] \leftarrow k$$
$$U[k] \leftarrow U[k] - 1$$

To analyse the time required by this process, we use "$U[k]$" to denote the value *originally* stored in $U[k]$ since all these values are set to 0 during the process. It is tempting to choose any of the instructions in the inner loop as a barometer. For each value of k, these instructions are executed $U[k]$ times. The total number of times they are executed is therefore $\sum_{k=1}^{s} U[k]$. But this sum is equal to n, the number of integers to sort, since the sum of the number of times that each element appears gives the total number of elements. If indeed these instructions could serve as a barometer, we would conclude that this process takes a time in the exact order of n. A simple example is sufficient to convince us that this is not necessarily the case. Suppose $U[k] = 1$ when k is a perfect square and $U[k] = 0$ otherwise. This would correspond to sorting an array T containing exactly once each perfect square between 1 and n^2, using $s = n^2$ pigeon-holes. In this case, the process clearly takes a time in $\Omega(n^2)$ since the outer loop is executed s times. Therefore, it cannot be that the time taken is in $\Theta(n)$. This proves that the choice of the instructions in the inner loop as a barometer was incorrect. The problem arises because we can only neglect the time spent initializing and controlling loops provided we make sure to include something even if the loop is executed zero times.

The correct and detailed analysis of the process is as follows. Let a be the time needed for the test $U[k] \neq 0$ each time round the inner loop and let b be the time taken by one execution of the instructions in the inner loop, including the implicit sequencing operation to go back to the test at the beginning of the loop. To execute the inner loop completely for a given value of k takes a time $t_k = (1 + U[k])a + U[k]b$, where we add 1 to $U[k]$ before multiplying by a to take account of the fact that the test is performed each time round the loop *and* one more time to determine that the loop has been completed. The crucial thing is that this time is not zero even when $U[k] = 0$. The complete process takes a time $c + \sum_{k=1}^{s}(d + t_k)$, where c and d are new constants to take account of the time needed to initialize and control the outer loop, respectively. When simplified, this expression yields $c + (a + d)s + (a + b)n$. We conclude that the process takes a time in $\Theta(n + s)$. Thus the time depends on two independent parameters n and s;

it cannot be expressed as a function of just one of them. It is easy to see that the initialization phase of pigeon-hole sorting (Section 2.7.2) also takes a time in $\Theta(n + s)$, unless *virtual initialization* is used—see the end of Section 5.1—in which case a time in $\Theta(n)$ suffices for that phase. In any case, this sorting technique takes a time in $\Theta(n + s)$ in total to sort n integers between 1 and s. If you prefer, the maximum rule can be invoked to state that this time is in $\Theta(\max(n, s))$. Hence, pigeon-hole sorting is worthwhile but only provided s is small enough compared to n. For instance, if we are interested in the time required as a function only of the number of elements to sort, this technique succeeds in astonishing linear time if $s \in O(n)$ but it chugs along in quadratic time when $s \in \Theta(n^2)$.

Despite the above, the use of a barometer is appropriate to analyse pigeon-hole sorting. Our problem was that we did not choose the proper barometer. Instead of the instructions *inside* the inner loop, we should have used the inner-loop *test* "$U[k] \neq 0$" as a barometer. Indeed, no instructions in the process are executed more times than this test is performed, which is the definition of a barometer. It is easy to show that this test is performed exactly $n + s$ times, and therefore the correct conclusion about the running time of the process follows immediately without need to introduce meaningless constants.

In conclusion, the use of a barometer is a handy tool to simplify the analysis of many algorithms, but this technique should be used with care.

4.4 Supplementary examples

In this section, we study several additional examples of analyses of algorithms involving loops, recursion, and the use of barometers.

Selection sort

Selection sorting, encountered in Section 2.4, provides a good example of the analysis of *nested* loops.

```
procedure select(T[1 .. n])
    for i ← 1 to n − 1 do
        minj ← i; minx ← T[i]
        for j ← i + 1 to n do
            if T[j] < minx then minj ← j
                              minx ← T[j]
        T[minj] ← T[i]
        T[i] ← minx
```

Although the time spent by each trip round the inner loop is not constant—it takes longer when $T[j] < minx$—this time is bounded above by some constant c (that takes the loop control into account). For each value of i, the instructions in the inner loop are executed $n − (i + 1) + 1 = n − i$ times, and therefore the time taken by the inner loop is $t(i) \leq (n − i)c$. The time taken for the i–th trip round the outer loop is bounded above by $b + t(i)$ for an appropriate constant b that takes account of the elementary operations before and after the inner loop and of the loop control for the outer loop. Therefore, the total time spent by the algorithm is bounded above by

$$\sum_{i=1}^{n-1} b + (n-i)c = \sum_{i=1}^{n-1} (b+cn) - c\sum_{i=1}^{n-1} i$$

$$= (n-1)(b+cn) - cn(n-1)/2$$

$$= \frac{1}{2}cn^2 + \left(b - \frac{1}{2}c\right)n - b,$$

which is in $O(n^2)$. Similar reasoning shows that this time is also in $\Omega(n^2)$ in all cases, and therefore selection sort takes a time in $\Theta(n^2)$ to sort n items.

The above argument can be simplified, obviating the need to introduce explicit constants such as b and c, once we are comfortable with the notion of a barometer instruction. Here, it is natural to take the innermost test "**if** $T[j] < minx$" as a barometer and count the exact number of times it is executed. This is a good measure of the total running time of the algorithm because none of the loops can be executed zero times (in which case loop control could have been more time-consuming than our barometer). The number of times that the test is executed is easily seen to be

$$\sum_{i=1}^{n-1}\sum_{j=i+1}^{n} 1 = \sum_{i=1}^{n-1} (n-i)$$

$$= \sum_{k=1}^{n-1} k = n(n-1)/2.$$

Thus the number of times the barometer instruction is executed is in $\Theta(n^2)$, which automatically gives the running time of the algorithm itself.

Insertion sort

We encountered insertion sorting also in Section 2.4.

```
procedure insert(T[1..n])
    for i ← 2 to n do
        x ← T[i]; j ← i - 1
        while j > 0 and x < T[j] do T[j + 1] ← T[j]
                                    j ← j - 1
        T[j + 1] ← x
```

Unlike selection sorting, we saw in Section 2.4 that the time taken to sort n items by insertion depends significantly on the original order of the elements. Here, we analyse this algorithm in the worst case; the average-case analysis is given in Section 4.5. To analyse the running time of this algorithm, we choose as barometer the number of times the **while** loop condition ($j > 0$ **and** $x < T[j]$) is tested.

Suppose for a moment that i is fixed. Let $x = T[i]$, as in the algorithm. The worst case arises when x is less than $T[j]$ for every j between 1 and $i-1$, since in this case we have to compare x to $T[i-1], T[i-2], ..., T[1]$ before we leave the **while** loop because $j = 0$. Thus the **while** loop test is performed i times in the worst case. This worst case happens for every value of i from 2 to n when the array is initially sorted into descending order. The barometer test is thus performed $\sum_{i=2}^{n} i = n(n+1)/2 - 1$ times in total, which is in $\Theta(n^2)$. This shows that insertion sort also takes a time in $\Theta(n^2)$ to sort n items in the worst case.

Euclid's algorithm

Recall from Section 2.7.4 that Euclid's algorithm is used to compute the greatest common divisor of two integers.

> **function** $Euclid(m, n)$
>   **while** $m > 0$ **do**
> $t \leftarrow m$
> $m \leftarrow n \bmod m$
> $n \leftarrow t$
>   **return** n

The analysis of this loop is slightly more subtle than those we have seen so far because clearly measurable progress occurs not every time round the loop but rather every other time. To see this, we first show that for any two integers m and n such that $n \geq m$, it is always true that $n \bmod m < n/2$.

◇ If $m > n/2$, then $1 \leq n/m < 2$, and so $n \div m = 1$, which implies that
  $n \bmod m = n - m \times (n \div m) = n - m < n - n/2 = n/2$.

◇ If $m \leq n/2$, then $n \bmod m < m \leq n/2$.

Assume without loss of generality that $n \geq m$ since otherwise the first trip round the loop swaps m and n (because $n \bmod m = n$ when $n < m$). This condition is preserved each time round the loop because $n \bmod m$ is never larger than m. If we assume that arithmetic operations are elementary, which is reasonable in many situations, the total time taken by the algorithm is in the exact order of the number of trips round the loop. Let us determine an upper bound on this number as a function of n. Consider what happens to m and n after we go round the loop *twice*, assuming the algorithm does not stop earlier. Let m_0 and n_0 denote the original value of the parameters. After the first trip round the loop, m becomes $n_0 \bmod m_0$. After the second trip round the loop, n takes up that value. By the observation above, n has become smaller than $n_0/2$. In other words, the value of n is at least halved after going round the loop twice. By then it is still the case that $n \geq m$ and therefore the same reasoning applies again: if the algorithm has not stopped earlier, two additional trips round the loop will make the value of n at least twice as small again. With some experience, the conclusion is now immediate: the loop is entered at most roughly $2 \lg n$ times.

Formally, it is best to complete the analysis of Euclid's algorithm by treating the **while** loop as if it were a recursive algorithm. Let $t(\ell)$ be the maximum number of times the algorithm goes round the loop on inputs m and n when $m \leq n \leq \ell$. If $n \leq 2$, we go round the loop either zero times (if $m = 0$) or one time. Otherwise, either we go round the loop less than twice (if $m = 0$ or m divides n exactly), or at least twice. In the latter case, the value of n is at least halved—and thus it becomes at most $\ell \div 2$—and that of m becomes no larger than the new value of n. Therefore it takes no more than $t(\ell \div 2)$ additional trips round the loop to complete the calculation. This yields the following recurrence.

$$t(\ell) \leq \begin{cases} 1 & \text{if } \ell \leq 2 \\ 2 + t(\ell \div 2) & \text{otherwise} \end{cases}$$

This is a special case of Equation 4.2 and the techniques of Section 4.7 apply equally well to conclude that $t(\ell) \in O(\log \ell)$, which proves that Euclid's algorithm runs in a time linear in the *size* of its input provided it is reasonable to consider all arithmetic operations as elementary. It is interesting to know that this algorithm performs least well on inputs of any given size when m and n are two consecutive numbers from the Fibonacci sequence.

You may wonder why we used $t(\ell)$ to bound the number of times the algorithm goes round the loop on inputs m and n when $m \leq n \leq \ell$ rather than defining t directly as a function of n, the larger of the two operands. It would seem more natural to define $t(n)$ as the maximum number of times the algorithm goes round the loop on inputs m and n when $m \leq n$. The problem is that this definition would not allow us to conclude that $t(n) \leq 2 + t(n \div 2)$ from the fact that n is at least halved after two trips round the loop. For example, $t(13) = 5$ with $Euclid(8, 13)$ as worst case, whereas $t(13 \div 2) = t(6) = 2$. This happens because two trips round the loop after a call on $Euclid(8, 13)$ leaves us *not* with $n = 6$ but with $n = 5$ (and $m = 3$), and indeed $t(13) \leq 2 + t(5)$ since $t(5) = 3$ (precisely with $Euclid(3, 5)$ as worst case). The source of the problem is that the "more natural" definition for t does not yield a nondecreasing function since $t(5) > t(6)$, and thus the existence of some $n' \leq n \div 2$ such that $t(n) \leq 2 + t(n')$ does not imply that $t(n) \leq 2 + t(n \div 2)$. Instead, all we can say is that $t(n) \leq 2 + \max\{t(n') \mid n' \leq n \div 2\}$, an awkward recurrence to work with. To summarize, we defined function t the way we did precisely so that it is obviously nondecreasing, yet it provides an upper bound on the time taken on any specific instance.

The Towers of Hanoi

The Towers of Hanoi provide us with another example of the analysis of recursive algorithms. It is said that after creating the world, God set on Earth three rods made of diamond and 64 rings of gold. These rings are all different in size. At the creation they were threaded on the first rod in order of size, the largest at the bottom and the smallest at the top. God also created a monastery close by the rods. The monks' task in life is to transfer all the rings onto the second rod. The only operation permitted is to move a single ring from one rod to another in such a way that no ring is ever placed on top of another smaller one. When the monks have finished their task, according to the legend, the world will come to an end. This is probably the most reassuring prophecy ever made concerning the end of the world, for if the monks manage to move one ring per second, working night and day without ever resting nor ever making a mistake, their work will still not be finished 500 000 million years after they began. This is more than 25 times the estimated age of the Universe!

The problem can obviously be generalized to an arbitrary number n of rings. For example, with $n = 3$, we obtain the solution given in Figure 4.1. To solve the general problem, we need only realize that to transfer the m smallest rings from rod i to rod j (where $1 \le i \le 3$, $1 \le j \le 3$, $i \ne j$ and $m \ge 1$), we can first transfer the smallest $m - 1$ rings from rod i to rod $k = 6 - i - j$, next transfer the m–th ring from rod i to rod j, and finally retransfer the $m - 1$ smallest rings from rod k to rod j. Here is a formal description of this algorithm; to solve the original instance, all you have to do (!) is to call it with the arguments $(64, 1, 2)$.

> **procedure** $Hanoi(m, i, j)$
> $\quad$ {Moves the m smallest rings from rod i to rod j}
> $\quad$ **if** $m > 0$ **then** $Hanoi(m - 1, i, 6 - i - j)$
> $\quad\quad\quad\quad\quad$ **write** i " $\rightarrow$ " j
> $\quad\quad\quad\quad\quad$ $Hanoi(m - 1, 6 - i - j, j)$

To analyse the execution time of this algorithm, we use the instruction **write** as a barometer. Let $t(m)$ denote the number of times it is executed on a call of $Hanoi(m, \cdot, \cdot)$. By inspection of the algorithm, we obtain the following recurrence:

$$t(m) = \begin{cases} 0 & \text{if } m = 0 \\ 2t(m - 1) + 1 & \text{otherwise,} \end{cases} \tag{4.3}$$

from which the technique of Section 4.7 yields $t(m) = 2^m - 1$; see Example 4.7.6. Since the number of executions of the **write** instruction is a good measure of the time taken by the algorithm, we conclude that it takes a time in $\Theta(2^n)$ to solve the problem with n rings. In fact, it can be proved that the problem with n rings cannot be solved in less than $2^n - 1$ moves and therefore this algorithm is optimal if one insists on printing the entire sequence of necessary moves.

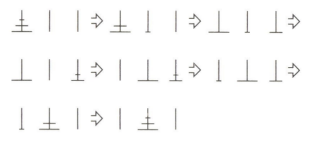

Figure 4.1. The Towers of Hanoi

Computing determinants

Yet another example of analysis of recursion concerns the recursive algorithm for calculating a determinant. Recall that the determinant of an $n \times n$ matrix can be computed from the determinants of n smaller $(n - 1) \times (n - 1)$ matrices obtained by deleting the first row and some column of the original matrix. Once the n sub-determinants are calculated, the determinant of the original matrix is obtained very quickly. In addition to the recursive calls, the dominant operation needed consists of creating the n submatrices whose determinants are to be calculated. This takes a time in $\Theta(n^3)$ if it is implemented in a straightforward way, but a time in $\Theta(n)$ suffices if pointers are used instead of copying elements. Therefore, the total time $t(n)$ needed to calculate the determinant of an $n \times n$ matrix by the recursive algorithm is given by the recurrence $t(n) = nt(n-1) + h(n)$ for $n \geq 2$, where $h(n) \in \Theta(n)$. This recurrence cannot be handled by the techniques of Section 4.7. However we saw in Problem 1.31 that constructive induction applies to conclude that $t(n) \in \Theta(n!)$, which shows that this algorithm is very inefficient. The same conclusion holds if we are less clever and need $h(n) \in \Theta(n^3)$. Recall from Section 2.7.1 that the determinant can be calculated in a time in $\Theta(n^3)$ by Gauss–Jordan elimination, and even faster by *another* recursive algorithm of the divide-and-conquer family. More work is needed to analyse these algorithms if the time taken for arithmetic operations is taken into account.

4.5 Average-case analysis

We saw that insertion sort takes quadratic time in the worst case. On the other hand, it is easy to show that it succeeds in linear time in the *best* case. It is natural to wonder about its efficiency *on the average*. For the question to make sense, we must be precise about the meaning of "on the average". This requires us to assume an a priori probability distribution on the instances that our algorithm may be asked to solve. The conclusion of an average-case analysis may depend crucially on this assumption, and such analysis may be misleading if in fact our assumption turns out not to correspond with the reality of the application that uses the algorithm. This important issue was discussed at more length in Section 2.4, and we shall come back to it in Section 10.7. Most of the time, average-case analyses are performed under the more or less realistic assumption that all instances of any given size are equally likely. For sorting problems, it is simpler to assume also that all the elements to be sorted are distinct.

Suppose we have n distinct elements to sort by insertion and all $n!$ permutations of these elements are equally likely. To determine the time taken on average by the algorithm, we could add the times required to sort each of the possible permutations, and then divide by $n!$ the answer thus obtained. An alternative approach, easier in this case, is to analyse directly the time required by the algorithm, reasoning probabilistically as we proceed. For any i, $2 \leq i \leq n$, consider the subarray $T[1..i]$. The *partial rank* of $T[i]$ is defined as the position it would occupy if the subarray were sorted. For example, the partial rank of $T[4]$ in $[3, 6, 2, \mathbf{5}, 1, 7, 4]$ is 3 because $T[1..4]$ once sorted is $[2, 3, \mathbf{5}, 6]$. Clearly, the partial rank of $T[i]$ does not depend on the order of the elements in subarray $T[1..i-1]$. It is easy to show that if all $n!$ permutations of $T[1..n]$ are equally likely, then the partial rank of $T[i]$ is equally likely to take any value between 1 and i, independently for all values of i.

Suppose now that i is fixed, $2 \leq i \leq n$, and that we are about to enter the **while** loop. Inspection of the algorithm shows that subarray $T[1..i-1]$ contains the same elements as before the algorithm was called, although they are now in sorted order, and $T[i]$ still has its original value since it has not yet been moved. Therefore the partial rank of $T[i]$ is equally likely to be any value between 1 and i.

Let k be this partial rank. We choose again as barometer the number of times the **while** loop condition ($j > 0$ **and** $x < T[j]$) is tested. By definition of partial rank, and since $T[1 .. i - 1]$ is sorted, this test is performed exactly $i - k + 1$ times. Because each value of k between 1 and i has probability $1/i$ of occurring, the average number of times the barometer test is performed for any given value of i is

$$c_i = \frac{1}{i} \sum_{k=1}^{i} (i - k + 1) = \frac{i + 1}{2}.$$

These events are independent for different values of i. The total average number of times the barometer test is performed when sorting n items is therefore

$$\sum_{i=2}^{n} c_i = \sum_{i=2}^{n} \frac{i + 1}{2} = \frac{(n - 1)(n + 4)}{4},$$

which is in $\Theta(n^2)$. We conclude that insertion sorting makes on the average about half as many comparisons as in the worst case, but this number is still quadratic.

4.6 Amortized analysis

Worst-case analysis is sometimes overly pessimistic. Consider for instance a process P that has side effects, which means that P modifies the value of global variables. As a result of side effects, two successive identical calls on P could take a substantially different amount of time. The easy thing to do when analysing an algorithm that uses P as subalgorithm would be to analyse P in the worst case, and assume the worst happens each time P is called. This approach yields a correct answer assuming we are satisfied with an analysis in O notation—as opposed to Θ notation—but the answer could be pessimistic. Consider for instance the following loop.

> **for** $i \leftarrow 1$ **to** n **do** P

If P takes a time in $\Theta(\log n)$ in the worst case, it is correct to conclude that the loop takes a time in $O(n \log n)$, but it may be that it is much faster *even in the worst case*. This could happen if P cannot take a long time ($\Omega(\log n)$) unless it has been called many times previously, each time at small cost. It could be for instance that P takes constant time on the average, in which case the entire loop would be performed in linear time.

The meaning of "on the average" here is entirely different from what we encountered in Section 4.5. Rather than taking the average over all possible inputs, which requires an assumption on the probability distribution of instances, we take the average over *successive* calls. Here the times taken by the various calls are highly dependent, whereas we implicitly assumed in Section 4.5 that each call was independent from the others. To prevent confusion, we shall say in this context that each call on P takes *amortized* constant time rather than saying that it takes constant time on the average.

Saying that a process takes amortized constant time means that there exists a constant c (depending only on the implementation) such that for any positive

n and any sequence of n calls on the process, the total time for those calls is bounded above by cn. Therefore, excessive time is allowed for one call only if very short times have been registered previously, *not* merely if further calls would go quickly. Indeed, if a call were allowed to be expensive on the ground that it prepares for much quicker later calls, the expense would be wasted should that call be the final one.

Consider for instance the time needed to get a cup of coffee in a common coffee room. Most of the time, you simply walk into the room, grab the pot, and pour coffee into your cup. Perhaps you spill a few drops on the table. Once in a while, however, you have the bad luck to find the pot empty, and you must start a fresh brew, which is considerably more time-consuming. While you are at it, you may as well clean up the table. Thus, the algorithm for getting a cup of coffee takes substantial time in the worst case, yet it is quick in the amortized sense because a long time is required only after several cups have been obtained quickly. (For this analogy to work properly, we must assume somewhat unrealistically that the pot is full when the first person walks in; otherwise the very first cup would consume too much time.)

A classic example of this behaviour in computer science concerns storage allocation with occasional need for "garbage collection". A simpler example concerns updating a binary counter. Suppose we wish to manage the counter as an array of bits representing the value of the counter in binary notation: array $C[1..m]$ represents $\sum_{j=1}^{m} 2^{m-j} C[j]$. For instance, array $[0, 1, 1, 0, 1, 1]$ represents 27. Since such a counter can only count up to $2^m - 1$, we shall assume that we are happy to count modulo 2^m. (Alternatively, we could produce an error message in case of overflow.) Here is the algorithm for adding 1 to the counter.

> **procedure** *count*$(C[1..m])$
>   {This procedure assumes $m \geq 1$
>   and $C[j] \in \{0, 1\}$ for each $1 \leq j \leq m$}
> $j \leftarrow m + 1$
>   **repeat**
> $j \leftarrow j - 1$
> $C[j] \leftarrow 1 - C[j]$
>   **until** $C[j] = 1$ **or** $j = 1$

Called on our example $[0, 1, 1, 0, 1, 1]$, the array becomes $[0, 1, 1, 0, 1, 0]$ the first time round the loop, $[0, 1, 1, 0, 0, 0]$ the second time, and $[0, 1, 1, 1, 0, 0]$ the third time (which indeed represents the value 28 in binary); the loop then terminates with $j = 4$ since $C[4]$ is now equal to 1. Clearly, the algorithm's worst case occurs when $C[j] = 1$ for all j, in which case it goes round the loop m times. Therefore, n calls on *count* starting from an all-zero array take total time in $O(nm)$. But do they take a time in $\Theta(nm)$? The answer is negative, as we are about to show that *count* takes constant amortized time. This implies that our n calls on *count* collectively take a time in $\Theta(n)$, with a hidden constant that does not depend on m. In particular, counting from 0 to $n = 2^m - 1$ can be achieved in a time linear in n, whereas careless worst-case analysis of *count* would yield the correct but pessimistic conclusion that it takes a time in $O(n \log n)$.

There are two main techniques to establish amortized analysis results: the potential function approach and the accounting trick. Both techniques apply best to analyse the number of times a barometer instruction is executed.

Potential functions

Suppose the process to be analysed modifies a database and its efficiency each time it is called depends on the current state of that database. We associate with the database a notion of "cleanliness", known as the *potential function* of the database. Calls on the process are allowed to take more time than average provided they clean up the database. Conversely, quick calls are allowed to mess it up. This is precisely what happens in the coffee room! The analogy holds even further: the faster you fill up your cup, the more likely you will spill coffee, which in turn means that it will take longer when the time comes to clean up. Similarly, the faster the process goes when it goes fast, the more it messes up the database, which in turn requires more time when cleaning up becomes necessary.

Formally, we introduce an integer-valued potential function Φ of the state of the database. Larger values of Φ correspond to dirtier states. Let ϕ_0 be the value of Φ on the initial state; it represents our standard of cleanliness. Let ϕ_i be the value of Φ on the database after the i–th call on the process, and let t_i be the time needed by that call (or the number of times the barometer instruction is performed). We define the *amortized time* taken by that call as

$$\hat{t}_i = t_i + \phi_i - \phi_{i-1}.$$

Thus, $\hat{t}_i$ is the actual time required to carry out the i–th call on the process plus the increase in potential caused by that call. It is sometimes better to think of it as the actual time minus the *de*crease in potential, as this shows that operations that clean up the database will be allowed to run longer without incurring a penalty in terms of their amortized time.

Let T_n denote the total time required for the first n calls on the process, and denote the total *amortized* time by $\hat{T}_n$.

$$
\begin{aligned}
\hat{T}_n &= \sum_{i=1}^{n} \hat{t}_i = \sum_{i=1}^{n} (t_i + \phi_i - \phi_{i-1}) \\
&= \sum_{i=1}^{n} t_i + \sum_{i=1}^{n} \phi_i - \sum_{i=1}^{n} \phi_{i-1} \\
&= T_n + \phi_n + \phi_{n-1} + \cdots + \phi_1 \\
&\qquad - \phi_{n-1} - \cdots - \phi_1 - \phi_0 \\
&= T_n + \phi_n - \phi_0
\end{aligned}
$$

Therefore

$$T_n = \hat{T}_n - (\phi_n - \phi_0).$$

The significance of this is that $T_n \leq \hat{T}_n$ holds for all n provided ϕ_n never becomes smaller than ϕ_0. In other words, the total amortized time is always an upper bound on the total actual time needed to perform a sequence of operations, as long as the database is never allowed to become "cleaner" than it was initially. (This shows that overcleaning can be harmful!) This approach is interesting when the actual time varies significantly from one call to the next, whereas the amortized time is nearly invariant. For instance, a sequence of operations takes linear time when the amortized time per operation is constant, regardless of the actual time required for each operation.

The challenge in applying this technique is to figure out the proper potential function. We illustrate this with our example of the binary counter. A call on *count* is increasingly expensive as the rightmost zero in the counter is farther to the left. Therefore the potential function that immediately comes to mind would be m minus the largest j such that $C[j] = 0$. It turns out, however, that this choice of potential function is not appropriate because a single operation can mess up the counter arbitrarily (adding 1 to the counter representing $2^k - 2$ causes this potential function to jump from 0 to k). Fortunately, a simpler potential function works well: define $\Phi(C)$ as the number of bits equal to 1 in C. Clearly, our condition that the potential never be allowed to decrease below the initial potential holds since the initial potential is zero.

What is the amortized cost of adding 1 to the counter, in terms of the number of times we go round the loop? There are three cases to consider.

◇ If the counter represents an even integer, we go round the loop once only as we flip the rightmost bit from 0 to 1. As a result, there is one more bit set to 1 than there was before. Therefore, the actual cost is 1 trip round the loop, and the increase in potential is also 1. By definition, the amortized cost of the operation is $1 + 1 = 2$.

◇ If all the bits in the counter are equal to 1, we go round the loop m times, flipping all those bits to 0. As a result, the potential drops from m to 0. Therefore, the amortized cost is $m - m = 0$.

◇ In all other cases, each time we go round the loop we decrease the potential by 1 since we flip a bit from 1 to 0, except for the last trip round the loop when we increase the potential by 1 since we flip a bit from 0 to 1. Thus, if we go round the loop k times, we decrease the potential $k - 1$ times and we increase it once, for a net decrease of $k - 2$. Therefore, the amortized cost is $k - (k - 2) = 2$.

In conclusion, the amortized cost of adding 1 to a binary counter is always exactly equivalent to going round the loop twice, except that it costs nothing when the counter cycles back to zero. Since the actual cost of a sequence of operations is never more than the amortized cost, this proves that the total number of times we go round the loop when incrementing a counter n times in succession is at most $2n$ provided the counter was initially set to zero. (This analysis would fail if the time to initialize the counter were taken into account, much as if we had taken account of the time to brew the first pot of coffee in the morning.)

The accounting trick

This technique can be thought of as a restatement of the potential function approach, yet it is easier to apply in some contexts. The classic use of the accounting trick serves to analyse the efficiency of the disjoint set structures described in Section 5.9. The actual analysis of those structures is however omitted as it reaches beyond the scope of this book.

Suppose you have already guessed an upper bound τ on the time spent in the amortized sense whenever process P is called, and you wish to prove that your intuition was correct (τ may depend on various parameters, such as the instance size). To use the accounting trick, you must set up a virtual bank account, which initially contains zero tokens. Each time P is called, an allowance of τ tokens is deposited in the account; each time the barometer instruction is executed, you must pay for it by spending one token from the account. The golden rule is never to allow the account to become overdrawn. This insures that long operations are permitted only if sufficiently many quick ones have already taken place. Therefore, it suffices to show that the golden rule is obeyed to conclude that the actual time taken by any sequence of operations never exceeds its amortized time, and in particular any sequence of s operations takes a time that is at most τs.

To analyse our example of a binary counter, we allocate two tokens for each call on *count* (this is our initial guess) and we spend one token each time *count* goes round its loop. The key insight again concerns the number of bits set to 1 in the counter. We leave it for the reader to verify that each call on *count* increases (decreases) the amount available in the bank account precisely by the increase (decrease) it causes in the number of bits set to 1 in the counter (unless the counter cycles back to zero, in which case less tokens are spent). In other words, if there were i bits set to 1 in the counter before the call and $j > 0$ bits afterwards, the number of tokens available in the bank account once the call is completed has increased by $j - i$ (counting a negative increase as a decrease). Consequently, the number of tokens in the account is always exactly equal to the number of bits currently set to 1 in the counter (unless the counter has cycled, in which case there are more tokens in the account). This proves that the account is never overdrawn since the number of bits set to 1 cannot be negative, and therefore each call on *count* costs at most two tokens in the amortized sense. We shall use this technique in Section 5.8 to analyse the amortized efficiency of binomial heaps.

4.7 Solving recurrences

The indispensable last step when analysing an algorithm is often to solve a recurrence equation. With a little experience and intuition most recurrences can be solved by intelligent guesswork. However, there exists a powerful technique that can be used to solve certain classes of recurrence almost automatically. This is the main topic of this section: the technique of the *characteristic equation*.

4.7.1 Intelligent guesswork

This approach generally proceeds in four stages: calculate the first few values of the recurrence, look for regularity, guess a suitable general form, and finally prove by mathematical induction (perhaps constructive induction) that this form is correct.

Consider the following recurrence.

$$T(n) = \begin{cases} 0 & \text{if } n = 0 \\ 3T(n \div 2) + n & \text{otherwise} \end{cases} \qquad (4.4)$$

One of the first lessons experience will teach you if you try solving recurrences is that discontinuous functions such as the floor function (implicit in $n \div 2$) are hard to analyse. Our first step is to replace $n \div 2$ with the better-behaved "$n/2$" with a suitable restriction on the set of values of n that we consider initially. It is tempting to restrict n to being even since in that case $n \div 2 = n/2$, but recursively dividing an even number by 2 may produce an odd number larger than 1. Therefore, it is a better idea to restrict n to being an exact power of 2. Once this special case is handled, the general case follows painlessly in asymptotic notation from the smoothness rule of Section 3.4.

First, we tabulate the value of the recurrence on the first few powers of 2.

n	1	2	4	8	16	32
$T(n)$	1	5	19	65	211	665

Each term in this table but the first is computed from the previous term. For instance, $T(16) = 3 \times T(8) + 16 = 3 \times 65 + 16 = 211$. But is this table useful? There is certainly no obvious pattern in this sequence! What regularity is there to look for?

The solution becomes apparent if we keep more "history" about the value of $T(n)$. Instead of writing $T(2) = 5$, it is more useful to write $T(2) = 3 \times 1 + 2$. Then,

$$T(4) = 3 \times T(2) + 4 = 3 \times (3 \times 1 + 2) + 4 = 3^2 \times 1 + 3 \times 2 + 4.$$

We continue in this way, writing n as an explicit power of 2.

n	$T(n)$
1	1
2	$3 \times 1 + 2$
2^2	$3^2 \times 1 + 3 \times 2 + 2^2$
2^3	$3^3 \times 1 + 3^2 \times 2 + 3 \times 2^2 + 2^3$
2^4	$3^4 \times 1 + 3^3 \times 2 + 3^2 \times 2^2 + 3 \times 2^3 + 2^4$
2^5	$3^5 \times 1 + 3^4 \times 2 + 3^3 \times 2^2 + 3^2 \times 2^3 + 3 \times 2^4 + 2^5$

The pattern is now obvious.

$$\begin{aligned} T(2^k) &= 3^k 2^0 + 3^{k-1} 2^1 + 3^{k-2} 2^2 + \cdots 1\, 2^{k-1} + 3^0 2^k \\ &= \sum_{i=0}^{k} 3^{k-i} 2^i = 3^k \sum_{i=0}^{k} (2/3)^i \\ &= 3^k \times (1 - (2/3)^{k+1})/(1 - 2/3) \qquad \text{(Proposition 1.7.10)} \\ &= 3^{k+1} - 2^{k+1} \end{aligned} \qquad (4.5)$$

It is easy to check this formula against our earlier tabulation. By induction (not *mathematical* induction), we are now convinced that Equation 4.5 is correct.

Nevertheless, we saw in Section 1.6 that induction is not always to be trusted. Therefore, the analysis of our recurrence when n is a power of 2 is incomplete until we prove Equation 4.5 by mathematical induction. This easy exercise is left to the reader.

With hindsight, Equation 4.5 could have been guessed with just a little more intuition. For this it would have been enough to tabulate the value of $T(n) + in$ for small values of i, such as $-2 \leq i \leq 2$.

n	1	2	4	8	16	32
$T(n) - 2n$	−1	1	11	49	179	601
$T(n) - n$	0	3	15	57	195	633
$T(n)$	1	5	19	65	211	665
$T(n) + n$	2	7	23	73	227	697
$T(n) + 2n$	3	9	27	81	243	729

This time, it is immediately apparent that $T(n) + 2n$ is an exact power of 3, from which Equation 4.5 is readily derived.

What happens when n is not a power of 2? Solving recurrence 4.4 exactly is rather difficult. Fortunately, this is unnecessary if we are happy to obtain the answer in asymptotic notation. For this, it is convenient to rewrite Equation 4.5 in terms of $T(n)$ rather than in terms of $T(2^k)$. Since $n = 2^k$ it follows that $k = \lg n$. Therefore

$$T(n) = T(2^{\lg n}) = 3^{1+\lg n} - 2^{1+\lg n}.$$

Using the fact that $3^{\lg n} = n^{\lg 3}$ (which is easily seen by taking the binary logarithm on both sides of the equation; see Problem 1.15) it follows that

$$T(n) = 3n^{\lg 3} - 2n \tag{4.6}$$

when n is a power of 2. Using conditional asymptotic notation, we conclude that $T(n) \in \Theta(n^{\lg 3} \mid n$ is a power of 2). Since $T(n)$ is a nondecreasing function (a fact easily proven by mathematical induction) and $n^{\lg 3}$ is a smooth function, it follows from Section 3.4 that $T(n) \in \Theta(n^{\lg 3})$ unconditionally.

In practice, you will never need this kind of guesswork to solve a recurrence such as Equation 4.4 because the techniques we are about to study can solve it automatically in a few minutes. However, there are recurrences for which those techniques are powerless, and intelligent guesswork can always be used as last resort.

4.7.2 Homogeneous recurrences

We begin our study of the *technique of the characteristic equation* with the resolution of homogeneous linear recurrences with constant coefficients, that is recurrences of the form

$$a_0 t_n + a_1 t_{n-1} + \cdots + a_k t_{n-k} = 0 \tag{4.7}$$

where the t_i are the values we are looking for. In addition to Equation 4.7, the values of t_i on k values of i (usually $0 \le i \le k - 1$ or $1 \le i \le k$) are needed to determine the sequence. These *initial conditions* will be considered later. Until then, Equation 4.7 typically has infinitely many solutions. This recurrence is

⋄ *linear* because it does not contain terms of the form $t_{n-i}t_{n-j}$, t_{n-i}^2, and so on;

⋄ *homogeneous* because the linear combination of the t_{n-i} is equal to zero; and

⋄ *with constant coefficients* because the a_i are constants.

Consider for instance our now familiar recurrence for the Fibonacci sequence.

$$f_n = f_{n-1} + f_{n-2}$$

This recurrence easily fits the mould of Equation 4.7 after obvious rewriting.

$$f_n - f_{n-1} - f_{n-2} = 0$$

Therefore, the Fibonacci sequence corresponds to a homogeneous linear recurrence with constant coefficients with $k = 2$, $a_0 = 1$ and $a_1 = a_2 = -1$.

Before we even start to look for solutions to Equation 4.7, it is interesting to note that any linear combination of solutions is itself a solution. In other words, if f_n and g_n satisfy Equation 4.7, so $\sum_{i=0}^{k} a_i f_{n-i} = 0$ and similarly for g_n, and if we set $t_n = c f_n + d g_n$ for arbitrary constants c and d, then t_n is also a solution to Equation 4.7. This is true because

$$a_0 t_n + a_1 t_{n-1} + \cdots + a_k t_{n-k}$$
$$= a_0(c f_n + d g_n) + a_1(c f_{n-1} + d g_{n-1}) + \cdots + a_k(c f_{n-k} + d g_{n-k})$$
$$= c(a_0 f_n + a_1 f_{n-1} + \cdots + a_k f_{n-k}) + d(a_0 g_n + a_1 g_{n-1} + \cdots + a_k g_{n-k})$$
$$= c \times 0 + d \times 0 = 0.$$

This rule generalizes to linear combinations of any number of solutions.

Trying to solve a few easy examples of recurrences of the form of Equation 4.7 (*not* the Fibonacci sequence) by intelligent guesswork suggests looking for solutions of the form

$$t_n = x^n$$

where x is a constant as yet unknown. If we try this guessed solution in Equation 4.7, we obtain

$$a_0 x^n + a_1 x^{n-1} + \cdots + a_k x^{n-k} = 0.$$

This equation is satisfied if $x = 0$, a trivial solution of no interest. Otherwise, the equation is satisfied if and only if

$$a_0 x^k + a_1 x^{k-1} + \cdots + a_k = 0.$$

This equation of degree k in x is called the *characteristic equation* of the recurrence 4.7 and

$$p(x) = a_0 x^k + a_1 x^{k-1} + \cdots + a_k$$

is called its *characteristic polynomial*.

Recall that the fundamental theorem of algebra states that any polynomial $p(x)$ of degree k has exactly k roots (not necessarily distinct), which means that it can be factorized as a product of k monomials

$$p(x) = \prod_{i=1}^{k} (x - r_i)$$

where the r_i may be complex numbers. Moreover, these r_i are the only solutions of the equation $p(x) = 0$.

Consider any root r_i of the characteristic polynomial. Since $p(r_i) = 0$ it follows that $x = r_i$ is a solution to the characteristic equation and therefore r_i^n is a solution to the recurrence. Since any linear combination of solutions is also a solution, we conclude that

$$t_n = \sum_{i=1}^{k} c_i r_i^n \tag{4.8}$$

satisfies the recurrence for any choice of constants $c_1, c_2, \ldots, c_k$. The remarkable fact, which we do not prove here, is that Equation 4.7 has *only* solutions of this form *provided all the r_i are distinct*. In this case, the k constants can be determined from k initial conditions by solving a system of k linear equations in k unknowns.

Example 4.7.1. (Fibonacci)   Consider the recurrence

$$f_n = \begin{cases} n & \text{if } n = 0 \text{ or } n = 1 \\ f_{n-1} + f_{n-2} & \text{otherwise} \end{cases}$$

First we rewrite this recurrence to fit the mould of Equation 4.7.

$$f_n - f_{n-1} - f_{n-2} = 0$$

The characteristic polynomial is

$$x^2 - x - 1$$

whose roots are

$$r_1 = \tfrac{1 + \sqrt{5}}{2} \text{ and } r_2 = \tfrac{1 - \sqrt{5}}{2}.$$

The general solution is therefore of the form

$$f_n = c_1 r_1^n + c_2 r_2^n. \tag{4.9}$$

It remains to use the initial conditions to determine the constants c_1 and c_2. When $n = 0$, Equation 4.9 yields $f_0 = c_1 + c_2$. But we know that $f_0 = 0$. Therefore,

$c_1 + c_2 = 0$. Similarly, when $n = 1$, Equation 4.9 together with the second initial condition tell us that $f_1 = c_1 r_1 + c_2 r_2 = 1$. Remembering that the values of r_1 and r_2 are known, this gives us two linear equations in the two unknowns c_1 and c_2.

$$
\begin{array}{rcrcl}
c_1 & + & c_2 & = & 0 \\
r_1\,c_1 & + & r_2\,c_2 & = & 1
\end{array}
$$

Solving these equations, we obtain

$$c_1 = \tfrac{1}{\sqrt{5}} \text{ and } c_2 = -\tfrac{1}{\sqrt{5}}.$$

Thus

$$f_n = \frac{1}{\sqrt{5}}\left[\left(\frac{1+\sqrt{5}}{2}\right)^n - \left(\frac{1-\sqrt{5}}{2}\right)^n\right],$$

which is de Moivre's famous formula for the Fibonacci sequence. Notice how much easier the technique of the characteristic equation is than the approach by constructive induction that we saw in Section 1.6.4. It is also more precise since all we were able to discover with constructive induction was that "f_n grows exponentially in a number close to ϕ"; now we have an exact formula.   □

If it surprises you that the solution of a recurrence with integer coefficients and initial conditions involves irrational numbers, try Problem 4.31 for an even bigger surprise!

Example 4.7.2.   Consider the recurrence

$$
t_n = \begin{cases}
0 & \text{if } n = 0 \\
5 & \text{if } n = 1 \\
3t_{n-1} + 4t_{n-2} & \text{otherwise}
\end{cases}
$$

First we rewrite the recurrence.

$$t_n - 3t_{n-1} - 4t_{n-2} = 0$$

The characteristic polynomial is

$$x^2 - 3x - 4 = (x+1)(x-4)$$

whose roots are $r_1 = -1$ and $r_2 = 4$. The general solution is therefore of the form

$$t_n = c_1(-1)^n + c_2\, 4^n.$$

The initial conditions give

$$
\begin{array}{rcrclcl}
c_1 & + & c_2 & = & 0 & & n = 0 \\
-c_1 & + & 4c_2 & = & 5 & & n = 1
\end{array}
$$

Solving these equations, we obtain $c_1 = -1$ and $c_2 = 1$. Therefore

$$t_n = 4^n - (-1)^n.$$

□

The situation becomes slightly more complicated when the characteristic polynomial has multiple roots, that is when the k roots are not all distinct. It is still true that Equation 4.8 satisfies the recurrence for any values of the constants c_i, but *this is no longer the most general solution*. To find other solutions, let

$$p(x) = a_0 x^k + a_1 x^{k-1} + \cdots + a_k$$

be the characteristic polynomial of our recurrence, and let r be a multiple root. By definition of multiple roots, there exists a polynomial $q(x)$ of degree $k - 2$ such that $p(x) = (x - r)^2 q(x)$. For every $n \geq k$ consider the n–th degree polynomials

$$u_n(x) = a_0 x^n + a_1 x^{n-1} + \cdots + a_k x^{n-k} \text{ and}$$

$$v_n(x) = a_0 n x^n + a_1 (n - 1) x^{n-1} + \cdots + a_k (n - k) x^{n-k}.$$

Observe that $v_n(x) = x \times u'_n(x)$, where $u'_n(x)$ denotes the derivative of $u_n(x)$ with respect to x. But $u_n(x)$ can be rewritten as

$$u_n(x) = x^{n-k} p(x) = x^{n-k}(x - r)^2 q(x) = (x - r)^2 \times [x^{n-k} q(x)].$$

Using the rule for computing the derivative of a product of functions, we obtain that the derivative of $u_n(x)$ with respect to x is

$$u'_n(x) = 2(x - r)x^{n-k} q(x) + (x - r)^2 [x^{n-k} q(x)]'.$$

Therefore $u'_n(r) = 0$, which implies that $v_n(r) = r \times u'_n(r) = 0$ for all $n \geq k$. In other words,

$$a_0 n r^n + a_1 (n - 1) r^{n-1} + \cdots + a_k (n - k) r^{n-k} = 0.$$

We conclude that $t_n = nr^n$ is also a solution to the recurrence. This is a genuinely new solution in the sense that it cannot be obtained by choosing appropriate constants c_i in Equation 4.8.

More generally, if root r has multiplicity m, then $t_n = r^n$, $t_n = nr^n$, $t_n = n^2 r^n, \ldots, t_n = n^{m-1} r^n$ are all distinct solutions to the recurrence. The general solution is a linear combination of these terms and of the terms contributed by the other roots of the characteristic polynomial. To summarize, if $r_1, r_2, \ldots, r_\ell$ are the ℓ distinct roots of the characteristic polynomial and if their multiplicities are $m_1, m_2, \ldots, m_\ell$, respectively, then

$$t_n = \sum_{i=1}^{\ell} \sum_{j=0}^{m_i - 1} c_{ij} n^j r_i^n$$

is the general solution to Equation 4.7. Again, the constants c_{ij}, $1 \leq i \leq \ell$ and $0 \leq j \leq m_i - 1$, are to be determined by the k initial conditions. There are k such constants because $\sum_{i=1}^{\ell} m_i = k$ (the sum of the multiplicities of the distinct roots is equal to the total number of roots). For simplicity, we shall normally label the constants $c_1, c_2, \ldots, c_k$ rather than using two indexes.

Example 4.7.3.   Consider the recurrence

$$t_n = \begin{cases} n & \text{if } n = 0, 1 \text{ or } 2 \\ 5t_{n-1} - 8t_{n-2} + 4t_{n-3} & \text{otherwise} \end{cases}$$

First we rewrite the recurrence.

$$t_n - 5t_{n-1} + 8t_{n-2} - 4t_{n-3} = 0$$

The characteristic polynomial is

$$x^3 - 5x^2 + 8x - 4 = (x - 1)(x - 2)^2.$$

The roots are therefore $r_1 = 1$ of multiplicity $m_1 = 1$ and $r_2 = 2$ of multiplicity $m_2 = 2$, and the general solution is

$$t_n = c_1 1^n + c_2 2^n + c_3 n 2^n.$$

The initial conditions give

$$\begin{array}{rcrcrcll} c_1 & + & c_2 & & & = & 0 & n = 0 \\ c_1 & + & 2c_2 & + & 2c_3 & = & 1 & n = 1 \\ c_1 & + & 4c_2 & + & 8c_3 & = & 2 & n = 2 \end{array}$$

Solving these equations, we obtain $c_1 = -2$, $c_2 = 2$ and $c_3 = -\frac{1}{2}$. Therefore

$$t_n = 2^{n+1} - n 2^{n-1} - 2.$$

$\square$

4.7.3 Inhomogeneous recurrences

The solution of a linear recurrence with constant coefficients becomes more difficult when the recurrence is not homogeneous, that is when the linear combination is not equal to zero. In particular, it is no longer true that any linear combination of solutions is a solution. We begin with a simple case. Consider the following recurrence.

$$a_0 t_n + a_1 t_{n-1} + \cdots + a_k t_{n-k} = b^n p(n) \tag{4.10}$$

The left-hand side is the same as before, but on the right-hand side we have $b^n p(n)$, where

◇ b is a constant; and

◇ $p(n)$ is a polynomial in n of degree d.

Example 4.7.4.   Consider the recurrence

$$t_n - 2t_{n-1} = 3^n. \tag{4.11}$$

In this case, $b = 3$ and $p(n) = 1$, a polynomial of degree 0. A little cunning allows us to reduce this example to the homogeneous case with which we are now familiar. To see this, first multiply the recurrence by 3, obtaining

$$3t_n - 6t_{n-1} = 3^{n+1}.$$

Now replace n by $n - 1$ in this recurrence to get

$$3t_{n-1} - 6t_{n-2} = 3^n. \tag{4.12}$$

Finally, subtract Equation 4.12 from 4.11 to obtain

$$t_n - 5t_{n-1} + 6t_{n-2} = 0, \tag{4.13}$$

which can be solved by the method of Section 4.7.2. The characteristic polynomial is

$$x^2 - 5x + 6 = (x - 2)(x - 3)$$

and therefore all solutions are of the form

$$t_n = c_1 2^n + c_2 3^n. \tag{4.14}$$

However, it is no longer true that an arbitrary choice of constants c_1 and c_2 in Equation 4.14 produces a solution to the recurrence even when initial conditions are not taken into account. Worse: even the basic solutions $t_n = 2^n$ and $t_n = 3^n$, which are of course solutions to Equation 4.13, are not solutions to the original recurrence given by Equation 4.11. What is going on? The explanation is that Equations 4.11 and 4.13 are *not* equivalent: Equation 4.13 can be solved given arbitrary values for t_0 and t_1 (the initial conditions), whereas our original Equation 4.11 implies that $t_1 = 2t_0 + 3$. The general solution to the original recurrence can be determined as a function of t_0 by solving two linear equations in the unknowns c_1 and c_2.

$$\begin{aligned} c_1 + \ c_2 &= \ t_0 & n = 0 \\ 2c_1 + 3c_2 &= 2t_0 + 3 & n = 1 \end{aligned} \tag{4.15}$$

Solving these, we obtain $c_1 = t_0 - 3$ and $c_2 = 3$. Therefore, the general solution is

$$t_n = (t_0 - 3) 2^n + 3^{n+1}$$

and thus $t_n \in \Theta(3^n)$ regardless of the initial condition.

Provided $t_0 \geq 0$, an easy proof by mathematical induction based on Equation 4.11 shows that $t_n \geq 0$ for all $n \geq 0$. Therefore, it is immediate from Equation 4.14 that $t_n \in O(3^n)$: there is no need to solve for the constants c_1 and c_2 to reach this conclusion. However, this equation alone is not sufficient to conclude that $t_n \in \Theta(3^n)$ because it could have been a priori that $c_2 = 0$. Nevertheless, it turns out that the value of c_2 can be obtained directly, with no need to set up System 4.15 of linear equations. This suffices to conclude that $t_n \in \Theta(3^n)$ whatever the value of t_0 (even if it is negative). To see this, substitute Equation 4.14 into the original recurrence.

$$\begin{aligned} 3^n &= t_n - 2t_{n-1} \\ &= (c_1 2^n + c_2 3^n) - 2(c_1 2^{n-1} + c_2 3^{n-1}) \\ &= c_2 3^{n-1} \end{aligned}$$

Regardless of the initial condition, we conclude that $c_2 = 3$.   □

In the examples that follow, we sometimes set up a system of linear equations to determine all the constants that appear in the general solution, whereas at other times we determine only the necessary constants by substituting the general solution into the original recurrence.

Example 4.7.5.   We wish to find the general solution of the following recurrence.

$$t_n - 2t_{n-1} = (n+5)\,3^n \qquad n \geq 1 \tag{4.16}$$

The manipulation needed to transform this into a homogeneous recurrence is slightly more complicated than with Example 4.7.4. We must

a. write down the recurrence,

b. replace n in the recurrence by $n-1$ and then multiply by -6, and

c. replace n in the recurrence by $n-2$ and then multiply by 9, successively obtaining

$$
\begin{array}{rrcl}
t_n & -\;2t_{n-1} & = & (n+5)\,3^n \\
& -\;6t_{n-1} \;+\; 12t_{n-2} & = & -6\,(n+4)\,3^{n-1} \\
& 9t_{n-2} \;-\; 18t_{n-3} & = & 9\,(n+3)\,3^{n-2}.
\end{array}
$$

Adding these three equations, we obtain a homogeneous recurrence

$$t_n - 8t_{n-1} + 21t_{n-2} - 18t_{n-3} = \;\; 0.$$

The characteristic polynomial is

$$x^3 - 8x^2 + 21x - 18 = (x-2)(x-3)^2$$

and therefore all solutions are of the form

$$t_n = c_1\,2^n + c_2\,3^n + c_3\,n\,3^n. \tag{4.17}$$

Once again, any choice of values for the constants c_1, c_2 and c_3 in Equation 4.17 provides a solution to the homogeneous recurrence, but the original recurrence imposes restrictions on these constants because it requires that $t_1 = 2t_0 + 18$ and $t_2 = 2t_1 + 63 = 4t_0 + 99$. Thus, the general solution is found by solving the following system of linear equations.

$$
\begin{array}{rcll}
c_1 \;+\; c_2 & = & t_0 & n = 0 \\
2c_1 \;+\; 3c_2 \;+\; 3c_3 & = & 2t_0 + 18 & n = 1 \\
4c_1 \;+\; 9c_2 \;+\; 18c_3 & = & 4t_0 + 99 & n = 2
\end{array}
$$

This implies that $c_1 = t_0 - 9$, $c_2 = 9$ and $c_3 = 3$. Therefore, the general solution to Equation 4.16 is

$$t_n = (t_0 - 9)\,2^n + (n+3)\,3^{n+1}$$

and thus $t_n \in \Theta(n3^n)$ regardless of the initial condition.

Alternatively, we could substitute Equation 4.17 into the original recurrence. After simple manipulation, we obtain

$$(n+5)\,3^n = c_3\,n\,3^{n-1} + (2c_3 + c_2)\,3^{n-1}.$$

Equating the coefficients of $n3^n$ yields $1 = c_3/3$ and thus $c_3 = 3$. The fact that c_3 is strictly positive suffices to establish the exact order of t_n, with no need to solve for the other constants. Once c_3 is known, however, the value of c_2 is just as easy to obtain by equating the coefficients of 3^n: $c_2 = 15 - 2c_3 = 9$.   □

Looking back on Examples 4.7.4 and 4.7.5, we see that part of the characteristic polynomial comes from the left-hand side of Equation 4.10 and the rest from the right-hand side. The part that comes from the left-hand side is exactly as if the equation had been homogeneous: $(x - 2)$ for both examples. The part that comes from the right-hand side is a result of our manipulation.

Generalizing, we can show that to solve Equation 4.10 it is sufficient to use the following characteristic polynomial.

$$(a_0 x^k + a_1 x^{k-1} + \cdots + a_k) (x - b)^{d+1}$$

(Recall that d is the degree of polynomial $p(n)$.) Once this polynomial is obtained, proceed as in the homogeneous case, except that some of the equations needed to determine the constants are obtained not from the initial conditions but from the recurrence itself.

Example 4.7.6.   The number of movements of a ring required in the Towers of Hanoi problem (see Section 4.4) is given by Equation 4.3.

$$t(m) = \begin{cases} 0 & \text{if } m = 0 \\ 2t(m-1)+1 & \text{otherwise} \end{cases}$$

This can be written as

$$t(m) - 2t(m-1) = 1, \tag{4.18}$$

which is of the form of Equation 4.10 with $b = 1$ and $p(n) = 1$, a polynomial of degree 0. The characteristic polynomial is therefore

$$(x - 2)(x - 1)$$

where the factor $(x - 2)$ comes from the left-hand side of Equation 4.18 and the factor $(x - 1)$ from its right-hand side. The roots of this polynomial are 1 and 2, both of multiplicity 1, so all solutions of this recurrence are of the form

$$t(m) = c_1 1^m + c_2 2^m. \tag{4.19}$$

We need two initial conditions to determine the constants c_1 and c_2. We know that $t(0) = 0$; to find the second initial condition we use the recurrence itself to calculate

$$t(1) = 2t(0) + 1 = 1.$$

This gives us two linear equations in the unknown constants.

$$
\begin{array}{ccccccl}
c_1 & + & c_2 & = & 0 & \quad m = 0 \\
c_1 & + & 2c_2 & = & 1 & \quad m = 1
\end{array}
$$

From this, we obtain the solution $c_1 = -1$ and $c_2 = 1$ and therefore

$$t(m) = 2^m - 1.$$

If all we want is to determine the exact order of $t(m)$, there is no need to calculate the constants in Equation 4.19. This time we do not even need to substitute Equation 4.19 into the original recurrence. Knowing that $t(m) = c_1 + c_2 2^m$ is sufficient to conclude that $c_2 > 0$ and thus $t(m) \in \Theta(2^m)$. For this, note that $t(m)$, the number of movements of a ring required, is certainly neither negative nor a constant since clearly $t(m) \geq m$. □

Example 4.7.7.   Consider the recurrence

$$t_n = 2t_{n-1} + n.$$

This can be rewritten

$$t_n - 2t_{n-1} = n, \quad {}^{=1^n p(1)} \; (x-2)(x-1)^2 = 0$$

which is of the form of Equation 4.10 with $b = 1$ and $p(n) = n$, a polynomial of degree 1. The characteristic polynomial is thus

$$(x - 2)(x - 1)^2$$

with roots 2 (multiplicity 1) and 1 (multiplicity 2). All solutions are therefore of the form

$$t_n = c_1 2^n + c_2 1^n + c_3 n 1^n. \tag{4.20}$$

Provided $t_0 \geq 0$, and therefore $t_n \geq 0$ for all n, we conclude immediately that $t_n \in O(2^n)$. Further analysis is required to assert that $t_n \in \Theta(2^n)$.

If we substitute Equation 4.20 into the original recurrence, we obtain

$$\begin{aligned} n &= t_n - 2t_{n-1} \\ &= (c_1 2^n + c_2 + c_3 n) - 2(c_1 2^{n-1} + c_2 + c_3(n-1)) \\ &= (2c_3 - c_2) - c_3 n \end{aligned}$$

from which we read directly that $2c_3 - c_2 = 0$ and $-c_3 = 1$, regardless of the initial condition. This implies that $c_3 = -1$ and $c_2 = -2$. At first we are disappointed because it is c_1 that is relevant to determining the exact order of t_n as given by Equation 4.20, and we obtained the other two constants instead. However, those constants turn Equation 4.20 into

$$t_n = c_1 2^n - n - 2. \tag{4.21}$$

Provided $t_0 \geq 0$, and therefore $t_n \geq 0$ for all n, Equation 4.21 implies that c_1 must be strictly positive. Therefore, we are entitled to conclude that $t_n \in \Theta(2^n)$ with no need to solve explicitly for c_1. Of course, c_1 can now be obtained easily from the initial condition if so desired.

Alternatively, all three constants can be determined as functions of t_0 by setting up and solving the appropriate system of linear equations obtained from Equation 4.20 and the value of t_1 and t_2 computed from the original recurrence.   □

By now, you may be convinced that, for all practical purposes, there is no need to worry about the constants: the exact order of t_n can always be read off directly from the general solution. Wrong! Or perhaps you think that the constants obtained by the simpler technique of substituting the general solution into the original recurrence are always sufficient to determine its exact order. Wrong again! Consider the following example.

Example 4.7.8.   Consider the recurrence

$$t_n = \begin{cases} 1 & \text{if } n = 0 \\ 4t_{n-1} - 2^n & \text{otherwise} \end{cases}$$

First rewrite the recurrence as

$$t_n - 4t_{n-1} = -2^n,$$

which is of the form of Equation 4.10 with $b = 2$ and $p(n) = -1$, a polynomial of degree 0. The characteristic polynomial is thus

$$(x - 4)(x - 2)$$

with roots 4 and 2, both of multiplicity 1. All solutions are therefore of the form

$$t_n = c_1 4^n + c_2 2^n. \tag{4.22}$$

You may be tempted to assert without further ado that $t_n \in \Theta(4^n)$ since that is clearly the dominant term in Equation 4.22.

   If you are in less of a hurry, you may wish to substitute Equation 4.22 into the original recurrence to see what comes out.

$$\begin{aligned} -2^n &= t_n - 4t_{n-1} \\ &= c_1 4^n + c_2 2^n - 4(c_1 4^{n-1} + c_2 2^{n-1}) \\ &= -c_2 2^n \end{aligned}$$

Therefore, $c_2 = 1$ regardless of the initial condition. Knowledge of c_2 is not directly relevant to determining the exact order of t_n as given by Equation 4.22. Unlike the previous example, however, nothing conclusive about c_1 can be asserted from the mere fact that c_2 is positive. Even if we had found that c_2 is negative, we still could not immediately conclude anything concerning c_1 because this time there is no obvious reason to believe that t_n must be positive.

   All else having failed, we are forced to determine all the constants. We could set up the usual system of two linear equations in two unknowns obtained from Equation 4.22 and the values of t_0 and t_1, but why throw away the knowledge we have already acquired about the value of c_2? We know that $t_n = c_1 4^n + 2^n$. Substituting the initial condition $t_0 = 1$ yields $1 = c_1 + 1$ and therefore $c_1 = 0$. The conclusion is that the exact solution for the recurrence is simply $t_n = 2^n$, and that the previous assertion that $t_n \in \Theta(4^n)$ was incorrect! Note however that t_n would be in $\Theta(4^n)$ if any larger value of t_0 were specified as initial condition since in general $c_1 = t_0 - 1$. On the other hand, with an initial condition $t_0 < 1$, t_n takes negative values that grow exponentially fast. This example illustrates the importance of the initial condition for some recurrences, whereas previous examples had shown that the asymptotic behaviour of many recurrences is not affected by the initial condition, at least when $t_0 \geq 0$.   □

A further generalization of the same type of argument allows us finally to solve recurrences of the form

$$a_0 t_n + a_1 t_{n-1} + \cdots + a_k t_{n-k} = b_1^n p_1(n) + b_2^n p_2(n) + \cdots \qquad (4.23)$$

where the b_i are distinct constants and the $p_i(n)$ are polynomials in n respectively of degree d_i. Such recurrences are solved using the following characteristic polynomial:

$$(a_0 x^k + a_1 x^{k-1} + \cdots + a_k)(x - b_1)^{d_1+1} (x - b_2)^{d_2+1} \cdots,$$

which contains one factor corresponding to the left-hand side and one factor corresponding to each term on the right-hand side. Once the characteristic polynomial is obtained, the recurrence is solved as before.

Example 4.7.9.   Consider the recurrence

$$t_n = \begin{cases} 0 & \text{if } n = 0 \\ 2t_{n-1} + n + 2^n & \text{otherwise} \end{cases}$$

First rewrite the recurrence as

$$t_n - 2t_{n-1} = n + 2^n,$$

which is of the form of Equation 4.23 with $b_1 = 1$, $p_1(n) = n$, $b_2 = 2$ and $p_2(n) = 1$. The degree of $p_1(n)$ is $d_1 = 1$ and the degree of $p_2(n)$ is $d_2 = 0$. The characteristic polynomial is

$$(x - 2)(x - 1)^2(x - 2),$$

which has roots 1 and 2, both of multiplicity 2. All solutions to the recurrence therefore have the form

$$t_n = c_1 1^n + c_2 n 1^n + c_3 2^n + c_4 n 2^n. \qquad (4.24)$$

We conclude from this equation that $t_n \in O(n2^n)$ without calculating the constants, but we need to know whether or not $c_4 > 0$ to determine the exact order of t_n. For this, substitute Equation 4.24 into the original recurrence, which gives

$$n + 2^n = (2c_2 - c_1) - c_2 n + c_4 2^n.$$

Equating the coefficients of 2^n, we obtain immediately that $c_4 = 1$ and therefore $t_n \in \Theta(n2^n)$. Constants c_1 and c_2 are equally easy to read off if desired. Constant c_3 can then be obtained from Equation 4.24, the value of the other constants, and the initial condition $t_0 = 0$.

Alternatively, all four constants can be determined by solving four linear equations in four unknowns. Since we need four equations and we have only one initial condition, we use the recurrence to calculate the value of three other points: $t_1 = 3$, $t_2 = 12$ and $t_3 = 35$. This gives rise to the following system.

c_1			+	c_3			= 0	$n = 0$
c_1	+	c_2	+	$2c_3$	+	$2c_4$	= 3	$n = 1$
c_1	+	$2c_2$	+	$4c_3$	+	$8c_4$	= 12	$n = 2$
c_1	+	$3c_2$	+	$8c_3$	+	$24c_4$	= 35	$n = 3$

Solving this system yields $c_1 = -2$, $c_2 = -1$, $c_3 = 2$ and $c_4 = 1$. Thus we finally obtain

$$t_n = n2^n + 2^{n+1} - n - 2.$$

$\square$

4.7.4 Change of variable

It is sometimes possible to solve more complicated recurrences by making a change of variable. In the following examples, we write $T(n)$ for the term of a general recurrence, and t_i for the term of a new recurrence obtained from the first by a change of variable. Be sure to study Example 4.7.13, which is among the most important recurrences for algorithmic purposes.

Example 4.7.10.   Reconsider the recurrence we solved by intelligent guesswork in Section 4.7.1, but only for the case when n is a power of 2.

$$T(n) = \begin{cases} 1 & \text{if } n = 1 \\ 3T(n/2) + n & \text{if } n \text{ is a power of 2, } n > 1 \end{cases}$$

To transform this into a form that we know how to solve, we replace n by 2^i. This is achieved by introducing a new recurrence t_i, defined by $t_i = T(2^i)$. This transformation is useful because $n/2$ becomes $(2^i)/2 = 2^{i-1}$. In other words, our original recurrence in which $T(n)$ is defined as a function of $T(n/2)$ gives way to one in which t_i is defined as a function of t_{i-1}, precisely the type of recurrence we have learned to solve.

$$t_i = T(2^i) = 3T(2^{i-1}) + 2^i$$
$$= 3t_{i-1} + 2^i$$

Once rewritten as

$$t_i - 3t_{i-1} = 2^i,$$

this recurrence is of the form of Equation 4.10. The characteristic polynomial is

$$(x - 3)(x - 2)$$

and hence all solutions for t_i are of the form

$$t_i = c_1 3^i + c_2 2^i.$$

We use the fact that $T(2^i) = t_i$ and thus $T(n) = t_{\lg n}$ when $n = 2^i$ to obtain

$$T(n) = c_1 3^{\lg n} + c_2 2^{\lg n}$$
$$= c_1 n^{\lg 3} + c_2 n \tag{4.25}$$

when n is a power of 2, which is sufficient to conclude that

$$T(n) \in O(n^{\lg 3} \mid n \text{ is a power of 2}).$$

However, we need to show that c_1 is strictly positive before we can assert something about the *exact* order of $T(n)$.

We are now familiar with two techniques to determine the constants. For the sake of the exercise, let us apply each of them to this situation. The more direct approach, which does not always provide the desired information, is to substitute the solution provided by Equation 4.25 into the original recurrence. Noting that $(1/2)^{\lg 3} = 1/3$, this yields

$$
\begin{aligned}
n = T(n) - 3T(n/2) \\
= (c_1 n^{\lg 3} + c_2 n) - 3(c_1 (n/2)^{\lg 3} + c_2 (n/2)) \\
= -c_2 n/2
\end{aligned}
$$

and therefore $c_2 = -2$. Even though we did not obtain the value of c_1, which is the more relevant constant, we are nevertheless in a position to assert that it must be strictly positive, for otherwise Equation 4.25 would falsely imply that $T(n)$ is negative. The fact that

$$
T(n) \in \Theta(n^{\lg 3} \mid n \text{ is a power of 2}) \tag{4.26}
$$

is thus established. Of course, the value of c_1 would now be easy to obtain from Equation 4.25, the fact that $c_2 = -2$, and the initial condition $T(1) = 1$, but this is not necessary if we are satisfied to solve the recurrence in asymptotic notation. Moreover we have learned that Equation 4.26 holds regardless of the initial condition, provided $T(n)$ is positive.

The alternative approach consists of setting up two linear equations in the two unknowns c_1 and c_2. It is guaranteed to yield the value of both constants. For this, we need the value of $T(n)$ on two points. We already know that $T(1) = 1$. To obtain another point, we use the recurrence itself: $T(2) = 3T(1) + 2 = 5$. Substituting $n = 1$ and $n = 2$ in Equation 4.25 yields the following system.

$$
\begin{array}{rcrclc}
c_1 & + & c_2 & = & 1 & \qquad n = 1 \\
3c_1 & + & 2c_2 & = & 5 & \qquad n = 2
\end{array}
$$

Solving these equations, we obtain $c_1 = 3$ and $c_2 = -2$. Therefore

$$
T(n) = 3n^{\lg 3} - 2n
$$

when n is a power of 2, which is of course exactly the answer we obtained in Section 4.7.1 by intelligent guesswork. $\square$

Example 4.7.11.   Consider the recurrence

$$
T(n) = 4T(n/2) + n^2
$$

when n is a power of 2, $n \geq 2$. We proceed as in the previous example.

$$
\begin{aligned}
t_i = T(2^i) &= 4T(2^{i-1}) + (2^i)^2 \\
&= 4t_{i-1} + 4^i
\end{aligned}
$$

We rewrite this in the form of Equation 4.10.

$$
t_i - 4t_{i-1} = 4^i
$$

The characteristic polynomial is $(x - 4)^2$ and hence all solutions are of the form

$$t_i = c_1 4^i + c_2 i 4^i.$$

In terms of $T(n)$, this is

$$T(n) = c_1 n^2 + c_2 n^2 \lg n. \tag{4.27}$$

Substituting Equation 4.27 into the original recurrence yields

$$n^2 = T(n) - 4T(n/2) = c_2 n^2$$

and thus $c_2 = 1$. Therefore

$$T(n) \in \Theta(n^2 \log n \mid n \text{ is a power of 2}),$$

regardless of initial conditions (even if $T(1)$ is negative).   □

Example 4.7.12.   Consider the recurrence

$$T(n) = 2T(n/2) + n \lg n$$

when n is a power of 2, $n \geq 2$. As before, we obtain

$$t_i = T(2^i) = 2T(2^{i-1}) + i 2^i$$
$$= 2t_{i-1} + i 2^i$$

We rewrite this in the form of Equation 4.10.

$$t_i - 2t_{i-1} = i 2^i$$

The characteristic polynomial is $(x - 2)(x - 2)^2 = (x - 2)^3$ and hence all solutions are of the form

$$t_i = c_1 2^i + c_2 i 2^i + c_3 i^2 2^i.$$

In terms of $T(n)$, this is

$$T(n) = c_1 n + c_2 n \lg n + c_3 n \lg^2 n. \tag{4.28}$$

Substituting Equation 4.28 into the original recurrence yields

$$n \lg n = T(n) - 2T(n/2) = (c_2 - c_3) n + 2c_3 n \lg n,$$

which implies that $c_2 = c_3$ and $2c_3 = 1$, and thus $c_2 = c_3 = \frac{1}{2}$. Therefore

$$T(n) \in \Theta(n \log^2 n \mid n \text{ is a power of 2}),$$

regardless of initial conditions.   □

Remark: In the preceding examples, the recurrence given for $T(n)$ only applies when n is a power of 2. It is therefore inevitable that the solution obtained should be in conditional asymptotic notation. In each case, however, it is sufficient to add the condition that $T(n)$ is eventually nondecreasing to be able to conclude that the asymptotic results obtained apply unconditionally for all values of n. This follows from the smoothness rule (Section 3.4) since the functions $n^{\lg 3}$, $n^2 \log n$ and $n \log^2 n$ are smooth.

Example 4.7.13.   We are now ready to solve one of the most important recurrences for algorithmic purposes. This recurrence is particularly useful for the analysis of divide-and-conquer algorithms, as we shall see in Chapter 7. The constants $n_0 \geq 1$, $\ell \geq 1$, $b \geq 2$ and $k \geq 0$ are integers, whereas c is a strictly positive real number. Let $T : \mathbb{N} \to \mathbb{R}^+$ be an eventually nondecreasing function such that

$$T(n) = \ell\, T(n/b) + cn^k \qquad n > n_0 \qquad (4.29)$$

when n/n_0 is an exact power of b, that is when $n \in \{bn_0, b^2 n_0, b^3 n_0, \ldots\}$. This time, the appropriate change of variable is $n = b^i n_0$.

$$\begin{aligned} t_i = T(b^i n_0) &= \ell\, T(b^{i-1} n_0) + c(b^i n_0)^k \\ &= \ell\, t_{i-1} + c\, n_0^k\, b^{ik} \end{aligned}$$

We rewrite this in the form of Equation 4.10.

$$t_i - \ell\, t_{i-1} = (c n_0^k)\,(b^k)^i$$

The right-hand side is of the required form $a^i p(i)$ where $p(i) = c n_0^k$ is a constant polynomial (of degree 0) and $a = b^k$. Thus, the characteristic polynomial is $(x - \ell)(x - b^k)$ whose roots are ℓ and b^k. From this, it is tempting (but false in general!) to conclude that all solutions are of the form

$$t_i = c_1 \ell^i + c_2\,(b^k)^i. \qquad (4.30)$$

To write this in terms of $T(n)$, note that $i = \log_b(n/n_0)$ when n is of the proper form, and thus $d^i = (n/n_0)^{\log_b d}$ for arbitrary positive values of d. Therefore,

$$\begin{aligned} T(n) &= (c_1/n_0^{\log_b \ell})\, n^{\log_b \ell} + (c_2/n_0^k)\, n^k \\ &= c_3\, n^{\log_b \ell} + c_4\, n^k \end{aligned} \qquad (4.31)$$

for appropriate new constants c_3 and c_4. To learn about these constants, we substitute Equation 4.31 into the original recurrence.

$$\begin{aligned} c n^k &= T(n) - \ell\, T(n/b) \\ &= c_3\, n^{\log_b \ell} + c_4\, n^k - \ell\,(c_3\,(n/b)^{\log_b \ell} + c_4\,(n/b)^k) \\ &= \left(1 - \frac{\ell}{b^k}\right) c_4\, n^k \end{aligned}$$

Therefore $c_4 = c/(1 - \ell/b^k)$. To express $T(n)$ in asymptotic notation, we need to keep only the dominant term in Equation 4.31. There are three cases to consider, depending whether ℓ is smaller than, bigger than or equal to b^k.

◇ If $\ell < b^k$ then $c_4 > 0$ and $k > \log_b \ell$. Therefore the term $c_4 n^k$ dominates Equation 4.31. We conclude that $T(n) \in \Theta(n^k \mid (n/n_0)$ is a power of $b)$. But n^k is a smooth function and $T(n)$ is eventually nondecreasing by assumption. Therefore $T(n) \in \Theta(n^k)$.

◇ If $\ell > b^k$ then $c_4 < 0$ and $\log_b \ell > k$. The fact that c_4 is negative implies that c_3 is positive, for otherwise Equation 4.31 would imply that $T(n)$ is negative, contrary to the specification that $T : \mathbb{N} \to \mathbb{R}^+$. Therefore the term $c_3 n^{\log_b \ell}$ dominates Equation 4.31. Furthermore $n^{\log_b \ell}$ is a smooth function and $T(n)$ is eventually nondecreasing. Therefore $T(n) \in \Theta(n^{\log_b \ell})$.

◇ If $\ell = b^k$, however, we are in trouble because the formula for c_4 involves a division by zero! What went wrong is that in this case the characteristic polynomial has a single root of multiplicity 2 rather than two distinct roots. Therefore Equation 4.30 does *not* provide the general solution to the recurrence. Rather, the general solution in this case is

$$t_i = c_5 (b^k)^i + c_6 i (b^k)^i.$$

In terms of $T(n)$, this is

$$T(n) = c_7 n^k + c_8 n^k \log_b(n/n_0) \tag{4.32}$$

for appropriate constants c_7 and c_8. Substituting this into the original recurrence, our usual manipulation yields a surprisingly simple $c_8 = c$. Therefore, $c n^k \log_b n$ is the dominant term in Equation 4.32 because c was assumed to be strictly positive at the beginning of this example. Since $n^k \log n$ is smooth and $T(n)$ is eventually nondecreasing, we conclude that $T(n) \in \Theta(n^k \log n)$.

Putting it all together,

$$T(n) \in \begin{cases} \Theta(n^k) & \text{if } \ell < b^k \\ \Theta(n^k \log n) & \text{if } \ell = b^k \\ \Theta(n^{\log_b \ell}) & \text{if } \ell > b^k \end{cases} \tag{4.33}$$

Problem 4.44 gives a generalization of this example.   □

Remark: It often happens in the analysis of algorithms that we derive a recurrence in the form of an *in*equality. For instance, we may get

$$T(n) \le \ell T(n/b) + cn^k \qquad n > n_0$$

when n/n_0 is an exact power of b, instead of Equation 4.29. What can we say about the asymptotic behaviour of such a recurrence? First note that we do not have enough information to determine the *exact* order of $T(n)$ because we are given only an upper bound on its value. (For all we know, it could be that $T(n) = 1$ for all n.) The best we can do in this case is to analyse the recurrence in terms of the O notation. For this we introduce an auxiliary recurrence patterned after the original but defined in terms of an equation (not an inequation). In this case

$$\hat{T}(n) = \begin{cases} T(n_0) & \text{if } n = n_0 \\ \ell \, \hat{T}(n/b) + cn^k & \text{if } n/n_0 \text{ is a power of } b, \ n > n_0. \end{cases}$$

This new recurrence falls under the scope of Example 4.7.13, except that we have no evidence that $\hat{T}(n)$ is eventually nondecreasing. Therefore Equation 4.33 holds for $\hat{T}(n)$, provided we use conditional asymptotic notation to restrict n/n_0 to being a power of b. Now, it is easy to prove by mathematical induction that $T(n) \leq \hat{T}(n)$ for all $n \geq n_0$ such that n/n_0 is a power of b. But clearly if

$$f(n) \in \Theta(t(n) \mid P(n))$$

and $g(n) \leq f(n)$ for all n such that $P(n)$ holds, then $g(n) \in O(t(n) \mid P(n))$. Therefore, our conclusion about the conditional asymptotic behaviour of $\hat{T}(n)$ holds for $T(n)$ as well, provided we replace Θ by O. Finally, whenever we know that $T(n)$ is eventually nondecreasing, we can invoke the smoothness of the functions involved to conclude that Equation 4.33 holds unconditionally for $T(n)$, provided again we replace Θ by O. The solution of our recurrence is thus

$$T(n) \in \begin{cases} O(n^k) & \text{if } \ell < b^k \\ O(n^k \log n) & \text{if } \ell = b^k \\ O(n^{\log_b \ell}) & \text{if } \ell > b^k \end{cases}$$

We shall study further recurrences involving inequalities in Section 4.7.6.

So far, the changes of variable we have used have all been of the same logarithmic nature. Rather different changes of variable are sometimes useful. We illustrate this with one example that comes from the analysis of the divide-and-conquer algorithm for multiplying large integers (see Section 7.1).

Example 4.7.14.   Consider an eventually nondecreasing function $T(n)$ such that

$$T(n) \leq T(\lfloor n/2 \rfloor) + T(\lceil n/2 \rceil) + T(1 + \lceil n/2 \rceil) + cn \tag{4.34}$$

for all sufficiently large n, where c is some positive real constant. As explained in the remark following the previous example, we have to be content here to analyse the recurrence in terms of the O notation rather than the Θ notation.

Let $n_0 \geq 1$ be large enough that $T(m) \geq T(n)$ for all $m \geq n \geq n_0/2$ and Equation 4.34 holds for all $n > n_0$. Consider any $n > n_0$. First observe that

$$\lfloor n/2 \rfloor \leq \lceil n/2 \rceil < 1 + \lceil n/2 \rceil,$$

which implies that

$$T(\lfloor n/2 \rfloor) \leq T(\lceil n/2 \rceil) \leq T(1 + \lceil n/2 \rceil).$$

Therefore, Equation 4.34 gives rise to

$$T(n) \le 3T(1 + \lceil n/2 \rceil) + cn.$$

Now make a change of variable by introducing a new function $\hat{T}$ such that $\hat{T}(n) = T(n + 2)$ for all n. Consider again any $n > n_0$.

$$\begin{aligned}
\hat{T}(n) = T(n + 2) &\le 3T(1 + \lceil (n + 2)/2 \rceil) + c(n + 2) \\
&\le 3T(2 + \lceil n/2 \rceil) + 2cn \quad \text{(because } n + 2 \le 2n\text{)} \\
&= 3\hat{T}(\lceil n/2 \rceil) + 2cn
\end{aligned}$$

In particular,

$$\hat{T}(n) \le 3\hat{T}(n/2) + dn \qquad n > n_0$$

when n/n_0 is a power of 2, where $d = 2c$. This is a special case of the recurrence analysed in the remark following Example 4.7.13, with $\ell = 3$, $b = 2$ and $k = 1$. Since $\ell > b^k$, we obtain $\hat{T}(n) \in O(n^{\lg 3})$. Finally, we use one last time the fact that $T(n)$ is eventually nondecreasing: $T(n) \le T(n + 2) = \hat{T}(n)$ for any sufficiently large n. Therefore any asymptotic upper bound on $\hat{T}(n)$ applies equally to $T(n)$, which concludes the proof that $T(n) \in O(n^{\lg 3})$.   □

4.7.5 Range transformations

When we make a change of variable, we transform the domain of the recurrence. Instead, it may be useful to transform the range to obtain a recurrence in a form that we know how to solve. Both transformations can sometimes be used together. We give just one example of this approach.

Example 4.7.15.   Consider the following recurrence, which defines $T(n)$ when n is a power of 2.

$$T(n) = \begin{cases} 1/3 & \text{if } n = 1 \\ n\,T^2(n/2) & \text{otherwise} \end{cases}$$

The first step is a change of variable: let t_i denote $T(2^i)$.

$$\begin{aligned}
t_i = T(2^i) &= 2^i\,T^2(2^{i-1}) \\
&= 2^i\,t_{i-1}^2
\end{aligned}$$

At first glance, none of the techniques we have seen applies to this recurrence since it is not linear; furthermore the coefficient 2^i is not a constant. To transform the range, we create yet another recurrence by using u_i to denote $\lg t_i$.

$$\begin{aligned}
u_i = \lg t_i &= i + 2 \lg t_{i-1} \\
&= i + 2u_{i-1}
\end{aligned}$$

This time, once rewritten as

$$u_i - 2u_{i-1} = i,$$

the recurrence fits Equation 4.10. The characteristic polynomial is

$$(x - 2)(x - 1)^2$$

and thus all solutions are of the form

$$u_i = c_1 2^i + c_2 1^i + c_3 i 1^i.$$

Substituting this solution into the recurrence for u_i yields

$$
\begin{aligned}
i &= u_i - 2u_{i-1} \\
&= c_1 2^i + c_2 + c_3 i - 2(c_1 2^{i-1} + c_2 + c_3 (i - 1)) \\
&= (2c_3 - c_2) - c_3 i
\end{aligned}
$$

and thus $c_3 = -1$ and $c_2 = 2c_3 = -2$. Therefore, the general solution for u_i, if the initial condition is not taken into account, is $u_i = c_1 2^i - i - 2$. This gives us the general solution for t_i and $T(n)$.

$$t_i = 2^{u_i} = 2^{c_1 2^i - i - 2}$$

$$T(n) = t_{\lg n} = 2^{c_1 n - \lg n - 2} = \frac{2^{c_1 n}}{4n}$$

We use the initial condition $T(1) = 1/3$ to determine c_1: $T(1) = 2^{c_1}/4 = 1/3$ implies that $c_1 = \lg(4/3) = 2 - \lg 3$. The final solution is therefore

$$T(n) = \frac{2^{2n}}{4n\, 3^n}.$$

$\square$

4.7.6 Asymptotic recurrences

When recurrences arise in the analysis of algorithms, they are often not as '"clean" as

$$S(n) = \begin{cases} a & \text{if } n = 1 \\ 4S(n \div 2) + bn & \text{if } n > 1 \end{cases} \tag{4.35}$$

for specific positive real constants a and b. Instead, we usually have to deal with something less precise, such as

$$T(n) = 4T(n \div 2) + f(n) \tag{4.36}$$

when n is sufficiently large, where all we know about $f(n)$ is that it is in the exact order of n, and we know nothing specific about the initial condition that defines $T(n)$ except that it is positive for all n. Such an equation is called an *asymptotic recurrence*. Fortunately, the asymptotic solution of a recurrence such as Equation 4.36 is virtually always identical to that of the simpler Equation 4.35. The general technique to solve an asymptotic recurrence is to "sandwich" the function it defines between two recurrences of the simpler type. When both simpler recurrences have the same asymptotic solution, the asymptotic recurrence must have the same solution as well. We illustrate this with our example.

For arbitrary positive real constants a and b, define the recurrence

$$T_{a,b}(n) = \begin{cases} a & \text{if } n = 1 \\ 4\,T_{a,b}(n \div 2) + bn & \text{if } n > 1. \end{cases}$$

The now-familiar techniques apply to find

$$T_{a,b}(n) = (a + b)n^2 - bn$$

provided n is a power of 2. Since n is a smooth function and $T_{a,b}(n)$ is nondecreasing (an easy proof by mathematical induction), it follows that $T_{a,b}(n) \in \Theta(n^2)$ regardless of the (positive) values of a and b. There is in fact no need to solve the recurrence explicitly as the result of Example 4.7.13 applies directly once it is established that $T_{a,b}(n)$ is nondecreasing.

To achieve our goal, it suffices to prove the existence of four positive real constants r, s, u and v such that

$$T_{r,s}(n) \leq T(n) \leq T_{u,v}(n) \tag{4.37}$$

for all $n \geq 1$. Since both $T_{r,s}(n)$ and $T_{u,v}(n)$ are in the exact order of n^2, it will follow that $T(n) \in \Theta(n^2)$ as well. One interesting benefit of this approach is that $T_{a,b}(n)$ is nondecreasing for any fixed positive values of a and b, which makes it possible to apply the smoothness rule. On the other hand, this rule could not have been invoked to simplify directly the analysis of $T(n)$ by restricting our attention to the case when n is a power of 2 because Equation 4.36 does not provide enough information to be able to assert that $T(n)$ is nondecreasing.

We still have to prove the existence of r, s, u and v. For this, note that $T_{a,a}(n) = a\,T_{1,1}(n)$ for all a and $T_{a,b}(n) \leq T_{a',b'}(n)$ when $a \leq a'$ and $b \leq b'$ (two more easy proofs by mathematical induction). Let c and d be positive real constants and let n_0 be an integer sufficiently large that $cn \leq f(n) \leq dn$ and

$$T(n) = 4\,T(n \div 2) + f(n)$$

for all $n > n_0$.   Choose $r = \min(T(n)/T_{1,1}(n) \mid 1 \leq n \leq n_0)$, $s = \min(r,c)$, $u = \max(T(n)/T_{1,1}(n) \mid 1 \leq n \leq n_0)$ and $v = \max(u,d)$. By definition,

$$T(n) \geq r\,T_{1,1}(n) = T_{r,r}(n) \geq T_{r,s}(n)$$

and

$$T(n) \leq u\,T_{1,1}(n) = T_{u,u}(n) \leq T_{u,v}(n)$$

for all $n \leq n_0$. This forms the basis of the proof by mathematical induction that Equation 4.37 holds. For the induction step, consider an arbitrary $n > n_0$ and assume by the induction hypothesis that $T_{r,s}(m) \le T(m) \le T_{u,v}(m)$ for all $m < n$. Then,

$$T(n) = 4T(n \div 2) + f(n)$$
$$\le 4T(n \div 2) + dn$$
$$\le 4T_{u,v}(n \div 2) + dn \quad \text{by the induction hypothesis}$$
$$\le 4T_{u,v}(n \div 2) + vn \quad \text{since } d \le v$$
$$= T_{u,v}(n).$$

The proof that $T_{r,s}(n) \le T(n)$ is similar, which completes the argument.

Example 4.7.16.   The important class of recurrences solved in Example 4.7.13 can be generalized in a similar way. Consider a function $T : \mathbb{N} \to \mathbb{R}^+$ such that

$$T(n) = \ell\, T(n \div b) + f(n)$$

for all sufficiently large n, where $\ell \ge 1$ and $b \ge 2$ are constants, and $f(n) \in \Theta(n^k)$ for some $k \ge 0$. For arbitrary positive real constants x and y, define

$$T_{x,y}(n) = \begin{cases} x & \text{if } n = 1 \\ \ell\, T_{x,y}(n \div b) + yn^k & \text{if } n > 1. \end{cases}$$

It is easy to show by mathematical induction that $T_{x,y}(n)$ is nondecreasing. Therefore, Example 4.7.13 applies to its analysis with the same result in Θ notation regardless of the value of x and y. Finally, we can show with the approach used above that our original function $T(n)$ must be sandwiched between $T_{r,s}(n)$ and $T_{u,v}(n)$ for appropriate choices of r, s, u and v. The conclusion is that

$$T(n) \in \begin{cases} \Theta(n^k) & \text{if } \ell < b^k \\ \Theta(n^k \log n) & \text{if } \ell = b^k \\ \Theta(n^{\log_b \ell}) & \text{if } \ell > b^k \end{cases}$$

exactly as was the case with the more specific recurrence given in Example 4.7.13. Moreover, if all we know about $f(n)$ is that it is in the order of n^k, rather than knowing its exact order, we are still entitled to reach the same conclusion concerning $T(n)$, except that Θ must be replaced by O throughout. (This is subtly different from the situation investigated in the remark following Example 4.7.13.)   □

4.8 Problems

Problem 4.1.   How much time does the following "algorithm" require as a function of n?

```
ℓ ← 0
for i ← 1 to n do
    for j ← 1 to n² do
        for k ← 1 to n³ do
            ℓ ← ℓ + 1
```

Express your answer in Θ notation in the simplest possible form. You may consider that each individual instruction (including loop control) is elementary.

Problem 4.2.   How much time does the following "algorithm" require as a function of n?

$$\ell \leftarrow 0$$
$$\textbf{for } i \leftarrow 1 \textbf{ to } n \textbf{ do}$$
$$\quad \textbf{for } j \leftarrow 1 \textbf{ to } i \textbf{ do}$$
$$\quad\quad \textbf{for } k \leftarrow j \textbf{ to } n \textbf{ do}$$
$$\quad\quad\quad \ell \leftarrow \ell + 1$$

Express your answer in Θ notation in the simplest possible form. You may consider that each individual instruction (including loop control) is elementary.

Problem 4.3.   Consider the loop

$$\textbf{for } i \leftarrow 1 \textbf{ to } m \textbf{ do } P$$

which is part of a larger algorithm that works on an instance of size n. Let t be the time needed for each execution of P, which we assume independent of i for the sake of this problem (but t could depend on n). Prove that this loop takes a time in $\Theta(mt)$ provided t is bounded below by some constant and provided there exists a threshold n_0 such that $m \geq 1$ whenever $n \geq n_0$. (Recall that we saw in Section 4.2.2 that the desired conclusion would not hold without those restrictions.)

Problem 4.4.   Prove by mathematical induction that the values of i and j at the end of the k–th iteration of *Fibiter* in Section 4.2.2 are f_{k-1} and f_k, respectively, where f_n denotes the n–th Fibonacci number.

Problem 4.5.   Consider the following algorithm to compute binomial coefficients.

$$\textbf{function } C(n, k)$$
$$\quad \textbf{if } k = 0 \textbf{ or } k = n \textbf{ then return } 1$$
$$\quad \textbf{else return } C(n - 1, k - 1) + C(n - 1, k)$$

Analyse the time taken by this algorithm under the (unreasonable) assumption that the addition $C(n - 1, k - 1) + C(n - 1, k)$ can be carried out in constant time once both $C(n - 1, k - 1)$ and $C(n - 1, k)$ have been obtained recursively. Let $t(n)$ denote the worst time that a call on $C(n, k)$ may take for all possible values of k, $0 \leq k \leq n$. Express $t(n)$ in the simplest possible form in Θ notation.

Problem 4.6.   Consider the following "algorithm".

$$\textbf{procedure } DC(n)$$
$$\quad \textbf{if } n \leq 1 \textbf{ then return}$$
$$\quad \textbf{for } i \leftarrow 1 \textbf{ to } 8 \textbf{ do } DC(n \div 2)$$
$$\quad \textbf{for } i \leftarrow 1 \textbf{ to } n^3 \textbf{ do } dummy \leftarrow 0$$

Write an asymptotic recurrence equation that gives the time $T(n)$ taken by a call of $DC(n)$. Use the result of Example 4.7.16 to determine the exact order of $T(n)$ in the simplest possible form. Do *not* reinvent the wheel here: apply Example 4.7.16 directly. The complete solution of this problem should not take more than 2 or 3 lines!

Note: This is how easy it is to analyse the running time of most divide-and-conquer algorithms; see Chapter 7.

Problem 4.7.   Rework Problem 4.6 if the constant 8 that appears in the middle line of algorithm DC is replaced by 9.

Problem 4.8.   Rework Problem 4.6 if the constant 8 that appears in the middle line of algorithm DC is replaced by 7.

Problem 4.9.   Consider the following "algorithm".

> **procedure** *waste*(n)
> > **for** $i \leftarrow 1$ **to** n **do**
> > > **for** $j \leftarrow 1$ **to** i **do**
> > > > write i, j, n
> > **if** $n > 0$ **then**
> > > **for** $i \leftarrow 1$ **to** 4 **do**
> > > > *waste*$(n \div 2)$

Let $T(n)$ stand for the number of lines of output generated by a call of *waste*(n). Provide a recurrence equation for $T(n)$ and use the result of Example 4.7.16 to determine the exact order of $T(n)$ in the simplest possible form. (We are *not* asking you to solve the recurrence exactly.)

Problem 4.10.   Prove by mathematical induction that if $d_0 = n$ and $d_\ell \le d_{\ell-1}/2$ for all $\ell \ge 1$, then $d_\ell \le n/2^\ell$ for all $\ell \ge 0$. (This is relevant to the analysis of the time taken by binary search; see Section 4.2.4.)

Problem 4.11.   Consider the following recurrence for $n \ge 1$.

$$\hat{t}(n) = \begin{cases} c & \text{if } n = 1 \\ \hat{t}(n \div 2) + b & \text{otherwise} \end{cases}$$

Use the technique of the characteristic equation to solve this recurrence when n is a power of 2. Prove by mathematical induction that $\hat{t}(n)$ is an eventually nondecreasing function. Use the smoothness rule to show that $\hat{t}(n) \in \Theta(\log n)$. Finally, conclude that $t(n) \in O(\log n)$, where $t(n)$ is given by Equation 4.2. Can we conclude from Equation 4.2 that $t(n) \in \Theta(\log n)$? Why or why not?

Problem 4.12.   Prove that the initialization phase of pigeon-hole sorting (Section 2.7.2) takes a time in $\Theta(n + s)$.

Problem 4.13.   We saw in Section 4.2.4 that binary search can find an item in a sorted array of size n in a time in $O(\log n)$. Prove that in the worst case a time in $\Omega(\log n)$ is required. On the other hand, what is the time required in the best case?

Problem 4.14.   How much time does insertion sorting take to sort n distinct items in the *best* case? State your answer in asymptotic notation.

Problem 4.15.   We saw in Section 4.4 that a good barometer for the worst-case analysis of insertion sorting is the number of times the **while** loop condition is tested. Show that this barometer is also appropriate if we are concerned with the best-case behaviour of the algorithm (see Problem 4.14).

Problem 4.16.   Prove that Euclid's algorithm performs least well on inputs of any given size when computing the greatest common divisor of two consecutive numbers from the Fibonacci sequence.

Problem 4.17.   Give a nonrecursive algorithm to solve the Towers of Hanoi problem (see Section 4.4). It is cheating simply to rewrite the recursive algorithm using an explicit stack to simulate the recursive calls!

Problem 4.18.   Prove that the Towers of Hanoi problem with n rings cannot be solved with fewer than $2^n - 1$ movements of rings.

Problem 4.19.   Give a procedure similar to algorithm *count* from Section 4.6 to increase an m-bit binary counter. This time, however, the counter should remain all ones instead of cycling back to zero when an overflow occurs. In other words, if the current value represented by the counter is v, the new value after a call on your algorithm should be $\min(v + 1, 2^m - 1)$. Give the amortized analysis of your algorithm. It should still take constant amortized time for each call.

Problem 4.20.   Prove Equation 4.6 from Section 4.7.1 by mathematical induction when n is a power of 2. Prove also by mathematical induction that the function $T(n)$ defined by Equation 4.4 is nondecreasing (for all n, not just when n is a power of 2).

Problem 4.21.   Consider arbitrary positive real constants a and b. Use intelligent guesswork to solve the following recurrence when $n \geq 1$.

$$t(n) = \begin{cases} a & \text{if } n = 1 \\ nt(n-1) + bn & \text{otherwise.} \end{cases}$$

You are allowed a term of the form $\sum_{i=1}^{n} 1/i!$ in your solution. Prove your answer by mathematical induction. Express $t(n)$ in Θ notation in the simplest possible form. What is the value of $\lim_{n \to \infty} t(n)/n!$ as a function of a and b? (Note: $\sum_{i=1}^{\infty} 1/i! = e - 1$, where $e = 2.7182818\ldots$ is the base of the natural logarithm.) Although we determined the asymptotic behaviour of this recurrence in Problem 1.31 using constructive induction, note that this time we have obtained a more precise formula for $t(n)$. In particular, we have obtained the limit of $t(n)/n!$ as n tends to infinity. Recall that this problem is relevant to the analysis of the recursive algorithm for calculating determinants.

Problem 4.22.   Solve the recurrence of Example 4.7.2 by intelligent guesswork. Resist the temptation to "cheat" by looking at the solution before working out this problem!

Problem 4.23.   Prove that Equation 4.7 (Section 4.7.2) has only solutions of the form

$$t_n = \sum_{i=1}^{k} c_i r_i^n$$

provided the roots $r_1, r_2, \ldots, r_k$ of the characteristic polynomial are distinct.

Problem 4.24.   Complete the solution of Example 4.7.7 by determining the value of c_1 as function of t_0.

Problem 4.25.   Complete the solution of Example 4.7.11 by determining the value of c_1 as function of t_0.

Problem 4.26.   Complete the solution of Example 4.7.12 by determining the value of c_1 as function of t_0.

Problem 4.27.   Complete the solution of Example 4.7.13 by showing that $c_8 = c$.

Problem 4.28.   Complete the remark that follows Example 4.7.13 by proving by mathematical induction that $T(n) \le \hat{T}(n)$ for all $n \ge n_0$ such that n/n_0 is a power of b.

Problem 4.29.   Solve the following recurrence exactly.

$$t_n = \begin{cases} n & \text{if } n = 0 \text{ or } n = 1 \\ 5t_{n-1} - 6t_{n-2} & \text{otherwise} \end{cases}$$

Express your answer as simply as possible using the Θ notation.

Problem 4.30.   Solve the following recurrence exactly.

$$t_n = \begin{cases} 9n^2 - 15n + 106 & \text{if } n = 0, 1 \text{ or } 2 \\ t_{n-1} + 2t_{n-2} - 2t_{n-3} & \text{otherwise} \end{cases}$$

Express your answer as simply as possible using the Θ notation.

Problem 4.31.   Consider the following recurrence.

$$t_n = \begin{cases} n & \text{if } n = 0 \text{ or } n = 1 \\ 2t_{n-1} - 2t_{n-2} & \text{otherwise} \end{cases}$$

Prove that $t_n = 2^{n/2} \sin(n\pi/4)$, not by mathematical induction but by using the technique of the characteristic equation.

Problem 4.32.   Solve the following recurrence exactly.

$$t_n = \begin{cases} n & \text{if } n = 0, 1, 2 \text{ or } 3 \\ t_{n-1} + t_{n-3} - t_{n-4} & \text{otherwise} \end{cases}$$

Express your answer as simply as possible using the Θ notation.

Problem 4.33. Solve the following recurrence exactly.

$$t_n = \begin{cases} n + 1 & \text{if } n = 0 \text{ or } n = 1 \\ 3t_{n-1} - 2t_{n-2} + 3 \times 2^{n-2} & \text{otherwise} \end{cases}$$

Express your answer as simply as possible using the Θ notation.

Problem 4.34. Solve the following recurrence exactly.

$$T(n) = \begin{cases} a & \text{if } n = 0 \text{ or } n = 1 \\ T(n-1) + T(n-2) + c & \text{otherwise} \end{cases}$$

Express your answer as simply as possible using the Θ notation and the golden ratio $\phi = (1 + \sqrt{5})/2$. Note that this is Recurrence 4.1 from Section 4.2.3 if $h(n) = c$, which represents the time taken by a call on *Fibrec(n)* if we count the additions at unit cost.

Problem 4.35. Solve the following recurrence exactly.

$$T(n) = \begin{cases} a & \text{if } n = 0 \text{ or } n = 1 \\ T(n-1) + T(n-2) + cn & \text{otherwise} \end{cases}$$

Express your answer as simply as possible using the Θ notation and the golden ratio $\phi = (1 + \sqrt{5})/2$. Note that this is Recurrence 4.1 from Section 4.2.3 if $h(n) = cn$, which represents the time taken by a call on *Fibrec(n)* if we do not count the additions at unit cost. Compare your answer to that of Problem 4.34, in which additions were counted at unit cost.

Problem 4.36. Solve the following recurrence exactly for n a power of 2.

$$T(n) = \begin{cases} 1 & \text{if } n = 1 \\ 4T(n/2) + n & \text{otherwise} \end{cases}$$

Express your answer as simply as possible using the Θ notation.

Problem 4.37. Solve the following recurrence exactly for n a power of 2.

$$T(n) = \begin{cases} 1 & \text{if } n = 1 \\ 2T(n/2) + \lg n & \text{otherwise} \end{cases}$$

Express your answer as simply as possible using the Θ notation.

Problem 4.38. Solve the following recurrence exactly for n a power of 2.

$$T(n) = \begin{cases} 1 & \text{if } n = 1 \\ 5T(n/2) + (n \lg n)^2 & \text{otherwise} \end{cases}$$

Express your answer as simply as possible using the Θ notation.

Problem 4.39. Solve the following recurrence exactly for n of the form 2^{2^k}.

$$T(n) = \begin{cases} 1 & \text{if } n = 2 \\ 2T(\sqrt{n}) + \lg n & \text{otherwise} \end{cases}$$

Express your answer as simply as possible using the Θ notation.

Problem 4.40. Solve the following recurrence exactly.

$$T(n) = \begin{cases} n & \text{if } n = 0 \text{ or } n = 1 \\ \sqrt{\frac{1}{2}T^2(n-1) + \frac{1}{2}T^2(n-2) + n} & \text{otherwise} \end{cases}$$

Express your answer as simply as possible using the Θ notation.

Problem 4.41. Solve the following recurrence exactly for n a power of 2.

$$T(n) = \begin{cases} 1 & \text{if } n = 1 \\ 3/2 & \text{if } n = 2 \\ \frac{3}{2}T(n/2) - \frac{1}{2}T(n/4) - 1/n & \text{otherwise} \end{cases}$$

Problem 4.42. Solve the following recurrence exactly.

$$t_n = \begin{cases} 0 & \text{if } n = 0 \\ 1/(4 - t_{n-1}) & \text{otherwise} \end{cases}$$

Problem 4.43. Solve the following recurrence exactly as a function of the initial conditions a and b.

$$T(n) = \begin{cases} a & \text{if } n = 0 \\ b & \text{if } n = 1 \\ (1 + T(n-1))/T(n-2) & \text{otherwise} \end{cases}$$

Problem 4.44. We saw in Example 4.7.13 the solution to an important recurrence that is particularly useful for the analysis of divide-and-conquer algorithms. In some cases, however, a more general result is required, and the technique of the characteristic equation does not always apply. Let $n_0 \geq 1$ and $b \geq 2$ be integers, and let a and d be real positive constants. Define

$$X = \{n \in \mathbb{N} \mid (\exists i \in \mathbb{N})[n = n_0 b^i]\}.$$

Let $f : X \to \mathbb{R}^{\geq 0}$ be an arbitrary function. Define the function $T : X \to \mathbb{R}^{\geq 0}$ by the recurrence

$$T(n) = \begin{cases} d & \text{if } n = n_0 \\ aT(n/b) + f(n) & \text{if } n \in X, n > n_0. \end{cases}$$

Let $p = \log_b a$. It turns out that the simplest way to express $T(n)$ in asymptotic notation depends on how $f(n)$ compares to n^p. In what follows, all asymptotic notation is implicitly conditional on $n \in X$. Prove that

1. If we set $f(n_0) = d$, which is of no consequence for the definition of T, the value of $T(n)$ is given by a simple summation when $n \in X$:

$$T(n) = \sum_{i=0}^{\log_b(n/n_0)} a^i f(n/b^i).$$

2. Let ε be any strictly positive real constant; then

$$T(n) \in \begin{cases} \Theta(n^p) & \text{if } f(n) \in O(n^p/(\log n)^{1+\varepsilon}) \\ \Theta(f(n)\log n \log\log n) & \text{if } f(n) \in \Theta(n^p/\log n) \\ \Theta(f(n)\log n) & \text{if } f(n) \in \Theta(n^p(\log n)^{\varepsilon-1}) \\ \Theta(f(n)) & \text{if } f(n) \in \Theta(n^{p+\varepsilon}). \end{cases}$$

The third alternative includes $f(n) \in \Theta(n^p)$ by choosing $\varepsilon = 1$.

3. As a special case of the first alternative, $T(n) \in \Theta(n^p)$ whenever $f(n) \in O(n^r)$ for some real constant $r < p$.

4. The first alternative can be generalized to include cases such as

$$f(n) \in O(n^p/((\log n)(\log\log n)^{1+\varepsilon}));$$

we also get $T(n) \in \Theta(n^p)$ if $f(n) \in O(n^p g(n))$ where $g(n)$ is nonincreasing and $\sum_{n \in X} g(n)$ converges.

5. The last alternative can be generalized to include cases such as

$$f(n) \in \Theta(n^{p+\varepsilon}\log n) \text{ or } f(n) \in \Theta(n^{p+\varepsilon}/\log n);$$

we also get $T(n) \in \Theta(f(n))$ if $f(n) \in \Omega(n^{p+\varepsilon})$ and if $f(n) \geq akf(n/b)$ for some constant $k > 1$ and all sufficiently large $n \in X$.

4.9 References and further reading

The Towers of Hanoi is the name given to a toy invented by the French mathematician Édouard Lucas in 1883: see Gardner (1959). Buneman and Levy (1980) and Dewdney (1984) give a solution to Problem 4.17.

Amortized analysis was popularized by Tarjan (1985).

The main mathematical aspects of the analysis of algorithms can be found in Greene and Knuth (1981). A number of techniques for analysing algorithms are given in Purdom and Brown (1985) and Rawlins (1992).

Several techniques for solving recurrences, including the characteristic equation and change of variable, are explained in Lueker (1980). For a more rigorous mathematical treatment see Knuth (1968) or Purdom and Brown (1985). The paper by Bentley, Haken and Saxe (1980) is particularly relevant for recurrences arising from the analysis of divide-and-conquer algorithms (see Chapter 7). Problem 4.44 comes partly from Verma (1994), which presents further general results.

Chapter 5

Some Data Structures

The use of well-chosen data structures is often a crucial factor in the design of efficient algorithms. Nevertheless, this book is not intended to be a manual on data structures. We assume the reader already has a good working knowledge of such basic notions as arrays, records, and the various structured data types obtained using pointers. We also suppose that the mathematical concepts of directed and undirected graphs are reasonably familiar, and that the reader knows how to represent such objects efficiently on a computer.

The chapter begins with a brief review of the more important aspects of these elementary data structures. The review includes a summary of their essential properties from the point of view of algorithmics. For this reason even readers who know the basic material well should skim the first few sections. The last three sections of the chapter introduce the less elementary notions of *heaps* and *disjoint sets*. Chosen because they will be used in subsequent chapters, these structures also offer interesting examples of the analysis of algorithms. Most readers will probably need to read the sections concerning these less familiar data structures quite thoroughly.

5.1 Arrays, stacks and queues

An *array* is a data structure consisting of a fixed number of items of the same type. (We shall talk about *items* or *elements*, indifferently.) On a machine, these are usually stored in contiguous storage cells. In a one-dimensional array, access to any particular item is obtained by specifying a single *subscript* or *index*. For instance, we might declare a one-dimensional array of integers as follows.

tab: **array** [1..50] **of** *integers*

Here *tab* is an array of 50 integers indexed from 1 to 50; *tab*[1] refers to the first item of the array, *tab*[50] to the last. It is natural to think of the items as being arranged from left to right, so we may also refer to $tab[1]$ as the left-hand item, and so on. We often omit to specify the type of the items in the array when the context makes this obvious.

From the point of view that interests us in this book, the essential property of an array is that we can calculate the address of any given item in constant time. For example, if we know that the array tab above starts at address 5000, and that integer variables occupy 4 bytes of storage each, then the address of the item with index k is easily seen to be $4996 + 4k$. Even if we think it worthwhile to check that k does indeed lie between 1 and 50, the time required to compute the address can still be bounded by a constant. It follows that the time required to read the value of a single item, or to change such a value, is in $O(1)$: in other words, we can treat such operations as elementary.

On the other hand, any operation that involves all the items of an array will tend to take longer as the size of the array increases. Suppose we are dealing with an array of some variable size n; that is, the array consists of n items. Then an operation such as initializing every item, or finding the largest item, usually takes a time proportional to the number of items to be examined. In other words, such operations take a time in $\Theta(n)$. Another common situation is where we want to keep the values of successive items of the array in order—numerical, alphabetic, or whatever. Now whenever we decide to insert a new value we have to open up a space in the correct position, either by copying all the higher values one position to the right, or else by copying all the lower values one position to the left. Whichever tactic we adopt (and even if we sometimes do one thing, sometimes the other), in the worst case we may have to shift $n/2$ items. Similarly, deleting an element may require us to move all or most of the remaining items in the array. Again, therefore, such operations take a time in $\Theta(n)$.

A one-dimensional array provides an efficient way to implement the data structure called a *stack*. Here items are added to the structure, and subsequently removed, on a last-in-first-out (LIFO) basis. The situation can be represented using an array called *stack*, say, whose index runs from 1 to the maximum required size of the stack, and whose items are of the required type, along with a counter. To set the stack empty, the counter is given the value zero; to add an item to the stack, the counter is incremented, and then the new item is written into $stack[counter]$; to remove an item, the value of $stack[counter]$ is read out, and then the counter is decremented. Tests can be added to ensure that no more items are placed on the stack than were provided for, and that items are not removed from an empty stack. Adding an item to a stack is usually called a **push** operation, while removing one is called **pop**.

The data structure called a *queue* can also be implemented quite efficiently in a one-dimensional array. Here items are added and removed on a first-in-first-out (FIFO) basis; see Problem 5.2. Adding an item is called an **enqueue** operation, while removing one is called **dequeue**. For both stacks and queues, one disadvantage of using an implementation in an array is that space usually has to be allocated at the outset for the maximum number of items envisaged; if ever this space is not sufficient, it is difficult to add more, while if too much space is allocated, waste results.

The items of an array can be of any fixed-length type: this is so that the address of any particular item can be easily calculated. The index is almost always an integer. However, other so-called ordinal types can be used. For instance,

> *lettab***: array** ['a' . . 'z'] **of** value

is one possible way of declaring an array of 26 values, indexed by the letters from 'a' to 'z'. It is not permissible to index an array using real numbers, nor do we allow an array to be indexed by structures such as strings or sets. If such things are allowed, accessing an array item can no longer be considered an elementary operation. However a more general data structure called an *associative table*, described in Section 5.6, *does* allow such indexes.

The examples given so far have all involved one-dimensional arrays, that is, arrays whose items are accessed using just one index. Arrays with two or more indexes can be declared in a similar way. For instance,

> *matrix***: array** [1 . . 20, 1 . . 20] **of** *complex*

is one possible way to declare an array containing 400 items of type *complex*. A reference to any particular item, such as *matrix*[5, 7], now requires two indexes. The essential point remains, however, that we can calculate the address of any given item in constant time, so reading or modifying its value can be taken to be an elementary operation. Obviously if both dimensions of a two-dimensional array depend on some parameter n, as in the case of an $n \times n$ matrix, then operations such as initializing every item of the array, or finding the largest item, now take a time in $\Theta(n^2)$.

We stated above that the time needed to initialize all the items of an array of size n is in $\Theta(n)$. Suppose however we do not need to initialize each item, but simply to know whether it has been initialized or not, and if so to obtain its value. Provided we are willing to use rather more space, the technique called *virtual initialization* allows us to avoid the time spent setting all the entries in the array. Suppose the array to be virtually initialized is $T[1 . . n]$. Then we also need two auxiliary arrays of integers the same size as T, and an integer counter. Call these auxiliary arrays $a[1 . . n]$ and $b[1 . . n]$, say, and the counter *ctr*. At the outset we simply set *ctr* to zero, leaving the arrays a, b and T holding whatever values they happen to contain.

Subsequently *ctr* tells us how many elements of T have been initialized, while the values $a[1]$ to $a[ctr]$ tell us which these elements are: $a[1]$ points to the element initialized first, $a[2]$ to the element initialized second, and so on; see Figure 5.1, where three items of the array T have been initialized. Furthermore, if $T[i]$ was the k–th element to be initialized, then $b[i] = k$. Thus the values in a point to T and the values in b point to a, as in the figure.

To test whether $T[i]$ has been assigned a value, we first check that $1 \le b[i] \le ctr$. If not, we can be sure that $T[i]$ has not been initialized. Otherwise we are not sure whether $T[i]$ has been initialized or not: it could be just an accident that $b[i]$ has a plausible value. However if $T[i]$ really *has* been assigned a value, then it was the $b[i]$–th element of the array to be initialized. We can check this by testing whether

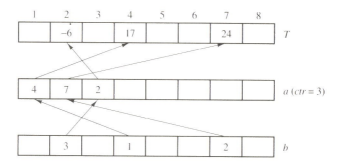

Figure 5.1. A virtually initialized array

$a[b[i]] = i$. Since the first *ctr* values of the array *a* certainly have been initialized, and $1 \leq b[i] \leq ctr$, it cannot be an accident if $a[b[i]] = i$, so this test is conclusive: if it is satisfied, then $T[i]$ has been initialized, and if not, not.

To assign a value to $T[i]$ for the first time, increment the counter *ctr*, set $a[ctr]$ to *i*, set $b[i]$ to *ctr*, and load the required value into $T[i]$. On subsequent assignments to $T[i]$, of course, none of this is necessary. Problem 5.3 invites you to fill in the details. The extra space needed to use this technique is a constant multiple of the size of *T*.

5.2 Records and pointers

While an array has a fixed number of items of the same type, a *record* is a data structure comprising a fixed number of items, often called *fields* in this context, that are possibly of different types. For example, if the information about a person that interests us consists of their name, age, weight and sex, we might want to use a data structure of the following form.

> **type** *person* = **record**
>   *name*: *string*
>   *age*: *integer*
>   *weight*: *real*
>   *male*: *Boolean*

Now if *Fred* is a variable of this type, we use the *dot notation* to refer to the fields; for example, *Fred. name* is a string and *Fred. age* is an integer.

An array can appear as an item of a record, and records can be kept in arrays. If we declare, for example,

> *class*: **array** [1..50] **of** *person*

then the array *class* holds 50 records. The attributes of the seventh member of the class are referred to as *class*[7]. *name*, *class*[7]. *age*, and so on. As with arrays, provided a record holds only fixed-length items, the address of any particular item can be calculated in constant time, so consulting or modifying the value of a field may be considered as an elementary operation.

Many programming languages allow records to be created and destroyed dynamically. (Some languages allow this for arrays, too, but it is less common.) This is one reason why records are commonly used in conjunction with pointers. A declaration such as

type *boss* = ↑*person*

says that *boss* is a pointer to a record whose type is *person*. Such a record can be created dynamically by a statement such as

boss ← **new** *person*.

Now *boss*↑ (note that here the arrow follows the name) means "the record that *boss* points to". To refer to the fields of this record, we use *boss*↑.*name*, *boss*↑.*age*, and so on. If a pointer has the special value **nil**, then it is not currently pointing to any record.

5.3 Lists

A *list* is a collection of items of information arranged in a certain order. Unlike arrays and records, the number of items in a list is generally not fixed, nor is it usually bounded in advance. The corresponding data structure should allow us to determine, for example, which is the first item in the structure, which is the last, and which are the predecessor and the successor (if they exist) of any given item. On a machine, the storage corresponding to any given item of information is often called a *node*. Besides the information in question, a node may contain one or more pointers. Such a structure is frequently represented graphically by boxes and arrows, as in Figure 5.2. The information attached to a node is shown inside the corresponding box, and the arrows show links from a node to its successor.

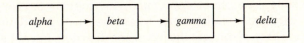

Figure 5.2. A list

Lists are subject to a number of operations: we might want to insert an additional node, to delete a node, to copy a list, to count the number of elements it contains, and so on. The various computer implementations commonly used differ in the quantity of storage required, and in the ease of carrying out certain operations. Here we content ourselves with mentioning the best-known techniques.

Implemented as an array by the declaration

type *list* = **record**
    counter: 0.. *maxlength*
    value: **array** [1.. *maxlength*] **of** *information*

the items of a list occupy the slots *value*[1] to *value*[*counter*], and the order of the items is the same as the order of their indexes in the array. Using this implementation, we can find the first and the last items of the list rapidly, as we can the predecessor and the successor of a given item. On the other hand, as we saw in Section 5.1, inserting a new item or deleting one of the existing items requires a worst-case number of operations in the order of the current size of the list. It was noted there, however, that this implementation is particularly efficient for the important structure known as the stack; and a stack can be considered as a kind of list where addition and deletion of items are allowed only at one designated end of the list. Despite this, such an implementation of a stack may present the major disadvantage of requiring that all the storage potentially required be reserved throughout the life of the program.

On the other hand, if pointers are used to implement a list structure, the nodes are usually records with a form similar to the following:

> **type** *list* = ↑*node*
> **type** *node* = **record**
>   *value*: *information*
>   *next*: ↑*node*

where each node except the last includes an explicit pointer to its successor. The pointer in the last node has the special value **nil**, indicating that it goes nowhere. In this case, provided a suitable programming language is used, the storage needed to represent the list can be allocated and recovered dynamically as the program proceeds. Hence two or more lists may be able to share the same space; furthermore there is no need to know a priori how long any particular list will get.

Even if additional pointers are used to ensure rapid access to the first and last items of the list, it is difficult when this representation is used to examine the k-th item, for arbitrary k, without having to follow k pointers and thus to take a time in $O(k)$. However, once an item has been found, inserting a new node or deleting an existing node can be done rapidly by copying or changing just a few fields. In our example, a single pointer is used in each node to designate its successor. It is therefore easy to traverse the list in one direction, but not in the other. If a higher storage overhead is acceptable, it suffices to add a second pointer to each node to allow the list to be traversed rapidly in either direction.

Elementary programming books are rife with variations on this theme. Lists may be circular, with the last item pointing back to the first, or they may have a special, different head cell, containing for example the number of nodes in the list. However we shall have no use for such structures in this book.

5.4 Graphs

Intuitively speaking, a *graph* is a set of nodes joined by a set of lines or arrows. Consider Figure 5.3 for instance. We distinguish directed and undirected graphs. In a directed graph the nodes are joined by arrows called *edges*. In the example of Figure 5.3 there exists an edge from *alpha* to *gamma* and another from *gamma* to *alpha*. Nodes *beta* and *delta*, however, are joined only in the direction indicated. In the case of an undirected graph, the nodes are joined by lines with no direction indicated, also called edges. In both directed and undirected graphs, sequences of edges may form *paths* and *cycles*. A graph is *connected* if you can get from any node to any other by following a sequence of edges; in the case of a directed graph, you are allowed to go the wrong way along an arrow. A directed graph is *strongly connected* if you can get from any node to any other by following a sequence of edges, but this time respecting the direction of the arrows.

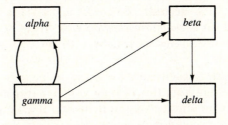

Figure 5.3. A directed graph

There are never more than two arrows joining any two given nodes of a directed graph, and if there *are* two arrows, they must go in opposite directions; there is never more than one line joining any two given nodes of an undirected graph. Formally, a graph is therefore a pair $G = \langle N, A \rangle$, where N is a set of nodes and A is a set of edges. An edge from node a to node b of a directed graph is denoted by the ordered pair (a, b), whereas an edge joining nodes a and b in an undirected graph is denoted by the set $\{a, b\}$. (Remember that a set is an *unordered* collection of elements; see Section 1.4.2.) For example, Figure 5.3 is an informal representation of the graph $G = \langle N, A \rangle$ where

$$N = \{alpha, beta, gamma, delta\}$$

$$A = \{(alpha, beta), (alpha, gamma), (beta, delta),$$
$$(gamma, alpha), (gamma, beta), (gamma, delta)\}.$$

There are at least two obvious ways to represent a graph on a computer. The first uses an *adjacency matrix*.

type *adjgraph* = **record**
    value: **array** $[1 .. nbnodes]$ **of** *information*
    adjacent: **array** $[1 .. nbnodes, 1 .. nbnodes]$ **of** *Boolean*

If the graph includes an edge from node i to node j, then *adjacent*$[i, j] = $ *true*; otherwise *adjacent*$[i, j] = $ *false*. In the case of an undirected graph, the matrix is necessarily symmetric.

With this representation it is easy to see whether or not there is an edge between two given nodes: to look up a value in an array takes constant time. On the other hand, should we wish to examine all the nodes connected to some given node, we have to scan a complete row of the matrix, in the case of an undirected graph, or both a complete row and a complete column, in the case of a directed graph. This takes a time in $\Theta(nbnodes)$, the number of nodes in the graph, independent of the number of edges that enter or leave this particular node. The space required to represent a graph in this fashion is quadratic in the number of nodes.

A second possible representation is the following.

type *lisgraph* = **array** [1 . . *nbnodes*] **of**
                  record
                  value: *information*
                  neighbours: *list*

Here we attach to each node i a list of its neighbours, that is, of those nodes j such that an edge from i to j (in the case of a directed graph), or between i and j (in the case of an undirected graph), exists. If the number of edges in the graph is small, this representation uses less storage than the one given previously. It may also be possible in this case to examine all the neighbours of a given node in less than *nbnodes* operations on the average. On the other hand, determining whether a direct connection exists between two given nodes i and j requires us to scan the list of neighbours of node i (and possibly of node j too, in the case of a directed graph), which is less efficient than looking up a Boolean value in an array.

5.5 Trees

A *tree* (strictly speaking, a *free tree*) is an acyclic, connected, undirected graph. Equivalently, a tree may be defined as an undirected graph in which there exists exactly one path between any given pair of nodes. Since a tree is a kind of graph, the same representations used to implement graphs can be used to implement trees. Figure 5.4(a) shows two trees, each of which has four nodes. You can easily verify that these are the only distinct trees with four nodes; see Problem 5.7. Trees have a number of simple properties, of which the following are perhaps the most important:

◇ A tree with n nodes has exactly $n - 1$ edges.

◇ If a single edge is added to a tree, then the resulting graph contains exactly one cycle.

◇ If a single edge is removed from a tree, then the resulting graph is no longer connected.

In this book we shall most often be concerned with *rooted trees*. These are trees in which one node, called the *root*, is special. When drawing a rooted tree, it is customary to put the root at the top, like a family tree, with the other edges coming down from it. Figure 5.4(b) illustrates four different rooted trees, each with four nodes. Again, you can easily verify that these are the only rooted trees with four nodes that exist. When there is no danger of confusion, we shall use the simple term "tree" instead of the more correct "rooted tree", since almost all our examples are of this kind.

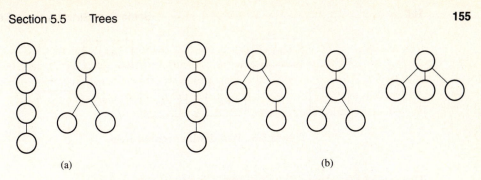

(a)   (b)

Figure 5.4. (a) Trees, and (b) Rooted trees with 4 nodes

Extending the analogy with a family tree, it is customary to use such terms as "parent" and "child" to describe the relationship between adjacent nodes. Thus in Figure 5.5, *alpha*, the root of the tree, is the *parent* of *beta* and *gamma*; *beta* is the parent of *delta*, *epsilon* and *zeta*, and the *child* of *alpha*; while *epsilon* and *zeta* are the *siblings* of *delta*. An *ancestor* of a node is either the node itself (this is not the same as the everyday definition), or its parent, its parent's parent, and so on. Thus both *alpha* and *zeta* are ancestors of *zeta*. A *descendant* of a node is defined analogously, again including the node itself.

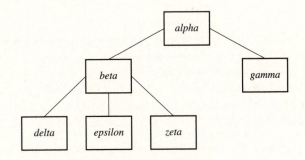

Figure 5.5. A rooted tree

A *leaf* of a rooted tree is a node with no children; the other nodes are called *internal nodes*. Although nothing in the definition indicates this, the branches of a rooted tree are often considered to be ordered from left to right: in the previous example *beta* is situated to the left of *gamma*, and—by analogy with a family tree once again—*delta* is called the *eldest* sibling of *epsilon* and *zeta*. The two trees in Figure 5.6 may therefore be considered distinct.

On a computer, any rooted tree may be represented using nodes of the following type.

type *treenode*1 = **record**
    value: *information*
    eldest-child, *next-sibling*: ↑ *treenode*1

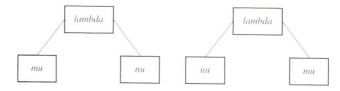

Figure 5.6. Two distinct rooted trees

The rooted tree shown in Figure 5.5 would be represented as in Figure 5.7, where the arrows show the direction of the pointers used in the computer representation, not the direction of edges in the tree (which is, of course, an undirected graph). We emphasize that this representation can be used for *any* rooted tree; it has the advantage that all the nodes can be represented using the same **record** structure, no matter how many children or siblings they have. However many operations are inefficient using this minimal representation: it is not obvious how to find the parent of a given node, for example (but see Problem 5.10).

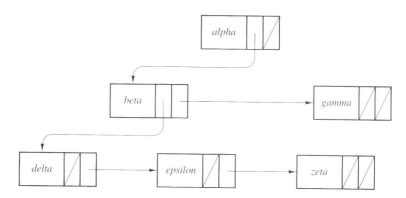

Figure 5.7. Possible computer representation of a rooted tree

Another representation suitable for *any* rooted tree uses nodes of the type

    type *treenode2* = **record**
        value: *information*
        parent: ↑ *treenode2*

where now each node contains only a single pointer leading to its parent. This representation is about as economical with storage space as one can hope to be, but it is inefficient unless all the operations on the tree involve starting from a node and going up, never down. (For an application where this is exactly what we need, see Section 5.9.) Moreover it does not represent the order of siblings.

    A suitable representation for a particular application can usually be designed by starting from one of these general representations and adding supplementary pointers, for example to the parent or to the eldest sibling of a given node. In this way we can speed up the operations we want to perform efficiently at the price of an increase in the storage needed.

We shall often have occasion to use *binary trees*. In such a tree, each node can have 0, 1, or 2 children. In fact, we almost always assume that a node has two pointers, one to its left and one to its right, either of which can be **nil**. When we do this, although the metaphor becomes somewhat strained, we naturally tend to talk about the left child and the right child, and the position occupied by a child is significant: a node with a left child but no right child can never be the same as a node with a right child but no left child. For instance, the two binary trees in Figure 5.8 are not the same: in the first case b is the left child of a and the right child is missing, whereas in the second case b is the right child of a and the left child is missing.

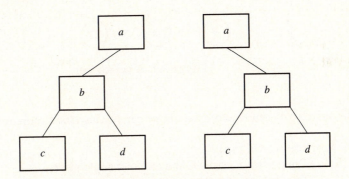

Figure 5.8. Two distinct binary trees

If each node of a rooted tree can have no more than k children, we say it is a k-*ary tree*. There are several ways of representing a k-ary tree on a computer. One obvious representation uses nodes of the following type.

> **type** *k-ary-node* = **record**
>   *value*: *information*
>   *child*: **array** [1 .. k] **of** ↑*k-ary-node*

In the case of a binary tree we can also define

> **type** *binary-node* = **record**
>   *value* : *information*
>   *left-child*, *right-child* : ↑*binary-node*

It is also sometimes possible, as we shall see in the following section, to represent a k-ary tree using an array without any explicit pointers.

A binary tree is a *search tree* if the value contained in every internal node is greater than or equal to the values contained in its left child or any of that child's descendants, and less than or equal to the values contained in its right child or any of that child's descendants. Figure 5.9 gives an example of a search tree. The figure shows the value contained in each node. This structure is interesting because, as the name implies, it allows efficient searches for values in the tree. In the example, although the tree contains 7 items, we can find 27, say, with only 3 comparisons. The first, with the value 20 stored at the root, tells us that 27 is in the right subtree (if it is anywhere); the second, with the value 34 stored at the root of the right subtree, tells us to look down to the left; and the third finds the value we seek.

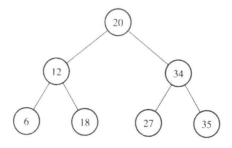

Figure 5.9. A search tree

The search procedure sketched above can be described more formally as follows.

function *search*(x, r)
    {The pointer r points to the root of a search tree.
    The function searches for the value x in this tree
    and returns a pointer to the node containing x.
    If x is missing, the function returns **nil**.}
    if r = **nil then** {x is not in the tree}
             return nil
    else if $x = r\uparrow.$ *value* **then return** r
    else if $x < r\uparrow.$ *value* **then return** *search*$(x, r\uparrow.left\text{-}child)$
    else return *search*$(x, r\uparrow. right\text{-}child)$

Here we suppose that the search tree is composed of nodes of the type *binary-node* defined above. For efficiency it may be better to rewrite the algorithm avoiding the recursive calls, although some compilers automatically remove this so-called tail recursion. Problem 5.11 invites you to do this.

It is simple to update a search tree, that is, to delete a node or to add a new value, without destroying the search tree property. However, if this is done carelessly, the resulting tree can become *unbalanced*. By this we mean that many of the nodes in the tree have only one child, not two, so its branches become long and stringy. When this happens, searching the tree is no longer efficient. In the worst case, every node in the tree may have exactly one child, except for a single leaf that has no children. With such an unbalanced tree, finding an item in a tree with n elements may involve comparing it with the contents of all n nodes.

A variety of methods are available to keep the tree balanced, and hence to guarantee that such operations as searches or the addition and deletion of nodes take a time in $O(\log n)$ in the worst case, where n is the number of nodes in the tree. These methods may also allow the efficient implementation of several additional operations. Among the older techniques are the use of AVL trees and 2–3 trees; more recent suggestions include red-black trees and splay trees. Since these concepts are not used in the rest of the book, here we only mention their existence.

Height, depth and level

It is easy to confuse the terms used to describe the position of a node in a rooted tree. Height and level, for instance, are similar concepts, but not the same.

◇ The *height* of a node is the number of edges in the longest path from the node in question to a leaf.

◇ The *depth* of a node is the number of edges in the path from the root to the node in question.

◇ The *level* of a node is equal to the height of the root of the tree minus the depth of the node concerned.

Node	Height	Depth	Level
alpha	2	0	2
beta	1	1	1
gamma	0	1	1
delta	0	2	0
epsilon	0	2	0
zeta	0	2	0

Figure 5.10. Height, depth and level

For example, Figure 5.10 gives the height, depth and level for each node of the tree illustrated in Figure 5.5. Informally, if the tree is drawn with successive generations of nodes in neat layers, then the depth of a node is found by numbering the layers downwards from 0 at the root; the level of a node is found by numbering the layers upwards from 0 at the bottom; only the height is a little more complicated.

Finally we define the *height of the tree* to be the height of its root; this is also the depth of the deepest leaf and the level of the root.

5.6 Associative tables

An *associative table* is just like an array, except that the index is not restricted to lie between two prespecified bounds. For instance, if T is a table, you may use $T[1]$ and then $T[10^6]$ with no need to reserve one million storage cells for the table. Better still, you may use strings rather than numbers for the index, so $T["Fred"]$ is as legitimate as $T[1]$. Ideally, a table should not take much more space than is needed to write down the indexes used so far, together with space for the values stored in those table locations.

The convenience of tables comes at a price: unlike arrays, tables cannot be implemented so that each access is guaranteed to take constant time. The easiest way to implement a table is with a list.

```
type table_list = ↑table_node
type table_node = record
        index: index_type
        value: information
        next: ↑table_node
```

With this implementation, access to $T[\text{"Fred"}]$ is accomplished by marching through the list until "Fred" is found in the *index* field of a node or until the end of the list is reached. In the first case, the associated information is in the *value* field of the same node; in the second, we know that "Fred" is missing. New entries are created when needed; see Problem 5.12. This implementation is very inefficient. In the worst case, each request concerns a missing element, forcing us to explore the entire list at each access. A sequence of n accesses therefore requires a time in $\Omega(n^2)$ in the worst case. If up to m distinct indexes are used in those n accesses, $m \le n$, and if each request is equally likely to access any of those indexes, the average-case performance of this implementation is as bad as its worst case: $\Omega(mn)$. Provided the *index* fields can be compared with one another and with the requested index in unit time, *balanced trees* can be used to reduce this time to $O(n \log m)$ in the worst case; see Section 5.5. This is better, but still not good enough for one of the main applications for associative tables, namely compilers.

Just about every compiler uses an associative table to implement the *symbol table*. This table holds all the identifiers used in the program to be compiled. If *Fred* is an identifier, the compiler must be able to access relevant information such as its type and the level at which it is defined. Using tables, this information is simply stored in $T[\text{"Fred"}]$. The use of either implementation outlined above would slow a compiler down unacceptably when it dealt with programs containing a large number of identifiers. Instead, most compilers use a technique known as *hash coding*, or simply *hashing*. Despite a disastrous worst case, hashing performs reasonably well in practice most of the time.

Let U be the universe of potential indexes for the associative table to be implemented, and let $N \ll |U|$ be a parameter chosen as described below. A *hash function* is a function $h : U \rightarrow \{0, 1, 2, \dots, N - 1\}$. This function should efficiently disperse all the probable indexes: $h(x)$ should be different from $h(y)$ for most of the pairs $x \ne y$ likely to be used simultaneously. For instance $h(x) = x \bmod N$ is reasonably good for compiler purposes provided N is prime and x is obtained from the identifier's name using any standard integer representation of character strings, such as ASCII.

When $x \ne y$ but $h(x) = h(y)$, we say there is a *collision* between x and y. If collisions were very unlikely, we could implement the associative table T with an ordinary array $A[0 .. N - 1]$, using $A[h(x)]$ each time $T[x]$ is logically needed. The problem is that $T[x]$ and $T[y]$ are confused whenever x and y collide. Unfortunately, this is intolerable because the collision probability cannot be neglected unless $N \gg m^2$, where m is the number of different indexes actually used; see Problem 5.14. Many solutions for this difficulty have been proposed. The simplest is *list hashing* or *chaining*. Each entry of array $A[0..N-1]$ is of type *table_list*: $A[i]$ contains the list of all indexes that hash to value i, together with their relevant information. Figure 5.11 illustrates the situation after the following four requests to associative table T.

   $T[\text{"Laurel"}] \leftarrow 3$
   $T[\text{"Chaplin"}] \leftarrow 1$
   $T[\text{"Hardy"}] \leftarrow 4$
   $T[\text{"Keaton"}] \leftarrow 1$

In this example, $N = 6$, $h(\text{"Keaton"}) = 1$, $h(\text{"Laurel"}) = h(\text{"Hardy"}) = 2$ and $h(\text{"Chaplin"}) = 4$.

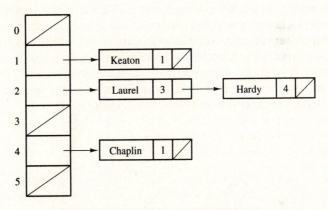

Figure 5.11. Illustration of hashing

The *load factor* of the table is m/N, where m is the number of distinct indexes used in the table and N is the size of the array used to implement it. If we suppose that every index, every value stored in the table and every pointer occupy a constant amount of space, the table takes space in $\Theta(N+m)$ and the average length of the ✓ lists is equal to the load factor. Thus increasing N reduces the average list length but increases the space occupied by the table. If the load factor is kept between $1/2$ and 1, the table occupies a space in $\Theta(m)$, which is optimal up to a small constant ✓ factor, and the average list length is less than 1, which is likely to imply efficient access to the table. It is tempting to improve the scheme by replacing the N collision lists by balanced trees, but this is not worthwhile if the load factor is kept small, unless it is essential to improve the worst-case performance.

   The load factor can be kept small by *rehashing*. With the compiler application in mind, for instance, the initial value of N is chosen so we expect small programs to use less than N different identifiers. We allow the load factor to be smaller than $1/2$ when the number of identifiers is small. Whenever more than N different identifiers are encountered, causing the load factor to exceed 1, it is time to double the size of the array used to implement the hash table. At that point, the hash function must be changed to double its range and every entry already in the table must be rehashed to its new position in a list of the larger array. Rehashing is expensive, but so infrequent that it does not cause a dramatic increase in the *amortized* time required per access to the table. Rehashing is repeated each time the load factor exceeds 1; after rehashing the load factor drops back to $1/2$.

Unfortunately, a small average list length does not guarantee a small average access time. The problem is that the longer a list is, the more likely it is that one of its elements will be accessed. Thus bad cases are more likely to happen than good ones. In the extreme scenario, there could be one list of length N and $N-1$ lists of length zero. Even though the average list length is 1, the situation is no better than when we used the simple *table_list* approach. If the table is used in a compiler, this would occur if all the identifiers of a program happened to hash to the same value. Although this is unlikely, it cannot be ruled out. Nevertheless, it can be proved that each access takes constant expected time in the amortized sense, provided rehashing is performed each time the load factor exceeds 1 and provided we make the unnatural assumption that every possible identifier is equally likely to be used. In practice, hashing works well most of the time even though identifiers are not chosen at random. Moreover, we shall see in Section 10.7.3 how to remove this assumption about the probability distribution of the instances to be handled and still have provably good expected performance.

5.7 Heaps

A heap is a special kind of rooted tree that can be implemented efficiently in an array without any explicit pointers. This interesting structure lends itself to numerous applications, including a remarkable sorting technique called *heapsort*, presented later in this section. It can also be used for the efficient representation of certain dynamic priority lists, such as the event list in a simulation or the list of tasks to be scheduled by an operating system.

A binary tree is *essentially complete* if each internal node, with the possible exception of one special node, has exactly two children. The special node, if there is one, is situated on level 1; it has a left child but no right child. Moreover, either all the leaves are on level 0, or else they are on levels 0 and 1, and no leaf on level 1 is to the left of an internal node at the same level. Intuitively, an essentially complete tree is one where the internal nodes are pushed up the tree as high as possible, the internal nodes on the last level being pushed over to the left; the leaves fill the last level containing internal nodes, if there is still any room, and then spill over onto the left of level 0. For example, Figure 5.12 illustrates an essentially complete binary tree containing 10 nodes. The five internal nodes occupy level 3 (the root), level 2, and the left side of level 1; the five leaves fill the right side of level 1 and then continue at the left of level 0.

If an essentially complete binary tree has height k, then there is one node (the root) on level k, there are two nodes on level $k-1$, and so on; there are 2^{k-1} nodes on level 1, and at least 1 and not more than 2^k on level 0. If the tree contains n

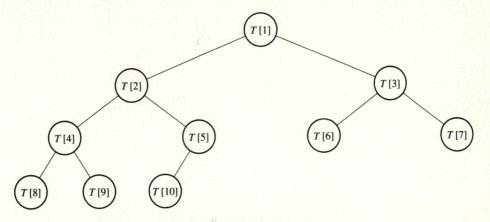

Figure 5.12. An essentially complete binary tree

nodes in all, counting both internal nodes and leaves, it follows that $2^k \le n < 2^{k+1}$. Equivalently, the height of a tree containing n nodes is $k = \lfloor \lg n \rfloor$, a result we shall use later.

This kind of tree can be represented in an array T by putting the nodes of depth k, from left to right, in the positions $T[2^k]$, $T[2^k+1], \ldots, T[2^{k+1}-1]$, with the possible exception of level 0, which may be incomplete. Figure 5.12 indicates which array element corresponds to each node of the tree. Using this representation, the parent of the node represented in $T[i]$ is found in $T[i \div 2]$ for $i > 1$ (the root $T[1]$ does not have a parent), and the children of the node represented in $T[i]$ are found in $T[2i]$ and $T[2i + 1]$, whenever they exist. The subtree whose root is in $T[i]$ is also easy to identify.

Now a *heap* is an essentially complete binary tree, each of whose nodes includes an element of information called the *value* of the node, and which has the property that the value of each internal node is greater than or equal to the values of its children. This is called the *heap property*. Figure 5.13 shows an example of a heap with 10 nodes. The underlying tree is of course the one shown in Figure 5.12, but now we have marked each node with its value. The heap property can be easily checked. For instance, the node whose value is 9 has two children whose values are 5 and 2: both children have a value less than the value of their parent. This same heap can be represented by the following array.

Since the value of each internal node is greater than or equal to the values of its children, which in turn have values greater than or equal to the values of *their* children, and so on, the heap property ensures that the value of each internal node is greater than or equal to the values of all the nodes that lie in the subtrees below it. In particular, the value of the root is greater than or equal to the values of all the other nodes in the heap.

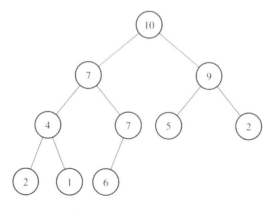

Figure 5.13. A heap

The crucial characteristic of this data structure is that the heap property can be restored efficiently if the value of a node is modified. If the value of a node increases to the extent that it becomes greater than the value of its parent, it suffices to exchange these two values, and then to continue the same process upwards in the tree if necessary until the heap property is restored. We say that the modified value has been *percolated* up to its new position in the heap. (This operation is often called *sifting up*, a curiously upside-down metaphor.) For example, if the value 1 in Figure 5.13 is modified so that it becomes 8, we can restore the heap property by exchanging the 8 with its parent 4, and then exchanging it again with its new parent 7, obtaining the result shown in Figure 5.14.

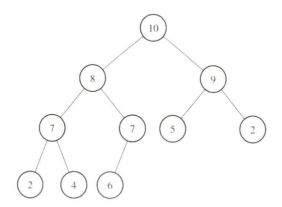

Figure 5.14. The heap, after percolating 8 to its place

If on the contrary the value of a node is decreased so that it becomes less than the value of at least one of its children, it suffices to exchange the modified value with the larger of the values in the children, and then to continue this process downwards in the tree if necessary until the heap property is restored. We say that the modified value has been *sifted down* to its new position. For example, if the 10 in the root of Figure 5.14 is modified to 3, we can restore the heap property by exchanging the 3 with its larger child, namely 9, and then exchanging it again with the larger of its new children, namely 5. The result we obtain is shown in Figure 5.15.

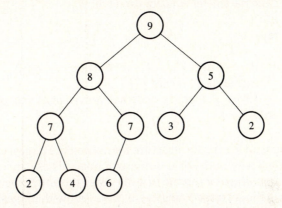

Figure 5.15. The heap, after sifting 3 down to its place

The following procedures describe more formally the basic processes for manipulating a heap. For clarity, they are written so as to reflect the preceding discussion as closely as possible. If you intend to use heaps for a "real" application, we encourage you to figure out how to avoid the inefficiency caused by our use of the "exchange" instruction.

procedure *alter-heap*$(T[1..n], i, v)$
    $\{T[1..n]$ is a heap. The value of $T[i]$ is set to v and the
    heap property is re-established. We suppose that $1 \le i \le n.\}$
    $x \leftarrow T[i]$
    $T[i] \leftarrow v$
    if $v < x$ **then** *sift-down*(T, i)
            else *percolate*(T, i)

procedure *sift-down*$(T[1..n], i)$
    $\{$This procedure sifts node i down so as to re-establish the heap
    property in $T[1..n]$. We suppose that T would be a heap if $T[i]$
    were sufficiently large. We also suppose that $1 \le i \le n.\}$
    $k \leftarrow i$
    repeat
        $j \leftarrow k$
        $\{$find the larger child of node $j\}$
        if $2j \le n$ **and** $T[2j] > T[k]$ **then** $k \leftarrow 2j$
        if $2j < n$ **and** $T[2j+1] > T[k]$ **then** $k \leftarrow 2j+1$
        exchange $T[j]$ and $T[k]$
        $\{$if $j = k$, then the node has arrived at its final position$\}$
    until $j = k$

procedure *percolate*($T[1 .. n], i$)
    {This procedure percolates node i so as to re-establish the heap
    property in $T[1 .. n]$. We suppose that T would be a heap if $T[i]$
    were sufficiently small. We also suppose that $1 \le i \le n$.
    The parameter n is not used here.}
    $k \leftarrow i$
    repeat
        $j \leftarrow k$
        if $j > 1$ **and** $T[j \div 2] < T[k]$ **then** $k \leftarrow j \div 2$
        exchange $T[j]$ and $T[k]$
        {if $j = k$, then the node has arrived at its final position}
    until $j = k$

The heap is an ideal data structure for finding the largest element of a set, removing it, adding a new node, or modifying a node. These are exactly the operations we need to implement dynamic priority lists efficiently: the value of a node gives the priority of the corresponding event, the event with highest priority is always found at the root of the heap, and the priority of an event can be changed dynamically at any time. This is particularly useful in computer simulations and in the design of schedulers for an operating system. Some typical procedures are illustrated below.

function *find-max*($T[1 .. n]$)
    {Returns the largest element of the heap $T[1 .. n]$}
    return $T[1]$

procedure *delete-max*($T[1 .. n]$)
    {Removes the largest element of the heap $T[1 .. n]$
    and restores the heap property in $T[1 .. n - 1]$}
    $T[1] \leftarrow T[n]$
    sift-down($T[1 .. n - 1], 1$)

procedure *insert-node*($T[1 .. n], v$)
    {Adds an element whose value is v to the heap $T[1 .. n]$
    and restores the heap property in $T[1 .. n + 1]$}
    $T[n + 1] \leftarrow v$
    percolate($T[1 .. n + 1], n + 1$)

It remains to be seen how to create a heap starting from an array $T[1 .. n]$ of elements in an undefined order. The obvious solution is to start with an empty heap and to add elements one by one.

procedure *slow-make-heap*($T[1 .. n]$)
    {This procedure makes the array $T[1 .. n]$ into a heap,
    albeit rather inefficiently}
    for $i \leftarrow 2$ **to** n **do** {*percolate*}($T[1 .. i], i$)

However this approach is not particularly efficient; see Problem 5.19. There exists a cleverer algorithm for making a heap. Suppose, for example, that our starting point is the following array:

1	6	9	2	7	5	2	7	4	10

represented by the tree in Figure 5.16a. We first make each of the subtrees whose roots are at level 1 into a heap; this is done by sifting down these roots, as illustrated in Figure 5.16b. The subtrees at the next higher level are then transformed into heaps, again by sifting down their roots. Figure 5.16c shows the process for the left subtree. The other subtree at level 2 is already a heap. This results in an essentially complete binary tree corresponding to the array:

1	10	9	7	7	5	2	2	4	6

It only remains to sift down its root to obtain the desired heap. The final process thus goes as follows:

10	1	9	7	7	5	2	2	4	6
10	7	9	1	7	5	2	2	4	6
10	7	9	4	7	5	2	2	1	6

The tree representation of the final form of the array is shown previously as Figure 5.13.

Here is a formal description of the algorithm.

> **procedure** *make-heap*($T[1 .. n]$)
> {This procedure makes the array $T[1 .. n]$ into a heap}
> **for** $i \leftarrow \lfloor n/2 \rfloor$ **downto** 1 **do** *sift-down*(T, i)

√ Theorem 5.7.1   *The algorithm constructs a heap in linear time.*

Proof   We give two proofs of this claim.

1. As a barometer we use the instructions in the **repeat** loop of the algorithm *sift-down*. To sift down a node at level r, clearly we make at most $r + 1$ trips round the loop. Now the height of a heap containing n nodes is $\lfloor \lg n \rfloor = k$, say. In the heap there are 2^{k-1} nodes at level 1 (not all of which are necessarily internal nodes), 2^{k-2} nodes at level 2 (all of which must be internal nodes), and so on, down to 1 node at level k, the root. When we apply *make-heap*, we sift down the value in each internal node. Hence if t is the total number of trips round the **repeat** loop, we have

$$
\begin{aligned}
t &\le 2 \times 2^{k-1} + 3 \times 2^{k-2} + \cdots + (k+1)2^0 \\
&< -2^k + 2^{k+1}\left(2^{-1} + 2 \times 2^{-2} + 3 \times 2^{-3} + \cdots\right) \\
&= 2^{k+2} - 2^k < 4n
\end{aligned}
$$

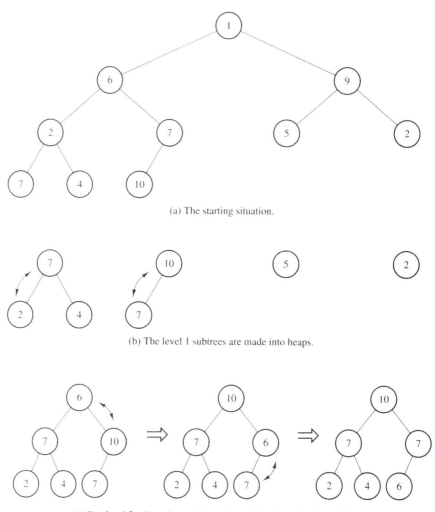

(a) The starting situation.

(b) The level 1 subtrees are made into heaps.

(c) One level 2 subtree is made into a heap (the other already is a heap).

Figure 5.16. Making a heap

where we used Proposition 1.7.12 to sum the infinite series. The required work is therefore in $O(n)$.

2. Let $t(k)$ be the time needed in the worst case to build a heap of height at most k. Assume that $k \geq 2$. To construct the heap, the algorithm first transforms each of the two subtrees attached to the root into heaps of height at most $k - 1$. (The right subtree could be of height $k - 2$.) The algorithm then sifts the root down a path whose length is at most k, which takes a time $s(k) \in O(k)$ in the worst case. We thus obtain the asymptotic recurrence

$$t(k) \leq 2t(k - 1) + s(k).$$

This is similar to Example 4.7.7, which yields $t(k) \in O(2^k)$. But a heap containing n elements is of height $\lfloor \lg n \rfloor$, hence it can be built in at most $t(\lfloor \lg n \rfloor)$ steps, which is in $O(n)$ because $2^{\lfloor \lg n \rfloor} \le n$. ∎

Williams invented the heap to serve as the underlying data structure for the following sorting algorithm.

> **procedure** *heapsort*($T[1..n]$)
>   {T is an array to be sorted}
>   *make-heap*(T)
>   **for** $i \leftarrow n$ **downto** 2 **do**
>   exchange $T[1]$ and $T[i]$
>   *sift-down*($T[1..i-1], 1$)

√ Theorem 5.7.2   *The algorithm takes a time in $O(n \log n)$ to sort n elements.*

Proof   Let $t(n)$ be the time taken to sort an array of n elements in the worst case. The *make-heap* operation takes a time linear in n, and the height of the heap that is produced is $\lfloor \lg n \rfloor$. The **for** loop is executed $n-1$ times. Each time round the loop, the "exchange" instruction takes constant time, and the *sift-down* operation then sifts the root down a path whose length is at most $\lg n$, which takes a time in the order of $\log n$ in the worst case. Hence

$$t(n) \in O(n) + (n-1)O(1) + (n-1)O(\log n) = O(n \log n).$$

∎

It can be shown that $t(n) \in \Theta(n \log n)$: the *exact* order of $t(n)$ is also $n \log n$, both in the worst case and on the average, supposing all initial permutations of the objects to be sorted to be equally likely. However this is more difficult to prove.

The basic concept of a heap can be improved in several ways. For applications that need *percolate* more often than *sift-down* (see for example Problem 6.16), it pays to have more than two children per internal node. This speeds up *percolate* (because the heap is shallower) at the cost of slowing down operations such as *sift-down* that must consider every child at each level. It is still possible to represent such heaps in an array without explicit pointers, but a little care is needed to do it correctly; see Problem 5.23.

For applications that tend to sift down an updated root node almost to the bottom level, it pays to ignore temporarily the new value stored at the root, choosing rather to treat this node as if it were empty, that is, as if it contained a value smaller than any other value in the tree. The empty node will therefore be sifted all the way down to a leaf. At this point, put the relevant value back into the empty leaf, and percolate it to its proper position. The advantage of this procedure is that it requires only one comparison at each level while the empty node is being sifted down, rather than two with the usual procedure. (This is because we must compare the children to each other, but we do not need to compare the greater child with its parent.) Experiments have shown that this approach yields an improvement over the classic *heapsort* algorithm.

We shall sometimes have occasion to use an *inverted heap*. By this we mean an essentially complete binary tree where the value of each internal node is less than or equal to the values of its children, and not greater than or equal as in the ordinary heap. In an inverted heap the smallest item is at the root. All the properties of an ordinary heap apply *mutatis mutandis*.

Although heaps can implement efficiently most of the operations needed to handle dynamic priority lists, there are some operations for which they are not suited. For example, there is no good way of searching for a particular item in a heap. In procedures such as *sift-down* and *percolate* above, we provided the address of the node concerned as one of the parameters of the procedure. Furthermore there is no efficient way of merging two heaps of the kind we have described. The best we can do is to put the contents of the two heaps side by side in an array, and then call procedure *make-heap* on the combined array.

As the following section will show, it is not hard to produce *mergeable heaps* at the cost of some complication in the data structures used. However in any kind of heap searching for a particular item is inefficient.

5.8 Binomial heaps

In an ordinary heap containing n items, finding the largest item takes a time in $O(1)$. Deleting the largest item or inserting a new item takes a time in $O(\log n)$. However merging two heaps that between them contain n items takes a time in $O(n)$. In this section we describe a different kind of heap, where finding the largest item still takes a time in $O(1)$ and deleting the largest item still takes a time in $O(\log n)$. However merging two of these new heaps only requires a time in $O(\log n)$, and inserting a new item—provided we look at the amortized cost, not the actual cost of each operation—only requires a time in $O(1)$.

We first define *binomial trees*. The i–th binomial tree B_i, $i \geq 0$ is defined recursively to consist of a root node with i children, where the j–th child, $1 \leq j \leq i$, is in turn the root of a binomial tree B_{j-1}. Figure 5.17 shows B_0 to B_4. It is easy to show by mathematical induction that the binomial tree B_i contains 2^i nodes, of which $\binom{i}{k}$ are at depth k, $0 \leq k \leq i$. Here $\binom{i}{k}$ is the binomial coefficient defined in Section 1.7.3. This, of course, is what gives binomial trees their name. We assume that each node in such a tree can store a value. Since the nodes have a variable number of children, they are probably best represented on a computer using the type *treenode*1 defined in Section 5.5.

To define a *binomial heap* we begin with a collection of binomial trees. Each binomial tree in the collection must be a different size, and furthermore each must have the heap property: the value stored at any internal node must be greater than or equal to the values of its children. This ensures that the largest item in the heap is in the root of one of its binomial trees. To complete the definition of a binomial heap, we add pointers to join each root to the next, in order of increasing size of the binomial trees. It is convenient to organize the roots in a doubly-linked list so that insertion or deletion of a root is easy. Finally we add a pointer to the root

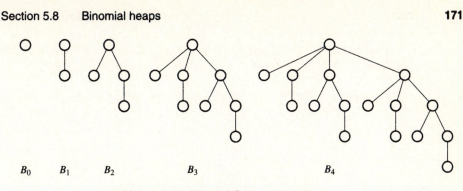

Figure 5.17. Binomial trees B_0 to B_4

containing the largest element in the heap. Figure 5.18 illustrates a binomial heap with 11 items. It is easy to see that a binomial heap containing n items comprises not more than $\lceil \lg n \rceil$ binomial trees.

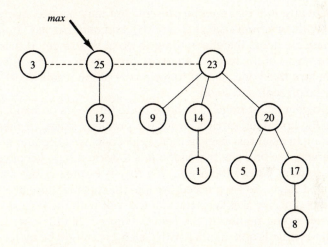

Figure 5.18. A binomial heap containing 11 items

Suppose we have two binomial trees B_i, the same size but possibly containing different values. Assume they both have the heap property. Then it is easy to combine them into a single binomial tree B_{i+1}, still with the heap property. Make the root with the smaller value into the $(i + 1)$–st child of the root with the larger value, and we are done. Figure 5.19 shows how two B_2's can be combined into a B_3 in this way. We shall call this operation *linking* two binomial trees. Clearly it takes a time in $O(1)$.

Next we describe how to merge two binomial heaps H_1 and H_2. Each consists of a collection of binomial trees arranged in increasing order of size. Begin by looking at any B_0's that may be present. If neither H_1 nor H_2 includes a B_0, there is nothing to do at this stage. If just one of H_1 and H_2 includes a B_0, keep it to form part of the result. Otherwise link the two B_0's from the two heaps into a B_1. Next

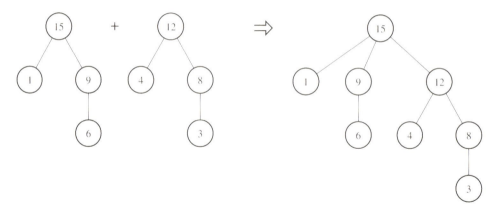

Figure 5.19. Linking two B_2's to make a B_3

look at any B_1's that may be present. We may have as many as three of them to deal with, one from each of H_1 and H_2, and one "carried" from the previous stage. If there are none, there is nothing to do at this stage. If there is just one, keep it to form part of the result. Otherwise link any two of the B_1's to form a B_2; should there be a third one, keep it to form part of the result. Next look at any B_2's that may be present, and so on.

In general, at stage i we have up to three B_i's on hand, one from each of H_1 and H_2, and one "carried" from the previous stage. If there are none, there is nothing to do at this stage; if there is just one, we keep it to form part of the result; otherwise we link any two of the B_i's to form a B_{i+1}, keeping the third, if there is one, to form part of the result. If a B_{i+1} is formed at this stage, it is "carried" to the next stage. As we proceed, we join the roots of those binomial trees that are to be kept, and we also keep track of the root with the largest value so as to set the corresponding pointer in the result. Figure 5.20 illustrates how a binomial heap with 6 elements and another with 7 elements might be merged to form a binomial heap with 13 elements.

The analogy with binary addition is close. There at each stage we have up to three 1s, one carried from the previous position, and one from each of the operands. If there are none, the result contains 0 in this position; if there is just one, the result contains a 1; otherwise two of the 1s generate a carry to the next position, and the result in this position is 0 or 1 depending whether two or three 1s were present initially.

If the result of a merge operation is a binomial heap comprising n items, it can be constructed in at most $\lceil \lg n \rceil + 1$ stages. Each stage requires at most one linking operation, plus the adjustment of a few pointers. Thus one stage can be done in a time in $O(1)$, and the complete merge takes a time in $O(\log n)$.

Finding the largest item in a binomial heap is simply a matter of returning the item indicated by the appropriate pointer. Clearly this can be done in a time in $O(1)$. Deleting the largest item of a binomial heap H is done as follows.

(i) Let B be the binomial tree whose root contains the largest item of H. Remove B

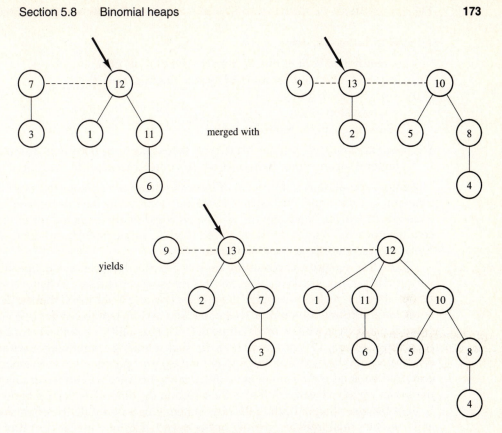

merged with

yields

Figure 5.20. Merging two binomial heaps

from H, joining any remaining constituents of H into a new binomial heap H_1.

(ii) Remove the root of B. Join the binomial trees that used to be the subtrees of this root into a new binomial heap H_2. (They are already in order of increasing size, as required.)

(iii) Merge H_1 and H_2 into a single binomial heap. This is the required result.

Here step (i) takes a time in $O(1)$, since it requires no more than the adjustment of a few pointers. Step (ii) takes a time in $O(\log n)$ because the root of any tree in H has at most $\lfloor \lg n \rfloor$ children; this exact time required depends on how the children are linked together. Step (iii) takes a time in $O(\log n)$ as we have just seen. Therefore the entire operation takes a time in $O(\log n)$.

Inserting a new item into a binomial heap H can be done as follows.

(i) Take the item to be inserted and convert it into a binomial tree containing just that one item. All that is required is to create a single node, and to initialize its value correctly. Call this new binomial tree B_0^*.

(ii) Set $i \leftarrow 0$.

(iii) If H includes a B_i, then

    – remove the root of this B_i from the list of roots of H;

    – link B_i^* and the B_i from H to form a binomial tree B_{i+1}^*;

    – set $i \leftarrow i + 1$; and

    – repeat step (iii).

    Otherwise go on to step (iv).

(iv) Insert the root of B_i^* into the list of roots belonging to H. If the item just inserted is larger than any other item in H, set H's pointer to point to the root of B_i^*.

The whole operation is reminiscent of incrementing a binary counter: most of the time step (iii) is executed just once or twice, but occasionally an insertion will cause a cascade of "carries" and step (iii) will be executed many times. As for the binary counter, however, we can do the required work in a time in $O(1)$ provided we are content to use amortized costs; see Section 4.6.

To do this, we use an accounting trick as described in Section 4.6. Specifically, we initially set up a virtual bank account containing zero tokens. Whenever a new binomial tree is created, we charge the process creating it one token that we deposit in the bank account. We assume that one token is sufficient to pay for one linking operation, which as we saw takes a time in $O(1)$, plus a little extra to pay for a small constant overhead. Whenever we perform such a linking operation, we withdraw one token from the bank account to pay for it, so the operation has zero amortized cost. Our bank account can never be overdrawn, because we can never link more trees than we have created. What is the effect on the binomial heap operations?

For the operation of finding the largest item, this accounting trick has no effect at all: no binomial trees are created or destroyed. Part of a merge operation consists of linking trees together. Apart from this, no trees are created or destroyed. As we just saw, linking (plus a little overhead) can be done at zero amortized cost. However the merge operation may also involve joining the roots of trees that were constituents of the original two heaps, and for which no linking has occurred. There may be up to $\lceil \lg n \rceil$ of these. The required work for each is in $O(1)$—only a few pointers have to be changed—so the total time required is in $O(\log n)$. Hence a merge operation still has an amortized cost in $O(\log n)$, despite the fact that the necessary linking operations have already been paid for.

To insert an extra item in a binomial heap, we begin in step (i) by creating a new binomial tree. When this tree is created, we charge one token that we deposit in the bank account. The rest of this step clearly takes a time in $O(1)$. Thus, even including the extra charge, the step can be carried out in a time in $O(1)$. Step (ii) is trivial. Every time we execute step (iii) we do one linking operation and adjust a small number of pointers. Since one binomial tree disappears during the linking operation, we can use one token from the bank account to pay for the whole step. The amortized cost of each execution of step (iii) is therefore zero. Step (iv) takes a time in $O(1)$. Pulling all this together, we see that the complete insertion operation can be carried out in an amortized time in $O(1)$, as we promised at the beginning of the section.

Even more elaborate data structures have been proposed to implement dynamic priority lists. Using *lazy binomial heaps*, which are just like binomial heaps except that we put off some housekeeping operations until they are absolutely necessary, two heaps can be merged in an amortized time in $O(1)$. The *Fibonacci heap* is another data structure that allows us to merge priority lists in constant amortized time. In addition, the value of a node in a Fibonacci heap can be increased and the node in question percolated to its new place in constant amortized time. We shall see in Problem 6.17 how useful this can be. Those heaps are based on *Fibonacci trees*; see Problem 5.29. The structure called a double-ended heap, or *deap*, allows both the largest and the smallest member of a set to be found efficiently.

5.9 Disjoint set structures

Suppose we have N objects numbered from 1 to N. We wish to group these into √disjoint sets, so that at any given time each object is in exactly one set. In each set √we choose one member to serve as a *label* for the set. For instance, if we decide to use the smallest object as the label, then we can refer to the set $\{2, 5, 7, 10\}$ simply as "set 2". Initially the N objects are in N different sets, each containing exactly one object. Thereafter, we execute a sequence of operations of two kinds:

◇ given some object, we *find* which set contains it, and return the label of this set; and

◇ given two different labels, we *merge* the contents of the two corresponding sets, and choose a label for the combined set.

Our problem is to represent this situation efficiently on a computer.

One possible representation is obvious. Suppose, as suggested above, we decide to use the smallest member of each set as the label. If we declare an array $set[1..N]$, it suffices to put the label of the set corresponding to each object in the appropriate array element. The two operations we want to perform can be implemented by the following procedures.

> **function** *find*1(x)
> {Finds the label of the set containing x}
> **return** $set[x]$

> **procedure** *merge*1(a, b)
> {Merges the sets labelled a and b; we assume $a \neq b$}
> $i \leftarrow \min(a, b)$
> $j \leftarrow \max(a, b)$
> **for** $k \leftarrow 1$ **to** N **do**
>   **if** $set[k] = j$ **then** $set[k] \leftarrow i$

Suppose we are to execute an arbitrary sequence of operations, of types *find* and *merge*, starting from the given initial situation. We do not know precisely in which order these operations will occur. However there will be n of type *find*, and not more than $N - 1$ of type *merge*, for after $N - 1$ *merge* operations all the objects are in the same set. For many applications n is comparable to N, too. If consulting or modifying one element of an array counts as an elementary operation, it is clear that *find*1 takes constant time, and that *merge*1 takes a time in $\Theta(N)$. The n *find* operations therefore take a time in $\Theta(n)$, while $N - 1$ *merge* operations take a time in $\Theta(N^2)$. If n and N are comparable, the whole sequence of operations takes a time in $\Theta(n^2)$.

Let us try to do better than this. Still using a single array, we can represent each set as a rooted tree, where each node contains a single pointer to its parent (as for the type *treenode2* in Section 5.5). We adopt the following scheme: if $set[i] = i$, then i is both the label of its set and the root of the corresponding tree; if $set[i] = j \neq i$, then j is the parent of i in some tree. The array

1	2	3	2	1	3	4	3	3	4

therefore represents the trees shown in Figure 5.21, which in turn represent the sets $\{1, 5\}$, $\{2, 4, 7, 10\}$ and $\{3, 6, 8, 9\}$. To merge two sets, we need now to change only a single value in the array; on the other hand, it is harder to find the set to which an object belongs.

> **function** *find2*(x)
>   {Finds the label of the set containing object x}
> $r \leftarrow x$
>   **while** $set[r] \neq r$ **do** $r \leftarrow set[r]$
>   **return** r

> **procedure** *merge2*(a, b)
>   {Merges the sets labelled a and b; we assume $a \neq b$}
>   **if** $a < b$ **then** $set[b] \leftarrow a$
>   **else** $set[a] \leftarrow b$

Now if each consultation or modification of an array element counts as an elementary operation, then the time needed to execute a *merge* operation is constant. However the time needed to execute a *find* operation is in $\Theta(N)$ in the worst case. When things go badly, therefore, executing an arbitrary sequence of n *find2* and $N - 1$ *merge2* operations starting from the initial situation can take a time in $\Theta(nN)$. If n is comparable to N as we assumed previously, this is $\Theta(n^2)$, and we have not gained anything over the use of *find1* and *merge1*. The problem arises because after k calls of *merge2* we may find ourselves confronted by a tree of height k, so each subsequent call on *find2* may take a time proportional to k. To avoid this, we must find a way to limit the height of the trees produced.

So far, we have chosen arbitrarily to use the smallest member of a set as its label. This means that when we merge two trees, the one that does *not* contain the smallest member of the resulting combined set becomes a subtree of the one that does. It would be better to arrange matters so it is always the tree whose height is least that becomes a subtree of the other. Suppose we have to merge two trees whose heights are respectively h_1 and h_2. Using this technique, the height of the resulting merged tree will be $\max(h_1, h_2)$ if $h_1 \neq h_2$, or $h_1 + 1$ if $h_1 = h_2$. As the following theorem shows, in this way the height of the trees does not grow as rapidly.

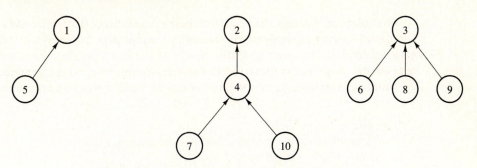

Figure 5.21. Tree representation for disjoint sets

Theorem 5.9.1   *Using the technique outlined above, after an arbitrary sequence of merge operations starting from the initial situation, a tree containing k nodes has a height at most $\lfloor \lg k \rfloor$.*

Proof The proof is by generalized mathematical induction on k, the number of nodes in the tree.

◇ *Basis*: The theorem is clearly true when $k = 1$, for a tree with only 1 node has height 0, and $0 \leq \lfloor \lg 1 \rfloor$.

◇ *Induction step*: Consider any $k > 1$. Assume the induction hypothesis that the theorem is true for all m such that $1 \leq m < k$. A tree containing k nodes can be obtained only by merging two smaller trees. Suppose these two smaller trees contain respectively a and b nodes, where we may assume without loss of generality that $a \leq b$. Now $a \geq 1$ since there is no way of obtaining a tree with 0 nodes starting from the initial situation, and $k = a + b$. It follows that $a \leq k/2$ and $b \leq k - 1$. Since $k > 1$, both $k/2 < k$ and $k - 1 < k$, and hence $a < k$ and $b < k$. Let the heights of the two smaller trees be h_a and h_b respectively, and let the height of the resulting merged tree be h_k. Two cases arise.

   – If $h_a \neq h_b$, then $h_k = \max(h_a, h_b) \leq \max(\lfloor \lg a \rfloor, \lfloor \lg b \rfloor)$, where we used the induction hypothesis twice to obtain the inequality. Since both a and b are less than k, it follows that $h_k \leq \lfloor \lg k \rfloor$.
   – If $h_a = h_b$, then $h_k = h_a + 1 \leq \lfloor \lg a \rfloor + 1$, again using the induction hypothesis. Now $\lfloor \lg a \rfloor \leq \lfloor \lg(k/2) \rfloor = \lfloor \lg(k) - 1 \rfloor = \lfloor \lg k \rfloor - 1$, and so $h_k \leq \lfloor \lg k \rfloor$.

Thus the theorem is true when $k = 1$, and its truth for $k = n > 1$ follows from its assumed truth for $k = 1, 2, \ldots, n - 1$. By the principle of generalized mathematical induction, the theorem is therefore true for all $k \geq 1$. ∎

The height of the trees can be maintained in an additional array $height[1 .. N]$ so that $height[i]$ gives the height of node i in its current tree. Whenever a is the label of a set, $height[a]$ therefore gives the height of the corresponding tree, and in fact these are the only heights that concern us. Initially, $height[i]$ is set to zero for each i. The procedure *find2* is unchanged, but we must modify *merge* appropriately.

procedure *merge3*(a, b)
    {Merges the sets labelled a and b; we assume $a \neq b$}
    if $height[a] = height[b]$
    then
        $height[a] \leftarrow height[a]+1$
        $set[b] \leftarrow a$
    else
        if $height[a] > height[b]$
        then $set[b] \leftarrow a$
        else $set[a] \leftarrow b$

If each consultation or modification of an array element counts as an elementary operation, the time needed to execute an arbitrary sequence of n *find2* and $N - 1$ *merge3* operations, starting from the initial situation, is in $\Theta(N + n \log N)$ in the worst case; assuming n and N are comparable, this is in the exact order of $n \log n$.

By modifying *find2*, we can make our operations faster still. When we are trying to determine the set that contains a certain object x, we first traverse the edges of the tree leading up from x to the root. Once we know the root, we can traverse the same edges again, this time modifying each node encountered on the way so its pointer now indicates the root directly. This technique is called *path compression*. For example, when we execute the operation *find*(20) on the tree of Figure 5.22a, the result is the tree of Figure 5.22b: nodes 20, 10 and 9, which lay on the path from node 20 to the root, now point directly to the root. The pointers of the remaining nodes have not changed.

This technique obviously tends to reduce the height of a tree and thus to accelerate subsequent *find* operations. On the other hand, the new *find* operation traverses the path from the node of interest to the root twice, and therefore takes about twice as long as before. Hence path compression may not be worthwhile if only a small number of *find* operations are performed. However, if many *find* operations are executed, then after a while we may expect, roughly speaking, that all the nodes involved will be attached directly to the roots of their respective trees, so the subsequent *finds* take constant time. A *merge* operation will perturb this situation only slightly, and not for long. Most of the time, therefore, both *find* and *merge* operations will require a time in $O(1)$, so a sequence of n of the former and $N - 1$ of the latter operations will take a time—nearly—in $O(n)$ when n and N are comparable. We see below how close we come to this ideal situation.

One small point remains to be cleared up. Using path compression, it is no longer true that the height of a tree whose root is a is given by $height[a]$. This is because path compression may change the height of a tree, but it does not affect the

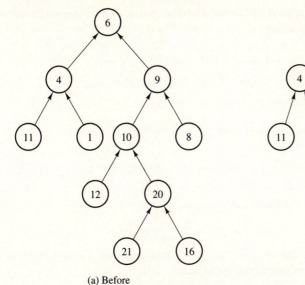

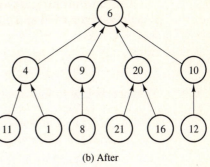

(b) After

(a) Before

Figure 5.22. Path compression

contents of the root node. However path compression can only reduce the height of a tree, never increase it, so if a is the root, it remains true that $height[a]$ is an upper bound on the height of the tree; see Problem 5.31. To avoid confusion we call this value the *rank* of the tree; the name of the array used in *merge3* should be changed accordingly. The *find* function is now as follows.

```
function find3(x)
    {Finds the label of the set containing object x}
    r ← x
    while set[r] ≠ r do r ← set[r]
    {r is the root of the tree}
    i ← x
    while i ≠ r do
        j ← set[i]
        set[i] ← r
        i ← j
    return r
```

From now on, when we use this combination of two arrays and of procedures *find3* and *merge3* to deal with disjoint sets of objects, we say we are using a *disjoint set structure*; see also Problems 5.32 and 5.33 for variations on the theme.

It is not easy to analyse the time needed for an arbitrary sequence of *find* and *merge* operations when path compression is used. In this book we content ourselves with giving the result. First we need to define two new functions $A(i, j)$ and $\alpha(i, j)$.

The function $A(i, j)$ is a slight variant of *Ackermann's function*; see Problem 5.38. It is defined for $i \geq 0$ and $j \geq 1$.

$$A(i, j) = \begin{cases} 2j & \text{if } i = 0 \\ 2 & \text{if } j = 1 \\ A(i - 1, A(i, j - 1)) & \text{otherwise} \end{cases}$$

The facts below follow easily from the definition:

$\diamond$ $A(1, 1) = 2$ and $A(1, j + 1) = A(0, A(1, j)) = 2A(1, j)$ for $j \geq 1$. It follows that $A(1, j) = 2^j$ for all j.

$\diamond$ $A(2, 1) = 2$ and $A(2, j + 1) = A(1, A(2, j)) = 2^{A(2,j)}$ for $j \geq 1$. Therefore $A(2, 1) = 2$, $A(2, 2) = 2^{A(2,1)} = 2^2 = 4$, $A(2, 3) = 2^{A(2,2)} = 2^{2^2} = 16$, $A(2, 4) = 2^{A(2,3)} = 2^{2^{2^2}} = 65536$, and in general

$$A(2, j) = 2^{\cdot^{\cdot^{2}}} \Big\} j \text{ 2s}$$

where the right-hand side contains j 2s altogether. Remember that exponentiation associates to the right, so

$$2^{2^{2^2}} = 2^{2^4} = 2^{16} = 65536.$$

$\diamond$ $A(3, 1) = 2$, $A(3, 2) = A(2, A(3, 1)) = 4$, $A(3, 3) = A(2, A(3, 2)) = 65536$,

$$A(3, 4) = A(2, A(3, 3)) = A(2, 65536) = 2^{\cdot^{\cdot^{2}}} \Big\}_{65536 \text{ 2s},}$$

and so on.

It is evident that the function A grows extremely fast.

Now the function $\alpha(i, j)$ is defined as a kind of inverse of A:

$$\alpha(i, j) = \min\{k \,|\, k \geq 1 \text{ and } A(k, 4\lceil i/j \rceil) > \lg j\}.$$

Whereas A grows very rapidly, α grows extremely slowly. To see this, observe that for any fixed j, $\alpha(i, j)$ is maximized when $i \leq j$, in which case $4\lceil i/j \rceil = 4$, so

$$\alpha(i, j) \leq \min\{k \,|\, k \geq 1 \text{ and } A(k, 4) > \lg j\}.$$

Therefore $\alpha(i, j) > 3$ only when

$$\lg j \geq A(3, 4) = 2^{\cdot^{\cdot^{2}}} \Big\}_{65536 \text{ 2s}}$$

which is huge. Thus for all except astronomical values of j, $\alpha(i, j) \leq 3$.

With a universe of N objects and the given initial situation, consider an arbitrary sequence of n calls of *find3* and $m \leq N - 1$ calls of *merge3*. Let $c = n + m$. Using the functions above, Tarjan was able to show that such a sequence can be executed in a time in $\Theta(c\alpha(c, N))$ in the worst case. (We continue to suppose, of course, that each consultation or modification of an array element counts as an elementary operation.) Since for all practical purposes we may suppose that $\alpha(c, N) \leq 3$, the time taken by the sequence of operations is essentially linear in c. However no known algorithm allows us to carry out the sequence in a time that is *truly* linear in c.

5.10 Problems

Problem 5.1.   You are to implement a stack of items of a given type. Give the necessary declarations and write three procedures respectively to initialize the stack, to add a new item, and to remove an item. Include tests in your procedures to prevent adding or removing too many items. Also write a function that returns the item currently at the top of the stack. Make sure this function behaves sensibly when the stack is empty.

Problem 5.2.   A queue can be represented using an array of items of the required type, along with two pointers. One gives the index of the item at the head of the queue (the next to leave), and the other gives the index of the item at the end of the queue (the last to arrive). Give the necessary declarations and write three procedures that initialize the queue, add a new item, and remove an item, respectively. If your array has space for n items, what is the maximum number of items that can be in the queue? How do you know when it is full, and when it is empty? Include tests in your procedures to prevent adding or removing too many items. Also write a function that returns the item currently at the head of the queue. Make sure this function behaves sensibly when the queue is empty.
Hint: As items are added and removed, the queue tends to drift along the array. When a pointer runs off the array, do not copy all the items to a new position, but rather let the pointer wrap around to the other end of the array.

Problem 5.3.   Fill in the details of the technique called virtual initialization described in Section 5.1 and illustrated in Figure 5.1. You should write three algorithms.

> **procedure** *init*
> {Virtually initializes $T[1..n]$}

> **procedure** *store*(i, v)
> {Sets $T[i]$ to the value v}

> **function** *val*(i)
> {Returns the value of $T[i]$ if this has been assigned;
> returns a default value (such as -1) otherwise}

A call on any of these (including *init*!) should take constant time in the worst case.

Problem 5.4.   What changes in your solution to Problem 5.3 if the index to the array T, instead of running from 1 to n, goes from n_1 to n_2, say?

Problem 5.5.   Without writing the detailed algorithms, sketch how to adapt virtual initialization to a two-dimensional array.

Problem 5.6.   Show in some detail how the directed graph of Figure 5.3 could be represented on a machine using (a) the *adjgraph* type of representation, and (b) the *lisgraph* type of representation.

Problem 5.7. Draw the three different trees with five nodes, and the six different trees with six nodes. Repeat the problem for rooted trees. For this problem the order of the branches of a rooted tree is immaterial. You should find nine rooted trees with five nodes, and twenty with six nodes.

Problem 5.8. Following Problem 5.7, how many rooted trees are there with six nodes if the order of the branches *is* taken into account?

Problem 5.9. Show how the four rooted trees illustrated in Figure 5.4b would be represented using pointers from a node to its eldest child and to its next sibling.

Problem 5.10. At the cost of one extra bit of storage in records of type *treenode*1, we can make it possible to find the parent of any given node. The idea is to use the *next-sibling* field of the rightmost member of a set of siblings to point to their common parent. Give the details of this approach. In a tree containing n nodes, how much time does it take to find the parent of a given node in the worst case? Does your answer change if you know that a node of the tree can never have more than k children?

Problem 5.11. Rewrite the algorithm *search* of Section 5.5 avoiding the recursive calls.

Problem 5.12. Give a detailed implementation of associative tables using lists of type *table_list* from Section 5.6. Your implementation should provide the following algorithms.

> **function** $init(T, x)$
> **function** $val(T, x)$
> **procedure** $set(T, x, y)$

These determine if $T[x]$ has been initialized, access its current value if it has one, and set $T[x]$ to y (either by creating entry $T[x]$ or by changing its value if it already exists), respectively.

Problem 5.13. Prove that a sequence of n accesses to an associative table implemented as in Problem 5.12 takes a time in $\Omega(n^2)$ in the worst case.

Problem 5.14. Prove that even if the array used to implement a hash table is of size $N = m^2$, where m is the number of elements to be stored in the table, the probability of collision is significant. Assume that the hash function sends each element to a random location in the array.

Problem 5.15. Prove that the cost of rehashing can be neglected even in the worst case, provided we perform an amortized analysis. In other words, show that accesses to the table can put enough tokens in the bank account to pay the complete cost of rehashing each time the load factor exceeds 1. Assume that both the choice of a new hash function and rehashing one entry in the table take constant time.

Problem 5.16.   Prove that if hashing is used to implement the symbol table of a compiler, if the load factor is kept below 1, and if we make the unnatural assumption that every possible identifier is equally likely to be used, the probability that any identifier collides with more than t others is less than $1/t$, for any integer t. Conclude that the average time needed for a sequence of n accesses to the table is in $O(n)$.

Problem 5.17.   Propose strategies other than chaining for handling collisions in a hash table.

Problem 5.18.   Sketch an essentially complete binary tree with (a) 15 nodes and (b) 16 nodes.

Problem 5.19.   In Section 5.7 we saw an algorithm for making a heap (*slow-make-heap*) that we described as "rather inefficient". Analyse the worst case for this algorithm, and compare it to the linear-time algorithm *make-heap*.

Problem 5.20.   Let $T[1..12]$ be an array such that $T[i]= i$ for each $i \leq 12$. Exhibit the state of the array after each of the following procedure calls. The calls are performed one after the other, each one except the first working on the array left by its predecessor.

> *make-heap*(T)
> *alter-heap*(T, 12, 10)
> *alter-heap*(T, 1, 6)
> *alter-heap*(T, 5, 8)

Problem 5.21.   Exhibit a heap T containing n distinct values, such that the following sequence results in a different heap.

> $m \leftarrow$ *find-max*($T[1..n]$)
> *delete-max*($T[1..n]$)
> *insert-node*($T[1..n-1], m$)

Draw the heap after each operation. You may choose n to suit yourself.

Problem 5.22.   Design an algorithm *find-in-heap*($T[1..n], x$) that looks for the value x in the heap T and returns either the index of x in the heap, if it is present, or 0 otherwise. What is the running time of your algorithm? Can you use the heap property to speed up the search, and if so, how?

Problem 5.23. (k-ary heaps)   In Section 5.7 we defined heaps in terms of an essentially complete *binary* tree. It should be clear that the idea can be generalized to essentially complete k-ary trees, for any $k \geq 2$. Show that we can map the nodes of a k-ary tree containing n nodes to the elements $T[0]$ to $T[n-1]$ of an array in such a way that the parent of the node represented in $T[i]$ is found in $T[(i-1) \div k]$ for $i > 0$, and the children of the node represented in $T[i]$ are found in $T[ik + 1], T[ik + 2], \ldots, T[(i + 1)k]$. Note that for binary trees, this is *not* the mapping we used in Section 5.7; there we used a mapping onto $T[1 .. n]$, not onto $T[0 .. n - 1]$.

Write procedures *sift-down* (T, k, i) and *percolate* (T, k, i) for these generalized heaps. What are the advantages and disadvantages of such generalized heaps? For an application where they may be useful, see Problem 6.16.

Problem 5.24.   For *heapsort*, what are the best and the worst initial arrangements of the elements to be sorted, as far as the execution time of the algorithm is concerned? Justify your answer.

Problem 5.25.   Prove that the binomial tree B_i defined in Section 5.8 contains 2^i nodes, of which $\binom{i}{k}$ are at depth k, $0 \le k \le i$.

Problem 5.26.   Prove that a binomial heap containing n items comprises at most $\lceil \lg n \rceil$ binomial trees, the largest of which contains $2^{\lfloor \lg n \rfloor}$ items.

Problem 5.27.   Consider the algorithm for inserting a new item into a binomial heap H given in Section 5.8. A simpler method would be to create a binomial tree B_0^* as in step (i) of the algorithm, make it into a binomial heap, and merge this new heap with H. Why did we prefer the more complicated algorithm?

Problem 5.28.   Using the accounting trick described in Section 5.8, what is the amortized cost of deleting the largest item from a binomial heap?

Problem 5.29.   **(Fibonacci trees)** It is convenient to define the Fibonacci tree F_{-1} to consist of a single node. Then the i-th Fibonacci tree F_i, $i \ge 0$, is defined recursively to consist of a root node with i children, where the j-th child, $1 \le j \le i$, is in turn the root of a Fibonacci tree F_{j-2}. Figure 5.23 shows F_0 to F_5. Prove that the Fibonacci tree F_i, $i \ge 0$, has f_{i+1} nodes, where f_k is the k-th member of the Fibonacci sequence; see Section 1.6.4.

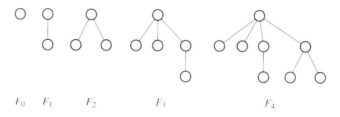

Figure 5.23. Fibonacci trees F_0 to F_4

Problem 5.30.   If each consultation or modification of an array element counts as an elementary operation, prove that the time needed to execute an arbitrary sequence of n operations of type *find2* and $N - 1$ operations of type *merge3* starting from the initial situation is in $\Theta(N + n \log N)$; this is $\Theta(n \log n)$ when n and N are comparable.

Problem 5.31.   When using path compression, we are content to use an array *rank* that gives us an upper bound on the height of a tree, rather than the exact height. Estimate how much time it would take to recompute the exact height of the tree after each path compression.

Problem 5.32.   In Section 5.9 we discussed merging two trees so the tree whose height is least becomes a subtree of the other. A second possible tactic is to ensure that the tree containing the smaller number of nodes always becomes a subtree of the other. Path compression does not change the number of nodes in a tree, so it is easy to store this value exactly, whereas we could not keep track efficiently of the exact height of a tree after path compression. Write a procedure *merge*4 to implement this tactic, and prove a result corresponding to Theorem 5.9.1.

Problem 5.33.   The root of a tree has no parent, and we never use the value of *rank* for a node that is not a root. Use this to implement a disjoint set structure with just one array of length N rather than two (*set* and *rank*).

Problem 5.34.   Let A be the variant of Ackermann's function defined in Section 5.9. Show that $A(i, 2) = 4$ for all i.

Problem 5.35.   Let A be the variant of Ackermann's function defined in Section 5.9. Show that $A(i + 1, j) \geq A(i, j)$ and $A(i, j + 1) \geq A(i, j)$ for all i and j.

Problem 5.36.   Let A be the variant of Ackermann's function defined in Section 5.9, and define $a(i, n)$ by

$$a(i, n) = \min\{j | A(i, j) > \lg n\}.$$

Show that $a(1, n)$ is in $O(\log \log n)$.

Problem 5.37.   Consider the function $\lg^*(n)$, the *iterated logarithm* of n. Informally, this is the number of times we need to apply the function $\lg$ to n to obtain a value less than or equal to 1. For example, $\lg 16 = 4$, $\lg 4 = 2$, and $\lg 2 = 1$; hence $\lg \lg \lg 16 = 1$, and so $\lg^* 16 = 3$. Slightly more formally, we may define $\lg^* n$ by

$$\lg^* n = \min\{k | \underbrace{\lg \lg \cdots \lg}_{k \text{ times}} n \leq 1\}.$$

The function $\lg^* n$ increases very slowly: $\lg^* n$ is 4 or less for every $n \leq 65536$. Let $a(i, n)$ be the function defined in the previous problem. Show that $a(2, n)$ is in $O(\lg^* n)$.

Problem 5.38.   Ackermann's function (the genuine thing this time) is defined by

$$A(i, j) = \begin{cases} j + 1 & \text{if } i = 0 \\ A(i - 1, 1) & \text{if } i > 0, j = 0 \\ A(i - 1, A(i, j - 1)) & \text{otherwise.} \end{cases}$$

Calculate $A(2, 5)$, $A(3, 3)$, and $A(4, 4)$.

5.11 References and further reading

For more information about data structures, consult Knuth (1968, 1973), Stone (1972), Horowitz and Sahni (1976), Standish (1980), Aho, Hopcroft and Ullman (1983), Tarjan (1983), Gonnet and Baeza-Yates (1984), Kingston (1990), Lewis and Denenberg (1991) and Wood (1993). Graphs and trees are presented from a mathematical standpoint in Berge (1958, 1970).

Virtual initialization comes from Exercise 2.12 in Aho, Hopcroft , and Ullman (1974). A variety of methods are available to keep search trees balanced; we did not explain them in this chapter because we shall not need them later. Among those, AVL trees, which come from Adel'son-Vel'skiĭ and Landis (1962), are described in detail in Knuth (1973); 2–3 trees come from Aho, Hopcroft and Ullman (1974); red-black trees are from Guibas and Sedgewick (1978); and splay trees, which offer good worst-case performance in the amortized sense, are from Sleator and Tarjan (1985). Read Tarjan (1983) too. Hash coding is treated in detail in Knuth (1973); many alternatives to chaining are given there.

The heap was introduced as a data structure for sorting by Williams (1964). Heaps with more than two children per internal node are from Johnson (1975, 1977); see Problems 5.23 and 6.16. The idea of speeding up *heapsort* by sifting nodes to the bottom before percolating them to their proper location is from Carlsson (1987a). For ideas on building heaps faster, consult McDiarmid and Reed (1989). See also Gonnet and Munro (1986) and Schaffer and Sedgewick (1993).

Binomial heaps are from Vuillemin (1978); see also Brown (1978) and Kozen (1992). Fibonacci heaps are from Fredman and Tarjan (1987), where it is shown that they can be used to speed up several classic network optimization algorithms of the sort we shall study in Chapter 6; see Problem 6.17 for one example. Double-ended heaps are from Carlsson (1986, 1987b), which are good sources of ideas on heaps in general.

The analysis of disjoint set structures involving Ackermann's function is from Tarjan (1975) but it is easier to read the subsequent account in Tarjan (1983). An earlier upper bound on the worst-case complexity of this problem was due to Hopcroft and Ullman (1973); it involved the lg* function of Problem 5.37. Galil and Italiano (1991) survey a number of proposed algorithms. In this book, we give only some of the possible uses for disjoint set structures; for more applications see Hopcroft and Karp (1971), Aho, Hopcroft and Ullman (1974, 1976) and Nelson and Oppen (1980). Ackermann's function is from Ackermann (1928).

Chapter 6

Greedy Algorithms

If greedy algorithms are the first family of algorithms that we examine in detail in this book, the reason is simple: they are usually the most straightforward. As the name suggests, they are shortsighted in their approach, taking decisions on the basis of information immediately at hand without worrying about the effect these decisions may have in the future. Thus they are easy to invent, easy to implement, and—when they work—efficient. However, since the world is rarely that simple, many problems cannot be solved correctly by such a crude approach.

Greedy algorithms are typically used to solve optimization problems. Examples later in this chapter include finding the shortest route from one node to another through a network, or finding the best order to execute a set of jobs on a computer. In such a context a greedy algorithm works by choosing the arc, or the job, that seems most promising at any instant; it never reconsiders this decision, whatever situation may arise later. There is no need to evaluate alternatives, nor to employ elaborate book-keeping procedures allowing previous decisions to be undone. We begin the chapter with an everyday example where this tactic works well.

6.1 Making change (1)

Suppose we live in a country where the following coins are available: dollars (100 cents), quarters (25 cents), dimes (10 cents), nickels (5 cents) and pennies (1 cent). Our problem is to devise an algorithm for paying a given amount to a customer using the smallest possible number of coins. For instance, if we must pay $2.89 (289 cents), the best solution is to give the customer 10 coins: 2 dollars, 3 quarters, 1 dime and 4 pennies. Most of us solve this kind of problem every day without thinking twice, unconsciously using an obvious greedy algorithm: starting with nothing, at every stage we add to the coins already chosen a coin of the largest value available that does not take us past the amount to be paid.

The algorithm may be formalized as follows.

function {*make-change*}(n): *set of coins*
    {Makes change for n units using the least possible
     number of coins. The constant C specifies the coinage}
    const $C = \{100, 25, 10, 5, 1\}$
    $S \leftarrow \varnothing$ {S is a set that will hold the solution}
    $s \leftarrow 0$ {s is the sum of the items in S}
    while $s \neq n$ **do**
        $x \leftarrow$ the largest item in C such that $s + x \leq n$
        if there is no such item **then**
            return "*no solution found*"
        $S \leftarrow S \cup$ {a coin of value x}
        $s \leftarrow s + x$
    return S

It is easy to convince oneself (but surprisingly hard to prove formally) that with the given values for the coins, and provided an adequate supply of each denomination is available, this algorithm always produces an optimal solution to our problem. However with a different series of values, or if the supply of some of the coins is limited, the greedy algorithm may not work; see Problems 6.2 and 6.4. In some cases it may choose a set of coins that is not optimal (that is, the set contains more coins than necessary), while in others it may fail to find a solution at all even though one exists (though this cannot happen if we have an unlimited supply of 1-unit coins).

The algorithm is "greedy" because at every step it chooses the largest coin it can, without worrying whether this will prove to be a sound decision in the long run. Furthermore it never changes its mind: once a coin has been included in the solution, it is there for good. As we shall explain in the following section, these are the characteristics of this family of algorithms.

For the particular problem of making change, a completely different algorithm is described in Chapter 8. This alternative algorithm uses dynamic programming. The dynamic programming algorithm always works, whereas the greedy algorithm may fail; however it is less straightforward than the greedy algorithm and (when both algorithms work) less efficient.

6.2 General characteristics of greedy algorithms

Commonly, greedy algorithms and the problems they can solve are characterized by most or all of the following features.

⋄ We have some problem to solve in an optimal way. To construct the solution of our problem, we have a set (or list) of candidates: the coins that are available, the edges of a graph that may be used to build a path, the set of jobs to be scheduled, or whatever.

⋄ As the algorithm proceeds, we accumulate two other sets. One contains candidates that have already been considered and chosen, while the other contains candidates that have been considered and rejected.

◇ There is a function that checks whether a particular set of candidates provides a *solution* to our problem, ignoring questions of optimality for the time being. For instance, do the coins we have chosen add up to the amount to be paid? Do the selected edges provide a path to the node we wish to reach? Have all the jobs been scheduled?

◇ A second function checks whether a set of candidates is *feasible*, that is, whether or not it is possible to complete the set by adding further candidates so as to obtain at least one solution to our problem. Here too, we are not for the time being concerned with optimality. We usually expect the problem to have at least one solution that can be obtained using candidates from the set initially available.

◇ Yet another function, the *selection function*, indicates at any time which of the remaining candidates, that have neither been chosen nor rejected, is the most promising.

◇ Finally an *objective function* gives the value of a solution we have found: the number of coins we used to make change, the length of the path we constructed, the time needed to process all the jobs in the schedule, or whatever other value we are trying to optimize. Unlike the three functions mentioned previously, the objective function does not appear explicitly in the greedy algorithm.

To solve our problem, we look for a set of candidates that constitutes a solution, and that optimizes (minimizes or maximizes, as the case may be) the value of the objective function. A greedy algorithm proceeds step by step. Initially the set of chosen candidates is empty. Then at each step we consider adding to this set the best remaining untried candidate, our choice being guided by the selection function. If the enlarged set of chosen candidates would no longer be feasible, we reject the candidate we are currently considering. In this case the candidate that has been tried and rejected is never considered again. However if the enlarged set is still feasible, then we add the current candidate to the set of chosen candidates, where it will stay from now on. Each time we enlarge the set of chosen candidates, we check whether it now constitutes a solution to our problem. When a greedy algorithm works correctly, the first solution found in this way is always optimal.

```
function greedy(C: set): set
    {C is the set of candidates}
    S ← ∅ {We construct the solution in the set S}
    while C ≠ ∅ and not solution(S) do
        x ← select(C)
        C ← C \ {x}
        if feasible(S ∪ {x}) then S ← S ∪ {x}
    if solution(S) then return S
            else return "there are no solutions"
```

It is clear why such algorithms are called "greedy": at every step, the procedure chooses the best morsel it can swallow, without worrying about the future. It never changes its mind: once a candidate is included in the solution, it is there for good; once a candidate is excluded from the solution, it is never reconsidered.

The selection function is usually related to the objective function. For example, if we are trying to maximize our profit, we are likely to choose whichever remaining candidate has the highest individual value. If we are trying to minimize cost, then we may select the cheapest remaining candidate, and so on. However, we shall see that at times there may be several plausible selection functions, so we have to choose the right one if we want our algorithm to work properly.

Returning for a moment to the example of making change, here is one way in which the general features of greedy algorithms can be equated to the particular features of this problem.

◇ The candidates are a set of coins, representing in our example 100, 25, 10, 5 and 1 units, with sufficient coins of each value that we never run out. (However the set of candidates must be finite.)

◇ The solution function checks whether the value of the coins chosen so far is *exactly* the amount to be paid.

◇ A set of coins is feasible if its total value *does not exceed* the amount to be paid.

◇ The selection function chooses the highest-valued coin remaining in the set of candidates.

◇ The objective function counts the number of coins used in the solution.

It is obviously more efficient to reject all the remaining 100-unit coins (say) at once when the remaining amount to be represented falls below this value. Using integer division to calculate how many of a particular value of coin to choose is also more efficient than proceeding by successive subtraction. If either of these tactics is adopted, then we can relax the condition that the available set of coins must be finite.

6.3 Graphs: Minimum spanning trees

Let $G = \langle N, A \rangle$ be a connected, undirected graph where N is the set of nodes and A is the set of edges. Each edge has a given nonnegative *length*. The problem is to find a subset T of the edges of G such that all the nodes remain connected when only the edges in T are used, and the sum of the lengths of the edges in T is as small as possible. Since G is connected, at least one solution must exist. If G has edges of length 0, then there may exist several solutions whose total length is the same but that involve different numbers of edges. In this case, given two solutions with equal total length, we prefer the one with least edges. Even with this proviso, the problem may have several different solutions of equal value. Instead of talking about length, we can associate a *cost* to each edge. The problem is then to find a subset T of the edges whose total cost is as small as possible. Obviously this change of terminology does not affect the way we solve the problem.

Let $G' = \langle N, T \rangle$ be the partial graph formed by the nodes of G and the edges in T, and suppose there are n nodes in N. A connected graph with n nodes must have at least $n - 1$ edges, so this is the minimum number of edges there can be in T. On the other hand, a graph with n nodes and more than $n - 1$ edges contains at least one cycle; see Problem 6.7. Hence if G' is connected and T has more than $n - 1$ edges, we can remove at least one of these without disconnecting G', provided we choose an edge that is part of a cycle. This will either decrease the total length of the edges in T, or else leave the total length the same (if we have removed an edge with length 0) while decreasing the number of edges in T. In either case the new solution is preferable to the old one. Thus a set T with n or more edges cannot be optimal. It follows that T must have exactly $n - 1$ edges, and since G' is connected, it must therefore be a tree.

The graph G' is called a *minimum spanning tree* for the graph G. This problem has many applications. For instance, suppose the nodes of G represent towns, and let the cost of an edge $\{a, b\}$ be the cost of laying a telephone line from a to b. Then a minimum spanning tree of G corresponds to the cheapest possible network serving all the towns in question, provided only direct links between towns can be used (in other words, provided we are not allowed to build telephone exchanges out in the country *between* the towns). Relaxing this condition is equivalent to allowing the addition of extra, auxiliary nodes to G. This may allow cheaper solutions to be obtained: see Problem 6.8.

At first sight, at least two lines of attack seem possible if we hope to find a greedy algorithm for this problem. Clearly our set of candidates must be the set A of edges in G. One possible tactic is to start with an empty set T, and to select at every stage the shortest edge that has not yet been chosen or rejected, regardless of where this edge is situated in G. Another line of attack involves choosing a node and building a tree from there, selecting at every stage the shortest available edge that can extend the tree to an additional node. Unusually, for this particular problem both approaches work! Before presenting the algorithms, we show how the general schema of a greedy algorithm applies in this case, and present a lemma for later use.

◇ The candidates, as already noted, are the edges in G.

◇ A set of edges is a solution if it constitutes a spanning tree for the nodes in N.

◇ A set of edges is feasible if it does not include a cycle.

◇ The selection function we use varies with the algorithm.

◇ The objective function to minimize is the total length of the edges in the solution.

We also need some further terminology. We say a feasible set of edges is *promising* if it can be extended to produce not merely a solution, but an optimal solution to our problem. In particular, the empty set is always promising (since an optimal solution always exists). Furthermore, if a promising set of edges is already a solution, then the required extension is vacuous, and this solution must itself be optimal. Next, we say that an edge *leaves* a given set of nodes if exactly one end of this edge is in the set. An edge can thus fail to leave a given set of nodes either because neither of its ends is in the set, or—less evidently—because both of them are. The following lemma is crucial for proving the correctness of the forthcoming algorithms.

Lemma 6.3.1   *Let $G = \langle N, A \rangle$ be a connected undirected graph where the length of each edge is given. Let $B \subset N$ be a strict subset of the nodes of G. Let $T \subseteq A$ be a promising set of edges such that no edge in T leaves B. Let v be the shortest edge that leaves B (or one of the shortest if ties exist). Then $T \cup \{v\}$ is promising.*

Proof   Let U be a minimum spanning tree of G such that $T \subseteq U$. Such a U must exist since T is promising by assumption. If $v \in U$, there is nothing to prove. Otherwise, when we add the edge v to U, we create exactly one cycle. (This is one of the properties of a tree: see Section 5.5.) In this cycle, since v leaves B, there necessarily exists at least one other edge, u say, that also leaves B, or the cycle could not close; see Figure 6.1. If we now remove u, the cycle disappears and we obtain a new tree V that spans G. However the length of v is by definition no greater than the length of u, and therefore the total length of the edges in V does not exceed the total length of the edges in U. Therefore V is also a minimum spanning tree of G, and it includes v. To complete the proof, it remains to remark that $T \subseteq V$ because the edge u that was removed leaves B, and therefore it could not have been an edge of T.   ∎

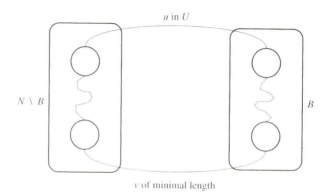

Figure 6.1. A cycle is created if we add edge v to U

6.3.1 Kruskal's algorithm

The set T of edges is initially empty. As the algorithm progresses, edges are added to T. So long as it has not found a solution, the partial graph formed by the nodes of G and the edges in T consists of several connected components. (Initially when T is empty, each node of G forms a distinct trivial connected component.) The elements of T included in a given connected component form a minimum spanning tree for the nodes in this component. At the end of the algorithm only one connected component remains, so T is then a minimum spanning tree for all the nodes of G.

To build bigger and bigger connected components, we examine the edges of G in order of increasing length. If an edge joins two nodes in different connected components, we add it to T. Consequently, the two connected components now form only one component. Otherwise the edge is rejected: it joins two nodes in the same connected component, and therefore cannot be added to T without forming a cycle (because the edges in T form a tree for each component). The algorithm stops when only one connected component remains.

To illustrate how this algorithm works, consider the graph in Figure 6.2. In increasing order of length the edges are: $\{1, 2\}, \{2, 3\}, \{4, 5\}, \{6, 7\}, \{1, 4\}, \{2, 5\}, \{4, 7\}, \{3, 5\}, \{2, 4\}, \{3, 6\}, \{5, 7\}$ and $\{5, 6\}$. The algorithm proceeds as follows.

Step		Edge considered	Connected components	
Initialization		—	$\{1\}\ \{2\}\ \{3\}\ \{4\}\ \{5\}\ \{6\}\ \{7\}$	7
1	*1*	$\{1, 2\}$	$\{1, 2\}\ \{3\}\ \{4\}\ \{5\}\ \{6\}\ \{7\}$	6
2	*2*	$\{2, 3\}$	$\{1, 2, 3\}\ \{4\}\ \{5\}\ \{6\}\ \{7\}$	5
3	*3*	$\{4, 5\}$	$\{1, 2, 3\}\ \{4, 5\}\ \{6\}\ \{7\}$	4
4	*3*	$\{6, 7\}$	$\{1, 2, 3\}\ \{4, 5\}\ \{6, 7\}$	3
5	*4*	$\{1, 4\}$	$\{1, 2, 3, 4, 5\}\ \{6, 7\}$	2
6	*4*	$\{2, 5\}$	rejected ← *since no connection, to lower # of groups*	
7	*4*	$\{4, 7\}$	$\{1, 2, 3, 4, 5, 6, 7\}$ *makes cycle*	1

value ↑   *# of groups ↓*

When the algorithm stops, T contains the chosen edges $\{1, 2\}, \{2, 3\}, \{4, 5\}, \{6, 7\}, \{1, 4\}$ and $\{4, 7\}$. This minimum spanning tree is shown by the heavy lines in Figure 6.2; its total length is 17.

Theorem 6.3.2   *Kruskal's algorithm finds a minimum spanning tree.*

Proof   The proof is by mathematical induction on the number of edges in the set T. We shall show that if T is promising at any stage of the algorithm, then it is still promising when an extra edge has been added. When the algorithm stops, T gives a solution to our problem; since it is also promising, this solution is optimal.

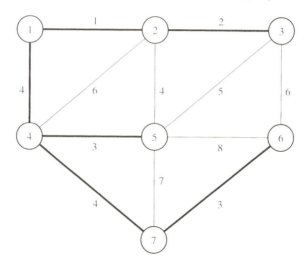

Figure 6.2. A graph and its minimum spanning tree

◇ *Basis*: The empty set is promising because G is connected and so a solution must exist.

◇ *Induction step*: Assume T is promising just before the algorithm adds a new edge $e = \{u, v\}$. The edges in T divide the nodes of G into two or more connected components; the node u is in one of these components, and v is in a different component. Let B be the set of nodes in the component that includes u. Now

  – the set B is a strict subset of the nodes of G (since it does not include v, for instance);
  – T is a promising set of edges such that no edge in T leaves B (for an edge in T either has both ends in B, or it has neither end in B, so by definition it does not leave B); and
  – e is one of the shortest edges that leaves B (for all the strictly shorter edges have already been examined, and either incorporated into T, or rejected because they had both ends in the same connected component).

Hence the conditions of Lemma 6.3.1 are fulfilled, and we conclude that the set $T \cup \{e\}$ is also promising.

This completes the proof by mathematical induction that the set T is promising at every stage of the algorithm, and hence that when the algorithm stops, T gives not merely a solution to our problem, but an optimal solution.   ∎

To implement the algorithm, we have to handle a certain number of sets, namely the nodes in each connected component. Two operations have to be carried out rapidly: *find*(x), which tells us in which connected component the node x is to be found, and *merge*(A, B), to merge two connected components. We therefore use disjoint set structures; see Section 5.9. For this algorithm it is preferable to represent the graph as a vector of edges with their associated lengths rather than as a matrix of distances; see Problem 6.9. Here is the algorithm.

> √ **function** *Kruskal*($G = \langle N, A \rangle$: *graph; length*: $A \to \mathbb{R}^+$): *set of edges*
>   {initialization}
>   Sort A by increasing length
> $n \leftarrow$ the number of nodes in N
> $T \leftarrow \varnothing$ {will contain the edges of the minimum spanning tree}
>   Initialize n sets, each containing a different element of N
>   {greedy loop}
>   **repeat**
> $e \leftarrow \{u, v\} \leftarrow$ shortest edge not yet considered
> $ucomp \leftarrow find(u)$
> $vcomp \leftarrow find(v)$
>   **if** $ucomp \neq vcomp$**then**
> $merge(ucomp, vcomp)$
> $T \leftarrow T \cup \{e\}$
>   **until** T contains $n - 1$ edges
>   **return** T

We can evaluate the execution time of the algorithm as follows. On a graph with n nodes and a edges, the number of operations is in

⋄ $\Theta(a \log a)$ to sort the edges, which is equivalent to $\Theta(a \log n)$ because $n - 1 \leq a \leq n(n-1)/2$;

⋄ $\Theta(n)$ to initialize the n disjoint sets;

⋄ $\Theta(2a\alpha(2a, n))$ for all the *find* and *merge* operations, where α is the slow-growing function defined in Section 5.9 (this follows from the results in Section 5.9 since there are at most $2a$ *find* operations and $n - 1$ *merge* operations on a universe containing n elements); and

⋄ at worst $O(a)$ for the remaining operations.

We conclude that the total time for the algorithm is in $\Theta(a \log n)$ because $\Theta(\alpha(2a, n)) \subset \Theta(\log n)$. Although this does not change the worst-case analysis, it is preferable to keep the edges in an inverted heap (see Section 5.7): thus the shortest edge is at the root of the heap. This allows the initialization to be carried out in a time in $\Theta(a)$, although each search for a minimum in the **repeat** loop now takes a time in $\Theta(\log a) = \Theta(\log n)$. This is particularly advantageous if the minimum spanning tree is found at a moment when a considerable number of edges remain to be tried. In such cases, the original algorithm wastes time sorting these useless edges.

6.3.2 Prim's algorithm

In Kruskal's algorithm the selection function chooses edges in increasing order of length without worrying too much about their connection to previously chosen edges, except that we are careful never to form a cycle. The result is a forest of trees that grows somewhat haphazardly, until finally all the components of the forest merge into a single tree. In Prim's algorithm, on the other hand, the minimum spanning tree grows in a natural way, starting from an arbitrary root. At each stage we add a new branch to the tree already constructed; the algorithm stops when all the nodes have been reached.

Let B be a set of nodes, and T a set of edges. Initially, B contains a single arbitrary node, and T is empty. At each step Prim's algorithm looks for the shortest possible edge $\{u, v\}$ such that $u \in B$ and $v \in N \setminus B$. It then adds v to B and $\{u, v\}$ to T. In this way the edges in T form at any instant a minimum spanning tree for the nodes in B. We continue thus as long as $B \neq N$. Here is an informal statement of the algorithm.

> **function** $Prim(G = \langle N, A \rangle$: *graph*; *length*: $A \to \mathbb{R}^+$): *set of edges*
>   {initialization}
> $T \leftarrow \varnothing$
> $B \leftarrow$ {an arbitrary member of N}
>   **while** $B \neq N$ **do**
>   find $e = \{u, v\}$ of minimum *length* such that
> $u \in B$ and $v \in N \setminus B$
> $T \leftarrow T \cup \{e\}$
> $B \leftarrow B \cup \{v\}$
>   **return** T

To illustrate the algorithm, consider once again the graph in Figure 6.2. We arbitrarily choose node 1 as the starting node. Now the algorithm might progress as follows.

Step	$\{u, v\}$	B
Initialization	—	{1}
1	{1,2}	{1,2}
2	{2,3}	{1,2,3}
3	{1,4}	{1,2,3,4}
4	{4,5}	{1,2,3,4,5}
5	{4,7}	{1,2,3,4,5,7}
6	{7,6}	{1,2,3,4,5,6,7}

When the algorithm stops, T contains the chosen edges {1,2}, {2,3}, {1,4}, {4,5}, {4,7} and {7,6}. The proof that the algorithm works is similar to the proof of Kruskal's algorithm.

> Theorem 6.3.3 *Prim's algorithm finds a minimum spanning tree.*

Proof   The proof is by mathematical induction on the number of edges in the set T. We shall show that if T is promising at any stage of the algorithm, then it is still promising when an extra edge has been added. When the algorithm stops, T gives a solution to our problem; since it is also promising, this solution is optimal.

⋄ *Basis*: The empty set is promising.

⋄ *Induction step*: Assume that T is promising just before the algorithm adds a new edge $e = \{u, v\}$. Now B is a strict subset of N (for the algorithm stops when $B = N$), T is a promising set of edges by the induction hypothesis, and e is by definition one of the shortest edges that leaves B. Hence the conditions of Lemma 6.3.1 are fulfilled, and $T \cup \{e\}$ is also promising.

This completes the proof by mathematical induction that the set T is promising at every stage of the algorithm. When the algorithm stops, T therefore gives an optimal solution to our problem.   ∎

To obtain a simple implementation on a computer, suppose the nodes of G are numbered from 1 to n, so that $N = \{1, 2, \ldots, n\}$. Suppose further that a symmetric matrix L gives the length of each edge, with $L[i, j] = \infty$ if the corresponding edge does not exist. We use two arrays. For each node $i \in N \setminus B$, *nearest*$[i]$ gives the node in B that is nearest to i, and *mindist*$[i]$ gives the distance from i to this nearest node. For a node $i \in B$, we set *mindist*$[i] = -1$. (In this way we can tell whether a node is in B or not.) The set B, arbitrarily initialized to $\{1\}$, is not represented explicitly; *nearest*[1] and *mindist*[1] are never used. Here is the algorithm.

```
function Prim(L[1 .. n, 1 .. n]): set of edges
    {initialization: only node 1 is in B}
    T ← ∅ {will contain the edges of the minimum spanning tree}
    for i = 2 to n do
        nearest[i] ← 1
        mindist[i] ← L[i, 1]
    {greedy loop}
    repeat n − 1 times
        min ← ∞
        for j ← 2 to n do
            if 0 ≤ mindist[j] < min then  min ← mindist[j]
                                          k ← j
        T ← T ∪ {{nearest[k], k}}
        mindist[k] ← −1 {add k to B}
        for j ← 2 to n do
            if L[j, k] < mindist[j] then
                                          mindist[j] ← L[j, k]
                                          nearest[j] ← k  return T
```

The main loop of the algorithm is executed $n-1$ times; at each iteration the enclosed **for** loops take a time in $\Theta(n)$. Thus Prim's algorithm takes a time in $\Theta(n^2)$.

We saw that Kruskal's algorithm takes a time in $\Theta(a \log n)$, where a is the number of edges in the graph. For a dense graph, a tends towards $n(n-1)/2$. In this case, Kruskal's algorithm takes a time in $\Theta(n^2 \log n)$, and Prim's algorithm is probably better. For a sparse graph, a tends towards n. In this case, Kruskal's algorithm takes a time in $\Theta(n \log n)$, and Prim's algorithm as presented here is probably less efficient. However Prim's algorithm, like Kruskal's, can be implemented using heaps. In this case—again like Kruskal's algorithm—it takes a time in $\Theta(a \log n)$. There exist other algorithms more efficient than either Prim's or Kruskal's; see Section 6.8.

6.4 Graphs: Shortest paths

Consider now a directed graph $G = \langle N, A \rangle$ where N is the set of nodes of G and A is the set of directed edges. Each edge has a nonnegative *length*. One of the nodes is designated as the *source* node. The problem is to determine the length of the shortest path from the source to each of the other nodes of the graph. As in Section 6.3 we could equally well talk about the *cost* of an edge instead of its length, and pose the problem of finding the cheapest path from the source to each other node.

This problem can be solved by a greedy algorithm often called *Dijkstra's algorithm*. The algorithm uses two sets of nodes, S and C. At every moment the set S contains those nodes that have already been chosen; as we shall see, the minimal distance from the source is already known for every node in S. The set C contains all the other nodes, whose minimal distance from the source is not yet known, and which are candidates to be chosen at some later stage. Hence we have the invariant property $N = S \cup C$. At the outset, S contains only the source itself; when the algorithm stops, S contains all the nodes of the graph and our problem is solved. At each step we choose the node in C whose distance to the source is least, and add it to S.

We shall say that a path from the source to some other node is *special* if all the intermediate nodes along the path belong to S. At each step of the algorithm, an array D holds the length of the shortest special path to each node of the graph. At the moment when we add a new node v to S, the shortest special path to v is also the shortest of all the paths to v. (We shall prove this later.) When the algorithm stops, all the nodes of the graph are in S, and so all the paths from the source to some other node are special. Consequently the values in D give the solution to the shortest path problem.

For simplicity, we again assume that the nodes of G are numbered from 1 to n, so $N = \{1, 2, \ldots, n\}$. We can suppose without loss of generality that node 1 is the source. Suppose also that a matrix L gives the length of each directed edge: $L[i, j] \geq 0$ if the edge $(i, j) \in A$, and $L[i, j] = \infty$ otherwise. Here is the algorithm.

√**function** $Dijkstra(L[1..n, 1..n])$: **array** $[2..n]$
    array $D[2..n]$
    {initialization}
    $C \leftarrow \{2, 3, \ldots, n\}$ $\{S = N \setminus C$ exists only implicitly$\}$
    for $i \leftarrow 2$ **to** n **do** $D[i] \leftarrow L[1, i]$
    {greedy loop}
    repeat $n - 2$ **times**
        $v \leftarrow$ some element of C minimizing $D[v]$
        $C \leftarrow C \setminus \{v\}$ {and implicitly $S \leftarrow S \cup \{v\}$}
        for each $w \in C$ **do**
            $D[w] \leftarrow \min(D[w], D[v] + L[v, w])$
    return D

The algorithm proceeds as follows on the graph in Figure 6.3.

Step	v *(select from C)*	C *(set of candidates)*	D *(distance)*
Initialization	—	{2,3,4,5}	[50,30,100,10]
1	*10* 5	{2,3,4}	[50,30,20,10]
2	*20* 4	{2,3}	[40,30,20,10]
3	*30* 3	{2}	[35,30,20,10]

(select min distance vertex w/)

Clearly D would not change if we did one more iteration to remove the last element of C. This is why the main loop is repeated only $n - 2$ times.

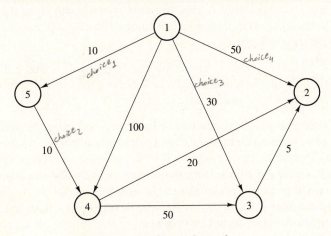

Figure 6.3. A directed graph

To determine not only the length of the shortest paths, but also where they pass, add a second array $P[2..n]$, where $P[v]$ contains the number of the node that precedes v in the shortest path. To find the complete path, follow the pointers P backwards from a destination to the source. The necessary modifications to the algorithm are simple:

◇ initialize $P[i]$ to 1 for $i = 2, 3, \ldots, n$;

◇ replace the contents of the inner **for** loop by

$$\textbf{if } D[w] > D[v] + L[v, w] \textbf{ then } D[w] \leftarrow D[v] + L[v, w]$$
$$P[w] \leftarrow v$$

The proof that the algorithm works is again by mathematical induction.

Theorem 6.4.1   *Dijkstra's algorithm finds the shortest paths from a single source to the other nodes of a graph.*

Proof   We prove by mathematical induction that

(a) if a node $i \neq 1$ is in S, then $D[i]$ gives the length of the shortest path from the source to i; and

(b) if a node i is not in S, then $D[i]$ gives the length of the shortest *special* path from the source to i.

◇ *Basis*: Initially only node 1, the source, is in S, so condition (a) is vacuously true. For the other nodes, the only special path from the source is the direct path, and D is initialized accordingly. Hence condition (b) also holds when the algorithm begins.

◇ *Induction hypothesis*: The induction hypothesis is that both conditions (a) and (b) hold just before we add a new node v to S. We detail separately the induction steps for conditions (a) and (b).

◇ *Induction step for condition (a)*: For every node already in S before the addition of v, nothing changes, so condition (a) is still true. As for node v, it will now belong to S. Before adding it to S, we must check that $D[v]$ gives the length of the shortest path from the source to v. By the induction hypothesis, $D[v]$ certainly gives the length of the shortest *special* path. We therefore have to verify that the shortest path from the source to v does not pass through any of the nodes that do not belong to S.

Suppose the contrary; that is, suppose that when we follow the shortest path from the source to v, we encounter one or more nodes (not counting v itself) that do not belong to S. Let x be the first such node encountered; see Figure 6.4. Now the initial segment of this path, as far as x, is a special path, so the distance to x is $D[x]$, by part (b) of the induction hypothesis. The total distance to v via x is certainly no shorter than this, since edge lengths are nonnegative. Finally $D[x]$ is not less than $D[v]$, since the algorithm chose v before x. Therefore the total distance to v via x is at least $D[v]$, and the path via x cannot be shorter than the shortest special path leading to v.

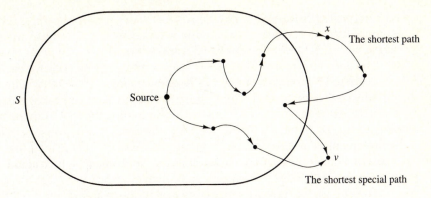

Figure 6.4. The shortest path to v cannot visit x

We have thus verified that when v is added to S, part (a) of the induction remains true.

◇ *Induction step for condition (b)*: Consider now a node w, different from v, which is not in S. When v is added to S, there are two possibilities for the shortest special path from the source to w: either it does not change, or else it now passes through v (and possibly through other nodes in S as well). In the second case, let x be the last node of S visited before arriving at w. The length of such a path is $D[x]+L[x,w]$. It seems at first glance that to compute the new value of $D[w]$ we should compare the old value of $D[w]$ with the values of $D[x]+L[x,w]$ for every node x in S (including v). However for every node x in S except v, this comparison was made when x was added to S, and $D[x]$ has not changed since then. Thus the new value of $D[w]$ can be computed simply by comparing the old value with $D[v]+L[v,w]$.

Since the algorithm does this explicitly, it ensures that part (b) of the induction also remains true whenever a new node v is added to S.

To complete the proof that the algorithm works, note that when the algorithm stops, all the nodes but one are in S (although the set S is not constructed explicitly). At this point it is clear that the shortest path from the source to the remaining node is a special path.   ∎

Analysis of the algorithm. Suppose Dijkstra's algorithm is applied to a graph with n nodes and a edges. Using the representation suggested up to now, the instance is given in the form of a matrix $L[1..n,1..n]$. Initialization takes a time in $O(n)$. In a straightforward implementation, choosing v in the **repeat** loop requires all the elements of C to be examined, so we look at $n-1, n-2, \ldots, 2$ values of D on successive iterations, giving a total time in $\Theta(n^2)$. The inner **for** loop does $n-2, n-3, \ldots, 1$ iterations, for a total also in $\Theta(n^2)$. The time required by this version of the algorithm is therefore in $\Theta(n^2)$.

If $a \ll n^2$, we might hope to avoid looking at the many entries containing ∞ in the matrix L. With this in mind, it could be preferable to represent the graph by an array of n lists, giving for each node its direct distance to adjacent nodes (like the type *lisgraph* of Section 5.4). This allows us to save time in the inner **for** loop, since we only have to consider those nodes w adjacent to v; but how are we to avoid taking a time in $\Omega(n^2)$ to determine in succession the $n - 2$ values taken by v?

The answer is to use an inverted heap containing one node for each element v of C, ordered by the value of $D[v]$. Thus the element v of C that minimizes $D[v]$ will always be found at the root. Initialization of the heap takes a time in $\Theta(n)$. The instruction "$C \leftarrow C \setminus \{v\}$" consists of eliminating the root from the heap, which takes a time in $O(\log n)$. As for the inner **for** loop, it now consists of looking, for each element w of C adjacent to v, to see whether $D[v] + L[v, w]$ is less than $D[w]$. If so, we must modify $D[w]$ and percolate w up the heap, which again takes a time in $O(\log n)$. This does not happen more than once for each edge of the graph.

To sum up, we have to remove the root of the heap exactly $n - 2$ times and to percolate at most a nodes, giving a total time in $\Theta((a + n)\log n)$. If the graph is connected, $a \geq n - 1$, and the time is in $\Theta(a \log n)$. The straightforward implementation is therefore preferable if the graph is dense, whereas it is preferable to use a heap if the graph is sparse. If $a \in \Theta(n^2 / \log n)$, the choice of representation may depend on the specific implementation. Problem 6.16 suggests a way to speed up the algorithm by using a k-ary heap with a well-chosen value of k; other, still faster algorithms are known; see Problem 6.17 and Section 6.8.

6.5 The knapsack problem (1)

This problem arises in various forms. In this chapter we look at the simplest version; a more difficult variant will be introduced in Section 8.4.

We are given n objects and a knapsack. For $i = 1, 2, \ldots, n$, object i has a positive weight w_i and a positive value v_i. The knapsack can carry a weight not exceeding W. Our aim is to fill the knapsack in a way that maximizes the value of the included objects, while respecting the capacity constraint. In this first version of the problem we assume that the objects can be broken into smaller pieces, so we may decide to carry only a fraction x_i of object i, where $0 \leq x_i \leq 1$. (If we are not allowed to break objects, the problem is much harder.) In this case, object i contributes $x_i w_i$ to the total weight in the knapsack, and $x_i v_i$ to the value of the load. In symbols, the problem can be stated as follows:

$$\text{maximize} \sum_{i=1}^{n} x_i v_i \quad \text{subject to} \sum_{i=1}^{n} x_i w_i \leq W$$

where $v_i > 0$, $w_i > 0$ and $0 \leq x_i \leq 1$ for $1 \leq i \leq n$. Here the conditions on v_i and w_i are constraints on the instance; those on x_i are constraints on the solution. We shall use a greedy algorithm to solve the problem. In terms of our general schema, the candidates are the different objects, and a solution is a vector $(x_1, \ldots, x_n)$ telling us what fraction of each object to include. A feasible solution is one that respects the constraints given above, and the objective function is the total value of the objects in the knapsack. What we should take as the selection function remains to be seen.

If $\sum_{i=1}^{n} w_i \leq W$, it is clearly optimal to pack all the objects in the knapsack. We can therefore assume that in any interesting instance of the problem $\sum_{i=1}^{n} w_i > W$. It is also clear that an optimal solution must fill the knapsack exactly, for otherwise we could add a fraction of one of the remaining objects and increase the value of the load. Thus in an optimal solution $\sum_{i=1}^{n} x_i w_i = W$. Since we are hoping to find a greedy algorithm that works, our general strategy will be to select each object in turn in some suitable order, to put as large a fraction as possible of the selected object into the knapsack, and to stop when the knapsack is full. Here is the algorithm.

```
function knapsack(w[1..n], v[1..n], W): array [1..n]
    {initialization}
    for i = 1 to n do x[i] ← 0
    weight ← 0
    {greedy loop}
    while weight < W do
        i ← the best remaining object {see below}
        if weight + w[i] ≤ W then x[i] ← 1
                                  weight ← weight + w[i]
                          else  x[i] ← (W − weight)/w[i]
                                weight ← W

    return x
```

There are at least three plausible selection functions for this problem: at each stage we might choose the most valuable remaining object, arguing that this increases the value of the load as quickly as possible; we might choose the lightest remaining object, on the grounds that this uses up capacity as slowly as possible; or we might avoid these extremes by choosing the object whose value per unit weight is as high as possible. Figures 6.5 and 6.6 show how these three different tactics work in one particular instance. Here we have five objects, and $W = 100$. If we select the objects in order of decreasing value, then we choose first object 3, then object 5, and finally we fill the knapsack with half of object 4. The value of the solution obtained in this way is $66 + 60 + 40/2 = 146$. If we select the objects in order of increasing weight, then we choose objects 1, 2, 3 and 4 in that order, and now the knapsack is full. The value of this solution is $20 + 30 + 66 + 40 = 156$. Finally if we select the objects in order of decreasing v_i/w_i, we choose first object 3, then object 1, next object 2, and finally we fill the knapsack with four-fifths of object 5. Using this tactic, the value of the solution is $20 + 30 + 66 + 0.8 \times 60 = 164$.

$$n = 5, W = 100$$

	1	2	3	4	5
w	10	20	30	40	50
v	20	30	66	40	60
v/w	2.0	1.5	2.2	1.0	1.2

if selection:
by v: (0 0 1 ½ 1)   146
by w: (1 1 1 1 0)   156   *values*
by v/w: (1 1 1 0 ⅘)   164

solution vector

Figure 6.5. An instance of the knapsack problem

This example shows that the solution obtained by a greedy algorithm that maximizes the value of each object it selects is not necessarily optimal, nor is the solution obtained by minimizing the weight of each object that is chosen. Fortunately the

Select:			x_i			Value
Max v_i	0	0	1	0.5	1	146
Min w_i	1	1	1	1	0	156
Max v_i/w_i	1	1	1	0	0.8	164

Figure 6.6. Three greedy approaches to the instance in Figure 6.5

following proof shows that the third possibility, selecting the object that maximizes the value per unit weight, does lead to an optimal solution.

Theorem 6.5.1 *If objects are selected in order of decreasing v_i/w_i, then algorithm knapsack finds an optimal solution.*

Proof Suppose without loss of generality that the available objects are numbered in order of decreasing value per unit weight, that is, that

$$v_1/w_1 \geq v_2/w_2 \geq \cdots \geq v_n/w_n .$$

Let $X = (x_1, \ldots, x_n)$ be the solution found by the greedy algorithm. If all the x_i are equal to 1, this solution is clearly optimal. Otherwise, let j be the smallest index such that $x_j < 1$. Looking at the way the algorithm works, it is clear that $x_i = 1$ when $i < j$, that $x_i = 0$ when $i > j$, and that $\sum_{i=1}^{n} x_i w_i = W$. Let the value of the solution X be $V(X) = \sum_{i=1}^{n} x_i v_i$.

Now let $Y = (y_1, \ldots, y_n)$ be any feasible solution. Since Y is feasible, $\sum_{i=1}^{n} y_i w_i \leq W$, and hence $\sum_{i=1}^{n} (x_i - y_i) w_i \geq 0$. Let the value of the solution Y be $V(Y) = \sum_{i=1}^{n} y_i v_i$. Now

$$V(X) - V(Y) = \sum_{i=1}^{n} (x_i - y_i) v_i = \sum_{i=1}^{n} (x_i - y_i) w_i \frac{v_i}{w_i}$$

When $i < j$, $x_i = 1$ and so $x_i - y_i$ is positive or zero, while $v_i/w_i \geq v_j/w_j$; when $i > j$, $x_i = 0$ and so $x_i - y_i$ is negative or zero, while $v_i/w_i \leq v_j/w_j$; and of course when $i = j$, $v_i/w_i = v_j/w_j$. Thus in every case $(x_i - y_i)(v_i/w_i) \geq (x_i - y_i)(v_j/w_j)$. Hence

$$V(X) - V(Y) \geq (v_j/w_j) \sum_{i=1}^{n} (x_i - y_i) w_i \geq 0 .$$

We have thus proved that no feasible solution can have a value greater than $V(X)$, so the solution X is optimal. ∎

Implementation of the algorithm is straightforward. If the objects are already sorted into decreasing order of v_i/w_i, then the greedy loop clearly takes a time in $O(n)$; the total time including the sort is therefore in $O(n \log n)$. As in Section 6.3.1, it may be worthwhile to keep the objects in a heap with the largest value of v_i/w_i at the root. Creating the heap takes a time in $O(n)$, while each trip round the greedy loop now takes a time in $O(\log n)$ since the heap property must be restored after the root is removed. Although this does not alter the worst-case analysis, it may be faster if only a few objects are needed to fill the knapsack.

6.6 Scheduling

In this section we present two problems concerning the optimal way to schedule jobs on a single machine. In the first, the problem is to minimize the average time that a job spends in the system. In the second, the jobs have deadlines, and a job brings in a certain profit only if it is completed by its deadline: our aim is to maximize profitability. Both these problems can be solved using greedy algorithms.

6.6.1 Minimizing time in the system

A single server, such as a processor, a petrol pump, or a cashier in a bank, has n customers to serve. The service time required by each customer is known in advance: customer i will take time t_i, $1 \le i \le n$. We want to minimize the average time that a customer spends in the system. Since n, the number of customers, is fixed, this is the same as minimizing the total time spent in the system by all the customers. In other words, we want to minimize

$$T = \sum_{i=1}^{n} (\text{time in system for customer } i).$$

Suppose for example we have three customers, with $t_1 = 5$, $t_2 = 10$ and $t_3 = 3$. There are six possible orders of service.

Order	T	
1 2 3 :	$5 + (5 + 10) + (5 + 10 + 3) = 38$	
1 3 2 :	$5 + (5 + 3) + (5 + 3 + 10) = 31$	
2 1 3 :	$10 + (10 + 5) + (10 + 5 + 3) = 43$	
2 3 1 :	$10 + (10 + 3) + (10 + 3 + 5) = 41$	
3 1 2 :	$3 + (3 + 5) + (3 + 5 + 10) = 29$	← optimal *sort t_i in increasing order SSF*
3 2 1 :	$3 + (3 + 10) + (3 + 10 + 5) = 34$	

In the first case, customer 1 is served immediately, customer 2 waits while customer 1 is served and then gets his turn, and customer 3 waits while both 1 and 2 are served and then is served last; the total time passed in the system by the three customers is 38. The calculations for the other cases are similar.

In this case, the optimal schedule is obtained when the three customers are served in order of increasing service time: customer 3, who needs the least time, is served first, while customer 2, who needs the most, is served last. Serving the customers in order of decreasing service time gives the worst schedule. However, one example is not a proof that this is always so.

To add plausibility to the idea that it may be optimal to schedule the customers in order of increasing service time, imagine a greedy algorithm that builds the optimal schedule item by item. Suppose that after scheduling service for customers $i_1, i_2, \ldots, i_m$ we add customer j. The increase in T at this stage is equal to the sum of the service times for customers i_1 to i_m (for this is how long customer j must wait before receiving service), plus t_j, the time needed to serve customer j. To minimize this, since a greedy algorithm never undoes its previous decisions, all we can do is to minimize t_j. Our greedy algorithm is therefore simple: at each step, add to the end of the schedule the customer requiring the least service among those who remain.

Theorem 6.6.1   *This greedy algorithm is optimal.*

Proof   Let $P = p_1 p_2 \cdots p_n$ be any permutation of the integers from 1 to n, and let $s_i = t_{p_i}$. If customers are served in the order P, then the service time required by the i-th customer to be served is s_i, and the total time passed in the system by all the customers is

$$T(P) = s_1 + (s_1 + s_2) + (s_1 + s_2 + s_3) + \cdots$$
$$= ns_1 + (n-1)s_2 + (n-2)s_3 + \cdots$$
$$= \sum_{k=1}^{n} (n - k + 1)s_k.$$

Suppose now that P does not arrange the customers in order of increasing service time. Then we can find two integers a and b with $a < b$ and $s_a > s_b$. In other words, the a-th customer is served before the b-th customer even though the former needs more service time than the latter; see Figure 6.7. If we exchange the positions of these two customers, we obtain a new order of service P', which is simply P with the integers p_a and p_b interchanged. The total time passed in the system by all the customers if schedule P' is used is

$$T(P') = (n - a + 1)s_b + (n - b + 1)s_a + \sum_{\substack{k=1 \\ k \neq a,b}}^{n} (n - k + 1)s_k.$$

The new schedule is preferable to the old because

$$T(P) - T(P') = (n - a + 1)(s_a - s_b) + (n - b + 1)(s_b - s_a)$$
$$= (b - a)(s_a - s_b) > 0.$$

The same result can be obtained less formally from Figure 6.7. Comparing schedules P and P', we see that the first $a - 1$ customers leave the system at exactly the same time in both schedules. The same is true of the last $n - b$ customers. Customer a now leaves when customer b used to, while customer b leaves earlier than customer a used to, because $s_b < s_a$. Finally those customers served in positions $a + 1$ to $b - 1$ also leave the system earlier, for the same reason. Overall, P' is therefore better than P.

Thus we can improve any schedule in which a customer is served before someone else who requires less service. The only schedules that remain are those obtained by putting the customers in order of nondecreasing service time. All such schedules are clearly equivalent, and therefore all optimal.   ∎

Implementing the algorithm is so straightforward that we omit the details. In essence all that is necessary is to sort the customers into order of nondecreasing service time, which takes a time in $O(n \log n)$. The problem can be generalized to a system with s servers, as can the algorithm: see Problem 6.20.

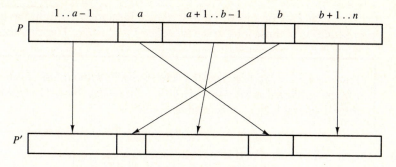

Figure 6.7. Exchanging two customers

6.6.2 Scheduling with deadlines

We have a set of n jobs to execute, each of which takes unit time. At any time $T = 1, 2, \ldots$ we can execute exactly one job. Job i earns us a profit $g_i > 0$ if and only if it is executed no later than time d_i.

For example, with $n = 4$ and the following values:

i	1	2	3	4
profit→ g_i	50	10	15	30
deadline→ d_i	2	1	2	1

the schedules to consider and the corresponding profits are

Sequence	Profit	Sequence	Profit	
1	50	2, 1	60	
2	10	2, 3	25	
3	15	3, 1	65	
4	30	4, 1	80	← optimum
1, 3	65	4, 3	45	

The sequence 3,2 for instance is not considered because job 2 would be executed at time $t = 2$, after its deadline $d_2 = 1$. To maximize our profit in this example, we should execute the schedule 4,1.

A set of jobs is *feasible* if there exists at least one sequence (also called feasible) that allows all the jobs in the set to be executed no later than their respective deadlines. An obvious greedy algorithm consists of constructing the schedule step by step, adding at each step the job with the highest value of g_i among those not yet considered, provided that the chosen set of jobs remains feasible.

In the preceding example we first choose job 1. Next, we choose job 4; the set $\{1, 4\}$ is feasible because it can be executed in the order 4,1. Next we try the set $\{1, 3, 4\}$, which turns out not to be feasible; job 3 is therefore rejected. Finally we try $\{1, 2, 4\}$, which is also infeasible, so job 2 is also rejected. Our solution—optimal in this case—is therefore to execute the set of jobs $\{1, 4\}$, which can only be done in the order 4,1. It remains to be proved that this algorithm always finds an optimal schedule and to find an efficient way of implementing it.

Let J be a set of k jobs. At first glance it seems we might have to try all the $k!$ permutations of these jobs to see whether J is feasible. Happily this is not the case.

> **Lemma 6.6.2**   *Let J be a set of k jobs. Suppose without loss of generality that the jobs are numbered so that $d_1 \le d_2 \le \cdots \le d_k$. Then the set J is feasible if and only if the sequence $1, 2, \ldots, k$ is feasible.*

Proof   The "if" is obvious. For the "only if", suppose the sequence $1, 2, \ldots, k$ is not feasible. Then at least one job in this sequence is scheduled after its deadline. Let r be any such job, so $d_r \le r - 1$. Since the jobs are scheduled in order of nondecreasing deadline, this means that at least r jobs have deadlines $r - 1$ or earlier. However these are scheduled, the last one will always be late. ∎

This shows that it suffices to check a single sequence, in order of nondecreasing deadlines, to know whether or not a set of jobs J is feasible.

> **Theorem 6.6.3**   *The greedy algorithm outlined earlier always finds an optimal schedule.*

Proof   Suppose the greedy algorithm chooses to execute a set of jobs I, and suppose the set J is optimal. Let S_I and S_J be feasible sequences, possibly including gaps, for the two sets of jobs in question. By rearranging the jobs in S_I and those in S_J, we can obtain two feasible sequences S_I' and S_J', which also may include gaps, such that every job common to I and J is scheduled at the same time in both sequences; see Figure 6.8.

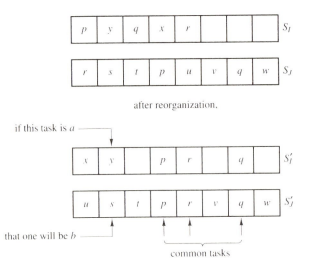

Figure 6.8. **Rearranging schedules to bring identical tasks together**

To see this, imagine that some job a occurs in both the feasible sequences S_I and S_J, where it is scheduled at times t_I and t_J respectively. If $t_I = t_J$ there is nothing to do. Otherwise, suppose $t_I < t_J$. Since the sequence S_J is feasible, it follows that the deadline for job a is no earlier than t_J. Modify sequence S_I as follows: if there is a gap in sequence S_I at time t_J, move job a back from time t_I into the gap at time t_J; if there is some job b scheduled in S_I at time t_J, exchange jobs a and b in sequence S_I. The resulting sequence is still feasible, since in either case a will be executed by its deadline, and in the second case moving job b to an earlier time can certainly do no harm. Now job a is scheduled at the same time t_J in both the modified sequence S_I and in S_J. A similar argument applies when $t_I > t_J$, except that in this case it is S_J that has to be modified.

Once job a has been treated in this way, it is clear that we never need to move it again. If sequences S_I and S_J have m jobs in common, therefore, after at most m modifications of either S_I or S_J we can ensure that all the jobs common to I and J are scheduled at the same time in both sequences. The resulting sequences S_I' and S_J' may not be the same if $I \neq J$. So suppose there is a time when the job scheduled in S_I' is different from that scheduled in S_J'.

◇ If some job a is scheduled in S_I' opposite a gap in S_J', a does not belong to J. The set $J \cup \{a\}$ is feasible, for we could put a in the gap, and it would be more profitable than J. This is impossible since J is optimal by assumption.

◇ If some job b is scheduled in S_J' opposite a gap in S_I', the set $I \cup \{b\}$ would be feasible, so the greedy algorithm would have included b in I. This is also impossible since it did not do so.

◇ The only remaining possibility is that some job a is scheduled in S_I' opposite a different job b in S_J'. In this case a does not appear in J and b does not appear in I. There are apparently three possibilities.

   – If $g_a > g_b$, one could substitute a for b in J and improve it. This is impossible because J is optimal.

   – If $g_a < g_b$, the greedy algorithm would have selected b before considering a since $(I \setminus \{a\}) \cup \{b\}$ would be feasible. This is also impossible since the algorithm did not include b in I.

   – The only remaining possibility is that $g_a = g_b$.

We conclude that for each time slot the sequences S_I' and S_J' either schedule no jobs, or the same job, or two different jobs yielding the same profit. The total profit from I is therefore equal to the profit from the optimal set J, so I is optimal too. ∎

For our first implementation of the algorithm, suppose without loss of generality that the jobs are numbered so that $g_1 \geq g_2 \geq \cdots \geq g_n$. The algorithm can be implemented more efficiently (and more easily) if we suppose further that $n > 0$ and $d_i > 0$, $1 \leq i \leq n$, and that additional storage is available at the front of the arrays d (that holds the deadlines) and j (in which we construct the solution). These additional cells are known as "sentinels". By storing an appropriate value in the sentinels we avoid repeated time-consuming range checks.

```
function sequence(d[0..n]): k, array [1..k]
    array j[0..n]
    {The schedule is constructed step by step in
     the array j. The variable k says how many jobs
     are already in the schedule.}
    d[0] ← j[0] ← 0 {sentinels}
    k ← j[1] ← 1 {job 1 is always chosen}
    {greedy loop}
    for i ← 2 to n do {decreasing order of g}
        r ← k
        while d[j[r]] > max(d[i], r) do r ← r − 1
        if d[i] > r then
            for m ← k step −1 to r + 1 do j[m + 1] ← j[m]
            j[r + 1] ← i
            k ← k + 1
    return k, j[1..k]
```

The k jobs in the array j are in order of increasing deadline. When job i is being considered, the algorithm checks whether it can be inserted into j at the appropriate place without pushing some job already in j past its deadline. If so, i is accepted; otherwise i is rejected. The exact values of the g_i are unnecessary provided the jobs are correctly numbered in order of decreasing profit. Figure 6.9 gives g_i and d_i for an example with six jobs, and Figure 6.10 illustrates how the algorithm works on this example. (Figure 6.10 calls it the "slow" algorithm since we shall shortly describe a better one.)

i	1	2	3	4	5	6
g_i	20	15	10	7	5	3
d_i	3	1	1	3	1	3

Figure 6.9. An example with six jobs

Analysis of the algorithm is straightforward. Sorting the jobs into order of decreasing profit takes a time in $\Theta(n \log n)$. The worst case for the algorithm is when this procedure turns out also to sort the jobs by order of decreasing deadline, and when they can all fit into the schedule. In this case, when job i is being considered the algorithm looks at each of the $k = i - 1$ jobs already in the schedule to find a place for the newcomer, and then moves them all along one position. In terms of the program above, there are $\sum_{k=1}^{n-1} k$ trips round the **while** loop and $\sum_{m=1}^{n-1} m$ trips round the inner **for** loop. The algorithm therefore takes a time in $\Omega(n^2)$.

A more efficient algorithm is obtained if we use a different technique to verify whether a given set of jobs is feasible. The new technique depends on the following lemma.

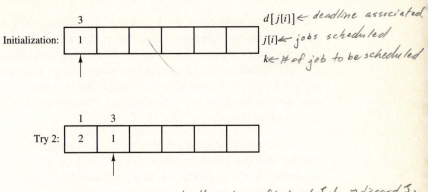

Initialization:

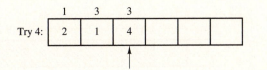

Try 2:

Try 3: unchanged *since J_3 deadline $=1$ ∴ conflict w/ Job$_2$ ⇒ discard J_3*

Try 4:

Try 5: unchanged *since J_5 deadline $=1$ ∴ conflict w/ Job$_2$ ⇒ discard J_5*

Try 6: unchanged *since J_6 deadline $=3$ ∴ conflict w/ Job$_4$ ⇒ discard J_6*

Optimal sequence: 2, 1, 4; value = 42

Figure 6.10. Illustration of the slow algorithm

Lemma 6.6.4   *A set of n jobs J is feasible if and only if we can construct a feasible sequence including all the jobs in J as follows. Start with an empty schedule of length n. Then for each job $i \in J$ in turn, schedule i at time t, where t is the largest integer such that $1 \le t \le \min(n, d_i)$ and the job to be executed at time t is not yet decided.*

In other words, starting with an empty schedule, consider each job in turn, and add it to the schedule being built as late as possible, but no later than its deadline. If a job cannot be scheduled in time to meet its deadline, then the set J is infeasible.

Proof   The "if" is obvious. For the "only if", note first that if a feasible sequence exists at all, then there exists a feasible sequence of length n. Since there are only n jobs to schedule, any longer sequence must contain gaps, and we can always move a job into an earlier gap without affecting the feasibility of the sequence.

When we try to add a new job, the sequence being built always contains at least one gap. Suppose we are unable to add a job whose deadline is d. This can happen only if all the slots from $t = 1$ to $t = r$ are already allocated, where $r = \min(n, d)$. Let $s > r$ be the smallest integer such that the slot $t = s$ is empty. The schedule already built therefore includes $s - 1$ jobs whose deadlines are earlier than s, no job with deadline exactly s, and possibly others with deadlines later than s. The job we are trying to add also has a deadline less than s. Hence J includes at least s jobs whose deadline is $s - 1$ or earlier. However these are scheduled, the last one is sure to be late.   ∎

The lemma suggests that we should consider an algorithm that tries to fill one by one the positions in a sequence of length n. For any position t, define $n_t = \max\{k \le t \mid \text{position } k \text{ is free}\}$. Also define certain sets of positions as follows: two positions i and j are in the same set if $n_i = n_j$; see Figure 6.11. For a given set K of positions, let $F(K)$ be the smallest member of K. Finally define a fictitious position 0 that is always free.

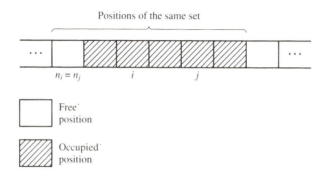

Figure 6.11. Sets of positions

As we assign new jobs to vacant positions, these sets merge to form larger sets: disjoint set structures are intended for just this purpose. We obtain an algorithm whose essential steps are the following:

 (i) Initialization: Each position $0, 1, 2, \ldots, n$ is in a different set and $F(\{i\}) = i$, $0 \le i \le n$.

(ii) Addition of a job with deadline d: Find the set that contains d; let this be set K. If $F(K) = 0$ reject the job; otherwise:

  – Assign the new job to position $F(K)$.

  – Find the set that contains $F(K) - 1$. Call this set L (it cannot be the same as K).

  – Merge K and L. The value of F for this new set is the old value of $F(L)$.

Figure 6.12 illustrates the working of this algorithm on the example given in Figure 6.9.

Initialization: $l = \min(6, \max(d_i)) = 3$

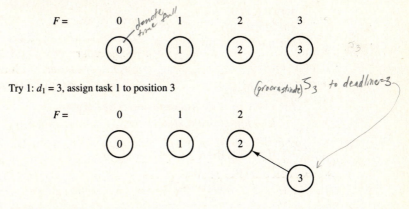

Try 1: $d_1 = 3$, assign task 1 to position 3

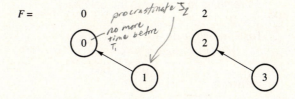

Try 2: $d_2 = 1$, assign task 2 to position 1

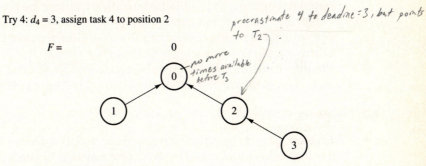

Try 3: $d_3 = 1$, no free position available since the F value is 0

Try 4: $d_4 = 3$, assign task 4 to position 2

Try 5: $d_5 = 1$, no free position available

Try 6: $d_6 = 3$, no free position available

Optimal sequence: 2, 4, 1; value = 42

Figure 6.12. Illustration of the fast algorithm

Here is a more precise statement of the fast algorithm. To simplify the description, we assume that the label of the set produced by a *merge* operation is necessarily the label of one of the sets that were merged. The schedule first produced may contain gaps; the algorithm ends by moving jobs forward to fill these.

```
function sequence2(d[1..n]): k, array [1..k]
    array j, F[0..n]
    {initialization}
    for i ← 0 to n do j[i] ← 0
                      F[i] ← i
                      initialize set {i}
    {greedy loop}
    for i ← 1 to n do {decreasing order of g}
        k ← find(min(n, d[i]))
        m ← F[k]
        if m ≠ 0 then
            j[m] ← i
            l ← find(m − 1)
            F[k] ← F[l]
            merge(k, l) {the resulting set has label k or l}
    {it remains to compress the solution}
    k ← 0
    for i ← 1 to n do
        if j[i] > 0 then  k ← k + 1
                          j[k] ← j[i]
    return k, j[1..k]
```

If the instance is given with the jobs already ordered by decreasing profit, so that an optimal sequence can be obtained merely by calling the preceding algorithm, most of the time will be spent manipulating disjoint sets. Since there are at most $2n$ *find* operations and n *merge* operations to execute, the required time is in $O(n\alpha(2n, n))$, where α is the slow-growing function of Section 5.9. This is essentially linear. If, on the other hand, the jobs are given in arbitrary order, then we have to begin by sorting them, and obtaining the initial sequence takes a time in $\Theta(n \log n)$.

6.7 Problems

Problem 6.1.   Is selection sort (see Section 2.4) a greedy algorithm? If so, what are the various functions involved (the function to check feasibility, the selection function, and so on)?

Problem 6.2.   The English coinage before decimalization included half-crowns (30 pence), florins (24 pence), shillings (12 pence), sixpences (6 pence), threepences (3 pence), and pennies (not to mention ha'pennies and farthings, worth respectively $\frac{1}{2}$ and $\frac{1}{4}$ pence). Show that with these coins the greedy algorithm of Section 6.1 does not necessarily produce an optimal solution, even when an unlimited supply of coins of each denomination is available.

Problem 6.3.   The Portuguese coinage includes coins for $1, 2\frac{1}{2}, 5, 10, 20, 25$ and 50 escudos. However prices are always for an integer number of escudos. Prove or give a counterexample: when an unlimited supply of coins of each denomination is available, the greedy algorithm of Section 6.1 always finds an optimal solution.

Problem 6.4.   Suppose the coinage includes the values given in Section 6.1, but you have run out of nickels. Show that using the greedy algorithm with the remaining values does not necessarily produce an optimal solution.

Problem 6.5.   Prove or give a counter-example: provided that each coin in the series is worth at least twice the next lower denomination, that the series includes a 1-unit coin, and that an unlimited supply of coins of each denomination is available, the greedy algorithm of Section 6.1 always finds an optimal solution.

Problem 6.6.   Suppose the available denominations are 1, p, $p^2, \ldots, p^n$, where $p > 1$ and $n \geq 0$ are integers. Prove or give a counter-example: with this series of denominations and an unlimited supply of coins of each denomination, the greedy algorithm of Section 6.1 always finds an optimal solution.

Problem 6.7.   Prove that a graph with n nodes and more than $n - 1$ edges must contain at least one cycle.

Problem 6.8.   Suppose the cost of laying a telephone cable from point a to point b is proportional to the Euclidean distance from a to b. A certain number of towns are to be connected at minimum cost. Find an example where it costs less to lay the cables via an exchange situated in between the towns than to use only direct links.

Problem 6.9.   What can you say about the time required by Kruskal's algorithm if, instead of providing a list of edges, the user supplies a matrix of distances, leaving to the algorithm the job of working out which edges exist?

Problem 6.10.   Suppose Kruskal's algorithm and Prim's algorithm are implemented as shown in Sections 6.3.1 and 6.3.2 respectively. What happens (a) in the case of Kruskal's algorithm (b) in the case of Prim's algorithm if by mistake we run the algorithm on a graph that is not connected?

Problem 6.11.   A graph may have several different minimum spanning trees. Is this the case for the graph in Figure 6.2? If so, where is this possibility reflected in the algorithms explained in Sections 6.3.1 and 6.3.2?

Problem 6.12.   The problem of finding a subset T of the edges of a connected graph G such that all the nodes remain connected when only the edges in T are used, and the sum of the lengths of the edges in T is as small as possible, still makes sense even if G may have edges with negative lengths. However, the solution may no longer be a tree. Adapt either Kruskal's algorithm or Prim's algorithm to work on a graph that may include edges of negative length.

Problem 6.13.   Show that Prim's algorithm can, like Kruskal's algorithm, be implemented using heaps. Show that it then takes a time in $\Theta(a \log n)$.

Problem 6.14.   In Dijkstra's algorithm, when we add a new node v to S, let w be a node not in S. Is it possible that the new shortest special path from the source to w should pass first by v and then by some other node of S?

Problem 6.15. Show by giving an explicit example that if the edge lengths can be negative, then Dijkstra's algorithm does not always work correctly. Is it still sensible to talk about shortest paths if negative distances are allowed?

Problem 6.16. In the analysis of the implementation of Dijkstra's algorithm that uses a heap, we saw that up to a nodes can be percolated, whereas less than n roots are eliminated. Eliminating the root has for effect to sift down the node that takes its place. In general, percolating up is somewhat quicker than sifting down, since at each level we compare the value of a node to the value of its parent, rather than making comparisons with both children. Using an k-ary heap (see Section 5.7 and Problem 5.23) may make percolation run faster still, at the cost of slowing down sifting. Let $k = \max(2, \lfloor a/n \rfloor)$. Show how to use a k-ary heap to calculate the shortest paths from a source to all the other nodes of a graph in a time in $O(a \log_k n)$. Note that this gives $O(n^2)$ if $a \approx n^2$ and $O(a \log n)$ if $a \approx n$. It therefore gives the best of both worlds.

Problem 6.17. A Fibonacci heap, mentioned in Section 5.8, has the following properties. A heap containing n items can be built in a time in $\Theta(n)$; finding the largest item, inserting a new item, increasing the value of an item and restoring the heap property, and merging two heaps all take an amortized time in $\Theta(1)$; and deleting any item, including in particular the largest, from a heap containing n items takes an amortized time in $O(\log n)$. An inverted Fibonacci heap is similar, except that the corresponding operations involve decreasing the value of an item, and finding or deleting the smallest item. Show how an inverted Fibonacci heap can be used to implement Dijkstra's algorithm in a time in $O(a + n \log n)$.

Problem 6.18. In Section 6.5 we assumed that we had available n objects numbered 1 to n. Suppose instead that we have n *types* of object available, with an adequate supply of each type. Formally, this simply replaces the old constraint $0 \le x_i \le 1$ by the looser constraint $x_i \ge 0$. Does the greedy algorithm of Section 6.5 still work? Is it still necessary?

Problem 6.19. Prove or give a counter-example: for the problem of scheduling with deadlines of Section 6.6.1, scheduling the customers in order of decreasing service time leads to the worst possible schedule.

Problem 6.20. As in Section 6.6.1 we have n customers. Customer i, $1 \le i \le n$, requires a known service time t_i. Without loss of generality, suppose the customers are numbered so that $t_1 \le t_2 \le \cdots \le t_n$. If there are s identical servers, prove that to minimize the total (and hence the average) time spent in the system by the customers, server j, $1 \le j \le s$, should serve customers $j, j + s, j + 2s, \ldots$ in that order.

Problem 6.21. Let $P_1, P_2, \ldots, P_n$ be n programs to be stored on a disk. Program P_i requires s_i kilobytes of storage, and the capacity of the disk is D kilobytes, where $D < \sum_{i=1}^{n} s_i$.

(a) We want to maximize the number of programs held on the disk. Prove or give a counter-example: we can use a greedy algorithm that selects programs in order of nondecreasing s_i.

(b) We want to use as much of the capacity of the disk as possible. Prove or give a counter-example: we can use a greedy algorithm that selects programs in order of nonincreasing s_i.

Problem 6.22.   Let $P_1, P_2, \ldots, P_n$ be n programs to be stored on a tape. Program P_i requires s_i kilobytes of storage; the tape is long enough to hold all the programs. We know how often each program is used: a fraction π_i of requests concern program i (and so $\sum_{i=1}^{n} \pi_i = 1$). Information is recorded along the tape at constant density, and the speed of the tape drive is also constant. After a program is loaded, the tape is rewound to the beginning. If the programs are held in the order $i_1, i_2, \ldots, i_n$ the average time required to load a program is therefore

$$\bar{T} = c \sum_{j=1}^{n} \left[\pi_{i_j} \sum_{k=1}^{j} s_{i_k} \right],$$

where the constant c depends on the recording density and the speed of the drive. We want to minimize $\bar{T}$ using a greedy algorithm. Prove or give a counter-example for each of the following: we can select the programs (a) in order of nondecreasing s_i; (b) in order of nonincreasing π_i; (c) in order of nonincreasing π_i / s_i.

Problem 6.23.   Suppose the two schedules S_I and S_J introduced in the proof of optimality in Section 6.6.2 are given in the form of arrays $SI[1 .. r]$ and $SJ[1 .. r]$, where $r = \max_{1 \leq i \leq n} d_i$. An array element holds i if job i is to be executed at the corresponding moment, and 0 represents a gap in the schedule. Write an algorithm that produces the schedules S_I' and S_J' in arrays SI and SJ respectively.

6.8 References and further reading

Edmonds (1971) introduced the notion of a greedy algorithm. A discussion of the greedy change-making algorithm can be found in Wright (1975) and Chang and Korsh (1976). We shall come back to this problem in Section 8.2, when we provide an algorithm that is slower, but that is guaranteed to return the optimal solution in all cases.

The problem of minimum spanning trees has a long history, which is discussed in Graham and Hell (1985). The first algorithm proposed (which we have not described) is due to Borůvka (1926). The algorithm to which Prim's name is attached was invented by Jarník (1930) and rediscovered by Prim (1957) and Dijkstra (1959). Kruskal's algorithm comes from Kruskal (1956). Other more sophisticated algorithms have been given by Yao (1975), Cheriton and Tarjan (1976) and Tarjan (1983); see also the next paragraph.

The implementation of Dijkstra's algorithm that takes a time in $O(n^2)$ is from Dijkstra (1959). The details of the improvement suggested in Problem 6.16, which uses k-ary heaps, can be found in Johnson (1977). Similar improvement for the minimum spanning tree problem is suggested in Johnson (1975). Faster algorithms for both these problems are given in Fredman and Tarjan (1987); in particular, use of the Fibonacci heap allows them to implement Dijkstra's algorithm in a time in $O(a + n \log n)$. Other ideas concerning shortest paths can be found in Tarjan (1983).

The solution to Problem 6.8 involves the notion of Steiner trees. The problem of finding a minimum Steiner tree is $\mathcal{NP}$–hard—see Section 12.5.5—and thus probably much harder than finding a minimum spanning tree. For more on this problem see Garey, Graham and Johnson (1977) and Winter (1987).

An important greedy algorithm that we have not discussed is used to derive optimal Huffman codes; see Schwartz (1964). Other greedy algorithms for a variety of problems are described in Horowitz and Sahni (1978).

Chapter 7

Divide-and-Conquer

> Divide-and-conquer is a technique for designing algorithms that consists of decomposing the instance to be solved into a number of smaller subinstances of the same problem, solving successively and independently each of these subinstances, and then combining the subsolutions thus obtained to obtain the solution of the original instance. Two questions that naturally spring to mind are "Why would anyone want to do this?" and "How should we solve the subinstances?" The efficiency of the divide-and-conquer technique lies in the answer to this latter question.

7.1 Introduction: Multiplying large integers

Consider again the problem of multiplying large integers. Recall that the classic algorithm (Figure 1.1) that most of us learn in school requires a time in $\Theta(n^2)$ to multiply n-figure numbers. We are so used to this algorithm that perhaps you never even questioned its optimality. Can we do better? Multiplication *à la russe* (Figure 1.2) offers no improvement in the running time. Another algorithm discussed in Section 1.2, which we called the "divide-and-conquer" technique (Figure 1.3), consisted of reducing the multiplication of two n-figure numbers to four multiplications of $\frac{n}{2}$-figure numbers. Unfortunately, the resulting algorithm does not yield any improvement over the classic multiplication algorithm either unless we are cleverer. To outperform the classic algorithm, and thus fully appreciate the virtues of divide-and-conquer, we must find a way to reduce the original multiplication not to four but to *three* half-size multiplications.

We illustrate the process with the example used in Section 1.2: the multiplication of 981 by 1234. First we pad the shorter operand with a nonsignificant zero to make it the same length as the longer one; thus 981 becomes 0981. Then we split each operand into two halves: 0981 gives rise to $w = 09$ and $x = 81$, and 1234 to $y = 12$ and $z = 34$. Notice that $981 = 10^2 w + x$ and $1234 = 10^2 y + z$. Therefore, the required product can be computed as

$$
\begin{aligned}
981 \times 1234 &= (10^2 w + x) \times (10^2 y + z) \\
&= 10^4 w y + 10^2 (w z + x y) + x z \\
&= 1080000 + 127800 + 2754 = 1210554.
\end{aligned}
$$

If you think we have merely restated the algorithm of Section 1.2 in more symbols, you are perfectly correct. The above procedure still needs four half-size multiplications: wy, wz, xy and xz.

The key observation is that there is no need to compute both wz and xy; all we really need is the *sum* of these two terms. Is it possible to obtain $wz + xy$ at the cost of a single multiplication? This seems impossible until we remember that we also need the values of wy and xz to apply the above formula. With this in mind, consider the product

$$
r = (w + x) \times (y + z) = wy + (wz + xy) + xz.
$$

After only one multiplication, we obtain the sum of all three terms needed to calculate the desired product. This suggests proceeding as follows.

$$
\begin{aligned}
p &= wy = 09 \times 12 &= 108 \\
q &= xz = 81 \times 34 &= 2754 \\
r &= (w + x) \times (y + z) &= 90 \times 46 = 4140,
\end{aligned}
$$

and finally

$$
\begin{aligned}
981 \times 1234 &= 10^4 p + 10^2 (r - p - q) + q \\
&= 1080000 + 127800 + 2754 = 1210554.
\end{aligned}
$$

Thus the product of 981 and 1234 can be reduced to *three* multiplications of two-figure numbers (09×12, 81×34 and 90×46) together with a certain number of shifts (multiplications by powers of 10), additions and subtractions.

To be sure, the number of additions—counting subtractions as if they were additions—is larger than with the original divide-and-conquer algorithm of Section 1.2. Is it worth performing four more additions to save one multiplication? The answer is no when we are multiplying small numbers like those in our example. However, it is worthwhile when the numbers to be multiplied are large, and it becomes increasingly so when the numbers get larger. When the operands are large, the time required for the additions and shifts becomes negligible compared to the time taken by a single multiplication. It thus seems reasonable to expect that reducing four multiplications to three will enable us to cut 25% of the computing time required for large multiplications. As we shall see, our saving will be significantly better.

To help grasp what we have achieved, suppose a given implementation of the classic multiplication algorithm requires a time $h(n) = cn^2$ to multiply two n-figure numbers, for some constant c that depends on the implementation. (This is a simplification since in reality the time required would have a more complicated form, such as $cn^2 + bn + a$.) Similarly, let $g(n)$ be the time taken by the divide-and-conquer algorithm to multiply two n-figure numbers, *not* counting the time needed to perform the three half-size multiplications. In other words, $g(n)$ is the time needed for the additions, shifts and various overhead operations. It is easy to implement these operations so that $g(n) \in \Theta(n)$. Ignore for the moment what happens if n is odd or if the numbers are not the same length.

If each of the three half-size multiplications is carried out by the classic algorithm, the time needed to multiply two n-figure numbers is

$$3h(n/2) + g(n) = 3c(n/2)^2 + g(n) = \tfrac{3}{4}cn^2 + g(n) = \tfrac{3}{4}h(n) + g(n). \checkmark$$

Because $h(n) \in \Theta(n^2)$ and $g(n) \in \Theta(n)$, the term $g(n)$ is negligible compared to $\tfrac{3}{4}h(n)$ when n is sufficiently large, which means that we have gained about 25% in speed compared to the classic algorithm, as we anticipated. Although this improvement is not to be sneezed at, we have not managed to change the order of the time required: the new algorithm still takes quadratic time.

To do better than this, we come back to the question posed in the opening paragraph: how should the subinstances be solved? If they are small, the classic algorithm may still be the best way to proceed. However, when the subinstances are sufficiently large, might it not be better to use our new algorithm *recursively*? The idea is analogous to profiting from a bank account that compounds interest payments! When we do this, we obtain an algorithm that can multiply two n-figure numbers in a time $t(n) = 3t(n/2) + g(n)$ when n is even and sufficiently large. This is similar to the recurrence we studied in Section 4.7.1 and Example 4.7.10; solving it yields $t(n) \in \Theta(n^{\lg 3} \mid n$ is a power of $2)$. We have to be content with conditional asymptotic notation because we have not yet addressed the question of how to multiply numbers of odd length; see Problem 7.1.

Since $\lg 3 \approx 1.585$ is smaller than 2, this algorithm can multiply two large integers much faster than the classic multiplication algorithm, and the bigger n, the more this improvement is worth having. A good implementation will probably not use base 10, but rather the largest base for which the hardware allows two "digits" to be multiplied directly. Recall that the performance of this algorithm and of the classic algorithm are compared empirically at the end of Section 2.7.3.

An important factor in the practical efficiency of this approach to multiplication, and indeed of any divide-and-conquer algorithm, is knowing when to stop dividing the instances and use the classic algorithm instead. Although the divide-and-conquer approach becomes more worthwhile as the instance to be solved gets larger, it may in fact be *slower* than the classic algorithm on instances that are too small. Therefore, a divide-and-conquer algorithm must avoid proceeding recursively when the size of the subinstances no longer justifies this. We come back to this issue in the next section.

For simplicity, several important issues have been swept under the rug so far. How do we deal with numbers of odd length? Even though both halves of the multiplier and the multiplicand are of size $n/2$, it can happen that their *sum* overflows and is of size 1 bigger. Therefore, it was slightly incorrect to claim that $r = (w + x) \times (y + z)$ involves a half-size multiplication. How does this affect the analysis of the running time? How do we multiply two numbers of different sizes? Are there arithmetic operations other than multiplication that we can handle more efficiently than by using classic algorithms?

Numbers of odd length are easily multiplied by splitting them as nearly down the middle as possible: an n-figure number is split into a $\lfloor n/2 \rfloor$-figure number and a $\lceil n/2 \rceil$-figure number. The second question is trickier. Consider multiplying 5678 by 6789. Our algorithm splits the operands into $w = 56$, $x = 78$, $y = 67$ and $z = 89$. The three half-size multiplications involved are

$$p = wy = 56 \times 67$$
$$q = xz = 78 \times 89, \text{ and}$$
$$r = (w + x) \times (y + z) = 134 \times 156.$$

The third multiplication involves *three*-figure numbers, and thus it is not really half-size compared with the original multiplication of four-figure numbers. However, the size of $w + x$ and $y + z$ cannot exceed $1 + \lceil n/2 \rceil$.

To simplify the analysis, let $t(n)$ denote the time taken by this algorithm in the worst case to multiply two numbers of size at most n (rather than exactly n). By definition, $t(n)$ is a nondecreasing function. When n is sufficiently large, our algorithm reduces the multiplication of two numbers of size at most n to three smaller multiplications $p = wy$, $q = xz$ and $r = (w + x) \times (y + z)$ of sizes at most $\lfloor n/2 \rfloor$, $\lceil n/2 \rceil$ and $1 + \lceil n/2 \rceil$, respectively, in addition to easy manipulations that take a time in $O(n)$. Therefore, there exists a positive constant c such that

$$t(n) \leq t(\lfloor n/2 \rfloor) + t(\lceil n/2 \rceil) + t(1 + \lceil n/2 \rceil) + cn$$

for all sufficiently large n. This is precisely the recurrence we studied in Example 4.7.14, which yields the now-familiar $t(n) \in O(n^{\lg 3})$. Thus it is always possible to multiply n-figure numbers in a time in $O(n^{\lg 3})$. A worst-case analysis of this algorithm shows that in fact $t(n) \in \Theta(n^{\lg 3})$, but this is of limited interest because even faster multiplication algorithms exist; see Problems 7.2 and 7.3.

Turning to the question of multiplying numbers of different size, let u and v be integers of size m and n, respectively. If m and n are within a factor of two of each other, it is best to pad the smaller operand with nonsignificant zeros to make it the same length as the other operand, as we did when we multiplied 981 by 1234. However, this approach is to be discouraged when one operand is much larger than the other. It could even be worse than using the classic multiplication algorithm! Without loss of generality, assume that $m \leq n$. The divide-and-conquer algorithm used with padding and the classic algorithm take time in $\Theta(n^{\lg 3})$ and $\Theta(mn)$, respectively, to compute the product of u and v. Considering that the hidden constant of the former is likely to be larger than that of the latter, we see that divide-and-conquer with padding is *slower* than the classic algorithm when $m < n^{\lg(3/2)}$, and thus in particular when $m < \sqrt{n}$.

Nevertheless, it is simple to combine both algorithms to obtain a truly better algorithm. The idea is to slice the longer operand v into blocks of size m and to use the divide-and-conquer algorithm to multiply u by each block of v, so that the divide-and-conquer algorithm is used to multiply pairs of operands of the same size. The final product of u and v is then easily obtained by simple additions and shifts. The total running time is dominated by the need to perform $\lceil n/m \rceil$ multiplications of m-figure numbers. Since each of these smaller multiplications takes a time in $\Theta(m^{\lg 3})$ and since $\lceil n/m \rceil \in \Theta(n/m)$, the total running time to multiply an n-figure number by an m-figure number is in $\Theta(nm^{\lg(3/2)})$ when $m \leq n$.

Multiplication is not the only interesting operation involving large integers. Modular exponentiation is crucial for modern cryptography; see Section 7.8. Integer division, modulo operations, and the calculation of the integer part of a square root can all be carried out in a time whose order is the same as that required for multiplication; see Section 12.4. Some other important operations, such as calculating the greatest common divisor, may well be inherently harder to compute; they are not treated here.

7.2 The general template

Multiplying large integers is not an isolated example of the benefit to be reaped from the divide-and-conquer approach. Consider an arbitrary problem, and let *adhoc* be a simple algorithm capable of solving the problem. We ask of *adhoc* that it be efficient on small instances, but its performance on large instances is of no concern. We call it the *basic subalgorithm*. The classic multiplication algorithm is an example of a basic subalgorithm.

The general template for divide-and-conquer algorithms is as follows.

> **function** $DC(x)$
>   **if** x is sufficiently small or simple **then return** $adhoc(x)$
>   decompose x into smaller instances $x_1, x_2, \ldots, x_\ell$
>   **for** $i \leftarrow 1$ **to** ℓ **do** $y_i \leftarrow DC(x_i)$
>   recombine the y_i 's to obtain a solution y for x
>   **return** y

Some divide-and-conquer algorithms do not follow this outline exactly: for instance, they could require that the first subinstance be solved before the second subinstance is formulated; see Section 7.5.

The number of subinstances, ℓ, is usually small and independent of the particular instance to be solved. When $\ell = 1$, it does not make much sense to "*decompose x into a smaller instance x_1*" and it is hard to justify calling the technique *divide*-and-conquer. Nevertheless, it does make sense to reduce the solution of a large instance to that of a smaller one. Divide-and-conquer goes by the name of *simplification* in this case; see Sections 7.3 and 7.7. When using simplification, it is sometimes possible to replace the recursivity inherent in divide-and-conquer by an iterative loop.

Implemented in a conventional language such as Pascal on a conventional machine that runs an unsophisticated compiler, an iterative algorithm is likely to be somewhat faster than the recursive version, although only by a constant multiplicative factor. On the other hand, it may be possible to save a substantial amount of storage in this way: for an instance of size n, the recursive algorithm uses a stack whose depth is often in $\Omega(\lg n)$ and in bad cases even in $\Omega(n)$.

For divide-and-conquer to be worthwhile, three conditions must be met. The decision when to use the basic subalgorithm rather than to make recursive calls must be taken judiciously, it must be possible to decompose an instance into subinstances and to recombine the subsolutions fairly efficiently, and the subinstances should as far as possible be of about the same size. Most divide-and-conquer algorithms are such that the size of the ℓ subinstances is roughly n/b for some constant b, where n is the size of the original instance. For example, our divide-and-conquer algorithm for multiplying large integers needs a time in $\Theta(n)$ to decompose the original instance into three subinstances of roughly half-size and to recombine the subsolutions: $\ell = 3$ and $b = 2$.

The running-time analysis of such divide-and-conquer algorithms is almost automatic, thanks to Examples 4.7.13 and 4.7.16. Let $g(n)$ be the time required by DC on instances of size n, not counting the time needed for the recursive calls. The total time $t(n)$ taken by this divide-and-conquer algorithm is something like

$$t(n) = \ell\, t(n \div b) + g(n)$$

provided n is large enough. If there exists an integer k such that $g(n) \in \Theta(n^k)$, then Example 4.7.16 applies to conclude that

$$
t(n) \in \begin{cases}
\Theta(n^k) & \text{if } \ell < b^k \\
\Theta(n^k \log n) & \text{if } \ell = b^k \\
\Theta(n^{\log_b \ell}) & \text{if } \ell > b^k.
\end{cases}
\tag{7.1}
$$

The techniques used in Section 4.7.6 and Example 4.7.14 generally apply to yield the same conclusion even if some of the subinstances are of a size that differs from $\lfloor n/b \rfloor$ by at most an additive constant, and in particular if some of the subinstances are of size $\lceil n/b \rceil$. As an example, our divide-and-conquer algorithm for large integer multiplication is characterized by $\ell = 3$, $b = 2$ and $k = 1$. Since $\ell > b^k$, the third case applies and we get immediately that the algorithm takes a time in $\Theta(n^{\lg 3})$ with no need to worry about the fact that two of the subinstances are of size $\lceil n/2 \rceil$ and $1 + \lceil n/2 \rceil$ rather than $\lfloor n/2 \rfloor$. In more complicated cases when $g(n)$ is not in the exact order of a polynomial, Problem 4.44 may apply.

It remains to see how to determine whether to divide the instance and make recursive calls, or whether the instance is so simple that it is better to invoke the basic subalgorithm directly. Although this choice does not affect the order of the execution time of the algorithm, we are also concerned to make the multiplicative constant hidden in the Θ notation as small as possible. With most divide-and-conquer algorithms, this decision is based on a simple *threshold*, usually denoted n_0. The basic subalgorithm is used to solve any instance whose size does not exceed n_0.

We return to the problem of multiplying large integers to see why the choice of threshold is important, and how to choose it. To avoid clouding the essential issues, we use a simplified recurrence formula for the running time of the divide-and-conquer algorithm for multiplying large integers:

$$t(n) = \begin{cases} h(n) & \text{if } n \leq n_0 \\ 3t(\lceil n/2 \rceil) + g(n) & \text{otherwise}, \end{cases}$$

where $h(n) \in \Theta(n^2)$ and $g(n) \in \Theta(n)$.

For the sake of argument, consider an implementation where $h(n) = n^2$ microseconds and $g(n) = 16n$ microseconds. Suppose we are given two 5000-figure numbers to multiply. If the divide-and-conquer algorithm proceeds recursively until it obtains subinstances of size 1, that is if $n_0 = 1$, it takes more than 41 seconds to compute the product. This is ridiculous, since the same numbers can be multiplied in 25 seconds using the classic algorithm. The classic algorithm slightly outperforms the divide-and-conquer algorithm even to multiply numbers with as many as 32 789 figures, when both algorithms require more than a quarter of an hour of computing time for a single multiplication! Must we conclude that divide-and-conquer allows us to go from a quadratic algorithm to an algorithm whose execution time is in $\Theta(n^{\lg 3})$, but only at the cost of an increase in the hidden constant so enormous that the new algorithm is never economic on instances of reasonable size? Fortunately not: to continue our example, 5000-figure numbers can be multiplied in just over 6 seconds, provided we choose the threshold n_0 intelligently; in this case $n_0 = 64$ is a good choice. With the same threshold, it takes hardly more than two minutes to multiply two 32 789-figure numbers.

Choosing the best threshold is complicated by the fact that the optimal value generally depends not only on the algorithm concerned, but also on the particular implementation. Moreover, there is in general no uniformly best value of the threshold. In our example it is best to use the classic algorithm to multiply 67-figure numbers whereas it is best to recur once to multiply 66-figure numbers. Thus 67 is better than 64 as threshold in the first case whereas the opposite is true in the second case. We shall in future abuse the term "optimal threshold" to mean *nearly optimal*.

So how shall we choose the threshold? Given a particular implementation, the optimal threshold can be determined empirically. We vary the value of the threshold and the size of the instances used for our tests and time the implementation on a number of cases. It is often possible to estimate an optimal threshold by tabulating the results of these tests or by drawing a few diagrams. However, changes in the value of the threshold over a certain range may have no effect on the efficiency of the algorithm when only instances of some specific size are considered. For instance, it takes exactly the same time to multiply two 5000-figure numbers when the threshold is set anywhere between 40 and 78, since any such value for the threshold causes the recursion to stop when subinstances reach size 40, down from size 79, at the 7th level of recursion. Nevertheless, these thresholds are not equivalent in general since 41-figure numbers take 17% longer to multiply with the threshold set to 40 rather than to 64. Therefore, it is usually not enough simply to vary the

threshold for an instance whose size remains fixed. This empirical approach may
require considerable amounts of computer (and human!) time. We once asked students in an algorithmics course to implement the divide-and-conquer algorithm
for multiplying large integers and to compare it with the classic algorithm. Several
groups tried to estimate the optimal threshold empirically, each group using in
the attempt more than 5000 dollars worth of machine time! On the other hand, a
purely theoretical calculation of the optimal threshold is rarely possible, given that
it varies from one implementation to another.

The hybrid approach, which we recommend, consists of determining theoretically the form of the recurrence equations, and then finding empirically the values
of the constants used in these equations for the implementation at hand. The optimal threshold can then be estimated by finding the size n of the instance for
which it makes no difference whether we apply the classic algorithm directly or
whether we go on for one more level of recursion; see Problem 7.8. This is why
we chose $n_0 = 64$: the classic multiplication algorithm requires $h(64) = 64^2 = 4096$
microseconds to multiply two 64–figure numbers, whereas if we use one level of
recursion in the divide-and-conquer approach, the same multiplication requires
$g(64) = 16 \times 64 = 1024$ microseconds in addition to three multiplications of 32-fig-
ure numbers by the classic algorithm, at a cost of $h(32) = 32^2 = 1024$ microseconds
each, for the same total of $3h(32) + g(64) = 4096$ microseconds.

One practical difficulty arises with this hybrid technique. Even though the classic multiplication algorithm requires quadratic time, it was an oversimplification to
state that $h(n) = cn^2$ for some constant c that depends on the implementation. It is
more likely that there exist three constants a, b and c such that $h(n) = cn^2 + bn + a$.
Although $bn + a$ becomes negligible compared to cn^2 when n is large, the classic algorithm is in fact used *precisely* on instances of moderate size. It is therefore
usually insufficient merely to estimate the higher-order constant c. Instead, it is
necessary to measure $h(n)$ a number of times for several different values of n to
estimate all the necessary constants. The same remark applies to $g(n)$.

7.3 Binary search

Binary searching predates computers. In essence, it is the algorithm used to look
up a word in a dictionary or a name in a telephone directory. It is probably the
simplest application of divide-and-conquer, so simple in fact that strictly speaking
this is an application of *simplification* rather than divide-and-conquer: the solution
to any sufficiently large instance is reduced to that of a single smaller one, in this
case of half size.

Let $T[1..n]$ be an array sorted into nondecreasing order; that is, $T[i] \le T[j]$
whenever $1 \le i \le j \le n$. Let x be some item. The problem consists of finding x
in the array T if indeed it is there. If x is not in the array, then instead we want to
find the position where it might be inserted. Formally, we wish to find the index
i such that $1 \le i \le n + 1$ and $T[i - 1] < x \le T[i]$, with the logical convention that
$T[0] = -\infty$ and $T[n + 1] = +\infty$. (By *logical* convention, we mean that these values
are not in fact present in the array.) The obvious approach to this problem is to
look sequentially at each element of T until we either come to the end of the array
or find an item no smaller than x.

```
function sequential(T[1..n], x)
    {Sequential search for x in array T}
    for i ← 1 to n do
        if T[i] ≥ x then return i
    return n + 1
```

This algorithm clearly takes a time in $\Theta(r)$, where r is the index returned. This is $\Omega(n)$ in the worst case and $O(1)$ in the best case. If we assume that the elements of T are distinct, that x is indeed somewhere in the array, and that it is to be found with equal probability at each possible position, then the average number of trips round the loop is $(n + 1)/2$; see Problem 7.9. On the average, therefore, as well as in the worst case, sequential search takes a time in $\Theta(n)$.

To speed up the search, we should look for x either in the first half of the array or in the second half. To find out which of these searches is appropriate, we compare x to an element in the middle of the array. Let $k = \lceil n/2 \rceil$. If $x \leq T[k]$, then the search for x can be confined to $T[1..k]$; otherwise it is sufficient to search $T[k + 1..n]$. To avoid repeated tests in each recursive call, it is better to verify at the outset if the answer is $n + 1$, that is if x lies to the right of T. We obtain the following algorithm, illustrated in Figure 7.1.

1	2	3	4	5	6	7	8	9	10	11	
−5	−2	0	3	8	8	9	12	12	26	31	$x \leq T[k]$?

i				k					j		no
						i		k	j		yes
						i	k	j			yes
				ik	j						no
				ij							$i = j$: stop

Figure 7.1. Binary search for $x = 12$ in $T[1..11]$

```
function binsearch(T[1..n], x)
    if n = 0 or x > T[n] then return n + 1
    else return binrec(T[1..n], x)
```

```
function binrec(T[i..j], x)
    {Binary search for x in subarray T[i..j]
     with the promise that T[i − 1] < x ≤ T[j]}
    if i = j then return i
    k ← (i + j) ÷ 2
    if x ≤ T[k] then return binrec(T[i..k], x)
              else return binrec(T[k + 1..j], x)
```

Let $t(m)$ be the time required for a call on $binrec(T[i..j], x)$, where $m = j - i + 1$ is the number of elements still under consideration in the search. The time required for a call on $binsearch(T[1..n], x)$ is clearly $t(n)$ up to a small additive constant.

When $m > 1$, the algorithm takes a constant amount of time in addition to one recursive call on $\lceil m/2 \rceil$ or $\lfloor m/2 \rfloor$ elements, depending whether or not $x \leq T[k]$. Therefore, $t(m) = t(m/2) + g(m)$ when m is even, where $g(m) \in O(1) = O(m^0)$. By our general analysis of divide-and-conquer algorithms, using Equation 7.1 with $\ell = 1$, $b = 2$ and $k = 0$, we conclude that $t(m) \in \Theta(\log m)$. Therefore, binary search can be accomplished in logarithmic time in the worst case. It is easy to see that this version of binary search also takes logarithmic time even in the best case.

Because the recursive call is dynamically at the end of the algorithm, it is easy to produce an iterative version.

> **function** $biniter(T[1..n], x)$
>   {Iterative binary search for x in array T}
>   **if** $x > T[n]$ **then return** $n + 1$
> $i \leftarrow 1$; $j \leftarrow n$
>   **while** $i < j$ **do**
>   { $T[i-1] < x \leq T[j]$ }
> $k \leftarrow (i + j) \div 2$
>   **if** $x \leq T[k]$ **then** $j \leftarrow k$
>   **else** $i \leftarrow k + 1$
>   **return** i

The analysis of this algorithm is identical to that of its recursive counterpart *binsearch*. Exactly the same array locations are probed (except when $n = 0$; see Problem 7.10), and the same sequences of values are assumed by i, j and k. Therefore, iterative binary search also takes logarithmic time in the worst case as well as in the best case. This algorithm can be modified to make it faster in the best case (constant time), at the cost of making it slightly slower (albeit still logarithmic) in the worst case, but this is to the detriment of average-case performance on large instances; see Problem 7.11.

7.4 Sorting

Let $T[1..n]$ be an array of n elements. Our problem is to sort these elements into ascending order. We have already seen that the problem can be solved by selection sorting and insertion sorting (Section 2.4), or by heapsort (Section 5.7). Recall that an analysis both in the worst case and on the average shows that the latter method takes a time in $\Theta(n \log n)$, whereas both the former methods take quadratic time. There are several classic algorithms for sorting that follow the divide-and-conquer template. It is interesting to note how different they are: significant freedom for creativity remains even after deciding to attempt solving a given problem by divide-and-conquer. We study two of them now—*mergesort* and *quicksort*—leaving yet another for Chapter 11.

7.4.1 Sorting by merging

The obvious divide-and-conquer approach to this problem consists of separating the array T into two parts whose sizes are as nearly equal as possible, sorting these parts by recursive calls, and then merging the solutions for each part, being careful to preserve the order. To do this, we need an efficient algorithm for merging two sorted arrays U and V into a single array T whose length is the sum of the lengths of U and V. This can be achieved more efficiently—and more easily—if additional storage is available at the end of both the arrays U and V to be used as a sentinel. (This technique works only if we can set the sentinel to a value guaranteed to be bigger than every element in U and V, which we denote below by "∞"; see Problem 7.13.)

> **procedure** $merge(U[1..m+1], V[1..n+1], T[1..m+n])$
> {Merges sorted arrays $U[1..m]$ and $V[1..n]$ into $T[1..m+n]$);
> $U[m+1]$ and $V[n+1]$ are used as sentinels}
> $i, j \leftarrow 1$
> $U[m+1], V[n+1] \leftarrow \infty$
> **for** $k \leftarrow 1$ **to** $m+n$ **do**
>   **if** $U[i] < V[j]$
>   **then** $T[k] \leftarrow U[i]$; $i \leftarrow i+1$
>   **else** $T[k] \leftarrow V[j]$; $j \leftarrow j+1$

The merge sorting algorithm is as follows, where we use insertion sort (*insert*) from Section 2.4 as the basic subalgorithm. For the sake of efficiency, it may be better if the intermediate arrays U and V are global variables.

> **procedure** $mergesort(T[1..n])$
>   **if** n is sufficiently small **then** $insert(T)$
>   **else**
>   **array** $U[1..1+\lfloor n/2 \rfloor], V[1..1+\lceil n/2 \rceil]$
> $U[1..\lfloor n/2 \rfloor] \leftarrow T[1..\lfloor n/2 \rfloor]$
> $V[1..\lceil n/2 \rceil] \leftarrow T[1+\lfloor n/2 \rfloor..n]$
> $mergesort(U[1..\lfloor n/2 \rfloor])$
> $mergesort(V[1..\lceil n/2 \rceil])$
> $merge(U, V, T)$

Figure 7.2 shows how merge sorting works.

This sorting algorithm illustrates well all the facets of divide-and-conquer. When the number of elements to be sorted is small, a relatively simple algorithm is used. On the other hand, when this is justified by the number of elements, *mergesort* separates the instance into two subinstances half the size, solves each of these recursively, and then combines the two sorted half-arrays to obtain the solution to the original instance.

Let $t(n)$ be the time taken by this algorithm to sort an array of n elements. Separating T into U and V takes linear time. It is easy to see that $merge(U, V, T)$ also takes linear time. Consequently, $t(n) = t(\lfloor n/2 \rfloor) + t(\lceil n/2 \rceil) + g(n)$, where $g(n) \in \Theta(n)$. This recurrence, which becomes $t(n) = 2t(n/2) + g(n)$ when n is even, is a special case of our general analysis for divide-and-conquer algorithms. Equation 7.1 applies with $\ell = 2$, $b = 2$ and $k = 1$. Since $\ell = b^k$, the second case applies to yield $t(n) \in \Theta(n \log n)$. Thus, the efficiency of *mergesort* is similar to that of *heapsort*. Merge sorting may be slightly faster in practice, but it requires significantly more

Array to be sorted

The array is split into two halves

One recursive call on *mergesort* for each half

One call on *merge*

The array is now sorted

Figure 7.2. *mergesort*

storage for the intermediate arrays U and V. Recall that *heapsort* can sort in-place, in the sense that it needs only a small constant number of working variables. Merge sorting can also be implemented in-place, but at the cost of such an increase in the hidden constant that this is only of theoretical interest; see Problem 7.14.

The merge sorting algorithm illustrates the importance of creating subinstances of roughly equal size when developing divide-and-conquer algorithms. Consider the following variation on *mergesort*.   (The dummy call to *badmergesort* ($V[1..1]$) is included only to stress similarity with the original *mergesort* algorithm.)

procedure *badmergesort*($T[1..n]$)
    if n is sufficiently small **then** *insert*(T)
    else
        array $U[1..n], V[1..2]$
        $U[1..n-1] \leftarrow T[1..n-1]$
        $V[1] \leftarrow T[n]$
        badmergesort($U[1..n-1]$)
        badmergesort($V[1..1]$)
        merge(U, V, T)

Let $\hat{t}(n)$ be the time needed to sort n elements with this modified algorithm. It is clear that $\hat{t}(n) = \hat{t}(n-1) + \hat{t}(1) + \hat{g}(n)$, where $\hat{g}(n) \in \Theta(n)$. This recurrence yields $\hat{t}(n) \in \Theta(n^2)$. Thus simply forgetting to balance the sizes of the subinstances can be disastrous for the efficiency of an algorithm obtained using divide-and-conquer. In fact, *badmergesort* is nothing but an inefficient implementation of insertion sort!

7.4.2 Quicksort

The sorting algorithm invented by Hoare, usually known as *quicksort*, is also based on the principle of divide-and-conquer. Unlike *mergesort*, most of the nonrecursive ✓ part of the work to be done is spent constructing the subinstances rather than combining their solutions. As a first step, this algorithm chooses as *pivot* one of the items in the array to be sorted. The array is then partitioned on either side of the pivot: elements are moved so that those greater than the pivot are to its right, whereas the others are to its left. If now the sections of the array on either side of the pivot are sorted independently by recursive calls of the algorithm, the final result is a completely sorted array, no subsequent merge step being necessary. To balance the sizes of the two subinstances to be sorted, we would like to use ✓ the median element as the pivot. (For a definition of the median, see Section 7.5.) Unfortunately, finding the median takes more time than it is worth. For this reason we simply use an arbitrary element of the array as the pivot, hoping for the best.

Designing a linear time pivoting algorithm is no challenge. However, it is crucial in practice that the hidden constant be small if *quicksort* is to be competitive with other sorting techniques such as *heapsort*. Suppose subarray $T[i..j]$ is to be pivoted around $p = T[i]$. One good way of pivoting consists of scanning the subarray just once, but starting at both ends. Pointers k and l are initialized to i and $j + 1$, respectively. Pointer k is then incremented until $T[k] > p$, and pointer l is decremented until $T[l] \leq p$. Now $T[k]$ and $T[l]$ are interchanged. This process continues as long as $k < l$. Finally, $T[i]$ and $T[l]$ are interchanged to put the pivot in its correct position.

```
procedure pivot(T[i..j]; var l)
    {Permutes the elements in array T[i..j] and returns a value l such
        that, at the end, i ≤ l ≤ j, T[k] ≤ p for all i ≤ k < l, T[l] = p,
        and T[k] > p for all l < k ≤ j, where p is the initial value of T[i]}
    p ← T[i]
    k ← i;  l ← j + 1
    repeat k ← k + 1 until T[k] > p or k ≥ j
    repeat l ← l - 1 until T[l] ≤ p
    while k < l do
        swap T[k] and T[l]
        repeat k ← k + 1 until T[k] > p
        repeat l ← l - 1 until T[l] ≤ p
    swap T[i] and T[l]
```

Now here is the sorting algorithm. To sort the entire array T, simply call *quicksort*$(T[1..n])$.

procedure *quicksort*($T[i..j]$)
    {Sorts subarray $T[i..j]$ into nondecreasing order}
    if $j - i$ is sufficiently small **then** *insert*($T[i..j]$)
    else
        pivot($T[i..j], l$)
        quicksort($T[i..l-1]$)
        quicksort($T[l+1..j]$)

Figure 7.3 shows how *pivot* and *quicksort* work.

Quicksort is inefficient if it happens systematically on most recursive calls that the subinstances $T[i..l-1]$ and $T[l+1..j]$ are severely unbalanced. In the worst case, for example if T is already sorted before the call to *quicksort*, we get $l = i$ each time, which means a recursive call on an instance of size 0 and another on an instance whose size is reduced only by 1. This gives rise to a recurrence similar to the one we encountered in the analysis of *badmergesort*, the unbalanced version of *mergesort*. Once again the running time is quadratic. Thus *quicksort* takes a time in $\Omega(n^2)$ in the worst case to sort n elements.

On the other hand, if the array to be sorted is initially in random order, it is likely that most of the time the subinstances to be sorted will be sufficiently well balanced. To determine the *average* time required by *quicksort* to sort an array of n items, we must make an assumption about the probability distribution of all n-item instances. The most natural assumption is that the elements of T are distinct and that each of the $n!$ possible initial permutations of the elements is equally likely. It must be stressed, however, that this assumption can be inadequate—or even plainly wrong—for some applications, in which case the analysis that follows does not apply. This is the case, for instance, if your application often needs to sort arrays that are already almost sorted.

Let $t(m)$ be the average time taken by a call on *quicksort*($T[i..j]$), where $m = j - i + 1$ is the number of elements in the subarray. In particular, *quicksort*($T[1..n]$) requires time $t(n)$ to sort all n elements of the array. By our assumption on the instance probability distribution, the pivot chosen by the algorithm when requested to sort $T[1..n]$ lies with equal probability in any position with respect to the other elements of T. Therefore, the value of l returned by the pivoting algorithm after the initial call *pivot*($T[1..n], l$) can be any integer between 1 and n, each value having equal probability $1/n$. This pivoting operation takes linear time $g(n) \in \Theta(n)$. It remains to sort recursively two subarrays of size $l - 1$ and $n - l$, respectively. It can be shown that the probability distribution on the subarrays is still uniform; see Problem 7.16. Therefore, the average time required to execute these recursive calls is $t(l-1)+t(n-l)$. Consequently,

$$t(n) = \frac{1}{n} \sum_{l=1}^{n} (g(n)+t(l-1)+t(n-l))$$

whenever n is large enough to warrant the recursive approach. In this formula, $\frac{1}{n}$ is the probability that any given value of l between 1 and n is returned by the top-level call to *pivot*, and $g(n)+t(l-1)+t(n-l)$ is the expected time to sort n elements conditional on this value of l being returned by that call.

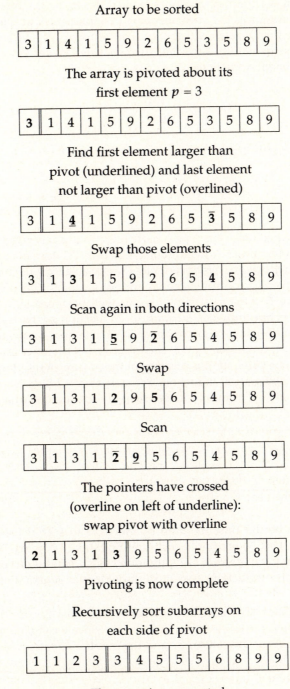

Figure 7.3. *quicksort*

To make the formula more explicit, let n_0 be the threshold above which the recursive approach is used, meaning that insertion sort is used whenever there are no more than n_0 elements to sort. Furthermore, let d be a constant (depending on the implementation) such that $g(n) \le dn$ whenever $n > n_0$. Taking $g(n)$ out of the summation, we have

$$t(n) \le dn + \frac{1}{n} \sum_{l=1}^{n} (t(l-1) + t(n-l)) \text{ for } n > n_0.$$

Noting that the term $t(k)$ appears twice for each $0 \le k \le n-1$, a little manipulation yields

$$t(n) \le dn + \frac{2}{n} \sum_{k=0}^{n-1} t(k) \text{ for } n > n_0. \tag{7.2}$$

An equation of this type is more difficult to analyse than the linear recurrences we saw in Section 4.7. In particular, Equation 7.1 does not apply this time. By analogy with *mergesort*, it is nevertheless reasonable to hope that $t(n)$ is in $O(n \log n)$: on the average the subinstances are not too badly unbalanced and the solution would be $O(n \log n)$ if they were as well balanced as with *mergesort*. Proving this conjecture provides a beautiful application of the technique of constructive induction (Section 1.6.4). To apply this technique, we postulate the existence of a constant c, unknown as yet, such that $t(n) \le c n \log n$ for all $n \ge 2$. We find an appropriate value for this constant in the process of proving its existence by generalized mathematical induction. We start at $n = 2$ because $n \log n$ is undefined or zero for smaller values of n; alternatively, we could start at $n = n_0 + 1$.

> **Theorem 7.4.1**   *Quicksort takes a time in $O(n \log n)$ to sort n elements on the average.*

Proof   Let $t(n)$ be the time required by *quicksort* to sort n elements on the average. Let d and n_0 be constants such that Equation 7.2 holds. We wish to prove that $t(n) \le c n \log n$ for all $n \ge 2$, provided c is a well-chosen constant. We proceed by constructive induction. Assume without loss of generality that $n_0 \ge 2$.

⋄ *Basis*: Consider any integer n such that $2 \le n \le n_0$. We have to show that $t(n) \le c n \log n$. This is easy since we still have complete freedom to choose the constant c and the number of basis cases is finite. It suffices to choose c at least as large as $t(n)/(n \log n)$. Thus, our first constraint on c is

$$c \ge \frac{t(n)}{n \log n} \text{ for all } n \text{ such that } 2 \le n \le n_0. \tag{7.3}$$

◇ *Induction step*: Consider any integer $n > n_0$. Assume the induction hypothesis that $t(k) \leq c\, k \log k$ for all k such that $2 \leq k < n$. We wish to constrain c so that $t(n) \leq c\, n \log n$ follows from the induction hypothesis. Let a stand for $t(0) + t(1)$. Starting with Equation 7.2,

$$t(n) \leq dn + \frac{2}{n} \sum_{k=0}^{n-1} t(k)$$

$$= dn + \frac{2}{n} \left(t(0) + t(1) + \sum_{k=2}^{n-1} t(k) \right)$$

$$\leq dn + \frac{2a}{n} + \frac{2}{n} \sum_{k=2}^{n-1} c\, k \log k \quad \text{by the induction hypothesis}$$

$$\leq dn + \frac{2a}{n} + \frac{2c}{n} \int_2^n x \log x \, dx \quad \text{(see Figure 7.4)}$$

$$= dn + \frac{2a}{n} + \frac{2c}{n} \left[\frac{x^2 \log x}{2} - \frac{x^2}{4} \right]_{x=2}^{n}$$

(recall that "log" denotes the natural logarithm)

$$< dn + \frac{2a}{n} + \frac{2c}{n} \left(\frac{n^2 \log n}{2} - \frac{n^2}{4} \right)$$

$$= dn + \frac{2a}{n} + c\, n \log n - \frac{cn}{2}$$

$$= c\, n \log n - \left(\frac{c}{2} - d - \frac{2a}{n^2} \right) n.$$

It follows that $t(n) \leq c\, n \log n$ provided $c/2 - d - 2a/n^2$ is nonnegative, which is equivalent to saying that $c \geq 2d + 4a/n^2$. Since we consider here only the case $n > n_0$, all is well provided

$$c \geq 2d + \frac{4a}{(n_0 + 1)^2}, \tag{7.4}$$

which is our second and final constraint on c.

Putting together the constraints given by Equations 7.3 and 7.4, it suffices to set

$$c = \max \left(2d + \frac{4\,(t(0) + t(1))}{(n_0 + 1)^2}, \ \max \left\{ \frac{t(n)}{n \log n} \,\Big|\, 2 \leq n \leq n_0 \right\} \right) \tag{7.5}$$

to conclude the proof by constructive induction that $t(n) \leq c\, n \log n$ for all $n \geq 2$, and therefore that $t(n) \in O(n \log n)$.

If you are puzzled or unconvinced, we urge you to work for yourself a proof by ordinary—as opposed to constructive—generalized mathematical induction that

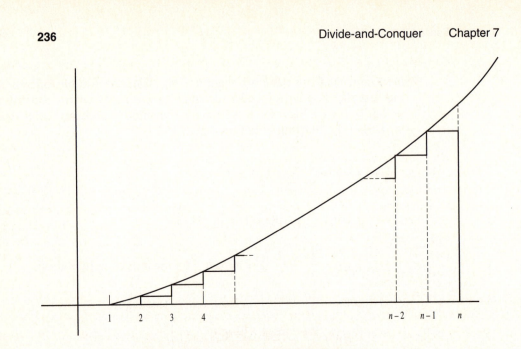

Figure 7.4. Summing monotonic functions

$t(n) \le c\, n \log n$ for all $n \ge 2$, this time using the explicit value for c given by Equation 7.5. ∎

Quicksort can therefore sort an array of n distinct elements in an average time in $O(n \log n)$. In practice, the hidden constant is smaller than those involved in heapsort or in merge sort. If an occasional long execution time can be tolerated, this is an excellent general-purpose sorting algorithm. Can *quicksort* be modified so as to take a time in $O(n \log n)$ even in the worst case? The answer is yes but no. Even if the median of $T[i..j]$ is chosen as pivot, which can be done in linear time as we shall see in Section 7.5, *quicksort* as described here still takes quadratic time in the worst case, which occurs if all the elements to be sorted are equal. A simple modification to the algorithm suffices to prevent this bad behaviour, although it is challenging to program it correctly and efficiently. For this, we need a new

procedure *pivotbis*$(T[i..j], p; \textbf{var } k, l)$

that partitions T into *three* sections using p as pivot: after pivoting, the elements in $T[i..k]$ are smaller than p, those in $T[k+1..l-1]$ are equal to p, and those in $T[l..j]$ are larger than p. The values of k and l are returned by *pivotbis*. After pivoting with a call on *pivotbis*$(T[i..j], T[i], k, l)$, it remains to call *quicksort* recursively on $T[i..k]$ and $T[l..j]$. With this modification, sorting an array of equal elements takes linear time. More interestingly, *quicksort* now takes a time in $O(n \log n)$ even in the worst case if the median of $T[i..j]$ is chosen as pivot in linear time. However, we mention this possibility only to point out that it should be shunned: the hidden constant associated with this "improved" version of quicksort is so large that it results in an algorithm worse than heapsort in every case!

7.5 Finding the median

Let $T[1..n]$ be an array of integers and let s be an integer between 1 and n. The s-th *smallest element* of T is defined as the element that would be in the s-th position if T were sorted into nondecreasing order. Given T and s, the problem of finding the s-th smallest element of T is known as the *selection* problem. In particular, the *median* of $T[1..n]$ is defined as its $\lceil n/2 \rceil$-th smallest element. When n is odd and the elements of T are distinct, the median is simply that element in T such that there are as many items in T smaller than it as there are items larger than it. For instance, the median of $[3, 1, 4, 1, 5, 9, 2, 6, 5]$ is 4 since 3, 1, 1 and 2 are smaller than 4 whereas 5, 9, 6 and 5 are larger.

What could be easier than to find the smallest element of T or to calculate the mean of all the elements? However, it is not obvious that the median can be found so easily. The naive algorithm for determining the median of $T[1..n]$ consists of sorting the array and then extracting its $\lceil n/2 \rceil$-th entry. If we use *heapsort* or *mergesort*, this takes a time in $\Theta(n \log n)$. Can we do better? To answer this question, we study the interrelation between finding the median and selecting the s-th smallest element.

It is obvious that any algorithm for the selection problem can be used to find the median: simply select the $\lceil n/2 \rceil$-th smallest. Interestingly, the converse holds as well. Assume for now the availability of an algorithm $median(T[1..n])$ that returns the median of T. Given an array T and an integer s, how could this algorithm be used to determine the s-th smallest element of T? Let p be the median of T. Now pivot T around p, much as for *quicksort*, but using the *pivotbis* algorithm introduced at the end of the previous section. Recall that a call on $pivotbis(T[i..j], p; \mathbf{var}\ k, l)$ partitions $T[i..j]$ into three sections: T is shuffled so the elements in $T[i..k]$ are smaller than p, those in $T[k+1..l-1]$ are equal to p, and those in $T[l..j]$ are larger than p. After a call on $pivotbis(T, p, k, l)$, we are done if $k < s < l$ as the s-th smallest element of T is then equal to p. If $s \le k$, the s-th smallest element of T is now the s-th smallest element of $T[1..k]$. Finally, if $s \ge l$, the s-th smallest element of T is now the $(s - l + 1)$-st smallest element of $T[l..n]$. In any case, we have made progress since either we are done, or the subarray to be considered contains less than half the elements, by virtue of p being the median of the original array.

There are strong similarities between this approach and binary searching (Section 7.3), and indeed the resulting algorithm can be programmed iteratively rather than recursively. The key idea is to use two variables i and j, initialized to 1 and n respectively, and to ensure that at every moment $i \le s \le j$ and the elements in $T[1..i-1]$ are smaller than those in $T[i..j]$, which are in turn smaller than those in $T[j+1..n]$. The immediate consequence of this is that the desired element resides in $T[i..j]$. When all the elements in $T[i..j]$ are equal, we are done.

Figure 7.5 illustrates the process. For simplicity, the illustration assumes *pivotbis* is implemented in a way that is intuitively simple even though a really efficient implementation would proceed differently.

Array in which to find 4th smallest element

| 3 | 1 | 4 | 1 | 5 | 9 | 2 | 6 | 5 | 3 | 5 | 8 | 9 |

Pivot array around its median $p = 5$ using *pivotbis*

| 3 | 1 | 4 | 1 | 2 | 3 | 5 | 5 | 5 | 9 | 6 | 8 | 9 |

Only part left of pivot is still relevant since $4 \leq 6$

| 3 | 1 | 4 | 1 | 2 | 3 | • | • | • | • | • | • | • |

Pivot that part around its median $p = 2$

| 1 | 1 | 2 | 3 | 4 | 3 | • | • | • | • | • | • | • |

Only part right of pivot is still relevant since $4 \geq 4$

| • | • | • | 3 | 4 | 3 | • | • | • | • | • | • | • |

Pivot that part around its median $p = 3$

| • | • | • | 3 | 3 | 4 | • | • | • | • | • | • | • |

Answer is 3 because the pivot is in the 4th position

Figure 7.5. Selection using the median

function *selection*$(T[1 .. n], s)$
{Finds the s-th smallest element in T, $1 \leq s \leq n$}
$i \leftarrow 1$; $j \leftarrow n$
repeat
{Answer lies in $T[i .. j]$}
$p \leftarrow median(T[i .. j])$
pivotbis$(T[i .. j], p, k, l)$
if $s \leq k$ **then** $j \leftarrow k$
else if $s \geq l$ **then** $i \leftarrow l$
else return p

By an analysis similar to that of binary search, the above algorithm selects the required element of T after going round the **repeat** loop a logarithmic number of times in the worst case. However, trips round the loop no longer take constant time, and indeed this algorithm cannot be used until we have an efficient way to find the median, which was our original problem. Can we modify the algorithm to avoid resort to the median?

First, observe that our algorithm still works regardless of which element of T is chosen as pivot (the value of p). It is only the *efficiency* of the algorithm that depends on the choice of pivot: using the median assures us that the number of elements still under consideration is at least halved each time round the **repeat** loop. If we are willing to sacrifice speed in the worst case to obtain an algorithm reasonably fast on the average, we can borrow another idea from quicksort and simply choose $T[i]$ as pivot. In other words, replace the first instruction in the loop with

$$p \leftarrow T[i].$$

This causes the algorithm to spend quadratic time in the worst case, for example if the array is in decreasing order and we wish to find the smallest element. Nevertheless, this modified algorithm runs in *linear* time on the average, under our usual assumption that the elements of T are distinct and that each of the $n!$ possible initial permutations of the elements is equally likely. (The analysis parallels that of *quicksort*; see Problem 7.18). This is much better than the time required on the average if we proceed by sorting the array, but the worst-case behaviour is unacceptable for many applications.

Happily, this quadratic worst case can be avoided without sacrificing linear behaviour on the average. The idea is that the number of trips round the loop remains logarithmic provided the pivot is chosen reasonably close to the median. A good *approximation* to the median can be found quickly with a little cunning. Consider the following algorithm.

> **function** *pseudomed*$(T[1 .. n])$
> {Finds an approximation to the median of array T}
> **if** $n \leq 5$ **then return** *adhocmed*(T)
> $z \leftarrow \lfloor n/5 \rfloor$
> **array** $Z[1 .. z]$
> **for** $i \leftarrow 1$ **to** z **do** $Z[i] \leftarrow$ *adhocmed*$(T[5i - 4 .. 5i])$
> **return** *selection*$(Z, \lceil z/2 \rceil)$

Here, *adhocmed* is an algorithm specially designed to find the median of at most five elements, which can be done in a time bounded above by a constant, and *selection*$(Z, \lceil z/2 \rceil)$ determines the exact median of array Z. Let p be the value returned by a call on *pseudomed*(T). How far from the true median of T can p be when $n > 5$?

As in the algorithm, let z be $\lfloor n/5 \rfloor$, the number of elements in the array Z created by the call on *pseudomed*(T). For each i between 1 and z, $Z[i]$ is by definition the median of $T[5i - 4 .. 5i]$, and therefore at least three elements out of the five in this subarray are less than or equal to it. Moreover, since p is the true median of Z, at least $z/2$ elements of Z are less than or equal to p. By transitivity ($T[j] \leq Z[i] \leq p$ implies that $T[j] \leq p$), at least $3z/2$ elements of T are less than or equal to p. Since $z = \lfloor n/5 \rfloor \geq (n - 4)/5$, we conclude that at least $(3n - 12)/10$ elements of T are less than or equal to p, and therefore at most the $(7n + 12)/10$ remaining elements of T are strictly larger than p. Similar reasoning applies to the number of elements of T that are strictly *smaller* than p.

Although p is probably not the exact median of T, we conclude that its rank is approximately between $3n/10$ and $7n/10$. To visualize how these factors arise, although nothing in the execution of the algorithm *pseudomed* really corresponds to this illustration, imagine as in Figure 7.6 that the elements of T are arranged in five rows, with the possible exception of at most four elements left aside. Now suppose each of the $\lfloor n/5 \rfloor$ columns as well as the middle row are sorted by magic, the smallest elements going to the top and to the left, respectively. The middle row corresponds to the array Z in the algorithm and the element in the circle corresponds to the median of this array, which is the value of p returned by the algorithm. Clearly, each of the elements in the box is less than or equal to p. The conclusion follows since the box contains approximately three-fifths of one-half of the elements of T.

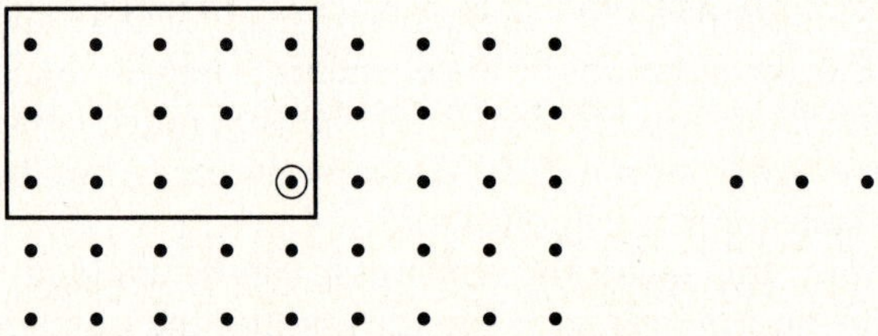

Figure 7.6. Visualization of the pseudomedian

We now analyse the efficiency of the *selection* algorithm presented at the beginning of this section when the first instruction in its **repeat** loop is replaced by

$$p \leftarrow pseudomed(T[i..j]) \, .$$

Let $t(n)$ be the time required in the worst case by a call on $selection(T[1..n], s)$. Consider any i and j such that $1 \leq i \leq j \leq n$. The time required to complete the **repeat** loop with these values for i and j is essentially $t(m)$, where $m = j - i + 1$ is the number of elements still under consideration. When $n > 5$, calculating $pseudomed(T)$ takes a time in $t(\lfloor n/5 \rfloor) + O(n)$ because the array Z can be constructed in linear time since each call to *adhocmed* takes constant time. The call to *pivotbis* also takes linear time. At this point, either we are finished or we have to go back round the loop with at most $(7n + 12)/10$ elements still to be considered. Therefore, there exists a constant d such that

$$t(n) \leq dn + t(\lfloor n/5 \rfloor) + \max\{t(m) \mid m \leq (7n + 12)/10\} \tag{7.6}$$

provided $n > 5$.

Equation 7.1 does not help us solve this recurrence, so once again we resort to constructive induction. This time, even guessing the answer in asymptotic notation requires insight. (Recall that the obvious try when we analysed *quicksort* was

$O(n \log n)$ because we had analysed *mergesort* already, and it worked; no such luck this time.) With some experience, the fact that $\frac{1}{5} + \frac{7}{10} < 1$ is a telltale that $t(n)$ may well be linear in n, which is clearly the best we could hope for; see Problem 7.19.

Theorem 7.5.1   *The selection algorithm used with pseudomed finds the s–th smallest among n elements in a time in $\Theta(n)$ in the worst case. In particular, the median can be found in linear time in the worst case.*

Proof   Let $t(n)$ and d be as above. Clearly, $t(n) \in \Omega(n)$ since the algorithm must look at each element of T at least once. Thus it remains to prove that $t(n) \in O(n)$. Let us postulate the existence of a constant c, unknown as yet, such that $t(n) \le cn$ for all $n \ge 1$. We find an appropriate value for this constant in the process of proving its existence by generalized mathematical induction. Constructive induction will also be used to determine the constant n_0 that separates the basis case from the induction step. For now, our only constraint is $n_0 \ge 5$ because Equation 7.6 only applies when $n > 5$. (We shall discover that the obvious choice $n_0 = 5$ does not work.)

⋄ *Basis*: Consider any integer n such that $1 \le n \le n_0$. We have to show that $t(n) \le cn$. This is easy since we still have complete freedom to choose the constant c and the number of basis cases is finite. It suffices to choose c at least as large as $t(n)/n$. Thus, our first constraint on c is

$$c \ge t(n)/n \text{ for all } n \text{ such that } 1 \le n \le n_0. \tag{7.7}$$

⋄ *Induction step*: Consider any integer $n > n_0$. Assume the induction hypothesis that $t(m) \le cm$ when $1 \le m < n$. We wish to constrain c so that $t(n) \le cn$ follows from the induction hypothesis. Starting with Equation 7.6, and because $1 \le (7n + 12)/10 < n$ when $n > n_0 \ge 5$,

$$t(n) \le dn + t(\lfloor n/5 \rfloor) + \max\{t(m) \mid m \le (7n + 12)/10\}$$

$$\le dn + cn/5 + (7n + 12)c/10 \quad \text{by the induction hypothesis}$$

$$= 9cn/10 + dn + 6c/5$$

$$= cn - (c/10 - d - 6c/5n)\,n.$$

It follows that $t(n) \le cn$ provided $c/10 - d - 6c/5n \ge 0$, which is equivalent to $(1 - 12/n)c \ge 10d$. This is possible provided $n \ge 13$ (so $1 - 12/n > 0$), in which case c must be no smaller than $10d/(1 - 12/n)$. Keeping in mind that $n > n_0$, any choice of $n_0 \ge 12$ is adequate, provided c is chosen accordingly. More precisely, all is well provided $n_0 \ge 12$ and

$$c \ge \frac{10d}{1 - \frac{12}{n_0+1}} \tag{7.8}$$

which is our second and final constraint on c and n_0. For instance, the induction step is correct if we take $n_0 = 12$ and $c \ge 130d$, or $n_0 = 23$ and $c \ge 20d$, or $n_0 = 131$ and $c \ge 11d$.

Putting together the constraints given by Equations 7.7 and 7.8, and choosing $n_0 = 23$ for the sake of definiteness, it suffices to set

$$c = \max(20d, \max\{t(m)/m \mid 1 \le m \le 23\})$$

to conclude the proof by constructive induction that $t(n) \le cn$ for all $n \ge 1$.   ∎

7.6 Matrix multiplication

Let A and B be two $n \times n$ matrices to be multiplied, and let C be their product. The classic matrix multiplication algorithm comes directly from the definition

$$C_{ij} = \sum_{k=1}^{n} A_{ik} B_{kj}.$$

Each entry in C is calculated in a time in $\Theta(n)$, assuming that scalar addition and multiplication are elementary operations. Since there are n^2 entries to compute, the product AB can be calculated in a time in $\Theta(n^3)$. ✓

Towards the end of the 1960s, Strassen caused a considerable stir by improving this algorithm. From an algorithmic point of view, this breakthrough is a landmark in the history of divide-and-conquer, even though the equally surprising algorithm for multiplying large integers (Section 7.1) was discovered almost a decade earlier. The basic idea behind Strassen's algorithm is similar to that earlier one. First we show that two 2×2 matrices can be multiplied using less than the eight scalar multiplications apparently required by the definition. Let

$$A = \begin{pmatrix} a_{11} & a_{12} \\ a_{21} & a_{22} \end{pmatrix} \quad \text{and} \quad B = \begin{pmatrix} b_{11} & b_{12} \\ b_{21} & b_{22} \end{pmatrix}$$

be two matrices to be multiplied. Consider the following operations, each of which involves just one multiplication.

$$\left. \begin{aligned}
m_1 &= (a_{21} + a_{22} - a_{11})(b_{22} - b_{12} + b_{11}) \\
m_2 &= a_{11} b_{11} \\
m_3 &= a_{12} b_{21} \\
m_4 &= (a_{11} - a_{21})(b_{22} - b_{12}) \\
m_5 &= (a_{21} + a_{22})(b_{12} - b_{11}) \\
m_6 &= (a_{12} - a_{21} + a_{11} - a_{22}) b_{22} \\
m_7 &= a_{22} (b_{11} + b_{22} - b_{12} - b_{21})
\end{aligned} \right\} \tag{7.9}$$

We leave the reader to verify that the required product AB is given by the following matrix.

$$C = \begin{pmatrix} m_2 + m_3 & m_1 + m_2 + m_5 + m_6 \\ m_1 + m_2 + m_4 - m_7 & m_1 + m_2 + m_4 + m_5 \end{pmatrix} \tag{7.10}$$

It is therefore possible to multiply two 2×2 matrices using only seven scalar multiplications. At first glance, this algorithm does not look very interesting: it uses a large number of additions and subtractions compared to the four additions that are sufficient for the classic algorithm.

If we now replace each entry of A and B by an $n \times n$ matrix, we obtain an algorithm that can multiply two $2n \times 2n$ matrices by carrying out seven multiplications of $n \times n$ matrices, as well as a number of additions and subtractions of $n \times n$ matrices. This is possible because the 2×2 algorithm does not rely on the commutativity of scalar multiplication. Given that large matrices can be added much faster than they can be multiplied, saving one multiplication more than compensates for the supplementary additions.

Let $t(n)$ be the time needed to multiply two $n \times n$ matrices by recursive use of Equations 7.9 and 7.10. Assume for simplicity that n is a power of 2. Since matrices can be added and subtracted in a time in $\Theta(n^2)$, $t(n) = 7t(n/2) + g(n)$, where $g(n) \in \Theta(n^2)$. This recurrence is another instance of our general analysis for divide-and-conquer algorithms. Equation 7.1 applies with $\ell = 7$, $b = 2$ and $k = 2$. Since $\ell > b^k$, the third case yields $t(n) \in \Theta(n^{\lg 7})$. Square matrices whose size is not a power of 2 are easily handled by padding them with rows and columns of zeros, at most doubling their size, which does not affect the asymptotic running time. Since $\lg 7 < 2.81$, it is thus possible to multiply two $n \times n$ matrices in a time in $O(n^{2.81})$, provided scalar operations are elementary.

Following Strassen's discovery, a number of researchers attempted to improve the constant ω such that it is possible to multiply two $n \times n$ matrices in a time in $O(n^\omega)$. The obvious thing to try first was to multiply two 2×2 matrices with *six* scalar multiplications. But in 1971 Hopcroft and Kerr proved this is impossible when the commutativity of multiplication cannot be used. The next thing to try was to find a way to multiply two 3×3 matrices with at most 21 scalar multiplications. This would yield a recursive algorithm to multiply $n \times n$ matrices in a time in $\Theta(n^{\log_3 21})$, asymptotically faster than Strassen's algorithm since $\log_3 21 < \log_2 7$. Unfortunately, this too is impossible.

Almost a decade passed before Pan discovered a way to multiply two 70×70 matrices with $143\,640$ scalar multiplications—compare this with the $343\,000$ required by the classic algorithm—and indeed $\log_{70} 143640$ is a tiny bit smaller than $\lg 7$. This discovery launched the so-called *decimal war*. Numerous algorithms, asymptotically more and more efficient, were discovered subsequently. For instance, it was known at the end of 1979 that matrices could be multiplied in a time in $O(n^{2.521813})$; imagine the excitement in January 1980 when this was improved to $O(n^{2.521801})$. The asymptotically fastest matrix multiplication algorithm known at the time of writing goes back to 1986 when Coppersmith and Winograd discovered that it is possible, at least in theory, to multiply two $n \times n$ matrices in a time in $O(n^{2.376})$. Because of the hidden constants involved, however, none of the algorithms found after Strassen's is of much practical use.

7.7 Exponentiation

Let a and n be two integers. We wish to compute the exponentiation $x = a^n$. For simplicity, we shall assume throughout this section that $n > 0$. If n is small, the obvious algorithm is adequate.

function $exposeq(a, n)$
   $r \leftarrow a$
   for $i \leftarrow 1$ **to** $n - 1$ **do** $r \leftarrow a \times r$
   return r

This algorithm takes a time in $\Theta(n)$ since the instruction $r \leftarrow a \times r$ is executed exactly $n - 1$ times, *provided the multiplications are counted as elementary operations*. However, on most computers, even small values of n and a cause this algorithm to produce integer overflow. For example, 15^{17} does not fit in a 64-bit integer.

If we wish to handle larger operands, we must take account of the time required for each multiplication. Let $M(q, s)$ denote the time needed to multiply two integers of sizes q and s. For our purpose, it does not matter whether we consider the size of integers in decimal digits, in bits, or in any other fixed basis larger than 1. Assume for simplicity that $q_1 \leq q_2$ and $s_1 \leq s_2$ imply that $M(q_1, s_1) \leq M(q_2, s_2)$. Let us estimate how much time our algorithm spends multiplying integers when $exposeq(a, n)$ is called. Let m be the size of a. First note that the product of two integers of size i and j is of size at least $i + j - 1$ and at most $i + j$; see Problem 7.24. Let r_i and m_i be the value and the size of r at the beginning of the i–th time round the loop. Clearly, $r_1 = a$ and therefore $m_1 = m$. Since $r_{i+1} = ar_i$, the size of r_{i+1} is at least $m + m_i - 1$ and at most $m + m_i$. The demonstration by mathematical induction that $im - i + 1 \leq m_i \leq im$ for all i follows immediately. Therefore, the multiplication performed the i–th time round the loop concerns an integer of size m and an integer whose size is between $im - i + 1$ and im, which takes a time between $M(m, im - i + 1)$ and $M(m, im)$. The total time $T(m, n)$ spent multiplying when computing a^n with $exposeq$ is therefore

$$\sum_{i=1}^{n-1} M(m, im - i + 1) \leq T(m, n) \leq \sum_{i=1}^{n-1} M(m, im) \quad (7.11)$$

where m is the size of a. This is a good estimate on the total time taken by $exposeq$ since most of the work is spent performing these multiplications.

If we use the classic multiplication algorithm (Section 1.2), then $M(q, s) \in \Theta(qs)$. Let c be such that $M(q, s) \leq c\,qs$.

$$T(m, n) \leq \sum_{i=1}^{n-1} M(m, im) \leq \sum_{i=1}^{n-1} c\,m\,im$$

$$= c\,m^2 \sum_{i=1}^{n-1} i < c\,m^2\,n^2$$

Thus, $T(m, n) \in O(m^2n^2)$. It is equally easy to show from Equation 7.11 that $T(m, n) \in \Omega(m^2n^2)$ and therefore $T(m, n) \in \Theta(m^2n^2)$; see Problem 7.25. On the other hand, if we use the divide-and-conquer multiplication algorithm described earlier in this chapter, $M(q, s) \in \Theta(sq^{\lg(3/2)})$ when $s \geq q$, and a similar argument yields $T(m, n) \in \Theta(m^{\lg 3}n^2)$.

The key observation for improving $exposeq$ is that $a^n = (a^{n/2})^2$ when n is even. This is interesting because $a^{n/2}$ can be computed about four times faster than a^n

with *exposeq*, and a single squaring (which is a multiplication) is sufficient to obtain the desired result from $a^{n/2}$. This yields the following recurrence.

$$a^n = \begin{cases} a & \text{if } n = 1 \\ (a^{n/2})^2 & \text{if } n \text{ is even} \\ a \times a^{n-1} & \text{otherwise} \end{cases}$$

For instance,

$$a^{29} = a\,a^{28} = a(a^{14})^2 = a\big((a^7)^2\big)^2 = \cdots = a\Big(\big(a(a\,a^2)^2\big)^2\Big)^2,$$

which involves only three multiplications and four squarings instead of the 28 multiplications required with *exposeq*. The above recurrence gives rise to the following algorithm.

> **function** *expoDC*(a, n)
>   **if** $n = 1$ **then return** a
>   **if** n is even **then return** $[expoDC(a, n/2)]^2$
>   **return** $a \times expoDC(a, n - 1)$

To analyse the efficiency of this algorithm, we first concentrate on the *number* of multiplications (counting squarings as multiplications) performed by a call on *expoDC*(a, n). Notice that the flow of control of the algorithm does not depend on the value of a, and therefore the number of multiplications is a function only of the exponent n; let us denote it by $N(n)$.

No multiplications are performed when $n = 1$, so $N(1) = 0$. When n is even, one multiplication is performed (the squaring of $a^{n/2}$) in addition to the $N(n/2)$ multiplications involved in the recursive call on *expoDC*$(a, n/2)$. When n is odd, one multiplication is performed (that of a by a^{n-1}) in addition to the $N(n-1)$ multiplications involved in the recursive call on *expoDC*$(a, n-1)$. Thus we have the following recurrence.

$$N(n) = \begin{cases} 0 & \text{if } n = 1 \\ N(n/2)+1 & \text{if } n \text{ is even} \\ N(n-1)+1 & \text{otherwise} \end{cases} \tag{7.12}$$

An unusual feature of this recurrence is that it does not give rise to an increasing function of n. For example,

$$N(15) = N(14)+1 = N(7)+2 = N(6)+3 = N(3)+4 = N(2)+5$$
$$\text{whereas } = N(1)+6 = 6$$
$$N(16) = N(8)+1 = N(4)+2 = N(2)+3 = N(1)+4 = 4.$$

This function is not even *eventually* nondecreasing; see Problem 7.26. Therefore, Equation 7.1 cannot be used directly.

To handle such a recurrence, it is useful to bound the function from above and below with nondecreasing functions. When $n > 1$ is odd,

$$N(n) = N(n-1)+1 = N((n-1)/2)+2 = N(\lfloor n/2 \rfloor)+2.$$

On the other hand, when n is even, $N(n) = N(\lfloor n/2 \rfloor) + 1$ since $\lfloor n/2 \rfloor = n/2$ in that case. Therefore,

$$N(\lfloor n/2 \rfloor) + 1 \leq N(n) \leq N(\lfloor n/2 \rfloor) + 2 \tag{7.13}$$

for all $n > 1$. Let N_1 and N_2 be functions defined by

$$N_i(n) = \begin{cases} 0 & \text{if } n = 1 \\ N_i(\lfloor n/2 \rfloor) + i & \text{otherwise} \end{cases} \tag{7.14}$$

for $i = 1$ and $i = 2$. Using Equation 7.13, it is easy to prove by mathematical induction that $N_1(n) \leq N(n) \leq N_2(n)$ for all n; see Problem 7.27. But now both N_1 and N_2 are nondecreasing (also an easy proof by mathematical induction). Moreover, $\lfloor n/2 \rfloor = n/2$ when $n > 1$ is a power of 2. Equation 7.1 applies to $N_1(n)$ and $N_2(n)$ with $\ell = 1$, $b = 2$ and $k = 0$ to yield that both these functions are in $\Theta(\log n)$. We conclude that $N(n)$ is in $\Theta(\log n)$ as well. Recall that *exposeq* required a number of multiplications in $\Theta(n)$ to perform the same exponentiation. Therefore, *expoDC* is more efficient than its rival using this criterion. It remains to be seen if it is also significantly better when the *time* spent on those multiplications is taken into account.

Let $M(q, s)$ denote again the time needed to multiply two integers of sizes q and s, and let $T(m, n)$ now denote the time spent multiplying by a call on $expoDC(a, n)$, where m is the size of a. Recall that the size of a^i is at most im. Inspection of the algorithm *expoDC* yields the following recurrence.

$$T(m, n) \leq \begin{cases} 0 & \text{if } n = 1 \\ T(m, n/2) + M(mn/2, mn/2) & \text{if } n \text{ is even} \\ T(m, n-1) + M(m, (n-1)m) & \text{otherwise} \end{cases} \tag{7.15}$$

As with the recurrence for N, this implies that

$$T(m, n) \leq T(m, \lfloor n/2 \rfloor) + M(m\lfloor n/2 \rfloor, m\lfloor n/2 \rfloor) + M(m, (n-1)m)$$

for all $n > 1$. If $M(q, s) \in \Theta(sq^{\alpha-1})$ for some constant α when $s \geq q$ ($\alpha = 2$ with the classic multiplication algorithm whereas $\alpha = \lg 3$ with divide-and-conquer multiplication), Problem 7.29 shows that $T(m, n) \in O(m^\alpha n^\alpha)$. A matching lower bound is easier to obtain. The last or next to last multiplication performed by $expoDC(a, n)$, depending whether n is even or odd, consists of squaring $a^{\lfloor n/2 \rfloor}$, an integer of size greater than $(m-1)\lfloor n/2 \rfloor$. This costs at least $M((m-1)\lfloor n/2 \rfloor, (m-1)\lfloor n/2 \rfloor)$, which is in $\Omega(((m-1)\lfloor n/2 \rfloor)^\alpha)$ and therefore in $\Omega(m^\alpha n^\alpha)$. We conclude that $T(m, n) \in \Theta(m^\alpha n^\alpha)$.

To summarize, the following table gives the time to compute a^n, where m is the size of a, depending whether we use *exposeq* or *expoDC*, and whether we use the classic or divide-and-conquer (D&C) multiplication algorithm.

	multiplication	
	classic	D&C
exposeq	$\Theta(m^2 n^2)$	$\Theta(m^{\lg 3} n^2)$
expoDC	$\Theta(m^2 n^2)$	$\Theta(m^{\lg 3} n^{\lg 3})$

It is interesting that nothing is gained—except perhaps a constant factor in speed—by being only half-clever: both *exposeq* and *expoDC* take a time in $\Theta(m^2 n^2)$ if the classic multiplication algorithm is used. This is true even though *expoDC* uses exponentially fewer multiplications than *exposeq*.

As for binary searching, the algorithm *expoDC* requires only one recursive call on a smaller instance. It is therefore an example of simplification rather than of divide-and-conquer. However, this recursive call is not at the dynamic end of the algorithm since a multiplication remains to be performed after it. This makes it harder to find an iterative version. Nevertheless, such an algorithm exists, corresponding intuitively to calculating $a^{29} = a^1 a^4 a^8 a^{16}$. We give it without further ado, noting that this simple version systematically makes two useless multiplications, including the very last squaring of x.

> **function** *expoiter*(a, n)
> $i \leftarrow n$; $r \leftarrow 1$; $x \leftarrow a$
>   **while** $i > 0$ **do**
>   **if** i is odd **then** $r \leftarrow rx$
> $x \leftarrow x^2$
> $i \leftarrow i \div 2$
>   **return** r

7.8 Putting it all together: Introduction to cryptography

Looking back at the previous section, it is disappointing that an exponential reduction in the number of multiplications required to compute a^n does not translate into a spectacular saving in running time. Nevertheless, there are applications for which it *is* reasonable to count all multiplications at the same cost. This is the case if we are interested in *modular* arithmetic, that is in the calculation of a^n modulo some third integer z. Recall that $x \bmod z$ denotes the remainder of the integer division of x by z. For instance, $25 \bmod 7 = 4$ because $25 = 3 \times 7 + 4$. If x and y are two integers between 0 and $z - 1$, and if z is an integer of size m, the modular multiplication $xy \bmod z$ involves one ordinary integer multiplication of two integers of size at most m, yielding an integer of size at most $2m$, followed by a division of the product by z, an integer of size m, to compute the remainder of the division. Therefore, the time taken by each modular multiplication is rather insensitive to the two numbers actually involved. Two elementary properties of modular arithmetic will be used; see Problem 7.30.

$$xy \bmod z = [(x \bmod z) \times (y \bmod z)] \bmod z$$

and

$$(x \bmod z)^y \bmod z = x^y \bmod z$$

Thus, *exposeq*, *expoDC* and *expoiter* can be adapted to compute $a^n \bmod z$ in modular arithmetic without ever having to manipulate integers larger than $\max(a, z^2)$. For this, it suffices to reduce modulo z after each multiplication. For example, *expoiter* gives rise to the following algorithm.

```
function expomod(a, n, z)
    {Computes a^n mod z}
    i ← n;  r ← 1;  x ← a mod z
    while i > 0 do
        if i is odd then r ← rx mod z
        x ← x^2 mod z
        i ← i ÷ 2
    return r
```

The analysis in the previous section applies *mutatis mutandis* to conclude that this algorithm needs only a number of modular multiplications in $\Theta(\log n)$ to compute $a^n \bmod z$. A more precise analysis shows that the number of modular multiplications is equal to the number of bits in the binary expansion of n, plus the number of these bits that are equal to 1; it is thus approximately equal to $\frac{3}{2} \lg n$ for a typical n. In contrast, the algorithm corresponding to *exposeq* requires $n - 1$ such multiplications for all n. For definiteness, say we wish to compute $a^n \bmod z$ where a, n and z are 200-digit numbers and that numbers of that size can be multiplied modulo z in one millisecond. Our algorithm *expomod* typically computes $a^n \bmod n$ in less than one second. The algorithm corresponding to *exposeq* would require roughly 10^{179} times the age of the Universe for the same task!

Impressive as this is, you may well wonder who needs to compute such huge modular exponentiations in real life. It turns out that modern *cryptography*, the art and science of secret communication over insecure channels, depends crucially on this. Consider two parties, whom we shall call Alice and Bob, and assume that Alice wishes to send some private message m to Bob over a channel susceptible to eavesdropping. To prevent others reading the message, Alice transforms it into a *ciphertext* c, which she sends to Bob. This transformation is the result of an *enciphering* algorithm whose output depends not only on the message m but also on another parameter k known as the *key*. Classically, this key is secret information that has to be established between Alice and Bob before secret communication can take place. From c and his knowledge of k, Bob can reconstruct Alice's actual message m. Such secrecy systems rely on the hope that an eavesdropper who intercepts c but does not know k will be unable to determine m from the available information.

This approach to cryptography has been used with more or less success throughout history. Its requirement that the parties must share secret information prior to communication may be acceptable to the military and diplomats, but not to the ordinary citizen. In the era of the electronic super-highway, it is desirable for any two citizens to be able to communicate privately without prior coordination. Can Alice and Bob communicate secretly in full view of a third party if they do not share a secret before the communication is established? The age of *public-key cryptography* was launched when the thought that this may be possible came to Diffie, Hellman and Merkle in the mid-seventies. Here, we present the amazingly simple solution discovered a few years later by Rivest, Shamir and Adleman, which became known as the *RSA cryptographic system* after the names of its inventors.

Consider two 100-digit prime numbers p and q chosen randomly by Bob; see Section 10.6.2 for an efficient algorithm capable of testing the primality of such large numbers. Let z be the product of p and q. Bob can compute z efficiently from p and q. However, no known algorithm can recompute p and q from z within the lifetime of the Universe, even using the fastest computer available at the time of writing. Let ϕ be $(p-1)(q-1)$. Let n be an integer chosen randomly by Bob between 1 and $z-1$ that has no common factors with ϕ. (It is not necessary for Bob to verify explicitly that n has the desired property because he will soon find out if it does not.) Elementary number theory tells us that there exists a unique integer s between 1 and $z-1$ such that $ns \bmod \phi = 1$. Moreover, s is easy to compute from n and ϕ—see Problem 7.31—and its existence is proof that n and ϕ have no common factors. If s does not exist, Bob has to choose randomly a new value for n; each attempt has a good probability of success. The key theorem is that $a^x \bmod z = a$ whenever $0 \leq a < z$ and $x \bmod \phi = 1$.

To allow Alice or anyone else to communicate with him privately, Bob makes public his choice of z and n, but he keeps s secret. Let m be a message that Alice wishes to transmit to Bob. Using standard encoding such as ASCII, Alice transforms her message into a bit string, which she interprets as a number a. Assume for simplicity that $0 \leq a \leq z-1$; otherwise she can slice her message m into chunks of appropriate size. Next, Alice uses algorithm *expomod* to compute $c = a^n \bmod z$, which she sends to Bob over an insecure channel. Using his private knowledge of s, Bob obtains a, and thus Alice's message m, with a call on *expomod*(c, s, z). This works because

$$c^s \bmod z = (a^n \bmod z)^s \bmod z = (a^n)^s \bmod z = a^{ns} \bmod z = a.$$

Now consider the eavesdropper's task. Assuming she has intercepted all communications between Alice and Bob, she knows z, n and c. Her purpose is to determine Alice's message a, which is the unique number between 0 and $z-1$ such that $c = a^n \bmod z$. Thus she has to compute the n-th *root* of c modulo z. No efficient algorithm is known for this calculation: modular exponentiations can be computed efficiently with *expomod* but it appears that the reverse process is infeasible. The best method known today is the obvious one: factorize z into p and q, compute ϕ as $(p-1)(q-1)$, use Problem 7.31 to compute s from n and ϕ, and compute $a = c^s \bmod z$ exactly as Bob would have done. Every step in this attack is feasible but the first: factorizing a 200-digit number is beyond the reach of current technology. Thus Bob's advantage in deciphering messages intended for him stems from the fact that he alone knows the factors of z, which are necessary to compute ϕ and s. This knowledge does not come from his factorizing skills but rather from the fact that he chose z's factors in the first place, and computed z from them.

At the time of writing, the safety of this cryptographic scheme has not been established mathematically: factorizing may turn out to be easy or not even necessary to break the scheme. Moreover, an efficient factorizing algorithm *is* known, but it requires the availability of a *quantum computer*, a device whose construction is beyond the reach of current technology; see Section 12.6. Nevertheless, the secret system we just described is widely considered to be one of the best inventions in the history of cryptography.

7.9 Problems

Problem 7.1. Consider an algorithm whose running time $t(n)$ on instances of size n is such that $t(n) = 3t(n/2) + g(n)$ when n is even and sufficiently large, where $g(n) \in O(n)$. This is the recurrence we encountered early in our study of the divide-and-conquer algorithm to multiply large integers in Section 7.1, before we had discussed how to handle operands of odd length. Recall that solving it yields $t(n) \in \Theta(n^{\lg 3} \mid n$ is a power of 2). Because $t(n) = 3t(n/2) + g(n)$ holds for all sufficiently large *even* values of n rather than merely when n is a power of 2, however, it may be tempting to conclude that $t(n) \in \Theta(n^{\lg 3} \mid n$ is even). Show that this conclusion could be premature without more information on the behaviour of $t(n)$ when n is odd. On the other hand, give a simple and natural condition on $t(n)$ that would allow the conclusion that it is in $\Theta(n^{\lg 3})$ unconditionally.

Problem 7.2. In Section 7.1 we saw a divide-and-conquer algorithm to multiply two n-figure integers in a time in $\Theta(n^{\lg 3})$. The key idea was to reduce the required multiplication to three half-size multiplications. Show that the operands to be multiplied can be separated into three parts rather than two, so as to obtain the required product after five multiplications of integers of size approximately $n/3$ rather than the nine submultiplications that would appear necessary at first sight. Analyse the efficiency of the divide-and-conquer algorithm suggested by this idea. Is it better than our algorithm from Section 7.1?

Problem 7.3. Generalize the algorithm suggested in Problem 7.2 by showing that the multiplication of two n-figure integers can be reduced to $2k - 1$ multiplications of integers about k times shorter, for any integer constant k. Conclude that there exists an algorithm A_α that can multiply two n-figure integers in a time in $O(n^\alpha)$ for every real number $\alpha > 1$.

Problem 7.4. Use a simple argument to prove that Problem 7.3 would be impossible if it required algorithm A_α to take a time in $\Theta(n^\alpha)$.

Problem 7.5. Continuing Problem 7.3, consider the following algorithm for multiplying large integers.

> **function** *supermul*(u, v)
>   {We assume for simplicity u and v are the same size}
> $n \leftarrow$ size of u and v
> $\alpha \leftarrow 1 + (\lg \lg n) / \lg n$
>   **return** $A_\alpha(u, v)$

At first glance this algorithm seems to multiply two n-figure integers in a time in $O(n \log n)$ since $n^\alpha = n \lg n$ when $\alpha = 1 + (\lg \lg n) / \lg n$. Find at least two fundamental errors in this analysis of *supermul*.

Problem 7.6. If you have not yet worked out Problems 4.6, 4.7 and 4.8, now is the time!

Problem 7.7. What happens to the efficiency of divide-and-conquer algorithms if, instead of using a threshold to decide when to revert to the basic subalgorithm, we recur at most r times, for some constant r, and then use the basic subalgorithm?

Problem 7.8. Let a and b be positive real constants. For each positive real number s, consider the function $f_s : \mathbb{R}^{\geq 0} \to \mathbb{R}^{\geq 0}$ defined by

$$f_s(x) = \begin{cases} ax^2 & \text{if } x \leq s \\ 3f_s(x/2) + bx & \text{otherwise} . \end{cases}$$

Prove by mathematical induction that if $u = 4b/a$ and if v is an arbitrary positive real constant, then $f_u(x) \leq f_v(x)$ for every positive real number x.
Note: The constant u was chosen so that $au^2 = 3a(u/2)^2 + bu$. This problem illustrates the rule according to which the optimal threshold in a divide-and-conquer algorithm can be estimated by finding the size n of the instance for which it makes no difference whether we apply the basic subalgorithm directly or whether we go on for one more level of recursion. Things are not so simple in practice because the size of subinstances cannot be halved indefinitely, but this rule remains an excellent guideline nevertheless.

Problem 7.9. Consider the sequential search algorithm *sequential* from Section 7.3 that finds some element x in array $T[1..n]$. Assuming the elements of T are distinct, that x is indeed somewhere in the array, and that it is to be found with equal probability at each possible position, prove that the average number of trips round the loop is $(n + 1)/2$.

Problem 7.10. The recursive algorithm *binsearch* for binary search (Section 7.3) handles search in an empty array $T[1..0]$ as a special case (explicit test for $n = 0$). Convince yourself that this test is not necessary in the iterative version *biniter*, regardless of the outcome of the comparison between x and $T[0]$, provided it is allowable to consult the value of $T[0]$ (meaning that there must be no range checks).

Problem 7.11. Quick inspection of the iterative binary search algorithm *biniter* in Section 7.3 shows what is apparently an inefficiency. Suppose T contains 17 distinct elements and $x = T[13]$. On the first trip round the loop, $i = 1$, $j = 17$, and $k = 9$. The comparison between x and $T[9]$ causes the assignment $i \leftarrow 10$ to be executed. On the second trip round the loop $i = 10$, $j = 17$, and $k = 13$. A comparison is then made between x and $T[13]$. This comparison could allow us to end the search immediately, but no test is made for equality, and so the assignment $j \leftarrow 13$ is carried out. Two more trips round the loop are necessary before we leave with $i = j = 13$. In contrast, algorithm *Binary_Search* from Section 4.2.4 leaves the loop immediately after it finds the element it is looking for.
Thus *biniter* systematically makes a number of trips round the loop in $\Theta(\log n)$, regardless of the position of x in T, whereas *Binary_Search* may make only one or two trips round the loop if x is favourably situated. On the other hand, a trip round

the loop in *Binary_Search* takes a little longer to execute on the average than a trip round the loop in *biniter*. To determine which algorithm is asymptotically better, analyse precisely the average number of trips round the loop that each makes. For simplicity, assume that T contains n distinct elements and that x appears in T, occupying each possible position with equal probability. Prove the existence of a constant c such that on the average *Binary_Search* saves at most c trips round the loop compared with *biniter*. In conclusion, which is the better algorithm when the instance is arbitrarily large?

Problem 7.12.   Let $T[1..n]$ be a sorted array of distinct integers, some of which may be negative. Give an algorithm that can find an index i such that $1 \leq i \leq n$ and $T[i] = i$, provided such an index exists. Your algorithm should take a time in $O(\log n)$ in the worst case.

Problem 7.13.   The use of sentinels in algorithm *merge* requires the availability of an additional cell in the arrays to be merged; see Section 7.4.1. Although this is not an issue when *merge* is used within *mergesort*, it can be a nuisance in other applications. More importantly, our merging algorithm can fail if it is not possible to guarantee that the sentinels are strictly greater than any possible value in the arrays to be merged.

(a) Give an example of arrays U and V that are sorted but where the result of *merge*(U, V, T) is not what it should be. What is the contents of T after this pathological call? (You are allowed the value ∞ in arrays U and V and you may wish to specify the values of U and V outside the bounds of the arrays.)

(b) Give a **procedure** for merging that does not use sentinels. Your algorithm must work correctly in linear time provided the arrays U and V are sorted prior to the call.

Problem 7.14.   In Section 7.4.1 we saw an algorithm *merge* capable of merging two sorted arrays U and V in linear time, that is, in a time in the exact order of the sum of the lengths of U and V. Find another merging algorithm that achieves the same goal, also in linear time, but without using an auxiliary array: the sections $T[1..k]$ and $T[k+1..n]$ of an array are sorted independently, and you have to sort the whole array $T[1..n]$ using only a fixed amount of additional storage.

Problem 7.15.   Rather than separate $T[1..n]$ into two half-size arrays for the purpose of merge sorting, we might choose to separate it into three arrays of size $n \div 3$, $(n+1) \div 3$ and $(n+2) \div 3$, to sort each of these recursively, and then to merge the three sorted arrays. Give a more formal description of this algorithm and analyse its execution time.

Problem 7.16.   Consider an array $T[1..n]$. As in the average-case analysis of *quicksort*, assume that the elements of T are distinct and that each of the $n!$ possible initial permutations of the elements is equally likely. Consider a call on *pivot*$(T[1..n], l)$. Prove that each of the $(l-1)!$ possible permutations of the elements in $T[1..l-1]$ is equally likely after the call. Prove the similar statement concerning $T[l+1, n]$.

Problem 7.17.   Give a linear-time algorithm for implementing *pivotbis* from Sections 7.4.2 and 7.5. Your algorithm should scan the array only once, and no auxiliary arrays should be used.

Problem 7.18.   Prove that the selection algorithm of Section 7.5 takes linear time on the average if we replace the first instruction in the **repeat** loop with " $p \leftarrow T[i]$ ". Assume that the elements of the array are distinct and that each of the possible initial permutations of the elements is equally likely.

Problem 7.19.   Let $a_1, a_2, \ldots, a_k$ be positive real numbers whose sum is strictly less than 1. Consider a function $f : \mathbb{N} \to \mathbb{R}^{\geq 0}$ such that

$$f(n) \leq f(\lfloor a_1 n \rfloor) + f(\lfloor a_2 n \rfloor) + \cdots + f(\lfloor a_k n \rfloor) + cn$$

for some positive c and all sufficiently large n. Prove by constructive induction that $f(n) \in O(n)$.
Would the above work in general if the a_i's sum to exactly 1? Justify your answer with an easy argument.

Problem 7.20.   An array T contains n elements. You want to find the m smallest, where m is much smaller than n. Would you

(a) sort T and pick the first m,

(b) call *select*(T, i) for $i = 1, 2, \ldots, m$, or

(c) use some other method?

   Justify your answer.

Problem 7.21.   The array T is as in the previous problem, but now you want the elements of rank $\lceil n/2 \rceil, \lceil n/2 \rceil + 1, \ldots, \lceil n/2 \rceil + m - 1$. Would you

(a) sort T and pick the appropriate elements,

(b) use *select* m times, or

(c) use some other method?

   Justify your answer.

Problem 7.22.   The number of additions and subtractions needed to calculate the product of two 2×2 matrices using Equations 7.9 and 7.10 seems at first to be 24. Show that this can be reduced to 15 by using auxiliary variables to avoid recalculating terms such as $m_1 + m_2 + m_4$.

Problem 7.23.   Assuming n is a power of 2, find the exact number of scalar additions and multiplications needed by Strassen's algorithm to multiply two $n \times n$ matrices. (Use the result of Problem 7.22.) Your answer will depend on the threshold used to stop making recursive calls. Bearing in mind what you learnt in Section 7.2, propose a threshold that minimizes the number of scalar operations.

Problem 7.24. We say that an integer x is of (decimal) size n if $10^{n-1} \leq x \leq 10^n - 1$. Prove that the product of two integers of size i and j is of size at least $i + j - 1$ and at most $i + j$. Prove that this rule applies equally well in any fixed basis $b \geq 2$, when we say that an integer x is of size n if $b^{n-1} \leq x \leq b^n - 1$.

Problem 7.25. Let $T(m, n)$ be the time spent multiplying when computing a^n with a call on *exposeq*(a, n), where m is the size of a; see Section 7.7. Use Equation 7.11 with $M(q, s) \in \Theta(qs)$ to conclude that $T(m, n) \in \Omega(m^2 n^2)$.

Problem 7.26. Consider the function $N(n)$ given by Equation 7.12, which counts the number of multiplications needed to compute a^n with algorithm *expoDC* from Section 7.7. We saw that $N(15) > N(16)$. Prove the existence of an infinity of integers n such that $N(n) > N(n + 1)$. Conclude that this function is not eventually nondecreasing.

Problem 7.27. Use Equations 7.12, 7.13 and 7.14 to prove that

$$N_1(n) \leq N(n) \leq N_2(n)$$

for all n and both $N_1(n)$ and $N_2(n)$ are nondecreasing functions.

Problem 7.28. Algorithm *expoDC* from Section 7.7 does not always minimize the number of multiplications—including squarings—to calculate a^n. For instance, it calculates a^{15} as $a(a(a\,a^2)^2)^2$, which requires six multiplications. Show that in fact a^{15} can be calculated with as few as five multiplications. Resist the temptation to use the formula $a^{15} = ((((a^2)^2)^2)^2)/a$ and claim that a division is just another form of multiplication!

Problem 7.29. Let $T(m, n)$ be given by Equation 7.15. This is the time spent multiplying when calling *expoDC*(a, n), where m is the size of a; see Section 7.7. If $M(q, s) \in \Theta(sq^{\alpha-1})$ for some constant α when $s \geq q$, prove that

$$T(m, n) \in O(m^\alpha n^\alpha).$$

Problem 7.30. Consider any integers x, y and z such that z is positive. Prove that

$$xy \bmod z = [(x \bmod z) \times (y \bmod z)] \bmod z$$

and

$$(x \bmod z)^y \bmod z = x^y \bmod z.$$

Hint: write x as $qz + r$, where $r = x \bmod z$ and $q = x \div z$.

Problem 7.31. Let u and v be two positive integers and let d be their greatest common divisor.

(a) Prove that there exist integers a and b such that $au + bv = d$.

[*Hint*: Suppose without loss of generality that $u \geq v$. If $u = v$, then $d = v$ and the result is immediate (take $a = 0$ and $b = 1$). Otherwise, let $w = u \bmod v$. Note that $v < u$ and $w < v$. First show that d is also the greatest common divisor of v and w, which is why Euclid's algorithm computes the greatest common divisor correctly. By mathematical induction, now let a' and b' be such that $a'v + b'w = d$. Finally take $a = b'$ and $b = a' - (u \div v)b'$. It remains to prove that $au + bv = d$ as desired.]

(b) Give an efficient algorithm to compute d, a and b from u and v. Your algorithm should not calculate d before starting work on a and b.
   [*Hint*: The hint above is relevant.]

(c) Consider two integers n and ϕ such that $\gcd(n, \phi) = 1$. Give an efficient algorithm to determine an integer s such that $ns \bmod \phi = 1$.
   [*Hint*: Using the previous subproblem, compute s and t such that $ns + t\phi = 1$.]

Problem 7.32.   In this problem, you are invited to work out a toy example of encipherment and decipherment using the RSA public-key cryptographic system; see Section 7.8. Assume Bob chooses his two "large" prime numbers to be $p = 19$ and $q = 23$. He multiplies them to obtain $z = 437$. Next, he chooses randomly $n = 13$. Compute $\phi = (p - 1)(q - 1)$ and use Problem 7.31 to find the unique s between 1 and $z - 1$ such that $ns \bmod \phi = 1$. Bob makes z and n public, but he keeps s secret.

Next, suppose Alice wishes to send cleartext message $m = 123$ to Bob. She looks up Bob's $z = 437$ and $n = 13$ in the public directory. Use *expomod* to compute the ciphertext $c = m^n \bmod z$. Alice sends c to Bob. Use Bob's secret s to decipher Alice's message: compute $c^s \bmod z$ with *expomod*. Is your answer $m = 123$ as it should be?

Of course, much bigger numbers would be used in real life.

Problem 7.33.   Consider the matrix
$$F = \begin{pmatrix} 0 & 1 \\ 1 & 1 \end{pmatrix}.$$

Let i and j be any two integers. What is the product of the vector (i, j) and the matrix F? What happens if i and j are two consecutive numbers from the Fibonacci sequence? Use this idea to invent a divide-and-conquer algorithm to calculate this sequence, and analyse its efficiency (1) counting all arithmetic operations at unit cost, and (2) counting a time in $\Theta(sq^{\alpha-1})$ to multiply integers of size q and s when $s \geq q$. Recall that the size of the n–th Fibonacci number is in $\Theta(n)$.

Problem 7.34.   Represent the polynomial $p(n) = a_0 + a_1 n + a_2 n^2 + \cdots + a_d n^d$ of degree d by an array $P[0 .. d]$ containing its coefficients. Suppose you already have an algorithm capable of multiplying a polynomial of degree k by a polynomial of degree 1 in a time in $O(k)$, as well as another algorithm capable of multiplying two polynomials of degree k in a time in $O(k \log k)$. Let $n_1, n_2, \ldots, n_d$ be integers. Give an efficient algorithm based on divide-and-conquer to find the unique polynomial $p(n)$ of degree d whose coefficient of highest degree is 1, such that $p(n_1) = p(n_2) = \ldots = p(n_d) = 0$. Analyse the efficiency of your algorithm.

Problem 7.35. Let $T[1..n]$ be an array of n integers. An integer is a *majority element* in T if it appears strictly more than $n/2$ times in T. Give an algorithm that can decide whether an array $T[1..n]$ contains a majority element, and if so find it. Your algorithm must run in linear time in the worst case.

Problem 7.36. Rework Problem 7.35 with the supplementary constraint that the only comparisons allowed between the elements of T are tests of equality. You may therefore not assume that an order relation exists between the elements.

Problem 7.37. If you could not manage Problem 7.36, try again but allow your algorithm to take a time in $O(n \log n)$ in the worst case.

Problem 7.38. are to organize a tournament involving n competitors. Each competitor must play exactly once against each possible opponent. Moreover, each competitor must play exactly one match every day, with the possible exception of a single day when he or she does not play at all.

(a) If n is a power of 2, give an algorithm to construct a timetable allowing the tournament to be finished in $n - 1$ days.

(b) For any integer $n > 1$ give an algorithm to construct a timetable allowing the tournament to be finished in $n - 1$ days if n is even, or in n days if n is odd. For example, Figure 7.7 gives possible timetables for tournaments involving five and six players.

		Player				
	Day	1	2	3	4	5
	1	2	1	–	5	4
	2	3	5	1	–	2
$(n = 5)$	3	4	3	2	1	–
	4	5	–	4	3	1
	5	–	4	5	2	3

		Player					
	Day	1	2	3	4	5	6
	1	2	1	6	5	4	3
	2	3	5	1	6	2	4
$(n = 6)$	3	4	3	2	1	6	5
	4	5	6	4	3	1	2
	5	6	4	5	2	3	1

Figure 7.7. Timetables for five and six players

Problem 7.39. You are given the Cartesian coordinates of n points in the plane. Give an algorithm capable of finding the closest pair of points in a time in $O(n \log n)$ in the worst case.

Problem 7.40.   Consider an array $T[1..n]$ and an integer k between 1 and n. Use simplification to design an efficient algorithm to interchange the first k and the last $n - k$ elements of T without making use of an auxiliary array. Analyse the running time of your algorithm.

Problem 7.41.   An *n-tally* is a circuit that takes n bits as input and produces $1 + \lfloor \lg n \rfloor$ bits as output. It counts (in binary) the number of bits equal to 1 among the inputs. For example, if $n = 9$ and the inputs are 011001011, the output is 0101. An (i, j)-*adder* is a circuit that has one i-bit input, one j-bit input, and one $[1 + \max(i, j)]$-bit output. It adds its two inputs in binary. For example, if $i = 3$, $j = 5$, and the inputs are 101 and 10111 respectively, the output is 011100. It is always possible to construct an (i, j)-adder using exactly $\max(i, j)$ 3-tallies. For this reason the 3-tally is often called a *full adder*.

(a) Using full adders and (i, j)-adders as primitive elements, show how to build an efficient n-tally.

(b) Give the recurrence, including the initial conditions, for the number of 3-tallies needed to build your n-tally. Do not forget to count the 3-tallies that are part of any (i, j)-adders you might have used.

(c) Using the Θ notation, give the simplest possible expression for the number of 3-tallies needed in the construction of your n-tally. Justify your answer.

Problem 7.42.   A *switch* is a circuit with two inputs, a control, and two outputs. It connects input A with output A and input B with output B, or input A with output B and input B with output A, depending on the position of the control; see Figure 7.8. Use these switches to construct a network with n inputs and n outputs able to implement any of the $n!$ possible permutations of the inputs. The number of switches used must be in $O(n \log n)$.

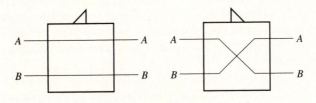

Figure 7.8. Switches

7.10 References and further reading

The algorithm for multiplying large integers in a time in $O(n^{1.59})$ is attributed to Karatsuba and Ofman (1962). A practical algorithm for the rapid multiplication of integers with up to 10,000 decimal digits is given in Pollard (1971). The fastest known algorithm, which can multiply two n-figure integers in a time in $O(n \log n \log \log n)$, is due to Schönhage and Strassen (1971); its details are spelled out in Brassard, Monet and Zuffellato (1986). A good survey of algorithms for large integer multiplication is given in the 1981 second edition of Knuth (1969), which includes the answer to Problems 7.2 and 7.3. See also Borodin and Munro (1975) and Turk (1982).

The technique to determine the optimal threshold at which to use the basic subalgorithm rather than continuing to divide the subproblems is original to Brassard and Bratley (1988). The solution to Problem 7.11 is also given in Brassard and Bratley (1988); it provides yet another nice application of the technique of constructive induction.

Quicksort is from Hoare (1962). *Mergesort* and *quicksort* are discussed in detail in Knuth (1973), which is a compendium of sorting techniques. Problem 7.14 was solved by Kronrod; see the solution to Exercise 18 of Section 5.2.4 of Knuth (1973). The algorithm linear in the worst case for selection and for finding the median is due to Blum, Floyd, Pratt, Rivest and Tarjan (1972).

The algorithm that multiplies two $n \times n$ matrices in a time in $O(n^{2.81})$ comes from Strassen (1969). Subsequent efforts to do better than Strassen's algorithm began with the proof by Hopcroft and Kerr (1971) that seven multiplications are necessary to multiply two 2×2 matrices in a noncommutative structure; the first positive success was obtained by Pan (1980), and the algorithm that is asymptotically the most efficient known at present is by Coppersmith and Winograd (1990).

The thought that secure communication over insecure channels can be achieved without prior agreement on a secret came independently to Merkle (1978) and Diffie and Hellman (1976). The RSA public-key cryptographic system described in Section 7.8, invented by Rivest, Shamir and Adleman (1978), was first published by Gardner (1977); be warned however that the challenge issued there was successfully taken up by Atkins, Graff, Lenstra and Leyland in April 1994 after eight months of calculation on more than 600 computers throughout the world. The efficient algorithm capable of breaking this system on a quantum computer is due to Shor (1994). For more information about cryptology, consult the introductory papers by Kahn (1966) and Hellman (1980) and the books by Kahn (1967), Denning (1983), Kranakis (1986), Koblitz (1987), Brassard (1988), Simmons (1992), Schneier (1994) and Stimson (1995). For an approach to cryptography that remains secure regardless of the eavesdropper's computing power, consult Bennett, Brassard and Ekert (1992). The natural generalization of Problem 7.28 is examined in Knuth (1969).

The solution to Problem 7.33 can be found in Gries and Levin (1980) and Urbanek (1980). Problem 7.39 is solved in Bentley (1980), but consult Section 10.9 for more on this problem. Problem 7.40 is solved in Gries (1981); see also Brassard and Bratley (1988).

Chapter 8

Dynamic Programming

In the previous chapter we saw that it is often possible to divide an instance into subinstances, to solve the subinstances (perhaps by dividing them further), and then to combine the solutions of the subinstances so as to solve the original instance. It sometimes happens that the natural way of dividing an instance suggested by the structure of the problem leads us to consider several overlapping subinstances. If we solve each of these independently, they will in turn create a host of identical subinstances. If we pay no attention to this duplication, we are likely to end up with an inefficient algorithm; if, on the other hand, we take advantage of the duplication and arrange to solve each subinstance only once, saving the solution for later use, then a more efficient algorithm will result. The underlying idea of dynamic programming is thus quite simple: avoid calculating the same thing twice, usually by keeping a table of known results that fills up as subinstances are solved.

Divide-and-conquer is a *top-down* method. When a problem is solved by divide-and-conquer, we immediately attack the complete instance, which we then divide into smaller and smaller subinstances as the algorithm progresses. Dynamic programming on the other hand is a *bottom-up* technique. We usually start with the smallest, and hence the simplest, subinstances. By combining their solutions, we obtain the answers to subinstances of increasing size, until finally we arrive at the solution of the original instance.

We begin the chapter with two simple examples of dynamic programming that illustrate the general technique in an uncomplicated setting. The following sections pick up the problems of making change, which we met in Section 6.1, and of filling a knapsack, encountered in Section 6.5.

8.1 Two simple examples

8.1.1 Calculating the binomial coefficient

Consider the problem of calculating the binomial coefficient

$$\binom{n}{k} = \begin{cases} 1 & \text{if } k = 0 \text{ or } k = n \\ \binom{n-1}{k-1} + \binom{n-1}{k} & \text{if } 0 < k < n \\ 0 & \text{otherwise.} \end{cases}$$

Suppose $0 \le k \le n$. If we calculate $\binom{n}{k}$ directly by

> **function** $C(n, k)$
>   **if** $k = 0$ **or** $k = n$ **then return** 1
>   **else return** $C(n - 1, k - 1) + C(n - 1, k)$

many of the values $C(i, j)$, $i < n$, $j < k$, are calculated over and over. For example, the algorithm calculates $C(5, 3)$ as the sum of $C(4, 2)$ and $C(4, 3)$. Both these intermediate results require us to calculate $C(3, 2)$. Similarly the value of $C(2, 2)$ is used several times. Since the final result is obtained by adding up a number of 1s, the execution time of this algorithm is sure to be in $\Omega\left(\binom{n}{k}\right)$. We met a similar phenomenon before in the algorithm *Fibrec* for calculating the Fibonacci sequence; see Section 2.7.5.

If, on the other hand, we use a table of intermediate results—this is of course *Pascal's triangle*—we obtain a more efficient algorithm; see Figure 8.1. The table should be filled line by line. In fact, it is not even necessary to store the entire table: it suffices to keep a vector of length k, representing the current line, and to update this vector from left to right. Thus to calculate $\binom{n}{k}$ the algorithm takes a time in $\Theta(nk)$ and space in $\Theta(k)$, if we assume that addition is an elementary operation.

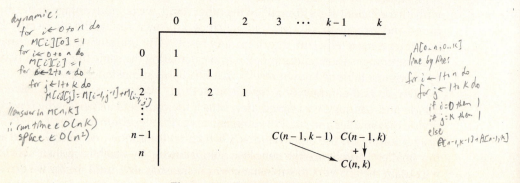

Figure 8.1. Pascal's triangle

8.1.2 The World Series

Imagine a competition in which two teams A and B play not more than $2n - 1$ games, the winner being the first team to achieve n victories. We assume that there are no tied games, that the results of each match are independent, and that for any given match there is a constant probability p that team A will be the winner, and hence a constant probability $q = 1 - p$ that team B will win.

Let $P(i, j)$ be the probability that team A will win the series given that they still need i more victories to achieve this, whereas team B still need j more victories if they are to win. For example, before the first game of the series the probability that team A will be the overall winner is $P(n, n)$: both teams still need n victories to win the series. If team A require 0 more victories, then in fact they have already won the series, and so $P(0, i) = 1$, $1 \le i \le n$. Similarly if team B require 0 more victories, then they have already won the series, and the probability that team A will be the overall winners is zero: so $P(i, 0) = 0$, $1 \le i \le n$. Since there cannot be a situation where both teams have won all the matches they need, $P(0, 0)$ is meaningless. Finally, since team A win any given match with probability p and lose it with probability q,

$$P(i, j) = pP(i - 1, j) + qP(i, j - 1), \quad i \ge 1, \ j \ge 1.$$

Thus we can compute $P(i, j)$ as follows.

function $P(i, j)$
    if $i = 0$ **then return** 1
    else if $j = 0$ **then return** 0
    else return $pP(i - 1, j) + qP(i, j - 1)$

Let $T(k)$ be the time needed in the worst case to calculate $P(i, j)$, where $k = i + j$. With this method, we see that

$$T(1) = c$$
$$T(k) \le 2T(k - 1) + d, \quad k > 1$$

where c and d are constants. Rewriting $T(k - 1)$ in terms of $T(k - 2)$, and so on, we find

$$T(k) \le 4T(k - 2) + 2d + d, \quad k > 2$$

$$\vdots$$

$$\le 2^{k-1}T(1) + (2^{k-2} + 2^{k-3} + \cdots + 2 + 1)d$$
$$= 2^{k-1}c + (2^{k-1} - 1)d$$
$$= 2^k(c/2 + d/2) - d.$$

$T(k)$ is therefore in $O(2^k)$, which is $O(4^n)$ if $i = j = n$. In fact, if we look at the way the recursive calls are generated, we find the pattern shown in Figure 8.2, which is identical to that obtained in the naive calculation of the binomial coefficient. To see this, imagine that any call $P(m, n)$ in the figure is replaced by $C(m + n, n)$.

Thus $P(i, j)$ is replaced by $C(i + j, j)$, $P(i - 1, j)$ by $C(i + j - 1, j)$, and $P(i, j - 1)$ by $C(i + j - 1, j - 1)$. Now the pattern of calls shown by the arrows corresponds to the calculation

$$C(i + j, j) = C(i + j - 1, j) + C(i + j - 1, j - 1)$$

of a binomial coefficient. The total number of recursive calls is therefore exactly $2\binom{i+j}{j} - 2$; see Problem 8.1. To calculate the probability $P(n, n)$ that team A will win given that the series has not yet started, the required time is thus in $\Omega\left(\binom{2n}{n}\right)$.

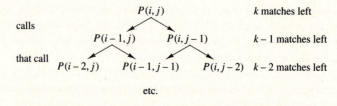

Figure 8.2. Recursive calls made by a call on $P(i, j)$

Problem 1.42 asks the reader to show that $\binom{2n}{n} \geq 4^n / (2n + 1)$. Combining these results, we see that the time required to calculate $P(n, n)$ is in $O(4^n)$ and in $\Omega(4^n / n)$. The method is therefore not practical for large values of n. (Although sporting competitions with $n > 4$ are the exception, this problem does have other applications!)

To speed up the algorithm, we proceed more or less as with Pascal's triangle: we declare an array of the appropriate size and then fill in the entries. This time, however, instead of filling the array line by line, we work diagonal by diagonal. Here is the algorithm to calculate $P(n, n)$.

```
function series(n, p)
    array P[0..n, 0..n]
    q ← 1 - p
    {Fill from top left to main diagonal}
    for s ← 1 to n do
        P[0, s] ← 1; P[s, 0] ← 0
        for k ← 1 to s - 1 do
            P[k, s - k] ← pP[k - 1, s - k] + qP[k, s - k - 1]
    {Fill from below main diagonal to bottom right}
    for s ← 1 to n do
        for k ← 0 to n - s do
            P[s + k, n - k] ← pP[s + k - 1, n - k] + qP[s + k, n - k - 1]
    return P[n, n]
```

Since the algorithm has to fill an $n \times n$ array, and since a constant time is required to calculate each entry, its execution time is in $\Theta(n^2)$. As with Pascal's triangle, it is easy to implement this algorithm so that storage space in $\Theta(n)$ is sufficient.

8.2 Making change (2)

Recall that the problem is to devise an algorithm for paying a given amount to a customer using the smallest possible number of coins. In Section 6.1 we described a greedy algorithm for this problem. Unfortunately, although the greedy algorithm is very efficient, it works only in a limited number of instances. With certain systems of coinage, or when coins of a particular denomination are missing or in short supply, the algorithm may either find a suboptimal answer, or not find an answer at all.

For example, suppose we live where there are coins for 1, 4 and 6 units. If we have to make change for 8 units, the greedy algorithm will propose doing so using one 6-unit coin and two 1-unit coins, for a total of three coins. However it is clearly possible to do better than this: we can give the customer his change using just two 4-unit coins. Although the greedy algorithm does not find this solution, it is easily obtained using dynamic programming.

As in the previous section, the crux of the method is to set up a table containing useful intermediate results that are then combined into the solution of the instance under consideration. Suppose the currency we are using has available coins of n different denominations. Let a coin of denomination i, $1 \le i \le n$, have value d_i units. We suppose, as is usual, that each $d_i > 0$. For the time being we shall also suppose that we have an unlimited supply of coins of each denomination. Finally suppose we have to give the customer coins worth N units, using as few coins as possible.

To solve this problem by dynamic programming, we set up a table $c[1..n, 0..N]$, with one row for each available denomination and one column for each amount from 0 units to N units. In this table $c[i, j]$ will be the minimum number of coins required to pay an amount of j units, $0 \le j \le N$, using only coins of denominations 1 to i, $1 \le i \le n$. The solution to the instance is therefore given by $c[n, N]$ if all we want to know is how many coins are needed. To fill in the table, note first that $c[i, 0]$ is zero for every value of i. After this initialization, the table can be filled either row by row from left to right, or column by column from top to bottom. To pay an amount j using coins of denominations 1 to i, we have in general two choices. First, we may choose not to use any coins of denomination i, even though this is now permitted, in which case $c[i, j] = c[i - 1, j]$. Alternatively, we may choose to use at least one coin of denomination i. In this case, once we have handed over the first coin of this denomination, there remains to be paid an amount of $j - d_i$ units. To pay this takes $c[i, j - d_i]$ coins, so $c[i, j] = 1 + c[i, j - d_i]$. Since we want to minimize the number of coins used, we choose whichever alternative is the better. In general therefore

$$c[i, j] = \min(c[i - 1, j], 1 + c[i, j - d_i]).$$

When $i = 1$ one of the elements to be compared falls outside the table. The same is true when $j < d_i$. It is convenient to think of such elements as having the value $+\infty$. If $i = 1$ and $j < d_1$, then both elements to be compared fall outside the table. In this case we set $c[i, j]$ to $+\infty$ to indicate that it is impossible to pay an amount j using only coins of type 1.

Figure 8.3 illustrates the instance given earlier, where we have to pay 8 units with coins worth 1, 4 and 6 units. For example, $c[3, 8]$ is obtained in this case as the smaller of $c[2, 8] = 2$ and $1 + c[3, 8 - d_3] = 1 + c[3, 2] = 3$. The entries elsewhere in the table are obtained similarly. The answer to this particular instance is that we can pay 8 units using only two coins. In fact the table gives us the solution to our problem for all the instances involving a payment of 8 units or less.

Amount:	0	1	2	3	4	5	6	7	8
$d_1 = 1$	0	1	2	3	4	5	6	7	8
$d_2 = 4$	0	1	2	3	1	2	3	4	2
$d_3 = 6$	0	1	2	3	1	2	1	2	2

Figure 8.3. Making change using dynamic programming

Here is a more formal version of the algorithm.

```
function coins(N)
    {Gives the minimum number of coins needed to make
     change for N units. Array d[1..n] specifies the coinage:
     in the example there are coins for 1, 4 and 6 units.}
    array d[1..n] = [1, 4, 6]
    array c[1..n, 0..N]
    for i ← 1 to n do c[i, 0] ← 0
    for i ← 1 to n do
        for j ← 1 to N do
            c[i, j] ← if i = 1 and j < d[i] then +∞
                      else if i = 1 then 1 + c[1, j - d[1]]    ← if have to use coin since smallest way available
                      else if j < d[i] then c[i - 1, j]        ← if can't use coin
                      else min(c[i - 1, j], 1 + c[i, j - d[i]]) ← if 2 ways, pick best
    return c[n, N]
```

If an unlimited supply of coins with a value of 1 unit is available, then we can always find a solution to our problem. If this is not the case, there may be values of N for which no solution is possible. This happens for instance if all the coins represent an even number of units, and we are required to pay an odd number of units. In such instances the algorithm returns the artificial result $+\infty$. Problem 8.9 invites the reader to modify the algorithm to handle a situation where the supply of coins of a particular denomination is limited.

Although the algorithm appears only to say how many coins are required to make change for a given amount, it is easy once the table c is constructed to discover exactly which coins are needed. Suppose we are to pay an amount j using coins of denominations $1, 2, \ldots, i$. Then the value of $c[i, j]$ says how many coins are needed. If $c[i, j] = c[i - 1, j]$, no coins of denomination i are necessary, and we move up to $c[i - 1, j]$ to see what to do next; if $c[i, j] = 1 + c[i, j - d_i]$, then we hand over one coin of denomination i, worth d_i, and move left to $c[i, j - d_i]$ to see what to do next. If $c[i - 1, j]$ and $1 + c[i, j - d_i]$ are both equal to $c[i, j]$, we may choose either course of action. Continuing in this way, we eventually arrive back at $c[0,0]$, and now there remains nothing to pay. This stage of the algorithm is essentially a greedy algorithm that bases its decisions on the information in the table, and never has to backtrack.

Analysis of the algorithm is straightforward. To see how many coins are needed to make change for N units when n different denominations are available, the algorithm has to fill up an $n \times (N + 1)$ array, so the execution time is in $\Theta(nN)$. To see which coins should be used, the search back from $c[n, N]$ to $c[0,0]$ makes $n - 1$ steps to the row above (corresponding to not using a coin of the current denomination) and $c[n, N]$ steps to the left (corresponding to handing over a coin). Since each of these steps can be made in constant time, the total time required is in $\Theta(n + c[n, N])$.

8.3 The principle of optimality

The solution to the problem of making change obtained by dynamic programming seems straightforward, and does not appear to hide any deep theoretical considerations. However it is important to realize that it relies on a useful principle called the *principle of optimality*, which in many settings appears so natural that it is invoked almost without thinking. This principle states that in an optimal sequence of decisions or choices, each subsequence must also be optimal. In our example, we took it for granted, when calculating $c[i, j]$ as the lesser of $c[i - 1, j]$ and $1 + c[i, j - d_i]$, that if $c[i, j]$ is the optimal way of making change for j units using coins of denominations 1 to i, then $c[i - 1, j]$ and $c[i, j - d_i]$ must also give the *optimal* solutions to the instances they represent. In other words, although the only value in the table that really interests us is $c[n, N]$, we took it for granted that all the other entries in the table must also represent optimal choices: and rightly so, for in this problem the principle of optimality applies.

Although this principle may appear obvious, it does not apply to every problem we might encounter. When the principle of optimality does *not* apply, it will probably not be possible to attack the problem in question using dynamic programming. This is the case, for instance, when a problem concerns the optimal use of limited resources. Here the optimal solution to an instance may not be obtained by combining the optimal solutions to two or more subinstances, if the resources used in these subsolutions add up to more than the total resources available.

For example, if the shortest route from Montreal to Toronto passes through Kingston, then that part of the journey from Montreal to Kingston must also follow the shortest possible route, as must the part of the journey from Kingston to Toronto. Thus the principle of optimality applies. However if the fastest way to drive from Montreal to Toronto takes us through Kingston, it does not necessarily follow that it is best to drive as fast as possible from Montreal to Kingston, and then to drive as fast as possible from Kingston to Toronto. If we use too much petrol on the first half of the trip, we may have to fill up somewhere on the second half, losing more time than we gained by driving hard. The sub-trips from Montreal to Kingston, and from Kingston to Toronto, are not independent, since they share a resource, so choosing an optimal solution for one sub-trip may prevent our using an optimal solution for the other. In this situation, the principle of optimality does not apply.

For a second example, consider the problem of finding not the shortest, but the longest simple route between two cities, using a given set of roads. A *simple* route is one that never visits the same spot twice, so this condition rules out infinite routes round and round a loop. If we know that the longest simple route from Montreal to Toronto passes through Kingston, it does *not* follow that it can be obtained by taking the longest simple route from Montreal to Kingston, and then the longest simple route from Kingston to Toronto. It is too much to expect that when these two simple routes are spliced together, the resulting route will also be simple. Once again, the principle of optimality does not apply.

Nevertheless, the principle of optimality applies more often than not. When it does, it can be restated as follows: the optimal solution to any nontrivial instance of a problem is a combination of optimal solutions to *some* of its subinstances. The difficulty in turning this principle into an algorithm is that it is not usually obvious which subinstances are relevant to the instance under consideration. Coming back to the example of finding the shortest route, how can we tell whether the subinstance consisting of finding the shortest route from Montreal to Ottawa is relevant when we want the shortest route from Montreal to Toronto? This difficulty prevents our using an approach similar to divide-and-conquer starting from the original instance and recursively finding optimal solutions to the relevant subinstances, and only to these. Instead, dynamic programming efficiently solves every subinstance to figure out which ones are in fact relevant; only then are these combined into an optimal solution to the original instance.

8.4 The knapsack problem (2)

As in Section 6.5, we are given a number of objects and a knapsack. This time, however, we suppose that the objects may *not* be broken into smaller pieces, so we may decide either to take an object or to leave it behind, but we may not take a fraction of an object. For $i = 1, 2, \ldots, n$, suppose that object i has a positive weight w_i and a positive value v_i. The knapsack can carry a weight not exceeding W. Our aim is again to fill the knapsack in a way that maximizes the value of the included objects, while respecting the capacity constraint. Let x_i be 0 if we elect not to take object i, or 1 if we include object i. In symbols the new problem may be stated as:

$$\text{maximize } \sum_{i=1}^{n} x_i v_i \quad \text{subject to } \sum_{i=1}^{n} x_i w_i \leq W$$

where $v_i > 0$, $w_i > 0$ and $x_i \in \{0, 1\}$ for $1 \leq i \leq n$. Here the conditions on v_i and w_i are constraints on the instance; those on x_i are constraints on the solution. Since the problem closely resembles the one in Section 6.5, it is natural to enquire first whether a slightly modified version of the greedy algorithm we used before will still work. Suppose then that we adapt the algorithm in the obvious way, so that it looks at the objects in order of decreasing value per unit weight. If the knapsack is not full, the algorithm should select a *complete* object if possible before going on to the next.

Unfortunately the greedy algorithm turns out not to work when x_i is required to be 0 or 1. For example, suppose we have three objects available, the first of which

not optimal

combine
∴ not simple

weighs 6 units and has a value of 8, while the other two weigh 5 units each and have a value of 5 each. If the knapsack can carry 10 units, then the optimal load includes the two lighter objects for a total value of 10. The greedy algorithm, on the other hand, would begin by choosing the object that weighs 6 units, since this is the one with the greatest value per unit weight. However if objects cannot be broken the algorithm will be unable to use the remaining capacity in the knapsack. The load it produces therefore consists of just one object with a value of only 8.

To solve the problem by dynamic programming, we set up a table $V[1..n, 0..W]$, with one row for each available object, and one column for each weight from 0 to W. In the table, $V[i, j]$ will be the maximum value of the objects we can transport if the weight limit is j, $0 \le j \le W$, and if we only include objects numbered from 1 to i, $1 \le i \le n$. The solution of the instance can therefore be found in $V[n, W]$.

The parallel with the problem of making change is close. As there, the principle of optimality applies. We may fill in the table either row by row or column by column. In the general situation, $V[i, j]$ is the larger (since we are trying to maximize value) of $V[i - 1, j]$ and $V[i - 1, j - w_i] + v_i$. The first of these choices corresponds to not adding object i to the load. The second corresponds to choosing object i, which has for effect to increase the value of the load by v_i and to reduce the capacity available by w_i. Thus we fill in the entries in the table using the general rule

$$V[i, j] = \max(V[i - 1, j], V[i - 1, j - w_i] + v_i).$$

For the out-of-bounds entries we define $V[0, j]$ to be 0 when $j \ge 0$, and we define $V[i, j]$ to be $-\infty$ for all i when $j < 0$. The formal statement of the algorithm, which closely resembles the function *coins* of the previous section, is left as an exercise for the reader; see Problem 8.11.

Figure 8.4 gives an example of the operation of the algorithm. In the figure there are five objects, whose weights are respectively 1, 2, 5, 6 and 7 units, and whose values are 1, 6, 18, 22 and 28. Their values per unit weight are thus 1.00, 3.00, 3.60, 3.67 and 4.00. If we can carry a maximum of 11 units of weight, then the table shows that we can compose a load whose value is 40.

object Weight limit:	0	1	2	3	4	5	6	7	8	9	10	11
1 $w_1 = 1, v_1 = 1$	0	1	1	1	1	1	1	1	1	1	1	1
2 $w_2 = 2, v_2 = 6$	0	1	6	7	7	7	7	7	7	7	7	7
3 $w_3 = 5, v_3 = 18$	0	1	6	7	7	18	19	24	25	25	25	25
4 $w_4 = 6, v_4 = 22$	0	1	6	7	7	18	22	24	28	29	29	40
5 $w_5 = 7, v_5 = 28$	0	1	6	7	7	18	22	28	29	34	35	40

Figure 8.4. The knapsack using dynamic programming

Just as for the problem of making change, the table V allows us to recover not only the value of the optimal load we can carry, but also its composition. In our example, we begin by looking at $V[5, 11]$. Since $V[5, 11] = V[4, 11]$ but $V[5, 11] \ne V[4, 11 - w_5] + v_5$, an optimal load cannot include object 5. Next $V[4, 11] \ne V[3, 11]$

but $V[4, 11] = V[3, 11 - w_4] + v_4$, so an optimal load must include object 4. Now $V[3, 5] \neq V[2, 5]$ but $V[3, 5] = V[2, 5 - w_3] + v_3$, so we must include object 3. Continuing thus, we find that $V[2, 0] = V[1, 0]$ and $V[1, 0] = V[0, 0]$, so the optimal load includes neither object 2 nor object 1. In this instance, therefore, there is only one optimal load, consisting of objects 3 and 4.

In this example the greedy algorithm would first consider object 5, since this has the greatest value per unit weight. The knapsack can carry one such object. Next the greedy algorithm would consider object 4, whose value per unit weight is next highest. This object cannot be included in the load without violating the capacity constraint. Continuing in this way, the greedy algorithm would look at objects 3, 2 and 1, in that order, finally ending up with a load consisting of objects 5, 2 and 1, for a total value of 35. Once again we see that the greedy algorithm does not work when objects cannot be broken.

Analysis of the dynamic programming algorithm is straightforward, and closely parallels the analysis of the algorithm for making change. We find that a time in $\Theta(nW)$ is necessary to construct the table V, and that the composition of the optimal load can then be determined in a time in $O(n + W)$.

8.5 Shortest paths

Let $G = \langle N, A \rangle$ be a directed graph; N is the set of nodes and A is the set of edges. Each edge has an associated nonnegative length. We want to calculate the length of the shortest path between each pair of nodes. Compare this to Section 6.4 where we were looking for the length of the shortest paths from one particular node, the source, to all the others.

As before, suppose the nodes of G are numbered from 1 to n, so $N = \{1, 2, \dots, n\}$, and suppose a matrix L gives the length of each edge, with $L[i, i] = 0$ for $i = 1, 2, \dots, n$, $L[i, j] \geq 0$ for all i and j, and $L[i, j] = \infty$ if the edge (i, j) does not exist.

The principle of optimality applies: if k is a node on the shortest path from i to j, then the part of the path from i to k, and the part from k to j, must also be optimal.

We construct a matrix D that gives the length of the shortest path between each pair of nodes. The algorithm initializes D to L, that is, to the direct distances between nodes. It then does n iterations. After iteration k, D gives the length of the shortest paths that only use nodes in $\{1, 2, \dots, k\}$ as intermediate nodes. After n iterations, D therefore gives the length of the shortest paths using any of the nodes in N as an intermediate node, which is the result we want. At iteration k, the algorithm must check for each pair of nodes (i, j) whether or not there exists a path from i to j passing through node k that is better than the present optimal path passing only through nodes in $\{1, 2, \dots, k - 1\}$. If D_k represents the matrix D after the k–th iteration (so $D_0 = L$), the necessary check can be implemented by

$$D_k[i, j] = \min(D_{k-1}[i, j], D_{k-1}[i, k] + D_{k-1}[k, j]),$$

where we use the principle of optimality to compute the length of the shortest path from i to j passing through k. We have also tacitly used the fact that an optimal path through k does not visit k twice.

At the k–th iteration the values in the k–th row and the k–th column of D do not change, since $D[k,k]$ is always zero. It is therefore not necessary to protect these values when updating D. This allows us to get away with using only a single $n \times n$ matrix D, whereas at first sight it might seem necessary to use two such matrices, one containing the values of D_{k-1} and the other the values of D_k, or even a matrix $n \times n \times n$.

The algorithm, known as *Floyd's algorithm*, follows.

function $Floyd(L[1..n, 1..n])$: **array** $[1..n, 1..n]$
    array $D[1..n, 1..n]$
    $D \leftarrow L$
    for $k \leftarrow 1$ **to** n **do**
        for $i \leftarrow 1$ **to** n **do**
            for $j \leftarrow 1$ **to** n **do**
                $D[i,j] \leftarrow \min(D[i,j], D[i,k]+D[k,j])$
    return D

Figure 8.5 gives an example of the way the algorithm works.

$$D_0 = L = \begin{pmatrix} 0 & 5 & \infty & \infty \\ 50 & 0 & 15 & 5 \\ 30 & \infty & 0 & 15 \\ 15 & \infty & 5 & 0 \end{pmatrix}$$

$$D_1 = \begin{pmatrix} 0 & 5 & \infty & \infty \\ 50 & 0 & 15 & 5 \\ 30 & 35 & 0 & 15 \\ 15 & 20 & 5 & 0 \end{pmatrix} \qquad D_2 = \begin{pmatrix} 0 & 5 & 20 & 10 \\ 50 & 0 & 15 & 5 \\ 30 & 35 & 0 & 15 \\ 15 & 20 & 5 & 0 \end{pmatrix}$$

$$D_3 = \begin{pmatrix} 0 & 5 & 20 & 10 \\ 45 & 0 & 15 & 5 \\ 30 & 35 & 0 & 15 \\ 15 & 20 & 5 & 0 \end{pmatrix} \qquad D_4 = \begin{pmatrix} 0 & 5 & 15 & 10 \\ 20 & 0 & 10 & 5 \\ 30 & 35 & 0 & 15 \\ 15 & 20 & 5 & 0 \end{pmatrix}$$

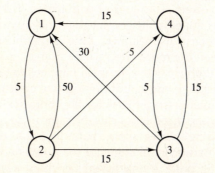

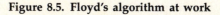

Figure 8.5. Floyd's algorithm at work

√It is obvious that this algorithm takes a time in $\Theta(n^3)$. We can also use Dijkstra's algorithm to solve the same problem; see Section 6.4. In this case we have to apply the algorithm n times, each time choosing a different node as the source. If we use the version of Dijkstra's algorithm that works with a matrix of distances, the total computation time is in $n \times \Theta(n^2)$, that is, in $\Theta(n^3)$. The order is the same as for Floyd's algorithm, but the simplicity of the latter means that it will probably have a smaller hidden constant and thus be faster in practice. Compilers are good at optimizing **for**-loops, too. On the other hand, if we use the version of Dijkstra's algorithm that works with a heap, and hence with lists of the distances to adjacent nodes, the total time is in $n \times \Theta((a + n)\log n)$, that is, in $\Theta((an + n^2)\log n)$, where a is the number of edges in the graph. If the graph is sparse ($a \ll n^2$), it may be preferable to use Dijkstra's algorithm n times; if the graph is dense ($a \approx n^2$), it is better to use Floyd's algorithm.

We usually want to know where the shortest path goes, not just its length. In this case we use a second matrix P, all of whose elements are initialized to 0. The innermost loop of the algorithm becomes

if $D[i,k]+D[k,j]< D[i,j]$ **then** $D[i,j] \leftarrow D[i,k]+D[k,j]$
$$P[i,j] \leftarrow k$$

When the algorithm stops, $P[i,j]$ contains the number of the last iteration that caused a change in $D[i,j]$. To recover the shortest path from i to j, look at $P[i,j]$. If $P[i,j]= 0$, then $D[i,j]$ never changed, and the shortest path is directly along the edge (i,j); otherwise, if $P[i,j]= k$, the shortest path from i to j passes through k. Look recursively at $P[i,k]$ and $P[k,j]$ to find any other intermediate nodes along the shortest path.

If we take the graph of Figure 8.5 as an example, P becomes

$$P = \begin{pmatrix} 0 & 0 & 4 & 2 \\ 4 & 0 & 4 & 0 \\ 0 & 1 & 0 & 0 \\ 0 & 1 & 0 & 0 \end{pmatrix}.$$

Since $P[1,3]= 4$, the shortest path from 1 to 3 passes through 4. Looking now at $P[1,4]$ and $P[4,3]$, we discover that between 1 and 4 we have to go via 2, but that from 4 to 3 we proceed directly. Finally we see that the trips from 1 to 2, and from 2 to 4, are also direct. The shortest path from 1 to 3 is thus 1, 2, 4, 3.

If we allow edges in the graph to have negative lengths, the notion of "shortest path" loses much of its meaning: if the graph includes a cycle whose total length is negative, then the more often we go round the negative cycle, the shorter our path will be! Problem 8.17 asks what happens to Floyd's algorithm if we give it a graph with negative edges, but no negative cycles. Even if a graph has negative cycles, it still makes sense to ask for the shortest simple paths. (Remember that a simple path is one that never visits the same node twice.) No efficient algorithm is known for finding shortest simple paths in graphs that may have edges of negative length. The situation is the same for the problem of finding longest simple paths, mentioned in Section 8.3: no efficient algorithm is known. These problems are both $\mathcal{NP}$–complete; see Chapter 12.

8.6 Chained matrix multiplication

Recall that the product C of a $p \times q$ matrix A and a $q \times r$ matrix B is the $p \times r$ matrix given by

$$c_{ij} = \sum_{k=1}^{q} a_{ik}b_{kj}, \qquad 1 \le i \le p, 1 \le j \le r.$$

Algorithmically, we can express this as

> **for** $i \leftarrow 1$ **to** p **do**
>> **for** $j \leftarrow 1$ **to** r **do**
>>> $C[i,j] \leftarrow 0$
>>> **for** $k \leftarrow 1$ **to** q **do**
>>>> $C[i,j] \leftarrow C[i,j] + A[i,k]B[k,j]$

from which it is clear that a total of pqr scalar multiplications are required to calculate the matrix product using this algorithm. (In this section we shall not consider the possibility of using a better matrix multiplication algorithm, such as Strassen's algorithm, described in Section 7.6.)

Suppose now we want to calculate the product of more than two matrices. Matrix multiplication is associative, so we can compute the matrix product

$$M = M_1 M_2 \cdots M_n$$

in a number of ways, which all give the same answer:

$$\begin{aligned}
M &= (\cdots ((M_1 M_2) M_3) \cdots M_n) \\
&= (M_1 (M_2 (M_3 \cdots (M_{n-1} M_n) \cdots))) \\
&= (\cdots ((M_1 M_2)(M_3 M_4)) \cdots),
\end{aligned}$$

and so on. However matrix multiplication is not commutative, so we are not allowed to change the order of the matrices in these arrangements.

The choice of a method of computation can have a considerable influence on the time required. Suppose, for example, that we want to calculate the product $ABCD$ of four matrices, where A is 13×5, B is 5×89, C is 89×3, and D is 3×34. To measure the efficiency of the different methods, we count the number of scalar multiplications involved. As programmed above, there will be an equal number of scalar additions, plus some housekeeping, so the number of scalar multiplications is a good indicator of overall efficiency. For instance, using $M = ((AB)C)D$, we calculate successively

$$\begin{array}{rl}
AB & 5785 \text{ multiplications} \\
(AB)C & 3471 \text{ multiplications} \\
((AB)C)D & 1326 \text{ multiplications}
\end{array}$$

for a total of $10\,582$ scalar multiplications. There are five essentially different ways of calculating the product in this case: when the product is expressed as $(AB)(CD)$, we do not differentiate between the method that calculates AB first and CD second, and the one that starts with CD and then calculates AB, since they both require the same number of multiplications. For each of these five methods, here is the corresponding number of scalar multiplications:

$$
\begin{array}{ll}
((AB)C)D & 10\,582 \\
(AB)(CD) & 54\,201 \\
(A(BC))D & 2\,856 \\
A((BC)D) & 4\,055 \\
A(B(CD)) & 26\,418
\end{array}
$$

The most efficient method is almost 19 times faster than the slowest.

To find directly the best way to calculate the product, we could simply parenthesize the expression in every possible fashion and count each time how many scalar multiplications are required. Let $T(n)$ be the number of essentially different ways to parenthesize a product of n matrices. Suppose we decide to make the first cut between the i–th and the $(i + 1)$–st matrices of the product, thus:

$$M = (M_1 M_2 \cdots M_i)(M_{i+1} M_{i+2} \cdots M_n).$$

There are now $T(i)$ ways to parenthesize the left-hand term and $T(n - i)$ ways to parenthesize the right-hand term. Any of the former may be combined with any of the latter, so for this particular value of i there are $T(i)T(n - i)$ ways of parenthesizing the whole expression. Since i can take any value from 1 to $n - 1$, we obtain finally the following recurrence for $T(n)$:

$$T(n) = \sum_{i=1}^{n-1} T(i)T(n - i).$$

Adding the obvious initial condition $T(1) = 1$, we can use the recurrence to calculate any required value of T. The following table gives some values of $T(n)$.

n	1	2	3	4	5	10	15
$T(n)$	1	1	2	5	14	4862	2674440

The values of $T(n)$ are called the *Catalan numbers*.

For each way that parentheses can be inserted in the expression for M, it takes a time in $\Omega(n)$ to count the number of scalar multiplications required (at least, if we do not try to be subtle). Since $T(n)$ is in $\Omega(4^n/n^2)$ (combine the results of Problems 8.24 and 1.42), finding the best way to calculate M using the direct approach requires a time in $\Omega(4^n/n)$. This method is therefore impracticable for large values of n: there are too many ways in which parentheses can be inserted for us to look at them all.

A little experimenting shows that none of the obvious greedy algorithms will allow us to compute matrix products in an optimal way; see Problem 8.20. Fortunately, the principle of optimality applies to this problem. For instance, if the best way of multiplying all the matrices requires us to make the first cut between the i–th and the $(i + 1)$–st matrices of the product, then both the subproducts $M_1 M_2 \cdots M_i$ and $M_{i+1} M_{i+2} \cdots M_n$ must also be calculated in an optimal way. This suggests that we should consider using dynamic programming. We construct a table m_{ij}, $1 \leq i \leq j \leq n$, where m_{ij} gives the optimal solution—that is, the required number of scalar multiplications—for the part $M_i M_{i+1} \cdots M_j$ of the required product. The solution to the original problem is thus given by m_{1n}.

Suppose the dimensions of the matrices are given by a vector $d[0..n]$ such that the matrix M_i, $1 \leq i \leq n$, is of dimension $d_{i-1} \times d_i$. We build the table m_{ij} diagonal by diagonal: diagonal s contains the elements m_{ij} such that $j - i = s$. The diagonal $s = 0$ therefore contains the elements m_{ii}, $1 \leq i \leq n$, corresponding to the "products" M_i. Here there is no multiplication to be done, so $m_{ii} = 0$ for every i. The diagonal $s = 1$ contains the elements $m_{i,i+1}$ corresponding to products of the ✓ form $M_i M_{i+1}$. Here we have no choice but to compute the product directly, which we can do using $d_{i-1} d_i d_{i+1}$ scalar multiplications, as we saw at the beginning of the section. Finally when $s > 1$ the diagonal s contains the elements $m_{i,i+s}$ corresponding to products of the form $M_i M_{i+1} \cdots M_{i+s}$. Now we have a choice: we can make the first cut in the product after any of the matrices $M_i, M_{i+1}, \ldots, M_{i+s-1}$. If we make the cut after M_k, $i \leq k < i + s$, we need m_{ik} scalar multiplications to calculate the left-hand term, $m_{k+1,i+s}$ to calculate the right-hand term, and then $d_{i-1} d_k d_{i+s}$ to multiply the two resulting matrices to obtain the final result. To find the optimum, we choose the cut that minimizes the required number of scalar multiplications.

Summing up, we fill the table m_{ij} using the following rules for $s = 0, 1, \ldots, n - 1$.

$$
\begin{aligned}
s = 0: \quad & m_{ii} && = 0 && i = 1, 2, \ldots, n \\
s = 1: \quad & m_{i,i+1} && = d_{i-1} d_i d_{i+1} && i = 1, 2, \ldots, n - 1 \\
1 < s < n: \quad & m_{i,i+s} && = \min_{i \leq k < i+s} (m_{ik} + m_{k+1,i+s} + d_{i-1} d_k d_{i+s}) && \\
& && && i = 1, 2, \ldots, n - s
\end{aligned}
$$

It is only for clarity that the second case need be written out explicitly, as it falls under the general case with $s = 1$.

To apply this to the example, we want to calculate the product $ABCD$ of four matrices, where A is 13×5, B is 5×89, C is 89×3, and D is 3×34. The vector d is therefore $(13, 5, 89, 3, 34)$. For $s = 1$, we find $m_{12} = 5785$, $m_{23} = 1335$ and $m_{34} = 9078$. Next, for $s = 2$ we obtain

$$
\begin{aligned}
m_{13} &= \min(m_{11} + m_{23} + 13 \times 5 \times 3, m_{12} + m_{33} + 13 \times 89 \times 3) \\
&= \min(1530, 9256) = 1530 \\
m_{24} &= \min(m_{22} + m_{34} + 5 \times 89 \times 34, m_{23} + m_{44} + 5 \times 3 \times 34) \\
&= \min(24208, 1845) = 1845.
\end{aligned}
$$

Finally for $s = 3$

$$
\begin{aligned}
m_{14} = \min(& m_{11} + m_{24} + 13 \times 5 \times 34, && \{k = 1\} \\
& m_{12} + m_{34} + 13 \times 89 \times 34, && \{k = 2\} \\
& m_{13} + m_{44} + 13 \times 3 \times 34) && \{k = 3\} \\
= \min(& 4055, 54201, 2856) = 2856.
\end{aligned}
$$

The complete array m is shown in Figure 8.6.

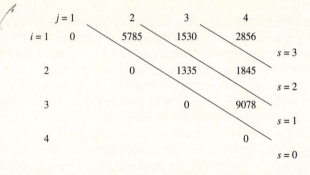

Figure 8.6. An example of the chained matrix multiplication algorithm

Once again, we usually want to know not just the number of scalar multiplications necessary to compute the product M, but also how to perform this computation efficiently. As in Section 8.5, we do this by adding a second array to keep track of the choices we have made. Let this new array be $bestk$. Now when we compute m_{ij}, we save in $bestk[i, j]$ the value of k that corresponds to the minimum term among those compared. When the algorithm stops, $bestk[1, n]$ tells us where to make the first cut in the product. Proceeding recursively on both the terms thus produced, we can reconstruct the optimal way of parenthesizing M. Problems 8.21 and 8.22 invite you to fill in the details.

For $s > 0$ there are $n - s$ elements to be computed in the diagonal s; for each of these we must choose between s possibilities given by the different values of k. The execution time of the algorithm is therefore in the exact order of

$$\sum_{s=1}^{n-1} (n - s)s = n \sum_{s=1}^{n-1} s - \sum_{s=1}^{n-1} s^2$$
$$= n^2(n - 1)/2 - n(n - 1)(2n - 1)/6$$
$$= (n^3 - n)/6,$$

where we used Propositions 1.7.14 and 1.7.15 to evaluate the sums. The execution time of the algorithm is thus in $\Theta(n^3)$, better algorithms exist.

8.7 Approaches using recursion

Although dynamic programming algorithms, such as the one just given for calculating m, are efficient, there is something unsatisfactory about the bottom-up approach. A top-down method, whether it be divide-and-conquer, stepwise refinement, or recursion, seems more natural, especially to one who has been taught always to develop programs in this way. A better reason is that the bottom-up approach leads us to compute values that might be completely irrelevant. It is tempting, therefore, to see whether we can achieve the same efficiency in a top-down version of the algorithm.

We illustrate this with the matrix multiplication problem described in the previous section. One simple line of attack is to replace the table m by a function fm, which is calculated as required. In other words, we would like to find a function

fm such that $fm(i, j) = m_{ij}$ for $1 \leq i \leq j \leq n$, but that can be calculated recursively, unlike the table m, which we calculated bottom-up.

Writing such a function is simple: all we have to do is to program the rules for calculating m.

> **function** $fm(i, j)$
>   **if** $i = j$ **then** {only one matrix is involved}
>   **return** 0
> $m \leftarrow \infty$
>   **for** $k \leftarrow i$ **to** $j - 1$ **do**
> $m \leftarrow \min(m, fm(i, k) + fm(k + 1, j) + d[i - 1]d[k]d[j])$
>   **return** m

$(M_i)(M_{i+1} \cdots M_j)$
$(M_i \cdot M_{i+1})(M_{i+2} \cdots M_j)$

Here the global array $d[0..n]$ gives the dimensions of the matrices involved, exactly as before. For all the relevant values of k the intervals $[i..k]$ and $[k + 1..j]$ concerned in the recursive calls involve less matrices than $[i..j]$. However each recursive call still involves at least one matrix (provided of course $i \leq j$ on the original call). Eventually therefore the recursion will stop. To find how many scalar multiplications are needed to calculate $M = M_1 M_2 \ldots M_n$, we simply call $fm(1, n)$.

To analyse this algorithm, let $T(s)$ be the time required to execute a call of $fm(i, i + s)$, where s is the number of matrix multiplications involved in the corresponding product. This is the same s used previously to number the diagonals of the table m. Clearly $T(0) = c$ for some constant c. When $s > 0$, we have to choose the smallest among s terms, each of the form

$$fm(i, k) + fm(k + 1, i + s) + d[i - 1]d[k]d[i + s], \quad i \leq k < i + s.$$

Let b be a constant such that we can execute two scalar multiplications, six scalar additions, a comparison with the previous value of the minimum, and any necessary housekeeping in a time b. Now the time required to evaluate one of these terms is $T(k - i) + T(i + s - k - 1) + b$. The total time $T(s)$ required to evaluate $fm(i, i + s)$ is therefore

$$T(s) = \sum_{k=i}^{i+s-1} (T(k - i) + T(i + s - k - 1) + b).$$

Writing $m = k - i$, this becomes

$$T(s) = \sum_{m=0}^{s-1} (T(m) + T(s - 1 - m) + b)$$

$$= sb + 2 \sum_{m=0}^{s-1} T(m).$$

Since this implies that $T(s) \geq 2T(s - 1)$, we see immediately that $T(s) \geq 2^s T(0)$, so the algorithm certainly takes a time in $\Omega(2^n)$ to find the best way to multiply n matrices. It therefore cannot be competitive with the algorithm using dynamic programming, which takes a time in $\Theta(n^3)$.

The algorithm can be speeded up if we are clever enough to avoid recursive calls when $d[i-1]d[k]d[i+s]$ is already greater than the previous value of the minimum. The improvement will depend on the instance, but is most unlikely to make an algorithm that takes exponential time competitive with one that only takes polynomial time.

To find an upper bound on the time taken by the recursive algorithm, we use constructive induction. Looking at the form of the recursion for T, and remembering that $T(s) \geq 2^s T(0)$, it seems possible that T might be bounded by a power of some constant larger than 2: so let us try proving $T(s) \leq a3^s$, for some appropriate constant a. Take this as the induction hypothesis, and assume it is true for all $m < s$. On substituting in the recurrence we obtain

$$T(s) \leq sd + 2 \sum_{m=0}^{s-1} a3^m$$
$$= sd + a3^s - a,$$

where we used Proposition 1.7.10 to compute the sum. Unfortunately, this does not allow us to conclude that $T(s) \leq a3^s$. However, if we adopt the tactic recommended in Section 1.6.4 and strengthen the induction hypothesis, things work better. As the strengthened induction hypothesis, suppose $T(m) \leq a3^m - b$ for $m < s$, where b is a new unknown constant. Now when we substitute into the recurrence we obtain

$$T(s) \leq sd + 2 \sum_{m=0}^{s-1} (a3^m - b)$$
$$= s(d - 2b) + a3^s - a.$$

This is sufficient to ensure that $T(s) \leq a3^s - b$ provided $b \geq d/2$ and $a \geq b$. To start the induction, we require that $T(0) \leq a - b$, which is satisfied provided $a \geq T(0) + b$. Summing up, we have proved that $T(s) \leq a3^m - b$ for all s provided $b \geq d/2$ and $a \geq T(0) + b$. The time taken by the recursive algorithm to find the best way of computing a product of n matrices is therefore in $O(3^n)$.

We conclude that a call on the recursive function $fm(1, n)$ is faster than naively trying all possible ways to parenthesize the desired product, which, as we saw, takes a time in $\Omega(4^n/n)$. However it is slower than the dynamic programming algorithm described previously. This illustrates a point made earlier in this chapter. To decide the best way to parenthesize the product $ABCDEFG$, say, fm recursively solves 12 subinstances, including the overlapping $ABCDEF$ and $BCDEFG$, both of which recursively solve $BCDEF$ from scratch. It is this duplication of effort that makes fm inefficient.

8.8 Memory functions

The algorithm in the previous section is not the first we have seen where a simple recursive formulation of a solution leads to an inefficient program, as common subinstances are solved independently more than once. Dynamic programming allows us to avoid this at the cost of complicating the algorithm. In dynamic programming, too, we may have to solve some irrelevant subinstances, since it is only later that we know exactly which subsolutions are needed. A top-down, recursive algorithm does not have this drawback. Can we perhaps combine the advantages of both techniques, and retain the simplicity of a recursive formulation without losing the efficiency offered by dynamic programming?

One easy way of doing this that works in many situations is to use a *memory function*. To the recursive program we add a table of the necessary size. Initially, all the entries in this table hold a special value to show they have not yet been calculated. Thereafter, whenever we call the function, we first look in the table to see whether it has already been evaluated with the same set of parameters. If so, we return the value in the table. If not, we go ahead and calculate the function. Before returning the calculated value, however, we save it at the appropriate place in the table. In this way it is never necessary to calculate the function twice for the same values of its parameters.

For the recursive algorithm *fm* of Section 8.7, let *mtab* be a table whose entries are all initialized to -1 (since the number of scalar multiplications required to compute a matrix product cannot be negative). The following reformulation of the function *fm*, which uses the table *mtab* as a global variable, combines the clarity of a recursive formulation with the efficiency of dynamic programming.

> **function** *fm-mem*(i, j)
>   **if** $i = j$ **then return** 0
>   **if** $mtab[i, j] \geq 0$ **then return** $mtab[i, j]$ ← lookup value already computed
> $m \leftarrow \infty$
>   **for** $k \leftarrow i$ **to** $j - 1$ **do** ← recursive calls
> $m \leftarrow \min(m, fm\text{-}mem(i, k) + fm\text{-}mem(k + 1, j)$
> $+ d[i - 1]d[k]d[j])$
> $mtab[i, j] \leftarrow m$ ← save computed value in table
>   **return** m

(marginalia: normal recursion brackets the m ← ∞ and for loop)

As pointed out in Section 8.7, this function may be speeded up by avoiding the recursive calls if $d[i - 1]d[k]d[j]$ is already larger than the previous value of m.

We sometimes have to pay a price for using this technique. We saw in Section 8.1.1, for instance, that we can calculate a binomial coefficient $\binom{n}{k}$ using a time in $\Theta(nk)$ and space in $\Theta(k)$. Implemented using a memory function, the calculation takes the same amount of time but needs space in $\Omega(nk)$; see Problem 8.26.

If we use a little more space—the space needed is only multiplied by a constant factor—we can avoid the initialization time needed to set all the entries of the table to some special value. This can be done using *virtual initialization*, described in Section 5.1. This is particularly desirable when only a few values of the function are to be calculated, but we do not know in advance which ones. For an example, see Section 9.1.

8.9 Problems

Problem 8.1.   Prove that the total number of recursive calls made during the computation of $C(n, k)$ using the algorithm of Section 8.1.1 is exactly $2\binom{n}{k} - 2$.

Problem 8.2.   Calculating the Fibonacci sequence affords another example of the kind of technique introduced in Section 8.1. Which algorithm in Section 2.7.5 uses dynamic programming?

Problem 8.3.   Prove that the time needed to calculate $P(n, n)$ using the function P of Section 8.1.2 is in $\Theta(4^n / \sqrt{n})$.

Problem 8.4.   Using the algorithm *series* of Section 8.1.2, calculate the probability that team A will win the series if $p = 0.45$ and if four victories are needed to win.

Problem 8.5.   Repeat the previous problem with $p = 0.55$. What should be the relation between the answers to the two problems?

Problem 8.6.   As in Problem 8.4, calculate the probability that team A will win the series if $p = 0.45$ and if four victories are needed to win. This time, however, calculate the required probability directly as the probability that team A will win 4 or more out of a series of 7 games. (Playing extra games after team A have won the series cannot change the result.)

Problem 8.7.   Adapt algorithm *series* of Section 8.1.2 to the case where team A win any given match with probability p and lose it with probability q, but there is also a probability r that the match is tied, so it counts as a win for nobody. Assume that n victories are still required to win the series. Of course we must have $p + q + r = 1$.

Problem 8.8.   Show that storage space in $\Theta(n)$ is sufficient to implement the algorithm *series* of Section 8.1.2.

Problem 8.9.   Adapt the algorithm *coins* of Section 8.2 so it will work correctly even when the number of coins of a particular denomination is limited.

Problem 8.10.   Rework the example illustrated in Figure 8.4, but renumbering the objects in the opposite order (so $w_1 = 7$, $v_1 = 28$, ..., $w_5 = 1$, $v_5 = 1$). Which elements of the table should remain unchanged?

Problem 8.11.   Write out the algorithm for filling the table V as described in Section 8.4.

Problem 8.12.   When $j < w_i$ in the algorithm for filling the table V described in Section 8.4, we take $V[i - 1, j - w_i]$ to be $-\infty$. Can the finished table contain entries that are $-\infty$? If so, what do they indicate? If not, why not?

Problem 8.13.   There may be more than one optimal solution to an instance of the knapsack problem. Using the table V described in Section 8.4, can you find all possible optimal solutions to an instance, or only one? If so, how? If not, why not?

Problem 8.14.   An instance of the knapsack problem described in Section 8.4 may have several different optimal solutions. How would you discover this? Does the table V allow you to recover more than one solution in this case?

Problem 8.15.   In Section 8.4 we assumed that we had available n objects numbered 1 to n. Suppose instead that we have n *types* of object available, with an adequate supply of each type. Formally, this simply replaces the constraint that x_i must be 0 or 1 by the looser constraint that x_i must be a nonnegative integer. Adapt the dynamic programming algorithm of Section 8.4 so it will handle this new problem.

Problem 8.16.   Adapt your algorithm of Problem 8.15 so it will work even when the number of objects of a given type is limited.

Problem 8.17.   Does Floyd's algorithm (see Section 8.5) work on a graph that has some edges whose lengths are negative, but that does not include a negative cycle? Justify your answer.

Problem 8.18. (Warshall's algorithm)   As for Floyd's algorithm (see Section 8.5) we are concerned with finding paths in a graph. In this case, however, the length of the edges is of no interest; only their existence is important. Let the matrix L be such that $L[i, j] = true$ if the edge (i, j) exists, and $L[i, j] = false$ otherwise. We want to find a matrix D such that $D[i, j] = true$ if there exists at least one path from i to j, and $D[i, j] = false$ otherwise. Adapt Floyd's algorithm for this slightly different case.
Note: We are looking for the *reflexive transitive closure* of the graph in question.

Problem 8.19.   Find a significantly better algorithm for the preceding problem in the case when the matrix L is symmetric, that is, when $L[i, j] = L[j, i]$.

Problem 8.20.   We (vainly) hope to find a greedy algorithm for the chained matrix multiplication problem; see Section 8.6. Suppose we are to calculate

$$M = M_1 M_2 \cdots M_n,$$

where matrix M_i is $d_{i-1} \times d_i$, $1 \le i \le n$. For each of the following suggested techniques, provide a counterexample where the technique does not work.

(a) First multiply the matrices M_i and M_{i+1} whose common dimension d_i is smallest, and continue in the same way.

(b) First multiply the matrices M_i and M_{i+1} whose common dimension d_i is largest, and continue in the same way.

(c) First multiply the matrices M_i and M_{i+1} that minimize the product $d_{i-1} d_i d_{i+1}$, and continue in the same way.

(d) First multiply the matrices M_i and M_{i+1} that maximize the product $d_{i-1} d_i d_{i+1}$, and continue in the same way.

Problem 8.21. Write out in detail the algorithm for calculating the values of m_{ij} described in Section 8.6.

Problem 8.22. Adapt your algorithm for the previous problem so that not only does it calculate m_{ij}, but it also says how the matrix product should be calculated to achieve the optimal value of m_{1n}.

Problem 8.23. What is wrong with the following simple argument? "The algorithm for calculating the values of m given in Section 8.6 has essentially to fill in the entries in just over half of an $n \times n$ table. Its execution time is thus clearly in $\Theta(n^2)$."

Problem 8.24. Let $T(n)$ be a Catalan number; see Section 8.6. Prove that

$$T(n) = \frac{1}{n} \binom{2n-2}{n-1}.$$

Problem 8.25. Prove that the number of ways to cut an n-sided convex polygon into $n-2$ triangles using diagonal lines that do not cross is $T(n-1)$, the $(n-1)$-st Catalan number; see Section 8.6. For example, a hexagon can be cut in 14 different ways, as shown in Figure 8.7.

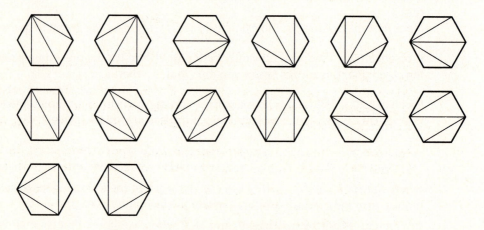

Figure 8.7. Cutting a hexagon into triangles

Problem 8.26. Show how to calculate (i) a binomial coefficient, and (ii) the function $series(n, p)$ of Section 8.1.2 using a memory function.

Problem 8.27. Show how to solve (i) the problem of making change, and (ii) the knapsack problem of Section 8.4 using a memory function.

Problem 8.28.   Consider the alphabet $\Sigma = \{a, b, c\}$. The elements of Σ have the following multiplication table, where the rows show the left-hand symbol and the columns show the right-hand symbol.

	a	b	c
a	b	b	a
b	c	b	a
c	a	c	c

Thus $ab = b$, $ba = c$, and so on. Note that the multiplication defined by this table is neither commutative nor associative.

Find an efficient algorithm that examines a string $x = x_1 x_2 \cdots x_n$ of characters of Σ and decides whether or not it is possible to parenthesize x in such a way that the value of the resulting expression is a. For instance, if $x = bbbba$, your algorithm should return "yes" because $(b(bb))(ba) = a$. This expression is not unique. For example, $(b(b(b(ba)))) = a$ as well. In terms of n, the length of the string x, how much time does your algorithm take?

Problem 8.29.   Modify your algorithm from the previous problem so it returns the number of different ways of parenthesizing x to obtain a.

Problem 8.30.   Let u and v be two strings of characters. We want to transform u into v with the smallest possible number of operations of the following three types: delete a character, add a character, or change a character. For instance, we can transform $abbac$ into $abcbc$ in three stages:

$$abbac \;\rightarrow\; abac \quad \text{(delete } b\text{)}$$
$$\rightarrow\; ababc \quad \text{(add } b\text{)}$$
$$\rightarrow\; abcbc \quad \text{(change } a \text{ into } c\text{).}$$

Show that this transformation is not optimal.
Write a dynamic programming algorithm that finds the minimum number of operations needed to transform u into v and tells us what these operations are. As a function of the lengths of u and v, how much time does your algorithm take?

Problem 8.31.   You have n objects that you wish to put in order using the relations "$<$" and "$=$". For example, with three objects 13 different orderings are possible.

$$a = b = c \quad a = b < c \quad a < b = c \quad a < b < c \quad a < c < b$$
$$a = c < b \quad b < a = c \quad b < a < c \quad b < c < a \quad b = c < a$$
$$c < a = b \quad c < a < b \quad c < b < a$$

Give a dynamic programming algorithm that can calculate, as a function of n, the number of different possible orderings. Your algorithm should take a time in $O(n^2)$ and space in $O(n)$.

Problem 8.32.   There are n trading posts along a river. At any of the posts you can rent a canoe to be returned at any other post downstream. (It is next to impossible to paddle against the current.) For each possible departure point i and each possible arrival point j the cost of a rental from i to j is known. However, it can happen that the cost of renting from i to j is higher than the total cost of a series of shorter rentals. In this case you can return the first canoe at some post k between i and j and continue your journey in a second canoe. There is no extra charge for changing canoes in this way.

Give an efficient algorithm to determine the minimum cost of a trip by canoe from each possible departure point i to each possible arrival point j. In terms of n, how much time is needed by your algorithm?

Problem 8.33. When we discussed binary search trees in Section 5.5, we mentioned that it is a good idea to keep them balanced. This is true provided all the nodes are equally likely to be accessed. If some nodes are more often accessed than others, however, an unbalanced tree may give better average performance. For example, the tree shown in Figure 8.8 is better than the one in Figure 5.9 if we are interested in minimizing the average number of comparisons with the tree and if the nodes are accessed with the following probabilities.

Node	6	12	18	20	27	34	35
Probability	0.2	0.25	0.05	0.1	0.05	0.3	0.05

More generally, suppose we have an ordered set $c_1 < c_2 < \cdots < c_n$ of n distinct keys. The probability that a request refers to key c_i is p_i, $1 \le i \le n$. Suppose for simplicity that every request refers to a key in the search tree, so $\sum_{i=1}^{n} p_i = 1$. Recall that the depth of the root of a tree is 0, the depth of its children is 1, and so on. If key c_i is held in a node at depth d_i, then $d_i + 1$ comparisons are necessary to find it. For a given tree the average number of comparisons needed is thus

$$C = \sum_{i=1}^{n} p_i(d_i + 1).$$

For example, the average number of comparisons needed with the tree in Figure 8.8 is

$$0.3 + (0.25 + 0.05) \times 2 + (0.2 + 0.1) \times 3 + (0.05 + 0.05) \times 4 = 2.2.$$

(a) Compute the average number of comparisons needed with the tree in Figure 5.9 and verify that the tree in Figure 8.8 is better.

(b) The tree in Figure 8.8 was obtained from the given probabilities using a simple algorithm. Can you guess what this is?

(c) Find yet another search tree for the same set of keys that is even more efficient on the average than Figure 8.8. What conclusion about algorithm design does this reinforce ?

Problem 8.34. Continuing Problem 8.33, design a dynamic programming algorithm to find an optimal binary search tree for a set of keys with given probabilities of access. How much time does your algorithm take as a function of the number of keys? Apply your algorithm to the instance given in Problem 8.33.

Hint: In any search tree where the nodes holding keys $c_i, c_{i+1}, \ldots, c_j$ form a subtree, let C_{ij} be the minimum average number of accesses made to these nodes. In particular, $C_{1,n}$ is the average number of accesses caused by a query to an optimal binary

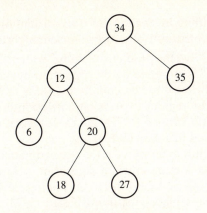

Figure 8.8. Another search tree

search tree and $C_{ii} = p_i$ for each i, $1 \le i \le n$. Invoke the principle of optimality to argue that

$$C_{ij} = \min_{i \le k \le j} (C_{i,k-1} + C_{k+1,j}) + \sum_{k=i}^{j} p_k$$

when $i < j$. Give a dynamic programming algorithm to compute C_{ij} for all $0 \le i \le j \le n$, and an algorithm to find the optimal binary search tree from the C_{ij}'s.

Problem 8.35.   Solve Problem 8.34 again. This time your algorithm to compute an optimal binary search tree for a set of n keys must run in a time in $O(n^2)$.
Hint: First prove that $r_{i,j-1} \le r_{ij} \le r_{i+1,j}$ for every $1 \le i \le j \le n$, where r_{ij} is the root of an optimal search subtree containing $c_i, c_{i+1}, \ldots, c_j$ for $1 \le i \le j \le n$ (ties are broken arbitrarily) and $r_{i,i-1} = i$, $1 \le i \le n$.

Problem 8.36.   As a function of n, how many binary search trees are there for n distinct keys?

Problem 8.37.   Recall that Ackermann's function $A(m, n)$, defined in Problem 5.38, grows extremely rapidly. Give a dynamic programming algorithm to calculate it. Your algorithm must consist simply of two nested loops and recursion is not allowed. Moreover, you are restricted to using a space in $O(m)$ to calculate $A(m, n)$. However you may suppose that a word of storage can hold an arbitrarily large integer.
Hint: Use two arrays *value*$[0..m]$ and *index*$[0..m]$ and make sure that *value*$[i] = A(i, index[i])$ at the end of each trip round the inner loop.

8.10 References and further reading

Several books cover dynamic programming. We mention only Bellman (1957), Bellman and Dreyfus (1962), Nemhauser (1966) and Laurière (1979).

The algorithm in Section 8.2 for making change is discussed in Wright (1975) and Chang and Korsh (1976). For more examples of solving knapsack problems using dynamic programming, see Hu (1981).

The algorithm in Section 8.5 for calculating all shortest paths is due to Floyd (1962). A theoretically more efficient algorithm is known: Fredman (1976) shows how to solve the problem in a time in $O(n^3 \sqrt[3]{\log \log n / \log n})$. The solution to Problem 8.18 is supplied by the algorithm in Warshall (1962). Both Floyd's and Warshall's algorithms are essentially the same as the earlier one in Kleene (1956) to determine the regular expression corresponding to a given finite automaton; see Hopcroft and Ullman (1979). All these algorithms with the exception of Fredman's are unified in Tarjan (1981).

The algorithm in Section 8.6 for chained matrix multiplication is described in Godbole (1973); a more efficient algorithm, able to solve the problem in a time in $O(n \log n)$, can be found in Hu and Shing (1982, 1984). Catalan numbers are discussed in many places, including Sloane (1973) and Purdom and Brown (1985). Memory functions are introduced in Michie (1968); for further details see Marsh (1970).

Problem 8.25 is discussed in Sloane (1973). A solution to Problem 8.30 is given in Wagner and Fischer (1974). Problem 8.31 suggested itself to the authors while grading an exam including a question resembling Problem 3.21: we were curious to know what proportion of all the possible answers was represented by the 69 different answers suggested by the students!

Problem 8.34 on the construction of optimal binary search trees comes from Gilbert and Moore (1959), where it is extended to the possibility that the requested key may not be in the tree. The improvement considered in Problem 8.35 comes from Knuth (1971, 1973) but a simpler and more general solution is given by Yao (1980), who also gives a sufficient condition for certain dynamic programming algorithms that run in cubic time to be transformable automatically into quadratic-time algorithms. The optimal search tree for the 31 most common words in English is compared in Knuth (1973) with the tree obtained using the obvious greedy algorithm suggested in Problem 8.33(b).

Important dynamic programming algorithms we have not mentioned include the one in Kasimi (1965) and Younger (1967) that takes cubic time to carry out the systematic analysis of any context-free language (see Hopcroft and Ullman 1979) and the one in Held and Karp (1962) that solves the travelling salesperson problem (see Sections 12.5.2 and 13.1.2) in a time in $O(n^2 2^n)$, much better than the time in $\Omega(n!)$ required by the naive algorithm.

Chapter 9

Exploring graphs

A great many problems can be formulated in terms of graphs. We have seen, for instance, the shortest route problem and the problem of the minimum spanning tree. To solve such problems, we often need to look at all the nodes, or all the edges, of a graph. Sometimes the structure of the problem is such that we need only visit some of the nodes, or some of the edges. Up to now the algorithms we have seen have implicitly imposed an order on these visits: it was a case of visiting the nearest node, or the shortest edge, and so on. In this chapter we introduce some general techniques that can be used when no particular order of visits is required.

√9.1 Graphs and games: An introduction

Consider the following game. It is one of the many variants of Nim, also known as the Marienbad game. Initially there is a heap of matches on the table between two players. The first player may remove as many matches as he likes, except that he must take at least one and he must leave at least one. There must therefore be at least two matches in the initial heap. Thereafter, each player in turn must remove at least one match and at most twice the number of matches his opponent just took. The player who removes the last match wins. There are no draws.

Suppose that at some stage in this game you find yourself in front of a pile of five matches. Your opponent has just picked up two matches, and now it is your turn to play. You may take one, two, three or four matches: however you may not take all five, since the rules forbid taking more than twice what your opponent just took. What should you do?

Most people playing this kind of game begin to run through the possibilities in their heads: "If I take four matches, that leaves just one for my opponent, which he can take and win; if I take three, that leaves two for my opponent, and again he can take them and win; if I take two, the same thing happens; but if I take just one, then he will have four matches in front of him of which he can only take one or two. In this case he doesn't win at once, so it is certainly my best move." By looking just one move ahead in this simple situation the player can determine what to do next. In a more complicated example, he may have several possible moves. To choose the best it may be necessary to consider not just the situation after his own move, but to look further ahead to see how his opponent can counter each possible move. And then he might have to think about his own move after each possible counter, and so on.

To formalize this process of looking ahead, we represent the game by a directed graph. Each node in the graph corresponds to a position in the game, and each edge corresponds to a move from one position to another. (In some contexts, for example in the reports of chess games, a move consists of an action by one player together with the reply from his opponent. In such contexts the term *half-move* is used to denote the action by just one player. In this book we stick to the simpler terminology and call each player's action a *move*.) A position in the game is not specified merely by the number of matches that remain on the table. It is also necessary to know the upper limit on the number of matches that may be taken on the next move. However it is not necessary to know whose turn it is to play, since the rules are the same for both players (unlike games such as 'fox and geese', where the players have different aims and forces). The nodes of the graph corresponding to this game are therefore pairs $\langle i, j \rangle$. In general, $\langle i, j \rangle$, $1 \leq j \leq i$, indicates that i matches remain on the table, and that any number of them between 1 and j may be taken on the next move. The edges leaving this position, that is, the moves that can be made, go to the j nodes $\langle i - k, \min(2k, i - k) \rangle$, $1 \leq k \leq j$. The node corresponding to the initial position in a game with n matches is $\langle n, n - 1 \rangle$, $n \geq 2$. The position $\langle 0, 0 \rangle$ loses the game: if a player is in this position when it is his turn to move, his opponent has just taken the last match and won.

Figure 9.1 shows part of the graph corresponding to this game. In fact, it is the part of the graph needed by the player in the example above who faces a heap of five matches of which he may take four: this is the position $\langle 5, 4 \rangle$. No positions of the form $\langle i, 0 \rangle$ appear except for the losing position $\langle 0, 0 \rangle$. Such positions cannot be reached in the course of a game, so they are of no interest. Similarly nodes $\langle i, j \rangle$ with j odd and $j < i - 1$ cannot be reached from any initial position, so they too are omitted. As we explain in a moment, the square nodes represent losing positions and the round nodes are winning positions. The heavy edges correspond to winning moves: in a winning position, choose one of the heavy edges to win. There are no heavy edges leaving a losing position, corresponding to the fact that such positions offer no winning move. We observe that the player who must move first in a game with two, three or five matches has no winning strategy, whereas he does have such a strategy in the game with four matches.

To decide which are the winning positions and which the losing positions, we start at the losing position $\langle 0, 0 \rangle$ and work back. This node has no successor, and a player who finds himself in this position loses the game. In any of the nodes $\langle 1, 1 \rangle$, $\langle 2, 2 \rangle$ or $\langle 3, 3 \rangle$, a player can make a move that puts his opponent in the losing position. These three nodes are therefore winning nodes. From $\langle 2, 1 \rangle$ the

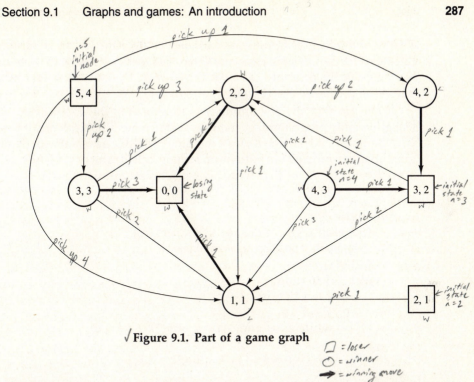

√ **Figure 9.1. Part of a game graph**

only possible move is to $\langle 1, 1 \rangle$. In position $\langle 2, 1 \rangle$ a player is therefore bound to put his opponent in a winning position, so $\langle 2, 1 \rangle$ itself is a losing position. A similar argument applies to the losing position $\langle 3, 2 \rangle$. Two moves are possible, but they both leave the opponent in a winning position, so $\langle 3, 2 \rangle$ itself is a losing position. From either $\langle 4, 2 \rangle$ or $\langle 4, 3 \rangle$ there is a move available that puts the opponent in a losing position, namely $\langle 3, 2 \rangle$; hence both these nodes are winning positions. Finally the four possible moves from $\langle 5, 4 \rangle$ all leave the opponent in a winning position, so $\langle 5, 4 \rangle$ is a losing position.

On a larger graph this process of labelling winning and losing positions can be continued backwards as required. The rules we have been applying can be summed up as follows: a position is a winning position if *at least one* of its successors is a losing position, for then the player can move to put his opponent in a losing position; a position is a losing position if *all* its successors are winning positions, for then the player cannot avoid leaving his opponent in a winning position. The following algorithm therefore determines whether a position is winning or losing.

function *recwin*(i, j)
　　{Returns *true* if and only if node $\langle i, j \rangle$ is winning;
　　we assume $0 \le j \le i$}
　　for $k \leftarrow 1$ **to** j **do**
　　　　if not *recwin*$(i - k, \min(2k, i - k))$
　　　　　　then return *true*
　　return *false*

This algorithm suffers from the same defect as algorithm *Fibrec* in Section 2.7.5: it calculates the same value over and over. For instance, *recwin*(5, 4) returns *false*, having called successively *recwin*(4, 2), *recwin*(3, 3), *recwin*(2, 2) and *recwin*(1, 1), but *recwin*(3, 3) too calls *recwin*(2, 2) and *recwin*(1, 1).

There are two obvious approaches to removing this inefficiency. The first, using dynamic programming, requires us to create a Boolean array G such that $G[i, j] = true$ if and only if $\langle i, j \rangle$ is a winning position. As usual with dynamic programming, we proceed in a bottom-up fashion, calculating $G[r, s]$ for $1 \le s \le r < i$, as well as the values of $G[i, s]$ for $1 \le s < j$, before calculating $G[i, j]$.

> **procedure** *dynwin*(*n*)
>   {For each $1 \le j \le i \le n$, sets $G[i, j]$ to *true*
>   if and only if position $\langle i, j \rangle$ is winning}
> $G[0, 0] \leftarrow false$
>   **for** $i \leftarrow 1$ **to** n **do**
>   **for** $j \leftarrow 1$ **to** i **do**
> $k \leftarrow 1$
>   **while** $k < j$ **and** $G[i - k, \min(2k, i - k)]$ **do**
> $k \leftarrow k + 1$
> $G[i, j] \leftarrow$ **not** $G[i - k, \min(2k, i - k)]$

In this context dynamic programming leads us to calculate wastefully some entries of the array G that are never needed. For instance, we know $\langle 15, 14 \rangle$ is a winning position as soon as we discover that its second successor $\langle 13, 4 \rangle$ is a losing position. It is no longer of interest to know whether the next successor $\langle 12, 6 \rangle$ is a winning or a losing position. In fact, only 28 nodes are really useful when we calculate $G[15, 14]$, although the dynamic programming algorithm determines 121 of them. About half this work can be avoided if we do not calculate $G[i, j]$ when j is odd and $j < i - 1$, since these nodes are never of interest, but there is no "bottom-up" reason for not calculating $G[12, 6]$. As usual, things get worse as the instance gets bigger: to solve the game with 248 matches it is sufficient to explore 1000 nodes, yet *dynwin* looks at more than 30 times this number.

The recursive algorithm given previously is inefficient because it recalculates the same value several times. Because of its top-down nature, however, it never calculates an unnecessary value. A solution that combines the advantages of both algorithms consists of using a memory function; see Section 8.8. This involves remembering which nodes have already been visited during the recursive computation using a global Boolean array $known[0..n, 0..n]$, where n is an upper bound on the number of matches to be used. The necessary initializations are as follows.

> $G[0, 0] \leftarrow false;$ $known[0, 0] \leftarrow true$
>   **for** $i \leftarrow 1$ **to** n **do**
>   **for** $j \leftarrow 1$ **to** i **do**
> $known[i, j] \leftarrow false$

Thereafter, to discover whether $\langle i, j \rangle$ is a winning or a losing position, call the following function.

mem function;
```
function nim(i, j)
    {For each 1 ≤ j ≤ i ≤ n, returns true
     if and only if position ⟨i, j⟩ is winning}
    if known[i, j] then return G[i, j]
    known[i, j] ← true
    for k ← 1 to j do
        if not nim(i − k, min(2k, i − k)) then
            G[i, j] ← true
            return true
    G[i, j] ← false
    return false
```

At first sight there is no particular reason to favour this approach over dynamic programming, because in any case we have to take the time to initialize the whole array $known[0 .. n, 0 .. n]$. However, virtual initialization (described in Section 5.1) allows us to avoid this, and to obtain a worthwhile gain in efficiency.

The game we have considered up to now is so simple that it can be solved without using the associated graph; see Problem 9.5. However the same principles apply to many other games of strategy. As before, a node of a directed graph corresponds to a particular position in the game, and an edge corresponds to a legal move between two positions. The graph is infinite if there is no a priori limit on the number of positions possible in the game. For simplicity, we shall suppose that the game is played by two players who move in turn, that the rules are the same for both players (we say the game is *symmetric*), and that chance plays no part in the outcome (the game is *deterministic*). The ideas we present can easily be adapted to more general contexts. We further suppose that no instance of the game can last forever and that no position in the game offers an infinite number of legal moves to the player whose turn it is. In particular, some positions in the game, called the *terminal positions*, offer no legal moves, and hence some nodes in the graph have no successors.

To determine a winning strategy in a game of this kind, we attach to each node of the graph a label chosen from the set *win*, *lose* and *draw*. The label refers to the situation of a player about to move in the corresponding position, assuming neither player will make an error. The labels are assigned systematically as follows. (In the simple example given earlier, no draws were possible, so the label *draw* was never used, and the rules stated there are incomplete.)

Labels
1. Label the terminal positions. The labels assigned depend on the game in question. For most games, if you find yourself in a terminal position, then there is no legal move you can make, and you have lost. However this is not always the case. If you cannot move because of a stalemate in chess, for example, the game is a draw. Also many games of the Nim family come in pairs, one where

the player who takes the last match wins, and one (called the *misère* version of the game) where the player who takes the last match loses.

2. A nonterminal position is a winning position if *at least one* of its successors is a losing position, for the player whose turn it is can leave his opponent in this losing position.

3. A nonterminal position is a losing position if *all* its successors are winning positions, for the player whose turn it is cannot avoid leaving his opponent in one of these winning positions.

4. Any other nonterminal position leads to a draw. In this case the successors must include at least one draw, possibly with some winning positions as well. The player whose turn it is can avoid leaving his opponent in a winning position, but cannot force him into a losing position.

Once these labels are assigned, a winning strategy can be read off from the graph.

In principle, this technique applies even to a game as complex as chess. At first sight, the graph associated with chess appears to contain cycles, since if two positions u and v of the pieces differ only by the legal move of a rook, say, the king not being in check, then we can move equally well from u to v and from v to u. However this problem disappears on closer examination. In the variant of Nim used as an example above, a position is defined not just by the number of matches on the table, but also by an invisible item of information giving the number of matches that can be picked up on the next move. Similarly, a position in chess is not defined simply by the position of the pieces. We also need to know whose turn it is to move, which rooks and kings have moved since the beginning of the game (to know if it is legal to castle), and whether some pawn has just moved two squares forward (to know if a capture *en passant* is possible). There are also rules explicitly designed to prevent a game dragging on forever. For example, a game is declared to be a draw after a certain number of moves in which no irreversible action (the movement of a pawn, or a capture) has taken place. Thanks to these and similar rules, there are no cycles in the graph corresponding to chess. However, they force us to include such items as the number of moves since the last irreversible action in the information defining a position.

Adapting the general rules given above, we can label each node as being a winning position for White, a winning position for Black, or a draw. Once constructed, this graph allows us in principle to play a perfect game of chess, that is, to win whenever it is possible, and to lose only when it is inevitable. Unfortunately— or perhaps fortunately for the game of chess—the graph contains so many nodes that it is out of the question to explore it completely, even with the fastest existing computers. The best we can do is to explore the graph near the current position, to see how the situation might develop, just like the novice who reasons, "If I do this, he will reply like that, and then I can do this", and so on. Even this technique is not without its subtleties, however. Should we look at *all* the possibilities offered by the current position, and then, for each of these, *all* the possibilities of reply?

Or should we rather pick a promising line of attack and follow it up for several moves to see where it leads? Different search strategies may lead to quite different results, as we describe shortly.

If we cannot hope to explore the whole graph for the game of chess, then we cannot hope to construct it and store it either. The best we can expect is to construct parts of the graph as we go along, saving them if they are interesting and throwing them away otherwise. Thus throughout this chapter we use the word "graph" in two different ways.

On the one hand, a graph may be a data structure in the storage of a computer. In this case, the nodes are represented by a certain number of bytes, and the edges are represented by pointers. The operations to be carried out are quite concrete: to "mark a node" means to change a bit in storage, to "find a neighbouring node" means to follow a pointer, and so on.

At other times, the graph exists only implicitly, as when we explore the abstract graph corresponding to the game of chess. This graph never really exists in the storage of the machine. Most of the time, all we have is a representation of the current position (that is, of the node we are in the process of visiting, for, as we saw, nodes correspond to positions of the pieces plus some extra information), and possibly representations of a small number of other positions. Of course we also know the rules of the game in question. In this case to "mark a node" means to take any appropriate measures that enable us to recognize a position we have already seen, or to avoid arriving at the same position twice. To "find a neighbouring node" means to change the current position by making a single legal move, for if it is possible to get from one position to another by making a single move, then an edge exists in the implicit graph between the two corresponding nodes.

Exactly similar considerations apply when we explore any large graph, as we shall see particularly in Section 9.6. However, whether the graph is a data structure or merely an abstraction that we can never manipulate as a whole, the techniques used to traverse it are essentially the same. In this chapter we therefore do not distinguish the two cases.

9.2 Traversing trees

We shall not spend long on detailed descriptions of how to explore a tree. We simply remind the reader that in the case of binary trees three techniques are often used. If at each node of the tree we visit first the node itself, then all the nodes in the left subtree, and finally all the nodes in the right subtree, we are traversing the tree in *preorder*; if we visit first the left subtree, then the node itself, and finally the right subtree, we are traversing the tree in *inorder*; and if we visit first the left subtree, then the right subtree, and lastly the node itself, we are traversing the tree in *postorder*. Preorder and postorder generalize in an obvious way to nonbinary trees.

These three techniques explore the tree from left to right. Three corresponding techniques explore the tree from right to left. Implementation of any of these techniques using recursion is straightforward.

√Lemma 9.2.1 *For each of the six techniques mentioned, the time $T(n)$ needed to explore a binary tree containing n nodes is in $\Theta(n)$.*

Proof Suppose that visiting a node takes a time in $O(1)$, that is, the time required is bounded above by some constant c. Without loss of generality we may suppose that $c \geq T(0)$. Suppose further that we are to explore a tree containing n nodes, $n > 0$; one of these nodes is the root, so if g of them lie in the left subtree, then there are $n - g - 1$ in the right subtree. Then

$$T(n) \leq \max_{0 \leq g \leq n-1} (T(g) + T(n - g - 1) + c), \qquad n > 0.$$

This is true whatever the order in which the left and right subtrees and the root are explored. We prove by constructive induction that $T(n) \leq an + b$, where a and b are appropriate constants, as yet unknown. If we choose $b \geq c$ the hypothesis is true for $n = 0$, because $c \geq T(0)$. For the induction step, let $n > 0$, and suppose the hypothesis is true for all $m, 0 \leq m \leq n - 1$. Then

$$T(n) \leq \max_{0 \leq g \leq n-1} (T(g) + T(n - g - 1) + c)$$

$$\leq \max_{0 \leq g \leq n-1} (ag + b + a(n - g - 1) + b + c)$$

$$\leq an + 3b - a.$$

Hence provided we choose $a \geq 2b$ we have $T(n) \leq an + b$, so the hypothesis is also true for $m = n$. This proves that $T(n) \leq an + b$ for every $n \geq 0$, and therefore $T(n)$ is in $O(n)$.

On the other hand it is clear that $T(n)$ is in $\Omega(n)$ since each of the n nodes is visited. Therefore $T(n)$ is in $\Theta(n)$. ∎

9.2.1 Preconditioning

If we have to solve several similar instances of the same problem, it may be worthwhile to invest some time in calculating auxiliary results that can thereafter be used to speed up the solution of each instance. This is *preconditioning*. Informally, let a be the time it takes to solve a typical instance when no auxiliary information is available, let b be the time it takes to solve a typical instance when auxiliary information *is* available, and let p be the time needed to calculate this extra information. To solve n typical instances takes time na without preconditioning and time $p + nb$ if preconditioning is used. Provided $b < a$, it is advantageous to use preconditioning when $n > p/(a - b)$.

From this point of view, the dynamic programming algorithm for making change given in Section 8.2 may be seen as an example of preconditioning. Once the necessary values c_{nj} have been calculated, we can make change quickly whenever this is required.

Even when there are few instances to be solved, precomputation of auxiliary information may be useful. Suppose we occasionally have to solve one instance from some large set of possible instances. When a solution is needed it must be provided very rapidly, for example to ensure sufficiently fast response for a real-time application. In this case it may well be impractical to calculate ahead of time and to store the solutions to all the relevant instances. On the other hand, it may be possible to calculate and store sufficient auxiliary information to speed up the solution of whatever instance comes along. Such an application of preconditioning may be of practical importance even if only one crucial instance is solved in the whole lifetime of the system: this may be just the instance that enables us, for example, to stop a runaway reactor.

As a second example of this technique we use the problem of determining ancestry in a rooted tree. Let T be a rooted tree, not necessarily binary. We say that a node v of T is an *ancestor* of node w if v lies on the path from w to the root of T. In particular, every node is its own ancestor, and the root is an ancestor of every node. (Those with a taste for recursive definitions may prefer the following: every node is its own ancestor, and, recursively, it is an ancestor of all the nodes of which its children are ancestors.) The problem is thus, given a pair of nodes (v, w) from T, to determine whether or not v is an ancestor of w. If T contains n nodes, any direct solution of this instance takes a time in $\Omega(n)$ in the worst case. However it is possible to precondition T in a time in $\Theta(n)$ so we can subsequently solve any particular instance of the ancestry problem in constant time.

We illustrate this using the tree in Figure 9.2. It contains 13 nodes. To precondition the tree, we traverse it first in preorder and then in postorder, numbering the nodes sequentially as we visit them. For a node v, let *prenum*$[v]$ be the number assigned to v when we traverse the tree in preorder, and let *postnum*$[v]$ be the number assigned during the traversal in postorder. In Figure 9.2 these numbers appear to the left and the right of the node, respectively.

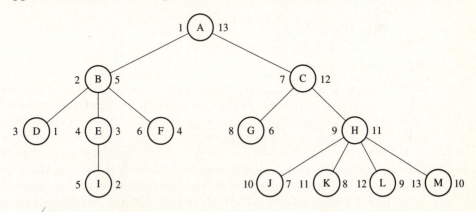

Figure 9.2. A rooted tree with preorder and postorder numberings

Let v and w be two nodes in the tree. In preorder we first number a node and then number its subtrees from left to right. Thus

$$prenum[v] \le prenum[w] \quad \Longleftrightarrow \quad \begin{array}{l} v \text{ is an ancestor of } w \text{ or} \\ v \text{ is to the left of } w \text{ in the tree.} \end{array}$$

In postorder we first number the subtrees of a node from left to right, and then we number the node itself. Thus

$$postnum[v] \geq postnum[w] \quad \Longleftrightarrow \quad v \text{ is an ancestor of } w \textbf{ or}$$
$$v \text{ is to the right of } w \text{ in the tree.}$$

It follows that

$$prenum[v] \leq prenum[w] \textbf{ and } postnum[v] \geq postnum[w]$$
$$\Longleftrightarrow v \text{ is an ancestor of } w.$$

Once the values of *prenum* and *postnum* have been calculated in a time in $\Theta(n)$, the required condition can be checked in a time in $\Theta(1)$.

√ 9.3 Depth-first search: Undirected graphs

Let $G = \langle N, A \rangle$ be an undirected graph all of whose nodes we wish to visit. Suppose it is somehow possible to mark a node to show it has already been visited.

To carry out a *depth-first* traversal of the graph, choose any node $v \in N$ as the starting point. Mark this node to show it has been visited. Next, if there is a node adjacent to v that has not yet been visited, choose this node as a new starting point and call the depth-first search procedure recursively. On return from the recursive call, if there is another node adjacent to v that has not been visited, choose this node as the next starting point, call the procedure recursively once again, and so on. When all the nodes adjacent to v are marked, the search starting at v is finished. If there remain any nodes of G that have not been visited, choose any one of them as a new starting point, and call the procedure yet again. Continue thus until all the nodes of G are marked. Here is the recursive algorithm.

```
procedure dfsearch(G)
    for each v ∈ N do mark[v] ← not-visited
    for each v ∈ N do
        if mark[v] ≠ visited then dfs(v)

procedure dfs(v)
    {Node v has not previously been visited}
    mark[v] ← visited
    for each node w adjacent to v do
        if mark[w] ≠ visited then dfs(w)
```

The algorithm is called depth-first search because it initiates as many recursive calls as possible before it ever returns from a call. The recursion stops only when exploration of the graph is blocked and can go no further. At this point the recursion "unwinds" so alternative possibilities at higher levels can be explored. If the graph corresponds to a game, this may be thought of intuitively as a search that explores the result of one particular strategy as many moves ahead as possible before looking around to see what alternative tactics might be available.

Consider for example the graph in Figure 9.3. If we suppose that the neighbours of a given node are examined in numerical order, and that node 1 is the first starting point, depth-first search of the graph progresses as follows:

1.	$dfs(1)$	initial call
2.	$dfs(2)$	recursive call
3.	$dfs(3)$	recursive call
4.	$dfs(6)$	recursive call
5.	$dfs(5)$	recursive call; progress is blocked
6.	$dfs(4)$	a neighbour of node 1 has not been visited
7.	$dfs(7)$	recursive call
8.	$dfs(8)$	recursive call; progress is blocked
9.	there are no more nodes to visit	

How much time is needed to explore a graph with n nodes and a edges? Since each node is visited exactly once, there are n calls of the procedure dfs. When we visit a node, we look at the mark on each of its neighbouring nodes. If the graph is represented so as to make the lists of adjacent nodes directly accessible (type *lisgraph* of Section 5.4), this work is proportional to a in total. The algorithm therefore takes a time in $\Theta(n)$ for the procedure calls and a time in $\Theta(a)$ to inspect the marks. The execution time is thus in $\Theta(\max(a, n))$. √

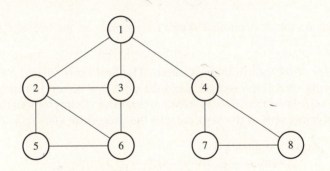

Figure 9.3. An undirected graph

Depth-first traversal of a connected graph associates a spanning tree to the graph. Call this tree T. The edges of T correspond to the edges used to traverse the graph; they are directed from the first node visited to the second. Edges not used in the traversal of the graph have no corresponding edge in T. The initial starting point of the exploration becomes the root of the tree. For example, the edges used in the depth-first search of the graph in Figure 9.3 described above are $\{1, 2\}$, $\{2, 3\}$, $\{3, 6\}$, $\{6, 5\}$, $\{1, 4\}$, $\{4, 7\}$ and $\{7, 8\}$. The corresponding directed edges, $(1, 2)$, $(2, 3)$, and so on, form a spanning tree for this graph. The root of the tree is node 1. The tree is illustrated in Figure 9.4. The broken lines in this figure correspond to edges of G not used in the depth-first search. It is easy to show that an edge of G with no corresponding edge in T necessarily joins some node v to one of its ancestors in T; see Problem 9.17.

If the graph being explored is not connected, a depth-first search associates to it not merely a single tree, but rather a forest of trees, one for each connected component of the graph. A depth-first search also provides a way to number the

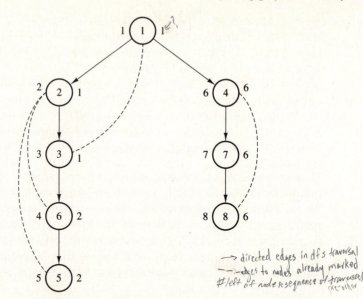

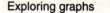

Figure 9.4. A depth-first search tree; *prenum* **on the left,** *highest* **on the right**

nodes of the graph being visited. The first node visited—the root of the tree—
is numbered 1, the second is numbered 2, and so on. In other words, the nodes of
the associated tree are numbered in preorder. To implement this, add the following
two statements at the beginning of the procedure *dfs*:

$$pnum \leftarrow pnum + 1$$
$$prenum[v] \leftarrow pnum$$

where *pnum* is a global variable initialized to zero. For example, the depth-first
search of the graph in Figure 9.3 described above numbers the nodes of the graph
as follows.

node	1	2	3	4	5	6	7	8
prenum	1	2	3	6	5	4	7	8

These are the numbers to the left of each node in Figure 9.4. Of course the tree
and the numbering generated by a depth-first search in a graph are not unique,
but depend on the chosen starting point and on the order in which neighbours are
visited.

9.3.1 Articulation points

A node v of a connected graph is an *articulation point* if the subgraph obtained by
deleting v and all the edges incident on v is no longer connected. For example,
node 1 is an articulation point of the graph in Figure 9.3; if we delete it, there
remain two connected components {2, 3, 5, 6} and {4, 7, 8}. A graph G is *biconnected*
(or *unarticulated*) if it is connected and has no articulation points. It is *bicoherent*
(or *isthmus-free*, or *2-edge-connected*) if each articulation point is joined by at least two

edges to each component of the remaining subgraph. These ideas are important in practice. If the graph G represents, say, a telecommunications network, then the fact that it is biconnected assures us that the rest of the network can continue to function even if the equipment in one of the nodes fails. If G is bicoherent, we can be sure the nodes will be able to communicate with one another even if one transmission line stops working.

To see how to find the articulation points of a connected graph G, look again at Figure 9.4. Remember that this figure shows *all* the edges of the graph G of Figure 9.3: those shown as solid lines form a spanning tree T, while the others are shown as broken lines. As we saw, these other edges only go from some node v to its ancestor in the tree, not from one branch to another. To the left of each node v is *prenum*[v], the number assigned by a preorder traversal of T.

To the right of each node v is a new number that we shall call *highest*[v]. Let w be the highest node in the tree that can be reached from v by following down zero or more solid lines, and then going up at most one broken line. Then define *highest*[v] to be *prenum*[w]. For instance, from node 7 we can go down one solid line to node 8, then up one broken line to node 4, and this is the highest node we can reach. Since *prenum*[4] = 6, we also have *highest*[7] = 6.

Because the broken lines do not cross from one branch to another, the highest node w reachable in this way must be an ancestor of v. (It cannot lie below v in the tree, because we can always get to v itself by not following any lines at all.) Among the ancestors of v, the highest up the tree is the one with the lowest value of *prenum*. If we have these values, it is therefore not necessary to know the exact level of each node: among the nodes we can reach, we simply choose the one that minimizes *prenum*.

Now consider any node v in T except the root. If v has no children, it cannot be an articulation point of G, for if we delete it the remaining nodes are still connected by the edges left in T. Otherwise, let x be a child of v. Suppose first that *highest*[x] < *prenum*[v]. This means that from x there is a chain of edges of G, not including the edge {v, x} (for we were not allowed to go *up* a solid line), that leads to some node higher up the tree than v. If we delete v, therefore, the nodes in the subtree rooted at x will not be disconnected from the rest of the tree. This is the case with node 3 in the figure, for example. Here *prenum*[3] = 3, and the only child of node 3, namely node 6, has *highest*[6] = 2 < *prenum*[3]. Therefore if we delete node 3, node 6 and its descendants will still be attached to one of the ancestors of node 3.

If on the other hand *highest*[x] ≥ *prenum*[v], then no chain of edges from x (again excluding the edge {v, x}) rejoins the tree higher than v. In this case, should v be deleted, the nodes in the subtree rooted at x will be disconnected from the rest of the tree. Node 4 in the figure illustrates this case. Here *prenum*[4] = 6, and the only child of node 4, namely node 7, has *highest*[7] = 6 = *prenum*[4]. Therefore if we delete node 4, no path from node 7 or from one of its descendants leads back above the deleted node, so the subtree rooted at node 7 will be detached from the rest of T.

Thus a node v that is not the root of T is an articulation point of G if and only if it has at least one child x with *highest*[x] ≥ *prenum*[v]. As for the root, it is evident that it is an articulation point of G if and only if it has more than one child; for in this case, since no edges cross from one branch to another, deleting the root disconnects the remaining subtrees of T.

It remains to be seen how to calculate the values of *highest*. Clearly this must be done from the leaves upwards. For example, from node 5 we can stay where we are, or go up to node 2; these are the only possibilities. From node 6 we can stay where we are, go up to node 2, or else go first down to node 5 and then to wherever is reachable from there; and so on. The values of *highest* are therefore calculated in postorder. At a general node v, *highest*[v] is the minimum (corresponding to the highest node) of three kinds of values: *prenum*[v] (we stay where we are), *prenum*[w] for each node w such that there is an edge $\{v, w\}$ in G with no corresponding edge in T (we go up a broken line), and *highest*[x] for every child x of v (we go down a solid line and see where we can get from there).

The complete algorithm for finding the articulation points of an undirected graph G is summarized as follows.

1. Carry out a depth-first search in G, starting from any node. Let T be the tree generated by this search, and for each node v of G, let *prenum*[v] be the number assigned by the search.

2. Traverse T in postorder. For each node v visited, calculate *highest*[v] as the minimum of
   (a) *prenum*[v];
   (b) *prenum*[w] for each node w such that there is an edge $\{v, w\}$ in G with no corresponding edge in T; and
   (c) *highest*[x] for every child x of v.

3. Determine the articulation points of G as follows.
   (a) The root of T is an articulation point if and only if it has more than one child.
   (b) Any other node v is an articulation point if and only if it has a child x such that *highest*[x] $\geq$ *prenum*[v].

It is not difficult to combine steps 1 and 2 of the above algorithm, calculating the values of both *prenum* and *highest* during the depth-first search of G.

√ 9.4 Depth-first search: Directed graphs

The algorithm is essentially the same as for undirected graphs, the difference residing in the interpretation of the word "adjacent". In a directed graph, node w is adjacent to node v if the directed edge (v, w) exists. If (v, w) exists but (w, v) does not, then w is adjacent to v but v is not adjacent to w. With this change of interpretation the procedures *dfs* and *search* from Section 9.3 apply equally well in the case of a directed graph.

The algorithm behaves quite differently, however. Consider a depth-first search of the directed graph in Figure 9.5. If the neighbours of a given node are examined in numerical order, the algorithm progresses as follows:

1. $dfs(1)$ initial call
2. $dfs(2)$ recursive call
3. $dfs(3)$ recursive call; progress is blocked
4. $dfs(4)$ a neighbour of node 1 has not been visited
5. $dfs(8)$ recursive call
6. $dfs(7)$ recursive call; progress is blocked
7. $dfs(5)$ new starting point
8. $dfs(6)$ recursive call; progress is blocked
9. there are no more nodes to visit

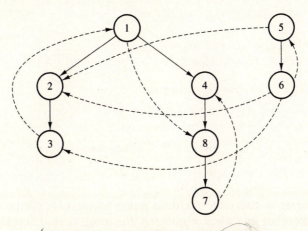

√**Figure 9.5. A directed graph**

An argument identical with the one in Section 9.3 shows that the time taken by this
√algorithm is also in $\Theta(\max(a, n))$. In this case, however, the edges used to visit all
the nodes of a directed graph $G = \langle N, A \rangle$ may form a forest of several trees even if √
G is connected. This happens in our example: the edges used, namely $(1, 2)$, $(2, 3)$,
$(1, 4)$, $(4, 8)$, $(8, 7)$ and $(5, 6)$, form the forest shown by the solid lines in Figure 9.6.

√**Figure 9.6. A depth-first search forest**

Let F be the set of edges in the forest, so that $A \setminus F$ is the set of edges of G that have no corresponding edge in the forest. In the case of an undirected graph, we saw that the edges of the graph with no corresponding edge in the forest necessarily join some node to one of its ancestors. In the case of a directed graph, however, three kinds of edge can appear in $A \setminus F$. These are shown by the broken lines in Figure 9.6.

1. Those like $(3, 1)$ or $(7, 4)$ lead from a node to one of its ancestors. *back edge ≈ dfs*

2. Those like $(1, 8)$ lead from a node to one of its descendants. *forward edge*

3. Those like $(5, 2)$ or $(6, 3)$ join one node to another that is neither its ancestor nor its descendant. Edges of this type are necessarily directed from right to left.

9.4.1 Acyclic graphs: Topological sorting *full*

Directed acyclic graphs can be used to represent a number of interesting relations. This class includes trees, but is less general than the class of all directed graphs. For example, a directed acyclic graph can be used to represent the structure of an arithmetic expression involving repeated subexpressions: thus Figure 9.7 represents the structure of the expression

$$(a + b)(c + d) + (a + b)(c - d).$$

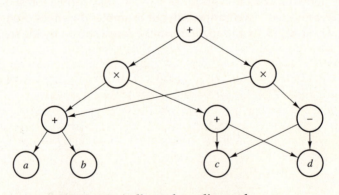

Figure 9.7. A directed acyclic graph

sense of nodes

These graphs also offer a natural representation for partial orderings, such as the relation of set-inclusion. Figure 9.8 illustrates part of another partial ordering defined on the positive integers: here there is an edge from node i to node j if and only if i is a proper divisor of j.

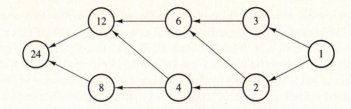

Figure 9.8. Another directed acyclic graph

Finally, directed acyclic graphs are often used to specify how a complex project develops over time. The nodes represent different stages of the project, from the initial state to final completion, and the edges correspond to activities that must be completed to pass from one stage to another. Figure 9.9 gives an example of this type of diagram.

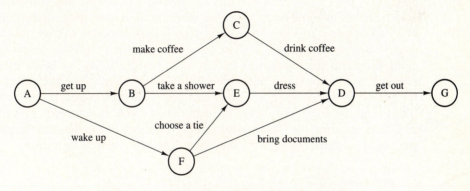

Figure 9.9. Yet another directed acyclic graph

Depth-first search can be used to detect whether a given directed graph is acyclic; see Problem 9.26. It can also be used to determine a *topological ordering* of the nodes of a directed acyclic graph. In this kind of ordering the nodes of the graph are listed in such a way that if there exists an edge (i, j), then node i precedes node j in the list. For example, for the graph of Figure 9.8, the natural order $1, 2, 3, 4, 6, 8, 12, 24$ is adequate; but the order $1, 3, 2, 6, 4, 12, 8, 24$ is also acceptable, as are several others. On the other hand, the order $1, 3, 6, 2, 4, 12, 8, 24$ will not do, because the graph includes an edge $(2, 6)$, and so 2 must precede 6 in the list.

Adapting the procedure *dfs* to make it into a topological sort is simple. Add an extra line

write v

at the end of the procedure *dfs*, run the procedure on the graph concerned, and then reverse the order of the resulting list of nodes.

To see this, consider what happens when we arrive at node v of a directed acyclic graph G using the modified procedure. Some nodes that must follow v in topological order may already have been visited while following a different path. In this case they are already on the list, as they should be since we reverse the list when the search is finished. Any node that must precede v in topological order either lies along the path we are currently exploring, in which case it is marked as visited but is not yet on the list, or else it has not yet been visited. In either case it will be added to the list after node v (again, correctly, for the list is to be reversed). Now the depth-first search explores the unvisited nodes that can be reached from v by following edges of G. In the topological ordering, these must come after v. Since we intend to reverse the list when the search is finished, adding them to the list during the exploration starting at v, and adding v only when this exploration is finished, gives us exactly what we want.

9.5 Breadth-first search

When a depth-first search arrives at some node v, it next tries to visit some neighbour of v, then a neighbour of this neighbour, and so on. When a breadth-first search arrives at some node v, on the other hand, it first visits all the neighbours of v. Only when this has been done does it look at nodes further away. Unlike depth-first search, breadth-first search is not naturally recursive. To underline the similarities and the differences between the two methods, we begin by giving a nonrecursive formulation of the depth-first search algorithm. Let *stack* be a data type allowing two operations, **push** and **pop**. The type is intended to represent a list of elements to be handled in the order "last come, first served" (often referred to as LIFO, standing for "last in, first out"). The function *top* denotes the element at the top of the stack. Here is the modified depth-first search algorithm.

```
procedure dfs2(v)
    P ← empty-stack
    mark[v] ← visited
    push v onto P
    while P is not empty do
        while there exists a node w adjacent to top(P)
                such that mark[w] ≠ visited
                do mark[w] ← visited
                    push w onto P {w is the new top(P)}
        pop P
```

Modifying the algorithm has not changed its behaviour. All we have done is to make explicit the stacking and unstacking of nodes that in the previous version was handled behind the scenes by the stack mechanism implicit in any recursive language.

For the breadth-first search algorithm, by contrast, we need a type *queue* that allows two operations **enqueue** and **dequeue**. This type represents a list of elements to be handled in the order "first come, first served" (or FIFO, for "first in, first out"). The function *first* denotes the element at the front of the queue. Here now is the breadth-first search algorithm.

```
procedure bfs(v)
    Q ← empty-queue
    mark[v] ← visited
    enqueue v into Q
    while Q is not empty do
        u ← first(Q)
        dequeue u from Q
        for each node w adjacent to u do
            if mark[w] ≠ visited then mark[w] ← visited
                enqueue w into Q
```

In both cases we need a main program to start the search.

```
procedure search(G)
    for each v ∈ N do mark[v] ← not-visited
    for each v ∈ N do
        if mark[v] ≠ visited then {dfs2 or bfs} (v)
```

For example, on the graph of Figure 9.3, if the search starts at node 1, and the neighbours of a node are visited in numerical order, breadth-first search proceeds as follows.

	Node visited	Q
1.	1	2,3,4
2.	2	3,4,5,6
3.	3	4,5,6
4.	4	5,6,7,8
5.	5	6,7,8
6.	6	7,8
7.	7	8
8.	8	—

(handwritten annotations: "unmarked adj. to N_1" at row 1; "dequeue" and "enqueue adj. to N_2" at row 2)

As for depth-first search, we can associate a tree with a breadth-first search. Figure 9.10 shows the tree generated by the search above. The edges of the graph with no corresponding edge in the tree are represented by broken lines; see Problem 9.30. In general, if the graph G being searched is not connected, the search generates a forest of trees, one for each connected component of G.

It is easy to show that the time required by a breadth-first search is in the same order as that required by a depth-first search, namely $\Theta(\max(a, n))$. If the appropriate interpretation of the word "adjacent" is used, the breadth-first search algorithm—again, exactly like the depth-first search algorithm—can be applied without modification to either directed or undirected graphs; see Problems 9.31 and 9.32.

Breadth-first search is most often used to carry out a partial exploration of an infinite (or unmanageably large) graph, or to find the shortest path from one point to another in a graph. Consider for example the following problem. The value 1 is given. To construct other values, two operations are available: multiplication by 2 and division by 3. For the second operation, the operand must be greater than 2

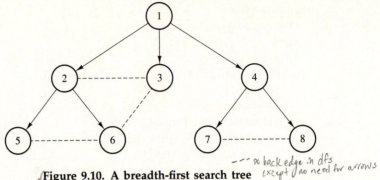

√Figure 9.10. A breadth-first search tree --- α back edge in dfs
except no need for arrows

(so we cannot reach 0), and any resulting fraction is dropped. If operations are executed from left to right, we may for instance obtain the value 10 as

$$10 = 1 \times 2 \times 2 \times 2 \times 2 \div 3 \times 2.$$

We want to obtain some specified value n. How should we set about it?

The problem can be represented as a search in the infinite directed graph of Figure 9.11. Here the given value 1 is in the node at top left. Thereafter each node is linked to the values that can be obtained using the two available operations. For example, from the value 16, we can obtain the two new values 32 (by multiplying 16 by 2) and 5 (by dividing 16 by 3, dropping the resulting fraction). For clarity, we have omitted links backwards to values already available, for instance from 8 to 2. These backwards links are nevertheless present in the real graph. The graph is infinite, for a sequence such as $1, 2, \ldots, 256, 512, \ldots$ can be continued indefinitely. It is not a tree, because node 42, for instance, can be reached from both 128 and 21. When the backwards links are included, it is not even acyclic.

To solve a given instance of the problem, that is, to find how to construct a particular value n, we search the graph starting at 1 until we find the value we are looking for. On this infinite graph, however, a depth-first search may not work. Suppose for example that $n = 13$. If we explore the neighbours of a node in the order "first multiplication by 2, then division by 3", a depth-first search visits successively nodes $1, 2, 4, \ldots$, and so on, heading off along the top branch and (since there is always a new neighbour to look at) never encountering a situation that forces it to back up to a previous node. In this case the search certainly fails. If on the other hand we explore the neighbours of a node in the order "first division by 3, then multiplication by 2", the search first runs down to node 12; from there it moves successively to nodes 24, 48, 96, 32, and 64, and from 64 it wanders off into the upper right-hand part of the graph. We may be lucky enough to get back to node 13 and thus find a solution to our problem, but nothing guarantees this. Even if we do, the solution found will be more complex than necessary. If you program this depth-first search on a computer, you will find in fact that you reach the given value 13 after 74 multiplication and division operations.

A breadth-first search, on the other hand, is sure to find a solution to the instance if there is one. If we examine neighbours in the order "first multiplication by 2,

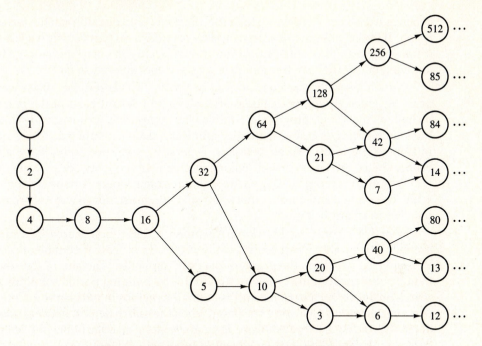

Figure 9.11. Multiplication by 2 and division by 3

then division by 3", a breadth-first search starting at 1 visits successively nodes $1, 2, \ldots, 16, 32, 5, 64, 10, 128, 21, 20, 3$, and so on. Not only are we sure to find the value we seek if it is in the graph, but also the solution obtained will use the smallest number of operations possible. In other words, the path found from 1 to the desired value n will be as short as possible. The same is true if we carry out the search looking at neighbours in the order "first division by 3, then multiplication by 2". Using either of these breadth-first searches, it is easy (even by hand) to discover several ways to produce the value 13 using just 9 operations. For example

$$13 = 1 \times 2 \times 2 \times 2 \times 2 \div 3 \times 2 \times 2 \times 2 \div 3.$$

Of course even a breadth-first search may fail. In our example, it may be that some values n are not present in the graph at all. (Having no idea whether this is true or not, we leave the question as an exercise for the reader.) In this case any search technique is certain to fail for the missing values. If a graph includes one or more nodes with an infinite number of neighbours, but no paths of infinite length, depth-first search may succeed where breadth-first search fails. Nevertheless this situation seems to be less common than its opposite.

9.6 Backtracking

As we saw earlier, various problems can be thought of in terms of abstract graphs. For example, we saw in Section 9.1 that we can use the nodes of a graph to represent positions in a game of chess, and edges to represent legal moves. Often the original problem translates to searching for a specific node, path or pattern in the associated graph. If the graph contains a large number of nodes, and particularly if it is infinite, it may be wasteful or infeasible to build it explicitly in computer storage before applying one of the search techniques we have encountered so far.

In such a situation we use an *implicit graph*. This is one for which we have available a description of its nodes and edges, so relevant parts of the graph can be built as the search progresses. In this way computing time is saved whenever the search succeeds before the entire graph has been constructed. The economy in storage space can also be dramatic, especially when nodes that have already been searched can be discarded, making room for subsequent nodes to be explored. If the graph involved is infinite, such a technique offers our only hope of exploring it at all. This section and the ones that follow detail some standard ways of organizing searches in an implicit graph.

In its basic form, backtracking resembles a depth-first search in a directed graph. The graph concerned is usually a tree, or at least it contains no cycles. Whatever its structure, the graph exists only implicitly. The aim of the search is to find solutions to some problem. We do this by building partial solutions as the search proceeds; such partial solutions limit the regions in which a complete solution may be found. Generally speaking, when the search begins, nothing is known about the solutions to the problem. Each move along an edge of the implicit graph corresponds to adding a new element to a partial solution, that is, to narrowing down the remaining possibilities for a complete solution. The search is successful if, proceeding in this way, a solution can be completely defined. In this case the algorithm may either stop (if only one solution to the problem is needed), or continue looking for alternative solutions (if we want to look at them all). On the other hand, the search is unsuccessful if at some stage the partial solution constructed so far cannot be completed. In this case the search backs up, exactly like a depth-first search, removing as it goes the elements that were added at each stage. When it gets back to a node with one or more unexplored neighbours, the search for a solution resumes.

9.6.1 The knapsack problem (3)

For a first example illustrating the general principle, we return to the knapsack problem described in Section 8.4. Recall that we are given a certain number of objects and a knapsack. This time, however, instead of supposing that we have n objects available, we shall suppose that we have n *types* of object, and that an adequate number of objects of each type are available. This does not alter the problem in any important way. For $i = 1, 2, \ldots, n$, an object of type i has a positive weight w_i and a positive value v_i. The knapsack can carry a weight not exceeding W. Our aim is to fill the knapsack in a way that maximizes the value of the included objects, while respecting the capacity constraint. We may take an object or to leave it behind, but we may not take a fraction of an object.

Suppose for concreteness that we wish to solve an instance of the problem involving four types of objects, whose weights are respectively 2, 3, 4 and 5 units, and whose values are 3, 5, 6 and 10. The knapsack can carry a maximum of 8

units of weight. This can be done using backtracking by exploring the implicit tree
shown in Figure 9.12.

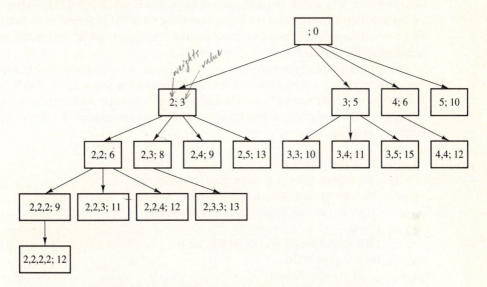

Figure 9.12. The implicit tree for a knapsack problem

Here a node such as $(2,3;8)$ corresponds to a partial solution of our problem.
The figures to the left of the semicolon are the weights of the objects we have
decided to include, and the figure to the right is the current value of the load.
Moving down from a node to one of its children corresponds to deciding which
kind of object to put into the knapsack next. Without loss of generality we may
agree to load objects into the knapsack in order of increasing weight. This is not
essential, and indeed any other order—by decreasing weight, for example, or by
value—would work just as well, but it reduces the size of the tree to be searched.
For instance, once we have visited node $(2,2,3;11)$ there is no point in later visiting
$(2,3,2;11)$.

Initially the partial solution is empty. The backtracking algorithm explores
the tree as in a depth-first search, constructing nodes and partial solutions as it
goes. In the example, the first node visited is $(2;3)$, the next is $(2,2;6)$, the third is
$(2,2,2;9)$ and the fourth $(2,2,2,2;12)$. As each new node is visited, the partial solution is extended. After visiting these four nodes, the depth-first search is blocked:
node $(2,2,2,2;12)$ has no unvisited successors (indeed no successors at all), since
adding more items to this partial solution would violate the capacity constraint.
Since this partial solution may turn out to be the optimal solution to our instance,
we memorize it.

The depth-first search now backs up to look for other solutions. At each step
back up the tree, the corresponding item is removed from the partial solution.
In the example, the search first backs up to $(2,2,2;9)$, which also has no unvisited
successors; one step further up the tree, however, at node $(2,2;6)$, two successors

remain to be visited. After exploring nodes $(2,2,3;11)$ and $(2,2,4;12)$, neither of which improves on the solution previously memorized, the search backs up one stage further, and so on. Exploring the tree in this way, $(2,3,3;13)$ is found to be a better solution than the one we have, and later $(3,5;15)$ is found to be better still. Since no other improvement is made before the search ends, this is the optimal solution to the instance.

Programming the algorithm is straightforward, and illustrates the close relation between recursion and depth-first search. Suppose the values of n and W, and of the arrays $w[1..n]$ and $v[1..n]$ for the instance to be solved are available as global variables. The ordering of the types of item is unimportant. Define a function *backpack* as follows.

> **function** *backpack*(i, r)
> {Calculates the value of the best load that can
>   be constructed using items of types i to n
>   and whose total weight does not exceed r}
> $b \leftarrow 0$
> {Try each allowed kind of item in turn}
> **for** $k \leftarrow i$ **to** n **do**
>   **if** $w[k] \leq r$ **then**
> $b \leftarrow \max(b, v[k] + backpack(k, r - w[k]))$
> **return** b

Now to find the value of the best load, call *backpack*$(1, W)$. Here each recursive call of *backpack* corresponds to extending the depth-first search one level down the tree, while the **for** loop takes care of examining all the possibilities at a given level. In this version of the program, the composition of the load being examined is given implicitly by the values of k saved on the recursive stack. It is not hard to adapt the program so that it gives the composition of the best load explicitly along with its value; see Problem 9.42.

9.6.2 The eight queens problem

For our second example of backtracking, consider the classic problem of placing eight queens on a chessboard in such a way that none of them threatens any of the others. Recall that a queen threatens the squares in the same row, in the same column, or on the same diagonals.

The most obvious way to solve this problem consists of trying systematically all the ways of placing eight queens on a chessboard, checking each time to see whether a solution has been obtained. This approach is of no practical use, even with a computer, since the number of positions we would have to check is $\binom{64}{8} = 4\,426\,165\,368$. The first improvement we might try consists of never putting more than one queen on any given row. This reduces the computer representation of the chessboard to a vector of eight elements, each giving the position of the queen in the corresponding row. For instance, the vector $(3,1,6,2,8,6,4,7)$ represents the position where the queen on row 1 is in column 3, the queen on row 2 is in column 1, and so on. This particular position is not a solution to our problem since the queens in rows 3 and 6 are in the same column, and also two pairs of queens lie on the same diagonal. Using this representation, we can write an algorithm using eight nested loops. (For the function *solution*, see Problem 9.43.)

```
program queens1
    for i₁ ← 1 to 8 do
        for i₂ ← 1 to 8 do
            · · ·
            for i₈ ← 1 to 8 do
                sol ← [i₁, i₂, ..., i₈]
                if solution(sol) then write sol
                                      stop
    write "there is no solution"
```

The number of positions to be considered is reduced to $8^8 = 16\,777\,216$, although in fact the algorithm finds a solution and stops after considering only $1\,299\,852$ positions.

Representing the chessboard by a vector prevents us ever trying to put two queens in the same row. Once we have realized this, it is natural to be equally systematic in our use of the columns. Hence we now represent the board by a vector of eight *different* numbers between 1 and 8, that is, by a permutation of the first eight integers. This yields the following algorithm.

```
program queens2
    sol ← initial-permutation
    while sol ≠ final-permutation and not solution(sol) do
        sol ← next-permutation
    if solution(sol) then write sol
                      else write "there is no solution"
```

There are several natural ways to generate systematically all the permutations of the first n integers. For instance, we can put each value in turn in the leading position and generate recursively, for each leading value, all the permutations of the remaining $n - 1$ elements. The following procedure shows how to do this. Here $T[1..n]$ is a global array initialized to $[1, 2, ..., n]$, and the initial call of the procedure is *perm*(1). This way of generating permutations is itself a kind of backtracking.

```
procedure perm(i)
    if i = n then use(T)  {T is a new permutation}
             else for j ← i to n do exchange T[i] and T[j]
                                    perm(i + 1)
                                    exchange T[i] and T[j]
```

This approach reduces the number of possible positions to $8! = 40\,320$. If the preceding algorithm is used to generate the permutations, only 2830 positions are in fact considered before the algorithm finds a solution. It is more complicated to generate permutations rather than all the possible vectors of eight integers between 1 and 8. On the other hand, it is easier to verify in this case whether a given position is a solution. Since we already know that two queens can neither be in the same row nor in the same column, it suffices to verify that they are not on the same diagonal.

Starting from a crude method that put the queens absolutely anywhere on the board, we progressed first to a method that never puts two queens in the same row, and then to a still better method that only considers positions where two queens can neither be in the same row nor in the same column. However, all these algorithms share an important defect: they never test a position to see if it is a solution until all the queens have been placed on the board. For instance, even the best of them makes 720 useless attempts to put the last six queens on the board when it has started by putting the first two on the main diagonal, where of course they threaten one another.

Backtracking allows us to do better than this. As a first step, we reformulate the eight queens problem as a tree searching problem. We say that a vector $V[1..k]$ of integers between 1 and 8 is *k-promising*, for $0 \le k \le 8$, if none of the k queens placed in positions $(1, V[1]), (2, V[2]), \ldots, (k, V[k])$ threatens any of the others. Mathematically, a vector V is k-promising if, for every pair of integers i and j between 1 and k with $i \neq j$, we have $V[i] - V[j] \notin \{i - j, 0, j - i\}$. For $k \le 1$, any vector V is k-promising. Solutions to the eight queens problem correspond to vectors that are 8-promising.

Let N be the set of k-promising vectors, $0 \le k \le 8$. Let $G = \langle N, A \rangle$ be the directed graph such that $(U, V) \in A$ if and only if there exists an integer k, $0 \le k < 8$, such that

◇ U is k-promising,

◇ V is $(k + 1)$-promising, and

◇ $U[i] = V[i]$ for every $i \in [1..k]$.

This graph is a tree. Its root is the empty vector corresponding to $k = 0$. Its leaves are either solutions ($k = 8$) or they are dead ends ($k < 8$) such as $[1, 4, 2, 5, 8]$: in such a position it is impossible to place a queen in the next row without threatening at least one of the queens already on the board. The solutions to the eight queens problem can be obtained by exploring this tree. We do not generate the tree explicitly so as to explore it thereafter, however. Rather, nodes are generated and abandoned during the course of the exploration. Depth-first search is the obvious method to use, particularly if we require only one solution.

This technique has two advantages over the algorithm that systematically tries each permutation. First, the number of nodes in the tree is less than $8! = 40\,320$. Although it is not easy to calculate this number theoretically, using a computer it is straightforward to count the nodes: there are 2057. In fact, it suffices to explore 114 nodes to obtain a first solution. Second, to decide whether a vector is k-promising, knowing that it is an extension of a $(k - 1)$-promising vector, we only need check the last queen to be added. This can be speeded up if we associate with each promising node the set of columns, of positive diagonals (at 45 degrees), and of negative diagonals (at 135 degrees) controlled by the queens already placed.

In the following procedure $sol[1..8]$ is a global array. To print all the solutions to the eight queens problem, call $queens(0, \varnothing, \varnothing, \varnothing)$.

> **procedure** $queens(k, col, diag45, diag135)$
> $\{sol[1..k]$ is k-promising,
> $col = \{sol[i] | 1 \le i \le k\}$,
> $diag45 = \{sol[i] - i + 1 | 1 \le i \le k\}$, and
> $diag135 = \{sol[i] + i - 1 | 1 \le i \le k\}\}$
>   **if** $k = 8$ **then** {an 8-promising vector is a solution}
>   **write** sol
>   **else** {explore $(k + 1)$-promising extensions of sol}
>   **for** $j \leftarrow 1$ **to** 8 **do**
>   **if** $j \notin col$ **and** $j - k \notin diag45$ **and** $j + k \notin diag135$
>   **then** $sol[k + 1] \leftarrow j$
> $\{sol[1..k + 1]$ is $(k + 1)$-promising$\}$
> $queens(k + 1, col \cup \{j\}$,
> $diag45 \cup \{j - k\}, diag135 \cup \{j + k\})$

It is clear that the problem generalizes to an arbitrary number of queens: how can we place n queens on an $n \times n$ "chessboard" in such a way that none of them threatens any of the others? As we might expect, the advantage to be gained by using backtracking instead of an exhaustive approach becomes more pronounced as n increases. For example, for $n = 12$ there are 479 001 600 possible permutations to be considered. Using the permutation generator given previously, the first solution to be found corresponds to the 4 546 044th position examined. On the other hand, the tree explored by the backtracking algorithm contains only 856 189 nodes, and a solution is obtained when the 262nd node is visited. The problem can be further generalized to placing "queens" in three dimensions on an $n \times n \times n$ board; see Problem 9.49.

9.6.3 The general template

Backtracking algorithms can be used even when the solutions sought do not necessarily all have the same length. Here is the general scheme.

> **procedure** $backtrack(v[1..k])$
> $\{v$ is a k-promising vector$\}$
>   **if** v is a solution **then write** v
> $\{$**else**$\}$ **for** each $(k + 1)$-promising vector w
>   such that $w[1..k] = v[1..k]$
>   **do** $backtrack(w[1..k + 1])$

The **else** should be present if and only if it is impossible to have two different solutions such that one is a prefix of the other.

Both the knapsack problem and the n queens problem were solved using depth-first search in the corresponding tree. Some problems that can be formulated in terms of exploring an implicit graph have the property that they correspond to an infinite graph. In this case it may be necessary to use breadth-first search to avoid the interminable exploration of some fruitless infinite branch. Breadth-first search is also appropriate if we have to find a solution starting from some initial position and taking as few steps as possible.

9.7 Branch-and-bound

Like backtracking, branch-and-bound is a technique for exploring an implicit directed graph. Again, this graph is usually acyclic or even a tree. This time, we are looking for the optimal solution to some problem. At each node we calculate a bound on the possible value of any solutions that might lie farther on in the graph. If the bound shows that any such solution must necessarily be worse than the best solution found so far, then we need not go on exploring this part of the graph.

In the simplest version, calculation of the bounds is combined with a breadth-first or a depth-first search, and serves only, as we have just explained, to prune certain branches of a tree or to close paths in a graph. More often, however, the calculated bound is also used to choose which open path looks the most promising, so it can be explored first.

In general terms we may say that a depth-first search finishes exploring nodes in inverse order of their creation, using a stack to hold nodes that have been generated but not yet explored fully. A breadth-first search finishes exploring nodes in the order of their creation, using a queue to hold those that have been generated but not yet explored. Branch-and-bound uses auxiliary computations to decide at each instant which node should be explored next, and a priority list to hold those nodes that have been generated but not yet explored. Remember that heaps are often ideal for holding priority lists; see Section 5.7. We illustrate the technique with two examples.

9.7.1 The assignment problem

In the *assignment problem*, n agents are to be assigned n tasks, each agent having exactly one task to perform. If agent i, $1 \le i \le n$, is assigned task j, $1 \le j \le n$, then the cost of performing this particular task will be c_{ij}. Given the complete matrix of costs, the problem is to assign agents to tasks so as to minimize the total cost of executing the n tasks.

For example, suppose three agents a, b and c are to be assigned tasks 1, 2 and 3, and the cost matrix is as follows:

	1	2	3
a	4	7	3
b	2	6	1
c	3	9	4

If we allot task 1 to agent a, task 2 to agent b, and task 3 to agent c, then our total cost will be $4 + 6 + 4 = 14$, while if we allot task 3 to agent a, task 2 to agent b, and task 1 to agent c, the cost is only $3 + 6 + 3 = 12$. In this particular example, the reader may verify that the optimal assignment is $a \to 2$, $b \to 3$, and $c \to 1$, whose cost is $7 + 1 + 3 = 11$.

The assignment problem has numerous applications. For instance, instead of talking about agents and tasks, we might formulate the problem in terms of buildings and sites, where c_{ij} is the cost of erecting building i on site j, and we want to minimize the total cost of the buildings. Other examples are easy to invent. In general, with n agents and n tasks, there are $n!$ possible assignments to consider, too many for an exhaustive search even for moderate values of n. We therefore resort to branch-and-bound.

Suppose we have to solve the instance whose cost matrix is shown in Figure 9.13. To obtain an upper bound on the answer, note that $a \rightarrow 1, b \rightarrow 2, c \rightarrow 3, d \rightarrow 4$ is one possible solution whose cost is $11 + 15 + 19 + 28 = 73$. The optimal solution to the problem cannot cost more than this. Another possible solution is $a \rightarrow 4, b \rightarrow 3, c \rightarrow 2, d \rightarrow 1$ whose cost is obtained by adding the elements in the other diagonal of the cost matrix, giving $40 + 13 + 17 + 17 = 87$. In this case the second solution is no improvement over the first. To obtain a lower bound on the solution, we can argue that whoever executes task 1, the cost will be at least 11; whoever executes task 2, the cost will be at least 12, and so on. Thus adding the smallest elements in each column gives us a lower bound on the answer. In the example, this is $11 + 12 + 13 + 22 = 58$. A second lower bound is obtained by adding the smallest elements in each row, on the grounds that each agent must do something. In this case we find $11 + 13 + 11 + 14 = 49$, not as useful as the previous lower bound. Pulling these facts together, we know that the answer to our instance lies somewhere in $[58..73]$.

	1	2	3	4
a	11	12	18	40
b	14	15	13	22
c	11	17	19	23
d	17	14	20	28

Figure 9.13. The cost matrix for an assignment problem

To solve the problem by branch-and-bound, we explore a tree whose nodes correspond to partial assignments. At the root of the tree, no assignments have been made. Subsequently, at each level we fix the assignment of one more agent. At each node we calculate a bound on the solutions that can be obtained by completing the corresponding partial assignment, and we use this bound both to close off paths and to guide the search. Suppose for example that, starting from the root, we decide first to fix the assignment of agent a. Since there are four ways of doing this, there are four branches from the root. Figure 9.14 illustrates the situation.

Here the figure next to each node is a lower bound on the solutions that can be obtained by completing the corresponding partial assignment. We have already seen how the bound of 58 at the root can be obtained. To calculate the bound for the node $a \rightarrow 1$, for example, note first that with this partial assignment task 1 will cost 11. Task 2 will be executed by b, c or d, so the lowest possible cost is 14. Similarly tasks 3 and 4 will also be executed by b, c or d, and their lowest possible costs will be 13 and 22 respectively. Thus a lower bound on any solution obtained by completing the partial assignment $a \rightarrow 1$ is $11 + 14 + 13 + 22 = 60$. Similarly for the node $a \rightarrow 2$, task 2 will be executed by agent a at a cost of 12, while tasks 1, 3

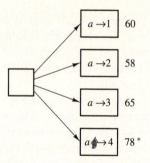

Figure 9.14. After assigning agent a + min (remaining)

and 4 will be executed by agents b, c and d at a minimum cost of 11, 13 and 22 respectively. Thus any solution that includes the assignment $a \rightarrow 2$ will cost at least $12 + 11 + 13 + 22 = 58$. The other two lower bounds are obtained similarly. Since we know the optimal solution cannot exceed 73, it is already clear that there is no point in exploring the node $a \rightarrow 4$ any further: any solution obtained by completing this partial assignment will cost at least 78, so it cannot be optimal. The asterisk on this node indicates that it is "dead". However the other three nodes are still alive. Node $a \rightarrow 2$ has the smallest lower bound. Arguing that it therefore looks more promising than the others, this is the one to explore next. We do this by fixing one more element in the partial assignment, say b. In this way we arrive at the situation shown in Figure 9.15.

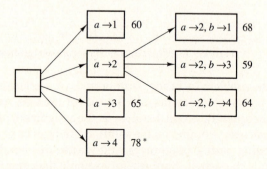

Figure 9.15. After assigning agent b

Again, the figure next to each node gives a lower bound on the cost of solutions that can be obtained by completing the corresponding partial assignment. For example, at node $a \rightarrow 2$, $b \rightarrow 1$, task 1 will cost 14 and task 2 will cost 12. The remaining tasks 3 and 4 must be executed by c or d. The smallest possible cost for task 3 is thus 19, while that for task 4 is 23. Hence a lower bound on the possible solutions is $14 + 12 + 19 + 23 = 68$. The other two new bounds are calculated similarly.

The most promising node in the tree is now $a \rightarrow 2$, $b \rightarrow 3$ with a lower bound of 59. To continue exploring the tree starting at this node, we fix one more element in the partial assignment, say c. When the assignments of a, b and c are fixed, however, we no longer have any choice about how we assign d, so the solution is complete. The right-hand nodes in Figure 9.16, which shows the next stage of our exploration, therefore correspond to complete solutions.

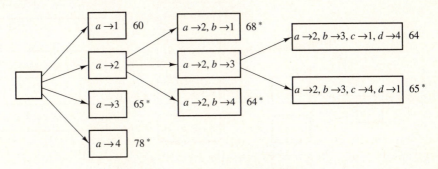

Figure 9.16. After assigning agent c

The solution $a \to 2$, $b \to 3$, $c \to 1$, $d \to 4$, with a cost of 64, is better than either of the solutions we found at the outset, and provides us with a new upper bound on the optimum. Thanks to this new upper bound, we can remove nodes $a \to 3$ and $a \to 2$, $b \to 1$ from further consideration, as indicated by the asterisks. No solution that completes these partial assignments can be as good as the one we have just found. If we only want one solution to the instance, we can eliminate node $a \to 2$, $b \to 4$ as well.

The only node still worth exploring is $a \to 1$. Proceeding as before, after two steps we obtain the final situation shown in Figure 9.17. The best solution found is $a \to 1$, $b \to 3$, $c \to 4$, $d \to 2$ with a cost of 61. At the remaining unexplored nodes the lower bound is greater than 61, so there is no point in exploring them further. The solution above is therefore the optimal solution to our instance.

The example illustrates that, although at an early stage node $a \to 2$ was the most promising, the optimal solution did not in fact come from there. To obtain our answer, we constructed just 15 of the 41 nodes (1 root, 4 at depth 1, 12 at depth 2, and 24 at depth 3) that are present in a complete tree of the type illustrated. Of the 24 possible solutions, only 6 (including the two used to determine the initial upper bound) were examined.

9.7.2 The knapsack problem (4)

As a second example, consider the knapsack problem; see Sections 8.4 and 9.6.1. Here we require to maximize $\sum_{i=1}^{n} x_i v_i$ subject to $\sum_{i=1}^{n} x_i w_i \le W$, where the v_i and w_i are all strictly positive, and the x_i are nonnegative integers. This problem too can be solved by branch-and-bound.

Suppose without loss of generality that the variables are numbered so that $v_i/w_i \ge v_{i+1}/w_{i+1}$. Then if the values of $x_1, \ldots, x_k$, $0 \le k < n$, are fixed, with $\sum_{i=1}^{k} x_i w_i \le W$, it is easy to see that the value obtainable by adding further items

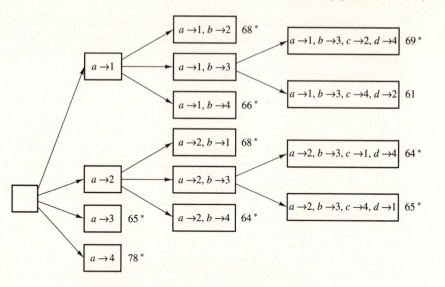

Figure 9.17. The tree completely explored

of types $k + 1, \ldots, n$ to the knapsack cannot exceed

$$\sum_{i=1}^{k} x_i v_i + \left(W - \sum_{i=1}^{k} x_i w_i \right) v_{k+1}/w_{k+1}.$$

Here the first term gives the value of the items already in the knapsack, while the second is a bound on the value that can be added.

To solve the problem by branch-and-bound, we explore a tree where at the root none of the values x_i is fixed, and then at each successive level the value of one more variable is determined, in numerical order of the variables. At each node we explore, we only generate those successors that satisfy the weight constraint, so each node has a finite number of successors. Whenever a node is generated we calculate an upper bound on the value of the solution that can be obtained by completing the partially specified load, and use these upper bounds to cut useless branches and to guide the exploration of the tree. We leave the details to the reader.

9.7.3 General considerations

The need to keep a list of nodes that have been generated but not yet completely explored, situated in several levels of the tree and preferably sorted in order of the corresponding bounds, makes branch-and-bound hard to program. The heap is an ideal data structure for holding this list. Unlike depth-first search and its related techniques, no elegant recursive formulation of branch-and-bound is available to the programmer. Nevertheless the technique is sufficiently powerful that it is often used in practical applications.

It is next to impossible to give any precise idea of how well the technique will perform on a given problem using a given bound. There is always a compromise to be made concerning the quality of the bound to be calculated. With a better bound we look at less nodes, and if we are lucky we may be guided to an optimum solution more quickly. On the other hand, we most likely spend more time at each node calculating the corresponding bound. In the worst case it may turn out that even an excellent bound does not let us cut any branches off the tree, so all the extra work at each node is wasted. In practice, however, for problems of the size encountered in applications, it almost always pays to invest the necessary time in calculating the best possible bound (within reason). For instance, one finds applications such as integer linear programming handled by branch-and-bound, the bound at each node being obtained by solving a related problem in linear programming with continuous variables.

9.8 The minimax principle

Whichever search technique we use, the awkward fact remains that for a game such as chess a complete search of the associated graph is out of the question. In this situation we have to be content with a partial search around the current position. This is the principle underlying an important heuristic called *minimax*. Although this heuristic does not allow us to be certain of winning whenever this is possible, it finds a move that may reasonably be expected to be among the best moves available, while exploring only part of the graph starting from some given position. Exploration of the graph is normally stopped before the terminal positions are reached, using one of several possible criteria, and the positions where exploration stopped are evaluated heuristically. In a sense, this is merely a systematic version of the method used by some human players that consists of looking ahead a small number of moves. Here we only outline the technique.

Suppose then that we want to play a good game of chess. The first step is to define a static evaluation function *eval* that attributes a value to each possible position. Ideally, the value of *eval*(u) should increase as the position u becomes more favourable to White. It is customary to give values not too far from zero to positions where neither side has a marked advantage, and large negative values to positions that favour Black. This evaluation function must take account of many factors: the number and the type of pieces remaining on both sides, control of the centre, freedom of movement, and so on. A compromise must be made between the accuracy of the function and the time needed to calculate it. When applied to a terminal position, the evaluation function should return $+\infty$ if Black has been mated, $-\infty$ if White has been mated, and 0 if the game is a draw. For example, an evaluation function that takes good account of the static aspects of the position, but that is too simplistic to be of real use, might be the following: for nonterminal positions, count 1 point for each white pawn, $3^1/4$ points for each white bishop or knight, 5 points for each white rook, and 10 points for each white queen; subtract a similar number of points for each black piece.

If the static evaluation function were perfect, it would be easy to determine the best move to make. Suppose it is White's turn to move in position u. The best move would be to the position v that maximizes *eval*(v) among all the successors of u.

$val \leftarrow -\infty$
for each position w that is a successor of u **do**
    if $eval(w) \geq val$ **then** $val \leftarrow eval(w)$
                      $v \leftarrow w$

This simplistic approach would not be very successful using the evaluation function suggested earlier, since it would not hesitate to sacrifice a queen to take a pawn!

If the evaluation function is not perfect, a better strategy for White is to assume that Black will reply with the move that minimizes the function $eval$, since the smaller the value of this function, the better the position is supposed to be for him. Ideally, Black would like a large negative value. We are now looking one move ahead. (Remember we agreed to call each action a move, avoiding the term "half-move".)

$val \leftarrow -\infty$
for each position w that is a successor of u **do**
    if w has no successor
        then $valw \leftarrow eval(w)$
        else $valw \leftarrow \min\{eval(x) | x$ is a successor of $w \}$
    if $valw \geq val$ **then** $val \leftarrow valw$
                $v \leftarrow w$

There is now no question of giving away a queen to take a pawn: which of course may be exactly the wrong rule to apply if it prevents White from finding the winning move. Maybe if he looked further ahead the gambit would turn out to be profitable. On the other hand, we are sure to avoid moves that would allow Black to mate immediately (provided we *can* avoid this).

To add more dynamic aspects to the static evaluation provided by $eval$, it is preferable to look several moves ahead. To look n moves ahead from position u, White should move to the position v given by

$val \leftarrow -\infty$
for each position w that is a successor of u **do**
    $B \leftarrow Black(w, n)$
    if $B \geq val$ **then** $val \leftarrow B$
               $v \leftarrow w$

where the functions $Black$ and $White$ are the following.

function $Black(w, n)$
    if $n = 0$ **or** w has no successor
        then return $eval(w)$
        else return $\min\{White(x, n - 1) | x$ is a successor of $w\}$

function $White(w, n)$
    if $n = 0$ **or** w has no successor
        then return $eval(w)$
        else return $\max\{Black(x, n - 1) | x$ is a successor of $w\}$

We see why the technique is called minimax. Black tries to minimize the advantage he allows to White, and White, on the other hand, tries to maximize the advantage he obtains from each move.

More generally, suppose Figure 9.18 shows part of the graph corresponding to some game. If the values attached to the nodes on the lowest level are obtained by applying the function *eval* to the corresponding positions, the values for the other nodes can be calculated using the minimax rule. In the example we suppose that player A is trying to maximize the evaluation function and that player B is trying to minimize it. If A plays to maximize his advantage, he will choose the second of the three possible moves. This assures him a value of at least 10; but see Problem 9.55.

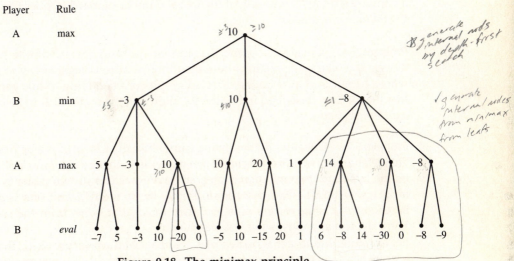

Figure 9.18. The minimax principle

The basic minimax technique can be improved in a number of ways. For example, it may be worthwhile to explore the most promising moves in greater depth. Similarly, the exploration of certain branches can be abandoned early if the information we have about them is already sufficient to show that they cannot possibly influence the value of nodes further up the tree. This second type of improvement, which we shall not describe in this book, is generally known as *alpha-beta pruning*.

9.9 Problems

Problem 9.1.   Add nodes $\langle 8,7 \rangle$, $\langle 7,6 \rangle$, $\langle 6,5 \rangle$ and their descendants to the graph of Figure 9.1.

Problem 9.2.   Can a winning position in the game described in Section 9.1 have more than one losing position among its successors? In other words, are there positions in which several different winning moves are available? Can this happen in the case of a winning initial position $\langle n, n-1 \rangle$?

Problem 9.3.   Suppose we change the rules of the game of Section 9.1 so that the player who is forced to take the last match *loses*. This is the *misère* version of the game. Suppose also that the first player must take at least one match and that he must leave at least two. Among the initial positions with three to eight matches, which are now winning positions for the first player?

Problem 9.4.   Modify the algorithm *recwin* of Section 9.1 so it returns an integer k, where $k = 0$ if the position is a losing position, and $1 \leq k \leq j$ if it is a winning move to take k matches.

Problem 9.5.   Prove that in the game described in Section 9.1 the first player has a winning strategy if and only if the initial number of matches does not appear in the Fibonacci sequence.

Problem 9.6.   Consider a game that cannot continue for an infinite number of moves, and where no position offers an infinite number of legal moves to the player whose turn it is. Let G be the directed graph corresponding to this game. Show that the method described in Section 9.1 allows *all* the nodes of G to be labelled as *win*, *lose* or *draw*.

Problem 9.7.   Consider the following game. Initially a heap of n matches is placed on the table between two players. Each player in turn may either (a) split any heap on the table into two unequal heaps, or (b) remove one or two matches from any heap on the table. He may not do both. He may only split one heap, and if he chooses to remove two matches, they must both come from the same heap. The player who removes the last match wins.

For example, suppose that during play we arrive at the position $\{5, 4\}$; that is, there are two heaps on the table, one of 5 matches, the other of 4. The player whose turn it is may move to $\{4, 3, 2\}$ or $\{4, 4, 1\}$ by splitting the heap of 5, to $\{5, 3, 1\}$ by splitting the heap of 4 (but not to $\{5, 2, 2\}$, since the new heaps must be unequal), or to $\{4, 4\}$, $\{4, 3\}$, $\{5, 3\}$ or $\{5, 2\}$ by taking one or two matches from either of the heaps.

Sketch the graph of the game for $n = 5$. If both play correctly, does the first or the second player win?

Problem 9.8.   Repeat the previous problem for the *misère* version of the game, where the player who takes the last match loses.

Problem 9.9.   Consider a game of the type described in Section 9.1. When we use a graph of winning and losing positions to describe such a game, we implicitly assume that both players will move intelligently so as to maximize their chances of winning. Can a player in a winning position lose if his opponent moves stupidly and makes an unexpected "error"?

Problem 9.10.   For any of the tree traversal techniques mentioned in Section 9.2, prove that a recursive implementation takes storage space in $\Omega(n)$ in the worst case.

Problem 9.11.   Show how any of the tree traversal techniques mentioned in Section 9.2 can be implemented so as to take only a time in $\Theta(n)$ and storage space in $\Theta(1)$, even when the nodes do not contain a pointer to their parents (in which case the problem is trivial).

Problem 9.12.   Generalize the concepts of preorder and postorder to arbitrary (nonbinary) trees. Assume the trees are represented as in Figure 5.7. Prove that both these techniques still run in a time in the order of the number of nodes in the tree to be traversed.

Problem 9.13.   In Section 9.2 we gave one way of preconditioning a tree so as to be able thereafter to verify rapidly whether one node is an ancestor of another. There exist several similar ways of arriving at the same result. Show, for example, that it can be done using a traversal in preorder followed by a traversal in inverted preorder, which visits first a node and then its subtrees from right to left.
If the trees are represented as in Figure 5.7, is this method more or less efficient than the one given in Section 9.2, or are they comparable?

Problem 9.14.   Show how a depth-first search progresses through the graph of Figure 9.3 if the starting point is node 6 and the neighbours of a given node are examined (a) in numerical order, and (b) in decreasing numerical order.
Exhibit the spanning tree and the numbering of the nodes of the graph generated by each of these searches.

Problem 9.15.   Analyse the running time of algorithm *dfs* if the graph to be explored is represented by an adjacency matrix (type *adjgraph* of Section 5.4) rather than by lists of adjacent nodes.

Problem 9.16.   Show how depth-first search can be used to find the connected components of an undirected graph.

Problem 9.17.   Let G be an undirected graph, and let T be the spanning tree generated by a depth-first search of G. Prove that an edge of G that has no corresponding edge in T cannot join nodes in different branches of the tree, but must necessarily join some node v to one of its ancestors in T.

Problem 9.18.   Prove or give a counterexample:
(a) if a graph is biconnected, then it is bicoherent;
(b) if a graph is bicoherent, then it is biconnected.

Problem 9.19.   Prove that a node v in a connected graph is an articulation point if and only if there exist two nodes a and b different from v such that every path joining a and b passes through v.

Problem 9.20.   Prove that for every pair of distinct nodes v and w in a biconnected graph, there exist at least two paths joining v and w that have no nodes in common except the starting and ending nodes.

Problem 9.21.   In the algorithm for finding the articulation points of an undirected graph given in Section 9.3.1, show how to calculate the values of both *prenum* and *highest* during the depth-first search of the graph, and implement the corresponding algorithm.

Problem 9.22.   The example in Section 9.3.1 finds the articulation points for the graph of Figure 9.3 using a depth-first search starting at node 1. Verify that the same articulation points are found if the search starts at node 6.

Problem 9.23.   Illustrate how the algorithm for finding the articulation points of an undirected graph given in Section 9.3.1 works on the graph of Figure 9.19, starting the search (a) at node 1, and (b) at node 3.

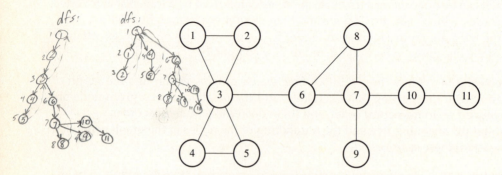

Figure 9.19. A graph with articulation points

Problem 9.24.   A graph is *planar* if it can be drawn on a sheet of paper so that none of the edges cross. Use depth-first search to design an algorithm capable of deciding in linear time if a given graph is planar.

Problem 9.25.   Illustrate the progress of the depth-first search algorithm on the graph of Figure 9.5 if the starting point is node 1 and the neighbours of a given node are examined in decreasing numerical order.

Problem 9.26.   Let F be the forest generated by a depth-first search on a directed graph $G = \langle N, A \rangle$. Prove that G is acyclic if and only if the set of edges of G with no corresponding edge in F includes no edge leading from a node to one of its ancestors in the forest.

Problem 9.27.   For the graph of Figure 9.8, what is the topological order obtained if we use the procedure suggested in Section 9.4.1, starting the depth-first search at node 1, and visiting the neighbours of a node in numerical order?

Problem 9.28.   What is wrong with the following argument? When we visit node v of a graph G using depth-first search, we immediately explore all the other nodes that can be reached from v by following edges of G. In the topological ordering, these other nodes must come later than v. Thus to obtain a topological ordering of the nodes, it suffices to add an extra line

>   **write** v

at the beginning of procedure *dfs*.

Problem 9.29.   A directed graph is *strongly connected* if there exist paths from u to v and from v to u for every pair of nodes u and v. If a directed graph is not strongly connected, the largest sets of nodes such that the induced subgraphs are strongly connected are called the *strongly connected components* of the graph. For example, the strongly connected components of the graph in Figure 9.5 are $\{1,2,3\}$, $\{5,6\}$ and $\{4,7,8\}$. Design an efficient algorithm based on depth-first search to find the strongly connected components of a graph.

Problem 9.30.   After a breadth-first search in an undirected graph G, let F be the forest of trees that is generated. If $\{u, v\}$ is an edge of G that has no corresponding edge in F (such an edge is represented by a broken line in Figure 9.10), show that the nodes u and v lie in the same tree in F, but neither u nor v is an ancestor of the other.

Problem 9.31.   Show how a breadth-first search progresses through the graph of Figure 9.5, assuming that the neighbours of a node are visited in numerical order, and that the necessary starting points are also chosen in numerical order.

Problem 9.32.   Sketch the forest generated by the search of Problem 9.31, showing the remaining edges of the graph as broken lines. How many kinds of "broken" edges are possible?

Problem 9.33.   Justify the claim that a depth-first search of the graph of Figure 9.11, starting at node 1 and visiting neighbours in the order "first division by 3, then multiplication by 2", works down to node 12 and then visits successively nodes 24, 48, 96, 32 and 64.

Problem 9.34.   List the first 15 nodes visited by a breadth-first search of the graph of Figure 9.11 starting at node 1 and visiting neighbours in the order "first division by 3, then multiplication by 2".

Problem 9.35.   Section 9.5 gives one way to produce the value 13, starting from 1 and using the operations multiplication by 2 and division by 3. Find another way to produce the value 13 using the same starting point and the same operations.

Problem 9.36.   A node p of a directed graph $G = \langle N, A \rangle$ is called a *sink* if for every node $v \in N$, $v \neq p$, the edge (v, p) exists, whereas the edge (p, v) does not exist. Write an algorithm that can detect the presence of a sink in G in a time in $O(n)$, where n is the number of nodes in the graph. Your algorithm should accept the graph represented by its adjacency matrix (type *adjgraph* of Section 5.4). Notice that a running time in $O(n)$ for this problem is remarkable given that the instance takes a space in $\Omega(n^2)$ merely to write down.

Problem 9.37. An *Euler path* in an undirected graph is a path where every edge appears exactly once. Design an algorithm that determines whether or not a given graph has an Euler path, and prints the path if so. How much time does your algorithm take?

Problem 9.38. Repeat Problem 9.37 for a directed graph.

Problem 9.39. In either a directed or an undirected graph, a path is said to be Hamiltonian if it passes exactly once through each node of the graph, without coming back to the starting node. In a directed graph, however, the direction of the edges in the path must be taken into account. Prove that if a directed graph is complete (that is, if each pair of nodes is joined in at least one direction) then it has a Hamiltonian path. Give an algorithm for finding such a path in this case.

Problem 9.40. Sketch the search tree explored by a backtracking algorithm solving the same instance of the knapsack problem as that in Section 9.6.1, but assuming this time that items are loaded in order of decreasing weight.

Problem 9.41. Solve the same instance of the knapsack problem as that in Section 9.6.1 by dynamic programming. You will need to work Problem 8.15 first.

Problem 9.42. Adapt the function *backpack* of Section 9.6.1 to give the composition of the best load as well as its value.

Problem 9.43. Let the vector $q[1..8]$ represent the positions of eight queens on a chessboard, with one queen in each row: if $q[i] = j$, $1 \le i \le 8$, $1 \le j \le 8$, the queen in row i is in column j. Write a function *solution*(q) that returns *false* if at least one pair of queens threaten each another, and returns *true* otherwise.

Problem 9.44. Given that the algorithm *queens*1 finds a solution and stops after trying 1 299 852 positions, solve the eight queens problem without using a computer.

Problem 9.45. Suppose the procedure *use*(T) called from the procedure *perm*(i) of Section 9.6 consists simply of printing the array T on a new line. Show the result of calling *perm*(1) when $n = 4$.

Problem 9.46. Suppose the procedure *use*(T) called from the procedure *perm*(i) of Section 9.6 takes constant time. How much time is needed, as a function of n, to execute the call *perm*(1)?
Rework the problem assuming now that *use*(T) takes a time in $\Theta(n)$.

Problem 9.47. For which values of n does the n queens problem have no solutions? Prove your answer.

Problem 9.48. How many solutions are there to the eight queens problem? How many *distinct* solutions are there if we do not distinguish solutions that can be transformed into one another by rotations and reflections?

Problem 9.49.   Investigate the problem of placing k "queens" on an $n \times n \times n$ three-dimensional board. Assume that a "queen" in three dimensions threatens positions in the same rows, columns or diagonals as herself in the obvious way. Clearly k cannot exceed n^2. Not counting the trivial case $n = 1$, what is the smallest value of n for which a solution with n^2 "queens" is possible?

Problem 9.50.   A Boolean array $M[1 .. n, 1 .. n]$ represents a square maze. In general, starting from a given point, you may move to adjacent points in the same row or the same column. If $M[i, j]$ is *true*, you may pass through point (i, j); if $M[i, j]$ is *false*, you may not pass through point (i, j). Figure 9.20 gives an example.
Give a backtracking algorithm that finds a path, if one exists, from $(1, 1)$ to (n, n). Without being completely formal—for instance, you may use statements such as "**for** each point v that is a neighbour of x **do** ..."—your algorithm must be clear and precise.

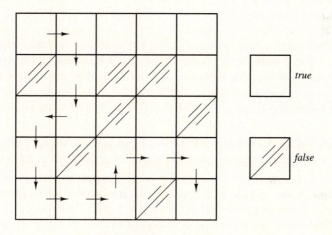

Figure 9.20. A maze

Problem 9.51.   The backtracking method suggested in Problem 9.50 illustrates the principle, but is very inefficient in practice. Find a much better way of solving the same problem.

Problem 9.52.   In Section 9.7 we calculated lower bounds for the nodes in the search tree by assuming that each unassigned task would be executed by the unassigned agent who could do it at least cost. This is like crossing out the rows and columns of the cost matrix corresponding to agents and tasks already assigned, and then adding the minimum elements from each remaining column. An alternative method of calculating bounds is to assume that each unassigned agent will perform the task he can do at least cost. This is like crossing out the rows and columns of the cost matrix corresponding to agents and tasks already assigned, and then adding the minimum elements from each remaining row. Show how a branch-and-bound algorithm for the instance in Section 9.7 proceeds using this second method of calculating lower bounds.

Problem 9.53. Use branch-and-bound to solve the assignment problems with the following cost matrices:

	1	2	3	4
a	94	1	54	68
b	74	10	88	82
c	62	88	8	76
d	11	74	81	21

(a)

	1	2	3	4	5
a	11	17	8	16	20
b	9	7	12	6	15
c	13	16	15	12	16
d	21	24	17	28	26
e	14	10	12	11	15

(b)

Problem 9.54. Four types of object are available, whose weights are respectively 7, 4, 3 and 2 units, and whose values are 9, 5, 3 and 1. We can carry a maximum of 10 units of weight. Objects may not be broken into smaller pieces. Determine the most valuable load that can be carried, using (a) dynamic programming, and (b) branch-and-bound. For part (a), you will need to work Problem 8.15 first.

Problem 9.55. Looking at the tree of Figure 9.18, we said that the player about to move in this position is assured a value of at least 10. Is this strictly true?

Problem 9.56. Let u correspond to the initial position of the pieces in the game of chess. What can you say about $White(u, 12345)$, besides the fact that it would take far too long to calculate in practice, even with a special-purpose computer? Justify your answer.

Problem 9.57. Three-dimensional tictactoe is played on a $4 \times 4 \times 4$ "board". As in ordinary tictactoe, players X and O mark squares alternately. The winner is the first to align four of his own marks in any direction, parallel to one side of the board or along a diagonal. There are 76 ways of winning. Devise an evaluation function for positions in this game, and use it to write a program to play the game against a human opponent.

9.10 References and further reading

There exist a number of books concerning graph algorithms or combinatorial problems that are often posed in terms of graphs. We mention in chronological order Christofides (1975), Lawler (1976), Reingold, Nievergelt and Deo (1977), Gondran and Minoux (1979), Even (1980), Papadimitriou and Steiglitz (1982), Tarjan (1983) and Melhorn (1984b). The mathematical notion of a graph is treated at length in Berge (1958, 1970).

Berlekamp, Conway and Guy (1982) give more versions of the game of Nim than most people will care to read. The game in Problem 9.7 is a variant of Grundy's game, also discussed by Berlekamp, Conway and Guy (1982). The book by Nilsson (1971) is a goldmine of ideas concerning graphs and games, the minimax technique, and alpha-beta pruning. Some algorithms for playing chess appear in Good (1968). A lively account of the first time a computer program beat the world backgammon champion is given in Deyong (1977). For a more technical description of this feat, consult Berliner (1980). In 1994, Garri Kasparov, the world chess champion, was beaten by a Pentium microcomputer. At the time of writing, humans are still unbeaten at the game of go.

A solution to Problem 9.11 is given in Robson (1973). To learn more about preconditioning, read Brassard and Bratley (1988). Many algorithms based on depth-first search can be found in Tarjan (1972), Hopcroft and Tarjan (1973) and Aho, Hopcroft and Ullman (1974, 1983). Problem 9.24 is solved in Hopcroft and Tarjan (1974). See also Rosenthal and Goldner (1977) for an efficient algorithm that, given an undirected graph that is connected but not biconnected, finds a smallest set of edges that can be added to make the graph biconnected.

The problem involving multiplying by 3 and dividing by 2 is reminiscent of Collatz's problem: see Problem E16 in Guy (1981). Backtracking is described in Golomb and Baumert (1965) and techniques for analysing its efficiency are given in Knuth (1975). The eight queens problem was invented by Bezzel in 1848; see the account of Ball (1967). Irving (1984) gives a particularly efficient backtracking algorithm to find all the solutions for the n queens problem. The problem can be solved in linear time with a divide-and-conquer algorithm due to Abramson and Yung (1989) provided we are happy with a single solution. We shall come back to this problem in Chapter 10. The three-dimensional n^2 queens problem mentioned in Problem 9.49 was posed by McCarty (1978) and solved by Allison, Yee and McGaughey (1989): there are no solutions for $n < 11$ but 264 solutions exist for $n = 11$.

Branch-and-bound is explained in Lawler and Wood (1966). The assignment problem is well known in operations research: see Hillier and Lieberman (1967). For an example of solving the knapsack problem by backtracking, see Hu (1981). Branch-and-bound is used to solve the travelling salesperson problem in Bellmore and Nemhauser (1968).

Chapter 10

Probabilistic Algorithms

10.1 Introduction

Imagine you are the heroine of a fairy tale. A treasure is hidden at a place described by a map that you cannot quite decipher. You have managed to reduce the search to two possible hiding-places, which are, however, a considerable distance apart. If you were at one or the other of these two places, you would immediately know whether it was the right one. It takes five days to get to either of the possible hiding-places, or to travel from one of them to the other. The problem is complicated by the fact that a dragon visits the treasure every night and carries part of it away to an inaccessible den in the mountains. You estimate it will take four more days' computation to solve the mystery of the map and thus to know with certainty where the treasure is hidden, but if you set out on a journey you will no longer have access to your computer. An elf offers to show you how to decipher the map if you pay him the equivalent of the treasure that the dragon can carry away in three nights. Should you accept the elf's offer?

Obviously it is preferable to give three nights' worth of treasure to the elf rather than allow the dragon four extra nights of plunder. If you are willing to take a calculated risk, however, you can do better. Suppose that x is the value of the treasure remaining today, and that y is the value of the treasure carried off every night by the dragon. Suppose further that $x > 9y$. Remembering it will take you five days to reach the hiding-place, you can expect to come home with $x - 9y$ if you wait four days to finish deciphering the map. If you accept the elf's offer, you can set out immediately and bring back $x - 5y$, of which $3y$ will go to pay the elf; you will thus have $x - 8y$ left. A better strategy is to toss a coin to decide which possible hiding-place to visit first, journeying on to the other if you find you have decided wrong. This gives you one chance out of two of coming home with $x - 5y$, and one chance out of two of coming home with $x - 10y$. Your expected profit is therefore $x - 7.5x$.

This fable can be translated into the context of algorithmics as follows: when an algorithm is confronted by a choice, it is sometimes preferable to choose a course of action at random, rather than to spend time working out which alternative is best. Such a situation arises when the time required to determine the optimal choice is prohibitive, compared to the time saved on the average by making this optimal choice.

The main characteristic of probabilistic algorithms is that the same algorithm may behave differently when it is applied twice to the same instance. Its execution time, and even the result obtained, may vary considerably from one use to the next. This can be exploited in a variety of ways. For example, a deterministic algorithm is never allowed to go astray (infinite loop, division by zero, etc.) because if it does so on a given instance, we can never solve this instance with that algorithm. By contrast, such behaviour is acceptable for a probabilistic algorithm provided it occurs with reasonably small probability on any given instance: if the algorithm gets stuck, simply restart it on the same instance for a fresh chance of success. Another bonus of this approach is that if there is more than one correct answer, several different ones may be obtained by running the probabilistic algorithm more than once; a deterministic algorithm always comes up with the same answer, although of course it can be programmed to seek several.

Another consequence of the fact that probabilistic algorithms may behave differently when run twice on the same input is that we shall sometimes allow them to yield erroneous results. Provided this happens with reasonably small probability on any given instance, it suffices to invoke the algorithm several times on the desired instance to build arbitrarily high confidence that the correct answer is obtained. By contrast, a deterministic algorithm that gives wrong answers on some inputs is worthless for most applications because it will *always* err on those inputs.

The analysis of probabilistic algorithms is often complex, requiring an acquaintance with results in probability and statistics beyond those introduced in Section 1.7.4. For this reason, a number of results are cited without proof in this chapter.

10.2 Probabilistic does not imply uncertain

Many probabilistic algorithms give probabilistic answers, that is answers that are not necessarily exact. There are critical applications for which such uncertain answers cannot be tolerated. Nevertheless, the error probability can often be brought down below that of a hardware error during the significantly longer time needed to compute the answer deterministically. Thus, paradoxically, it may happen that the uncertain answer given by a probabilistic algorithm is not only obtained faster but is actually more to be trusted than the "guaranteed" answer obtained by a deterministic algorithm! Moreover, there are problems for which no algorithm is known, be it deterministic or probabilistic, that can give the answer with certainty within a reasonable amount of time (even ignoring possible hardware errors), yet probabilistic algorithms can solve the problem quickly if an arbitrarily small error probability is tolerated. This is the case, for example, if you want to determine whether a 1000-digit number is prime or composite.

Two categories of probabilistic algorithms do not guarantee correctness of the result. *Numerical* algorithms yield a *confidence interval* of the form "With probability 90%, the correct answer is 59 plus or minus 3". The more time you allow such numerical algorithms, the more precise the interval is. Opinion polls provide a familiar example of this type of answer. Furthermore, they illustrate that a probabilistic algorithm can be much more efficient, albeit less precise, than the corresponding deterministic algorithm—a general election. Numerical algorithms are useful if you are satisfied with an approximation to the correct answer. By contrast, so-called *Monte Carlo* algorithms give the exact answer with high probability, although sometimes they provide a wrong answer. In general, you cannot tell if the answer provided by a Monte Carlo algorithm is correct, but you can reduce the error probability arbitrarily by allowing the algorithm more time. (For historical reasons, some authors use the term "Monte Carlo" for any probabilistic algorithm, and in particular for those we call "numerical".)

Not all probabilistic algorithms give probabilistic answers, however. Often, probabilistic choices are used only to guide the algorithm more quickly towards the desired solution, in which case the answer obtained is always correct. Furthermore, it may happen that any purported solution can be verified efficiently for correctness. If it is found to be wrong, the probabilistic algorithm should admit that it failed rather than respond incorrectly. Probabilistic algorithms that never give an incorrect answer are called *Las Vegas*. Once again, the possibility that the algorithm might admit failure is not dramatic: simply keep trying the algorithm on the desired input until it is successful.

Somewhat facetiously, we illustrate the difference between the various types of probabilistic algorithm by how they would answer the question: "When did Christopher Columbus discover America?" Called 5 times, a numerical probabilistic algorithm might answer

Between 1490 and 1500
Between 1485 and 1495
Between 1491 and 1501
Between 1480 and 1490
Between 1489 and 1499.

If we give the algorithm more time, we may reduce the probability of a false bracket (apparently 20% on our sample since the fourth answer was incorrect) or decrease the span of each bracket (11 years in our example), or both. When asked the same question, a Monte Carlo algorithm called 10 times might answer

1492, 1492, 1492, 1491, 1492, 1492, 357 B.C., 1492, 1492, 1492.

Again we have a 20% error rate on this sample, which could be made smaller by allowing the algorithm more time. Note that wrong answers are sometimes close to the correct answer, sometimes completely wrong. Finally, a Las Vegas algorithm called 10 times might answer

1492, 1492, Sorry!, 1492, 1492, 1492, 1492, 1492, Sorry!, 1492.

The algorithm never yields an incorrect answer, but it fails to provide an answer once in a while.

10.3 Expected versus average time

We make an important distinction between the words "average" and "expected". The *average* time of a deterministic algorithm was discussed in Section 2.4. It refers to the average time taken by the algorithm when each possible instance of a given size is considered equally likely. As we saw, average-case analysis can be misleading if in fact some instances are more likely than others. By contrast, the *expected* time of a probabilistic algorithm is defined on each individual instance: it refers to the mean time that it would take to solve the same instance over and over again. This is a robust notion that does not depend on the probability distribution on the instances to be solved because the probabilities involved are under direct control of the algorithm.

It is meaningful to talk about the average expected time and the worst-case expected time of a probabilistic algorithm. The latter, for example, refers to the expected time taken by the worst possible instance of a given size, *not* the time incurred if the worst possible probabilistic choices are unfortunately taken. Las Vegas algorithms can be more efficient than deterministic ones, but only with respect to expected time: it is always possible that misfortune will force a Las Vegas algorithm to take a long route to the solution. Nevertheless, the expected behaviour of Las Vegas algorithms can be much better than that of deterministic algorithms.

For example, we saw in Section 7.5 an algorithm that can find the median of an array in linear time in the worst case. In Section 10.7.2, we shall study a Las Vegas algorithm for the median whose worst-case expected time is also linear in the size of the instance. Its expected performance is considerably better than that of the algorithm from Section 7.5 *on each and every instance*. The only price to pay when using this Las Vegas algorithm is the unlikely possibility that it may occasionally take excessive time, independently of the instance at hand, due to nothing but bad luck.

A similar approach can be used to turn *quicksort* into an algorithm that sorts n elements in worst-case expected time in $O(n \log n)$, whereas the algorithm we saw in Section 7.4.2 requires a time in $\Omega(n^2)$ when the n elements are already sorted. Likewise, *universal hashing* provides access to a symbol table in constant expected time in the worst case, whereas classic hash coding is disastrous in the worst case; see Section 10.7.3. The main advantage of randomizing a deterministic algorithm that offers good average behaviour despite a bad worst case is to make it less vulnerable to an unexpected probability distribution of the instances that some application might give it to solve; see the end of Section 2.4 and Section 10.7.

10.4 Pseudorandom generation

Throughout this chapter, we suppose we have available a random number generator that can be called at unit cost. Let a and b be real numbers such that $a < b$. A call on *uniform*(a, b) returns a real number x chosen randomly in the interval $a \le x < b$. The distribution of x is uniform on the interval, and successive calls on the generator yield independent values of x. To generate random integers, we extend the notation to *uniform*$(i .. j)$, where i and j are integers, $i \le j$, and the call returns an integer k chosen randomly, uniformly and independently in the interval $i \leq k \leq j$. A useful special case is the function *coinflip*, which returns *heads* or *tails*, each with probability 50%. Note that *uniform*(a, b), *uniform*$(i . . j)$ and *coinflip* are easy to obtain even if only *uniform*$(0, 1)$ is directly available.

> **function** *uniform*(a, b)
>   **return** $a + (b - a) \times uniform(0, 1)$

> **function** *uniform*$(i . . j)$
>   **return** $\lfloor uniform(i, j + 1) \rfloor$

> **function** *coinflip*
>   **if** *uniform*$(0 . . 1) = 0$ **then return** *heads*
>   **else return** *tails*

Truly random generators are not usually available in practice. Moreover, it is not realistic to expect *uniform*$(0, 1)$ to take an arbitrary *real* value between 0 and 1. Most of the time *pseudorandom* generators are used instead: these are deterministic procedures able to generate long sequences of values that appear to have the properties of a random sequence. To start a sequence, we supply an initial value called a *seed*. The same seed always gives rise to the same sequence. To obtain different sequences, we may choose, for example, a seed that depends on the date or time. Most programming languages include such a generator, although some implementations should be used with caution. Using a good pseudorandom generator, the theoretical results obtained in this chapter concerning the efficiency and reliability of various probabilistic algorithms can generally be expected to hold. However, the impractical hypothesis that a genuinely random generator is available is crucial when we carry out the analysis.

The theory of pseudorandom generators is beyond the scope of this book, but the general principle is simple. Most generators are based on a pair of functions $f : X \to X$ and $g : X \to Y$, where X is a sufficiently large set and Y is the domain of pseudorandom values to be generated. We require both X and Y to be finite, which means that we can only hope to approximate the effect of *uniform*$(0, 1)$ by using a suitably large Y. On the other hand, $Y = \{0, 1\}$ is adequate for many applications: it corresponds to tossing a fair coin. To generate our pseudorandom sequence, let $s \in X$ be a seed. This seed defines a sequence

$$\begin{cases} x_0 = s \\ x_i = f(x_{i-1}) \text{ for all } i > 0. \end{cases}$$

Finally, the pseudorandom sequence $y_0, y_1, y_2, \ldots$ is defined by $y_i = g(x_i)$ for all $i \geq 0$. This sequence is necessarily periodic, with a period that cannot exceed the number of elements in X. Nevertheless, if X is sufficiently large and if f and g (and sometimes s) are chosen adequately, the period can be made very long, and the sequence may be for most practical purposes indistinguishable from a truly random sequence of elements of Y.

We give one simple example to illustrate this principle. Let p and q be two distinct large prime numbers, both congruent to 3 modulo 4, and let n be their product. Assume p and q are large enough that it is infeasible to factorize n. (At the time of writing, 100 digits each is considered sufficient; see Section 10.7.4.) Let X be the set of integers from 0 to $n - 1$ and let $Y = \{0, 1\}$. Define $f(x) = x^2 \bmod n$ and $g(x) = x \bmod 2$. Provided the seed is chosen uniformly at random among the elements of X that are relatively prime to n, it has been demonstrated that it is almost always infeasible to distinguish the sequence thus generated from a truly random binary sequence. For most practical algorithmic purposes, faster but less secure pseudorandom generators may be preferable. For instance, linear congruential pseudorandom generators of the form $f(x) = ax + b \bmod n$ for appropriate values of a, b and n are widely used.

10.5 Numerical probabilistic algorithms

Randomness was first used in algorithmics for the approximate solution of numerical problems. It was already in use in the secret world of atomic research during World War II, when this technique was given the code word "Monte Carlo" (a term still used by some authors to denote numerical probabilistic algorithms, but which we use with a different meaning in this book). A familiar example of a numerical probabilistic algorithm is simulation. This technique can be used, for example, to estimate the mean length of a queue in a system so complex that it is infeasible to get closed-form solutions or even numerical answers by deterministic methods. For certain real-life problems, computation of an exact solution is not possible even in principle, perhaps because of uncertainties in the experimental data to be used, or maybe because a digital computer can handle only binary or decimal values while the answer to be computed is irrational. For other problems, a precise answer exists but it would take too long to figure it out exactly.

The answer obtained by a numerical probabilistic algorithm is always approximate, but its expected precision improves as the time available to the algorithm increases. The error is usually inversely proportional to the square root of the amount of work performed, so that 100 times more work is needed to obtain one additional digit of precision.

10.5.1 Buffon's needle

In the eighteenth century, Georges Louis Leclerc, comte de Buffon, proved that if you throw a needle at random (in a random position and at a random angle, with uniform distribution) on a floor made of planks of constant width, if the needle is exactly half as long as the planks in the floor are wide and if the width of the cracks between the planks is zero, the probability that the needle will fall across a crack is $1/\pi$. This theorem may serve to predict approximately how many needles will fall across a crack if you drop n of them: the expectation is n/π. Figure 10.1 illustrates the fall of 22 needles, of which 8 fell across a crack; we would have expected 7 on the average since $\pi \approx {}^{22}/_{7}$. We assume the needles are dropped randomly and independently of one another: to preclude interference they should not stack up or even touch. It may be better to throw and pick up the same needle several times.

Figure 10.1. Buffon's needle

There is, however, an algorithmically more refreshing interpretation of Buffon's theorem. Instead of using it to predict the number of needles that will fall across a crack (admittedly of limited interest at best), why not use it "backwards" to estimate the value of π? Pretend for the moment that you do not have a good approximation for π but that you know Buffon's theorem. Imagine you drop a large number n of needles on your floor and count the number k of them that fall across a crack. You may now use n/k as an estimate for π. (You would be out of luck should $k = 0$, but this is overwhelmingly unlikely when n is large.) The more precise you want your estimate to be, the more needles you need to drop. In principle, you can get arbitrarily close to the exact value of π by dropping sufficiently many needles, or preferably by dropping the same needle a sufficient number of times to avoid interference. We carry out the precise analysis later in this section. In practice, this is not a useful "algorithm" because much better approximations of π can be obtained more efficiently by deterministic methods. Nevertheless, this approach to the "experimental determination of π" was taken up vigorously in the nineteenth century, making it one of the first probabilistic algorithms ever used.

We have seen that Buffon's theorem can serve to predict the number of needles that will fall across a crack and to estimate the value of π. A third possible use for this theorem is to estimate the width of the planks (in terms of the number of needle lengths). Remember that both previous applications took for granted that the needles are *precisely* half as long as the planks are wide. If this assumption fails, it is no longer true that n/k becomes arbitrarily close to π with overwhelming probability as we drop more and more needles. Let ω and λ be the width of the planks and the length of the needles, respectively. Buffon proved a more general theorem: provided $\omega \geq \lambda$, the probability that a randomly thrown needle will fall across a crack is $p = 2\lambda/\omega\pi$. In particular, $p = 1/\pi$ when $\lambda = \omega/2$, as we have supposed so far. Assume now that we know both π and the length of the needles precisely, but we do not have a ruler handy to measure the width of the planks. First we make sure that the needles are shorter than the planks are wide. In this (unlikely!) scenario, we can estimate the width of the planks with arbitrary precision by dropping a sufficiently large number n of needles and counting the number k that fall across a crack. Our estimate is simply $\omega \approx 2\lambda n / k\pi$. As always, the more needles we drop, the more precise our estimate is likely to be.

With high probability, the algorithms to estimate the value of π and the width of the planks return a value that converges to the correct answer as the number of needles dropped grows to infinity (provided the needles are half as long as the planks are wide in the first case, and both π and the length of the needles is known precisely in the second case). The natural question to ask is: How quickly do these algorithms converge? Alas, they are painfully slow: you need to drop 100 times more needles to obtain one more decimal digit in precision.

Convergence analysis for numerical probabilistic algorithms requires more knowledge of probability and statistics than we normally assume from our readers. Nevertheless, we proceed with a sketch of the basic approach for those who have the required background. We concentrate on the analysis of the algorithm for estimating π. For technical reasons, we first analyse how good k/n would be as an estimator for $1/\pi$. Consider an arbitrary small positive ε. We associate a random variable X_i with each needle: $X_i = 1$ if the i-th needle falls across a crack and $X_i = 0$ otherwise. By Buffon's theorem, $\Pr[X_i = 1] = 1/\pi$ for each i. The expectation and variance of X_i are $E(X_i) = 1/\pi$ and $\mathrm{Var}(X_i) = \frac{1}{\pi}(1 - \frac{1}{\pi})$, respectively. Now, let X denote the random variable corresponding to our estimate of $1/\pi$ after dropping n needles: $X = \sum_{i=1}^{n} X_i / n$. For any integer k between 0 and n

$$\Pr[X = k/n] = \binom{n}{k} \left(\frac{1}{\pi}\right)^k \left(1 - \frac{1}{\pi}\right)^{n-k}.$$

For instance, when $n = 22$, $\Pr[X = \frac{7}{22}] \approx 18\%$ and $\Pr[\frac{6}{22} \leq X \leq \frac{8}{22}]$ is just slightly above 50%. This random variable has expectation $E(X) = 1/\pi$ and variance $\mathrm{Var}(X) = \frac{1}{\pi}(1 - \frac{1}{\pi})/n$. By the Central Limit Theorem, the distribution of X is almost normal provided n is sufficiently large; see Section 1.7.4. Tables for the normal distribution tell us that

$$\Pr[\, |X - E(X)| < 1.645\sqrt{\mathrm{Var}(X)}\,] \approx 90\%.$$

Using our values for $E(X)$ and $\mathrm{Var}(X)$, we infer that $\Pr[\, |X - \frac{1}{\pi}| < \varepsilon] \geq 90\%$ when $\varepsilon > 1.645\sqrt{\frac{1}{\pi}(1 - \frac{1}{\pi})/n}$, and thus when $n > 0.588/\varepsilon^2$. Therefore, it suffices to drop at least $0.588/\varepsilon^2$ needles to obtain an absolute error in our estimate of $1/\pi$ that does not exceed ε nine times out of ten. This dependence on $1/\varepsilon^2$ explains why one additional digit of precision—which means that ε must be 10 times smaller—requires 100 times more needles. If we are not happy with a confidence interval that is reliable only nine times out of ten, another entry in the normal distribution table can be used. For example, the fact that

$$\Pr[\, |X - E(X)| < 2.576\sqrt{\mathrm{Var}(X)}\,] \approx 99\%$$

tells us that $\Pr[\,|X - \frac{1}{\pi}| < \varepsilon] \geq 99\%$ provided $\varepsilon > 2.576\sqrt{\frac{1}{\pi}(1 - \frac{1}{\pi})/n}$, which is satisfied when $n > 1.440/\varepsilon^2$. Thus a tenfold reduction in the probability of error is inexpensive compared to a one-figure increase in precision. In general, after we have decided how many needles to drop, there is a tradeoff between the number of digits that we output and the probability that those digits are correct.

Of course, we are interested in finding a confidence interval for our estimate of π, not of $1/\pi$. A straightforward calculation shows that if $|X - \frac{1}{\pi}| < \varepsilon$ then $|\frac{1}{X} - \pi| < \frac{\varepsilon\pi^2}{1-\varepsilon\pi}$. Moreover $9.8\varepsilon < \frac{\varepsilon\pi^2}{1-\varepsilon\pi} < 10\varepsilon$ when $\varepsilon < 0.00415$, which means intuitively that the same number of needles will provide one less decimal place concerning π than $1/\pi$, although the relative error is essentially the same because π is about 10 times bigger than $1/\pi$. Putting all this together, assuming we want an absolute error in our estimate for π that does not exceed $\varepsilon < 0.0415$ at least 99% of the time, it is sufficient to drop $144/\varepsilon^2$ needles. Slightly fewer needles suffice in the limit of small ε. This is nearly one and a half million needles even if we are satisfied that our estimate be within 0.01 of the exact value of π ninety-nine times out of one hundred! Did we ever claim this scheme was practical?

To summarize, the user of the algorithm should supply two parameters: the desired reliability ρ and precision ε. From those parameters, with the help of a table of the normal distribution, the algorithm determines the number n of needles that need to be thrown so the resulting estimate will be between $\pi - \varepsilon$ and $\pi + \varepsilon$ with probability at least ρ. For instance, the algorithm would choose n to be about one and a half million if the user supplied $\rho = 99\%$ and $\varepsilon = 0.01$. Finally, the algorithm drops n needles on the floor, counts the number k of them that fall across a crack, and announces: "The value of π is probably between $\frac{n}{k} - \varepsilon$ and $\frac{n}{k} + \varepsilon$". This answer will be correct a proportion ρ of the time if the experiment is repeated several times with the same values of ρ and ε.

There remains one subtlety if you want to implement a similar algorithm to estimate a value that you really do not know already: we needed the value of π for our convergence analysis! How can we determine the required number n of needles as a function of ρ and ε alone? One solution is to be overly conservative in our estimate of the variance of the random variables involved. The variance of X_i is $p(1 - p)$ when $X_i = 1$ with probability p and $X_i = 0$ otherwise, which is at most $^1/_4$ (the worst case is when $p = {}^1/_2$). If we determine n as if the variance of X_i were $^1/_4$, we will throw more needles than strictly necessary but the desired precision will be obtained with a reliability better than required. The algorithm can then estimate the actual reliability obtained using a table of Student's t distribution. The details can be found in any standard text on statistics. An alternative solution is to use a small sample of arbitrary size to get a first estimate of the required value, use this to make a better estimate of the sample size needed, take another sample, and so on. Again, the details are in any standard text.

10.5.2 Numerical integration

This brings us to the best-known numerical probabilistic algorithms: Monte Carlo integration, whose name is unfortunate since it is *not* an example of a Monte Carlo algorithm according to the terminology adopted in this book. Recall that if $f : \mathbb{R} \to \mathbb{R}^{\geq 0}$ is a continuous function and if $a \leq b$, then the area of the surface bounded by the curve $y = f(x)$, the x–axis and the vertical lines $x = a$ and $x = b$ is

$$I = \int_a^b f(x)\,\mathrm{d}x.$$

Now consider a rectangle of width $b - a$ and height $I/(b - a)$ placed as in Figure 10.2. The area of this rectangle is also I. Since the rectangle and the surface below the curve have the same area and the same width, they must have the same average height. We conclude that the average height of the curve between a and b is $I/(b - a)$. If we take a point below the x–axis to have negative height, this interpretation holds more generally for arbitrary continuous functions $f : \mathbb{R} \to \mathbb{R}$.

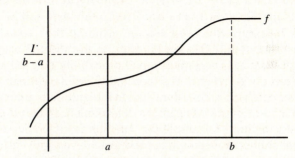

Figure 10.2. Numerical integration

After reading the previous section, a probabilistic algorithm to estimate the integral should immediately spring to mind: estimate the average height of the curve by random sampling and multiply the result by $b - a$.

> **function** $MCint(f, n, a, b)$
> $sum \leftarrow 0$
>   **for** $i \leftarrow 1$ **to** n **do**
> $x \leftarrow uniform(a, b)$
> $sum \leftarrow sum + f(x)$
>   **return** $(b - a) \times (sum/n)$

An analysis similar to that for Buffon's needle shows that the variance of the estimate calculated by this algorithm is inversely proportional to the number of sample points, and the distribution of the estimate is approximately normal when n is large. Therefore, the expected error in the estimate is again inversely proportional to $\sqrt{n}$, so that 100 times more work is needed to obtain one additional digit of precision.

Algorithm $MCint$ is hardly more practical than Buffon's method for estimating π; see Problem 10.3. A better estimate of the integral can generally be obtained by deterministic methods. Perhaps the simplest is similar in spirit to $MCint$ except that it estimates the average height by deterministic sampling at regular intervals.

```
function DETint(f, n, a, b)
    sum ← 0
    delta ← (b - a)/n
    x ← a + delta/2
    for i ← 1 to n do
        sum ← sum + f(x)
        x ← x + delta
    return sum × delta
```

In general, this deterministic algorithm needs many less iterations than Monte Carlo integration to obtain a comparable degree of precision. This is typical of most of the functions we may wish to integrate. However, to every deterministic integration algorithm, even the most sophisticated, there correspond continuous functions that can be constructed expressly to fool the algorithm. Consider for example the function $f(x) = \sin^2((100!)\pi x)$. Any call on $DETint(f, n, 0, 1)$ with $1 \le n \le 100$ returns the value zero, even though the true value of this integral is $1/2$. No function can play this kind of trick on the Monte Carlo integration algorithm, although there is an extremely small probability that the algorithm might make a similar error even when f is a thoroughly ordinary function.

A better reason to use Monte Carlo integration in practice arises when we have to evaluate a multiple integral. If a deterministic integration algorithm using some systematic method to sample the function is generalized to several dimensions, the number of sample points needed to achieve a given precision grows exponentially with the dimension of the integral to be evaluated. If 100 points are needed to evaluate a simple integral, then it will probably be necessary to use all 10 000 points of a 100×100 grid to achieve the same precision when a double integral is evaluated; one million points will be needed for a triple integral, and so on. With Monte Carlo integration, on the other hand, the dimension of the integral generally has little effect on the precision obtained, although the amount of work for each iteration is likely to increase slightly with the dimension. In practice, Monte Carlo integration is used to evaluate integrals of dimension four or higher because no other simple technique can compete. Nevertheless, there are better algorithms that are more complicated. For instance, the precision of the answer can be improved using hybrid techniques that are partly systematic and partly probabilistic. If the dimension is fixed, it may be preferable to choose points systematically so that they are well-spaced yet reasonable in number, a technique known as *quasi* Monte Carlo integration.

10.5.3 Probabilistic counting

How far can you count on an n-bit register? Using ordinary binary notation, you can count from 0 to $2^n - 1$. Is it possible to go farther? Clearly the register can assume no more than 2^n distinct values since that is the number of distinct ways to set n binary values. However, we might be able to go beyond 2^n if we are willing to skip intermediate values. For instance, we could count twice as far if we counted only even values. More precisely, let c denote our n-bit register. Sometimes we also use c to denote the integer represented in binary by the register. We wish to implement two procedures $init(c)$ and $tick(c)$, and one function $count(c)$ such that a call on $count(c)$ returns the number of calls to $tick(c)$ since the last call on $init(c)$. In other words, $init$ resets the counter to zero, $tick$ adds 1 to it, and $count$ asks for its current value. The algorithms should be able to maintain an arbitrarily large number of counters $c_1, c_2, \ldots$, and side-effects are not allowed: no information can be passed between calls, except through the register transmitted as an explicit parameter.

We suggested above that we could skip some values to count farther. However, this is nonsense if we insist on a *deterministic* counting strategy. Because side-effects are not allowed, there is no way $tick$ can add 1 to the counter every other call: the behaviour of $tick(c)$ must be determined completely from the current value of c. If there exists a value of c such that $tick(c)$ leaves c unchanged, the counter will stick at that point until $init(c)$ is called. (This is reasonable when the counter has reached its upper limit.) Since c can assume only 2^n different values, the counter is forced to reassume a previously held value after at most 2^n calls on $tick(c)$. Therefore, deterministically counting more than 2^n events in an n-bit register is impossible.

Provided we relax the requirement that $count$ should return the exact number of $tick$s since the last $init$, there is an obvious probabilistic strategy to count twice as far. The register is an ordinary binary counter, initialized to zero by a call on $init$. Each time $tick$ is called, flip a fair coin. If it comes up heads, add 1 to the register. If it comes up tails, however, do nothing. When $count$ is called, return twice the value stored in the register. Following a call on $init$, it is easy to prove that the expected value returned by $count$ after t calls to $tick$ is precisely t, even when t is odd. The variance can be shown to be reasonably small, so the estimate returned by $count$ is fairly accurate most of the time; see Problem 10.5.

We do not expect you to be impressed by the previous paragraph. Counting twice as far simply means up to $2^{n+1} - 2$, which could have been achieved deterministically if a single additional bit had been available in the register. We now show that probabilistic counting strategies can count *exponentially* farther: from 0 to $2^{2^n-1} - 1$. Thus, 8 bits are sufficient to count more than 5×10^{76} events! The idea is to keep in the register an estimate of the logarithm of the actual number of ticks. More precisely, $count(c)$ returns $2^c - 1$. We subtract 1 so that a count of 0 can be represented; moreover $count(0) = 0$ as it should since $init(c)$ sets c to 0. It remains to see how to implement $tick$.

Assume that $2^c - 1$ is a good estimate of the number of ticks since the last initialization. After an additional tick, a good estimate of the total number of ticks would be 2^c, but this is not of a form that can be represented with our strategy. To circumvent this, we add 1 to c with some probability p to be determined and we leave it unchanged otherwise. Thus, our estimate of the number of ticks becomes $2^{c+1} - 1$ with probability p, whereas it remains $2^c - 1$ with complementary probability $1 - p$. The expected value returned by $count(c)$ after this tick is therefore

$$(2^{c+1} - 1)\, p + (2^c - 1)\, (1 - p) = 2^c + 2^c p - 1$$

and we see that it suffices to set $p = 2^{-c}$ to obtain 2^c, the desired expected value for $count(c)$. (This reasoning is not rigorous; work Problem 10.6 for a proof that the expected value returned by $count$ is correct.) To summarize, we obtain the following algorithms.

procedure $init(c)$
    $c \leftarrow 0$

procedure $tick(c)$
    for $i \leftarrow 1$ **to** c **do**
        if $coinflip = heads$ **then return**
    $c \leftarrow c + 1$
    {The probability of overflow is too small to be worth checking}

function $count(c)$
    return $2^c - 1$

There is an additional advantage in keeping the logarithm of the actual count in c. We saw in the previous sections that numeric probabilistic algorithms keep the absolute error under control. When implementing a counter whose range is as large as 5×10^{76}, we are more likely to wish to keep the *relative* error under control. Fortunately a small absolute error in the logarithm of the number of ticks translates into a small relative error in the actual count. In particular, $count$ is guaranteed to give the exact answer when the number of ticks since initialization is 0 or 1. It can be proved by mathematical induction that the variance of $count$ after m ticks is $m(m-1)/2$. This is not so good, as it means that the standard deviation is roughly 70% of the actual number of counts: this process will distinguish a million from a billion, but not reliably one million from two millions.

Although there are applications for which such lack of precision is acceptable, no real application can possibly wish to count as many as 5×10^{76} events. Fortunately, the variance of the estimated count can be improved at the cost of not counting quite as far. For this, it suffices to keep track in the register of the logarithm in a basis smaller than 2. For example, we could use

$$count(c) = [(1 + \varepsilon)^c - 1]/\varepsilon \qquad (10.1)$$

for small ε. The division by ε is to keep the desirable property that $count$ always gives the exact answer after 0 or 1 ticks. Using $\varepsilon = {}^1/_{30}$, this allows counting up to more than 125 000 events in an 8-bit register with less than 24% relative error 95% of the time. Of course, the probability that $tick$ will increase c when called should no longer be 2^{-c}: it must be set appropriately; see Problem 10.8.

For an entirely different type of probabilistic counting, which saves time rather than storage, be sure to work Problem 10.12. Under some conditions, this algorithm can count approximately the number of elements in a set in a time that is in the order of the square root of that number.

10.6 Monte Carlo algorithms

There exist problems for which no efficient algorithm is known, whether it be deterministic or probabilistic, that is able to obtain a correct solution every time. A *Monte Carlo* algorithm occasionally makes a mistake, but it finds a correct solution with high probability whatever the instance considered. This is a stronger claim than saying that it works correctly on a majority of instances, only failing now and again in some special cases: there must be no instance on which the probability of error is high. However, no warning is usually given when the algorithm makes a mistake.

Let p be a real number such that $0 < p < 1$. We say that a Monte Carlo algorithm is *p-correct* if it returns a correct answer with probability at least p, whatever the instance considered. In some cases we shall allow p to depend on the instance size but never on the instance itself. The most interesting feature of Monte Carlo algorithms is that it is often possible to reduce the error probability arbitrarily at the cost of a slight increase in computing time. We call this *amplifying the stochastic advantage*. We shall study this general phenomenon in Section 10.6.4, but first we consider two examples. The first is of limited practical interest, but it has the advantage of simplicity. We use it to introduce the key notions. The second, on the other hand, is of unquestionable practical importance.

10.6.1 Verifying matrix multiplication

Consider three $n \times n$ matrices A, B and C. You suspect that $C = AB$. How can you verify whether or not this is so? The obvious approach is to multiply A and B, and to compare the result with C. Using a straightforward matrix multiplication algorithm, this takes a time in $\Theta(n^3)$. Strassen's algorithm is faster, and even faster matrix multiplication algorithms exist for very large n, but the asymptotically fastest algorithm currently known still requires a time in $\Omega(n^{2.37})$; see Section 7.6. Can we do better if we are willing to tolerate a small probability of error? Surprisingly, the answer is that for any fixed $\varepsilon > 0$, a time in $O(n^2)$ is sufficient to solve this problem with error probability at most ε. The constant hidden in the O notation, however, depends on ε.

Assume for the sake of argument that $C \neq AB$. Let $D = AB - C$. By assumption, D is not identically zero. Let i be an integer such that the i–th row of D contains at least one nonzero element. Consider any subset $S \subseteq \{1, 2, \ldots, n\}$. Let $\Sigma_S(D)$ denote the vector of length n obtained by adding pointwise the rows of D indexed by the elements of S; an empty sum is equal to 0. For instance, $\Sigma_{\{1,3,4\}}(D)$ is obtained by adding the first, third and fourth rows of D. Let S' be the same subset as S, except that $i \in S'$ if and only if $i \notin S$. Since the i–th row of D is not identically 0, $\Sigma_S(D)$ and $\Sigma_{S'}(D)$ cannot be simultaneously 0. Assume now that S is chosen randomly: for each j between 1 and n, decide by the flip of a fair coin whether or not to include j in S. Because $i \in S$ is as likely as $i \notin S$, the probability that $\Sigma_S(D) \neq 0$ is at least one-half.

On the other hand, $\Sigma_S(D)$ is always 0 if $C = AB$ since in this case $D = 0$. This suggests testing whether or not $C = AB$ by computing $\Sigma_S(D)$ for a randomly chosen subset S and comparing the result with 0. But how can this be done efficiently without first computing D (and hence AB)?

The solution is to consider $\Sigma_S(D)$ as a matrix multiplication of its own. Let X be a binary vector of length n such that $X_j = 1$ if $j \in S$ and $X_j = 0$ otherwise. It is straightforward to verify that $\Sigma_S(D) = XD$, provided we think of X as a $1 \times n$ matrix. Thus, our test corresponds to checking whether or not $X(AB - C)$ is 0, or equivalently whether or not $XAB = XC$, for a randomly chosen binary vector X. It appears at first that computing XAB should be even more time consuming than computing AB, but this is not the case. Remember from Section 8.6 that the time needed to compute a chained matrix multiplication depends crucially on the order in which the matrices are multiplied. In this case, it only takes a time in $\Theta(n^2)$ to compute XAB as $(XA)B$ because this is the time needed to multiply the $1 \times n$ matrix X with the $n \times n$ matrix A, and because the result, XA, is again a $1 \times n$ matrix that we can multiply with B in a time in $\Theta(n^2)$. This suggests the following algorithm.

> **function** *Freivalds*(A, B, C, n)
> **for** $j \leftarrow 1$ **to** n **do** $X_j \leftarrow uniform(0..1)$
> **if** $(XA)B = XC$ **then return** *true*
> **else return** *false*

From the discussion above, we know that this algorithm returns a correct answer with probability at least one-half on every instance: it is therefore $1/2$-correct by definition. It is not p-correct for any p smaller than $1/2$, however, because its error probability is exactly $1/2$ when C differs from AB in precisely one row: an incorrect answer is returned if and only if $X_i = 0$ where it is row i that differs between C and AB. Is this really interesting? Surely an error probability of 50% is intolerable in practice? Worse, an easier "algorithm" to achieve this error rate would be to flip a single fair coin and return *true* or *false* depending on the outcome without even looking at the three matrices in question! The key observation is that whenever *Freivalds*(A, B, C, n) returns *false*, you can be sure this answer is correct: the existence of a vector X such that XAB differs from XC allows you to conclude with certainty that $AB \neq C$. It is only when the algorithm returns *true* that you are not sure whether to believe it.

Consider for example the following 3×3 matrices.

$$A = \begin{pmatrix} 1 & 2 & 3 \\ 4 & 5 & 6 \\ 7 & 8 & 9 \end{pmatrix} \quad B = \begin{pmatrix} 3 & 1 & 4 \\ 1 & 5 & 9 \\ 2 & 6 & 5 \end{pmatrix} \quad C = \begin{pmatrix} 11 & 29 & 37 \\ 29 & 65 & 91 \\ 47 & 99 & 45 \end{pmatrix}$$

A call on *Freivalds*$(A, B, C, 3)$ could choose $X = (1, 1, 0)$, in which case XA is obtained by adding the first and second rows of A, thus $XA = (5, 7, 9)$. Continuing, we calculate $(XA)B = (40, 94, 128)$. This is compared to $XC = (40, 94, 128)$, which is obtained by adding the first and second rows of C. With this choice of X, *Freivalds* returns *true* since $XAB = XC$. Another call on *Freivalds* might choose $X = (0, 1, 1)$ instead. This time, the calculations are

$$XA = (11, 13, 15), \quad (XA)B = (76,166,236), \quad XC = (76,164,136),$$

and *Freivalds* returns *false*. We are luckier: the fact that $XAB \neq XC$ is conclusive proof that $AB \neq C$.

This suggests running *Freivalds*(A, B, C, n) several times on the same instance, using independent flips of the coin each time. Getting the answer *false* just once allows you to conclude that $AB \neq C$, regardless of how many times you get the answer *true*. Consider now the following algorithm, in which k is a new parameter.

function *RepeatFreivalds*(A, B, C, n, k)
    for $i \leftarrow 1$ **to** k **do**
        if *Freivalds*$(A, B, C, n) = false$ **then return** *false*
    return *true*

We are interested in the error probability of this new algorithm. Consider two cases. If in fact $C = AB$, each call on *Freivalds* necessarily returns *true* since there is no risk of randomly choosing an X such that $XAB \neq XC$, and thus *RepeatFreivalds* returns *true* after going k times round the loop. In this case, the error probability is zero. On the other hand, if in fact $C \neq AB$, the probability for each call on *Freivalds* that it will (incorrectly) return *true* is at most $^1/_2$. These probabilities multiply because the coin flips are independent from one call to the next. Therefore, the probability that k successive calls each return the wrong answer is at most 2^{-k}. But this is the only way for *RepeatFreivalds* to return an erroneous answer. We conclude that our new algorithm is $(1 - 2^{-k})$–correct. When $k = 10$, this is better than 99.9%-correct. Repeating 20 times brings the error probability below one in a million. Such a spectacularly rapid decrease in error probability is typical for Monte Carlo algorithms that solve decision problems—that is, problems for which the answer is either *true* or *false*—provided one of the answers, if obtained, is guaranteed to be correct.

Alternatively, Monte Carlo algorithms can be given an explicit upper bound on the tolerable error probability.

function *Freivaldsepsilon*$(A, B, C, n, \varepsilon)$
    $k \leftarrow \lceil \lg {}^1/_\varepsilon \rceil$
    return *RepeatFreivalds*(A, B, C, n, k)

An advantage of this version of the algorithm is that we can analyse its running time as a function simultaneously of the instance size and the error probability. In this case, the algorithm clearly takes a time in $\Theta(n^2 \log {}^1/_\varepsilon)$.

The algorithms in this section are of limited practical interest because it takes $3n^2$ scalar multiplications to compute XAB and XC, compared to n^3 to compute AB by the direct method. If we insist on an error probability no larger than one in a million, and if in fact $C = AB$, the 20 required runs of *Freivalds* perform $60n^2$ scalar multiplications, which does not improve on n^3 unless n is larger than 60. Nevertheless, this approach is potentially useful if very large matrix products have to be verified.

10.6.2 Primality testing

Perhaps the most famous Monte Carlo algorithm decides whether a given odd integer is prime or composite. No known algorithm can solve this problem with certainty in a reasonable time when the number to be tested has more than a few hundred decimal digits. Testing the primality of large numbers is more than a mathematical recreation: we saw in Section 7.8 that it is crucial for modern cryptology.

The story of probabilistic primality testing has its roots with Pierre de Fermat, the father of modern number theory. He stated the following theorem, sometimes known as Fermat's little theorem, in 1640.

Theorem 10.6.1 (Fermat)   *Let n be prime. Then*

$$a^{n-1} \bmod n = 1$$

for any integer a such that $1 \le a \le n - 1$.

For example, let $n = 7$ and $a = 5$. We have

$$a^{n-1} = 5^6 = 15625 = 2232 \times 7 + 1$$

and thus $a^{n-1} \bmod n = 1$ as it should. Now consider the contrapositive of Fermat's little theorem: if n and a are integers such that $1 \le a \le n - 1$ and if $a^{n-1} \bmod n \neq 1$ then n is not prime. An anecdotal example is provided by Fermat himself. In his quest for a formula that would yield only prime numbers, he formulated the hypothesis that $F_n = 2^{2^n} + 1$ is prime for all n. Observe that $F_0 = 3$, $F_1 = 5$, $F_2 = 17$, $F_3 = 257$ and $F_4 = 65537$ are all prime numbers. Unfortunately, $F_5 = 4294967297$ was a number too large for Fermat to attempt proving its primality. Nearly a century had to pass before Euler factorized $F_5 = 641 \times 6700417$, disproving Fermat's conjecture. Ironically, Fermat could have used his own theorem to reach the same conclusion. It would have been well within his reach to invent an efficient modular exponentiation algorithm similar to *expomod* and use it to compute $3^{F_5-1} \bmod F_5 = 3029026160 \neq 1$; see Section 7.8. Although tedious, this calculation involves nothing more than 32 successive modular squarings since $F_5 - 1 = 2^{32}$. From the contrapositive to his own theorem, Fermat would have known that F_5 is not prime.

This suggests the following probabilistic algorithm for primality testing. We assume $n \ge 2$.

```
function Fermat(n)
    a ← uniform(1 .. n − 1)
    if expomod(a, n − 1, n) = 1 then return true
                               else return false
```

From the above discussion, we know that n is composite whenever a call on *Fermat*(n) returns *false* because the existence of an a between 1 and $n - 1$ such that $a^{n-1} \bmod n \neq 1$ is sufficient to show this by Fermat's little theorem. It is remarkable that whenever this algorithm tells you n is composite, it provides no clue concerning its divisors. To the best of our current algorithmic knowledge, factorization is much harder than primality testing. Recall that the presumed difference in difficulty between these problems is crucial to the RSA cryptographic system described in Section 7.8: the easiness of primality testing is necessary for its implementation whereas the hardness of factorization is prerequisite to its safety.

What can we say, however, if *Fermat*(n) returns *true*? To conclude that n is prime, we would need the *converse* rather than the contrapositive to Fermat's theorem. This would say that $a^{n-1} \bmod n$ is never equal to 1 when n is composite and $1 \le a \le n - 1$. Unfortunately, this is not the case since $1^{n-1} \bmod n = 1$ for all $n \ge 2$. Moreover, $(n-1)^{n-1} \bmod n = 1$ for all odd $n \ge 3$ because $(n-1)^2 \bmod n = 1$. The smallest nontrivial counterexample to the converse is that $4^{14} \bmod 15 = 1$ despite the fact that 15 is composite. An integer a such that $2 \le a \le n - 2$ and $a^{n-1} \bmod n = 1$ is called a *false witness of primality* for n if in fact n is composite. Provided we modify Fermat's test to choose a randomly between 2 and $n - 2$, it can only fail on composite numbers when a false witness is chosen.

The good news is that false witnesses are rather few. Although only 5 among the 332 odd composite numbers smaller than 1000 boast no false witnesses, more than half of them have only two false witnesses and less than 16% of them have more than 15. Moreover, there are only 4490 false witnesses for all these composite numbers taken together. Compare this to 172 878, the total number of candidate witnesses that exist for the same set of numbers. The average error probability of Fermat's test on odd composite numbers smaller than 1000 is less than 3.3%. It is even smaller if we consider larger numbers.

The bad news is that there are composite numbers that admit a significant proportion of false witnesses. The worst case among composites smaller than 1000 is 561, which admits 318 false witnesses: this is more than half the potential witnesses. A more convincing case is made with a 15-digit number: *Fermat*(651693055693681) returns *true* with probability greater than 99.9965% despite the fact that this number is composite! More generally, for any $\delta > 0$ there are infinitely many composite numbers for which Fermat's test discovers compositeness with probability smaller than δ. In other words, Fermat's test is not p-correct for any fixed $p > 0$. Consequently, the error probability cannot be brought down below an arbitrarily small ε by repeating Fermat's test some fixed number of times according to the technique we saw in the previous section.

Fortunately, a slight modification in Fermat's test solves this difficulty. Let n be an odd integer greater than 4, and let s and t be integers such that $n - 1 = 2^s t$, where t is odd. Note that $s > 0$ since $n - 1$ is even. Let $B(n)$ be the set of integers defined as follows: $a \in B(n)$ if and only if $2 \le a \le n - 2$ and

$\diamond$ $a^t \bmod n = 1$, or

$\diamond$ there exists an integer i, $0 \le i < s$, such that $a^{2^i t} \bmod n = n - 1$.

This may seem complicated, but it is easy to implement efficiently. Provided n is odd and $2 \le a \le n - 2$, a call on *Btest*(a, n) returns *true* if and only if $a \in B(n)$.

```
function Btest(a, n)
    s ← 0; t ← n - 1
    repeat
        s ← s + 1; t ← t ÷ 2
    until t mod 2 = 1
    x ← expomod(a, t, n)
    if x = 1 or x = n - 1 then return true
    for i ← 1 to s - 1 do
        x ← x² mod n
        if x = n - 1 then return true
    return false
```

For example, let us see if 158 belongs to $B(289)$. We set $s = 5$ and $t = 9$ because $n - 1 = 288 = 2^5 \times 9$. Then we compute

$$x = a^t \bmod n = 158^9 \bmod 289 = 131.$$

The test is not finished since 131 is neither 1 nor $n - 1 = 288$. Next, we successively square x (modulo n) up to 4 times ($s - 1 = 4$) to see if we obtain 288.

$$
\begin{aligned}
a^{2t} \bmod n &= 131^2 \bmod 289 &= 110 \\
a^{2^2 t} \bmod n &= 110^2 \bmod 289 &= 251 \\
a^{2^3 t} \bmod n &= 251^2 \bmod 289 &= 288
\end{aligned}
$$

At this point we stop because we have found that $a^{2^i t} \bmod n = n - 1$ for $i = 3 < s$, and we conclude that $158 \in B(289)$.

An extension of Fermat's theorem shows that $a \in B(n)$ for all $2 \le a \le n - 2$ when n is prime. On the other hand, we say that n is a *strong pseudoprime* to the base a and that a is a *strong false witness* of primality for n whenever $n > 4$ is an odd composite number and $a \in B(n)$. For instance, we just saw that 158 is a strong false witness of primality for 289 since $289 = 17^2$ is composite. This yields a better test than Fermat's because strong false witnesses are automatically false witnesses with respect to Fermat's test, but not conversely. In fact, strong false witnesses are much rarer than Fermat false witnesses. For instance, 4 is a false witness of primality for 15, but it is not a strong false witness because $4^7 \bmod 15 = 4$. We also saw that 561 admits 318 false witnesses, but only 8 of these are strong false witnesses. Considering all odd composites smaller than 1000, the average probability of randomly selecting a strong false witness is less than 1%; more than 72% of these composites do not admit even one strong false witness. The superiority of the strong test is best illustrated by the fact that every odd composite integer between 5 and 10^{13} fails to be a strong pseudoprime to at least one of the bases 2, 3, 5, 7 or 61. In other words, five calls on *Btest* are sufficient to decide *deterministically* on the primality of any integer up to 10^{13}. Most importantly, unlike Fermat's test, there is a guarantee that the proportion of strong false witnesses is small *for every odd composite*. More precisely, we have the following theorem.

> Theorem 10.6.2   *Consider an arbitrary odd $n > 4$.*
>
> ◇ *If n is prime, then $B(n) = \{a \mid 2 \leq a \leq n - 2\}$.*
> ◇ *If n is composite, then $|B(n)| \leq (n - 9)/4$.*

Consequently, $Btest(a, n)$ always returns *true* when n is a prime larger than 4 and $2 \leq a \leq n - 2$, whereas it returns *false* with probability better than $3/4$ when n is a composite odd integer larger than 4 and a is chosen randomly between 2 and $n - 2$. In other words, the following Monte Carlo algorithm is $3/4$-correct for primality testing; it is known as the Miller–Rabin test.

> **function** *MillRab*(n)
> {This algorithm should only be called if $n > 4$ is odd}
> $a \leftarrow uniform(2 .. n - 2)$
> **return** $Btest(a, n)$

Because the answer *false* is guaranteed to be correct, the technique we saw in the previous section applies to reduce the error probability very rapidly.

> **function** *RepeatMillRab*(n, k)
> {This algorithm should only be called if $n > 4$ is odd}
> **for** $i \leftarrow 1$ **to** k **do**
>   **if** *MillRab*$(n) =$ *false* **then return** *false*
> **return** *true*

This algorithm always returns the correct answer when $n > 4$ is prime. When $n > 4$ is an odd composite, each call on *MillRab* has probability at most $1/4$ of hitting a strong false witness and erroneously returning *true*. Since the only way for *RepeatMillRab* to return *true* in this case is to randomly hit k strong false witnesses in a row, this happens with probability at most 4^{-k}. For instance, it suffices to take $k = 10$ to reduce the error probability below one in a million. In conclusion, *RepeatMillRab*$(\cdot, k)$ is a $(1 - 4^{-k})$-correct Monte Carlo algorithm for primality testing.

How much time does it take to decide on the primality of n with an error probability bounded by ε? We must repeat the Miller–Rabin test k times where $4^{-k} \leq \varepsilon$, which is the same as $2^{2k} \geq 1/\varepsilon$. This is achieved with $k = \lceil \frac{1}{2} \lg 1/\varepsilon \rceil$. Each call on *MillRab* involves one modular exponentiation, with t as exponent, and $s - 1$ modular squarings. We know from Section 7.8 that the exponentiation requires a number of modular multiplications and squarings in $O(\log t)$. Counting squarings as multiplications, and since $\lg n > \lg(n - 1) = \lg 2^s t = s + \lg t$, the time required by a call on *MillRab* is dominated by a number of modular multiplications in $O(\log n)$. If these are performed according to the classic algorithm, each of them takes a time in $O(\log^2 n)$ because we reduce modulo n after each multiplication.

Putting it all together, the total time to decide the primality of n with error probability bounded by ε is thus in $O(\log^3 n \lg 1/\varepsilon)$. This is entirely reasonable in practice for thousand-digit numbers and error probability less than 10^{-100}.

10.6.3 Can a number be probably prime?

Assume you run the Miller–Rabin test 10 times on some odd number n, and you obtain the answer "*true*" each time. What can you conclude? We saw that if n were composite, this could occur with probability at most $4^{-10} = 2^{-20}$, which is less than one in a million. It may be tempting to conclude that "n is prime, except with probability 2^{-20} of error". However, such a statement is nonsense: any given integer larger than 1 is either prime or composite! The best we can say is: "I believe n to be prime; otherwise I have observed a phenomenon whose probability of occurrence was less than one in a million". Moreover, even this toned down statement must be taken with a grain of salt if the witnesses for the test were obtained by a pseudorandom generator rather than being truly random: perhaps n is composite and we failed to find a witness not because we were unlucky but rather because the pseudorandom generator was defective; see Section 10.4. Nevertheless, such failure is unlikely if a good generator is used and we shall not worry further about this possibility.

Since it is impossible to ever be sure that a given number is prime with this Monte Carlo algorithm—only composite numbers can be certified—and since it is the primes that are relevant for cryptographic purposes, you may wonder if it is worth risking a "false prime" to save computing time. If your life depended on the primality of a given number, would you not spend the time necessary to certify its primality with the best available deterministic method? Say you have the choice between running *RepeatMillRab*$(n, 150)$ or a more sophisticated method that takes significantly more time but guarantees a correct answer. Which approach would be least likely to lead you into error? As discussed in Section 10.2, the sophisticated method is more likely to be wrong, despite its claims, because the probability of an undetected hardware error during its longer computing time is likely to be higher than $4^{-150} \approx 10^{-100}$. Moreover, you can be more confident that your implementation of the Miller–Rabin test is error-free than you can about the more complicated algorithm. Thus we reach the paradoxical conclusion that a probable prime, whatever meaning you give to this phrase, may be more reliable than a number whose primality was "proved" deterministically! Note however that there are probabilistic methods that can produce *certified* random primes in less time than it takes to find probabilistic primes with repeated use of the Miller–Rabin test. Because these methods are guaranteed to return a prime, they belong to the class of Las Vegas algorithms.

The importance of interpreting the outcome of a Monte Carlo algorithm correctly is best illustrated if you wish to *generate* an ℓ-digit number that is probably prime, perhaps for cryptographic purposes. The obvious algorithm is to keep choosing random ℓ-digit odd integers until one is found that passes a sufficient number of rounds of the Miller–Rabin test. More precisely, consider the following algorithm, which should only be used with $\ell > 1$.

function *randomprime*(ℓ, k)
   repeat
       {Choose odd n randomly between $10^{\ell-1}$ and $10^{\ell} - 1$}
       $n \leftarrow 1 + 2 \times uniform(10^{\ell-1}/2 \mathinner{\ldotp\ldotp} 10^{\ell}/2 - 1)$
   until *RepeatMillRab*(n, k)
   return n

What can we say about the outcome of this algorithm? We already know that we cannot claim that the number obtained is prime with probability at least $1 - 4^{-k}$. Nevertheless, it does make sense to investigate the average number of "false primes" (a euphemism for "composite") produced if we run the algorithm m times. It is tempting to conclude from the discussion above that the answer is "at most $4^{-k} m$ because our error probability on each of the m numbers produced is at most 4^{-k}". For example, if we call *randomprime*$(1000, 5)$ one million times, we would expect less than 1000 composites among the million 1000-digit numbers thus produced (because $4^{-5}10^6 \approx 977$). It would suffice to call *randomprime*$(1000, 10)$ instead to bring this expected number below 1 at the cost of less than doubling the running time. This conclusion is correct, but only because the expected error probability of the Miller–Rabin test on a randomly selected odd composite is much less than $^1/_4$. However, the simple reasoning is wrong!

The problem is that a large random odd number is much more likely to be composite than prime. Therefore, a call on *randomprime* is likely to use *RepeatMillRab* to test many composite numbers before a prime number is tested, if indeed this ever happens. The probability of error inherent in each call of *RepeatMillRab* on composite numbers will accumulate. Even if each call is likely to find that its number is composite, the probability that one of the calls will err—causing *randomprime* to return this composite by mistake—is not negligible if many composites are tested before a prime is hit by chance. For the sake of argument, consider what would happen if the error probability of the Miller–Rabin test were exactly $^1/_4$ on every odd composite and if we called *randomprime*$(1000, 5)$. Each time round the **repeat** loop, one of three things happens.

◇ If the randomly chosen number n is prime, *RepeatMillRab*$(n, 5)$ is sure to return *true*, ending the loop; *randomprime* correctly returns a prime number in this case.

◇ If the randomly chosen number n is composite, there is a probability exactly $4^{-5} = 1/1024$ that *RepeatMillRab*$(n, 5)$ will return *true*, ending the loop; *randomprime* erroneously returns a composite number in this case.

◇ Otherwise, the algorithm goes back round the loop with the random choice of another 1000-digit odd number.

The probability that a random 1000-digit odd number is prime is roughly one in a thousand; see Problem 10.19. Hence the first two cases above are nearly equiprobable while the third case is overwhelmingly the most probable. As a result, the loop in *randomprime* is just as likely to end for either of the possible reasons, so it returns composite numbers approximately as often as it does primes! (Once again, the performance of *randomprime* will be much better in reality because in fact the error probability of *MillRab* is substantially smaller than $1/4$ on most composite numbers.)

10.6.4 Amplification of stochastic advantage

Both Monte Carlo algorithms studied so far have a useful property: one of the possible answers is always correct when obtained. One guarantees that a given number is composite, the other that a given matrix product is incorrect. We say such algorithms are *biased*. Thanks to this property, it is easy to reduce the error probability arbitrarily by repeating the algorithm a suitable number of times. The occurrence of even a single "guaranteed" answer is enough to produce certainty; a large number of identical probabilistic answers, on the other hand, increases confidence that the correct answer has been obtained. This is known as *amplification of the stochastic advantage*.

Assume we have an *un*biased Monte Carlo algorithm whose error probability is nonzero regardless of the instance to be solved and of the answer returned. Is it still possible to decrease the error probability arbitrarily by repeating the algorithm? The answer is that it depends on the original error probability. For simplicity, let us concentrate on algorithms that solve decision problems; but see Problem 10.22. Consider a Monte Carlo algorithm about which all you know is that it is p-correct. The first obvious remark is that amplification of the stochastic advantage is impossible in general unless $p > 1/2$ because there is always the worthless $1/2$-correct "algorithm"

> **function** *stupid*(x)
>   **if** *coinflip* = *heads* **then return** *true*
>   **else return** *false*

whose stochastic "advantage" cannot be amplified. Provided $p \geq 1/2$, define the *advantage* of a p-correct Monte Carlo algorithm to be $p - 1/2$. Any Monte Carlo algorithm whose advantage is positive can be turned into one whose error probability is as small as we wish. We begin with an example.

Let *MC* be a $3/4$-correct unbiased Monte Carlo algorithm to solve some decision problem. Consider the following algorithm, which calls *MC*(x) three times and returns the most frequent answer.

> **function** *MC3*(x)
> $t \leftarrow MC(x);\ u \leftarrow MC(x);\ v \leftarrow MC(x)$
>   **if** $t = u$ **or** $t = v$ **then return** t
>   **else return** u

What is the error probability of *MC3*? Let R and W denote the right and wrong answers, respectively. We know that t, u and v each have probability at least $3/4$ to be R, independently of one another. Assume for simplicity that this probability is exactly $^3/_4$ since algorithm $MC3$ would clearly be even better if the error probability of MC were smaller than $^1/_4$. There are eight possible outcomes for the three calls on MC, whose probabilities are summarized in the following table.

t	u	v	prob	$MC3$
R	R	R	27/64	R
R	R	W	9/64	R
R	W	R	9/64	R
R	W	W	3/64	W
W	R	R	9/64	R
W	R	W	3/64	W
W	W	R	3/64	W
W	W	W	1/64	W

Adding the probabilities associated with rows 1, 2, 3 and 5, we conclude that $MC3$ is correct with probability 27/32, which is better than 84%.

More generally, let MC be a Monte Carlo algorithm to solve some decision problem whose advantage is $\varepsilon > 0$. Consider the following algorithm, which calls MC k times and returns the most frequent answer.

```
function RepeatMC(x, k)
    T, F ← 0
    for i ← 1 to k do
        if MC(x) then T ← T + 1
                 else F ← F + 1
    if T > F then return true else return false
```

What is the error probability of $RepeatMC$? To find out, we associate a random variable X_i with each call to MC: $X_i = 1$ if the correct answer is obtained and $X_i = 0$ otherwise. By assumption, $\Pr[X_i = 1] \geq \frac{1}{2} + \varepsilon$ for each i. Assume for simplicity that this probability is exactly $\frac{1}{2} + \varepsilon$ since otherwise $RepeatMC$ would be even better. Assume also that k is odd to avoid the risk of a tie ($T = F$) in the majority vote; see Problem 10.23. The expectation and variance of X_i are $E(X_i) = \frac{1}{2} + \varepsilon$ and $\text{Var}(X_i) = (\frac{1}{2} + \varepsilon)(\frac{1}{2} - \varepsilon) = \frac{1}{4} - \varepsilon^2$, respectively. Now, let $X = \sum_{i=1}^{k} X_i$ be the random variable that corresponds to the number of correct answers in k trials. For any integer i between 0 and k

$$\Pr[X = i] = \binom{k}{i} \left(\tfrac{1}{2} + \varepsilon\right)^i \left(\tfrac{1}{2} - \varepsilon\right)^{k-i}, \tag{10.2}$$

and X has expectation $E(X) = (\frac{1}{2} + \varepsilon) k$ and variance $\text{Var}(X) = (\frac{1}{4} - \varepsilon^2) k$. We are interested in $\Pr[X \leq k/2]$, which is the error probability of $RepeatMC$.

Given specific values for ε and k, we can calculate this probability with the dynamic programming algorithm given in Section 8.1.2 for the World Series, or compute it as $\sum_{i=0}^{k \div 2} \Pr[X = i]$ using Equation 10.2. Better still, we can use the formula in

Problem 10.25. However, it is more convenient to use the Central Limit Theorem, which says that the distribution of X is almost normal when k is large; in practice, $k = 30$ is large enough. Assume for instance that you want an error probability smaller than 5%. Tables for the normal distribution tell us that

$$\Pr[\, X < E(X) - 1.645 \sqrt{\text{Var}(X)} \,] \approx 5\%.$$

To obtain $\Pr[X \leq k/2] < 5\%$ it suffices that

$$k/2 < E(X) - 1.645 \sqrt{\text{Var}(X)}.$$

Using our values for $E(X)$ and $\text{Var}(X)$, this condition translates to

$$k > 2.706 \left(\frac{1}{4\varepsilon^2} - 1 \right). \tag{10.3}$$

For instance, if $\varepsilon = 5\%$, Equation 10.3 tells us that it "suffices" to run a 55%-correct unbiased Monte Carlo algorithm 269 times and take the most frequent answer to obtain a 95%-correct algorithm. (Equation 10.3 gives $k > 267.894$ but we took $k = 269$ rather than 268 because we wanted k to be odd; see Problem 10.23.) In other words, this repetition translates a 5% advantage into a 5% error probability. An exact calculation shows that the resulting error probability is just above 4.99%, illustrating the precision of the normal approximation for such large values of k. This demonstrates the handicap of unbiased Monte Carlo algorithms: running a 55%-correct *biased* algorithm just 4 times reduces the error probability to about 4.1% since $0.45^4 \approx 0.041$.

Equation 10.3 shows that the number of repetitions necessary to achieve a given confidence level (95% in this case) depends strongly on the advantage ε of the original algorithm. An advantage 10 times smaller would necessitate about 100 times more repetitions for the same reliability. On the other hand, it is not much more expensive to obtain considerably more confidence in the final answer. For instance, had we wanted an error probability 10 times smaller, we would have used

$$\Pr[\, X < E(X) - 2.576 \sqrt{\text{Var}(X)} \,] \approx \tfrac{1}{2}\%$$

to conclude that it is sufficient to repeat a $(\tfrac{1}{2} + \varepsilon)$-correct unbiased Monte Carlo algorithm $6.636\,(\frac{1}{4\varepsilon^2} - 1)$ times to make it 99.5%-correct. This is not even two and a half times more expensive than achieving 95%-correctness. A combinatorial argument shows that to bring the error probability below δ for an unbiased Monte Carlo algorithm whose advantage is ε, the number of repetitions necessary is proportional to $1/\varepsilon^2$, as we saw, but also to $\log {}^1/_\delta$. See Problems 10.24 and 10.25 for details.

10.7 Las Vegas algorithms

Las Vegas algorithms make probabilistic choices to help guide them more quickly to a correct solution. Unlike Monte Carlo algorithms, they never return a wrong answer. There are two main categories of Las Vegas algorithms. They may use randomness to guide their search in such a way that a correct solution is guaranteed even if unfortunate choices are made: it will only take longer if this happens. Alternatively, they may allow themselves to take wrong turns that bring them to a dead end, rendering it impossible to find a solution in this run of the algorithm.

Las Vegas algorithms of the first kind are often used when a known deterministic algorithm to solve the problem of interest runs much faster on the average than in the worst case. *Quicksort* from Section 7.4.2 provides the most famous example; see Section 10.7.2. Incorporating an element of randomness allows a Las Vegas algorithm to reduce, and sometimes even to eliminate, this difference between good and bad instances. It is not a case of preventing the occasional occurrence of the algorithm's worst-case behaviour, but rather of breaking the link between the occurrence of such behaviour and the particular instance to be solved.

Recall from Section 2.4 that analysing the average efficiency of an algorithm may sometimes give misleading results. The reason is that any analysis of the average case must be based on a hypothesis about the probability distribution of the instances to be handled. A hypothesis that is correct for a given application of the algorithm may prove disastrously wrong for a different application. Suppose, for example, that *quicksort* is used as a subalgorithm inside a more complex algorithm. We saw in Section 7.4.2 that it takes an average time in $\Theta(n \log n)$ to sort n items provided the instances to be sorted are chosen randomly. This analysis no longer bears any relation to reality if in fact we give the algorithm only instances that are already almost sorted. In general, such deterministic algorithms are vulnerable to an unexpected probability distribution of the instances that some particular application might give them to solve: even if the catastrophic worst-case instances are few in number, they could be the most relevant for that application, causing a spectacular degradation in performance. Las Vegas algorithms free us from worrying about such situations by evening out the time required on different instances of a given size.

The performance of these Las Vegas algorithms is not better than that of the corresponding deterministic algorithm when we consider the average over all instances of a given size. With high probability, instances that took a long time deterministically are now solved much faster, but instances on which the deterministic algorithm was particularly good are slowed down to average by the Las Vegas algorithm. Thus, these Las Vegas algorithms "steal" time from the "rich" instances—those that were solved quickly by the deterministic algorithm—to give it to the "poor" instances. We call this the *Robin Hood effect*, and illustrate it in Sections 10.7.2 and 10.7.3. This is interesting when we consider deterministic algorithms that are not significantly faster than average in the best case, so nothing much is lost by slowing them down to average, but that suffer from a few painfully bad cases.

The other category of Las Vegas algorithms now and again make choices that bring them to a dead end. We ask that these algorithms be capable of recognizing this predicament, in which case they simply admit failure. Such behaviour would be intolerable from a deterministic algorithm as it would mean that it is unable to solve the instance considered. However, the probabilistic nature of Las Vegas algorithms makes this admission of failure acceptable provided it does not occur with overwhelming probability: simply rerun the same algorithm on the same instance for a fresh chance of success when failure occurs. There are practical problems for which willingness to risk failure allows an efficient Las Vegas algorithm when no deterministic algorithms are known to be efficient; see Section 10.7.4. Although no guaranteed upper bound can be set on the time it will take to obtain an answer if the algorithm is restarted whenever it fails, this time may be reasonable with high probability. These algorithms should not be confused with those, such as the simplex algorithm for linear programming, that are extremely efficient for the great majority of instances to be handled, but catastrophic for a few instances: a Las Vegas algorithm should have good expected performance whatever the instance to be solved.

When a Las Vegas algorithm is allowed to fail, it is more convenient to represent it in the form of a **procedure** rather than a **function**. This allows for a return parameter *success*, set to *true* if a solution is obtained and *false* otherwise. The typical call to solve instance x is $LV(x, y, success)$, where the return parameter y receives the solution whenever *success* is set to *true*. For convenience, we write

> **return** *success* ← *true*

as a shortcut for

> *success* ← *true*
> **return**

and similarly with **return** *success* ← *false*.

Let $p(x)$ be the probability of success of the algorithm each time it is asked to solve instance x. For an algorithm to deserve the name "Las Vegas", we require that $p(x) > 0$ for every instance x. This ensures that a solution will be found eventually if we keep repeating the algorithm. It is even better if there exists a constant $\delta > 0$ such that $p(x) \geq \delta$ for every instance x since otherwise the expected number of repetitions before success could grow arbitrarily with the instance size.

Consider the following algorithm.

> **function** *RepeatLV* (x)
>   **repeat**
> $LV(x, y, success)$
>   **until** *success*
>   **return** y

Since each call on $LV(x)$ has probability $p(x)$ of being successful, the expected number of trips round the loop is $1/p(x)$. A more interesting parameter is the expected time $t(x)$ before *RepeatLV* (x) is successful. One may think at first that this is simply $1/p(x)$ multiplied by the expected time taken by each call on $LV(x)$.

However, a correct analysis must consider separately the expected time taken by $LV(x)$ in case of success and in case of failure. Let these expected times be denoted by $s(x)$ and $f(x)$, respectively. Neglecting the time taken by the control of the **repeat** loop, $t(x)$ is given by a case analysis.

◊ With probability $p(x)$, the first call on $LV(x)$ succeeds after expected time $s(x)$.

◊ With probability $1 - p(x)$, the first call on $LV(x)$ fails after expected time $f(x)$. After this we are back to the starting point, still an expected time $t(x)$ away from success. The total expected time in this case is thus $f(x)+t(x)$.

Therefore, $t(x)$ is given by a simple recurrence

$$t(x) = p(x)s(x) + (1 - p(x))(f(x)+t(x)),$$

which is easily solved to yield

$$t(x) = s(x) + \frac{1 - p(x)}{p(x)} f(x). \tag{10.4}$$

Some Las Vegas algorithms allow fine-tuning of various parameters. Turning a knob here, for instance, will decrease both the expected time in case of either success or failure (which is good) and the probability of success (which is bad). When this happens, Equation 10.4 is the key to optimizing the overall performance of the algorithm. We illustrate this in Section 10.7.1 with a return to the eight queens problem. Section 10.7.4 gives a more sophisticated and useful example of a Las Vegas algorithm that may fail occasionally, but for which there is a better strategy than to restart the entire computation in case of failure.

10.7.1 The eight queens problem revisited

The eight queens problem provides an instructive example of a Las Vegas algorithm that benefits from being allowed to fail. Recall that the backtracking technique used in Section 9.6.2 involves systematically exploring the nodes of the implicit tree formed by the so-called k-promising vectors. Using this technique, we obtain the first solution after examining only 114 of the 2057 nodes in the tree. This is not bad, but the algorithm does not take into account one important fact: there is nothing systematic about the positions of the queens in most of the solutions. On the contrary, the queens seem more to have been positioned haphazardly.

This observation suggests a greedy Las Vegas algorithm that places queens randomly on successive rows, only taking care never to place a new queen in a position that is threatened by one already placed. Since this is a greedy algorithm, no attempt is made to relocate previous queens when there is no possibility left for the next queen: this is a dead end. As a result, the algorithm either ends successfully if it manages to place all the queens on the board or fails if there is no square in which the next queen can be added. The greedy approach makes the algorithm easier than backtracking to understand and to implement by hand— even though the actual code is longer—but it also entails a possibility of failure. Does this simplicity come at the expense of efficiency? We shall see that nothing could be farther from the truth. The algorithm uses the same sets *col*, *diag*45 and *diag*135 as in Section 9.6.2 to help determine which positions are still available in the current row.

```
procedure queensLV (var sol[1..8], success)
    array ok[1..8] {will hold available positions}
    col, diag45, diag135 ← ∅
    for k ← 0 to 7 do
        {sol[1..k] is k-promising; let's place the (k + 1)−st queen}
        nb ← 0 {to count the number of possibilities}
        for j ← 1 to 8 do
            if j ∉ col and j − k ∉ diag45 and j + k ∉ diag135
            then {column j is available for the (k + 1)−st queen}
                nb ← nb + 1
                ok[nb]← j
        if nb = 0 then return success ← false
        j ← ok[uniform(1..nb)]
        col ← col ∪ {j}
        diag45 ← diag45 ∪ {j − k}
        diag135 ← diag135 ∪ {j + k}
        sol[k + 1]← j
        {end of for loop in k}
    return success ← true
```

To analyse this algorithm, we need to determine its probability p of success, the average number s of nodes that it explores in the case of success, and the average number f of nodes that it explores in the case of failure. Clearly $s = 9$, counting the 0-promising empty vector and the 8-promising solution. Using a computer we can calculate $p \approx 0.1293$ and $f \approx 6.971$. A solution is therefore obtained more than one time out of eight by proceeding in a completely random fashion! The expected number of nodes explored if we repeat the algorithm until a success is finally obtained is given by Equation 10.4: $s + \frac{1-p}{p} f \approx 55.93$, less than half the number of nodes explored by systematic backtracking.

We can do better still. The Las Vegas algorithm is too defeatist: as soon as it detects a failure it starts all over from the beginning. The backtracking algorithm, on the other hand, makes a systematic search for a solution that we know has nothing systematic about it. A judicious combination of these two algorithms first places a number of queens on the board in a random way, and then uses backtracking to try and add the remaining queens, without, however, reconsidering the positions of the queens that were placed randomly.

An unfortunate random choice of the positions of the first few queens can make it impossible to add all the others. This happens, for instance, if the first two queens are placed in positions 1 and 3, respectively. The more queens we place randomly, the smaller the average time needed by the subsequent backtracking stage, whether it fails or succeeds, but the greater the probability of failure. This is the "fine-tuning knob" mentioned previously. Let *stopLV* denote the number of queens we place randomly before moving on to the backtracking phase, $0 \le stopLV \le 8$.

The modified algorithm is similar to *queensLV*, except that we must include the declaration of an inner **procedure** *backtrack* (see below), the loop in k goes from 0 to *stopLV* − 1, and we replace the last line (**return** *success* ← *true*) by

$$backtrack(stopLV, col, diag45, diag135, success).$$

This calls the backtracking phase provided the loop did not terminate prematurely in failure. The **procedure** *backtrack* looks like algorithm *queens* of Section 9.6.2 except that it has an additional parameter *success* and that it returns immediately after either finding the first solution or finding that there are none, whichever is the case.

To set the fine-tuning knob in its optimal position, we need to determine the probability p of success, the expected number s of nodes explored in the case of success and the expected number f of nodes explored in the case of failure for each possible value for *stopLV*. Equation 10.4 can then be used to determine the expected number t of nodes explored if the algorithm is repeated until it eventually finds a solution. These numbers, obtained by exploring the entire backtracking tree with the help of a computer, are summarized in Figure 10.3. The case *stopLV* = 0 corresponds to using the deterministic algorithm directly.

stopLV	p	s	f	t
0	1.0000	114.00	—	114.00
1	1.0000	39.63	—	39.63
2	0.8750	22.53	39.67	28.20
3	0.4931	13.48	15.10	29.01
4	0.2618	10.31	8.79	35.10
5	0.1624	9.33	7.29	46.92
6	0.1357	9.05	6.98	53.50
7	0.1293	9.00	6.97	55.93
8	0.1293	9.00	6.97	55.93

Figure 10.3. Fine-tuning a Las Vegas algorithm

Although a purely probabilistic approach (*stopLV* = 8) is better than pure determinism (*stopLV* = 0), a mixture of both is better still. The most entertaining compromise when the algorithm is performed by hand is to place the first three queens at random (*stopLV* = 3) and to continue by backtracking: this fails essentially every other time, but it is very quick whether it succeeds nor not. Try it, it's fun!

The number of nodes explored is a good measure of the amount of work expounded by the algorithm, but it may not give a complete picture of the situation. To ease our minds, we implemented algorithm *queensLV* on a workstation. Pure backtracking finds the first solution in 0.45 millisecond, whereas an average of 0.14 millisecond is sufficient if the first two queens are placed at random before backtracking. This is more than three times faster. However, it takes 0.21 millisecond on the average if the first three queens are placed at random, only twice as good as pure backtracking. If all the queens are placed in a random way, we lose: it takes on the average almost one millisecond to find a solution, twice the time needed deterministically. This disappointing result is easily explained: the time needed to generate pseudorandom values cannot be neglected. It turns out that 71% of the time spent solving the eight queens problem when all the queens are placed randomly is used generating pseudorandom values. Even though our performance might have been better had we used a faster—albeit less sophisticated—generator, should we conclude that the benefits of randomness are likely to be offset by the overhead of pseudorandom generation?

Once again, the eight queens problem generalizes to an arbitrary number n of queens. The advantage gained by using the probabilistic approach becomes more convincing as n increases. We tried the algorithm on the 39 queens problem. Pure deterministic backtracking needs to explore more than 10^{10} nodes before it finds the first solution: 11 402 835 415 nodes to be exact. By comparison, the Las Vegas algorithm succeeds with probability roughly 21% if it places the first 29 queens randomly, after exploring only about 100 nodes whether it fails or succeeds. On the average, less than 500 nodes are explored before success is reached if the algorithm is restarted after each failure. This is more than 20 million times better than pure backtracking. Furthermore, the improvement persists when time on a real computer is considered: it takes approximately 41 hours of uninterrupted computation on our workstation to solve the problem by pure deterministic backtracking, whereas the Las Vegas algorithm finds one solution every 8.5 milliseconds. If the pure greedy Las Vegas algorithm is used, the success rate is roughly one in 135 trials, but each attempt is so fast that a solution is found about every 150 milliseconds on the average, still nearly one million times faster than pure backtracking.

If we want one solution to the n queens problem for a specific value of n, it is obviously silly to analyse exhaustively all the possibilities to discover the optimal value of *stopLV*, and then to apply the Las Vegas algorithm accordingly. Empirical evidence suggests that the Las Vegas algorithm greatly outperforms pure backtracking provided we place almost all—but not quite all—the queens randomly. For example, the expected number of nodes explored is minimized if we place 88 queens at random for the 100 queens problem and 983 for the 1000 queens problem. Even if we do not use the best possible value for *stopLV*, we obtain our solution reasonably quickly if we are not too far off. Moreover, many different solutions can be obtained easily by calling the algorithm repeatedly.

10.7.2 Probabilistic selection and sorting

We return to the problem of finding the k–th smallest element in an array T of n elements. We saw in Section 7.5 an algorithm that can solve this problem in a time in $\Theta(n)$ in the worst case, independently of the value of k. In particular, choosing $k = \lceil n/2 \rceil$ provides a linear worst-case time algorithm to find the median of an array.

Recall that this algorithm begins by partitioning the elements of the array on either side of a pivot, and that then, like binary search, it restricts its attention to the relevant subarray. The process is repeated until all the elements still under consideration are equal, perhaps because there is only one left, in which case we have found the desired value. A fundamental principle of the divide-and-conquer technique suggests that the nearer the pivot is to the median of the elements, the more efficient the algorithm will be. Despite this, there is no question of choosing the exact median as the pivot: this would cause an infinite recursion, as finding the median is a special case of the selection problem under consideration. Thus we choose a suboptimal pivot known as the pseudomedian. This avoids the infinite recursion, but choosing the pseudomedian is still relatively costly.

On the other hand, we also saw a simpler approach that uses as pivot the first element that remains under consideration. This assures us of a linear execution time on the average, but with the risk that the algorithm will take quadratic time in the worst case. Despite this prohibitive worst case, the simpler algorithm has the advantage of a much smaller hidden constant on account of the time saved by not calculating the pseudomedian. Any simple deterministic strategy for choosing the pivot is likely to result in quadratic worst-case time for finding the median, and conversely linear worst-case algorithms seem to require a large hidden constant. The decision whether it is more important to have efficient execution in the worst case or on the average must be taken in the light of the particular application. If we decide to aim for speed on the average thanks to the simpler deterministic algorithm, we must make sure that the instances to be solved are indeed chosen randomly according to the uniform distribution. A bad probability distribution of the instances could spell disaster.

For the execution time to depend only on the number of elements but not on the actual instance, it suffices to choose the pivot randomly among the elements still under consideration. The resulting algorithm is very similar to *selection* from Section 7.5.

> **function** *selectionLV* $(T[1..n], s)$
>   {Finds the s–th smallest element in T, $1 \le s \le n$}
> $i \leftarrow 1$; $j \leftarrow n$
>   **repeat**
>   {Answer lies in $T[i..j]$}
> $p \leftarrow T[uniform(i..j)]$
> $pivotbis(T[i..j], p, k, l)$
>   **if** $s \le k$ **then** $j \leftarrow k$
>   **else if** $s \ge l$ **then** $i \leftarrow l$
>   **else return** p

The analysis requested in Problem 7.18 applies *mutatis mutandis* to conclude that the expected time taken by this probabilistic selection algorithm is linear, independently of the instance to be solved. Thus its efficiency is not affected by the peculiarities of the application in which the algorithm is used. It is always possible that some particular execution of the algorithm will take quadratic time, but the probability that this will happen becomes increasingly negligible as n gets larger, and, to repeat, this unlikely occurrence is no longer linked to specific instances.

To sum up, we started with an algorithm that is excellent when we consider its average execution time on all the instances of some particular size but that is inefficient on certain specific instances. Using the probabilistic approach, we transformed this algorithm into a Las Vegas algorithm that is efficient with high probability, whatever the instance considered. Thus we reap the benefits of both deterministic algorithms seen in Section 7.5: expected linear time on all instances, with a small hidden constant.

We once asked the students in an algorithmics course to implement the selection algorithm of their choice. The only algorithms they had seen in class were those in Section 7.5. Since the students did not know which instances would be used to test their programs—and suspecting the worst of their professors—none of them took the risk of using a deterministic algorithm with quadratic worst case. Three students, however, thought of using the probabilistic approach. This idea allowed them to beat their colleagues hands down: their programs took an average of 300 milliseconds to solve the trial instance, whereas the majority of the deterministic algorithms took between 1500 and 2600 milliseconds. Moreover, their programs were much simpler—and thus less likely to contain subtle errors—than their colleagues'.

The same approach can be used to turn *quicksort* into an algorithm that sorts n elements in worst-case expected time in $O(n \log n)$, whereas the algorithm we saw in Section 7.4.2 requires a time in $\Omega(n^2)$ when the array to be sorted is already sorted. The randomized version of *quicksort* is as follows. To sort the entire array T, simply call *quicksortLV*$(T[1 .. n])$.

> **procedure** *quicksortLV*$(T[i .. j])$
>   {Sorts subarray $T[i .. j]$ into nondecreasing order}
>   **if** $j - i$ is sufficiently small **then** *insert*$(T[i .. j])$
>   **else**
> $p \leftarrow T[uniform(i .. j)]$
> $pivotbis(T[i .. j], p, k, l)$
> $quicksortLV(T[i .. k])$
> $quicksortLV(T[l, j])$

10.7.3 Universal hashing

Recall from Section 5.6 that associative tables, such as those used to keep track of identifiers in compilers, are usually implemented using hashing. This gives expected constant time per access to the table provided the symbols in the table are random. Unfortunately, this says nothing about the performance of hashing on nonrandom instances. If hashing is used to implement the symbol table in a compiler, for example, the assumption that all possible identifiers are equally likely is unreasonable (thank goodness!). Consequently, such average-case analysis can be misleading and the probability of bad cases may be significantly higher than expected.

More importantly, certain programs will inevitably cause more collisions than expected through no fault of the unlucky programmer. These programs will compile slowly every time they are submitted because the hash function is fixed once and for all in the compiler. Conventional wisdom has it that things will even out from a systems perspective: some programs will take more time to compile than expected, but others will go faster. At the end of the day, compilation will have been efficient on the average. This viewpoint is inherently unfair. If each program

is compiled many times, it is always the same few programs that will require substantially more time than expected. In a real sense, these programs are paying the
price for all other programs to compile quickly. Las Vegas hashing allows us to
retain the efficiency of hashing on the average, without arbitrarily favouring some
programs at the expense of others. This is the Robin Hood effect at its best: each
program is given its fair share of the benefits to be reaped by hashing. Also, each
program will once in a while pay the price of overall efficiency by taking more time
than expected. Moreover, the good expected performance of Las Vegas hashing can
be proved mathematically without assumptions on the probability distribution of
the access sequences to the table.

The basic idea of Las Vegas hashing is for the compiler to choose the hash
function randomly at the beginning of each compilation and again whenever rehashing becomes necessary. This ensures that collision lists remain reasonably
well-balanced with high probability, whatever the set of identifiers in the program
to be compiled. As a result, a program that causes a large number of collisions during one compilation will probably be luckier the next time it is compiled. But what
do we mean by "choose the hash function randomly"?

The answer lies in a technique known as *universal hashing*. Let U be the universe
of potential indexes for the associative table, such as the set of all possible identifiers
if we are implementing a compiler, and let $B = \{0, 1, 2, \ldots, N - 1\}$ be the set of
indexes in the hash table. Consider any two distinct x and y in U. Suppose first
that $h : U \to B$ is a function chosen randomly among all the functions from U to
B according to the uniform distribution. Then the probability that $h(x) = h(y)$
is $1/N$. This is because $h(y)$ could take any of the N values from B with equal
probability; in particular the value attributed to $h(x)$ would also be chosen for
$h(y)$ with probability $1/N$. However, U is usually large and there are far too many
functions from U into B for it to be reasonable to choose one at random according
to the uniform distribution.

Consider now a set H of functions from U to B, and consider again any two
distinct x and y in U. Suppose that $h : U \to B$ is a function chosen randomly
from the members of H according to the uniform distribution. We say that H is a
universal₂ class of hash functions if the probability that $h(x) = h(y)$ is at most $1/N$.
In other words, we require that the probability of $h(x) = h(y)$ be small no matter
which distinct values of x and y are considered, provided the choice of h is made
independently of those values. We saw that the set of all functions from U to B is
universal₂, but too large to be useful. Universal classes are interesting because they
can be reasonably small, so that a random function can be chosen in practice from
such a class according to the uniform distribution. Moreover, the functions can be
evaluated efficiently. We give below one explicit example of such a universal₂ class
of hash functions, but first let us see how good they are at solving the compilation
problem.

Let H be a universal₂ class of hash functions from U to B. Let x and y be any
two distinct identifiers. By definition of universality, if h is chosen randomly in H
according to the uniform distribution, the probability of collision between x and
y is at most $1/N$. Now consider a program with m distinct identifiers and let x
be any one of those. For each of the $m - 1$ identifiers other than x, the probability

of collision with x is at most $1/N$. Therefore, the expected number of identifiers in collision with x is at most $(m-1)/N$, which is less than the load factor. Since this is true for each x and since we keep the load factor below 1 by rehashing when necessary, each access to the hash table takes constant expected time in the worst case. Therefore, n requests to the hash table take expected time in $\Theta(n)$ in the worst case. Compare this with a time in $\Omega(n^2)$ required in the worst case for classic hashing. As usual with Las Vegas algorithms, "the worst case" refers to the worst possible set of requests to the table, not the worst possible random choices made by the compiler.

Several efficient universal$_2$ classes of hash functions are known. We give one example. Assume for simplicity that $U = \{0, 1, 2, \ldots, a-1\}$ and $B = \{0, 1, 2, \ldots, N-1\}$. (Identifiers must be transformed into integers using any standard integer representation of character strings, such as ASCII.) Let p be a prime number at least as large as a. Let i and j be two integers. Define $h_{ij} : U \rightarrow B$ by

$$h_{ij}(x) = ((ix + j) \bmod p) \bmod N.$$

Then, $H = \{h_{ij} \mid 1 \le i < p \text{ and } 0 \le j < p\}$ is a universal$_2$ class of hash functions from U to B. Randomly choosing a function in H is as simple as choosing two integers smaller than p. Moreover, the value of $h_{ij}(x)$ can be calculated efficiently, especially if we choose N to be a power of 2, which simplifies the second modulo operation.

10.7.4 Factorizing large integers

Let n be an integer greater than 1. The *factorization* problem consists of finding the unique decomposition of n into a product of prime factors. The problem of *splitting* consists of finding one nontrivial divisor of n, provided n is composite. Factorizing reduces to splitting and primality testing: to factorize n, we are done if n is prime; otherwise, find a nontrivial divisor m and recursively factorize m and n/m.

The naive splitting algorithm is trial division, which finds the smallest prime divisor of n. It is useless to look for a divisor larger than $\sqrt{n}$ because if $m > \sqrt{n}$ divides n, then so does n/m, which is smaller than $\sqrt{n}$.

```
function trialdiv(n)
    for m ← 2 to ⌊√n⌋ do
        if m divides n then return m
    {If the loop fails to find a divisor, n is prime}
    return n {a prime number is its own smallest prime divisor}
```

This algorithm takes a time in $\Omega(\sqrt{n})$ in the worst case, which is of no practical use even on medium-size integers: counting just one nanosecond for each trip round the loop, it would take thousands of years to split a hard composite number with forty or so decimal digits, where "hard" means that the number is the product of two primes of roughly equal size.

The largest hard composite number that has been factorized at the time of writing spans 129 decimal digits. This factorization was the key to meeting the RSA cryptographic challenge mentioned in Section 7.10. Recall that it required eight months of calculation on more than 600 computers throughout the world. It is estimated that this would have taken 5000 years of uninterrupted calculation if a single workstation that can run one million instructions per second had been used. Although this effort is staggering, success would not have been possible without a sophisticated algorithm. Indeed, when the challenge was issued in 1977, it was estimated that the fastest computer then available running the best algorithm known at the time would have completed the calculation after two million times the age of the Universe! In this section we give but a glimpse of the basic idea behind the successful algorithm.

Efficient splitting algorithms rest on the following theorem, whose easy proof is left as an exercise.

Theorem 10.7.1 *Let n be a composite integer. Let a and b be distinct integers between 1 and $n - 1$ such that $a + b \neq n$. If $a^2 \bmod n = b^2 \bmod n$ then $\gcd(a + b, n)$ is a nontrivial divisor of n.*

Consider $n = 2537$ for example. Let $a = 2012$ and $b = 1127$. Note that $a^2 = 1595n + 1629$ and $b^2 = 500n + 1629$, which shows that both a^2 and b^2 are equal to 1629 modulo n. Since $a \neq b$ and $a + b \neq n$, the theorem says that $\gcd(a + b, n) = \gcd(3139, 2537) = 43$ is a nontrivial divisor of n, which indeed it is. This suggests an approach to splitting n: find two distinct numbers between 1 and $n - 1$ that have the same square modulo n but whose sum is not n, and use Euclid's algorithm to compute the greatest common divisor of their sum with n. This is fine provided such numbers always exist when n is composite and provided we can find them efficiently.

The first question is quickly disposed of. Provided n has at least two distinct prime divisors, $a^2 \bmod n$ admits at least four distinct "square roots" in arithmetic modulo n for any a relatively prime to n. Continuing our example, 1629 admits exactly four square roots modulo 2537, namely 525, 1127, 1410 and 2012. These roots come in pairs: $525 + 2012 = 1127 + 1410 = 2537$. Any two of them will do provided they are not from the same pair.

So how can we find a and b with the desired property? This is where randomness enters the game. Let k be an integer to be specified later. An integer is *k-smooth* if all its prime divisors are among the k smallest prime numbers. For instance, $120 = 2^3 \times 3 \times 5$ is 3-smooth but $35 = 5 \times 7$ is not. When k is small, k-smooth integers can be factorized efficiently by trial division. In its first phase, the Las Vegas splitting algorithm chooses an integer x randomly between 1 and $n - 1$, and computes $y = x^2 \bmod n$. If y is k-smooth, both x and the factorization of y are kept in a table. Otherwise, another x is chosen randomly. This process is repeated until we have found $k + 1$ different integers for which we know the factorization of their squares modulo n.

Still continuing our example with $n = 2537$, let us take $k = 7$. We are thus concerned only with the primes 2, 3, 5, 7, 11, 13 and 17. A first integer $x = 1769$ is chosen randomly. We calculate its square modulo n: $x^2 = 1233n + 1240$ and thus $y = 1240$. An attempt to factorize $1240 = 2^3 \times 5 \times 31$ fails since 31 is not divisible by any of the admissible primes. A second attempt with $x = 2455$ is luckier: its square modulo n is $1650 = 2 \times 3 \times 5^2 \times 11$. Each attempt succeeds with probability roughly 20% in this small example. Continuing thus until 8 successes have been recorded, we obtain the following table.

$$
\begin{array}{llll}
x_1 &=& 2455 & y_1 = 1650 = 2 \times 3 \times 5^2 \times 11 \\
x_2 &=& 970 & y_2 = 2210 = 2 \times 5 \times 13 \times 17 \\
x_3 &=& 1105 & y_3 = 728 = 2^3 \times 7 \times 13 \\
x_4 &=& 1458 & y_4 = 2295 = 3^3 \times 5 \times 17 \\
x_5 &=& 216 & y_5 = 990 = 2 \times 3^2 \times 5 \times 11 \\
x_6 &=& 80 & y_6 = 1326 = 2 \times 3 \times 13 \times 17 \\
x_7 &=& 1844 & y_7 = 756 = 2^2 \times 3^3 \times 7 \\
x_8 &=& 433 & y_8 = 2288 = 2^4 \times 11 \times 13
\end{array}
$$

This is used to form a $(k+1) \times k$ matrix M over $\{0, 1\}$. Each row corresponds to one success; each column corresponds to one of the admissible primes. The entry M_{ij} is set to 0 if the j–th prime appears to an even power (including zero) in the factorization of y_i; otherwise $M_{ij} = 1$. For example $M_{3,1} = 1$ because the first prime, 2, occurs to the odd power 3 in y_3, and $M_{3,2} = 0$ because the second prime, 3, occurs to the even power 0. Continuing our example, we obtain the following matrix.

$$
M = \begin{pmatrix}
1 & 1 & 0 & 0 & 1 & 0 & 0 \\
1 & 0 & 1 & 0 & 0 & 1 & 1 \\
1 & 0 & 0 & 1 & 0 & 1 & 0 \\
0 & 1 & 1 & 0 & 0 & 0 & 1 \\
1 & 0 & 1 & 0 & 1 & 0 & 0 \\
1 & 1 & 0 & 0 & 0 & 1 & 1 \\
0 & 1 & 0 & 1 & 0 & 0 & 0 \\
0 & 0 & 0 & 0 & 1 & 1 & 0
\end{pmatrix}
$$

Since this matrix contains more rows than columns, the rows cannot be linearly independent: there must exist a nonempty set of rows that add up to the all-zero vector in arithmetic modulo 2. Such a set can be found by Gauss–Jordan elimination, although more efficient methods are available when k is large, especially for very sparse matrices such as those obtained by this factorization algorithm when n is large. In our example, there are seven different solutions, such as rows 1, 2, 4 and 8, or rows 1, 3, 4, 5, 6 and 7. Consider now what happens if the y_i's corresponding to the selected rows are multiplied. Our two examples yield

$$
\begin{array}{lll}
y_1 y_2 y_4 y_8 &=& 2^6 \times 3^4 \times 5^4 \times 11^2 \times 13^2 \times 17^2, \text{ and} \\
y_1 y_3 y_4 y_5 y_6 y_7 &=& 2^8 \times 3^{10} \times 5^4 \times 7^2 \times 11^2 \times 13^2 \times 17^2,
\end{array}
$$

respectively. The exponents in those products are necessarily even by construction. Thus one square root of these products is obtained by halving each of the powers.

In arithmetic modulo n, a square root of the same product can also be obtained by multiplying the corresponding x_i's since each $y_i = x_i^2 \bmod n$. In our example the two approaches to calculating a square root modulo n of $y_1 y_2 y_4 y_8$ yield

$$
\begin{aligned}
a &= 2^3 \times 3^2 \times 5^2 \times 11 \times 13 \times 17 && \bmod 2537 &= 2012 \\
b &= 2455 \times 970 \times 1458 \times 433 && \bmod 2537 &= 1127.
\end{aligned}
$$

As we saw earlier, it suffices to calculate the greatest common divisor of $a + b$ and n to obtain a nontrivial divisor of n. In general, this technique yields two integers a and b between 1 and $n - 1$ such that $a^2 \bmod n = b^2 \bmod n$. There is no guarantee, however, that $a \neq b$ and $a + b \neq n$. Indeed, use of $y_1 y_3 y_4 y_5 y_6 y_7$ instead of $y_1 y_2 y_4 y_8$ results in

$$
\begin{aligned}
a' &= 2^4 \times 3^5 \times 5^2 \times 7 \times 11 \times 13 \times 17 && \bmod 2537 &= 1973 \\
b' &= 2455 \times 1105 \times 1458 \times 216 \times 80 \times 1844 && \bmod 2537 &= 564,
\end{aligned}
$$

which is worthless because $a' + b' = n$. Nevertheless, it can be proved that this entire process succeeds with probability at least 50% unless $\gcd(a, n)$ is a nontrivial divisor of n, which is just as good for splitting purposes; see Problem 10.41. Contrary to the n queens problem, however, we should not restart from scratch in case of failure. Why throw out so much good work? Instead, we look for other sets of rows of M that add up to zero in arithmetic modulo 2. If this still fails, we find a few more pairs $\langle x_i, y_i \rangle$ and try again with the resulting enlarged matrix.

It remains to determine what value of k should be used to optimize the performance of this approach. The larger this parameter, the higher the probability that $x^2 \bmod n$ will be k-smooth when x is chosen randomly. On the other hand, the smaller this parameter, the faster we can carry out a test of k-smoothness and factorize the k-smooth values that are found, and the fewer such values we require. Finding the optimal compromise calls for deep number theory. Let

$$
L = e^{\sqrt{\log n \log \log n}},
$$

let b be an arbitrary positive real number and let $t = L^{1/2b}$. It can be shown that if $k \approx L^b$, about one x in t is such that $x^2 \bmod n$ is k-smooth. Since each unsuccessful attempt requires k divisions and since it takes $k + 1$ successes to build the matrix, this phase requires an expected number of trial divisions approximately in $O(tk^2) = O(L^{2b+(1/2b)})$, which is minimized at $O(L^2)$ with $b = 1/2$. Finding a set of rows that add up to the zero vector takes a time in $O(k^3) = O(L^{3b})$ if Gauss–Jordan elimination is used (again, it is possible to do better than this), which is negligible compared to the time needed to build the matrix if $b = 1/2$. The final calculation of a greatest common divisor by Euclid's algorithm is completely negligible. Thus, if we take $k \approx \sqrt{L}$, the algorithm splits n after an expected number of divisions that is approximately in $O(L^2)$. If n is an average 100 decimal digit number, $L^2 \approx 5 \times 10^{30}$ whereas $\sqrt{n} \approx 7 \times 10^{49}$, which is more than 10^{19} times bigger. This illustrates how much better this algorithm is than trial division. This comparison is not entirely fair since the hidden constant for trial division is smaller, but even 10^{30} picoseconds is about twice the estimated age of the Universe.

Several improvements make the algorithm more practical. If instead of choosing x at random between 1 and $n - 1$, we choose it so that $x^2 \bmod n$ is more likely to be k-smooth, we reduce the number of trials before the $k + 1$ required relations are obtained. Randomness plays a fundamental role in this algorithm because no deterministic approach for finding so many good x's has been proved efficient. Nevertheless, there are unproved heuristics that work so well in practice that it would be silly to use the "pure" algorithm outlined above. The simplest of these is to choose the x's slightly larger than $\sqrt{n}$; see Problem 10.42. Another heuristic, the *quadratic sieve*, operates in a time in $O(L)$. The successful factorization of a hard 129-digit number mentioned at the beginning of this section was performed with the somewhat more sophisticated "double large prime multiple polynomial variation of the quadratic sieve". Other interesting factorization techniques are the elliptic curve method and the number field sieve; they involve rather deep number theory.

10.8 Problems

Problem 10.1.   You have a coin biased so that each toss produces *heads* with probability p and *tail* with complementary probability $q = 1 - p$. Assume that each toss of the coin is independent from previous tosses: the probability of getting *heads* at any given toss is exactly p, regardless of previous outcomes. Unfortunately you do not know the value of p. Design a simple process by which you can use this coin to generate a perfectly unbiased sequence of random bits.

Problem 10.2.   In Section 10.5.1, we saw that it "suffices" to drop about one and a half million needles on the floor to estimate π within 0.01 ninety-five times out of one hundred. This was achieved by dropping needles that are half as long as the planks in the floor are wide. Our estimate of π was n/k, where n is the number of needles dropped and k is the number that fall across a crack. Show that we can improve this "algorithm" by dropping needles twice as long and producing $n/2k$ as estimate of π. How many of these needles need we drop to have probability at least 95% of obtaining the correct value of π within 0.01?

Problem 10.3.   Yet another probabilistic approach for estimating the value of π is to use Monte Carlo integration to estimate the area of a quarter circle of radius 2. In other words, we can use the relation

$$\pi = \int_{x=0}^{2} \sqrt{4 - x^2}\, dx.$$

How many random values of x must we use to have probability at least 95% of obtaining the correct value of π within 0.01?

Problem 10.4.   Write a computer program to simulate Buffon's experiment to estimate the value of π. The challenge is that you are not allowed to use the value of π in your program. If you do not see why this is a difficulty, try it!

Problem 10.5.   Consider the simplest probabilistic counting strategy, in which the register is incremented with probability $^1/_2$ at each *tick*, and *count* returns twice the value held in the register; see Section 10.5.3. Prove that the expected value returned by this strategy is exactly the number of *tick*s. What is the variance of the value returned? Interpret this variance in terms of a confidence interval.

Problem 10.6.   In this problem, we analyse rigorously the probabilistic counting algorithm of Section 10.5.3. Prove that the expected value returned by a call on *count* after a call on *init* followed by m calls on *tick* is m, provided we ignore the unlikely possibility that the register may overflow. To do this, let $p_m(i)$ denote the probability that the register holds value i after m calls on *tick*, in which case *count* would return $2^i - 1$. Clearly, $p_0(0) = 1$, $p_m(0) = 0$ for all $m > 0$, and $p_m(i) = 0$ for all $i > m$. The register holds value i after m ticks either if it held value $i - 1$ after $m - 1$ ticks (with probability $p_{m-1}(i - 1)$) and it increased by 1 with the next tick (with probability $2^{-(i-1)}$), or if it held value i already after $m - 1$ ticks (with probability $p_{m-1}(i)$) and it kept its value on the next tick (with probability $1 - 2^{-i}$). Therefore

$$p_m(i) = 2^{-(i-1)} p_{m-1}(i - 1) + (1 - 2^{-i}) p_{m-1}(i)$$

for all $1 \le i \le m$. The expected value returned by *count* after m ticks is

$$E(m) = \sum_{i=0}^{m} (2^i - 1) p_m(i).$$

You have to prove by mathematical induction that $E(m) = m$ for all $m \ge 0$.

Problem 10.7.   Continuing Problem 10.6, prove that the variance of the value returned by a call on *count* after a call on *init* followed by m calls on *tick* is $m(m - 1)/2$. Interpret this in terms of a confidence interval.

Problem 10.8.   Consider the modified probabilistic counting algorithm specified by Equation 10.1. Determine the probability under which *tick(c)* should increment c. Do you get 2^{-c} as you should when $\varepsilon = 1$? Rework this problem if the division by ε is removed from Equation 10.1. What would be terribly wrong in this case?
Note: In practice the 2^n relevant probabilities would be precomputed and kept in an array, which makes the approach interesting only if a large number of registers is needed or if the context of Problem 10.10 applies.

Problem 10.9.   Continuing Problem 10.8, what is the variance of the value returned by *count* after m ticks when Equation 10.1 is followed? Give your answer as a function of m and ε. Interpret it in terms of a confidence interval.

Problem 10.10.   Smart cards provide an interesting application for the probabilistic counting technique of Section 10.5.3. *Write-only* memories are technologically easier to implement than ordinary read-write memories. Write-only bits are initialized to 0 at the factory. They can be read at will, and they can be flipped to 1, but they cannot be reset to 0. Prove that it is impossible to count more than n events in an n-bit write-only register by any deterministic technique. Show however that it is possible to count up to $2^n - 1$ events by probabilistic methods. In other words, probabilistic counting and a write-only register cover the same ground as deterministic counting and an ordinary register of the same length.

Problem 10.11.   A room contains 25 strangers; would you be willing to bet at even odds that at least two of them share the same birthday?

Problem 10.12.   Let X be a finite set whose cardinality n we would like to know. Unfortunately, n is too large for it to be practical simply to count the elements one by one. Suppose, on the other hand, that we are able to choose elements from X randomly according to the uniform distribution with a call on $uniform(X)$. Consider the following algorithm.

```
function card(X)
    k ← 0
    S ← ∅
    a ← uniform(X)
    repeat
        k ← k + 1
        S ← S ∪ {a}
        a ← uniform(X)
    until a ∈ S
    return k²/2
```

Prove that this algorithm returns an unbiased estimate of the number n of elements in X and that it runs in an expected time in $\Theta(\sqrt{n})$ if calls on $uniform(X)$ and operations involving set S can be carried out at unit cost. If you cannot prove this rigorously (it's hard!), give a convincing argument that it is reasonable to believe that the number of elements in the set is roughly the square of the number of independent draws in X before the first repetition occurs. It might help you to work Problems 5.14 and 10.11 first.

Problem 10.13.   The probabilistic counting algorithm in Problem 10.12 is efficient in terms of time, but it may be impractical in terms of storage because of the need to keep track of set S. Make the best of pseudorandom generation to modify the algorithm so that it takes constant storage without increasing its running time by more than a small constant factor. This is one of the rare instances where using a truly random generator would be a hindrance rather than a help, although we pay a price: the correctness of the modified algorithm can no longer be proved mathematically.

Problem 10.14.   Find an efficient Monte Carlo algorithm to decide, given two $n \times n$ matrices A and B, whether or not B is the inverse of A. In terms of n and the acceptable error probability ε, how much time does your algorithm require?

Problem 10.15.   Show that strong false witnesses of primality are automatically false witnesses with respect to Fermat's test; see Section 10.6.2.
Hint: Use the fact that $(n-1)^2 \bmod n = 1$.

Problem 10.16.   Prove Theorem 10.6.2.

Problem 10.17.   The algorithm *randomprime* of Section 10.6.3 generates probable random primes by repeatedly choosing random odd integers until one is found that passes enough rounds of the Miller–Rabin test. Explain how the result differs if instead we choose a random odd starting point and successively increase it by 2 until a number is obtained that passes the same number of rounds of the same test.

Problem 10.18.   We saw that 561 is the worst case for Fermat's primality test among all odd composites smaller than 1000. This is true provided we consider the error probability of the test. However, there is one odd composite smaller than 1000 that admits even more false witnesses than 561. Which is it? How many of these false witnesses are also strong false witnesses?

Problem 10.19.   The *prime number theorem* asserts that the number of prime numbers smaller than n is approximately $n/\log n$. (Recall that "log" denotes the natural logarithm.) This approximation is fairly accurate. For instance, there are 50 847 478 primes smaller than 10^9 whereas $n/\log n \approx 48\,254\,942$ when $n = 10^9$. Estimate the probability that an odd 1000-digit integer chosen randomly according to the uniform distribution is prime.
Hint: The number of 1000-digit primes is equal to the number of primes less than 10^{1000} minus the number of primes less than 10^{999}.

Problem 10.20.   Consider the following nonterminating program.

```
program printprimes
    print 2, 3
    n ← 5
    repeat
        if RepeatMillRab(n, ⌊lg n⌋) then print n
        n ← n + 2
    adnauseam
```

Clearly, every prime number will eventually be printed by this program. One might also expect composite numbers to be produced erroneously once in a while. Prove that this is unlikely to happen. More precisely, prove that the probability is better than 99% that no composite number larger than 100 will *ever* be produced, regardless of how long the program is allowed to run.
Note: This figure of 99% is very conservative as it would still hold even if *MillRab*(n) had a flat 25% chance of failure on each composite integer.

Problem 10.21.   In Section 10.6.2 we saw a Monte Carlo algorithm to decide primality that is always correct when given a prime number and that is correct with probability at least $3/4$ when given a composite number. The running time of the algorithm on input n is in $O(\log^3 n)$. Find a Monte Carlo algorithm that is always correct when given a composite number and that is correct with probability at least $1/2$ when given a prime number. Your algorithm must run in a time in $O(\log^k n)$ for some constant k.

Problem 10.22.   In Section 10.6.4, we studied amplification of the stochastic advantage of unbiased Monte Carlo algorithms for decision problems. Here, we investigate the situation for problems that have more than two potential answers. For general problems, instances may have more than one *correct* answer. Think for example of the eight queens problem or the problem of finding an arbitrary nontrivial divisor of a composite integer. When such problems are solved by probabilistic algorithms, it may happen that different correct answers are obtained when the same algorithm is run several times on the same input. We saw in Section 10.7 that this is a virtue for Las Vegas algorithms, but it can be catastrophic when unbiased Monte Carlo algorithms are concerned.

Recall that a Monte Carlo algorithm is p-correct if it returns a correct answer with probability at least p, whatever the instance considered. The potential difficulty is that even though a p-correct algorithm returns a correct answer with high probability when p is large, it could happen that one systematic wrong answer is returned more often than any given correct answer. In this case, amplification of the stochastic advantage by majority voting would decrease the probability of being correct! Show that if algorithm MC is 75%-correct, it may happen that $MC3$ is not even 71%-correct, where $MC3$ returns the most frequent answer of three calls on MC, as in Section 10.6.4. (Ties are broken arbitrarily.) For what value of k could $RepeatMC(\cdot, k)$ be less than 50%-correct even though MC is 75%-correct?

Problem 10.23.   Let MC be a p-correct unbiased Monte Carlo algorithm and consider algorithm $RepeatMC(\cdot, k)$ from Section 10.6.4, which runs MC k times and produces the most frequent answer. A problem occurs if k is even in the case of a tie. The code for $RepeatMC$ in Section 10.6.4 returns *false* in this case (since $T = F$). This degrades the probability of correctness on instances for which the correct answer is *true*. A better solution would be to flip a fair coin in case of a tie to decide which answer to return. Prove that if $RepeatMC$ is modified along this line, the probability that $RepeatMC(\cdot, k)$ returns the correct answer when k is even is exactly equal to the probability that $RepeatMC(\cdot, k-1)$ returns the correct answer. Conclude that it is never a good idea to repeat an unbiased Monte Carlo algorithm an even number of times for the purpose of amplifying the stochastic advantage.

Problem 10.24.   Let ε and δ be two positive real numbers such that $\varepsilon + \delta < 1/2$. Let MC be a $(\frac{1}{2} + \varepsilon)$-correct unbiased Monte Carlo algorithm for a decision problem. Using only elementary combinatorial arguments, prove that $RepeatMC(\cdot, k)$ is $(1 - \delta)$-correct provided $k \geq \frac{1}{2\varepsilon^2} \log 1/\delta$. In other words, it suffices to repeat a Monte Carlo algorithm whose advantage is ε this number k of times to obtain a Monte Carlo algorithm whose error probability is at most δ. (Recall that "log" denotes the natural logarithm.) This formula is overly conservative. It suggests repeating a 55%-correct unbiased Monte Carlo algorithm about 600 times to achieve 95%-correctness whereas we saw in Section 10.6.4 that 269 repetitions are sufficient. *Hint*: Use Equation 10.2 and the fact that $-2/\lg(1 - 4\varepsilon^2) < (\log 2)/2\varepsilon^2$.

Problem 10.25.   Continuing Problem 10.24, prove that if an unbiased Monte Carlo algorithm whose advantage is ε is repeated $k = 2m - 1$ times and if the most frequent answer is kept, the resulting algorithm is $(1 - \delta)$-correct, where

$$\delta = \frac{1}{2} - \varepsilon \sum_{i=0}^{m-1} \binom{2i}{i} \left(\tfrac{1}{4} - \varepsilon^2\right)^i \leq \frac{(1 - 4\varepsilon^2)^m}{4\varepsilon\sqrt{\pi m}}. \tag{10.5}$$

The first part of this formula is useful to calculate the exact error probability resulting from amplification of stochastic advantage. A good upper bound on the number of repetitions necessary to go from advantage ε to error probability δ can be obtained quickly from the second part. For instance, it tells us it is sufficient to repeat a 55%-correct algorithm 303 times to achieve 95%-correctness. This is better than 600 times as suggested by the formula in Problem 10.24 but not as good as 269, which we obtain with the Central Limit Theorem using tables for the normal distribution. Nevertheless, this method has the advantage of not requiring availability of those tables and it holds even for small values of k, when the Central Limit Theorem is inappropriate.

Problem 10.26.   Following Problem 7.36, give a $^1/_2$-correct biased Monte Carlo algorithm to decide if an array T contains a majority element. Your algorithm should run in linear time and the only comparisons allowed between the elements of T are tests of equality. Note that the only merit of this algorithm is simplicity since the deterministic algorithm requested in Problem 7.36 solves the problem in linear time with a very small hidden constant.

Problem 10.27.   Show that the problem of primality can be solved by a Las Vegas algorithm whose expected running time is in $O(\log^k n)$ for some constant k. You may take for granted the Monte Carlo algorithm required by Problem 10.21.

Problem 10.28.   In the spirit of Problem 10.27, let A and B be two biased Monte Carlo algorithms for solving the same decision problem. Algorithm A is p-correct but its answer is guaranteed when it is *true*; algorithm B is q-correct but its answer is guaranteed when it is *false*. Show how to combine A and B into a Las Vegas algorithm $LV(x, y, success)$ to solve the same problem. One call on LV should not take significantly more time than a call on A followed by a call on B. If your Las Vegas algorithm succeeds with probability at least r whatever the instance, what is the best value of r you can obtain?

Problem 10.29.   Let X be a finite set whose elements are easy to enumerate and let Y be a nonempty subset of X of unknown cardinality. Assume you can decide, given $x \in X$, whether or not $x \in Y$. How would you choose a random element of Y according to the uniform distribution? The obvious solution is to make a first pass through X to count the number n of elements in Y, then choose a random integer $k \leftarrow uniform(1..n)$, and finally locate the k–th element of Y by going through X again, unless you kept the elements of Y in an array during the first pass through X. Surprisingly, this problem can be solved with a single pass through X, without additional storage, and without first counting the elements in Y. Consider the following algorithm.

```
function draw(X, Y)
    n ← 0
    for each x ∈ X do
        if x ∈ Y then n ← n + 1
                        if uniform(1 .. n) = n then z ← x
    if n > 0 then return z
            else return "Error! Y is empty!"
```

Prove by mathematical induction on the number of elements in Y that this algorithm finds an element of Y randomly according to the uniform distribution. Modify algorithm *queensLV* from Section 10.7.1 to incorporate this technique, choosing randomly according to the uniform distribution among the positions still open for the next queen even though we do not know a priori how many there are. This makes the algorithm more elegant but less efficient because it requires more calls to the pseudorandom generator.

Problem 10.30.   Work by hand the Las Vegas algorithm for the eight queens problem. Place the first 3 queens randomly on the first 3 rows and try to complete the solution by backtracking. Start over if you fail. As we said, your probability of success is roughly 50% on each attempt. Solve the problem by hand with pure backtracking as well. Which method led you to a solution faster?

Problem 10.31.   Implement on a computer the Las Vegas algorithm for the n queens problem that places the first *stopLV* queens randomly before it tries to complete the partial solution by backtracking. Experiment with solving the 39 queens problem with different values of *stopLV*. Find one solution each for the 100 queens and the 1000 queens problems.

Problem 10.32.   Prove that if the symbol table of a compiler is implemented with universal hashing and if the load factor is kept smaller than 1, the probability that any identifier is in collision with more than t others is less than $1/t$, for any integer t. Conclude that the average time needed for a sequence of n accesses to the table is in $O(n)$. Compare this result with that of Problem 5.16.

Problem 10.33.   Let U be a set with a elements. How many functions are there from U into $\{0, 1, 2, \ldots, N-1\}$? How many bits does it take to write down a description of one of these functions on the average?

Problem 10.34.   Prove that the class of hash functions given at the end of Section 10.7.3 is universal$_2$.

Problem 10.35.   Find applications of universal hashing that have nothing to do with compilation nor even with the implementation of an associative table.

Problem 10.36.   Normally, the elements of a list are scattered all round the store of your computer. A *compact* list of length n is implemented by two arrays $val[1 .. n]$ and $ptr[1 .. n]$, and one integer *head*. The first element of the list is in $val[head]$, the next is in $val[ptr[head]]$, and so on. In general, if $val[i]$ is not the last element of the list, $ptr[i]$ gives the index in val of the following element. The end of the list is marked by $ptr[i] = 0$. Consider now a compact list whose elements are in nondecreasing order. Let x be an element. The problem is to locate x within the list. Binary search is not possible because there is no direct means of finding the middle of a list, be it compact or not.

(a) Prove that any deterministic algorithm for this problem requires a time in $\Omega(n)$ in the worst case.

(b) Devise a Las Vegas algorithm capable of solving this problem in expected time in $O(\sqrt{n})$ in the worst case.

Hint: Look at $\sqrt{n}$ randomly chosen points in the list and start your search at the largest of those points that is not larger than the target x. What do you do if all your points are larger than the target?

Problem 10.37.   Prove Theorem 10.7.1.

Problem 10.38.   Find an x different from those given in Section 10.7.4 such that $1000 \leq x \leq 2000$ and x^2 mod 2537 is 7-smooth.

Problem 10.39.   In Section 10.7.4 we saw two solutions to the problem of finding a nonempty set of rows of matrix M that add up to the zero vector in arithmetic modulo 2. Find the other five solutions. For each one, determine if it leads to a nontrivial divisor of $n = 2537$.

Problem 10.40.   Let n be a composite number that has at least two distinct prime divisors and let a be relatively prime to n. Prove that a^2 mod n admits at least four distinct square roots in arithmetic modulo n.

Problem 10.41.   Let n be a composite number that has at least two distinct prime divisors and let $\langle a, b \rangle$ be the first pair obtained by the Las Vegas splitting algorithm of Section 10.7.4. Prove that either $\gcd(a, n)$ or $\gcd(a + b, n)$ is a nontrivial divisor of n with probability at least 50%.
Hint: If $\gcd(a, n) = 1$ then $\gcd(x_i, n) = 1$ for each x_i that entered into building b. Take one arbitrary such x_i. We know from Problem 10.40 that $y_i = x_i^2$ mod n has at least four distinct square roots modulo n, including x_i. Show that if any root other than x_i and $n - x_i$ had been randomly chosen instead of x_i, the splitting would have been successful. Conclude as required.

Problem 10.42.   At the end of Section 10.7.4, we claimed that we expect the probability that x^2 mod n be k-smooth to improve if x is chosen slightly larger than $\sqrt{n}$, rather than being chosen randomly between 1 and $n - 1$. Give a convincing intuitive reason to support this assertion.
Hint: Show that the binary length of $\lceil \sqrt{n} \rceil^2$ mod n is at most about half that of a random square modulo n. What about the length of $(\lceil \sqrt{n} \rceil + i)^2$ mod n for small i?

10.9 References and further reading

Early historic examples of probabilistic algorithms are traced back to "primitive" cultures by Shallit (1992). The term "Monte Carlo", introduced into the literature by Metropolis and Ulam (1949), was already in use in the secret world of atomic research during World War II, in particular in Los Alamos, New Mexico. Recall that "Monte Carlo" is often used to describe any probabilistic algorithm, contrary to the usage in this book. The term "Las Vegas" was introduced by Babai (1979) to distinguish probabilistic algorithms that reply correctly when they reply at all from those that occasionally make a mistake.

Two encyclopaedic sources of techniques for generating pseudorandom numbers are Knuth (1969) and Devroye (1986). The former includes tests for trying to distinguish a pseudorandom sequence from one that is truly random. The solution to Problem 10.1 is from von Neumann (1951). We used the highly recommended pseudorandom generator given by L'Écuyer (1988, 1990) in our experiments with the n queens problem. A more interesting generator from a cryptographic point of view is given by Blum and Micali (1984); this article and the one by Yao (1982) introduce the notion of an *unpredictable generator*, which can pass any statistical test that can be carried out in polynomial time. The generator described at the end of Section 10.4 is from Blum, Blum and Shub (1986). More references on this subject can be found in Brassard (1988). General techniques are given in Vazirani (1986, 1987) to cope with generators that are partly under the control of an adversary.

The experiment devised by Georges Louis Leclerc (1777), comte de Buffon, was carried out several times in the nineteenth century; see for instance Hall (1873). The process by which it can be used to estimate π is analysed in detail in Solomon (1978). A standard text on mathematical statistics and data analysis is Rice (1988). For an early text on numeric probabilistic algorithms, consult Sobol' (1974). The point is made in Fox (1986) that pure Monte Carlo methods are not specially good for numerical integration with a *fixed* dimension: it is preferable to choose your points systematically so they are well spaced, a technique known as quasi Monte Carlo. Probabilistic counting is from Morris (1978); see Flajolet (1985) for a detailed analysis. A solution to Problem 10.12 is given in Brassard and Bratley (1988) but beware that it is incorrect in the first two printings: the correct analysis was provided to the authors by Philippe Flajolet. For a cryptographic application, see Kaliski, Rivest and Sherman (1988). Yet a different flavour of probabilistic counting is discussed in Flajolet and Martin (1985). Numeric probabilistic algorithms designed to solve problems from linear algebra are discussed in Curtiss (1956), Vickery (1956), Hammersley and Handscomb (1965) and Carasso (1971). A guide to simulation is provided by Bratley, Fox and Schrage (1983).

The Monte Carlo algorithm to verify matrix multiplication is from Freivalds (1979); see also Freivalds (1977). The Monte Carlo primality test presented here is equivalent to the one in Rabin (1976, 1980*b*); it draws on previous work of Miller (1976). Another Monte Carlo test for primality was discovered independently by Solovay and Strassen (1977). The expected number of false witnesses of primality for a random composite integer is investigated in Erdős and Pomerance (1986); see also Monier (1980). The fact that it suffices to test strong pseudoprimality to bases 2, 3, 5, 7 and 61 to decide deterministically if an integer up to 10^{13} is prime was discovered by Claude Goutier. The proof that Fermat's test can be arbitrarily bad follows from Alford, Granville and Pomerance (1994). The discussion on the generation of random primes is from Beauchemin, Brassard, Crépeau, Goutier and Pomerance (1988); see also Kim and Pomerance (1989) and Damgård, Landrock and Pomerance (1993). Efficient methods to generate certified random primes are given by Couvreur and Quisquater (1982) and Maurer (1995). A theoretical solution to Problem 10.21 is given in Goldwasser and Kilian (1986) and Adleman and Huang (1992). For more information on tests of primality and their implementation, consult Williams (1978), Lenstra (1982), Adleman, Pomerance and Rumely (1983), Kranakis (1986), Cohen and Lenstra (1987), Koblitz (1987) and Bressoud (1989). More information on general number theory can be found in the classic Hardy and Wright (1938).

The Las Vegas approach to the eight queens problem was suggested to the authors by Manuel Blum. Further investigations were carried out by Pageau (1993). For more background on the problem, consult the references given in Section 9.10. The term "Robin Hood" appeared in Celis, Larson and Munro (1985) in a deterministic context. An early (1970) linear expected time probabilistic median finding algorithm is attributed to Floyd: see Exercise 5.3.3.13 in Knuth (1973). It predates the classic worst-case linear time deterministic algorithm described in Section 7.5. A probabilistic algorithm capable of finding the i–th smallest among n elements in an expected number of comparisons in $n + i + O(\sqrt{n})$ is given in Rivest and Floyd (1973). Universal hashing was invented by Carter and Wegman (1979); see also Wegman and Carter (1981). An early integer factorization algorithm of Pollard (1975) has a probabilistic flavour. The probabilistic integer factorization algorithm discussed here is from Dixon (1981), but it is based on ideas put forward by Kraitchik (1926); see also Pomerance (1982). The history of the quadratic sieve factorization algorithm is given by Pomerance (1984) and the double prime variation used to take up the RSA challenge is from Lenstra and Manasse (1991). The factorization algorithm based on elliptic curves is discussed in Lenstra (1987). The number field sieve is described in Lenstra, Lenstra, Manasse and Pollard (1993). See also Koblitz (1987) and Bressoud (1989). The technique for searching in an ordered list comes from Janko (1976); see Problem 10.36. A detailed analysis of this technique is given in Bentley, Stanat and Steele (1981), where it is also proven that an expected time in $\Omega(\sqrt{n})$ is required in the worst case to solve this problem by any probabilistic algorithm.

Several interesting probabilistic algorithms have not been discussed in this chapter. We close by mentioning a few of them. Given the cartesian coordinates of points in the plane, Rabin (1976) gives an algorithm capable of finding the closest pair in expected linear time; contrast this with Problem 7.39. A Monte Carlo algorithm is given in Schwartz (1978) to decide whether a multivariate polynomial over an infinite domain is identically zero and to test whether two such polynomials are identical. Consult Zippel (1979) for sparse polynomial interpolation probabilistic algorithms. Rabin (1980a) gives an efficient probabilistic algorithm for computing roots of arbitrary polynomials over any finite field as well as an efficient probabilistic algorithm for factorizing polynomials over arbitrary finite fields and for finding irreducible polynomials. A very elegant Las Vegas algorithm for finding square roots modulo a prime number is due to Peralta (1986); see also Brassard and Bratley (1988). A rare example of an unbiased Monte Carlo algorithm for a decision problem, which can decide efficiently whether a given integer is a perfect number and whether a pair of integers is amicable, is described in Bach, Miller and Shallit (1986).

Chapter 11

Parallel Algorithms

Elsewhere in this book, we implicitly assume that our algorithms will be executed on a machine that can do only one calculation at once. Of course, any modern machine overlaps computation with input/output operations such as waiting for a key to be struck, or printing a file. Many of them also overlap different arithmetic operations when computing an expression, so that additions, for example, may be carried out in parallel with multiplications. However we have not so far considered the possibility that the machine might be able to compute several dozen, or even several hundred, different expressions at the same time. If we allow this possibility, then we may hope, if we are both clever and lucky, to speed up some of our algorithms by a similar factor.

Computers that can perform such parallel computations are not yet on every desk. However their numbers are increasing, and interest in *parallel algorithms*, that take advantage of this ability, is widespread. Research in this area is so active that it would be unrealistic to try to mention all the areas where parallel techniques are being studied. In this chapter we therefore present only an introductory selection of parallel algorithms that illustrate some fundamental techniques.

We first describe more precisely the machine we have in mind when designing such algorithms. Next we illustrate one or two basic techniques, and discuss what we mean by an efficient parallel algorithm. Finally we give a small number of examples from the fields of graph theory, expression evaluation and sorting.

11.1 A model for parallel computation

The basic model of ordinary, sequential computation, on what is sometimes called a *von Neumann machine*, is so widely accepted that we have not found it necessary in this book to define it more precisely. Everyone accepts that such a machine executes one instruction at a time, on one item of data at a time, following a program stored in the machine's memory. The fact that in reality every modern machine incorporates a certain degree of parallelism, that enables it, for example, to perform a limited number of arithmetic operations in parallel, to fetch the next instruction while the last is still being executed, or to overlap input and output with computation, is essentially irrelevant to the conceptual model. Similarly, most programming languages, like the informal language we use in this book, assume that the computer executes one instruction at a time on just one variable.

In the area of parallel computation, working machines are relatively few and their architectures are diverse, and no consensus exists as to which theoretical model of computation is best. For example, it is not obvious what it might imply in practice if we choose a model that allows several processors to assign new values to the same variable in parallel. Practical constraints will probably prevent such parallel assignments from being executed truly simultaneously. Should we therefore suppose that the variable now has the last value assigned to it, and if so, can we tell which this last assignment is? Or if truly simultaneous assignments *are* possible, what is the result of assigning different values simultaneously to the same variable? Such considerations lead some people to prefer a model that forbids multiple parallel assignments to the same variable.

Again, suppose we have an array that is being changed by a number of parallel processors, with one processor for each array element. If we want to model some such instruction as "stop when all the array elements are zero", how much time should we suppose is necessary to implement this instruction? Certainly each processor can see immediately that its own element is zero; but what should we suppose is the mechanism required to check *every* element? Do the processors have to exchange messages with one another, is there an extra layer of processors for overall control, or how exactly is a decision to be reached?

For these and similar reasons, there is no clear answer to the question of which model of parallel computation is in general the best. In this book we use a popular model called the *parallel random-access machine*, or p-ram. This model is certainly the most natural one to use, and it is easy to understand, but it is not very close to existing machines. The reader should therefore be warned that adapting the algorithms in this chapter for use on a real machine may not be straightforward. Section 11.11 contains pointers to more realistic parallel computers.

In the p-ram model a number of ordinary, sequential processors are assumed to share a global memory. Each processor has the usual set of arithmetic and logical instructions that it can execute in parallel with whatever is happening on the other processors. However we assume that the processors do not all set off doing different things, but that they all execute the same program supplied from some central control point, albeit possibly on different items of data. Furthermore the processors are synchronized to the extent that they are all working on the same instruction at the same time. For obvious reasons such a model is also called a *single-instruction multiple-data-stream* model. For the time being we shall not define more precisely what we mean by this, relying on the examples to clarify the basically simple idea.

Each processor has access to the whole of the global memory. At each step, it may either read from or write to no more than one storage location. For our purposes, we shall further assume that while any number of processors may read from the same storage location in the same step, no two of them may write simultaneously into the same location, nor may a processor write into a location that is being read. We thus avoid having to decide what happens if two or more processors try to write different values into the same location, or if a value changes as it is being read. A model defined in this way is called a *concurrent-read, exclusive-write*, or CREW model. Other possible models that we shall not consider for the moment are the EREW (exclusive-read, exclusive-write) and CRCW (concurrent-read, concurrent-write) models, defined in the obvious way. Nobody seems to have found a use for an exclusive-read, concurrent-write model.

When analysing parallel algorithms in the following sections, we make the crucial assumption that an access to memory in our hypothetical CREW p-ram, whether for reading or for writing, can be made in constant time, regardless of the number of processors in use. This assumption is not true in practice. Since it is not feasible to provide direct links in hardware from all the processors to all the storage locations, the average time required to perform a memory access on a real system increases as the number of processors goes up; furthermore, some patterns of memory access are faster than others. In fact it is not true that even a single processor can access every address in an arbitrarily large memory in constant time. For simplicity, however, we ignore this complication in this book.

For simplicity, too, we ignore most of the problems raised by the overall control of the parallel machine. To describe our parallel algorithms, we use statements of the general form

for $x \in S$ **in parallel do** *statement*(x).

This is interpreted to mean that we assign a processor to each element x of the set S, and then carry out the instructions in *statement*(x) for every such element in parallel, using x as the data, and computing on the assigned processor. We suppose that the processors are numbered in sequence, and that the elements of the set S can also be numbered in some straightforward way, so that assigning a particular processor to x can be done in constant time. Variants of this form of instruction will be used without further explanation if their meaning is clear. For instance,

for $1 \leq i \leq 10$ **in parallel do** *statement*(i)

means that *statement*(i) is to be executed in parallel for $i = 1, 2, \ldots, 10$.

We have to be careful that the *statement* to be executed respects our (so far ill-defined) requirement that the processors "are all working on the same instruction at the same time". For example, we do not allow the *statement* to be a function call, since this might lead to quite different actions on the part of each processor. However assignment instructions, array accesses, and so forth are generally acceptable. We allow conditional instructions, too, but not loops whose length depends on the data. Our requirement is thus becoming a little clearer: by "the same instruction" we mean more or less "the same machine instruction", not "the same statement in some high-level language". However we accept that, in the case of conditional instructions, for instance, some of the processors may actually execute the instruction while others may skip past it.

If a computation requires that p processors be used, we may further suppose
✓ that a time in $\Theta(\log p)$ is required before the computation begins to send them the
necessary instructions and set them to work. This is easily achieved if initially one
processor is active, and then at each time step every active processor activates one
other, so the number of active processors doubles at each step. However in the
following paragraphs we do not take explicit account of this initialization time.

✓ 11.2 Some basic techniques

11.2.1 Computing with a complete binary tree

This simple technique is best illustrated by an example. Suppose we want to
compute the sum of n integers. To make life simple, suppose too that n is a power
of 2; should this not be the case, merely add dummy, zero elements as required.
These n elements are placed at the leaves of a complete binary tree, as illustrated
in Figure 11.1. Now in the first step, the sums of the elements lying beneath each
internal node at level 1 are calculated in parallel; in the second step, the sums of the
elements lying beneath each internal node at level 2 are calculated in parallel; and
so on, until at the $(\lg n)$–th step the value obtained at the root gives the solution to
our problem.

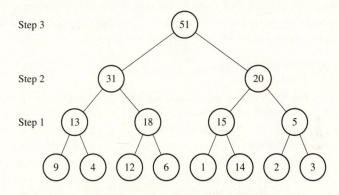

Figure 11.1. Computing with a complete binary tree

More formally, let $n = 2^k$, and let T be an array indexed from 1 to $2n - 1$. This
array can be used to store a complete binary tree with $2n - 1$ nodes, with the root
in $T[1]$ and the children of node $T[i]$ in nodes $T[2i]$ and $T[2i+1]$, just like a heap.
Let the n elements to be summed be placed initially in the leaves of the tree, that
is, in nodes $T[n]$ to $T[2n - 1]$. Now the algorithm for calculating the sum of these
n elements is as follows.

> **function** $parsum(T, n)$
> {Calculates the sum $T[n] + \cdots + T[2n - 1]$}
> **for** $i \leftarrow \lg n - 1$ **downto** 0 **do**
> **for** $2^i \leq j \leq 2^{i+1} - 1$ **in parallel do**
> $T[j] \leftarrow T[2j] + T[2j + 1]$
> **return** $T[1]$

Here the only synchronization required is that all the parallel computations for a particular value of i should be completed before those for the next value of i begin. During one trip round the loop on i, each processor involved performs two memory accesses to read its operands, one addition, and a final memory access to store the result. Since we assume that a memory access takes constant time, the total work required from each processor also takes constant time. Finally, because the processors work in parallel, all the work required in one trip round the outer loop can be executed in constant time. The algorithm makes $\lg n$ trips round the loop, so the total time required is in $\Theta(\log n)$. It is evident that the maximum number of processors ever required to operate simultaneously is $n/2$.

The same technique can clearly be applied to such problems as finding the product, the maximum or the minimum of n elements, or deciding if they are all zero.

11.2.2 Pointer doubling

In its simplest form, the pointer-doubling algorithm applies to lists of items. Suppose we have a list L of n items, each containing a pointer to its successor. Let the successor to item i be $s[i]$. If item k is the last element of the list, then $s[k]$ is the special pointer **nil**. For our first example, we wish to calculate for each item i the distance $d[i]$ from that item to the end of the list. We suppose as many processors are available as there are elements in L, so we can associate a separate processor to each list item. Now the algorithm is as follows.

> **procedure** *pardist*(L)
> {Initialization}
> **for** each item $i \in L$ **in parallel do**
>   **if** $s[i] = $ **nil then** $d[i] \leftarrow 0$
>   **else** $d[i] \leftarrow 1$
> {Main loop}
> **repeat** $\lceil \lg n \rceil$ **times**
>   **for** each item $i \in L$ **in parallel do**
>   **if** $s[i] \neq$ **nil then**
> $d[i] \leftarrow d[i] + d[s[i]]$
> $s[i] \leftarrow s[s[i]]$

Figure 11.2 illustrates the progress of this algorithm on a list of 7 elements. As written, the pointer fields in the original list are changed, and the list structure is destroyed. If this is undesirable, copy the pointers in the initialization phase of the algorithm, and then work with the copies.

Here the synchronization required is more subtle than in the previous example. There is no problem with simultaneous attempts to write to the same location, since each processor only assigns values to d and s in its own item. In the model we adopted we do not have to worry about simultaneous attempts to read the same location. However we *do* have to worry about values changing before we have time to read them. When several processors are executing the instruction $d[i] \leftarrow d[i] + d[s[i]]$ in parallel, for instance, the synchronization must be tight enough to ensure that the processor assigned to item i reads the necessary value of

Key: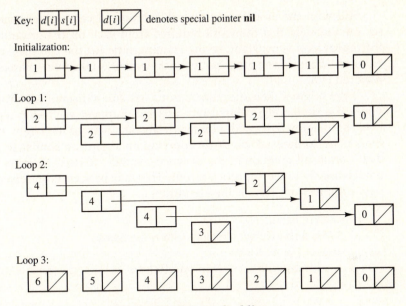

Figure 11.2. Pointer doubling

$d[s[i]]$ before the processor assigned to item $s[i]$ changes its value of d. The safest way to ensure this for every i is to insist that *all* the reads necessary to evaluate the right-hand sides are executed before any new values of the left-hand sides are written. Similarly, in the instruction $s[i] \leftarrow s[s[i]]$, the reads necessary to evaluate the right-hand sides must all occur before any new values of the left-hand sides are written. The requirement stated above, that all the processors should be working on the same instruction at the same time, now has to be interpreted more strictly, with synchronization at the machine instruction level.

When the algorithm stops, $s[i] = $ **nil** for every item i in L. To see this, observe that the pointers are "doubled" at each execution of the statement $s[i] \leftarrow s[s[i]]$. More precisely, $s[i]$ originally points to the element following i in L; after one execution of this statement, $s[i]$ points to the element originally two places along from i; after two executions of the statement, it points to the element originally four places along; and so on. When a pointer goes off the end of the list we give it the special value **nil**. Since there are n elements in L, it suffices to "double" the pointers $\lceil \lg n \rceil$ times to be sure they all go off the end. (For the case when n is unknown, see Problem 11.21.)

To see that the computed values of $d[i]$ are correct, observe that at the beginning of each iteration, if we add the values of d for all the items in the sublist headed by item i (of course, using the current values of s), we obtain the distance from i to the end of the original list L. Now at each iteration the pointer $s[i]$ is modified so as to omit i's immediate successor from this sublist. However the value of d for this immediate successor is added to $d[i]$, so the same condition is still true at the beginning of the next iteration.

Still with the assumption that all memory accesses take constant time, we see immediately that the work required from each processor on one iteration of the **repeat** loop is constant, so the running time for the complete algorithm is in $\Theta(\log n)$. There is one processor per list element, so the total number of processors required is n.

If the original data structure is not a list, but a disjoint set structure (see Section 5.9), a similar algorithm can be applied. Suppose each set is represented by a tree, as in Figure 5.21, with pointers from each item to its parent, except that the roots point to themselves. Now applying an algorithm similar to *pardist*, except that it omits all mention of the distances d, will "flatten" the trees so every item points directly to the appropriate root. This may be seen as an extreme example of path compression. Here is the algorithm.

> **procedure** *flatten*(*D*)
>   {*D* is a disjoint set structure with n elements}
>   **repeat** $\lceil \lg n \rceil$ **times**
>   **for each item** $i \in D$ **in parallel do**
> $s[i] \leftarrow s[s[i]]$

Variations on the theme of pointer doubling are used for many other simple computations. Suppose, for example, that each item i in a list L has a value $v[i]$, and let $\circ$ be a binary, associative operator that takes these values as operands. Consider the following variant of procedure *pardist*.

> **procedure** *paroper*(*L*)
>   {Initialization}
>   **for each item** $i \in L$ **in parallel do**
> $d[i] \leftarrow v[i]$
>   {Main loop}
>   **repeat** $\lceil \lg n \rceil$ **times**
>   **for each item** $i \in L$ **in parallel do** $\leftarrow \in O(1) \Rightarrow \in (\lg n)$
>   **if** $s[i] \neq$ **nil then**
> $\rightarrow d[i] \leftarrow d[i] \circ d[s[i]]$
> $\rightarrow s[i] \leftarrow s[s[i]]$

Let x_i be the value of v for the i-th item in the list, $1 \leq i \leq n$. (This is *not* the same as $v[i]$. In the case of x_i, the suffix indicates that we want the value of the i-th item in the original list; in the case of $v[i]$ the index is a pointer to an item, not its position in the list.) Define $X_{i,j}$ by

$$X_{i,j} = x_i \circ x_{i+1} \circ \cdots \circ x_j,$$

that is, as the generalized product of the i-th to the j-th elements of L. Then it is not difficult to prove (see Problem 11.3) that when the algorithm terminates, the value of d for the first element of L is $X_{1,n}$, the value of d for the second element of L is $X_{2,n}$, and so on, along to the last element of L whose value of d is $X_{n,n} = x_n$. Figure 11.3 illustrates the operation of the algorithm on a list of seven elements where the operator $\circ$ is ordinary addition.

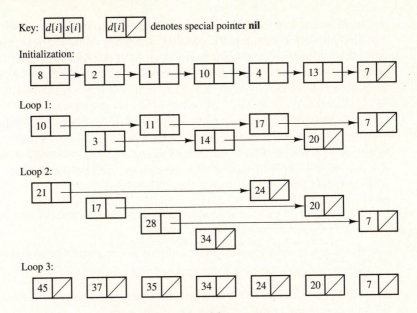

Figure 11.3. Algorithm *paroper*

By choosing an appropriate operator, several useful computations can be performed. Taking ∘ as addition, as in the example of Figure 11.3, gives us the sum of the elements of L. When the algorithm stops, this sum is returned as the value of d in the first element of L. The product of the elements of L, their maximum or their minimum can be computed similarly. More imaginative schemes are also possible. For instance, if each $d[i]$ is initialized to be a pointer to the item i itself, and ∘ is an operator which, given two pointers, returns a pointer to the item with the larger value of v, then *paroper* can be used to obtain a pointer to the element of L with the largest value, not merely the value itself. For a further development of this theme, see Problem 11.5.

The analysis of *paroper* is exactly like that of *pardist*. The running time of the algorithm, provided the operator ∘ can be treated as elementary, is in $\Theta(\log n)$, and the number of processors required is n.

√11.3 Work and efficiency

It seems likely that a parallel algorithm that takes t seconds to execute on, say, 20 processors, is doing more computation than one that takes the same time using only 5 processors, which in turn is doing more than an ordinary sequential algorithm also taking t seconds. For this reason we define the *work* performed by an algorithm, whether sequential or parallel, to be the product pt of p, the number of processors it uses, and t, the running time. (Since for many algorithms the number of processors needed during the computation varies, it can be argued that the work performed would be better measured by $\sum it_i$, where t_i is the time during which exactly i processors are active. However this makes the implicit assumption that the unused processors are freed to do something else. In any case, it is more involved than we need at present.) It is easily seen that for a parallel algorithm this work is the time needed to simulate the parallel algorithm using a single processor which, at each step of the computation, imitates each parallel processor in turn. If we have two algorithms A and B for the same problem that require work w_a and w_b respectively to obtain a solution, we say that A is *work-efficient* with respect to B if $w_a \in O(w_b)$.

In Section 12.5.1 we shall see that an ordinary, sequential algorithm is generally regarded as efficient if its running time for a problem of size n is in $O(n^k)$ for some constant k. For a parallel algorithm to be regarded as efficient, on the other hand, we usually expect it to satisfy two constraints, one on the number of processors required, and one on the running time. These are

⋄ the number of processors required to solve an instance of size n should be in $O(n^a)$ for some constant a, and

⋄ the time required to solve an instance of size n should be in $O(\log^b n)$ for some constant b.

We say that an efficient parallel algorithm takes a polynomial number of processors and *polylogarithmic* time.

A parallel algorithm is *optimal* if it is work-efficient with respect to the best possible sequential algorithm. It may sometimes be called optimal if it is work-efficient with respect to the best *known* sequential algorithm. In this case, however, it is preferable to say that the corresponding problem has *optimal speed-up*. We shall see in Chapter 12 that there are many problems for which no known efficient (that is, polynomial-time) sequential algorithm exists. For such problems we cannot expect to find an efficient parallel solution (that is, one that uses a polynomial number of processors and polylogarithmic time): see Problem 11.6. On the other hand, there are many problems for which an efficient sequential algorithm is known, but for which no efficient parallel algorithm has yet been discovered. It is believed, but not proved, that some problems that can be solved by an efficient sequential algorithm have no efficient parallel solution.

Take the technique described in Section 11.2.1 as an example. We saw there that we can compute the sum of n elements stored in an array using $n/2$ processors and a time in $\Theta(\log n)$. The work required by that algorithm is therefore in $(n/2) \times \Theta(\log n) = \Theta(n \log n)$. Since the sum of n elements can clearly be obtained in $\Theta(n)$ operations by straightforward addition on a sequential processor, the parallel algorithm, although it is efficient, is not optimal. Similarly the techniques described in Section 11.2.2 allow us to carry out a variety of operations (calculating the distance to the end of a list of n elements, finding the sum or the maximum of the list elements, etc.) in a time in $\Theta(\log n)$ using n processors. Here again the work required is in $\Theta(n \log n)$. Since these operations can be carried out by a single sequential processor in a time in $\Theta(n)$, these algorithms, too, are not optimal.

If we look more closely at the algorithm to compute the sum of n elements using a binary tree, one possible reason for its being less than optimal is immediately apparent. In the first trip round the main loop, $n/2$ processors are required, and this determines the resources needed by the algorithm; for in the second trip round the loop only $n/4$ processors do useful work, in the third only $n/8$ are needed, and so on, so that most of the time, most of the processors are idle. This suggests that we may be able to use less processors without this having a catastrophic effect on the computing time.

Suppose then we have only $p < n/2$ processors available. One way to proceed is to divide the n numbers whose sum we require to calculate into p groups, $p - 1$ of which contain $\lceil n/p \rceil$ numbers, while the last contains the remaining $n - (p - 1)\lceil n/p \rceil$ numbers. The last group may thus contain less than $\lceil n/p \rceil$ members, but it cannot contain more. Now assign one of the available processors to each group, and set each processor to calculating the sum of its group. Although the processors work in parallel, the individual calculations can be straightforward, sequential computations taking $\Theta(\lceil n/p \rceil)$ operations. Because the processors work in parallel, the total time required for this stage is also in $\Theta(\lceil n/p \rceil)$. The problem is now reduced to finding the sum of the p group sums, and this can be solved by the unmodified balanced tree technique using $p/2$ processors in a time in $\Theta(\log p)$. Overall, the modified algorithm using $p < n/2$ processors thus takes a time in $\Theta(\lceil n/p \rceil + \log p)$.

In particular, if we take $p = n/\log n$ we obtain an algorithm that can find the sum of n numbers in a time in $\Theta(\log n)$. We have thus reduced the number of processors required by a factor of $(\log n)/2$ without changing the order of the running time. The work done by the modified algorithm is in $\Theta(p \times \log n) = \Theta(n)$. Clearly no sequential algorithm can do better than this, so the modified algorithm is an optimal parallel algorithm.

In general, we may not be so fortunate. For example, dividing the items of a list into groups is harder than dividing the items of an array. For the former, we may have to begin by scanning the whole list; for the latter, a simple calculation using the array indexes is usually sufficient. Nevertheless, using a similar technique we can always reduce the number of processors required by a parallel algorithm. Suppose we have an algorithm that runs in time t using p processors on a problem of size n, but that we only have $q < p$ processors available. (Here t, p and q are functions of n.) How should we proceed?

As before, we divide the p processors into q groups, and use one of the q available processors to simulate each group. There will be $q - 1$ groups containing $\lceil p/q \rceil$ processors, and a last group containing no more processors than the others, and maybe less. Next, suppose the original algorithm carries out steps $1, 2, \ldots$, where the p processors execute each step independently, but have to be synchronized between steps. In the modified algorithm using only q processors, at step 1 one of these simulates in turn each processor in the first group; a second simulates in turn each processor in the second group; and so on. Since there are $\lceil p/q \rceil$ processors or less to simulate in each group, the simulation of step 1 using q processors takes $\lceil p/q \rceil$ times longer than the original step 1, and so on for the other steps. Thus the complete computation using q processors takes $\lceil p/q \rceil$ times longer than the complete computation using p processors. In symbols, the modified algorithm takes a time in $\Theta(\lceil p/q \rceil t)$. (Remember that p, q and t may be functions of the size n of the instance.) Since $p/q \le \lceil p/q \rceil < 2p/q$ when $p > q$, we have proved the following theorem.

√

> **Theorem 11.3.1 (Brent)** *If there exists a parallel algorithm that takes time $t(n)$ to solve a problem of size n using $p(n)$ processors, then for any $q(n) < p(n)$ there is a modified algorithm that can solve the same problem using only $q(n)$ processors in a time in $\Theta(p(n)t(n)/q(n))$.*

Here the original algorithm does work in $\Theta(p(n)t(n))$ and the modified algorithm does work in $\Theta((p(n)t(n)/q(n))\times q(n)) = \Theta(p(n)t(n))$, so in terms of work we have neither gained nor lost by the modification: the modified algorithm is work-efficient with respect to the original algorithm. We can thus reduce the number of processors used by an algorithm without altering its efficiency. In particular, if the original algorithm is optimal, so is the modified algorithm. Of course the algorithm using less processors will usually take longer to finish, even though the work performed is the same.

11.4 Two examples from graph theory

√11.4.1 Shortest paths

We have already encountered variants of this problem in Sections 6.4 and 8.5. We repeat the details briefly. Let $G = \langle N, A \rangle$ be a directed graph. The nodes of G are numbered from 1 to n, and a matrix L gives the length of each edge, with $L[i, i] = 0$, $L[i, j] \geq 0$ if $i \neq j$, and $L[i, j] = \infty$ if the edge (i, j) does not exist. We want to calculate the length of the shortest path between each pair of nodes. We now give a parallel algorithm for this problem. It is interesting to compare this to algorithm *Floyd* of Section 8.5.

The parallel algorithm constructs a matrix D that gives the length of the shortest path between each pair of nodes. It initializes D to L, that is, to the direct distances between nodes, and then does $\lceil \lg n \rceil$ iterations. After iteration k, D gives the length of the shortest paths that use not more than 2^k edges, or, equivalently, not more than $2^k - 1$ intermediate nodes. Since the edge lengths are nonnegative, the shortest paths we are looking for must be simple: that is, they cannot visit the same node twice. They therefore use at most $n - 1$ edges. Hence after $\lceil \lg n \rceil$ iterations, D gives the result we want.

At iteration k, the algorithm must check for each pair of nodes (i, j) whether or not there exists a new path from i to j using more than 2^{k-1} and no more than 2^k edges that is better than the present optimal path that uses no more than 2^{k-1} edges. Any such new path has a "middle" node m defined so that neither the part of the path from i to m, nor the part from m to j, uses more than 2^{k-1} edges. The optimal lengths of these parts are therefore the current values of $D[i, m]$ and $D[m, j]$ respectively. Since the principle of optimality applies, to check whether an improved new path from i to j exists, it suffices to compare the length of the best existing path with $D[i, m]+D[m, j]$ for each possible value of m. Then we simply choose the minimum. Here is the algorithm.

procedure *parpaths*($L[1..n, 1..n]$): **array** $[1..n, 1..n]$
  array $D[1..n, 1..n], T[1..n, 1..n, 1..n]$
  for all i, j **in parallel do** $D[i, j] \leftarrow L[i, j]$ ← *need n^2 processor for const time*
  repeat $\lceil \lg n \rceil$ **times** ← *since shortest paths double in length*
    for all i, j, m **in parallel do** ← *need n^3 parallel processes for const time*
      $T[i, m, j] \leftarrow D[i, m] + D[m, j]$
    for all i, j **in parallel do** ← n^2
      $D[i, j] \leftarrow \min(\underbrace{D[i, j]}_{1}, \underbrace{T[i, 1, j], T[i, 2, j], \ldots, T[i, n, j]}_{n})$ ← *$\frac{n}{2}$ proc $\Rightarrow n^2(\frac{n}{2})$ proc*
  return D
                                                              ⇒ *$n+1$ →use min like person* ∴ $\frac{n^2(n+1)}{2}$

Here the array T stores path lengths to avoid conflicts between reading and writing in the last **for** statement. There is no conflict between reading the old value of $D[i, j]$ and writing its new value in this statement, since this is done by the same processor. The variables i, j and m range from 1 to n.

Analysis of the algorithm is straightforward. The first **for** statement can be executed in constant time using n^2 processors. Within the **repeat** statement, the first **for** statement can be executed in constant time using n^3 processors. The minimum of $n + 1$ elements can be calculated in a time in $\Theta(\log n)$ using $\Theta(n/\log n)$ proces-? sors, as described in Section 11.2.1. There are n^2 such minima to be computed in parallel, so one iteration of the second **for** statement can be executed in a time in $\Theta(\log n)$ using $\Theta(n^3/\log n)$ processors. Finally the **repeat** statement is executed $\lceil \lg n \rceil$ times, so the complete algorithm can be executed in a time in $\Theta(\log^2 n)$ using $\Theta(n^3)$ processors. ∴ *efficient*

It is easy to show that the number of processors can be reduced to $\Theta(n^3/\log n)$ while keeping the same order for the time: see Problem 11.8. However this is still not optimal.

11.4.2 Connected components [1]

Let $G = \langle N, A \rangle$ be an undirected graph. As usual, we suppose that the nodes of G are numbered from 1 to n. Let the matrix L be such that $L[i, j] = true$ if the edge (i, j) exists, and $L[i, j] = false$ otherwise. Since the graph is undirected, $L[i, j] = L[j, i]$ for every pair of nodes (i, j). We want to find the connected components of the graph G. Problem 9.16 asks the reader to find a sequential algorithm for this problem. Here we describe a parallel algorithm.

In outline, the algorithm proceeds by forming disjoint sets (see Section 5.9) of nodes known to be connected, merging these into larger sets, and so on, until finally the nodes in each connected component of the graph are in a single set. As in Section 5.9 we represent these disjoint sets by rooted trees. With each node of G we associate an entry in the vector $set[1..n]$. If $set[i] = i$, then i is both the label of a set and the root of the corresponding tree; if $set[i] = j \neq i$, then node i is in the set whose label is j but is not the root of the tree. Note that in this application

(a) the trees are always "flattened"; that is, each node (including the root itself) points directly to the root; and

(b) the label of the set, that is, the node at the root of the tree, is always the lowest-numbered node in the set.

We begin by describing just one iteration of the parallel algorithm that merges disjoint sets. To illustrate the operation of the algorithm, suppose for example that we have a graph with 19 nodes, and that by some means or other we have reached the situation shown in Figure 11.4. Here nodes 1, 2 and 3 are in the set labelled 1, nodes 4 and 5 are in the set labelled 4, and so on. In terms of our representation, this means that $set[1] = set[2] = set[3] = 1$, $set[4] = set[5] = 4$, and so on. The nodes in any given set are already known to be connected, but there are also some connections not yet taken into account. These are indicated by dotted edges in Figure 11.4. Thus for example node 3 is connected to node 7 and node 4 is connected to node 8; in other words, $L[3,7] = true$, $L[4,8] = true$, and so on, while for instance $L[3,4] = false$ because nodes 3 and 4 are not connected. Connections between nodes in the same set are omitted, as they are no longer of interest.

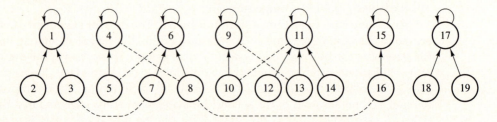

Figure 11.4. Merging sets: initial situation

In the description of the algorithm, we need three arrays $S[1..n, 1..n]$, $T[1..n]$ and $oldT[1..n]$. The first step of the parallel merging algorithm can now be specified as follows.

{Step 1}
for all i, j **in parallel do**
    if $L[i,j]$ **and** $set[i] \neq set[j]$ **then** $S[i,j] \leftarrow set[j]$
                        else $S[i,j] \leftarrow \infty$
for all i **in parallel do** $T[i] \leftarrow \min(S[i,1], S[i,2], \ldots, S[i,n])$
for all i **in parallel do**
    if $T[i] = \infty$ **then** $T[i] \leftarrow set[i]$

Here and throughout this section the variables i and j range from 1 to n.

The effect of this step is that for each node i, $T[i]$ now points to the root of a set. If node i is connected to nodes in other sets besides its own, then $T[i]$ points to the root of one of these other sets: in fact, to the one with the lowest number. If node i has no connections outside its own set, then $T[i] = set[i]$.

Applying step 1 to the situation in Figure 11.4 yields the situation in Figure 11.5, where the connections between nodes are now omitted, and the arrows show the values of T obtained. All the arrows point to root nodes. Thus, for instance, node 1, which has no connections outside its own set, has $T[1] = set[1] = 1$. Node 3, which is connected to node 8, a node not in its own set, points to the root of this other set, namely node 6. A slightly more complicated case is provided by node 8. This is connected to both nodes 4 and 16, neither of which is in the same set as node 8. Thus $T[8]$ must point either to the root of the set containing node 4, or to the root of the set containing node 16, that is, to either node 4 or node 15. Since the algorithm chooses the lowest-numbered root, we obtain $T[8] = 4$.

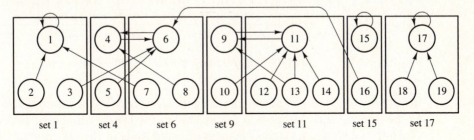

Figure 11.5. Merging sets: after step 1

The second step of the merging algorithm is as follows.

> {Step 2}
> **for** all i, j **in parallel do**
>   **if** $set[j] = i$ **and** $T[j] \neq i$ **then** $S[i, j] \leftarrow T[j]$
>   **else** $S[i, j] \leftarrow \infty$
> **for** all i **in parallel do** $T[i] \leftarrow \min(S[i, 1], S[i, 2], \dots, S[i, n])$
> **for** all i **in parallel do**
>   **if** $T[i] = \infty$ **then** $T[i] \leftarrow set[i]$

If node i is not the label of a set, there is no node j with $set[j] = i$, so this step simply sets $T[i] \leftarrow set[i]$. If on the other hand i is a label, the algorithm examines all the values of $T[j]$ for which j is a node in set i, and for which $T[j] \neq i$, that is, $T[j]$ points to a different set. It then chooses the smallest among these. If there are no such values $T[i] \leftarrow set[i]$, that is, the label node i points to itself. This only happens if none of the nodes in set i is connected to a node in a different set.

After step 2 is applied to the situation in Figure 11.5, we obtain the situation illustrated in Figure 11.6. The arrows now show the new values of T. Every node that is not a label points to the root of its own set, and arrows between sets only join root nodes.

Consider this directed graph, which we shall call H: its nodes are the nodes of G, but its edges are specified by the pointers T. It is redrawn in Figure 11.7 to make its structure clearer. Tracing through the algorithm, we see that if one of the initial sets has no connection to any other (that is, if it includes every node in some connected component of the graph G), then after steps 1 and 2 the pointers T simply reproduce the initial set structure. This is the case of set 17 in the example. The other nodes of H form one or more connected components, each of which resembles a pair of trees whose roots are joined in a cycle. In the example one pair of trees has nodes 1 and 6 as its roots, and the other has nodes 9 and 11.

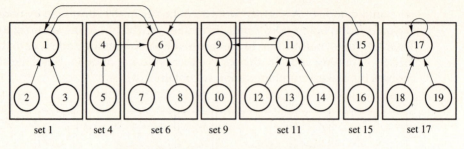

Figure 11.6. Merging sets: after step 2

To see why this is so, consider a component of H formed by the fusion of two or more of the original sets. Suppose a is the label of the lowest-numbered set involved. Since the label of a set is the lowest-numbered node in the set, this means that a is in fact the lowest-numbered node in the given component of H. Now $T[a] = b$, where b is the label of a set different from a, since at step 2 of the algorithm we choose pointers across different sets whenever possible. Furthermore $T[b] = a$, since if set a is connected to set b, then set b is connected to set a (because the graph G is undirected), and $T[b]$ is chosen in step 2 to be as small as possible. Hence $T[a] = b$ and $T[b] = a$ and these two nodes form a cycle. All the remaining nodes in this component of H must be joined to either node a or node b by a chain of one or more pointers T, so they form two trees, one with a as root, and the other with b as root.

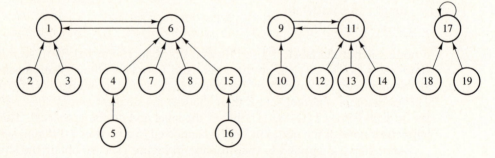

Figure 11.7. Merging sets: the graph H

The third and final step of the algorithm uses the pointer-doubling technique to flatten these double trees, rather as in Section 11.2.2. The only subtlety is that if we "double" the pointer of a node sufficiently often, we are sure that it will point to one of the pair of roots, but we cannot be sure which. In the example, if we "double" the pointer from node 5, it will point to node 6; all subsequent doublings leave this unchanged. If we double the pointer from node 4, it will point to node 1; again, subsequent doublings do not alter this. However if the two roots are nodes a and b, we have seen that before any pointer doubling $T[a] = b$ and $T[b] = a$. Suppose we save the original values of T in the array $oldT$. After a sufficient number of doublings the pointer from node i points to one of the pair of roots, and now we can use the values in $oldT$ to find the other. Comparing, we can choose the root with the lower number. As pointed out above, this is the lowest-numbered node in this component of H.

In a component of H that has only a single root, say a, at the outset $T[a] = a$, so the above technique, while unnecessary, does no harm. Since the whole graph G contains n nodes, no component of H can contain more than this. Whether for a single or a double tree, $\lceil \lg n \rceil$ pointer doublings are therefore enough to ensure that every node points to a root.

Here is the third step of the algorithm.

```
{Step 3}
for all i in parallel do oldT[i] ← T[i]
repeat ⌈lg n⌉ times
    for all i in parallel do T[i] ← T[T[i]]
for all i in parallel do set[i] ← min(T[i], oldT[T[i]])
```

Suppose some connected component of G is initially represented by more than one disjoint set. After execution of steps 1, 2 and 3, some of these will have been merged into larger ones. In fact, each set representing only part of a connected component of G must be linked to at least one other set representing a different part of the same component. Hence such sets must at worst be merged two by two. In other words, in the worst case the number of disjoint sets representing the same connected component of G is halved by the application of steps 1, 2 and 3.

The complete parallel algorithm for finding the connected components of an undirected graph G with n nodes can therefore be specified as follows. First, each node of G is put into a separate disjoint set. Steps 1, 2 and 3 are then iterated $\lceil \lg n \rceil$ times. Since the number of disjoint sets representing the same connected component of G is at least halved at each iteration, this is sure to make all the possible merges even if G has only a single connected component. When the algorithm stops, the remaining disjoint sets therefore represent different components of G. Here is the algorithm.

```
procedure concomps(L[1..n, 1..n]): array [1..n]
{L is the Boolean adjacency matrix of an undirected
  graph G. The algorithm returns a vector representing a
  disjoint set structure, where each disjoint set corresponds
  to a connected component of G.}
    array set[1..n], S[1..n, 1..n], T[1..n], oldT[1..n]
    for all i in parallel do set[i] ← i
    repeat ⌈lg n⌉ times
        Step 1
        Step 2
        Step 3
    return set
```

Analysis of the algorithm

Analysis of the algorithm is straightforward. First, since the three steps are iterated $\lceil \lg n \rceil$ times, and since each execution of step 3 causes the pointer-doubling statement to be executed $\lceil \lg n \rceil$ times, the running time of the algorithm is in $\Omega(\log^2 n)$, no matter how many processors are available.

Now the first **for** statement of step 1 can be executed in constant time with n^2 processors. In the second **for** statement of this step, the minimum of n values in an array can be found in a time in $\Theta(\log n)$ by the techniques of Section 11.2.1 using $\Theta(n)$ processors. There are n such minima to be calculated, so the **for** statement can be executed in a time in $\Theta(\log n)$ using $\Theta(n^2)$ processors. The third **for** statement can be executed in constant time using n processors. Thus overall step 1 can be executed in a time in $\Theta(\log n)$ using n^2 processors. It is easy to check that there are no write conflicts during this step. The analysis of step 2 exactly parallels that of step 1.

As for step 3, the first and last statements can be executed in constant time with n processors, while the **repeat** statement, as we saw, takes a time in $\Theta(\log n)$ and can be executed with n processors. Again, there are no write conflicts.

Pulling these facts together, we see that algorithm *concomps* can be executed in a time in $\Theta(\log^2 n)$ using $\Theta(n^2)$ processors. The work performed is in $\Theta(n^2\log^2 n)$, which is not optimal. Indeed, it can easily be improved. The critical points in the algorithm that determine the number of processors needed are the calculations of n minima in steps 1 and 2. Using the result of Problem 11.2, we see that one minimum can in fact be calculated in a time in $\Theta(\log n)$ using a number of processors in $\Theta(n/\log n)$; the n minima required can thus be calculated in the same time using $\Theta(n^2/\log n)$ processors. With this improvement algorithm *concomps* can be executed in a time in $\Theta(\log^2 n)$ using $\Theta(n^2/\log n)$ processors. However this is still not optimal.

The algorithm can be further improved by taking advantage of the fact that, as the computation progresses, the number of disjoint sets to be handled decreases, and less processors are needed. Space does not permit us to describe this improvement in detail. However it leads to a parallel algorithm for the connected components problem that still takes a time in $\Theta(\log^2 n)$, but now using only $\Theta(n^2/\log^2 n)$ processors. The work performed by this improved algorithm is in $\Theta(n^2)$. Since no sequential algorithm that uses the adjacency matrix of the graph G can do better than this, the improved parallel algorithm is optimal.

11.5 Parallel evaluation of expressions

There is a considerable literature on this subject, that we cannot hope to summarize here. Instead we give just one example of how to compute simple expressions in parallel. The example chosen is easy to explain; nonetheless the solution technique has a pleasing novelty.

Suppose we are looking for a parallel algorithm to evaluate simple arithmetic expressions, whose operands are constants, and that involve only the four operators $+, -, \times$ and $/$. Throughout this section, we assume that these four arithmetic operations are elementary, that is, they can be computed in constant time. For simplicity, we suppose that the expression to be evaluated is given in the form of an *expression tree*: this is a binary tree where each internal node represents one of the four available operators, and each leaf represents an operand. Figure 11.8 shows such a tree, corresponding to the expression

$$((7 - (21/3)) \times 3) + ((9 \times (10 - 8)) + 6).$$

We further suppose that the leaves of the tree are numbered from left to right around the bottom of the tree, again as illustrated in Figure 11.8. The x to the right of each internal node in this figure will be explained later. If the tree has n leaves (operands), then of course it has $n - 1$ internal nodes (operators). In the example, $n = 8$.

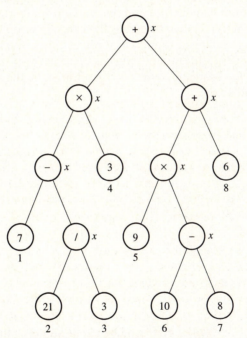

Figure 11.8. A binary expression tree

The obvious way to evaluate such an expression tree in parallel is to assign one processor to each internal node, and to use an algorithm with the following form.

> **repeat**
> > **for** each internal node i **in parallel do**
> > > **if** the values of the children of i are known **then**
> > > > compute the value of i
> > > > remove i's children from the tree
> **until** only one node is left

The number of iterations needed is equal to the height of the expression tree. In the worst case, however, a binary tree with n leaves can have height $n - 1$, and this simple algorithm does not produce any parallelism at all! Only one processor does useful work at each iteration, so the computation could just as well be carried out on a sequential machine; see Problem 11.10.

To speed things up, the processors must do something useful even before both their children have been evaluated. Hence we look for something a processor can do when the value of at least one of its children is known. To this end, we associate a function $f(x)$ with each internal node of the tree. Initially, every internal node is associated with the function x, as illustrated in Figure 11.8. The meaning of these functions is that, when a processor at some node has calculated a value x, the value it transmits up the tree is not x but $f(x)$. Consider for example the fragment of tree shown in Figure 11.9a. Here the processor assigned to internal node A receives one value from its left child and one value from its right child, multiplies them to obtain an answer x, then transmits the value $f(x)$ up the tree to node B. In its turn the processor attached to node B receives this value from its left child A and the value 9 from its right child C (which is a leaf, corresponding to a constant operand), adds them to obtain an answer x, then transmits the value $g(x)$ up the tree to its parent. And so on.

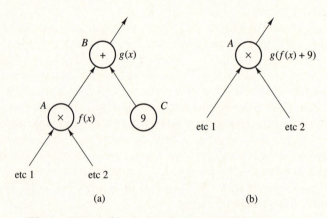

Figure 11.9. A fragment of an expression tree

Even before receiving a value from node A, however, the processor at node B can do useful work reconstructing the expression tree. Because the value of node B's right-hand child is known, it can modify the function stored at node A and remove node B and its child (the right-hand one, in this case) from the tree. The result is shown in Figure 11.9b. If, when it calculates a value x, the processor at node A transmits $g(f(x)+9)$ directly to B's parent, bypassing B and its right-hand child, the result obtained at the root of the tree does not change.

There is nothing special about the operator + in the node B, nor about the value 9 that we gave to its right-hand child C. In general, if node B holds the operator $\circ$, where $\circ$ is any of $+, -, \times$ or $/$, and if the value of its right child is any constant k, then B can replace A's function by $g(f(x) \circ k)$ and cut itself and its right child out of the expression tree. If the constant k is B's left child and the node A is B's right child, B should replace A's function by $g(k \circ f(x))$. This is important because the operators $-$ and $/$ are not commutative. Minor adjustments take care of the cases when A is a leaf (take $f(x)$ to be the constant function that returns the value of the operand at A), or when B is the root of the tree (the final value of the tree is the value that would normally be transmitted up to the next level).

The operation described above is called a *cut*. In the example, the leaf C and its parent B were cut from the tree. It is important for what follows to see that a cut can be performed in constant time. The manipulation of pointers in the tree can certainly be done in constant time: only three pointers are involved in the operation. It is less evident that the function associated with a node can be updated quickly. For instance, if in the example nodes A and B had both been created by a preceding series of cut operations, the functions $f(x)$ and $g(x)$ might already—or so it appears—be quite complex, so that substituting f into g to obtain $g(f(x) \circ k)$ would be no trivial matter.

Fortunately, if the only operators permitted are $+, -, \times$ and $/$, the functions that can be obtained in this way all have the form $(ax + b)/(cx + d)$. To see this, note first that the initial function at each internal node, namely x, can be represented with $a = d = 1$ and $b = c = 0$. If $f(x) = (ax + b)/(cx + d)$, then $f(x) + k = ((a + kc)x + (b + kd))/(cx + d)$, and so on for the seven other operations involving a function $f(x)$ and a constant k. Finally if $f(x) = (a_1x + b_1)/(c_1x + d_1)$ and $g(x) = (a_2x + b_2)/(c_2x + d_2)$, then $g(f(x)) = (a_3x + b_3)/(c_3x + d_3)$, where $a_3 = a_1a_2 + b_2c_1$ and there are equally simple expressions for b_3, c_3 and d_3; see Problem 11.11. Hence to represent any function associated with an internal node we keep just the four corresponding constants a, b, c and d. Provided these constants are not too large, the representation of any functional composition of the form $g(f(x) \circ k)$ or $g(k \circ f(x))$ can then be computed in constant time when required. Furthermore, when the value of x becomes available, $f(x)$ too can be computed in constant time. (The proviso is necessary because in a complicated expression tree the constants a, b, c and d can grow exponentially. However we shall not consider this possibility here.)

The last consideration before we state the algorithm for evaluating expressions is that only three nodes are involved in a cut operation. In Figure 11.9, these are the nodes A, B and C. Pointers, values and associated functions are read and changed for these three nodes and no others. It is therefore possible to execute a cut operation elsewhere in the tree in parallel with the operation on A, B and C, provided none of these is also involved in the second operation. Moreover, let A, B and C be the nodes involved in one cut operation, and A', B' and C' be the nodes involved in another, with C and C' being the two leaves involved. Remember that the leaves of the expression tree are numbered in order round the tree. Then it is a sufficient condition for the operations not to interfere with one another—that is, for the sets $\{A, B, C\}$ and $\{A', B', C'\}$ to be disjoint—if C and C' are nonconsecutive leaves that are either both left children or both right children. Problem 11.12 asks the reader to prove this.

The complete parallel algorithm for evaluating simple expressions can now be stated as follows. We assume that one processor is allocated to each internal node of the expression tree.

> **function** *peval*(*T* : *expression tree*)
> {Evaluate an expression tree with n leaves and
> $n - 1$ internal nodes. The leaves are initially numbered
>   in order round the base of the tree.}
>   **for** each internal node of T **in parallel do**
>   initialize the function $f(x)$ to x
>   **repeat** $\lceil \lg n \rceil$ **times**
>   **for** each internal node of T **in parallel do**
>   **if** the left child is an odd-numbered leaf, cut it
>   **if** the right child is an odd-numbered leaf, cut it
>   **if** either child is now a leaf, renumber it
>   **return** the value of the remaining leaf

We first cut all the odd-numbered leaves that are left children. By the remarks above, this can be done in parallel without the cut operations interfering with one another. Next we cut all the odd-numbered leaves that are right children. Again, this can be done in parallel. Since every odd-numbered leaf is either a left or a right child, all of them have now been removed, and only the $\lfloor n/2 \rfloor$ even-numbered leaves remain. These are renumbered by dividing their numbers by 2, ready for the next iteration. Since each iteration removes at least half the leaves from the expression tree, after $\lceil \lg n \rceil$ iterations only one leaf remains. The value of this leaf is the value of the expression.

Figure 11.10 illustrates one iteration of this process when applied to the expression tree of Figure 11.8. The first half of the figure shows the state of the tree after the odd-numbered left leaves have been cut, and the second half the state after the odd-numbered right leaves have been cut. It is readily seen that if the leaf numbers are now halved, the tree will be ready for the next iteration. The reader may verify that the second iteration reduces the tree to three nodes (one internal node and two leaves), while the third reduces it to a single node holding the value of the original expression, namely 24.

Because a cut can be performed in constant time, the algorithm described above is easily seen to take a time in $\Theta(\log n)$ using $\Theta(n)$ processors. The work performed is in $\Theta(n \log n)$, so the algorithm is not optimal. As in previous examples, after one iteration only half the processors are still useful, after two iterations only a quarter, and so on. At the cost of additional complexity, we may take advantage of this to reduce the number of processors required to $\Theta(n/\log n)$ without increasing the time required beyond $\Theta(\log n)$. The improved algorithm does work in $\Theta(n)$, and is therefore optimal.

The form of input required for the above algorithm (an expression tree with the leaves numbered from left to right) may be thought a little unusual. Although we omit all details here, we note that if the expression to be calculated is not in the required form, but is stored instead as a string (that is, an array of characters),

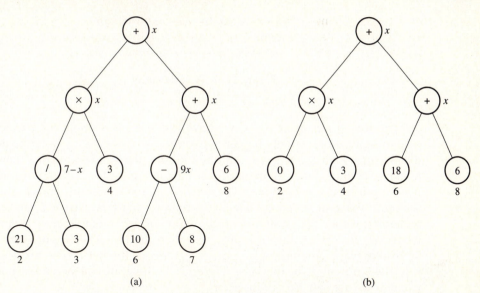

Figure 11.10. (a) **Left children cut** (b) **Right children cut**

then the numbered expression tree can be obtained in a time in $\Theta(\log n)$ using $\Theta(n/\log n)$ processors: exactly the same orders as for the evaluation algorithm. Transforming the input into the required form is therefore not a bottleneck.

11.6 Parallel sorting networks

Before we attack the problem of parallel sorting using a CREW p-ram, we digress for a moment to look at an interesting class of networks that are able to sort their inputs.

We begin by defining a *comparator*. This is a circuit with two inputs and two outputs, which we shall represent as shown in Figure 11.11. By convention we suppose that the inputs are on the left and the outputs on the right. If as shown in the figure the two inputs are x_1 and x_2 and the two outputs are y_1 and y_2, then $y_1 = \min(x_1, x_2)$ and $y_2 = \max(x_1, x_2)$. In other words, the larger input sinks to the lower output, while the smaller input floats up to the upper output. In the sequel it will be convenient to suppose that the inputs are exchanged when $x_1 \le x_2$. Thus two equal inputs are notionally exchanged, although of course this has no visible effect. Clearly a single comparator is able to sort two inputs. We shall suppose that this sorting operation can be carried out in constant time. We also assume that any number of comparators whose inputs and outputs are disjoint can operate in parallel. Comparators meeting these requirements are easy to build in practice.

More generally, we want to design networks that can sort n inputs. If any vector $(x_1, x_2, \ldots, x_n)$ is applied to the inputs of such a network, then the output vector $(y_1, y_2, \ldots, y_n)$ will be a permutation of the inputs such that $y_1 \le y_2 \le \cdots \le y_n$. If we denote such a network by S_n, then S_1 requires no

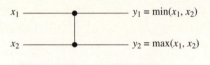

Figure 11.11. A comparator

comparators at all, while S_2, as we have just seen, is a single comparator. One way to build progressively bigger networks is to design S_{n+1} in terms of S_n, so that starting with S_1 or S_2 we can build all the networks we want. There are at least two obvious ways to do this, illustrated in Figure 11.12. Both networks have $n + 1$ inputs and $n + 1$ outputs. The network on the left corresponds to sorting by selection: the largest element falls to the bottom, and then we use S_n to sort the n remaining values. The network on the right corresponds to sorting by insertion: we use S_n to sort the first n inputs, and then the $(n + 1)$–st input is inserted in its correct place. Interestingly, when we compare the networks obtained in this way, they turn out to be the same. Figure 11.13 illustrates the network S_5 obtained whether we use selection or insertion.

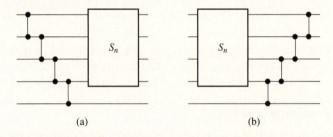

(a)   (b)

Figure 11.12. Selection and insertion sorting networks

There are two useful measures of the quality of our networks. First, we can simply count the number of comparators needed to build S_n. This is called the *size* of the network. In the example S_5 contains 10 comparators, and it is evident that in general S_n will contain $\sum_{i=1}^{n-1} = n(n - 1)/2$ comparators. The second measure of interest is the time the network takes to sort its inputs. We assumed that a comparator takes a constant time to operate, but of course it cannot fire before its inputs are ready. We define the *depth* of a network to be the maximum number of comparators through which an input must pass before it arrives at an output. The depth of the network in Figure 11.13 is 7. Comparators in the same vertical line can all operate at once, while successive lines must be executed from left to right. In this case input 2 passes through 7 comparators. In general it is easy to see that a network S_n designed in this way has depth $2n - 3$ when $n \geq 2$. If each phase takes constant time, the time required to sort n elements using this type of parallel sorting network is proportional to the depth of the network, and is therefore in $\Theta(n)$.

In the following sections we shall see how to improve this design.

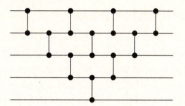

Figure 11.13. A network for sorting five inputs

11.6.1 The zero-one principle

To prove our sorting networks work as they should, we shall use the following somewhat surprising proposition, known as the *zero-one principle*.

Proposition 11.6.1   *A sorting network with n inputs correctly sorts any set of values on its inputs if and only if it correctly sorts all the 2^n input vectors consisting only of zeros and ones.*

Proof   The "only if" part of the proposition is obvious. To prove the "if" part, let $f : \mathbb{R} \to \mathbb{R}$ be any nondecreasing function, so that $f(x) \leq f(y)$ whenever $x \leq y$. Suppose the sorting network under consideration correctly sorts all the 2^n input vectors consisting only of zeros and ones, but that there is some vector $(x_1, x_2, \ldots, x_n)$ of inputs that it sorts incorrectly. Notice that even an incorrect sorting network produces a permutation of its inputs. Let the (incorrect) output vector from this set of inputs be $(y_1, y_2, \ldots, y_n)$, and let y_i be any element of this vector such that $y_i > y_{i+1}$. Such an element necessarily exists since the vector is incorrectly sorted.

  Now consider what would happen if instead of $(x_1, x_2, \ldots, x_n)$ we applied the input vector $(f(x_1), f(x_2), \ldots, f(x_n))$ to the network. Because f is nondecreasing, $f(x_i) \leq f(x_j)$ whenever $x_i \leq x_j$. Thus the values $f(x_i)$ propagate through the sorting network in exactly the same way as the values x_i : whenever two values of x were interchanged, now the two corresponding values of $f(x)$ are exchanged. (This is why we required the comparators to exchange two equal values.) The output vector of the sorting network would therefore be $(f(y_1), f(y_2), \ldots, f(y_n))$, since the network would perform exactly the same permutation of its inputs as before.

  Finally let f be the function defined as follows: $f(x) = 0$ when $x < y_i$, and $f(x) = 1$ otherwise. Now the input vector $(f(x_1), f(x_2), \ldots, f(x_n))$ is a vector consisting solely of zeros and ones. In the output vector $f(y_i) = 1$ and $f(y_{i+1}) = 0$, because $y_{i+1} < y_i$. The output vector would therefore be incorrectly sorted, contradicting the assumption that the network correctly sorts all input vectors containing only zeros and ones. It follows that no such input vector as $(x_1, x_2, \ldots, x_n)$ can exist: the network correctly sorts *any* input vector, and our proof of the zero-one principle is complete.   ∎

11.6.2 Parallel merging networks

We need one more tool before returning to sorting networks. For any positive integer n, a *merging network F_n* is a network built of comparators, with two groups of n inputs and a single group of $2n$ outputs. Provided each of the two groups of inputs is already sorted, then each input appears on one of the outputs, and the outputs are also sorted. (Compare this to the description of merging in Section 7.4.1.) For instance, Figure 11.14 shows an F_4 network, illustrating how the inputs are transmitted to the outputs.

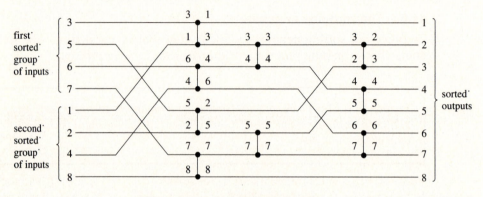

Figure 11.14. A merging network

For simplicity, suppose from now on that n is a power of 2. A single comparator can serve as F_1. From this base we can create merging networks F_2, F_4, and so on, always designing F_{2n} in terms of F_n. This is another example of the divide-and-conquer technique discussed in Chapter 7. Figure 11.15 shows how it is done. Suppose the two groups of inputs are $(w_1, w_2, \ldots, w_n)$ and $(x_1, x_2, \ldots, x_n)$ and the outputs are $(y_1, y_2, \ldots, y_{2n})$. We merge the odd-numbered inputs $(w_1, w_3, \ldots, w_{n-1})$ from the first group with the odd-numbered inputs $(x_1, x_3, \ldots, x_{n-1})$ from the second group using one merge network F_n, and we merge the even-numbered inputs $(w_2, w_4, \ldots, w_n)$ from the first group with the even-numbered inputs $(x_2, x_4, \ldots, x_n)$ from the second group using another. Call the outputs of these two merges $(v_1, v_2, \ldots, v_{2n})$, numbering the outputs from the odd-numbered merge before those from the even-numbered merge. Now permute the outputs v_i so that, from top to bottom, they are in the order $(v_1, v_{n+1}, v_2, v_{n+2}, \ldots, v_n, v_{2n})$. This permutation is the so-called *perfect shuffle*: if you cut a pack of $2n$ cards exactly in half and then riffle them together so that cards fall alternately from each half, this is the order you obtain. Finally install comparators between what are now outputs 2 and 3, 4 and 5, $\ldots$, $2n - 2$ and $2n - 1$. The output on the right is the desired sorted vector $(y_1, y_2, \ldots, y_{2n})$.

An argument exactly analogous to the one given above shows that the zero-one principle also holds for merging networks. Hence to prove the proposed network works, we first show that it works when the inputs w and x consist solely of zeros and ones, and then invoke the zero-one principle to conclude that it works for any

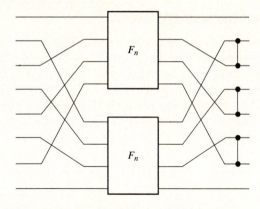

Figure 11.15. Designing F_{2n} in terms of F_n

inputs. The argument is by mathematical induction. For the basis of the induction, it is obvious that F_1, a single comparator, works correctly. For the induction step, suppose all the networks $F_1, F_2, \ldots, F_n$ have been shown to work correctly. Consider what our proposed F_{2n} does when the input vector w consists of r zeros followed by $n - r$ ones, and x consists of s zeros followed by $n - s$ ones. (Remember that both groups of inputs must already be sorted.) Since by the induction hypothesis the networks F_n work correctly, the output $(v_1, v_2, \ldots, v_n)$ of the upper merging network consists of $\lceil r/2 \rceil + \lceil s/2 \rceil$ zeros followed by the appropriate number of ones, while the output $(v_{n+1}, v_{n+2}, \ldots, v_{2n})$ of the lower merging network consists of $\lfloor r/2 \rfloor + \lfloor s/2 \rfloor$ zeros followed by ones. If r and s are both even, then after shuffling the outputs from the two merging networks, the $2n$ lines from top to bottom hold $r + s$ zeros followed by ones; the final column of comparators is unnecessary, but does no harm. If just one of r and s is odd, then after shuffling the outputs from the two merging networks the $2n$ lines from top to bottom again hold $r + s$ zeros followed by ones; as before the final column of comparators is unnecessary. If both r and s are odd, however, then after shuffling the outputs from the two merging networks the values on the lines from top to bottom are $r + s - 1$ zeros, 1 one, 1 zero, and then ones. This time the comparator between lines $r + s$ and $r + s + 1$ is necessary to finish the sort. The proposed F_{2n} therefore correctly sorts any inputs consisting solely of zeros and ones; by the zero-one principle, it correctly sorts any inputs.

Figure 11.14 was obtained in this way, except that the network has been cleaned up to remove some redundant crossings of the lines.

To compute the size $s(n)$ of the network F_n obtained using this construction we use the recurrence

$$s(2n) = 2s(n) + n/2 - 1$$

that is immediate from Figure 11.15. The initial condition is $s(1) = 1$. Using the methods of Section 4.7 it follows easily that $s(n) = 1 + n \lg n$. It is equally easy to show that the depth of the network F_n is $1 + \lg n$.

11.6.3 Improved sorting networks

We can now use divide-and-conquer to design sorting networks S_n that are a considerable improvement on those seen at the beginning of Section 11.6. Figure 11.16 shows how this is done: two networks S_n are used to sort separately the first and the last n inputs, and then a merging circuit F_n is used to complete the sort. A proof that the network S_{2n} works correctly if the two smaller networks S_n also work is scarcely necessary. The divide-and-conquer approach stops at S_2, that consists of a single comparator.

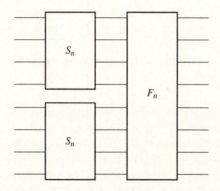

Figure 11.16. An improved sorting network

It is easy to show that the sorting networks obtained in this way use a number of comparators in $\Theta(n \log^2 n)$ and that the time they require to sort their inputs is in $\Theta(\log^2 n)$. For obvious reasons the networks described above are called odd-even merging and sorting networks. They were discovered by Batcher in 1964. These sorting networks are not optimal. Anticipating a little, we shall see in the next chapter that *any* algorithm that sorts n elements by making comparisons between them must make at least $\lceil \lg n! \rceil$ in the worst case. Thus any sorting network for n elements must include at least $\lceil \lg n! \rceil$ comparators. For example, any sorting network for 16 elements must contain at least 45 comparators. The odd-even sorting network S_{16} contains 63 comparators. A different network is known that uses only 60 comparators. It seems there is still room for progress! Concerning depth, too, the odd-even sorting network is not optimal: for 16 inputs, the odd-even sorting network has depth 10, but a different network is known that has depth 9. A class of sorting networks with depth in $\Theta(\log n)$ and size in $\Theta(n \log n)$ is known to exist, but has not yet yielded networks that are useful in practice.

11.7 Parallel sorting

The previous sections describe how to perform parallel sorting using a network of comparators. If each comparator is simulated by a processor, we obtain an algorithm that can be executed on a CREW p-ram. Such an algorithm can sort n items in a time in $\Theta(\log^2 n)$ using $\Theta(n \log^2 n)$ processors. (This follows directly from the result of Problem 11.17.) In this section we sketch a sorting algorithm due to Cole that can be executed on a CREW p-ram, and that sorts n items in a time in $\Theta(\log n)$ using a number of processors in $\Theta(n)$. The work performed is therefore in $\Theta(n \log n)$. As we shall see in Section 12.2.1, this parallel algorithm is therefore optimal, at least as far as sorting by comparison is concerned.

Throughout this section we assume for simplicity that we have n distinct items to be sorted into ascending order, where n is a power of 2; otherwise we add the necessary number of dummy elements. In essence, Cole's parallel algorithm is a tree-based merge sort. It may be helpful to compare this with the ordinary sequential merge sort described in Section 7.4.1. The algorithm uses a complete binary tree with n leaves. Initially one of the items to be sorted is placed at each leaf. Then the computation proceeds up the tree, level by level, from the leaves to the root. At each internal node the sorted subsets of items produced by its children are merged. Suppose such a merge can be carried out in a time in $\Theta(M(n))$, and that all the merges at the same level of the tree can be performed in parallel. As there are $\lg n$ levels of internal nodes in the tree, the whole sorting procedure can therefore be carried out in a time in $\Theta(M(n)\log n)$.

If we have no additional information about two sorted sequences each containing m items, it can be proved that with m processors the time required to merge the sequences is in $\Omega(\log \log m)$. Using such an approach, we would expect a tree-based merge sort to take a time at least in $\Omega(\log n \log \log n)$. Cole's idea was to provide just the additional information needed for it to be possible to merge two sorted sequences in a time in $O(1)$, so the overall algorithm runs in a time in $O(\log n)$.

The following section groups some necessary definitions, and then we outline the algorithm.

11.7.1 Preliminaries

There are n items to be sorted. As the algorithm progresses, various subsets of these n items are stored in ascending order in sorted arrays. In what follows, since all the arrays of interest are sorted, we simply call them arrays, taking for granted that the items they contain are ordered. We use lower-case letters to name items, and capital letters to name arrays.

Let a, b and c be three items, with $a < c$. We say that b is *between* a and c if $a \le b < c$. We also say that a and c *straddle* b.

Let L be an array of items. If a is an item in L, then the *rank* of a in L is defined straightforwardly: the smallest item in L has rank 1, the next smallest has rank 2, and so on. We tacitly suppose that every array L is extended by two invisible items, namely $-\infty$ with rank 0, and $+\infty$ with rank $|L| + 1$. This allows us to define the rank of an item from one array with respect to another (sometimes called the *cross-rank*) as follows. Let L and J be two arrays, and let b be an item in J. If a and c are the two consecutive items of L that straddle b (these necessarily exist because of the presence of the two invisible items in L), then the rank of b in L is defined to be the same as the rank of a in L. We denote by J/L the set of ranks in L of all the items in J.

Again, let J and L be two arrays of items, and now let a and b be two consecutive items of L (including the invisible items). We define the interval *induced* by these items to be $[a, b)$. An item x belongs to this interval if $a \le x < b$, that is, if a and b straddle x. We say that L *covers* J if each interval induced by consecutive items of L contains at most three items from J. (This time the invisible items in J are *not* included.) For example, if L contains the items 10, 20 and 30, while J contains 1, 7, 22, 23, 26, and 35, then L covers J: the interval induced by the items $-\infty$ and 10 from L contains two items from J, the interval induced by 10 and 20 contains none, and so on. However if K contains the items 11, 12, 14, 17, 22, and 41, L does not cover K because the interval induced by the items 10 and 20 from L contains more than three items from K.

We use the symbol & to denote the operation of merging two sorted arrays. Suppose L covers J and M covers K. Contrary to what one might hope, it is not necessarily true that $L\&M$ covers $J\&K$; see Problem 11.19. Finally, for any array L, $r(L)$ denotes the array obtained by taking every fourth item in L. If L contains less than four items, $r(L)$ is empty.

11.7.2 The key idea

We now give an informal account of the method of merging two arrays in a time in $O(1)$. Let J, K and L be three sorted arrays, and suppose L covers both J and K. The situation is illustrated in Figure 11.17. Since L covers J, each interval induced by two consecutive items of L, including those induced by the invisible items, contains at most three items of J; the same is true for K. If we know the ranks J/L, K/L, L/J and L/K, it is easy to determine which items are in which interval.

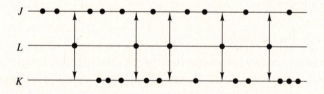

Figure 11.17. Merging J and K with help from L.

The items from J that lie in the first interval induced by L can be merged with those from K that also lie in the first interval in a time in $O(1)$ because there are at most six of them altogether. The same is true of the items from J and K that lie in the second interval induced by L, and so on. If we have enough processors, all these merges of at most six items can be performed in parallel, so they can all be finished in a time in $O(1)$. To obtain $J\&K$, all that remains is to concatenate the results of merging the intervals separately. With enough processors, this too can be done in constant time. Thus the whole merge can be completed in constant time.

We call this operation *merging with help*. In the example above, arrays J and K are said to be merged with help from L.

11.7.3 The algorithm

The n items to be sorted are placed initially at the leaves of a complete binary tree. At a typical internal node v of this tree the task is to compute L_v, an array containing all the items in the subtree rooted at v. At each stage in the computation at node v an array A_v contains a subset of the items in L_v; A_v is recalculated at each stage. More precisely, let $A_v(t)$ be the array at hand at the start of stage t, $t = 0, 1, \ldots$, and let $A_v(t + 1)$ be the array created during the stage. In general $A_v(t + 1)$ is twice the size of $A_v(t)$, until finally $A_v(t + 1) = L_v$. A node v at which $A_v(t) \neq L_v$ is said to be *active*, while a node at which $A_v(t) = L_v$ is called *complete*. Arrays associated with node v's children are given the suffixes x and y: it does not matter which suffix refers to which child. At each stage three other arrays are involved: $B_v(t)$ is an array transmitted up the tree to v's parent, and $B_x(t)$ and $B_y(t)$ are two arrays received from v's children.

As a first approximation, the computation performed during each stage at each internal node v comprises the following three phases (see Figure 11.18):

1. Compute the array $B_v(t) \leftarrow r(A_v(t))$, and send it up the tree to v's parent.

2. Read the two arrays $B_x(t)$ and $B_y(t)$ that v's children have just sent up the tree.

3. Compute $A_v(t + 1) \leftarrow B_x(t) \& B_y(t)$. This merge operation is performed in constant time as outlined above with help from array $A_v(t)$, which, as we shall see, covers both $B_x(t)$ and $B_y(t)$.

There are differences in the three phases according to whether node v is active or complete. However for our present purposes it is unnecessary to give the details; it is sufficient to note that

⋄ at stage 0 nodes at level 1 read the values sent by their children, which are leaves, merge these two values, and become complete;

⋄ three stages after a node becomes complete, its parent in turn becomes complete.

Since there are $\lg n$ levels of internal nodes in the tree, we conclude that the algorithm has $3 \lg n - 2$ stages.

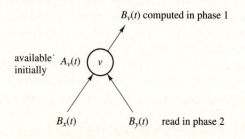

$B_v(t)$ computed in phase 1

available initially $A_v(t)$ v

$B_x(t)$ $B_y(t)$ read in phase 2

Figure 11.18. Stage t at node v

It remains to prove that the merges required by phase 3 of each stage can be performed in a time in $O(1)$. Combined with the above result, this will show that the complete algorithm runs in a time in $O(\log n)$.

11.7.4 A sketch of the details

To show that at any internal node v with children x and y, and at any stage t, the arrays $B_x(t)$ and $B_y(t)$ can be merged in a time in $O(1)$ with help from $A_v(t)$, two things have to be proved: first, that $A_v(t)$ covers both $B_x(t)$ and $B_y(t)$; and second, that the ranks $A_v(t)/B_x(t)$, $A_v(t)/B_y(t)$, $B_x(t)/A_v(t)$ and $B_x(t)/A_v(t)$ are known or can be obtained quickly.

It is fairly straightforward to prove the required covering property. A lengthy but not difficult argument then shows that the required ranks can all be obtained in a time in $O(1)$ provided we allocate a processor to each item in the array $A(t)$ at every active node, another to each item in the array $B(t)$ at every active node, and finally another to each item in the array $A(t + 1)$ at every active node. All the operations required by a single stage of the algorithm can therefore be carried out in a time in $O(1)$ provided there are enough processors available to allocate one to each item in each of the arrays $A(t)$, $B(t)$ and $A(t + 1)$ at each active node.

For a node v, the size of the array $A_v(t)$ at v is one-quarter the size of the arrays $A_x(t)$ and $A_y(t)$ at its children, provided the children are not yet complete. Hence the total size of the arrays $A(t)$ at v's level is one-eighth the size of the arrays $A(t)$ at its children's level, provided the children are not complete. (There are twice as many children as parents.) Although we have not given the details, this is also true at the stage when the children first become complete. At the second stage when the children are complete, the size of $A_v(t)$ at v is one-half the size of $A_x(t)$ and $A_y(t)$ at its children, so the total size of these arrays at v's level is one-quarter the size at the children's level; similarly, at the third stage when the children are complete, the total size of the arrays $A(t)$ at v's level is one-half the total size of these arrays at the children's level.

Since there can never be more than n items in all the arrays $A(t)$ at the same level, the total number of items in all the arrays $A(t)$ throughout the whole tree cannot exceed the maximum of three values: $n + n/8 + n/16 + \cdots = 8n/7$ when there are n items at the level whose nodes have just become complete, $n + n/4 + n/32 + \cdots = 9n/7$ one stage later, and $n + n/2 + n/16 + \cdots = 11n/7$ one stage later still. Hence the total size of all the arrays $A(t)$ is bounded by $11n/7$. Similarly it can be shown that the total size of all the arrays $B(t)$, and hence the total size of all the arrays $A(t + 1)$ at active nodes, is not greater than $8n/7$. The total number of items in all the arrays $A(t)$, $B(t)$ and $A(t + 1)$ at every active node is therefore not greater than $27n/7$.

We conclude finally that the algorithm can be executed in a time in $O(1)$ using a number of processors in $O(n)$. The algorithm as described is without write conflicts, although simultaneous reads may occur.

11.8 Some remarks on EREW and CRCW p-rams

Throughout this chapter we have assumed that our algorithms are to be executed on a CREW p-ram, that is, on a machine that allows several processors to read the same storage location simultaneously, but that does not permit simultaneous writing to the same location. It seems intuitively likely that such a machine should be more powerful than an EREW p-ram, and less powerful than a CRCW p-ram. We now give two simple examples to confirm this intuition.

To show that a CREW p-ram can outperform an EREW p-ram, consider the following problem. A binary tree contains n nodes, each node i except the root being linked to its parent by a pointer $p[i]$. At the root, the pointer p has the special value **nil**. Each node i also has a second pointer $r[i]$. We want to set the value of r at every node so that it points to the root of the tree. Consider the following parallel algorithm for doing this.

> **procedure** *find-root*(T)
>   {T is a binary tree with n nodes}
>   **for** every ordered pair (i, j) **in parallel do**
>   **if** $p[j] =$ **nil then** $r[i] \leftarrow j$

Here i and j range from 1 to n, so we need n^2 processors to execute the **if** statement in parallel for every pair of nodes. Assuming these are available, the statement can be executed in parallel for every pair of nodes on a CREW p-ram. When evaluating the condition, n processors read the value of $p[j]$ for every j; however concurrent reads are allowed, so this causes no problem. As for the assignment statement, only one processor for each value of i finds that the condition comes out true, so only one processor for each value of i assigns a value to $r[i]$. There are therefore no write conflicts. The operations involved are elementary, so the algorithm can be executed in a time in $O(1)$ using n^2 CREW processors.

On the other hand, a simple argument shows that no algorithm for an EREW processor can produce the required result in a time in $O(1)$, no matter how many processors are available. For at each step on such a machine, an item of information stored in memory can be read, and therefore copied, by at most one processor. Hence the number of storage locations that contain this item of information can at most double at each step. In the problem above, the identity of the root is known initially to at most one node. To copy this information and store it in all n nodes therefore require at least $\lceil \lg n \rceil$ steps. Thus any algorithm for the problem using EREW processors requires a time in $\Omega(\log n)$.

A second simple problem will serve to show that a CRCW machine can outperform a CREW machine. The problem is to find the maximum of n numbers stored in an array $A[1..n]$. Consider the following algorithm.

> **function** *find-max*$(A[1..n])$
>   **array** $M[1..n]$ **of** *Boolean*
>   **for** $1 \le i \le n$ **in parallel do** $M[i] \leftarrow true$
>   **for** all ordered pairs (i, j) **in parallel do**
>   **if** $A[i] < A[j]$ **then** $M[i] \leftarrow false$
>   **for** $1 \le i \le n$ **in parallel do**
>   **if** $M[i]$ **then** $max \leftarrow A[i]$
>   **return** max

As before i and j range from 1 to n, so we need n^2 processors to execute the first **if** statement in parallel for every pair of items in the array A. Assuming these are available, the statement can be executed in a time in $O(1)$. Here, however, as many as $n-1$ processors may try to write to $M[i]$ simultaneously. The machine must therefore permit concurrent write operations. Note that if several processors are involved, they all try to write the same value, namely *false*. This additional constraint is often imposed on the CRCW model. After execution of the first **if** statement, $M[i]$ is *true* if and only if $A[i]$ is equal to the largest value in A. (There may be several such items.) Finally the second **if** statement writes this maximum value to *max*. Again, several processors may try to write to *max* simultaneously, but if they do, then they all try to write the same value. This statement too can be executed in a time in $O(1)$. Hence the whole algorithm can be executed in a time in $O(1)$ on a CRCW p-ram using n^2 processors.

Although the argument is not simple in this case, it can be proved that any algorithm (such as the ones described earlier in the chapter) for finding the maximum of n elements using a CREW p-ram must take a time in $\Omega(\log n)$, no matter how many processors are available. Hence a CRCW p-ram is more powerful than a CREW p-ram.

11.9 Distributed computation

In Section 11.1 we defined a model of parallel computation, called the single-instruction multiple-data-stream model, in which the processors are more or less synchronized. Suppose we relax this restriction, and allow each processor to work on its own data at its own speed using its own program. When it has something interesting to report it sends a message to its colleagues, and sometimes it may receive messages from them. This is the *multiple-instruction multiple-data-stream* model. The two models are often called the SIMD and MIMD models, respectively.

With the SIMD model, although it is not a logical necessity, it is usually convenient to keep the processors involved in the execution of a parallel algorithm close together, perhaps even in the same physical piece of equipment. Otherwise the overhead involved in keeping them synchronized may be prohibitive. Once the restrictions are relaxed, however, there is no longer any reason why all the processors involved in the execution of a parallel algorithm should be at the same site. If messages are exchanged relatively infrequently, the processors can be anywhere in the world, and the messages can be sent by electronic mail. Executing a parallel algorithm in this way is an example of *distributed computing*. Two striking examples of this technique involve respectively factorizing large integers, and the travelling salesperson problem.

For the first example, consider the Las Vegas algorithm for factorizing large integers described in Section 10.7.4. This depends essentially on finding a sufficient number of integers with a special property (their squares modulo n must be k-smooth—see the description of the algorithm in Section 10.7.4), where the candidates are chosen randomly. If several processors are available, it is obviously possible to have one of them collect the necessary integers, while the others sift possible candidates. Each processor can work independently of the others, except perhaps for some arrangement to avoid unnecessary duplication of effort. When a suitable integer is found, the processor concerned can send a message to the keeper of the collection with the new information, until eventually enough suitable integers are found. If finding a suitable integer is a relatively rare event, electronic mail is quite fast enough to provide the message path.

Using this kind of technique, Lenstra and Manasse designed an experiment that involved recruiting volunteers with access to the Internet, supplying them with the necessary programs, and collecting results as they were acquired. The experiment began in the summer of 1987 using the elliptic curve method of factorization, not described in this book. In 1988 they changed to a variant of the quadratic sieve algorithm outlined in Section 10.7.4. Their programs were designed to run on a workstation during periods when it would otherwise have been idle—overnight or at weekends, for example—so the computing power used was essentially free. They estimate that they had access to the equivalent of some 1000 million instructions per second of sustained computing power, allowing them to factorize 100-digit integers in about a week. They expected the required computing time to roughly double for each extra three digits added to the size of the number to be factorized. See Section 10.7.4 for a recent example of an even more impressive success on a number with 129 digits.

In the case of the travelling salesperson problem, all the existing efficient computer programs are based on a scheme that involves finding suitable cutting planes. (It does not matter if you don't know what these are.) Again, several processors can be used to search for cutting planes independently. In 1993 a team of four people solved a 4461-city problem after computing for 28 nights in parallel on a network of 75 machines. They estimated that the computation involved would have taken nearly two years had it been executed on a single workstation.

11.10 Problems

Problem 11.1.   Prove that algorithm *flatten* is correct.

Problem 11.2.   Show that the minimum of n elements stored in an array can be found in a time in $\Theta(\log n)$ using $\Theta(n / \log n)$ processors.

Problem 11.3.   With the definitions of Section 11.2.2, prove that when algorithm *paroper* terminates, the value of d for the first element of L is $X_{1,n}$, the value of d for the second element of L is $X_{2,n}$, and so on, the value of d for the last element being $X_{n,n}$.

Problem 11.4.   Write an algorithm similar to *paroper* of Section 11.2.2 except that when it terminates the value of d for the first element of L is $X_{1,1}$, the value of d for the second element of L is $X_{1,2}$, and so on, the value of d for the last element being $X_{1,n}$.

Problem 11.5.   Write an algorithm similar to *paroper* of Section 11.2.2 except that it takes two parameters: a list and a value. Assume that the operator ∘ takes three parameters, not two. Two of these are pointers to list items and the third is a value k. When both list items have values less than or equal to k, ∘ returns a pointer to the item with the larger value; when only one item has a value less than or equal to k,

∘ returns a pointer to this item; when neither item has a value less than or equal to k, ∘ returns **nil**. Your algorithm should return a pointer to an item in the list whose value is k if there is one; otherwise it should return a pointer to the item with the largest value not exceeding k. This is a kind of "binary search" on a linked list, which cannot be done sequentially.

Problem 11.6. Show that if we have an efficient parallel algorithm (using a polynomial number of processors and taking polylogarithmic time) for some problem, then we can find an efficient sequential algorithm (taking polynomial time) for the same problem.

Problem 11.7. Show that if $p > q$ then $p/q \leq \lceil p/q \rceil < 2p/q$.

Problem 11.8. Show that algorithm *parpaths* can be executed using $\Theta(n^3/\log n)$ processors taking a time in $\Theta(\log^2 n)$.

Problem 11.9. Draw figures to illustrate the progress of algorithm *concomps* on the graph of Figure 11.19.

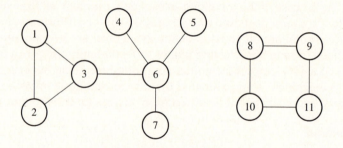

Figure 11.19. A graph

Problem 11.10. Give an example of an expression with five operands that requires four iterations of the naive algorithm of Section 11.5 to evaluate.

Problem 11.11. If $f(x) = (a_1 x + b_1)/(c_1 + d_1)$, $g(x) = (a_2 x + b_2)/(c_2 + d_2)$ and $g(f(x)) = (a_3 x + b_3)/(c_3 + d_3)$, find expressions for a_3, b_3, c_3 and d_3 in terms of a_1, a_2, b_1, b_2, etc.

Problem 11.12. Show that two cut operations (see Section 11.5) involving leaves C and C' do not interfere with one another if C and C' are nonconsecutive leaves of the expression tree, and either they are both left children or both right children.

Problem 11.13. Draw the expression

$$7 \times (4 + (64/(10 - (3 \times (13 - (6 + 5))))))$$

as an expression tree with the leaves numbered from left to right, and illustrate the operation of the parallel evaluation algorithm of Section 11.5 on this tree.

Problem 11.14.   State and prove a zero-one principle for merging networks.

Problem 11.15.   Show that the size and depth of the merging networks F_n described in Section 11.6.2 are $1 + n \lg n$ and $1 + \lg n$ respectively.

Problem 11.16.   In Section 11.6.2 we showed how to build merging networks F_n when n is a power of 2. Extend this by showing how to build a merging network F_n for any $n > 0$. In terms of n, what are the size and the depth of the resulting networks?

Problem 11.17.   Show that the size and depth of the sorting networks S_n described in Section 11.6.3 are $n - 1 + n(\lg^2 n - \lg n)/4$ and $(\lg^2 n + \lg n)/2$ respectively.

Problem 11.18.   Consider the networks defined as follows for $n \geq 2$. The network contains $n(n-1)/2$ comparators arranged like bricks in a wall as illustrated in Figure 11.20: there are $\lceil n/2 \rceil$ comparators between inputs 1 and 2, $\lfloor n/2 \rfloor$ comparators between or behind these between inputs 2 and 3, $\lceil n/2 \rceil$ more directly under the first group between inputs 3 and 4, and so on. Prove that these networks are valid sorting networks. In terms of n, what is their depth?

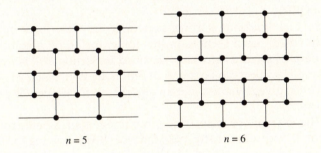

$n = 5$ $n = 6$

Figure 11.20. Two networks

Problem 11.19.   Let J, K, L and M be four sorted arrays such that L covers J and M covers K, where covering is defined in Section 11.7.1. Give an example showing that $L\&M$ does not necessarily cover $J\&K$.

Problem 11.20.   Point out where simultaneous read operations may occur in Cole's parallel merge sort.

Problem 11.21.   Suppose we want to write an algorithm like *pardist* of Section 11.2.2, using pointer doubling, but on a list of unknown length. Instead of repeating the doubling step $\log n$ times, we might try to use some construct such as the following.

```
repeat
    the doubling step
until s[i]= s[s[i]] for every i in L
```

This poses a problem for the overall control of our parallel machine: how can every processor be made aware that the loop has ended? Show how this can be done for (a) an EREW p-ram, (b) a CREW p-ram, and (c) a CRCW p-ram. How much time is required to test loop termination in each case?

11.11 References and further reading

Introductory books on parallel algorithms include Gibbons and Rytter (1988) and Akl (1989). Lakshmivarahan and Dhall (1990) have a useful chapter on multi-processors and multicomputers. Leighton (1992) is concerned about relationships between the architecture of commercially available machines and efficient parallel algorithms for a wide variety of problems. Reif (1993) is more advanced.

Brent's theorem is from Brent (1974). The parallel algorithm for finding short-est paths described in Section 11.4.1 essentially follows Kučera (1982). The parallel algorithm for finding connected components of a graph described in Section 11.4.2 is from Hirschberg, Chandra and Sarwate (1979). The optimal algorithm men-tioned but not described at the end of this section can be found in Chin, Lam and Chen (1982). More parallel algorithms for graph problems are presented in Quinn and Deo (1984).

The example of parallel evaluation of simple arithmetic expressions given in Section 11.5 follows Gibbons and Rytter (1988). There is more on this subject in Brent (1974).

Several kinds of sorting networks are described in Batcher (1968), and Knuth (1973) has a section on this topic, including a solution to Problem 11.18. The parallel sorting algorithm sketched in Section 11.7 is from Cole (1988). More on parallel sorting can be found in Bitton, DeWitt, Hsiao and Menon (1984), while Akl (1985) gives twenty different algorithms for particular parallel machine archi-tectures.

The example of factorizing large integers using electronic mail presented in Section 11.9 is from Lenstra and Manasse (1990). Solving the travelling salesperson problem for a network of 4461 cities was described by Vašek Chvátal in a talk in October 1993. To gain a better appreciation of the kinds of parallel machine architectures currently in use, see Duncan (1990), a tutorial that reviews alternative approaches to parallel processing. One particular successful design is described in Tucker and Robertson (1988).

Chapter 12

Computational Complexity

Up to now we have been interested in *algorithmics*, which is concerned with the systematic design and analysis of specific algorithms, each more efficient than its predecessors, to solve some given problem. However, a book on algorithmics is incomplete without an introduction to its sister craft: *computational complexity*. This field, which runs in parallel with algorithmics, considers globally all possible algorithms able to solve a given problem. This includes algorithms that have never even been thought of.

Using algorithmics, we can prove by giving and analysing an explicit algorithm that the problem under study can be solved in a time in $O(f(n))$ for some function $f(n)$ that we aim to reduce as much as possible. Using complexity, on the other hand, we try to find a function $g(n)$ as large as possible for which we can prove that *any* algorithm capable of solving our problem correctly on all of its instances must necessarily take a time in $\Omega(g(n))$. We call such a function $g(n)$ a *lower bound* on the complexity of the problem. Our satisfaction is complete when $f(n) \in \Theta(g(n))$ since then we know we have found the most efficient algorithm possible, except perhaps for changes in the hidden multiplicative constant. Unfortunately, such happiness does not come often in the current state of our ignorance. Nevertheless, we can now and then find even the exact number of times that a given operation—such as a comparison—is required to solve the problem. In this chapter we introduce just a few of the principal techniques and concepts used in the study of computational complexity: information-theoretic arguments, adversary arguments, reduction and $\mathcal{NP}$–completeness. We shall also see that complexity techniques can be useful for the design of algorithms.

12.1 Introduction: A simple example

Consider the game of twenty questions as an introductory example. Your friend chooses a positive integer no larger than one million, which you are to guess. You are allowed a maximum of 20 yes/no questions. Your friend must be able to decide unambiguously whether to answer "yes" or "no" to each of your questions. For instance you may ask "Is your number a prime?" If you are familiar with this game, you will use a divide-and-conquer approach to solve this riddle, halving with each question the number of candidates for the mystery number. Thus your first question will be "Is your number between 1 and 500 000?" It is elementary to show that you always find the answer within your allowed 20 questions in this way because one million is less than 2^{20}.

Finding this algorithm, which shows that 20 questions are *sufficient* to solve the problem, was a matter for algorithmics. Whether or not 20 questions are *necessary*, on the other hand, is the concern of complexity. It is easy to show that our algorithm will use all its 20 questions on most mystery numbers. Nevertheless, we cannot conclude from the failure of this specific algorithm consistently to solve the riddle with less than 20 questions that this cannot be done with a cleverer algorithm. The techniques we are about to study, particularly information-theoretic arguments and adversary arguments, allow us to prove in a snap that 20 questions are in fact necessary. However, this problem is sufficiently simple that we can solve it with an elementary approach.

Let S_i be the set of candidates for the mystery number after the i-th question has been asked, and let $k_i = |S_i|$ be the number of remaining candidates. Initially, S_0 contains all the positive integers up to one million, and therefore $k_0 = 10^6$. Let Q_i be the i-th question, which may depend on the answers to previous questions, and let $Q_i(n)$ denote the answer to that question if the mystery number is n. Let Y_i be $\{n \in S_{i-1} \mid Q_i(n) = \text{"yes"}\}$ and let N_i be $\{n \in S_{i-1} \mid Q_i(n) = \text{"no"}\}$. It is clear that $Y_i \cap N_i = \emptyset$ and $Y_i \cup N_i = S_{i-1}$. Therefore, $|S_{i-1}| = |Y_i| + |N_i|$, which implies that at least one of Y_i or N_i contains $\lceil k_{i-1}/2 \rceil$ numbers or more. Since the mystery number can be any of the candidates, we cannot rule out the possibility that your friend's answer to Q_i will result in your keeping the larger of Y_i or N_i as the set of remaining candidates S_i. This is true regardless of how clever you are in your choice of questions. Hence, it is possible that $k_i \geq \lceil k_{i-1}/2 \rceil$ for each i. Since $k_0 = 10^6$, it may be that $k_1 \geq 500\,000$, hence it may be that $k_2 \geq 250\,000$, and so on. Continuing in this way, we find that $k_{19} \geq 2$ is possible. We conclude that at least two candidates may remain for the mystery number after 19 questions, and thus 20 questions are necessary to solve the riddle in the worst case.

12.2 Information-theoretic arguments

This technique applies to a variety of problems, particularly those involving comparisons between items. A *decision tree* is a way to represent the working of an algorithm on all possible data of a given size. Formally, it is a rooted binary tree. Each internal node of the tree contains a test of some sort on the data. Each leaf contains an output, which we call the *verdict*. A *trip* through the tree consists of starting from the root and asking the question that is found there. If the answer is "yes", the trip continues recursively in the left subtree; otherwise it continues recursively in the right subtree. The trip ends when it reaches a leaf; the verdict found there is the outcome of the trip.

Consider again the game of 20 questions, but assume for simplicity that the mystery number is known to be between 1 and 6. You will obviously not need all 20 questions. How many do you really need? Figure 12.1 gives a decision tree for this game. If the mystery number is $n = 5$, for example, your first question is "Is $n \leq 3$?" and you continue in the right subtree because the answer is "no" (thus you know that $n \in \{4,5,6\}$). There, you find the question "Is $n \leq 5$?" and you continue to the left since the answer is "yes" (so you know that $n \in \{4,5\}$). Finally, you ask the question "Is $n \leq 4$?" and reach the correct right-hand verdict "$n = 5$" from the answer "no".

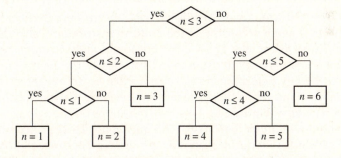

Figure 12.1. A decision tree for the game of three questions

This is relevant because to any deterministic algorithm to play the game there corresponds a decision tree, provided there is a limit to the number of questions the algorithm may ask. Conversely, any such decision tree can be thought of as an algorithm. Assume for simplicity that decision trees are *pruned* in the sense that all the leaves are accessible from the root by making some consistent sequence of decisions. Though wasteful, it is allowable to ask a question whose answer is determined by the sequence of questions and answers leading to that question. For example, one may ask whether $A \leq C$ in a node reached after learning that $A \leq B$ and $B \leq C$: we shall see in Figure 12.5 that this behaviour may occur in natural algorithms. Recall that the height of the tree is the distance from the root to the most distant leaf. Since one question is asked for each internal node on that path, and since this leaf can be reached when processing at least one input, the height of the tree corresponds to the number of questions asked in the worst case. Moreover, the tree must have at least one leaf for each possible verdict. (Problem 12.5 illustrates the fact that there may be more leaves than distinct verdicts in general.)

Come back now to the question of playing the original game of twenty questions, but with only 19 questions. Any solution would give rise to a decision tree of height at most 19 that must have at least one million leaves. This is impossible because the decision tree is binary, any binary tree of height k has at most 2^k leaves (see Problem 12.1), and 2^{19} is less than one million. We conclude immediately that the game of twenty questions cannot be solved with 19 questions in the worst case.

Decision trees can also be used to analyse the complexity of a problem on the average rather than in the worst case. Let T be a binary tree. Define the *average height* of T as the sum of the depths of all the leaves divided by the number of leaves. For example, the decision tree of Figure 12.1 has average height $(3 + 3 + 2 + 3 + 3 + 2)/6 = 8/3$. Just as the height of a pruned decision tree gives the worst-case performance of the corresponding algorithm, its average height gives the average-case performance, provided each verdict is equally likely and each possible verdict appears exactly once as a leaf of the tree. Continuing our simplified example, if each integer between 1 and 6 is equally likely to be the mystery number, the algorithm corresponding to Figure 12.1 asks 8/3 questions on the average. Can one do better? Can the average-case performance be improved, perhaps if one is willing to ask more questions than required on a few instances?

The following theorem tells us that if the mystery number is randomly chosen between 1 and 6 according to the uniform distribution, any algorithm to play the game must ask at least $\lg 6 \approx 2.585$ questions on the average, no matter how many questions it may ask in some cases. But clearly the average number of questions asked by any deterministic algorithm must be an integer divided by 6 since the number of questions is an integer for each of the 6 equiprobable verdicts. The solution given in Figure 12.1 asks 16/6 questions on the average. Any improvement would ask no more than $15/6 = 2.5$ questions. This is ruled out since $\lg 6 > 15/6$. We conclude that our decision tree provides an optimal algorithm when the mystery number is between 1 and 6, both in the worst case and on the average. Similarly, 20 questions are necessary in the worst case for the original game with one million verdicts, and no algorithm can ask less than $\lg 10^6 \approx 19.93$ questions on the average if all verdicts are equally likely.

Theorem 12.2.1   *Any binary tree with k leaves has an average height of at least $\lg k$.*

Proof   Let T be a binary tree with k leaves. Define $H(T)$ as the sum of the depths of the leaves. For example, $H(T) = 16$ for the tree in Figure 12.1. By definition, the average height of T is $H(T)/k$, and thus our goal is to prove that $H(T) \geq k \lg k$. The root of T can have 0, 1 or 2 children; see Figure 12.2. In the first case, the root is the only leaf in the tree: $k = 1$ and $H(T) = 0$. In the second case, the single child is the root of a subtree A, which also has k leaves. The distance from any leaf to the root of T is one more than the distance from the same leaf to the root of A, so $H(T) = H(A) + k$. In the third case, T is composed of a root and of two subtrees A and B with i and $k - i$ leaves, respectively, for some $1 \leq i < k$. By a similar argument we obtain this time $H(T) = H(A) + H(B) + k$.

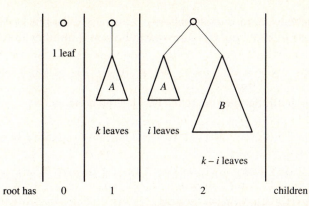

Figure 12.2. Minimizing the average height of a binary tree with k leaves

For $k \geq 1$, define $h(k)$ as the smallest value possible for $H(X)$ when X is a binary tree with k leaves. In particular, $H(T) \geq h(k)$. Clearly, $h(1) = 0$. If we define $h(0) = 0$, the preceding discussion and the principle of optimality used in dynamic programming lead to

$$h(k) = \min_{0 \leq i \leq k} (h(i) + h(k - i) + k)$$

for every $k > 1$. At first sight this recurrence is not well founded since it defines $h(k)$ in terms of itself when we take $i = 0$ or $i = k$ in the minimum. However it is impossible that $h(k) = h(k) + k$, so those terms cannot yield the minimum. We can thus reformulate the recurrence that defines $h(k)$.

$$h(k) = \begin{cases} 0 & \text{if } k \leq 1 \\ k + \min_{1 \leq i \leq k-1} (h(i) + h(k - i)) & \text{otherwise} \end{cases}$$

We now prove by mathematical induction that $h(k) \geq k \lg k$ for all $k \geq 1$. The base $k = 1$ is immediate. Let $k > 1$. Assume the induction hypothesis that $h(j) \geq j \lg j$ for every positive integer j smaller than k. By definition,

$$h(k) = k + \min_{1 \leq i \leq k-1} (h(i) + h(k - i)).$$

By the induction hypothesis,

$$h(k) \geq k + \min_{1 \leq i \leq k-1} (i \lg i + (k - i) \lg(k - i)).$$

To have available the tools of real analysis for function minimization, let $g : [1, k - 1] \to \mathbb{R}$ be defined as $g(x) = x \lg x + (k - x) \lg(k - x)$. Calculating the derivative gives $g'(x) = \lg x - \lg(k - x)$, which is zero if and only if $x = k - x$. Since the second derivative is positive, $g(x)$ attains its minimum at $x = k/2$. This minimum is $g(k/2) = k \lg k - k$. But the minimum value attained by

$g(i)$ when i is an integer between 1 and $k - 1$ cannot be less than the minimum value of $g(x)$ when x is allowed to be a real number in the same range. Therefore,

$$\min_{i \in [1..k-1]} g(i) \geq \min_{x \in [1,k-1]} g(x) \geq k \lg k - k.$$

Putting it all together we reach the desired conclusion:

$$H(T) \geq h(k) \geq k + \min_{i \in [1..k-1]} g(i) \geq k \lg k,$$

and thus the average height of T, which is $H(T)/k$, is at least $\lg k$. ∎

12.2.1 The complexity of sorting

What is the minimum number of comparisons needed to sort n items? For simplicity we count only comparisons between the items to be sorted, ignoring those that may be made to control the loops in our program. We saw in Section 2.7.2 that the answer is "none"! Indeed, pigeonhole sorting does not need any comparisons provided enough storage space is available. However, it is useful only in special circumstances. To make the question interesting, we restrict our attention to *comparison-based* sorting algorithms: the only operation allowed on the items to be sorted consists of comparing them pairwise to determine whether they are equal and, if not, which is the greater. In particular, arithmetic is disallowed on the items to be sorted. Note that pigeonhole sorting performs implicit arithmetic because indexing in an array involves adding the index to the array's base address. The difference between allowing arithmetic on the items and restricting the algorithm to comparing them is similar to the difference between hash coding and binary search.

Our question is thus: what is the minimum number of comparisons needed in any algorithm for sorting n items by comparison? Although the theorems in this section hold even if we consider probabilistic sorting algorithms, we shall for simplicity confine our discussion to deterministic algorithms. We resort once again to decision trees. A decision tree for sorting n items is *valid* if to each possible order relation between the items to be sorted it associates a verdict compatible with this relation. For example, Figure 12.3 is a valid decision tree for sorting A, B and C.

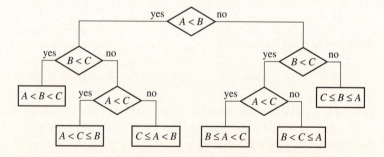

Figure 12.3. A valid decision tree for sorting three items

Every valid decision tree for sorting n items gives rise to an *ad hoc* sorting algorithm for the same number of items. For example, to the decision tree of Figure 12.3 there corresponds the following algorithm.

procedure *adhocsort3*($T[1..3]$)
   $A \leftarrow T[1]$; $B \leftarrow T[2]$; $C \leftarrow T[3]$
   if $A < B$ **then if** $B < C$ **then** {already sorted}
                           else if $A < C$ **then** $T \leftarrow A, C, B$
                                  else $T \leftarrow C, A, B$
              else if $B < C$ **then if** $A < C$ **then** $T \leftarrow B, A, C$
                                  else $T \leftarrow B, C, A$
                    else $T \leftarrow C, B, A$

Similarly, to every deterministic algorithm for sorting by comparison there corresponds, for each value of n, a decision tree that is valid for sorting n items. Figures 12.4 and 12.5 give the trees corresponding to the insertion sorting algorithm (Section 2.4) and to *heapsort* (Section 5.7) when three items are to be sorted. The annotations on the trees are intended to help follow the progress of the corresponding algorithms. Notice that *heapsort* sometimes makes unnecessary comparisons. For instance, if $B \leq A < C$, the decision tree of Figure 12.5 first tests whether $B > A$ (answer: no), and then whether $C > A$ (answer: yes). It would now be possible to establish the correct verdict. Nevertheless, *heapsort* asks again whether $B > A$ before reaching its conclusion. To avoid unreachable nodes in the decision tree, we did not include the leaf that would correspond to the contradictory answer "yes" to this useless question; the tree is therefore pruned. Thus *heapsort* is not optimal insofar as the number of comparisons is concerned. This situation does not occur with the decision tree of Figure 12.4, but beware of appearances: it occurs much more frequently with the insertion sorting algorithm than with *heapsort* when the number of items to be sorted increases.

As with the game of twenty questions, the height of the decision tree corresponding to any algorithm for sorting n items by comparison gives the number of comparisons carried out by this algorithm in the worst case. For example, a possible worst case for sorting three items by insertion is encountered if the array is already in descending order $C < B < A$; in this case the three comparisons "$B < A$?", "$C < A$?" and "$C < B$?" on the path from the root to the appropriate verdict in the decision tree all have to be made.

The decision trees we have seen for sorting three items are all of height 3. Can we find a valid decision tree for sorting three items whose height is less? If so, we shall have an ad hoc algorithm for sorting three items that is more efficient in the worst case. Try it: you will soon see that it cannot be done. The reason is that any correct sorting algorithm must be able to produce at least six different verdicts when $n = 3$ since this is the number of permutations of three items. In the worst case, solving the three-item sorting problem in less than three comparisons is just as impossible—and for the same reason—as guessing an integer between 1 and 6 with less than three questions.

More generally, any valid decision tree for sorting n items must contain at least $n!$ leaves, and thus it must have height at least $\lceil \lg n! \rceil$ and average height

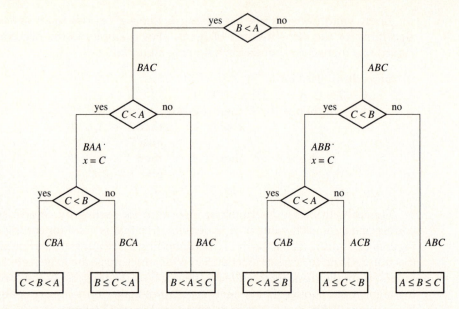

Figure 12.4. The three-item insertion sort decision tree

at least lg n! by Problem 12.1 and Theorem 12.2.1. This translates directly into the complexity of sorting: any algorithm that sorts n items by comparisons must make at least $\lceil \lg n! \rceil$ comparisons in the worst case and lg n! on the average, provided all verdicts are equally likely. Since each comparison must take at least some constant amount of time and since lg $n! \in \Theta(n \log n)$ by Problem 3.24, it follows that it takes a time in $\Omega(n \log n)$ to sort n items both in the worst case and on the average, no matter which comparison-based sorting algorithm is used. Thus we see that *quicksort* is optimal on the average, even though its worst-case performance is pitiful; see Section 7.4.2.

We have proved that any deterministic algorithm for sorting by comparison must make at least $\lceil \lg n! \rceil$ comparisons in the worst case when sorting n items. Beware of making complexity arguments such as these say things they do not say. In particular, the decision tree argument does *not* imply that it is always possible to sort n items with as few as $\lceil \lg n! \rceil$ comparisons in the worst case. In fact, it has been proved that 30 comparisons are necessary and sufficient in the worst case for sorting 12 items, yet $\lceil \lg 12! \rceil = 29$.

In the worst case, the insertion sorting algorithm makes 66 comparisons when sorting 12 items, whereas *heapsort* makes 59, of which the first 18 are made during construction of the heap. Hence they are both far from optimal. However, it can be shown that *heapsort* never makes much more than twice the optimal number of comparisons, whereas insertion sorting becomes arbitrarily bad when the number of items to be sorted becomes large. Even better than *heapsort* from this standpoint is *mergesort*, which makes a number of comparisons that is essentially optimal; see Problem 12.7. Do not believe that optimizing the number of comparisons is

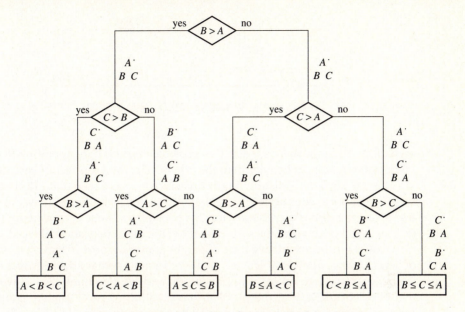

Figure 12.5. The three-item *heapsort* decision tree

a goal in itself, however: sorting by *binary insertion* makes as few comparisons as *mergesort*, yet this requires a quadratic amount of data movement—and hence time—in the worst case. (This is like insertion sorting except that the point at which each successive item is to be inserted is determined by binary rather than sequential search.)

12.2.2 Complexity to the rescue of algorithmics

Sometimes, techniques developed for computational complexity are useful for the design of efficient algorithms. We illustrate this with a classic mindtwister. We are given 12 coins and told that either they are all identical in weight or else 11 of them are identical and one is different. Our task is to decide whether all the coins are the same, and if not to find the odd coin and say whether it is lighter or heavier than the others. To this end, we are given a balance scale. The only operation allowed is to put some coins on the left-hand pan, some others on the right-hand pan, and to see whether the weights are the same or whether the scale tilts one way or the other. Figure 12.6 illustrates weighing two sets of four coins and finding that the left-hand side is heavier than the right-hand side. To make the problem challenging, we are restricted to using the scale only three times. We recommend putting down the book and trying to find a solution on your own. Even if you succeed, you may find the discussion below interesting.

   Any algorithm to solve this problem can be represented by a decision tree. Each internal node specifies which coins are in each pan of the scale and each leaf gives a verdict such as "coin D is heavier". The tree must be of height at most 3 since we are not allowed to make more than three measurements. How many verdicts must we accommodate? One possible verdict is that all the coins are identical; for

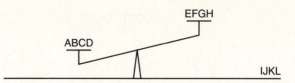

Figure 12.6. Weighing ABCD against EFGH

each of the 12 coins, there are also two possible verdicts corresponding to that coin being either lighter or heavier than the others. The total number of verdicts is thus $1 + 12 \times 2 = 25$. This is disquieting at first since we have seen that a decision tree of height 3 cannot accommodate more than $2^3 = 8$ verdicts. Fortunately, our decision tree is ternary rather than binary for this problem because each measurement has three possible outcomes: the scale may tilt to the left, it may stay balanced, or it may tilt to the right. Just as binary trees of height k have at most 2^k leaves, ternary trees of height k have at most 3^k leaves. All is well since a ternary decision tree of height 3 can accommodate up to $3^3 = 27$ verdicts and we need only 25. Nevertheless, this does not prove that the problem has a solution: recall that 30 comparisons are required in the worst case to sort 12 items even though $\lceil \lg 12! \rceil = 29$. See also Problem 12.12.

   Decision trees are useful for finding the solution because they help us avoid false starts. The key insight is that there must remain at most $3^2 = 9$ possible verdicts for each of the three potential outcomes of the first measurement. Otherwise, there would be no hope of solving the problem in the worst case with only two additional measurements. Note also that it is pointless to use the scale with a different number of coins on each pan: no useful information can be extracted if the pan tilts to the side containing more coins. Therefore, we first use the scale to compare two sets of k coins, for some $1 \le k \le 6$. If the scale stays balanced, the odd coin can be any of the $12 - 2k$ remaining coins, which leaves $25 - 4k$ possible verdicts, counting the possibility that all the coins are the same. If the scale tilts to one side, on the other hand, it could be because one of the coins on that side is heavier or because one of the coins on the other side is lighter, leaving $2k$ possible verdicts. As we have seen, there is no hope of solving the problem if there remain more than 9 possible verdicts after the first measurement. Thus, we need simultaneously $25 - 4k \le 9$ and $2k \le 9$. The only integer solution to these equations is $k = 4$. This reasoning still does not prove that a solution can be found if we start by comparing two sets of four coins, but it does tell us that there is no point trying anything else.

   There are two cases to consider after the first measurement: either one set weighs more than the other or the two sets weigh the same. In either case, the second measurement must be such that at most three verdicts remain possible after its outcome becomes known. This is because the final measurement cannot distinguish between more than three possibilities. If one set is found heavier than the other in the first measurement, reasoning similar to the above shows that the second measurement must involve either 5 or 6 of the 8 coins used in the first measurement. Knowing this, it is easy to fill in the details and work out exactly the last two measurements.

The situation is more interesting if both sets weigh the same in the first measurement: we are left with what looks like the original problem, except that we have four coins rather than twelve and we are allowed only two measurements rather than three. Using information-theoretic arguments yet again, it does not take long to realize that this scaled-down version of the problem has no solution (Problem 12.13), and it seems at first that this nails the coffin on the original problem as well. What saves us is that we are allowed to use some of the eight coins that participated in the first measurement even though we know the coin we are looking for is not among them. Since information-theoretic arguments tell us we cannot succeed if we don't use at least one of those initial coins, we know we have to try this if we are to succeed at all. At this point, not much challenge is left and we invite you to work Problem 12.11 for the details.

12.3 Adversary arguments

Given a problem, we wish to prove a lower bound on the time required in the worst case by any algorithm that solves it correctly on all instances. Throughout this section, we shall assume for simplicity that the algorithms are deterministic, although probabilistic algorithms can be taken into account with more careful arguments. The idea behind adversary arguments is to start the algorithm on an input that is initially unspecified, except for its size. Whenever the algorithm probes the input, a malevolent dæmon, known as the adversary, answers in a way that will force the algorithm to work hard. The dæmon must be consistent in the sense that there must always exist at least one input that would cause the algorithm to see exactly the dæmon's answers on each of its probes. The dæmon's goal is to keep the algorithm uncertain of the correct answer for as long as possible. If the algorithm claims to know the answer before it has probed the input a sufficient number of times, the dæmon must be able to exhibit a possible input that is consistent with all its answers to the algorithm's probes, yet whose correct solution is different from the output of the algorithm. Since this could have been the actual input for the algorithm, the latter can be mistaken unless it probes the input sufficiently in the worst case.

Consider again the game of twenty questions introduced in Section 12.1. The honest way for your friend to play the game is for her to choose a number between 1 and one million even before you ask your first question. If she is sneaky, however, she may delay her choice for as long as possible, making it depend on your actual questions. Her goal is to answer each question in a way that is consistent with previous answers, but also in a way that forces you to ask as many questions as possible. When you ask question Q_i, she forms the sets N_i and Y_i described in Section 12.1, and answers "yes" if and only if Y_i contains more elements than N_i. She is forced to decide on her mystery number only when there remains a unique candidate. In this way, no matter which strategy you use, your friend makes sure that you never do better than halve the number of candidates with each question. Should you claim to know the answer after fewer than 20 questions, more than one candidate remains, so at least one number different from your output is consistent with all the information you have. Your friend could then "prove" you wrong by pretending she had chosen her number from the beginning to be one of those.

Once information-theoretic arguments are well understood, they are easier to use than adversary arguments to prove that 20 questions are required in the worst case to play this game. However, there are problems for which information-theoretic arguments are powerless, whereas adversary arguments can be used. We now give three such examples. The first two are elementary, whereas the third is more involved.

12.3.1 Finding the maximum of an array

Consider an array $T[1 .. n]$ of integers. We assume $n > 0$. Our task is to find the index of a maximum value attained by the array. For example, if $n = 7$ and $T = [2, 7, 1, 8, 2, 8, 1]$, both 4 and 6 are correct answers since $T[4] = T[6] = 8$ is the largest value in the array. As with comparison-based sorting (Section 12.2.1), the only operation allowed on the items is to compare them pairwise. The obvious algorithm performs exactly $n - 1$ comparisons.

> **function** $maxindex(T[1 .. n])$
> $m \leftarrow T[1]; \ k \leftarrow 1$
>   **for** $i \leftarrow 2$ **to** n **do**
>   **if** $T[i] > m$ **then** $m \leftarrow T[i]$
> $k \leftarrow i$
>   **return** k

Is it possible to do better?

If we try to use an information-theoretic argument, we find that any decision tree for this problem must accommodate n possible verdicts. Since the tree is binary, it must have height at least $\lceil \lg n \rceil$. Therefore, any comparison-based algorithm to find the maximum must perform at least $\lceil \lg n \rceil$ comparisons in the worst case. This is a far cry from $n - 1$, the best we know how to achieve. Can adversary arguments provide a tighter lower bound?

Consider an arbitrary comparison-based algorithm for this problem. Let it run on an array $T[1 .. n]$, as yet unspecified. The dæmon answers any question concerning a comparison between items as if $T[i]$ were equal to i for all i. Each time the algorithm asks "Is $T[i] < T[j]$?" for $i \neq j$, we say that the smaller of i and j has "lost a comparison". Assume the algorithm performs less than $n - 1$ comparisons before it outputs the answer k. Let j be an integer different from k, $1 \leq j \leq n$, that has not lost any comparisons. Such a j exists since by assumption at most $n - 2$ comparisons have been performed and each comparison makes at most one new loser. At this point, the dæmon can claim that the algorithm is wrong. For this, it pretends that $T[i] = i$ for each $i \neq j$ but that $T[j] = n + 1$. Indeed, $T[k] = k$ is not maximum in this array, yet the answers obtained by the algorithm are consistent with it. This completes the proof that $n - 1$ comparisons are necessary to solve the maximum problem with any comparison-based algorithm.

This result does not hold if arithmetic is allowed on the items in addition to comparisons. To do better, compute $a = \sum_{i=1}^{\ell} n^{T[i]}$ and $b = \sum_{i=\ell+1}^{n} n^{T[i]}$, where

$\ell = \lceil n/2 \rceil$. If there is an item x in $T[1 .. \ell]$ that is larger than any item in $T[\ell + 1 .. n]$, then $a > b$ because

$$\sum_{i=1}^{\ell} n^{T[i]} \ge n^x > \tfrac{1}{2} n \times n^{x-1} \ge \sum_{i=\ell+1}^{n} n^{T[i]}.$$

Similarly, $a < b$ if the maximum of T is in the second half. If the maximum appears in both halves, any relation between a and b is possible. Thus, a single comparison between a and b suffices to determine whether the maximum is in the first or the second half of T. Proceeding as with binary search allows us to find the answer after at most $\lceil \lg n \rceil$ comparisons. Of course, it would be silly to use this approach in practice since it trades inexpensive comparisons for a larger number of time-consuming arithmetic operations.

12.3.2 Testing graph connectivity

Consider an algorithm that tests whether or not an undirected graph with n vertices, $n \ge 2$, is connected. The only questions allowed are of the form "Is there an edge between vertices i and j?" We know from Section 9.3 that this problem can be solved by depth-first search, which takes a time in $O(n^2)$ in the worst case. Can it be solved faster by a more sophisticated algorithm? Information-theoretic arguments are useless with this problem because there are only two possible verdicts: either the graph is connected or it is not. Thus the decision tree has height at least 1, which says that the algorithm must ask at least one question. Big deal!

To devise an adversary argument, the dæmon splits the vertex set into two subsets V and W of sizes $\lfloor n/2 \rfloor$ and $\lceil n/2 \rceil$, respectively. Whenever the algorithm asks whether or not there is an edge between vertices i and j, the dæmon says "yes" if and only if both vertices belong to the same subset. If the algorithm claims to know the answer before inquiring about the presence of each potential edge whose endpoints are in not in the same subset, the dæmon can prove it wrong as follows. If the algorithm claims the graph is connected, the dæmon shows the disconnected graph that has an edge between vertices i and j if and only if these vertices are in the same subset. This graph is disconnected because there are no paths between vertices in V and vertices in W. On the other hand, if the algorithm claims the graph is disconnected, the dæmon shows the connected graph obtained in the same way, but throwing in one additional edge between V and W that has not been queried by the algorithm. Such an edge exists by the assumption that the algorithm did not query all the potential edges of this type. Clearly, the dæmon produces a graph consistent with the algorithm's queries that is connected if and only if the algorithm said it was not. This proves that any algorithm that does not ask at least $\lfloor n/2 \rfloor \times \lceil n/2 \rceil \in \Omega(n^2)$ questions in the worst case cannot be correct. Therefore, depth-first search is optimal in the worst case up to the hidden multiplicative constant.

Do not conclude that it is enough to ask $\lfloor n/2 \rfloor \times \lceil n/2 \rceil$ questions to solve the problem in general. One difficulty is that the algorithm does not know which strategy the dæmon will use, and even if it did, it would not know how the vertex set was split between V and W. In fact, it can be shown by a more sophisticated adversary argument that in the worst case each of the $n(n-1)/2$ potential edges must be queried by any correct algorithm; see Problem 12.16.

12.3.3 The median revisited

We saw in Section 7.5 that a number of comparisons in $O(n)$ is sufficient to find the median of an array $T[1..n]$ of integers. Clearly a time in $\Omega(n)$ is also necessary because when all the items are distinct we must look at each of them at least once. With any comparison-based algorithm, the trivial lower bound on the exact number of comparisons is thus $\lceil n/2 \rceil$ because each comparison looks at only two items and all of them must be looked at. Can we find a more interesting lower bound?

Assume for simplicity that n is odd and $n \geq 3$. We shall prove that at least $3(n-1)/2$ comparisons are necessary for any comparison-based algorithm to locate the median in the worst case. If the algorithm does not make this many comparisons, the dæmon can force it to give an incorrect answer. Without loss of generality, we assume the algorithm never compares an item with itself; if it did, the dæmon would respond with the only reasonable answer. We assume also that each item of T is involved in at least one comparison requested by the algorithm. Otherwise, it is impossible for the algorithm to locate the median with certainty, and the dæmon's task would be easy. This is true because we shall see that the dæmon never sets two items of T to the same value.

Initially, the dæmon sets each entry in T to "uninitialized". As the algorithm makes comparisons, the dæmon changes these values. Some items of T are set to values between 1 and n, whereas others are set to values between $3n+1$ and $4n$. We call those values "low" and "high", respectively. The dæmon makes sure there are always as many low items as there are high. Intuitively, low items will be smaller than the median and high items will be larger. However, the dæmon may change the values of T whenever it wishes, provided the answers it gave to the algorithm previously are still valid. Thus one of the formerly low or high items may turn out to be the median in the end. Each time the algorithm asks for a comparison that involves $T[i]$ and $T[j]$, there are three possibilities.

◇ If both $T[i]$ and $T[j]$ are uninitialized, the dæmon sets $T[i]$ to i and $T[j]$ to $3n+j$. Thus, $T[i]$ becomes low and $T[j]$ becomes high.

◇ If only one of $T[i]$ and $T[j]$ is initialized, there are five subcases.

  – If a single item of T remains uninitialized, the dæmon sets its value to $2n$, which is neither low nor high. This item becomes the *provisional median*: all the low items are smaller, all the high items are larger, and there are as many low as there are high items. However, the median may prove to be elsewhere in the end.

  – Otherwise, if $T[i]$ is low, the dæmon sets $T[j]$ to the high value $3n+j$. To restore the balance between low and high items, it selects an arbitrary uninitialized $T[k]$ and sets it to the low value k.

- If $T[j]$ is low, the dæmon acts as in the previous subcase with i and j interchanged.

- If $T[i]$ is high, the dæmon sets $T[j]$ to the low value j. To restore the balance between low and high items, it selects an arbitrary uninitialized $T[k]$ and sets it to the high value $3n + k$.

- If $T[j]$ is high, the dæmon acts as in the previous subcase with i and j interchanged.

◇ Otherwise, both $T[i]$ and $T[j]$ are initialized. If they are both low or if one is low and the other is the provisional median, we say of the smaller that "it has lost a comparison"; if they are both high or if one is high and the other is the provisional median, we say of the larger that "it has lost a comparison". Neither loses a comparison if one is low and the other is high.

Finally, the dæmon answers the algorithm's request for a comparison in accordance with the current values of $T[i]$ and $T[j]$.

Now assume the algorithm makes less than $3(n-1)/2$ comparisons before it outputs its guess of the median. Because items of T become initialized in pairs, except for the provisional median, and because we assumed that each item is involved in at least one comparison, exactly $(n-1)/2$ comparisons were of the first or second type above. Consequently, less than $\frac{3}{2}(n-1) - \frac{1}{2}(n-1) = n-1$ comparisons involved two items already initialized. Since items can lose a comparison only in this case, at least one item in addition to the provisional median never lost a comparison. Call it $T[i]$. Assume without loss of generality that it is low. By the definition of losing a comparison, the dæmon never had to admit to the algorithm that this item is smaller than any other low item or than the provisional median. Therefore, no contradiction appears if the dæmon changes its mind and increases $T[i]$, provided it keeps it smaller than any high item. This gives the dæmon a choice of keeping $T[i] = i$ so that the provisional median is indeed the final median, or of resetting $T[i] = 2n + 1$ so $T[i]$ becomes the final median. Whichever answer was returned by the algorithm, the dæmon can thus exhibit an array T with a different median even though it is consistent with all the answers seen by the algorithm. This proves that the algorithm is incorrect unless it makes at least $3(n-1)/2$ comparisons in the worst case.

12.4 Linear reductions

We saw that any algorithm for sorting by comparison takes a minimum time in $\Omega(n \log n)$ to sort n items, both on the average and in the worst case. On the other hand, we know that *heapsort* and *mergesort* both solve the problem in a time in $O(n \log n)$. Except for the value of the multiplicative constant, the question of the complexity of sorting by comparison is therefore settled: a time in $\Theta(n \log n)$ is both necessary and sufficient for sorting n items. Unfortunately, it does not often happen in the present state of our ignorance that the bounds derived from algorithmics and complexity meet so satisfactorily.

Because it is so difficult to determine the exact complexity of most of the problems we meet in practice, we often have to be content to compare the relative difficulty of different problems. We say that a problem *reduces* to another if we can efficiently transform instances of the first problem into instances of the second in such a way that solving the transformed instance yields the answer to the original instance. Suppose we prove that a certain number of problems are equivalent in the sense that they each reduce to one another. As a result, these problems all have about the same complexity: any algorithmic improvement in the method of solution of one of them now automatically yields, at least in theory, a more efficient algorithm for all the others. From a negative point of view, if these problems have all been studied independently in the past, and if all the efforts to find an efficient algorithm for any one of them have failed, then the fact that the problems are equivalent makes it even more unlikely that such an algorithm exists. Section 12.5 goes into this second motivation in more detail.

We encountered an example of reduction already: in Section 10.7.4 we saw that factorization reduces to splitting and primality testing. Similarly, both splitting and primality testing obviously reduce to factorization because they are immediately solved once the number under consideration has been factorized as a product of prime numbers. Even though we do not know the exact complexity of these problems, this says that factorization is of similar difficulty to the combined tasks of splitting and primality testing.

Another simple example concerns multiplying and squaring large integers. We saw in Section 7.1 that it is possible to multiply two n-figure numbers in a time in $O(n^{1.59})$, which improves on the classic quadratic-time algorithm. Can we do better? We saw in Problems 7.2 and 7.3 that the answer is "yes": we can multiply in a time in $O(n^\alpha)$ for any real number $\alpha > 1$, although the hidden multiplicative constant grows when α becomes smaller. Even better, Schönhage and Strassen discovered a multiplication algorithm that takes a time in $O(n \log n \log \log n)$. Is *this* the best possible? Finding a better algorithm is a matter for algorithmics; proving that this algorithm is optimal is a concern for complexity. Unfortunately, no nontrivial lower bound on the complexity of multiplication is known. Multiplying two n-figure numbers obviously requires a time in $\Omega(n)$ because each digit of the operands must be looked at. For all we know a yet undiscovered multiplication algorithm may exist that meets this bound by multiplying in a time in $O(n)$.

Consider now the apparently simpler problem of squaring large integers. Could *it* be handled in linear time whereas multiplication cannot? Even though the exact complexity of squaring is as elusive as that of multiplication, there is one thing we know how to prove: up to a small multiplicative constant, they require the same time. Therefore, one of them can be solved in linear time if and only if they both can. More interestingly, any significant algorithmic improvement on the art of squaring would yield a better multiplication algorithm. Intuitively, this follows from two formulas that relate the problems to one another.

$$x^2 \quad = x \times x$$

$$x \times y \quad = \frac{(x + y)^2 - (x - y)^2}{4}$$

From these formulas we see that one squaring cannot be harder than one multiplication, which is no big surprise, whereas one multiplication cannot be much harder than two squarings.

Formally, we prove the computational equivalence of these problems by exhibiting two algorithms. Each solves one problem by calling on an arbitrary algorithm for the other. These algorithms could be used to teach one operation to someone who only knows how to perform the other.

function *square*(x)
   return *mult*(x, x)

function *mult*(x, y)
   return ($square$($x + y$)$-square$($x - y$))$/4$

Let $M(n)$ and $S(n)$ be respectively the time needed to multiply and to square integers of size at most n. The first algorithm makes it plain that $S(n) \leq M(n)+c$ for a small constant c that takes account of the overhead in *square* over and above the time it spends inside *mult*. Therefore, $S(n) \in O(M(n))$.

The second algorithm must be analysed with slightly more care because $x + y$ can be one digit longer than x and y. Assume without loss of generality that $x \geq y$ to avoid worrying about the possibility that $x - y$ might be negative. Thus

$$M(n) \leq S(n + 1)+S(n)+f(n), \qquad\qquad (12.1)$$

where $f(n)$ is the time needed to perform the addition, subtractions and division by 4 required by the algorithm, in addition to the overhead in *mult*. We know already that additions and subtractions can be performed in linear time. Division by 4 is trivial if the numbers are represented in binary and it can be done in linear time even if another base is used; see Problem 12.21. Thus $f(n) \in O(n)$ is negligible since both $M(n)$ and $S(n)$ are in $\Omega(n)$. However, Equation 12.1 is not sufficient to conclude that $M(n) \in O(S(n))$. Consider what would happen if the squaring algorithm were so inept as to take a time in $\Theta(n!)$ to square an n-figure number. In this case, multiplication of two numbers of that size could take a time in $\Theta((n + 1)!)$, which is about n times bigger than the time spent to square one such number. Nevertheless, $M(n) \in O(S(n))$ does follow from a reasonable assumption; see Theorem 12.4.4 below. Thus we conclude that the problems of integer multiplication and squaring have the same complexity up to a multiplicative factor.

What can we say about other elementary arithmetic operations such as integer division and taking a square root? Everyday experience leads us to believe that the second of these problems, and probably also the first, is genuinely more difficult than multiplication. This turns out not to be true. Under reasonable assumptions, it takes the same time to multiply two n-figure numbers, to compute the quotient when a $2n$-figure number is divided by an n-figure number, and to compute the integer part of the square root of an n-figure number. This is brought about by exotic formulas such as

$$x^2 = \cfrac{1}{\cfrac{1}{x} - \cfrac{1}{x+1}} - x$$

$$\tfrac{1}{x} \approx \sqrt{x + \sqrt{x+1} - \sqrt{x-1}} - \sqrt{x - \sqrt{x+1} + \sqrt{x-1}}$$

and classic techniques such as Newton's method to find zeros of functions. Work Problems 12.27 and 12.28 for more detail.

In addition to its usefulness for complexity purposes, the fact that one multiplication reduces to two squarings is interesting from an algorithmic point of view: it provides an instructive example of preconditioning; see Section 9.2. Pretend for the sake of argument that you are a Roman and that you know no other notation for numbers. If you must frequently multiply numbers between 1 and 1000, you may find it worthwhile to compile a multiplication table once and for all. However, this table will span more than half a million entries even if you only compile the product of x and y when $x \geq y$. A better solution is to compile a table of values for $x^2/4$ for all x between 1 and 2000. (You will have to invent a pseudo-Roman symbol to denote one-quarter.) Once you have this table, you can perform any required multiplication with one addition and two subtractions, together with two table look-ups.

12.4.1 Formal definitions

> **Definition 12.4.1** *Let* A *and* B *be two problems. We say that* A *is* linearly reducible *to* B*, denoted* A $\leq^\ell$ B*, if the existence of an algorithm for* B *that works in a time in* $O(t(n))$ *for an arbitrary function* $t(n)$ *implies that there exists an algorithm for* A *that also works in a time in* $O(t(n))$*. When* A $\leq^\ell$ B *and* B $\leq^\ell$ A *both hold, we say that* A *and* B *are* linearly equivalent *and write* A $\equiv^\ell$ B*.*

Intuitively, A $\leq^\ell$ B means that someone who knows how to handle problem B can easily be taught how to handle problem A as well. It follows from Problem 3.10 that linear reductions are transitive: if A $\leq^\ell$ B and B $\leq^\ell$ C, then A $\leq^\ell$ C. Linear equivalences are also transitive, in addition to being reflexive and symmetric.

Formally, we prove A $\leq^\ell$ B by exhibiting an algorithm that solves an instance of A by transforming it into one or more instances of problem B. The conclusion that A $\leq^\ell$ B follows immediately if the required instances for problem B are the same size as the original instance of problem A, if a constant number of them are required, and if the amount of work in addition to solving those instances is not larger (up to a multiplicative constant) than the time required to solve problem B. For example, we saw that one integer squaring reduces to a single multiplication of the same size plus a constant amount of work. Thus integer squaring linearly reduces to integer multiplication.

The situation is more complicated when solving instances of size n of problem A involves instances of problem B of a different size or when it involves a number of instances of problem B that is not bounded by a constant. For example, one integer multiplication reduces to two integer squarings, one of which can be of a slightly larger size. To handle such situations precisely, we must derive a formula for the time taken by the reduction algorithm to solve an instance of size n of problem A as a function of the time required to solve problem B on instances of arbitrary size. Equation 12.1 is typical of this approach. To conclude the desired relation between the times taken to solve both problems, however, it is usually necessary to make assumptions that involve the concept of smoothness introduced in Section 3.4 and other concepts introduced below.

Recall that function $f : \mathbb{N} \to \mathbb{R}^{\geq 0}$ is smooth if it is eventually nondecreasing and if $f(bn) \in O(f(n))$ for every integer $b \geq 2$. We extend this definition to algorithms and problems.

Definition 12.4.2   *An* algorithm *is* smooth *if it takes a time in* $\Theta(t(n))$ *for some smooth function* $t(n)$. *A* problem *is* smooth *if any reasonable algorithm that solves it is smooth. (By "reasonable" we mean that the algorithm is not purposely slower than necessary; see below.)*

Even though a smooth function must be eventually nondecreasing by definition, this does not imply that the actual time taken by a specific implementation of a smooth algorithm must also be given by an eventually nondecreasing function. Consider for example the modular exponentiation algorithm *expomod* of Section 7.8. It takes longer with this algorithm to compute a $(2^k - 1)$–st power than a 2^k-th power for any large k, and thus the actual time taken by any reasonable implementation of this algorithm is *not* an eventually nondecreasing function of the exponent. Nevertheless, this algorithm *is* smooth because it takes a time in $\Theta(\log n)$ to compute an n–th power, counting the multiplications at unit cost, and $\log n$ is a smooth function. The restriction that the algorithm be reasonable in the definition of a smooth problem is necessary because any problem that can be solved at all can be solved by an algorithm that takes a time in $\Omega(2^n)$—begin the algorithm by a useless loop that counts from 1 to 2^n—and such an algorithm cannot be smooth; see Problem 12.22. Another example of an unreasonable algorithm would be one that sorts n items by systematically trying all $n!$ permutations until one is found that is sorted: this is unreasonable because there exist obvious sorting algorithms that are much more efficient.

Definition 12.4.3   *A function* $t : \mathbb{N} \to \mathbb{R}^{\geq 0}$ *is* at least quadratic *if* $t(n) \in \Omega(n^2)$. *It is* strongly quadratic *if it is eventually nondecreasing and if* $t(an) \geq a^2 t(n)$ *for every positive integer* a *and every sufficiently large integer* n. *At least and strongly* linear *functions are defined similarly. These notions extend to algorithms and problems as in the case of smooth functions.*

It is easy to show that strongly quadratic functions are at least quadratic. Most of the theorems that follow are stated conditionally on a "reasonable" assumption, such as A $\leq^\ell$ B assuming B is smooth. This can be interpreted literally as meaning that A $\leq^\ell$ B follows under the assumption that B is smooth. From a more practical point of view it also means that, for any smooth function $t(n)$, the existence of an algorithm for B that works in a time in $O(t(n))$ implies that there exists an algorithm for A that also works in a time in $O(t(n))$. Moreover, all these theorems are constructive: the algorithm for A follows from the algorithm for B and the proof of the corresponding theorem.

We are now in a position to state precisely and demonstrate the linear equivalence between integer squaring and multiplication.

Theorem 12.4.4 *Let* **SQR** *and* **MLT** *be the problems consisting of squaring an integer of size* n *and of multiplying two integers of size* n, *respectively. Under the assumption that* **SQR** *is smooth, the two problems are linearly equivalent.*

Proof   We argued previously that both problems must be at least linear. Let $M(n)$ and $S(n)$ respectively be the times needed to multiply and to square operands of size at most n. We saw that there exist a constant c and a function $f(n) \in O(n)$ such that $S(n) \leq M(n)+c$ and $M(n) \leq S(n+1)+S(n)+f(n)$. Because $M(n)$ is at least linear, $M(n) \geq c$ for all sufficiently large n. Therefore, $S(n) \leq 2M(n)$, also for all sufficiently large n, which implies by definition that $S(n) \in O(M(n))$ and thus **SQR** $\leq^\ell$ **MLT**.

For the other direction, assume that $S(n) \in \Theta(s(n))$ for some smooth function $s(n)$. Let a, b_1 and b_2 be appropriate constants such that $s(2n) \leq as(n)$, $S(n) \leq b_1 s(n)$ and $s(n) \leq b_2 S(n)$ for all sufficiently large n. Because any smooth function is eventually nondecreasing by definition,

$$S(n+1) \leq b_1 s(n+1) \leq b_1 s(2n) \leq b_1 as(n) \leq b_1 ab_2 S(n)$$

for all sufficiently large n. Because $f(n) \in O(n)$ and $S(n) \in \Omega(n)$, there exists a constant d such that $f(n) \leq dS(n)$ for all sufficiently large n. Putting it all together, we conclude that

$$M(n) \leq S(n+1)+S(n)+f(n) \leq (b_1 ab_2 + 1 + d)\, S(n)$$

for all sufficiently large n, and thus $M(n) \in O(S(n))$ and **MLT** $\leq^\ell$ **SQR** by definition. ∎

We give more examples of linear reductions below, and we suggest others in the exercises. In Section 12.5.2, we shall study the notion of *polynomial* reduction, which is coarser than that of linear reduction, but easier to use because it does not require the notions introduced in Definitions 12.4.2 and 12.4.3. It is also more general.

12.4.2 Reductions among matrix problems

Recall that an $m \times n$ matrix is *square* if $m = n$. An *upper triangular* matrix is a square matrix M whose entries below the diagonal are all zero: $M_{ij} = 0$ when $i > j$. The *transpose* of an $m \times n$ matrix M is the $n \times m$ matrix M^t defined by $M^t_{ij} = M_{ji}$. A matrix M is *symmetric* if it is equal to its own transpose, which implies that it must be square. A square matrix M is *nonsingular* if there exists a matrix N such that $M \times N = I$, the identity matrix; this matrix N is called the *inverse* of M and is denoted M^{-1}.

We saw in Section 7.6 that a time in $O(n^{2.81})$—or even $O(n^{2.376})$—is sufficient to multiply two arbitrary $n \times n$ matrices, contrary to intuition that suggests that this problem inevitably requires a time in $\Omega(n^3)$. Is it possible that the multiplication of upper triangular matrices could be carried out significantly faster than the multiplication of arbitrary square matrices? How about symmetric matrices? More interestingly, experience might well lead us to believe that inverting nonsingular matrices should be inherently more difficult than multiplying them.

We denote the problems of multiplying arbitrary square matrices, multiplying upper triangular square matrices, multiplying symmetric matrices and inverting nonsingular upper triangular matrices, by MQ, MT, MS and IT, respectively. We shall prove under reasonable assumptions that these four problems are linearly equivalent. The problem of inverting an *arbitrary* nonsingular matrix is also linearly equivalent to these problems, but the proof of this is more difficult and it requires a stronger assumption; see Problem 12.31. Note however that the resulting algorithm is numerically unstable. Consequently, we can invert any nonsingular $n \times n$ matrix in a time in $O(n^{2.376})$—at least in theory. Moreover, any new algorithm to multiply upper triangular or symmetric matrices more efficiently will also provide a new, more efficient algorithm for inverting arbitrary nonsingular matrices.

In what follows we measure the complexity of algorithms that manipulate $n \times n$ matrices in terms of n, referring for example to an algorithm that runs in a time in $\Theta(n^2)$ as quadratic. Formally speaking, this is incorrect because the running time should be given as a function of the *size* of the instance, so a time in $\Theta(n^2)$ is really linear. All the problems considered are at least quadratic in the worst case because any algorithm that solves them must look at each entry of the matrix or matrices concerned. We proceed to prove the linear equivalence of our matrix problems by a sequence of reductions: we prove that $\text{MT} \leq^\ell \text{MQ}$, $\text{MS} \leq^\ell \text{MQ}$, $\text{MQ} \leq^\ell \text{MT}$, $\text{MQ} \leq^\ell \text{MS}$, $\text{MQ} \leq^\ell \text{IT}$ and $\text{IT} \leq^\ell \text{MQ}$. This implies that $\text{MQ} \equiv^\ell \text{MT}$, $\text{MQ} \equiv^\ell \text{MS}$ and $\text{MQ} \equiv^\ell \text{IT}$. The equivalence of all four problems follows immediately by the transitivity of linear equivalences.

Theorem 12.4.5 $\text{MT} \leq^\ell \text{MQ}$ *and* $\text{MQ} \leq^\ell \text{MS}$.

Proof   Any algorithm that can multiply two arbitrary square matrices can be used directly for multiplying upper triangular and symmetric matrices.   ∎

Theorem 12.4.6   MQ$\leq^{\ell}$ MT, *assuming* MT *is smooth.*

Proof   Suppose there exists an algorithm able to multiply two $n \times n$ upper triangular matrices in a time in $O(t(n))$, where $t(n)$ is a smooth function. Let A and B be two arbitrary $n \times n$ matrices to be multiplied. Consider the following product of $3n \times 3n$ upper triangular matrices

$$\begin{pmatrix} 0 & A & 0 \\ 0 & 0 & 0 \\ 0 & 0 & 0 \end{pmatrix} \times \begin{pmatrix} 0 & 0 & 0 \\ 0 & 0 & B \\ 0 & 0 & 0 \end{pmatrix} = \begin{pmatrix} 0 & 0 & AB \\ 0 & 0 & 0 \\ 0 & 0 & 0 \end{pmatrix}$$

where "0" denotes the $n \times n$ matrix all of whose entries are zero. This product shows us how to obtain the desired result AB by a reduction to one larger multiplication of upper triangular matrices. The time required for this operation is in $O(n^2)$ for the preparation of the two upper triangular matrices and the extraction of AB from their product, plus $O(t(3n))$ for the multiplication of the two upper triangular matrices. By the smoothness assumption, $t(3n) \in O(t(n))$. Because $t(n)$ is at least quadratic, $t(n) \in \Omega(n^2)$ and thus $n^2 \in O(t(n))$. Consequently, the total time required to multiply arbitrary $n \times n$ matrices is in $O(n^2 + t(3n))$, which is the same as $O(t(n))$.   ∎

Theorem 12.4.7   MQ$\leq^{\ell}$ MS, *assuming* MS *is smooth.*

Proof   This is similar to the proof of Theorem 12.4.6: we reduce the multiplication of two arbitrary $n \times n$ matrices A and B to a multiplication of $2n \times 2n$ symmetric matrices.

$$\begin{pmatrix} 0 & A \\ A^t & 0 \end{pmatrix} \times \begin{pmatrix} 0 & B^t \\ B & 0 \end{pmatrix} = \begin{pmatrix} AB & 0 \\ 0 & A^t B^t \end{pmatrix}$$

We leave the details to the reader. Note that the product of two symmetric matrices is not necessarily symmetric.   ∎

Theorem 12.4.8   MQ$\leq^{\ell}$ IT, *assuming* IT *is smooth.*

Proof   Suppose there exists an algorithm able to invert a nonsingular $n \times n$ upper triangular matrix in a time in $O(t(n))$, where $t(n)$ is a smooth function. Let A and B

be two arbitrary $n \times n$ matrices to be multiplied. Consider the following product of $3n \times 3n$ upper triangular matrices

$$\begin{pmatrix} I & A & 0 \\ 0 & I & B \\ 0 & 0 & I \end{pmatrix} \times \begin{pmatrix} I & -A & AB \\ 0 & I & -B \\ 0 & 0 & I \end{pmatrix} = \begin{pmatrix} I & 0 & 0 \\ 0 & I & 0 \\ 0 & 0 & I \end{pmatrix}$$

where I is the $n \times n$ identity matrix. This product shows us how to obtain the desired product AB by inverting the first of the upper triangular matrices above: the result appears in the upper right corner of the inverse.

$$\begin{pmatrix} I & A & 0 \\ 0 & I & B \\ 0 & 0 & I \end{pmatrix}^{-1} = \begin{pmatrix} I & -A & AB \\ 0 & I & -B \\ 0 & 0 & I \end{pmatrix}$$

As in the proof of Theorem 12.4.6, this entire operation takes a time in $O(n^2 + t(3n))$, which is the same as $O(t(n))$.   ■

It remains to prove that $\mathsf{IT} \leq^\ell \mathsf{MQ}$, which is the most interesting of these reductions. For this it is useful to introduce yet another problem: $\mathsf{IT2}$ is the problem of inverting nonsingular upper triangular matrices whose size is a power of 2.

Lemma 12.4.9 $\mathsf{IT} \leq^\ell \mathsf{IT2}$, *assuming* $\mathsf{IT2}$ *is smooth.*

Proof   Suppose there exists an algorithm able to invert a nonsingular $m \times m$ upper triangular matrix in a time in $O(t(m) \mid m$ is a power of 2), where $t(m)$ is a smooth function. Let A be a nonsingular $n \times n$ upper triangular matrix for arbitrary n. Let m be the smallest power of 2 not smaller than n. Let B be the $m \times m$ upper triangular matrix such that $B_{ij} = A_{ij}$ for $1 \leq i \leq n$ and $1 \leq j \leq n$, $B_{ii} = 1$ for $n < i \leq m$ and $B_{ij} = 0$ otherwise:

$$B = \begin{pmatrix} A & 0 \\ 0 & I \end{pmatrix}$$

where the 0's are rectangular zero matrices of the proper size so that B is $m \times m$ and I is the $(m - n) \times (m - n)$ identity matrix. It is easy to verify that the inverse of A can be read off directly as the $n \times n$ submatrix in the upper left corner of B^{-1}. Thus the calculation of A^{-1} takes a time that is in $O(t(m))$ for inverting B, plus something in $O(n^2)$ to prepare matrix B and read the answer from B^{-1}. Because $t(m)$ is a smooth function and m is even, $t(m) = t(2(m/2)) \leq ct(m/2)$ for an appropriate constant c, provided n is sufficiently large. Because smooth functions are eventually nondecreasing and $m/2 < n$, $t(m/2) \leq t(n)$, again provided n is sufficiently large. It follows that $t(m) \leq ct(n)$. Thus matrix A can be inverted in a time in $O(ct(n) + n^2)$. This is the same as $O(t(n))$ because $t(n)$ is at least quadratic.   ■

Lemma 12.4.10   IT2$\leq^{\ell}$ MQ, *assuming* MQ *is strongly quadratic.*

Proof   Let A be a nonsingular $n \times n$ upper triangular matrix to be inverted, where n is a power of 2. If $n = 1$, inversion is trivial. Otherwise decompose A into three submatrices B, C and D, each of size $\frac{n}{2} \times \frac{n}{2}$, defined by

$$A = \begin{pmatrix} B & C \\ 0 & D \end{pmatrix}.$$

Note that B and D are upper triangular whereas C is arbitrary. Similarly let F, G and H be unknown $\frac{n}{2} \times \frac{n}{2}$ matrices such that

$$A^{-1} = \begin{pmatrix} F & G \\ 0 & H \end{pmatrix}.$$

The lower left submatrix is zero because the inverse of a nonsingular upper triangular matrix is upper triangular; see Problem 12.30. The product of A and A^{-1} should be the identity matrix.

$$\begin{pmatrix} B & C \\ 0 & D \end{pmatrix} \times \begin{pmatrix} F & G \\ 0 & H \end{pmatrix} = \begin{pmatrix} BF & BG + CH \\ 0 & DH \end{pmatrix} = \begin{pmatrix} I & 0 \\ 0 & I \end{pmatrix}$$

Therefore, $BF = DH = I$, which implies that B and D are nonsingular and that $F = B^{-1}$ and $H = D^{-1}$. Moreover, $BG + CH = 0$, and thus $G = -B^{-1}CH = -B^{-1}CD^{-1}$. Putting it all together, the inverse of A is obtained from the inverses of B and D after two matrix multiplications to compute $-B^{-1}CD^{-1}$:

$$A^{-1} = \begin{pmatrix} B^{-1} & -B^{-1}CD^{-1} \\ 0 & D^{-1} \end{pmatrix}.$$

Since both B and D are nonsingular upper triangular matrices half the size of A, this suggests a divide-and-conquer algorithm to compute A^{-1} via two recursive calculations of inverses, two matrix multiplications, and some additional bookkeeping operations that take a negligible time $g(n) \in O(n^2)$.

   Let $I(n)$ be the time spent by this algorithm to compute the inverse of an $n \times n$ upper triangular matrix when n is a power of 2. Let $M(n)$ be the time we need to multiply two $n \times n$ arbitrary matrices. From the above discussion, $I(n) \leq 2I(n/2) + 2M(n/2) + g(n)$ when n is a power of 2 larger than 1. By the assumption that MQ is strongly quadratic, $M(n) \in \Theta(t(n))$ for some strongly quadratic function $t(n)$. Let a, b and c be constants such that $g(n) \leq an^2$, $t(n) \geq bn^2$ and $M(n) \leq ct(n)$ for all sufficiently large n. Constant b exists because all strongly quadratic functions are at least quadratic by Problem 12.23. By the definition of strongly quadratic, $t(n) \geq 4t(n/2)$ and thus $t(n/2) \leq \frac{1}{4}t(n)$. It follows from all these formulas that

$$
\begin{aligned}
I(n) &\leq 2I(n/2) + 2M(n/2) + g(n) \\
&\leq 2I(n/2) + 2ct(n/2) + an^2 \\
&\leq 2I(n/2) + \left(\frac{c}{2} + \frac{a}{b}\right)t(n) \\
&\leq 2I(n/2) + dt(n)
\end{aligned}
\tag{12.2}
$$

for all $n \geq n_0$ that are powers of 2, for appropriate constants d and n_0. Without loss of generality, we may choose n_0 to be a power of 2.

It remains to prove that $I(n) \in O(t(n) \mid n$ is a power of 2). For this we use constructive induction to determine a constant u such that $I(n) \leq ut(n)$ for all $n \geq n_0$ that are powers of 2. The basis of the induction is established provided we choose $u \geq I(n_0)/t(n_0)$. For the induction step, consider any $n > n_0$ that is a power of 2 and assume the partially specified induction hypothesis that $I(n/2) \leq ut(n/2)$. By Equation 12.2, the induction hypothesis, and the fact that $t(n/2) \leq \frac{1}{4}t(n)$,

$$
\begin{aligned}
I(n) &\leq 2I(n/2) + dt(n) \\
&\leq 2ut(n/2) + dt(n) \\
&\leq \left(\frac{u}{2} + d\right)t(n).
\end{aligned}
$$

This shows that $I(n) \leq ut(n)$ provided $\frac{u}{2} + d \leq u$, which is the same as $u \geq 2d$. In conclusion, $I(n) \leq ut(n)$ holds for all $n \geq n_0$ that are powers of 2 provided we choose $u \geq \max(I(n_0)/t(n_0), 2d)$. This completes the proof that $I(n) \in O(t(n) \mid n$ is a power of 2), and thus that IT2 $\leq^\ell$ MQ assuming MQ is strongly quadratic.

The reduction used in this proof is different from the reductions seen previously in the sense that a single inversion of an upper triangular matrix involves a large number of matrix multiplications if those implied by the recursive calls are counted. The linearity of the reduction is possible only because most of the implied multiplications are performed on matrices much smaller than the one we seek to invert.   ■

Theorem 12.4.11   IT $\leq^\ell$ MQ, *assuming* MQ *is strongly quadratic.*

Proof   This is almost immediate from the two preceding lemmas. The only technical problem is that we need the assumption that IT2 is smooth to apply Lemma 12.4.9, and this is not a consequence of Lemma 12.4.10 even if MQ is strongly quadratic. All is well nevertheless because the proof of Lemma 12.4.10 makes do with the multiplication of matrices of size $\frac{n}{2} \times \frac{n}{2}$ to invert an upper triangular matrix of size $n \times n$, when n is a power of 2. Equation 12.2 can thus be refined as

$$
I(n) \leq 2I(n/2) + \hat{d}t(n/2)
$$

and from there it follows that there exists a constant $\hat{u}$ such that $I(n) \leq \hat{u}t(n/2)$ provided n is a sufficiently large power of 2. The proof of Lemma 12.4.9 then goes through without needing $t(n)$ to be smooth: it is enough that $t(n)$ be eventually nondecreasing, which it is by virtue of being strongly quadratic. We leave the details to the reader. ∎

12.4.3 Reductions among shortest path problems

In this section $\mathbb{R}^\infty$ denotes $\mathbb{R}^{\geq 0} \cup \{\infty\}$, with the natural conventions that $x + \infty = \infty$ and $\min(x, \infty) = x$ for all $x \in \mathbb{R}^\infty$.

Let X, Y and Z be three sets of nodes. Let $f : X \times Y \rightarrow \mathbb{R}^\infty$ and $g : Y \times Z \rightarrow \mathbb{R}^\infty$ be two functions representing the cost of going directly from one node to another. An infinite cost represents the absence of a direct link. Denote by $f \times g$ the function $h : X \times Z \rightarrow \mathbb{R}\infty$ defined for every $x \in X$ and $z \in Z$ by

$$h(x, z) = \min_{y \in Y}(f(x, y) + g(y, z)).$$

This is the minimum cost of going from x to z passing through exactly one node in Y. Notice the analogy between this definition and ordinary matrix multiplication: addition and multiplication are replaced by the minimum operation and addition, respectively.

The preceding notation becomes particularly interesting when the sets X, Y and Z, and also the functions f and g, coincide. In this case $f \times f$, which we shall write f^2, gives the minimum cost of going from one node of X to another (possibly the same) while passing through exactly one intermediate node (still possibly the same). Similarly, $\min(f, f^2)$ gives the minimum cost of going from one node of X to another either directly or by passing through exactly one intermediate node. The meaning of f^i is similar for any $i > 0$. It is natural to define f^0 as the cost of going from one node to another while staying in the same place.

$$f^0(x, y) = \begin{cases} 0 & \text{if } x = y \\ \infty & \text{otherwise} \end{cases}$$

The minimum cost of going from one node to another without restrictions on the number of nodes on the path, which we write $f^\star$, is therefore

$$f^\star(x, y) = \min_{i \geq 0} f^i(x, y).$$

This definition apparently implies an infinite computation; it is not even immediately clear that $f^\star$ is well defined. However, f never takes negative values. Any path that passes twice through the same node can therefore be shortened by taking out the loop thus formed, without increasing the cost of the resulting path. Consequently, it suffices to consider only those paths whose length is less than the number n of nodes in X. We thus have that

$$f^\star(x, y) = \min_{0 \leq i < n} f^i(x, y). \tag{12.3}$$

The straightforward algorithm for calculating $f \times g$ takes a time in $\Theta(n^3)$ if the three sets of nodes concerned are of cardinality n and if we count additions and comparisons at unit cost. Unfortunately, there is no obvious way of adapting to this problem Strassen's algorithm for ordinary matrix multiplication (see Section 7.6). The difficulty is that Strassen's algorithm does subtractions, which are the reverse of additions; there is no equivalent to this operation in the present context since ordinary additions are replaced by taking the minimum, which is not a reversible operation. Algorithms that are asymptotically faster than $\Theta(n^3)$ are known for this problem, but they are quite complicated and have only theoretical advantages; see Section 12.8.

Equation 12.3 yields a direct algorithm for calculating $f^\star$ in n times the time needed for a single calculation of the type $f \times g$. This is a time in $\Theta(n^4)$ if the straightforward algorithm is used. Thus, computing $f^\star$ for a given function f seems at first sight to need more time than calculating a simple product $f \times g$. However, we saw in Section 8.5 a dynamic programming algorithm for calculating shortest paths in a graph, namely Floyd's algorithm. This is nothing other than the calculation of $f^\star$. Thus it *is* possible to get away with a time in $\Theta(n^3)$ after all. Could it be that the problems of calculating $f \times g$ and $f^\star$ are of the same complexity? Surprisingly, the answer is yes: these two problems are linearly equivalent. The existence of algorithms asymptotically more efficient than $\Theta(n^3)$ for solving the problem of calculating $f \times g$ therefore implies that Floyd's algorithm for calculating shortest routes is not optimal, at least in theory.

Here we are content to state the main theorem formally and relegate its proof to the exercises. Assuming f and g are defined on the same domain, denote by MUL and TRC the problems consisting of calculating $f \times g$ and $f^\star$, respectively. (TRC stands for "transitive reflexive closure"). For simplicity, time complexities will be measured as a function of the number of nodes; an algorithm such as Floyd's, for example, is considered cubic because it takes a time in $\Theta(n^3)$ even though this is improper from a formal viewpoint because the size of an n-node instance is in $\Theta(n^2)$ if it is provided as a matrix of distances.

Theorem 12.4.12   MUL $\equiv^\ell$ TRC, *assuming both problems are smooth and assuming* MUL *is strongly quadratic.*

Proof   Work Problems 12.32 and 12.33.   ∎

When the range of the cost functions is restricted to $\{0, \infty\}$, calculating $f^\star$ comes down to determining for each pair of nodes whether or not there is a path joining them. We saw in Problem 8.18 that Warshall's algorithm solves this problem in a time in $\Theta(n^3)$. Let MULB and TRCB be the problems consisting of calculating $f \times g$ and $f^\star$, respectively, when the cost functions are restricted in this way. It is clear that MULB $\leq^\ell$ MUL and TRCB $\leq^\ell$ TRC since the general algorithms can also be used to solve instances of the restricted problems. Furthermore, the proof that

$MUL \equiv^{\ell} TRC$ can easily be adapted to show that $MULB \equiv^{\ell} TRCB$ under similar assumptions. This is interesting because of the following theorem, which involves the problem MQ of ordinary square matrix multiplication, which we studied in Section 12.4.2.

Theorem 12.4.13 $MULB \leq^{\ell} MQ$.

Proof   Let $f \times g$ be an instance of size n of problem MULB. Assume without loss of generality that the underlying sets of nodes are $\{1, 2, \ldots, n\}$. Define two $n \times n$ matrices A and B by

$$A_{ij} = \begin{cases} 0 & \text{if } f(i,j) = \infty \\ 1 & \text{if } f(i,j) = 0 \end{cases}$$

and similarly for B with respect to function g. Intuitively, $A_{ij} = 1$ if and only if there is a direct f-link between nodes i and j. By the definition of ordinary matrix multiplication, $(AB)_{ij}$ counts the number of ways to reach node j from node i by going first through an f-link and then through a g-link. Therefore,

$$(f \times g)(i,j) = \begin{cases} \infty & \text{if } (AB)_{ij} = 0 \\ 0 & \text{otherwise.} \end{cases}$$

Thus, one $n \times n$ ordinary matrix multiplication is all that is needed to solve an instance of size n of problem MULB.   ∎

Strassen's algorithm can therefore be used to solve problems MULB and TRCB in a time in $O(n^{2.81})$, thus showing that Warshall's algorithm is not optimal. However using Strassen's algorithm requires a number of *arithmetic* operations in $O(n^{2.81})$; the time in $O(n^3)$ taken by Warshall's algorithm counts only *Boolean* operations as elementary.

An interesting situation occurs when we consider *symmetric* versions of the problems studied in this section. These correspond to problems on undirected graphs. A cost function $f : X \times X \to \mathbb{R}\infty$ is symmetric if $f(u, v) = f(v, u)$ for every $u, v \in X$. Each of the four problems discussed earlier has a symmetric version that arises when the cost functions involved are symmetric; call them MULS, TRCS, MULBS and TRCBS. Inspired by Theorem 12.4.7, which shows that ordinary matrix multiplication is not easier when symmetric matrices are involved, it is tempting to conjecture that the same holds with shortest path problems. Indeed, the proof of Theorem 12.4.7 applies *mutatis mutandis* to prove that $MUL \equiv^{\ell} MULS$ and $MULB \equiv^{\ell} MULBS$. However, the analogy breaks down when it comes to TRCBS. A moment's thought will convince you that this is just a fancy name for the problem of finding the connected components in an undirected graph, which is easily solved in a time in $O(n^2)$ by depth-first search. On the other hand, no algorithm is known that can solve MULB so quickly. But recall that $TRCB \equiv^{\ell} MULB$. Thus it seems that TRCB is genuinely harder than its symmetric version TRCBS. For the same reason, it seems that MULBS is genuinely harder than TRCBS. This is odd in a sense because the naive algorithm stemming directly from Equation 12.3 would require that we solve n instances of MULBS to solve a single instance of TRCBS.

12.5 Introduction to $\mathcal{NP}$–completeness

There exist many real-life, practical problems for which no efficient algorithm is known, but whose intrinsic difficulty no one has yet managed to prove. Among these are such famous problems as the travelling salesperson, optimal graph colouring, the knapsack problem, Hamiltonian cycles, integer programming, finding the longest simple path in a graph, and satisfying a Boolean formula: some of these are described below. Should we blame algorithmics or complexity? Maybe there do in fact exist efficient algorithms for these problems. After all, computer science is a relative newcomer: it is certain that new algorithmic techniques remain to be discovered. On the other hand perhaps these problems are intrinsically hard but we lack the techniques to prove this.

This section presents a remarkable result: an efficient algorithm to solve any one of the problems listed in the previous paragraph would automatically provide us with efficient algorithms for all of them. We do not know whether these problems are easy or hard to solve, but we do know that they are all of similar complexity. The practical importance of these problems ensured that each of them separately has been the object of sustained efforts to find an efficient method of solution. For this reason it is widely conjectured that such algorithms do not exist. If you have a problem to solve and you can show that it is computationally equivalent to one of those mentioned previously, you may take this as convincing evidence—but no proof—that your problem is hard in the worst case. At least you will be certain that at the moment nobody else knows how to solve your problem efficiently.

At the heart of this theory lies the idea that there may be problems that are genuinely hard to solve, yet for which the validity of any purported solution can be verified efficiently. Consider the *Hamiltonian cycle problem* as an example. Given an undirected graph $G = \langle N, A \rangle$, the problem is to find a path that starts with some node, visits each node exactly once, and returns to the starting node. We say that the graph is Hamiltonian if such a cycle exists. This problem is believed to be hard. However, it is obviously easy to verify whether a sequence of nodes defines a Hamiltonian cycle. Another example is factorization. Given a composite number, it may be hard to find a nontrivial divisor, but any purported divisor can be verified easily. It may seem obvious that it is genuinely easier for many problems to verify the validity of a purported solution than to find one from scratch. The greatest embarrassment of modern computational complexity theory is that we do not know how to prove this.

12.5.1 The classes $\mathcal{P}$ and $\mathcal{NP}$

Before going further it will help to define what we mean by an efficient algorithm. Does this mean it takes a time in $O(n \log n)$? $O(n^2)$? $O(n^{2.81})$? It all depends on the problem to be solved. A sorting algorithm that takes a time in $\Theta(n^2)$ is inefficient, whereas an algorithm for matrix multiplication that takes a time in $O(n^2 \log n)$ would be an astonishing breakthrough. So we might be tempted to say that an algorithm is efficient if it is better than the obvious straightforward algorithm, or maybe if it is the best possible algorithm to solve our problem. However, this definition would be fuzzy and awkward to work with, and in some cases "the best possible algorithm" does not even exist; see Problem 12.34. Moreover, there are problems for which even the best possible algorithm takes an exorbitant amount of time even on small instances. Might it not be reasonable to admit that such problems are inherently intractable rather than claiming that clever algorithms are efficient even though they are too slow to be used in practice?

For our present purposes we answer this question by stipulating that an algorithm is *efficient* if there exists a polynomial $p(n)$ such that the algorithm can solve any instance of size n in a time in $O(p(n))$. We say of such algorithms that they are *polynomial-time*. This definition is motivated by the comparison in Section 2.6 between an algorithm that takes a time in $\Theta(2^n)$ and one that only requires a time in $\Theta(n^3)$, and also by some of the examples given in Section 2.7. An exponential-time algorithm becomes rapidly useless in practice, whereas generally speaking a polynomial-time algorithm allows us to solve much larger instances.

This notion of efficiency should be taken with a grain of salt. Given two algorithms requiring a time in $\Theta(n^{\lg \lg n})$ and in $\Theta(n^{10})$, respectively, the first is inefficient according to our definition because it is not polynomial-time. However, it will beat the polynomial-time algorithm on all instances of size less than 10^{300}, assuming the hidden constants are similar. In fact, it is not reasonable to assert that an algorithm requiring a time in $\Theta(n^{10})$ is efficient in practice. Nonetheless, to decree that $\Theta(n^3)$ is efficient whereas $\Theta(n^4)$ is not, for example, would be rather too arbitrary. Moreover, even a linear-time algorithm may be unusable in practice if the hidden multiplicative constant is too large, whereas an algorithm that takes exponential time in the worst case may be very quick on most instances. Nevertheless, there are significant technical advantages to considering the class of all polynomial-time algorithms. In particular, all reasonable deterministic single-processor models of computation can be simulated on each other with at most a polynomial slow-down. Therefore, the notion of polynomial-time computability is robust: it does not depend on which model you prefer, unless you use possibly more powerful models such as probabilistic or quantum computers. Furthermore, the fact that sums, products and composition of polynomials are polynomials will be useful.

In this section, all our analyses for the time taken by an algorithm will be "up to a polynomial". This means that we do not hesitate to count at unit cost an operation that really takes a polynomial amount of time. For example, we may count additions and multiplications at unit cost even on operands whose size grows with the size of the instance being solved, provided this growth is bounded by some polynomial. This is allowable because we only wish to distinguish polynomial-time algorithms from those that are not polynomial-time, and because it takes polynomial time to execute a polynomial number of polynomial-time operations; see Problem 12.35. On the other hand, we would not count at unit cost arithmetic that involves operands of size exponentially larger than the instance. If the algorithm needs such large operands, it must break them into sections, keep them in an array, and spend the required time to carry out multiprecision arithmetic; such an algorithm cannot be polynomial-time.

Our goal is to distinguish problems that can be solved efficiently from those that cannot. For technical reasons we concentrate on the study of *decision* problems.

For these, the answer is either *yes* or *no*, or equivalently either *true* or *false*. For example, "Find a Hamiltonian cycle in G" is not a decision problem, but "Is graph G Hamiltonian?" is. A decision problem can be thought of as defining a set X of instances on which the correct answer is "yes". We call these the *yes-instances*; any other instance is a *no-instance*. We say that a correct algorithm that solves a decision problem *accepts* the yes-instances and *rejects* the no-instances.

Definition 12.5.1 $\mathcal{P}$ *is the class of decision problems that can be solved by a polynomial-time algorithm.*

For simplicity we do not allow probabilistic algorithms in this definition, even those of the Las Vegas variety whose answers are guaranteed correct. This is one more reason to take the definition with a grain of salt: there may be decision problems that can be solved in expected polynomial time, but only by probabilistic algorithms; such problems are not in $\mathcal{P}$ according to the definition.

The theory of $\mathcal{NP}$– completeness is concerned with the notion of polynomially *verifiable* properties. Intuitively, a decision problem X is efficiently verifiable if an omniscient being could produce convincing evidence that $x \in X$ whenever this is so. Given this evidence, you should be able to verify efficiently that indeed $x \in X$ without further interactions with the being. However, if in fact $x \notin X$, you should not be falsely convinced that $x \in X$ regardless of what the being tells you. Consider the problem of deciding if a graph is Hamiltonian as an example. Although this problem is believed to be difficult, it is efficiently verifiable: if the being exhibits a Hamiltonian cycle you can easily verify that it is correct. On the other hand, nothing the being could show you—with the possible exception of a shotgun— would convince you that the graph is Hamiltonian if it is not.

Consider a decision problem X. Let Q be a set, arbitrary for the time being, which we call the *proof space* for X. A *proof system* for X is a set F of pairs $\langle x, q \rangle$. For any $x \in X$ there must exist at least one $q \in Q$ such that $\langle x, q \rangle \in F$; on the other hand no such q must exist when $x \notin X$. Thus, it suffices for the being to show you some $q \in Q$ such that $\langle x, q \rangle \in F$ to convince you that $x \in X$. Seeing this q will convince you that x is a yes-instance since no such q would exist should x be a no-instance. Moreover, the being can always come up with such a q for yes-instances because they always exist by definition. Formally, F is a subset of $X \times Q$ such that

$$(\forall x \in X)\,(\exists q \in Q)\,[\langle x, q \rangle \in F].$$

Any q such that $\langle x, q \rangle \in F$ is called a *proof* or a *certificate* that $x \in X$. We did not specify explicitly in the above formal definition that

$$(\forall x \notin X)\,(\forall q \in Q)\,[\langle x, q \rangle \notin F]$$

because it is implicit in the requirement that F must be a subset of $X \times Q$.

For example, if X is the set of all Hamiltonian graphs, we may take Q as the set of sequences of graph nodes, and define $\langle G, \sigma \rangle \in F$ if and only if the sequence of nodes σ specifies a Hamiltonian cycle in graph G.

For another example, if X is the set of all composite numbers, we may take $Q = \mathbb{N}$ as the proof space and

$$F = \{\langle n, q \rangle \mid 1 < q < n \text{ and } q \text{ divides } n\}$$

as the proof system. This proof system is not unique. Another possibility would be

$$F' = \{\langle n, q \rangle \mid 1 < q < n \text{ and } \gcd(q, n) \neq 1\}.$$

Still more proof systems for the same problem may come from the discussion in Section 10.6.2, which shows that certificates that a number is composite may be of no help in factorizing it.

The class $\mathcal{NP}$ corresponds to the decision problems that have an *efficient* proof system, which means that each yes-instance must have at least one *succinct* certificate, whose validity can be verified quickly.

Definition 12.5.2 $\mathcal{NP}$ *is the class of decision problems* X *that admit a proof system* $F \subseteq X \times Q$ *such that there exists a polynomial* $p(n)$ *and a polynomial-time algorithm* A *such that*

- ⋄ *For all* $x \in X$ *there exists a* $q \in Q$ *such that* $\langle x, q \rangle \in F$ *and moreover the size of* q *is at most* $p(n)$, *where* n *is the size of* x.

- ⋄ *For all pairs* $\langle x, q \rangle$, *algorithm* A *can verify whether or not* $\langle x, q \rangle \in F$. *In other words,* $F \in \mathcal{P}$.

Both examples above fit this definition. A Hamiltonian cycle in a graph, if it exists, takes less space to describe than the graph itself, and it can be verified in linear time whether a sequence of nodes defines a Hamiltonian cycle. Similarly, any nontrivial factor of a composite number is smaller than the number itself, and a single division is sufficient to verify its validity. Thus both these problems are in $\mathcal{NP}$.

An important word of caution is required before we proceed: you may be tempted to think that the letters $\mathcal{NP}$ stand for "non polynomial". Wrong! This would be silly because (1) any problem that can be solved in polynomial time is automatically in $\mathcal{NP}$ (Theorem 12.5.3), and (2) we do not know how to prove the existence of even a single problem in $\mathcal{NP}$ that cannot be solved in polynomial time, though we conjecture that they exist. In fact, $\mathcal{NP}$ stand for "nondeterministic polynomial-time" as we shall see in Section 12.5.6.

Another potentially slippery point is that the definition of $\mathcal{NP}$ is asymmetric: we require the existence of succinct certificates for each yes-instance but there is no such requirement for no-instances. Even though the set of all Hamiltonian graphs is clearly in $\mathcal{NP}$, there is no such evidence for the set of all *non*-Hamiltonian graphs. Indeed, what kind of succinct evidence could convince you efficiently that a graph is *not* Hamiltonian when this is so? It is conjectured that no such evidence can exist in general and thus that the set of all non-Hamiltonian graphs is not in $\mathcal{NP}$. Problem 12.36 offers a surprise along these lines.

Our first theorem establishes a relation between $\mathcal{P}$ and $\mathcal{NP}$.

Theorem 12.5.3 $\mathcal{P} \subseteq \mathcal{NP}$.

Proof   Intuitively, this is because there is no need for help from an omniscient being when we can handle our decision problem ourselves. Formally, consider an arbitrary decision problem $X \in \mathcal{P}$. Let $Q = \{0\}$ be a trivial proof space. Define

$$F = \{\langle x,0\rangle \mid x \in X\}.$$

Clearly, any yes-instance admits one succinct "certificate", namely 0, and no-instances have no certificates at all. Moreover, it suffices to verify that $x \in X$ and $q = 0$ in order to establish that $\langle x,q\rangle \in F$. This can be done in polynomial time precisely because we assumed that $X \in \mathcal{P}$.   ∎

The central open question is whether or not the set inclusion in Theorem 12.5.3 is proper. Is it possible that $\mathcal{P} = \mathcal{NP}$? If this were the case, any property that can be verified in polynomial time given a certificate could also be decided in polynomial time from scratch. Although this seems very unlikely, no one has yet been able to settle the question. In the remainder of this section, we shall study the consequences of the *conjecture* that

$$\mathcal{P} \neq \mathcal{NP}.$$

For this, we need a notion of reduction that allows us to compare the intrinsic difficulty of problems in $\mathcal{NP}$ and to discover that there are problems in $\mathcal{NP}$ that are as hard as anything else in $\mathcal{NP}$. Such problems, which are called $\mathcal{NP}-complete$, can be solved in polynomial time if and only if all the other problems in $\mathcal{NP}$ can, which is the same as saying $\mathcal{P} = \mathcal{NP}$. Thus, under the conjecture that $\mathcal{P} \neq \mathcal{NP}$, we know that $\mathcal{NP}-$complete problems cannot be solved in polynomial time.

12.5.2 Polynomial reductions

The notion of linear reduction and of linear equivalence considered in Section 12.4 is interesting for problems that can be solved in quadratic or cubic time. However, it is too restrictive when we consider problems for which the best known algorithms take exponential time. For this reason we introduce a different kind of reduction.

Definition 12.5.4   *Let* A *and* B *be two problems. We say that* A *is polynomially Turing reducible to* B *if there exists an algorithm for solving* A *in a time that would be polynomial if we could solve arbitrary instances of problem* B *at unit cost. This is denoted* A $\leq_T^p$ B. *When* A $\leq_T^p$ B *and* B $\leq_T^p$ A *both hold, we say that* A *and* B *are polynomially Turing equivalent and we write* A $\equiv_T^p$ B.

In other words, the algorithm for solving problem A may make whatever use it chooses of an imaginary algorithm that can solve problem B at unit cost. This imaginary algorithm is sometimes called an *oracle*. As in the linear case, a reduction proof usually takes the form of an explicit algorithm to solve one problem by calling on an arbitrary algorithm for the other problem. Again, this could be used to teach someone who only knows how to solve one problem how to solve the other. Again too, polynomial reductions are transitive: if $A \leq_T^p B$ and $B \leq_T^p C$, then $A \leq_T^p C$. Unlike linear reductions, however, we allow the first algorithm to take a polynomial amount of time, still counting the calls to the second algorithm at unit cost, and to call the second algorithm a polynomial number of times on arbitrary instances of size polynomial in the size of the original instance.

As a first example, we prove the polynomial equivalence of two versions of the Hamiltonian cycle problem. Let HAM and HAMD denote the problems of finding a Hamiltonian cycle in a graph if one exists and of deciding whether or not a graph is Hamiltonian, respectively. We allow an algorithm for HAM to return an arbitrary answer when presented with a non-Hamiltonian graph. The following theorem says that it is not significantly harder to find a Hamiltonian cycle than to decide if a graph is Hamiltonian.

Theorem 12.5.5 $\text{HAM} \equiv_T^p \text{HAMD}$.

Proof   First we prove the obvious direction: $\text{HAMD} \leq_T^p \text{HAM}$. Consider the following algorithm.

> **function** $HamD(G : \text{graph})$
> $\sigma \leftarrow Ham(G)$
> **if** σ defines a Hamiltonian cycle in G
>   **then return** *true*
>   **else return** *false*

This algorithm solves HAMD correctly provided algorithm *Ham* solves problem HAM correctly: by definition of HAM, algorithm *Ham* must return a Hamiltonian cycle in G provided one exists, in which case *HamD* will correctly return *true*. Conversely, if the graph is not Hamiltonian, the output σ returned by *Ham* cannot be a Hamiltonian cycle, and thus *HamD* will correctly return *false*. It is clear that *HamD* takes polynomial time provided we count the call on *Ham* at unit cost.

Consider now the interesting direction: $\text{HAM} \leq_T^p \text{HAMD}$. We are to *find* a Hamiltonian cycle assuming we know how to *decide* if such cycles exist. The idea is to consider each edge in turn. For each, we ask if the graph would still be Hamiltonian if this edge were removed. We keep the edge only if its removal would make the graph non-Hamiltonian; otherwise we remove it before we proceed with the next edge. The resulting graph will still be Hamiltonian since we never make a change that would destroy this property. Moreover, it contains only the edges necessary to define a Hamiltonian cycle, for any additional edge could be removed without making the graph non-Hamiltonian, and hence it would have been removed when its turn came. Therefore, it suffices to follow the edges of the final graph to obtain a Hamiltonian cycle in the original graph. Here is a sketch of this greedy algorithm.

> **function** $Ham(G = \langle N, A \rangle)$
>   **if** $HamD(G) = false$ **then return** "No solution!"
>   **for each** $e \in A$ **do**
>   **if** $HamD(\langle N, A \setminus \{e\} \rangle)$ **then** $A \leftarrow A \setminus \{e\}$
> $\sigma \leftarrow$ sequence of nodes obtained by following
>   the unique cycle remaining in G

Clearly *Ham* takes polynomial time if we count each call on *HamD* at unit cost. ∎

Consider two problems A and B such that $A \leq_T^p B$. Let $p(n)$ be a polynomial such that the reduction algorithm for problem A never requires the solution of more than $p(n)$ instances of problem B when solving an instance of size n, and such that none of those instances is of size larger than $p(n)$. Such a polynomial must exist for otherwise the reduction algorithm would require more than polynomial time even counting the calls on the algorithm for B at unit cost. Assume now that there exists an algorithm *SolveB* capable of solving problem B in a time in $O(t(n))$ for some eventually nondecreasing function $t(n)$. We may now run the reduction algorithm to solve problem A, calling *SolveB* whenever necessary. The entire time spent inside *SolveB* will be in $O(p(n)t(p(n)))$ since no more than $p(n)$ calls on instances of size at most $p(n)$ will be necessary. Thus problem A can be solved in a time in $O(p(n)t(p(n))+q(n))$, where $q(n)$ is a polynomial that takes account of the time required by the reduction algorithm outside the calls on *SolveB*. Consider now what happens if $t(n)$ is a polynomial. In this case, $p(n)t(p(n))+q(n)$ is also a polynomial because sums, products and compositions of polynomials are polynomials. Thus we have the following fundamental theorem.

Theorem 12.5.6   *Consider two problems* A *and* B. *If* $A \leq_T^p B$ *and if* B *can be solved in polynomial time, then* A *can also be solved in polynomial time.*

Proof   This is immediate from the discussion above.   ∎

In particular, we know from Theorem 12.5.5 that a polynomial-time algorithm exists to find Hamiltonian cycles if and only if a polynomial-time algorithm exists to decide if a graph is Hamiltonian. By definition, the latter is equivalent to saying that HAMD $\in \mathcal{P}$ since HAMD is a decision problem. Therefore, the question of whether or not it is possible to find Hamiltonian cycles in polynomial time is equivalent to a question concerning membership in $\mathcal{P}$ despite the fact that the class $\mathcal{P}$ is defined only for decision problems. This is typical of many interesting problems, which are polynomially equivalent to a similar decision problem. We say of such problems that they are *decision-reducible*. It is precisely because decision-reducibility is commonplace that there is no severe lack of generality in defining $\mathcal{P}$ and $\mathcal{NP}$ as classes of decision problems. Whenever you are interested in a problem that is not a decision problem, chances are that you can find a similar decision problem that is polynomially equivalent. The problem that interests you can be solved in polynomial time if and only if the corresponding decision problem is in $\mathcal{P}$. See Problems 12.43, 12.45, 12.46 and 12.47 for more examples.

The restriction to decision problems allows us to introduce a simplified notion of polynomial reduction.

Definition 12.5.7 *Let X and Y be two decision problems defined on sets of instances I and J, respectively. Problem X is* polynomially many-one reducible *to problem Y if there exists a function $f : I \rightarrow J$ computable in polynomial time such that $x \in X$ if and only if $f(x) \in Y$ for any instance $x \in I$ of problem X. This is denoted $X \leq_m^p Y$ and function f is called the* reduction function. *When $X \leq_m^p Y$ and $Y \leq_m^p X$ both hold, we say that X and Y are* polynomially many-one equivalent *and we write $X \equiv_m^p Y$.*

In other words, the reduction function maps all yes-instances of problem X onto yes-instances of problem Y, and all no-instances of problem X onto no-instances of problem Y; see Figure 12.7. Note that a necessary condition for the reduction function f to be computable in polynomial time is that the size of $f(x)$ must be bounded above by some polynomial in the size of x for all $x \in I$. Many-one reductions are useful tools to establish Turing reductions: to decide if $x \in X$, it suffices to compute $y = f(x)$ and ask whether or not $y \in Y$. Thus we have the following theorem.

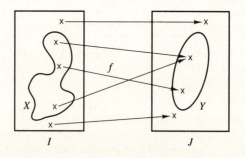

Figure 12.7. Many-one reduction

> **Theorem 12.5.8** *If X and Y are two decision problems such that $X \leq_m^p Y$, then $X \leq_T^p Y$.*

Proof Imagine solutions to problem Y can be obtained at unit cost by a call on *DecideY* and let f be the reduction function between X and Y computable in polynomial-time. Consider the following algorithm.

> **function** *DecideX*(x)
> $y \leftarrow f(x)$
>   **if** *DecideY*(y) **then return** *true*
>   **else return** *false*

By definition of the reduction function, this algorithm solves problem X. Because the reduction function is computable in polynomial time, it solves problem X in polynomial time, counting the call on *DecideY* at unit cost. ∎

This theorem is so useful that we shall often prove $X \leq_m^p Y$ in cases where we really need to establish $X \leq_T^p Y$. Beware that the converse of this theorem does not hold in general: it is possible for two decision problems X and Y that $X \leq_T^p Y$ yet $X \not\leq_m^p Y$; see Problems 12.38, 12.39 and 12.40.

  Consider for example the travelling salesperson problem. An instance of this problem consists of a graph with costs on the edges. The optimization problem, denoted **TSP**, consists of finding a tour in the graph that begins and ends at some node, after having visited each of the other nodes exactly once, and whose cost is the minimum possible; the answer is undefined if no such tour exists. To define an instance of the *decision* problem **TSPD**, a bound L is provided in addition to the graph: the question is to decide whether or not there exists a valid tour whose total cost does not exceed L. Problem 12.47 asks you to prove that this problem is decision-reducible: **TSP** $\equiv_T^p$ **TSPD**. Now we prove that the Hamiltonian cycle problem is polynomially reducible to the travelling salesperson problem. In fact, these problems are polynomially equivalent, but the reduction in the other direction is more difficult.

> **Theorem 12.5.9**   **HAMD** $\leq_m^p$ **TSPD**.

Proof Let $G = \langle N, A \rangle$ be a graph with n nodes. We would like to decide if it is Hamiltonian. Define $f(G)$ as the instance of **TSPD** consisting of the complete graph $H = \langle N, N \times N \rangle$, the cost function

$$c(u,v) = \begin{cases} 1 & \text{if } \{u,v\} \in A \\ 2 & \text{otherwise} \end{cases}$$

and the bound $L = n$. Any Hamiltonian cycle in G translates into a tour in H that has cost exactly n. On the other hand, if there are no Hamiltonian cycles in G, any tour in H must use at least one edge of cost 2, and thus be of total cost at least $n + 1$. Therefore, G is a yes-instance of HAMD if and only if $f(G) = \langle H, c, L \rangle$ is a yes-instance of TSPD. This proves that HAMD $\leq^p_m$ TSPD because function f is easy to compute in polynomial time. ∎

12.5.3 $\mathcal{NP}$-complete problems

As we saw, the fundamental question concerning the classes $\mathcal{P}$ and $\mathcal{NP}$ is whether the inclusion $\mathcal{P} \subseteq \mathcal{NP}$ is strict. Does there exist a problem that allows an efficient proof system but for which it is inherently difficult to discover certificates in the worst case? Our intuition and experience lead us to believe that it is generally more difficult to discover a proof than to verify it: progress in mathematics would be much faster were this not so. This intuition translates into the conjecture that $\mathcal{P} \neq \mathcal{NP}$. It is a cause of considerable chagrin to workers in the theory of complexity that they can neither prove nor disprove this conjecture. If indeed there exists a simple proof that $\mathcal{P} \neq \mathcal{NP}$, it has certainly not been easy to find!

On the other hand, one of the great successes of this theory is the demonstration that there exist a large number of practical problems in $\mathcal{NP}$ such that if any one of them were in $\mathcal{P}$ then the whole of $\mathcal{NP}$ would be equal to $\mathcal{P}$. The evidence that supports the conjecture $\mathcal{P} \neq \mathcal{NP}$ therefore also lends credence to the view that none of these problems can be solved by a polynomial-time algorithm in the worst case. Such problems are called $\mathcal{NP}$-complete. To be $\mathcal{NP}$-complete, a decision problem must belong to $\mathcal{NP}$ and it must be possible to polynomially reduce any other problem in $\mathcal{NP}$ to that problem.

Definition 12.5.10 *A decision problem X is $\mathcal{NP}$-complete if*

 ⋄ $X \in \mathcal{NP}$; *and*
 ⋄ $Y \leq^p_T X$ *for every problem* $Y \in \mathcal{NP}$.

Some authors replace the second condition by $Y \leq^p_m X$ or by other kinds of reduction. It is not known if this gives rise to a genuinely different class of $\mathcal{NP}$-complete problems.

What would happen if some $\mathcal{NP}$-complete problem X could be solved in polynomial time? Consider any other problem $Y \in \mathcal{NP}$. We have $Y \leq^p_T X$ by definition that X is $\mathcal{NP}$-complete. Therefore, Y can also be solved in polynomial time by Theorem 12.5.6. Thus any problem in $\mathcal{NP}$ belongs to $\mathcal{P}$, implying that $\mathcal{NP} \subseteq \mathcal{P}$. But we know $\mathcal{P} \subseteq \mathcal{NP}$, and therefore $\mathcal{P} = \mathcal{NP}$. This proves that if any $\mathcal{NP}$-complete problem can be solved in polynomial time, then so can all problems in $\mathcal{NP}$. Conversely, no $\mathcal{NP}$-complete problem can be solved in polynomial time under the assumption that $\mathcal{P} \neq \mathcal{NP}$.

How can we prove that a problem is $\mathcal{NP}$-complete? If we already have a pool of problems that have been shown to be $\mathcal{NP}$-complete, the following theorem is useful.

> **Theorem 12.5.11** *Let X be an $\mathcal{NP}$−complete problem. Consider a decision problem $Z \in \mathcal{NP}$ such that $X \leq_T^p Z$. Then Z is also $\mathcal{NP}$−complete.*

Proof   To be $\mathcal{NP}$−complete, Z must satisfy two conditions by Definition 12.5.10. The first is that $Z \in \mathcal{NP}$, which is in the statement of the theorem. For the second condition, consider an arbitrary $Y \in \mathcal{NP}$. Since X is $\mathcal{NP}$−complete and $Y \in \mathcal{NP}$, it follows that $Y \leq_T^p X$. By assumption, $X \leq_T^p Z$. By transitivity of polynomial reductions, $Y \leq_T^p Z$, which is what we had to prove to establish the $\mathcal{NP}$−completeness of Z. ∎

To prove that Z is $\mathcal{NP}$−complete, we choose an appropriate problem from the pool of problems already known to be $\mathcal{NP}$−complete, and show that it is polynomially reducible to Z, either many-one or in the sense of Turing. We must also show that $Z \in \mathcal{NP}$ by exhibiting an efficient proof system for Z. Several thousand $\mathcal{NP}$−complete problems have been enumerated in this way. For example, it suffices to prove that the Hamiltonian cycle problem is $\mathcal{NP}$−complete to conclude in the light of Theorem 12.5.9 that the travelling salesperson problem is $\mathcal{NP}$−complete as well.

This is all well and good once the process is under way, since the more problems there are in the pool, the more likely it is that we can find one that can be reduced without too much difficulty to some new problem. The trick, of course, is to get the ball rolling. What should we do at the outset when the pool is empty to prove for the very first time that some particular problem is $\mathcal{NP}$−complete? How do we even know that $\mathcal{NP}$−complete problems exist at all? This is the *tour de force* that Steven Cook and Leonid Levin managed to perform independently in the early 1970's, opening the way to the whole theory of $\mathcal{NP}$−completeness. The full proof of this result is technically difficult; in the rest of this section, we give a rough overview of the fundamental ideas behind it. Recall that Boolean formulas are reviewed in Section 1.4.1.

> **Definition 12.5.12** *A Boolean formula is* satisfiable *if there exists at least one way of assigning values to its variables so as to make it true. We denote by* **SAT** *the problem of deciding, given a Boolean formula, whether or not it is satisfiable.*

For example, $(p \vee q) \Rightarrow (p \wedge q)$ is satisfiable because it is *true* if we assign the value *true* to both p and q. This formula is satisfiable despite the fact that there exist other value assignments for the variables that make it *false*, such as $p = true$ and $q = false$. On the other hand, $(\neg p) \wedge (p \vee q) \wedge (\neg q)$ is not satisfiable because it remains *false* regardless of which Boolean values are assigned to p and q. Try it!

It is possible in principle to decide whether a Boolean formula is satisfiable by working out its value for every possible assignment to its Boolean variables. However this is impractical when the number n of Boolean variables involved is large, since there are 2^n possible assignments. No efficient algorithm to solve this problem is known. On the other hand, any assignment purporting to satisfy a Boolean formula is both succinct and easy to verify, which shows that SAT $\in \mathcal{NP}$.

Consider now a special case of Boolean formulas.

Definition 12.5.13 *A literal is either a Boolean variable or its negation. A* clause *is a literal or a disjunction of literals. A Boolean formula is in* conjunctive normal form (CNF) *if it is a clause or a conjunction of clauses. It is in* k–CNF *for some positive integer k if it is composed of clauses, each of which contains at most k literals.*

For notational simplicity, it is customary to represent disjunction (or) in such formulas by the symbol "$+$" and conjunction (and) by simply juxtaposing the operands as if it were arithmetic multiplication; negation is often denoted by a horizontal bar above the variable concerned.

Consider for example the following formulas.

$$(p + \overline{q} + r)\,(\overline{p} + q + r)\,q\,\overline{r}$$
$$(p + qr)\,(\overline{p} + q\,(q + r))$$
$$(p \Rightarrow q) \Longleftrightarrow (\overline{p} + q)$$

The first formula is composed of four clauses. It is in 3–CNF, and therefore in CNF, but not in 2–CNF. The second formula is not in CNF since neither $(p + qr)$ nor $(\overline{p} + q\,(q + r))$ is a clause. The third formula is also not in CNF since it contains operators other than conjunction, disjunction and negation.

Definition 12.5.14 SAT–CNF *is the restriction of problem* SAT *to Boolean formulas in CNF. For any positive k,* SAT–k–CNF *is the restriction of* SAT–CNF *to Boolean formulas in k–CNF.*

Clearly, those problems are in $\mathcal{NP}$. An efficient algorithm is known to solve SAT–2–CNF but even SAT–3–CNF is intractable to the best of our knowledge. This is not surprising as we shall see in Section 12.5.4 that this latter problem is $\mathcal{NP}$–complete.

The relevance of Boolean formulas in the context of $\mathcal{NP}$–completeness arises from their ability to simulate algorithms. Consider an arbitrary decision problem that can be solved by a polynomial-time algorithm A. Suppose the size of the instances is measured in bits. To every integer n there corresponds a Boolean formula $\Psi_n(A)$ in CNF that can be obtained efficiently. This formula contains a large number of variables, among which $x_1, x_2, \ldots, x_n$ correspond in a natural way to the bits of instances of size n for A. The Boolean formula is constructed so that there exists a way to satisfy it by choosing the values of its other Boolean variables if and only if algorithm A accepts the instance corresponding to the Boolean value of the x variables. For example, algorithm A accepts the instance 10010 if and only if formula $x_1 \overline{x}_2 \overline{x}_3 x_4 \overline{x}_5 \Psi_5(A)$ is satisfiable.

The proof that this Boolean formula exists and that it can be constructed efficiently poses difficult technical problems beyond the scope of this book. We content ourselves with mentioning that the formula $\Psi_n(A)$ contains among other things a distinct Boolean variable b_{it} for each bit i of storage that algorithm A may need to use when solving an instance of size n, and for each unit t of time taken by this computation. Once the variables $x_1, x_2, \ldots, x_n$ are fixed, the clauses of $\Psi_n(A)$ force the other Boolean variables to simulate the step-by-step execution of the algorithm on the corresponding instance.

Consider now an arbitrary problem $Y \in \mathcal{NP}$ whose proof space and efficient proof system are Q and F, respectively. Assume without loss of generality that there is a polynomial $p(n)$ such that for all $y \in Y$ there exists a certificate $q \in Q$ whose length is exactly $p(n)$, where n is the length of y. Assuming that we can solve instances of SAT–CNF at unit cost, we want to decide efficiently if $y \in Y$ for any given instance y. For this, consider algorithm A_y, whose specific purpose is to verify if its input is a certificate that $y \in Y$. In other words, $A_y(q)$ returns *true* if and only if $\langle y, q \rangle \in F$. This can be done efficiently by the assumption that proof system F is efficient. By definition, Boolean formula $\Psi_{p(n)}(A_y)$ is satisfiable if and only if there exists a q of length $p(n)$ such that A_y accepts input q. By definition of the proof system, this is equivalent to saying that $y \in Y$. Therefore, it suffices to decide whether or not $\Psi_{p(n)}(A_y)$ is satisfiable to know whether or not $y \in Y$. This shows how to reduce an arbitrary instance of problem Y to the satisfiability of a Boolean formula in CNF, and therefore $Y \leq_m^p$ SAT–CNF. We conclude that $Y \leq_T^p$ SAT–CNF for all problems Y in $\mathcal{NP}$. Remembering that SAT–CNF is itself in $\mathcal{NP}$, we obtain the following fundamental theorem.

Theorem 12.5.15 (Cook)   SAT–CNF *is* $\mathcal{NP}$−*complete.*

Armed with this first $\mathcal{NP}$−completeness result, we can now apply Theorem 12.5.11 to prove the $\mathcal{NP}$−completeness of other problems.

12.5.4   A few $\mathcal{NP}$−completeness proofs

We have just seen that SAT–CNF is $\mathcal{NP}$−complete. Let Z be some other decision problem in $\mathcal{NP}$. To show that Z too is $\mathcal{NP}$−complete, Theorem 12.5.11 applies and we need only prove SAT–CNF $\leq_T^p Z$. Thereafter, to show that some other W in $\mathcal{NP}$ is $\mathcal{NP}$−complete, we have the choice of proving SAT–CNF $\leq_T^p W$ or $Z \leq_T^p W$. Beware not to proceed backwards: it is the problem already known to be $\mathcal{NP}$–complete that must be reduced to the new problem, not the other way round. We illustrate this principle with a few examples.

> **Theorem 12.5.16**   SAT *is* $\mathcal{NP}$–*complete.*

Proof   We already know that SAT is in $\mathcal{NP}$. Since SAT–CNF is the only problem that we know to be $\mathcal{NP}$–complete so far, we must show that SAT–CNF $\leq_T^p$ SAT to apply Theorem 12.5.11. This is immediate since Boolean formulas in CNF are a special case of general Boolean formulas and it is easy to tell, given a Boolean formula, whether or not it is in CNF. Therefore any algorithm capable of solving SAT efficiently can be used directly to solve SAT–CNF.   ∎

> **Theorem 12.5.17**   SAT–3–CNF *is* $\mathcal{NP}$–*complete.*

Proof   We already know that SAT–3–CNF is in $\mathcal{NP}$. Because we now know two different $\mathcal{NP}$–complete problems, we have the choice of proving either SAT–CNF $\leq_T^p$ SAT–3–CNF or SAT $\leq_T^p$ SAT–3–CNF. Let us prove the former and proceed by many-one reduction: we prove SAT–CNF $\leq_m^p$ SAT–3–CNF. Consider an arbitrary Boolean formula Ψ in CNF. We are to construct efficiently a Boolean formula $\xi = f(\Psi)$ in 3–CNF that is satisfiable if and only if Ψ is satisfiable. Consider first the case when Ψ contains only one clause, which is a disjunction of k literals.

⋄ If $k \leq 3$, let $\xi = \Psi$, which is already in 3–CNF.

⋄ If $k = 4$, let ℓ_1, ℓ_2, ℓ_3 and ℓ_4 be literals such that Ψ is $\ell_1 + \ell_2 + \ell_3 + \ell_4$. Let u be a new Boolean variable. Take

$$\xi = (\ell_1 + \ell_2 + u)(\overline{u} + \ell_3 + \ell_4).$$

Note that if at least one of the ℓ_i's is *true* then Ψ is *true* and it is possible to select a truth value for u so that ξ is *true* also. Conversely, if all the ℓ_i's are *false* then Ψ is *false* and ξ is *false* whatever truth value is chosen for u. Therefore, given any fixed truth values for the ℓ_i's, Ψ is *true* if and only if ξ is satisfiable with a suitable choice of value for u.

⋄ More generally, if $k \geq 4$, let $\ell_1, \ell_2, \ldots, \ell_k$ be the literals such that Ψ is $\ell_1 + \ell_2 + \cdots + \ell_k$. Let $u_1, u_2, \ldots, u_{k-3}$ be new Boolean variables. Take

$$\xi = (\ell_1 + \ell_2 + u_1)(\overline{u}_1 + \ell_3 + u_2) \cdots (\overline{u}_{k-3} + \ell_{k-1} + \ell_k).$$

Again, given any fixed truth values for the ℓ_i's, Ψ is *true* if and only if ξ is satisfiable with a suitable choice of assignments for the u_i's.

If the formula Ψ consists of several clauses, treat each of them independently—using different u variables for each clause—and form the conjunction of all the expressions in 3–CNF thus obtained. For example, if

$$\Psi = (p + \overline{q} + r + s)\,(\overline{r} + s)\,(\overline{p} + s + \overline{x} + v + \overline{w})$$

we obtain

$$\xi = (p + \overline{q} + u_1)\,(\overline{u}_1 + r + s)\,(\overline{r} + s)\,(\overline{p} + s + u_2)\,(\overline{u}_2 + \overline{x} + u_3)\,(\overline{u}_3 + v + \overline{w}).$$

Because each clause is "translated" with the help of different u variables, and because the only way to satisfy Ψ is to satisfy each of its clauses with the same truth assignment for the Boolean variables, any satisfying assignment for Ψ gives rise to one for ξ and vice versa. In other words, Ψ is satisfiable if and only if ξ is. But ξ is in 3–CNF. This shows how to transform an arbitrary CNF formula efficiently into one in 3–CNF in a way that preserves satisfiability. Thus SAT–CNF $\leq_m^p$ SAT–3–CNF, which completes the proof that SAT–3–CNF is $\mathcal{NP}$–complete.   ∎

Definition 12.5.18   *Let G be an undirected graph and let k be an integer. A colouring of G is an assignment of colours to the nodes of G such that any two nodes joined by an edge are of different colours. It is a* k-colouring *if it uses no more than k distinct colours. The smallest k such that a k-colouring exists is called the graph's* chromatic number *and any such k-colouring is an* optimal colouring. *We define the following four problems.*

⋄ **3COL:** *Given a graph G, can G be painted with 3 colours?*

⋄ **COLD:** *Given a graph G and an integer k, can G be painted with k colours?*

⋄ **COLO:** *Given a graph G, find the chromatic number of G.*

⋄ **COLC:** *Given a graph G, find an optimal colouring of G.*

Problems 12.43 and 12.44 ask you to prove that these problems are polynomially equivalent: any one of them can be solved in polynomial time if and only if they all can. As we are about to prove that 3COL is $\mathcal{NP}$–complete, this is evidence that all four problems are hard.

Theorem 12.5.19   3COL *is* $\mathcal{NP}$–complete.

Proof   It is easy to see that 3COL is in $\mathcal{NP}$ since any purported 3-colouring can be verified efficiently. To show that 3COL is $\mathcal{NP}$–complete we shall prove this time that SAT–3–CNF $\leq_m^p$ 3COL. Given a Boolean formula Ψ in 3–CNF, we have to construct efficiently a graph G that can be painted with three colours if and only if Ψ is satisfiable. This reduction is considerably more complex than those we have seen so far.

Suppose for simplicity that every clause of the formula Ψ contains exactly three literals (see Problem 12.54). Let k be the number of clauses in Ψ. Suppose further without loss of generality that the Boolean variables appearing in Ψ are $x_1, x_2, \ldots, x_t$. The graph G we are about to build contains $3 + 2t + 6k$ nodes and $3 + 3t + 12k$ edges. Three special nodes of this graph are linked in a *control triangle* shown on top of Figure 12.8: call them T, F and C. Because each is linked to the other two, they must be a different colour in any valid colouring of the graph. When the time comes to paint G in three colours, imagine that the colours assigned to T and F represent the Boolean values *true* and *false*, respectively. We shall say that a node is coloured *true* if it is the same colour as T, and similarly for nodes coloured *false*. Any node coloured either *true* or *false* is called a *truth node*.

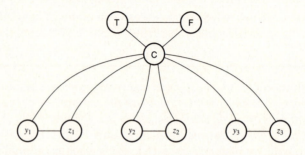

Figure 12.8. Graph representation of three Boolean variables

For each Boolean variable x_i of Ψ the graph contains two nodes y_i and z_i linked to each other and to the control node C. In any valid three-colouring of G, this forces y_i to be coloured either *true* or *false* and z_i to be the complementary colour. Think of the colour of node y_i as the truth assignment for Boolean variable x_i so the colour of node z_i corresponds to the truth value of $\overline{x}_i$. We may think of the y_i's and z_i's as corresponding to literals in the Boolean formula. For example, Figure 12.8 shows the part of the graph that we have constructed up to now if the formula is on three variables.

We still have to add 6 nodes and 12 edges for each clause in Ψ. These are added so that the graph will be colourable with three colours if and only if the choice of colours for $y_1, y_2, \ldots, y_t$ corresponds to an assignment of Boolean values to $x_1, x_2, \ldots, x_t$ that satisfies every clause. This is accomplished thanks to the *widget* illustrated in Figure 12.9. We say that a widget is *linked* to nodes a, b and c if these are the edge endpoints marked 1, 2 and 3. Each widget is also connected directly to nodes T and C by two other dangling edges. It can be verified by trying all eight possibilities that if the widget is linked only to truth nodes, then it can be painted with the colours assigned to the control triangle if and only if it is linked with at least one node coloured *true*. Thus, the widget can be used to simulate the disjunction of the three literals represented by the nodes to which it is joined. To complete the graph, it suffices to include one copy of the widget for each clause in Ψ. Each widget is linked to nodes chosen from the y_i's and z_i's so as to correspond to the three literals of the clause concerned. Any valid three-colouring of the graph provides a truth assignment for the Boolean formula and vice versa. Therefore, the graph can be painted with three colours if and only if Ψ is satisfiable. Because it can be constructed efficiently starting from any Boolean formula Ψ in 3–CNF, we conclude that SAT–3–CNF $\leq_m^p$ 3COL, and therefore that 3COL is $\mathcal{NP}$–complete. ∎

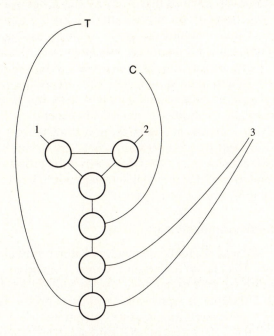

Figure 12.9. A widget

12.5.5 $\mathcal{NP}$–hard problems

To provide evidence that a problem cannot be solved efficiently, there is no need to prove that it belongs to $\mathcal{NP}$. We say that a problem X is $\mathcal{NP}$–*hard* if there is an $\mathcal{NP}$–complete problem Y that can be polynomially Turing reduced to it: $Y \leq_T^p X$. By definition of polynomial reductions, any polynomial-time algorithm for X would translate into one for Y. Since Y is $\mathcal{NP}$–complete, this would imply that $\mathcal{P} = \mathcal{NP}$, contrary to the generally accepted belief. Therefore, no $\mathcal{NP}$–hard problem can be solved in polynomial time in the worst case under the assumption that $\mathcal{P} \neq \mathcal{NP}$.

There are several reasons to study $\mathcal{NP}$–hardness rather than $\mathcal{NP}$–completeness. In particular, $\mathcal{NP}$–hard problems do not have to be decision problems. Consider for example the graph colouring problems stated in Definition 12.5.18. It is obvious that any efficient algorithm to find an optimal graph colouring (COLC) or to determine the chromatic number of a graph (COLO) can be used to determine efficiently whether a graph can be painted with three colours (3COL). In symbols, 3COL $\leq_T^p$ COLO $\leq_T^p$ COLC. It follows from the $\mathcal{NP}$–completeness of 3COL that both COLO and COLC are $\mathcal{NP}$–hard even though they are not $\mathcal{NP}$–complete because they are not decision problems. We shall see many $\mathcal{NP}$–hard problems that are not $\mathcal{NP}$–complete for this reason in Chapter 13.

The notion of $\mathcal{NP}$–hardness is interesting also for decision problems. There are decision problems that are known to be $\mathcal{NP}$–hard but believed not to be in $\mathcal{NP}$, and thus not $\mathcal{NP}$–complete. Consider for example the problem COLE of *exact* colouring: given a graph G and an integer k, can G be painted with k colours but no less? Again it is obvious that 3COL $\leq^p_T$ COLE because a graph is 3-colourable if and only if its chromatic number is either $0, 1, 2$ or 3. From the $\mathcal{NP}$–completeness of 3COL we conclude that the exact graph colouring problem is $\mathcal{NP}$–hard. However, this decision problem does not seem to be in $\mathcal{NP}$. Although any valid colouring of G with k colours can be used as a succinct certificate that G can be painted with k colours, it is hard to imagine what a succinct certificate that G *cannot* be painted with fewer colours would look like, and there are strong theoretical reasons to believe that such certificates do not exist in general.

Finally, $\mathcal{NP}$–hardness is often the only thing we really care to establish. Unless it should turn out that $\mathcal{P} = \mathcal{NP}$, it is not very useful in practice to know that a given problem belongs to $\mathcal{NP}$. Thus even if the problem considered is a decision problem and even if it is reasonable to expect it to be in $\mathcal{NP}$, why waste time and effort exhibiting a proof system for it?

12.5.6 Nondeterministic algorithms

The class $\mathcal{NP}$ was originally defined quite differently, although the definitions are equivalent. The classic definition involves the notion of nondeterministic algorithms, which we only sketch here. As we said earlier, the name $\mathcal{NP}$ arose from this other definition: it represents the class of problems that can be solved by a $\mathcal{N}$ondeterministic algorithm in $\mathcal{P}$olynomial time.

Although nondeterministic algorithms can be defined with respect to general problems, we concentrate again for simplicity on decision problems. In this context, nondeterministic algorithms terminate their execution with either **accept** or **reject**, two special instructions explained below, or they may loop forever. In addition, nondeterministic algorithms may use a special instruction

> **choose** n **between** i **and** j

whose effect is to set n to some integer value between i and j, inclusive. The actual value assigned to n is not specified by the algorithm, nor is it subject to the laws of probability. Thus nondeterministic algorithms should not be confused with probabilistic algorithms

The effect of the algorithm is determined by the existence or the nonexistence of sequences of nondeterministic choices that lead to an **accept** instruction. We are *not* concerned with how such sequences could be determined efficiently or how their nonexistence could be established. For this reason nondeterministic algorithms are only a mathematical abstraction that cannot be used directly in practice: we never program such an algorithm in the hope of running it efficiently on a real computer. In particular, it would be pointless to replace the **choose** instructions by probabilistic choices such as "$n \leftarrow uniform(i\,..\,j)$" because the probability of success could be infinitesimal in general. Thus we are not worried by the fact that, as we shall see, nondeterministic algorithms can solve $\mathcal{NP}$–complete problems in polynomial time.

Definition 12.5.20   *An* accepting computation *of the algorithm is a sequence of nondeterministic choices that leads to an* **accept** *instruction. The algorithm accepts input x if it has at least one accepting computation when run on x; otherwise it* rejects *the input. The algorithm solves* decision problem X *if it accepts every $x \in X$ and rejects every $x \notin X$.*

The time *taken by a nondeterministic algorithm on an instance that it accepts is defined as the shortest possible time that any accepting computation may cause it to run on this instance; the time is undefined on rejected instances. A nondeterministic algorithm* runs in polynomial time *if the time it takes on accepted instances is bounded by some polynomial in the size of the instance.*

Note that a nondeterministic algorithm accepts input x even if it has only one accepting computation to pit against many rejecting computations. Note also that there is no limit on how long a polynomial-time nondeterministic algorithm may run if the "wrong" nondeterministic choices are made or if it is run on a rejected instance; the algorithm may even loop forever in these cases. A computation may be arbitrarily long even on an accepted instance, provided the same instance also admits at least one polynomially bounded computation.

Consider for example the following nondeterministic algorithm to decide if a graph is Hamiltonian. It chooses a sequence of nodes nondeterministically in the hope of hitting a Hamiltonian cycle. Clearly, there exists at least one sequence of choices that leads to acceptance if and only if a Hamiltonian cycle exists. On the other hand, it would be pointless to try running the algorithm after replacing the nondeterministic choices by probabilistic ones.

```
procedure HamND(G = ⟨N, A⟩)
    {This algorithm assumes the graph contains at least 3 nodes}
    n ← |N|
    let the nodes be N = {v₁, v₂, ..., vₙ}
    S ← ∅
    x ← v₁
    for k ← 2 to n do
        choose i {between} 2 and n
        if i ∈ S or {x, vᵢ} ∉ A then reject
        x ← vᵢ
        S ← S ∪ {x}
    if {x, v₁} ∈ A then accept
                    else reject
```

Consider now an arbitrary problem $X \in \mathcal{NP}$ and let Q and F be its proof space and efficient proof system, respectively. Assume for simplicity that Q is the set of all binary strings. The relevance of nondeterministic algorithms is that, given any x, they can nondeterministically choose a $q \in Q$ such that $\langle x, q \rangle \in F$ provided such a q exists. This q can be chosen bit by bit, after a sequence of binary nondeterministic choices. In a sense, the algorithm uses its nondeterministic power to guess a certificate that $x \in X$ if one exists. After guessing q, the algorithm verifies deterministically whether or not $\langle x, q \rangle \in F$, and it accepts if this is so. This nondeterministic algorithm accepts each yes-instance because there is at least one sequence of binary nondeterministic choices that hits upon a proper certificate, yielding an accepting computation. On the other hand, no-instances cannot be accepted because $\langle x, q \rangle \notin F$ no matter which q is chosen when $x \notin X$. Moreover, this nondeterministic algorithm runs in polynomial time because the existence of a succinct certificate on yes-instances is guaranteed and because the test that $\langle x, q \rangle \in F$ can be performed in polynomial time by definition of $\mathcal{NP}$.

Formally, here is the polynomial-time nondeterministic algorithm to solve problem X. Note that it never halts on no-instances, which is allowed in the definition of polynomial-time for nondeterministic algorithms.

```
procedure XND(x)
q ← empty binary string
while ⟨x, q⟩ ∉ F do
    choose b between 0 and 1
    append bit b to the right of q
accept
```

Conversely, any decision problem that is solved in polynomial time by a nondeterministic algorithm belongs to $\mathcal{NP}$. For this we use the set of all possible sequences of nondeterministic choices as proof space. The proof system F is defined as the set of pairs $\langle x, \sigma \rangle$ such that x is a yes-instance and σ is a sequence of nondeterministic choices according to which the nondeterministic algorithm accepts input x. Because the nondeterministic algorithm runs in polynomial time, at least one of these accepting sequences is of polynomial length, so there is at least one succinct certificate for every yes-instance. Moreover, it is easy to verify in deterministic polynomial time that a given σ is a proper certificate that $x \in X$: it suffices to simulate the nondeterministic algorithm, except that sequence σ is consulted to decide deterministically how to proceed each time we come to a nondeterministic choice.

From the discussion above, we see that Definition 12.5.2 of $\mathcal{NP}$ is equivalent to saying that $\mathcal{NP}$ is the class of decision problems that are solved in polynomial time by nondeterministic algorithms. Again, this was the original definition from which $\mathcal{NP}$ got its name.

12.6 A menagerie of complexity classes

A fruitful approach in the study of computational complexity revolves around the notion of *complexity classes*. A complexity class consists of the set of all problems of some kind (decision problems for instance) that can be solved using a given model of computation without exceeding some given amount of resources. For example, P is the class of all decision problems that can be solved by deterministic algorithms in polynomial time and NP is the class of all decision problems that can be solved by nondeterministic algorithms in polynomial time. Many other complexity classes have been studied. Here we merely scratch the surface of this rich topic. Figure 12.10 summarizes the discussion below.

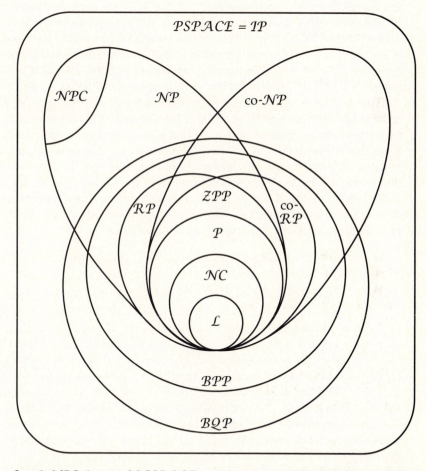

L and NPC denote $LOGSPACE$ and the class of NP-complete problems, respectively. This diagram is correct provided there are no NP-complete problems in BQP, which is believed but not proven. All the regions are conjectured to be nonempty, but only $LOGSPACE$ and $PSPACE$ are known to be different.

Figure 12.10. A menagerie of complexity classes

$\mathcal{PSPACE}$ is the class of all decision problems that can be solved using at most a polynomial number of bits of storage. More precisely, a decision problem belongs to $\mathcal{PSPACE}$ if there exists an algorithm A that solves it and a polynomial $p(n)$ such that the amount of storage needed by A on any instance x is no more than $p(n)$ bits, where n is the size of x. Because any algorithm can be transformed without significant slow-down into one that needs no more space than it uses time, it is clear that $\mathcal{P} \subseteq \mathcal{PSPACE}$. However, it is not known whether or not this inclusion is proper. This is even more embarrassing than our inability to prove that $\mathcal{P} \neq \mathcal{NP}$ because $\mathcal{NP} \subseteq \mathcal{PSPACE}$; see Problem 12.60. You guessed it: we do not know whether or not this latter inclusion is proper. Nevertheless, there are things that we do know about $\mathcal{PSPACE}$. There exist problems in $\mathcal{PSPACE}$ to which all other problems in $\mathcal{PSPACE}$ can be polynomially Turing reduced. Those $\mathcal{PSPACE}$–complete problems can be solved in polynomial time if and only if $\mathcal{P} = \mathcal{PSPACE}$. A surprising result is that nondeterminism does not buy much computing power when the limiting resource is storage: $\mathcal{PSPACE} = \mathcal{NPSPACE}$, where $\mathcal{NPSPACE}$ is the nondeterministic version of $\mathcal{PSPACE}$; see Problem 12.61.

Just as $\mathcal{PSPACE}$ is believed to lie beyond $\mathcal{P}$ and $\mathcal{NP}$, $\mathcal{LOGSPACE}$ is believed to be more restrictive than $\mathcal{P}$. This is the class of all decision problems that can be solved with an amount of storage that is no more than some constant times the logarithm of the instance size. For this definition to make sense, we assume that the instance is given in read-only storage, and we count only the number of additional bits of read/write storage needed to perform the calculation. Problem 12.62 asks you to prove that $\mathcal{LOGSPACE} \subseteq \mathcal{P}$, but we have to admit ignorance of whether or not this inclusion is proper. However, we *do* know that $\mathcal{LOGSPACE}$ is strictly included in $\mathcal{PSPACE}$. To summarize, we know that

$$\mathcal{LOGSPACE} \subseteq \mathcal{P} \subseteq \mathcal{NP} \subseteq \mathcal{PSPACE}$$

and at least one of these inclusions is strict. It is conjectured they all are.

If C is a complexity class of decision problems, we denote by *co-C* the class of decision problems whose complements are in C. In other words, if I is a set of instances and $X \subseteq I$ is a decision problem that belongs to C, then $I \setminus X$ belongs to *co-C*. For example, the set of Boolean formulas that are *not* satisfiable and the set of graphs that do *not* contain a Hamiltonian cycle belong to co-$\mathcal{NP}$. It is clear that $\mathcal{P}$ is a subset of both $\mathcal{NP}$ and co-$\mathcal{NP}$, and that $\mathcal{NP}$ and co-$\mathcal{NP}$ are both subsets of $\mathcal{PSPACE}$. The discussion just before Theorem 12.5.3 gives credence to the conjecture than $\mathcal{NP} \neq$ co-$\mathcal{NP}$, but this is not something we know how to prove. Nevertheless, it is known that $\mathcal{NP} =$ co-$\mathcal{NP}$ if and only if there exists an $\mathcal{NP}$–complete problem in co-$\mathcal{NP}$. Not many problems are known to be in $\mathcal{NP} \cap$ co-$\mathcal{NP}$ yet believed not to be in $\mathcal{P}$. Among those, we mention the set of prime numbers and the decision problem polynomially Turing equivalent to factorization given in Problem 12.48.

Probabilistic algorithms give rise to probabilistic complexity classes. For technical reasons, the formal definition of those classes restricts probabilistic algorithms to tossing fair coins rather than having access to *uniform*(a, b) for arbitrary real numbers a and b.

◇ Monte Carlo algorithms give rise to the class $\mathcal{BPP}$, which stands for *bounded-error probabilistic polynomial-time*. A decision problem belongs to $\mathcal{BPP}$ if there is a p-correct probabilistic algorithm that solves it in polynomial time for some $p > 1/2$. As we saw in Section 10.6.4, the error probability can be reduced below any desired threshold by repeating the algorithm some number of times and taking the most frequent answer.

◇ Las Vegas algorithms give rise to the class $\mathcal{ZPP}$, which stands for *zero-error probabilistic polynomial-time*. A decision problem belongs to $\mathcal{ZPP}$ if there is a probabilistic algorithm that solves it with no possibility of error in expected polynomial time.

◇ Between $\mathcal{BPP}$ and $\mathcal{ZPP}$ is the class $\mathcal{RP}$, which stands for *random polynomial-time*. A decision problem belongs to $\mathcal{RP}$ if there is a p-correct probabilistic algorithm that solves it in polynomial time for some $p > 0$ so that the correct answer is obtained with certainty on all no-instances. As we saw in Section 10.6.4, the error probability can be reduced below any desired threshold much more efficiently than with general $\mathcal{BPP}$ algorithms. It is conjectured that $\mathcal{RP} \neq \text{co-}\mathcal{RP}$.

The following relations between probabilistic and deterministic complexity classes hold.

$$\mathcal{P} \subseteq \mathcal{ZPP} \subseteq \mathcal{RP} \subseteq \mathcal{BPP} \subseteq \mathcal{PSPACE}$$

In addition, Problems 12.64 and 12.65 ask you to prove that $\mathcal{RP} \subseteq \mathcal{NP}$ and $\mathcal{ZPP} = \mathcal{RP} \cap \text{co-}\mathcal{RP}$. On the other hand, it is believed that neither $\mathcal{NP}$ nor $\mathcal{BPP}$ is a subset of the other.

When we defined $\mathcal{NP}$, we said we could think of it as the class of decision problems for which an omniscient being could convince you of the validity of any yes-instance by showing you a succinct certificate whose validity you could verify efficiently even though you may be unable to find the certificate yourself. It is natural to extend this notion to allow *interaction* with the being: it shows you something, you issue a challenge, it answers, you issue another challenge, and so on. A decision problem X belongs to the class $\mathcal{IP}$, which stands for *interactively provable*, if the being can convince you that $x \in X$ whenever this is so, but if you are almost certain to catch it lying if it tries to convince you that $x \in X$ when in fact this is not so. The entire interaction is required to take a time bounded by some polynomial in the size of the instance, assuming that the being answers instantly. See Problem 12.66 for an example. It is obvious that $\mathcal{NP} \subseteq \mathcal{IP}$ since the interaction could consist simply in the being showing you an $\mathcal{NP}$ certificate. Could it be that there are statements that can be proved interactively, but only if several rounds take place? In other words, is the inclusion $\mathcal{NP} \subseteq \mathcal{IP}$ strict? Although we do not know the answer for sure, it is a safe bet that this is so because one of the most striking recent results in computational complexity is that $\mathcal{IP} = \mathcal{PSPACE}$.

Parallel algorithms give rise to parallel complexity classes. Although there is a great number of these, we mention only the most popular. $\mathcal{NC}$ is the class of problems that can be solved by efficient parallel algorithms. Recall from Section 11.3 that this means that the problem can be solved in polylogarithmic time on a polynomial number of processors. (The class $\mathcal{NC}$ is named after its inventor Nicholas Pippenger: it stands for Nick's Class.) It is obvious that $\mathcal{NC} \subseteq \mathcal{P}$ because it is straightforward to simulate polynomially many processors working for polylogarithmic time on a single processor in polynomial time. It is also known that $\mathcal{LOGSPACE} \subseteq \mathcal{NC}$. Neither inclusion is known to be strict. The theory of $\mathcal{NP}$–completeness has a close parallel in the study of $\mathcal{NC}$: $\mathcal{P}$–complete problems are known to be in $\mathcal{P}$ but they are in $\mathcal{NC}$ if and only if $\mathcal{NC} = \mathcal{P}$. The problem of deciding, given a directed graph $G = \langle N, A \rangle$ and two nodes $u, v \in N$, whether or not there is a path from u to v is $\mathcal{P}$–complete, for example.

Finally, quantum computers give rise to a whole new collection of complexity classes. Although we do not explain in this book what a quantum computer is, think of a device that uses the superposition principle of quantum mechanics for computational purposes. This allows massive parallelism in a single piece of hardware. Quantum computing is reminiscent of classical probabilistic algorithms, except that sometimes the "probabilities" appear to go negative thanks to a phenomenon known as quantum interference. It is not known if quantum computers are genuinely more powerful than probabilistic machines. There is strong evidence that they are, because the factorization of large integers can be performed in polynomial time by quantum computers, whereas it is a task believed to be intractable with classical machines. On the other hand, there is strong evidence that quantum computers cannot solve $\mathcal{NP}$–complete problems in polynomial time. Furthermore, quantum computers are still the stuff of dreams: they lie beyond the reach of current technology. But for how long? Of all the quantum complexity classes, we mention only one: $\mathcal{BQP}$ is the class of decision problems that can be solved in polynomial time on a quantum computer so that the correct answer is obtained with probability at least p on all instances, for some $p > 1/2$. It is known that $\mathcal{BPP} \subseteq \mathcal{BQP} \subseteq \mathcal{PSPACE}$; both inclusions are believed to be strict, but neither has been proven so.

12.7 Problems

Problem 12.1. Prove by mathematical induction on the height that a binary tree of height k has at most 2^k leaves. Conclude that any binary tree with t leaves must have height at least $\lceil \lg t \rceil$.

Problem 12.2. Consider a positive integer k. Let $t = \lfloor \lg k \rfloor$ and $\ell = k - 2^t$. Prove that $h(k) = kt + 2\ell$, where $h(k)$ is the function used in the proof of Theorem 12.2.1. Give an intuitive interpretation of this formula in the context of the average height of a tree with k leaves.

Problem 12.3. Give the decision trees corresponding to the algorithms for sorting by selection (Section 2.4) and by merging (Section 7.4.1), and to *quicksort* (Section 7.4.2) for the case of three items. In the latter two cases, stop the recursive calls when only a single item remains to be "sorted".

Problem 12.4. Give a valid decision tree for sorting four items.

Problem 12.5.   Give a valid decision tree for determining the median of five items. Note that it has only 5 different verdicts, but many more leaves.

Problem 12.6.   Give exact formulas for the number of comparisons carried out in the worst case by the insertion and the selection sorting algorithms when sorting n items. How well do these algorithms perform compared with the information-theoretic lower bound $\lceil \lg 50! \rceil$ for $n = 50$?

Problem 12.7.   Prove that if n is a power of 2, *mergesort* makes $n \lg n - n + 1$ comparisons in the worst case when sorting n items. How does this compare with the information-theoretic lower bound $\lceil \lg n! \rceil$? Find the smallest power of 2 such that *mergesort* requires more comparisons than the information-theoretic lower bound when sorting this number of items.

Problem 12.8.   Continuing Problem 12.7, find an explicit formula for the number of comparisons performed in the worst case by *mergesort* in general, as a function of the number n of items to be sorted. Find the smallest positive integer such that *mergesort* requires more comparisons than the information-theoretic lower bound when sorting this number of items.

Problem 12.9.   Suppose we ask our sorting algorithm not merely to determine the order of the items but also to determine which ones, if any, are equal. For example, a verdict such as $A < B \le C$ is not acceptable: the algorithm must specify whether $B = C$ or $B < C$. Give an information-theoretic lower bound on the number of comparisons required in the worst case to handle n items. Rework this problem if there are three possible outcomes for each comparison: "$<$", "$=$" and "$>$".

Problem 12.10.   Let $T[1..n]$ be an array and $k \le n$ an integer. The problem consists of returning in descending order the k largest items of T. Prove by an information-theoretic argument that any comparison-based deterministic algorithm that solves this problem must make at least $\frac{k}{2} \lg \frac{n}{2}$ comparisons, both in the worst case and on the average. Conclude that this must take a time in $\Omega(k \log n)$. On the other hand, give an algorithm able to solve this problem in a time in $O(n \log k)$ and a space in $O(k)$ in the worst case. Your algorithm should make no more than one sequential pass through the array T. Justify your analysis of the time and space used by your algorithm.

Problem 12.11.   Give a complete decision tree for the 12-coin problem of Section 12.2.2. Each node of the tree should specify which coins are in each pan of the scale. The left child of an internal node gives the next measurement to make if the balance tilts to the left, as do the middle child if the scale is balanced and the right child if the balance tilts to the right. Omit the right-hand descendants of the root to make the tree smaller; these can be handled by symmetry. Refer to the coins as A, B, C, ..., L, so the root of the decision tree should read ABCD : EFGH in accordance with Figure 12.6 and the information-theoretic reasoning of Section 12.2.2.

Problem 12.12.   Continuing Problem 12.11, prove by an information-theoretic argument that the coin-and-balance problem cannot be solved using the scale only three times if we have 13 coins rather than 12. This is interesting because it seems possible at first sight that this problem could be solved: 13 coins generate 27 potential verdicts and a ternary tree of height 3 has 27 leaves to accommodate them all.

Problem 12.13.   Continuing Problems 12.11 and 12.12, prove that the *four*-coin problem cannot be solved with only two measurements unless an additional coin known to be of the "proper" weight is available.

Problem 12.14.   Use an adversary argument to prove that any comparison-based algorithm to decide if a target value appears among n possibilities must take a time in $\Omega(\log n)$ in the worst case, regardless of how cleverly the table of possibilities is arranged. In particular, this lower bound is achieved with binary search if the table is sorted. Could you have proved this result with an information-theoretic argument? How important was it to restrict our attention to comparison-based algorithms?

Problem 12.15.   Let $T[1..n]$ be a sorted array of distinct integers, some of which may be negative. Problem 7.12 asked you for an algorithm that can find an index i such that $1 \le i \le n$ and $T[i] = i$, provided such an index exists, in a time in $O(\log n)$ in the worst case. Use an information-theoretic argument to show that any comparison-based algorithm that solves this problem must take a time in $\Omega(\log n)$. On the other hand, prove by an adversary argument that any comparison-based algorithm that solves this problem would require a time in $\Omega(n)$ in the worst case were it not for the restriction that the items of T be distinct.

Problem 12.16.   Use an adversary argument to prove that any correct deterministic algorithm to decide if an undirected graph is connected must ask for each pair $\{i, j\}$ of vertices whether or not there is an edge between i and j. Assume as in Section 12.3.2 that the only questions about the graph that are allowed are of the form "Is there an edge between vertices i and j?"

Problem 12.17.   Consider the problem of determining whether an undirected graph with n vertices contains a path of length at least 2.

(a) Use an adversary argument to prove that any algorithm to solve this problem must take a time in $\Omega(n^2)$ in the worst case if it is restricted to asking questions of the form "Is there an edge between vertices i and j?" (This is the case if the graph is represented with an adjacency matrix: **type** *adjgraph* in Section 5.4.)

(b) Prove on the other hand that this problem can be solved in a time in $O(n)$ if the algorithm can ask at each vertex for the list of adjacent vertices. (This is the case if the graph is represented with adjacency lists: **type** *lisgraph* in Section 5.4.)

Problem 12.18.   We saw that any correct comparison-based algorithm for finding the median among n items must make at least $3(n-1)/2$ comparisons in the worst case. Use a much simpler adversary argument to prove that when all the items are distinct it is not possible to locate the median with certainty without looking at each item. On the other hand, show by an example that this is not true if the items are not distinct.

Problem 12.19.   The obvious algorithm to find both the minimum and the maximum items in an array of n items takes $2n - 3$ comparisons. Prove by an adversary argument that any comparison-based algorithm for this problem requires at least $\lceil 3n/2 \rceil - 2$ comparisons in the worst case. (Optional: find an algorithm that achieves this lower bound.)

Problem 12.20.   Show how to use a factorization algorithm to split composite numbers and to decide on the primality of arbitrary numbers. (This is not to say that the best primality test proceeds by factorization!)

Problem 12.21.   Assume that large integers are represented in decimal in an array. For example, $T[1..n]$ represents integer $\sum_{i=1}^{n} 10^{i-1} T[i]$. Give an algorithm to perform division by 4 of such integers in a time in $O(n)$. Analyse the time taken by your algorithm. Generalize it to bases other than 10.

Problem 12.22.   Prove that it is impossible for a function in $\Omega(2^n)$ to be smooth.

Problem 12.23.   Prove that any strongly quadratic function is at least quadratic; see Section 12.4.1.

Problem 12.24.   Continuing Problem 12.23, give an explicit example showing it was necessary to specify in the definition of a strongly quadratic function that it be eventually nondecreasing. Specifically, exhibit a function $t : \mathbb{N} \to \mathbb{R}^{\geq 0}$ such that $t(an) \geq a^2 t(n)$ for every positive integer a and every sufficiently large integer n, yet $t(n)$ is not at least quadratic.

Problem 12.25.   Give an explicit example of an eventually nondecreasing function that is at least quadratic but not strongly quadratic.

Problem 12.26.   A function $t : \mathbb{N} \to \mathbb{R}^{\geq 0}$ is *supra quadratic* if it is eventually nondecreasing and if there exists a positive ε such that $t(an) \geq a^{2+\varepsilon} t(n)$ for every positive integer a and every sufficiently large integer n. Show that $n^2 \log n$ is strongly quadratic but not supra quadratic.

Problem 12.27.   Let SQR, MLT and DIV be the problems consisting of squaring an integer of size n, of multiplying two integers of size n, and of determining the quotient when an integer of size $2n$ is divided by an integer of size n, respectively. Clearly, these problems are at least linear because any algorithm that solves them must take into account every bit of the operands involved. Assuming that the three problems are smooth and that MLT is strongly linear, prove that the three problems are linearly equivalent.
Hint: If $10^{n-1} \leq i \leq 10^n - 1$, its *pseudo-inverse* $i^\star$ is defined as $10^{2n-1} \div i$. For example, $36^\star = 27$ and $27^\star = 37$. (In practice we would probably not use base 10.) Let INV be the problem of computing the pseudo-inverse of an integer of size n.

Use INV in your chain of reductions. For example, prove that $i \div j \approx (i \times j^\star) \div 10^{2n-1}$ when i and j are integers of (decimal) size $2n$ and n, respectively, and show how to use this to conclude that DIV $\leq^\ell$ INV follows from MLT $\leq^\ell$ SQR $\leq^\ell$ INV.

Problem 12.28. Continuing Problem 12.27, let SQRT be the problem of finding the integer part of the square root of an integer of size n. Prove under suitable assumptions that SQRT and MLT are linearly equivalent. State explicitly the assumptions you need.

Problem 12.29. Denote by SU the problem of squaring a triangular matrix whose diagonal consists only of 1s. Prove that SU $\equiv^\ell$ MQ under suitable assumptions. What assumptions do you need?

Problem 12.30. Prove that the inverse of a nonsingular upper triangular matrix is upper triangular.

Problem 12.31. Denote by IQ the problem of inverting an arbitrary nonsingular matrix. Prove that IQ $\equiv^\ell$ MQ, assuming both IQ and MQ are supra quadratic; see Problem 12.26. Note that this reduction would *not* go through should an algorithm that is capable of multiplying $n \times n$ matrices in a time in $O(n^2 \log n)$ exist because this function is not supra quadratic.

Problem 12.32. Prove that MUL $\leq^\ell$ TRC, assuming TRC is smooth.

Problem 12.33. Prove that TRC $\leq^\ell$ MUL, assuming MUL is smooth and strongly quadratic.

Problem 12.34. Exhibit a decision problem for which you can prove that to any algorithm that solves it there corresponds another algorithm that solves it exponentially faster on all but finitely many instances.

Problem 12.35. Prove that it takes polynomial time to execute a polynomial number of polynomial-time operations.

Problem 12.36. The set of all composite numbers is obviously in $\mathcal{NP}$ since any nontrivial divisor of n is convincing evidence that n is composite. Recalling the asymmetry of $\mathcal{NP}$ mentioned just before Theorem 12.5.3, it is tempting to expect that the complementary set of all prime numbers is not in $\mathcal{NP}$. After all, it seems certain at first sight that there is no succinct way to prove that a number is prime: what could we possibly exhibit to prove the *non*existence of a nontrivial divisor? However, nothing is certain in this world except death and taxes: primality too is in $\mathcal{NP}$, although the notion of a certificate of primality is rather more subtle than that of a certificate of nonprimality. Your problem is to figure it out!
Hint: An odd integer $n > 2$ is prime if and only if there exists an integer x between 1 and $n - 1$ such that $x^{n-1} \bmod n = 1$ and $x^{(n-1)/p} \bmod n \neq 1$ for each prime divisor p of $n - 1$.

Problem 12.37. Prove that polynomial reductions are transitive. Consider any problems A, B and C such that A $\leq_T^p$ B and B $\leq_T^p$ C; prove that A $\leq_T^p$ C. Rework this problem with many-one reductions "$\leq_m^p$" with the restriction that A, B and C are decision problems.

Problem 12.38.   Exhibit two very simple decision problems X and Y such that $X \leq_T^p Y$, yet $X \nleq_m^p Y$.

Problem 12.39.   Exhibit two decision problems X and Y such that $X \leq_T^p Y$, yet there are good reasons to believe that $X \nleq_m^p Y$. To make this problem more interesting than Problem 12.38, your sets X and Y must be infinite and so must their complements.

Problem 12.40.   Following Problem 12.39, exhibit two decision problems X and Y such that $X \leq_T^p Y$, yet you can prove that $X \nleq_m^p Y$. Again, X and Y must be infinite and so must their complements.

Problem 12.41.   Consider two decision problems X and Y. Prove that if $X \in \mathcal{NP}$ and $Y \leq_m^p X$, then $Y \in \mathcal{NP}$.

Problem 12.42.   Continuing Problem 12.41, give convincing evidence that it is possible that $X \in \mathcal{NP}$ and $Y \leq_T^p X$, yet $Y \notin \mathcal{NP}$ even though Y is a decision problem.

Problem 12.43.   Prove that the problem of optimal graph colouring is decision-reducible. Specifically, consider the problems COLD, COLO and COLC introduced in Definition 12.5.18. Prove that these three problems are polynomially Turing equivalent.

Problem 12.44.   Continuing Problem 12.43, prove that problem 3COL, also introduced in Definition 12.5.18, is polynomially Turing equivalent to COLD, COLO and COLC. You may assume the result required in Problem 12.43 and you may use the fact that 3COL is $\mathcal{NP}$–complete.

Problem 12.45.   Given an undirected graph $G = \langle N, A \rangle$, a *clique* is a set of nodes such that there is an edge in the graph between any two nodes in the clique. (Sometimes a clique is defined as a maximal set having this property; we do not insist on this condition.) There are three natural problems concerning cliques.

◇ CLQD: Given a graph G and an integer k, does there exist a clique of size k in G?

◇ CLKO: Given a graph G, find the size of the largest clique in G.

◇ CLKC: Given a graph G, find a clique of maximum size in G.

Prove that the clique problem is decision-reducible: all three problems above are polynomially Turing equivalent.

Problem 12.46.   Prove that the problem of finding a satisfying assignment in a Boolean formula is decision-reducible: the problem of finding a satisfying assignment for a Boolean formula is polynomially reducible to the problem of deciding if such an assignment exists.

Problem 12.47.   Prove that the travelling salesperson problem is decision-reducible: TSP $\equiv_T^p$ TSPD. (These problems are defined just before Theorem 12.5.9.)

Problem 12.48.   Consider the decision problem

$$F = \{\langle n, d \rangle \mid n \in \mathbb{N}^+ \text{ and } n \text{ has a nontrivial divisor smaller than } d\}.$$

Prove that F is polynomially Turing equivalent to the factorization problem.

Problem 12.49.   Prove that any two $\mathcal{NP}$–complete problems are polynomially Turing equivalent.

Problem 12.50.   Prove that HAMD, the problem of deciding if a graph is Hamiltonian, is $\mathcal{NP}$–complete.

Problem 12.51.   Prove that COLD is $\mathcal{NP}$–complete; see Definition 12.5.18.

Problem 12.52.   Prove that 3COL is $\mathcal{NP}$–complete even if we restrict ourselves to planar graphs of degree not greater than 4; see Definition 12.5.18.

Problem 12.53.   Find a polynomial-time algorithm to solve SAT–2–CNF.

Problem 12.54.   Consider the problem of deciding the satisfiability of Boolean formulas in CNF such that each clause contains *exactly* three literals. Prove that this problem is $\mathcal{NP}$–complete by reducing SAT–3-CNF to it.

Problem 12.55.   Prove that CLQD, the decision version of the clique problem introduced in Problem 12.45, is $\mathcal{NP}$–complete.

Problem 12.56.   You are given a collection $x_1, x_2, \ldots, x_n$ of n integers. Your task is to decide whether or not there exists a set $X \subseteq \{1, 2, \ldots, n\}$ such that $\sum_{i \in X} x_i = \sum_{i \notin X} x_i$. This is known as the PARTITION problem.
(a) Prove that this problem is $\mathcal{NP}$–complete.
(b) Prove that it is decision-reducible: an oracle to solve the decision problem can be used in polynomial time to find an appropriate X whenever it exists.

Problem 12.57.   Prove that if $X \in \mathcal{NP}$ and Y is $\mathcal{NP}$–hard, then $X \leq_T^p Y$. In other words, $\mathcal{NP}$–hard problems are at least as hard as any problem in $\mathcal{NP}$.

Problem 12.58.   Give explicitly a nondeterministic algorithm that solves the problem of nonprimality in polynomial time.

Problem 12.59.   Continuing Problems 12.36 and 12.58, give explicitly a nondeterministic algorithm that solves the problem of primality in polynomial time. Analyse the running time of your algorithm.

Problem 12.60.   Prove that $\mathcal{NP} \subseteq \mathcal{PSPACE}$. For this note that a polynomial amount of storage is sufficient to enumerate all polynomially bounded potential certificates and to try each of them to see if at least one is adequate.

Problem 12.61.   Prove that $\mathcal{PSPACE} = \mathcal{NPSPACE}$. For this, show that if $s(n) \geq \lg n$ can be computed efficiently, any decision problem that can be solved with an amount of storage in $O(s(n))$ bits by a nondeterministic algorithm can also be solved with an amount of storage in $O(s^2(n))$ bits by a deterministic algorithm.

Problem 12.62.   Prove that $\mathcal{LOGSPACE} \subseteq \mathcal{P}$. For this, note that any deterministic algorithm that finds itself twice in the same configuration loops forever; there are only 2^s different configurations when only s bits of storage are available; and $2^{k \lg n} = n^k$.

Problem 12.63.   Assuming $\mathcal{NP} \neq$ co-$\mathcal{NP}$, prove that $\mathcal{NP}$–complete problems cannot belong to co-$\mathcal{NP}$.

Problem 12.64.   Prove that $\mathcal{RP} \subseteq \mathcal{NP}$. For this note that any sequence of probabilistic choices that leads an $\mathcal{RP}$ probabilistic algorithm to accept is convincing evidence that the instance considered is a yes-instance.

Problem 12.65.   Prove that $\mathcal{ZPP} = \mathcal{RP} \cap$ co-$\mathcal{RP}$. Note the similarity with Problem 10.28.

Problem 12.66.   Two graphs $G = \langle V, A \rangle$ and $H = \langle W, B \rangle$ are *isomorphic* if there is a correspondence between the vertices of G and those of H that preserves adjacency. Formally, G and H are isomorphic if there exists a bijective function $\sigma : V \rightarrow W$ such that $(v_1, v_2) \in A$ if and only if $(\sigma(v_1), \sigma(v_2)) \in B$ for all $v_1, v_2 \in V$. Even though no polynomial-time algorithm is known to decide whether or not two given graphs are isomorphic, this problem is obviously in $\mathcal{NP}$ since the function σ can serve as a certificate. However, it is believed that the problem of graph *non*isomorphism is not in $\mathcal{NP}$: what kind of succinct evidence could prove that two given graphs are not isomorphic? Nevertheless, your problem is to show that graph nonisomorphism belongs to the class $\mathcal{IP}$.

Hint: If in fact G and H are isomorphic and if you present me with a graph K chosen randomly among all graphs isomorphic to G, there is no way I can tell whether you produced K from G or from H.

12.8 References and further reading

Computational complexity is covered in detail by Papadimitriou (1994). An introduction for nonspecialists is given by Pippenger (1978). The proof by Wells that 30 comparisons are necessary in the worst case to sort 12 items is an early example of massive calculation: it took 60 hours on a then state-of-the-art MANIAC II computer. See Gonnet and Munro (1986) and Carlsson (1987a) for modifications of *heapsort* that make it come very close to being optimal for the worst-case number of comparisons. It is possible to sort in a time faster than $\Theta(n \log n)$ with the technique of fusion trees introduced by Fredman and Willard (1990) even if the items to be sorted are too large to use pigeonhole sorting; of course this sorting technique does not proceed by comparisons.

The notion of smooth problems and its application to linear reductions is original to Brassard and Bratley (1988). The linear reduction from integer division to integer multiplication is from Cook and Aanderaa (1969). For further information on reductions among arithmetic problems, consult Aho, Hopcroft and Ullman (1974). The reduction from the inversion of arbitrary nonsingular matrices to matrix multiplication is from Bunch and Hopcroft (1974). If f and g are cost functions as in Section 12.4.3, an algorithm asymptotically faster than the naive algorithm for calculating fg is given in Fredman (1976). The linear reduction from cost function multiplication to the calculation of transitive reflexive closures is from Fischer and Meyer (1971) and the converse reduction is from Furman (1970); together they prove Theorem 12.4.12. In the case of cost functions whose range is restricted to $\{0, +\infty\}$, Arlazarov, Dinic, Kronrod and Faradžev (1970) present an algorithm to calculate fg using a number of *Boolean* operations in $O(n^3 / \log n)$; Theorem 12.4.13 is from Fischer and Meyer (1971).

The theory of $\mathcal{NP}$–completeness originated with two fundamental papers: Cook (1971) proves that SAT–CNF is $\mathcal{NP}$–complete and Karp (1972) underlines the importance of this notion by presenting a large number of $\mathcal{NP}$–complete problems. To be historically exact, the original statement from Cook (1971) is that $X \leq_{\mathsf{T}}^p$ TAUT–DNF for every $X \in \mathcal{NP}$, where TAUT–DNF is concerned with tautologies in disjunctive normal form; however this problem is probably not $\mathcal{NP}$–complete because it does not belong to $\mathcal{NP}$ unless $\mathcal{NP} = $ co-$\mathcal{NP}$. A similar theory was developed independently by Levin (1973), who used tiling problems instead of tautologies. The idea that polynomial time is a fundamental concept came earlier to Cobham (1964) and Edmonds (1965). The uncontested authority in matters of $\mathcal{NP}$–completeness is Garey and Johnson (1979). A good introduction is also provided by Hopcroft and Ullman (1979).

The term "decision-reducible" was suggested to the authors by Papadimitriou; read Bellare and Goldwasser (1994) for more on the complexity of decision versus search. Decision-reducibility should not be confused with the better-known notion of self-reducibility according to which the solution of many problems can be reduced to solving the same problem on smaller instances. See Naik, Ogiwara and Selman (1993) for more detail on how decision-reducibility and self-reducibility relate.

Probabilistic complexity classes were investigated by Gill (1977); the class $\mathcal{RP}$ is from Adleman and Manders (1977). Interactive proofs and the class $\mathcal{IP}$ are from Goldwasser, Micali and Rackoff (1989); a similar idea was developed independently by Babai and Moran (1988). The first serious investigation of $\mathcal{NC}$ is from Pippenger (1979). Quantum computing originated with Benioff (1982), Feynman (1982, 1986) and Deutsch (1985); see also Deutsch and Jozsa (1992), Bernstein and Vazirani (1993), Lloyd (1993), Berthiaume and Brassard (1994), Brassard (1994), Shor (1994) and Simon (1994). An encyclopædic source of information on the menagerie of classical complexity classes is Johnson (1990); see also Papadimitriou (1994).

Many of the problems concerning polynomial reductions in Section 12.7 are solved in Karp (1972). Problem 12.34 is from Blum (1967). The fact that the set of primes is in $\mathcal{NP}$ (Problems 12.36 and 12.59) is from Pratt (1975); more succinct primality certificates are given by Pomerance (1987). Problems 12.48 and 12.63 are from Brassard (1979). Part of the solution to Problem 12.52 is from Stockmeyer (1973). Problem 12.61 is from Savitch (1970). Problem 12.66 is from Goldreich, Micali and Wigderson (1991).

Several important computational complexity techniques have gone unmentioned in this chapter. An algebraic approach to lower bounds is described in Aho, Hopcroft and Ullman (1974), Borodin and Munro (1975) and Winograd (1980). Although we do not know how to prove that there are no efficient algorithms for $\mathcal{NP}$-complete problems, there exist problems that are intrinsically difficult, as described in Aho, Hopcroft and Ullman (1974). These can be solved in theory, but it can be proved that no algorithm can solve them in practice when the instances are of moderate size, even if it is allowed to take a time comparable to the age of the Universe and as many bits of storage as there are elementary particles in the known Universe; see Stockmeyer and Chandra (1979). There also exist problems that cannot be solved by any algorithm, whatever the resources available; read Turing (1936), Gardner and Bennett (1979) and Hopcroft and Ullman (1979) for a discussion of these *undecidable* problems.

Chapter 13

Heuristic and

Approximate Algorithms

Knowing that a problem is hard to solve is instructive. It may even be useful if it stops you wasting time searching for an efficient algorithm that probably does not exist. However it does not make the problem go away. Sometimes you have to find some sort of solution to a problem whether it is hard or not. This is the realm of heuristic and approximate algorithms.

By a *heuristic algorithm*, often called simply a *heuristic*, we mean a procedure that may produce a good or even optimal solution to your problem if you are lucky, but that on the other hand may produce no solution or one that is far from optimal if you are not. A heuristic may be deterministic or probabilistic. The essential difference between a probabilistic heuristic and a Monte Carlo algorithm is that the latter must find a correct solution with positive (preferably high) probability whatever the instance considered. On the other hand, there may be instances for which a heuristic, probabilistic or not, will never find a solution. In some cases, a heuristic procedure may amount to little more than intelligent guesswork. One example that we have already seen is the minimax heuristic described in Section 9.8.

We reserve the term *approximate algorithm* for a procedure that always provides some kind of solution to your problem, though it may fail to find the optimal solution. To be useful, it must also be possible to calculate a bound either on the difference or else on the ratio between the optimal solution and the one produced by the approximate algorithm. The following sections illustrate various kinds of bounds that may be encountered.

Even when an exact algorithm is available, a good approximation algorithm may sometimes be useful. The data involved in a particular instance to be solved are often uncertain or inaccurate to a certain degree: the difficulty of gathering information in practical situations is such that it is rarely possible to achieve precision. If the error caused by using an approximation algorithm is less than the possible error caused by using inexact data, and if the approximation algorithm is more efficient than the exact algorithm, then for all practical purposes it may be preferable to use the former.

13.1 Heuristic algorithms

13.1.1 Colouring a graph

We encountered graph colouring problems in Section 12.5.4. Several related problems are formally defined in Definition 12.5.18. The particular problem that concerns us in this section is the following.

Let $G = \langle N, A \rangle$ be an undirected graph. We want to paint the nodes of G in such a way that no two adjacent nodes are the same colour. The problem asks what is the minimum number of colours required. This minimum is called the *chromatic number* of the graph. For instance, the graph of Figure 13.1 can be painted using only two colours, say red for nodes 1, 3 and 4, and blue for nodes 2 and 5. As we saw in Section 12.5.5, this problem is $\mathcal{NP}$–hard.

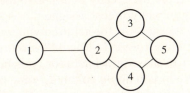

Figure 13.1. A graph to be coloured

An obvious greedy heuristic consists of choosing a colour and an arbitrary starting node, and then considering each node in turn. If a node can be painted with the first colour (in other words, if none of its neighbours has yet been painted), we do so. When no further nodes can be painted, we choose a new colour and a new starting node that has not yet been painted. Then we paint as many nodes as we can with this second colour. This time we paint a node if none of its neighbours has already been painted with the second colour; it doesn't matter whether one or more neighbours have already been painted with the first colour. If there are still unpainted nodes, we choose a third colour, paint as many nodes as we can with that, and so on.

In the example, if node 1 is painted red, we are not allowed to paint node 2 with the same colour. However nodes 3 and 4 can both be painted red, but then node 5 cannot be painted. If we start again at node 2 using blue paint, we can paint nodes 2 and 5 and finish the job using just two colours. This is an optimal solution to our example, since obviously no solution using just one colour is possible. Suppose, however, that we systematically consider the nodes in the order 1, 5, 2, 3, 4. Now we get a different answer: in this case nodes 1 and 5 can be painted red, then node 2 can be painted blue, but now nodes 3 and 4 require a third colour, since they already have both a red neighbour and a blue neighbour. In this case the result is not optimal. The greedy algorithm is therefore no more than a heuristic that may possibly, but not certainly, find an optimal solution.

Even though the heuristic may not find an optimal solution, we may hope that in practice it will be able to find a "good" solution, not too different from the optimum. Let us see whether this hope is justified.

First, it is not hard to show that for any graph G there is at least one ordering of the nodes that allows the greedy algorithm to find an optimal solution. In other words, whatever graph you are working on, there is always a chance you might be lucky and find an optimal solution. To see this, consider any graph G and suppose that an optimal solution requires k colours. Suppose further that by magic you are given a way of colouring G using just k colours. Number these k colours arbitrarily, and then number the nodes of G as follows. First number consecutively all the nodes of G that are painted with colour 1 in the optimal solution. Continue the sequence by numbering all those nodes that are painted with colour 2 in the optimal solution, and so on. When you finish colour k all the nodes will have been numbered. Between nodes of the same colour it doesn't matter which is numbered first.

Now if you apply the greedy heuristic to the graph G considering the nodes in order of the numbers you just assigned, it is sure to find an optimal solution. This may not be the same as the solution you were given to start with, however. For consider applying colour 1. You will certainly be able to paint all the nodes that had colour 1 in the original solution; maybe you will be able to paint some more as well. When you apply colour 2, some nodes that had this colour in the original solution may already be painted with colour 1. However there are sure to be one or more nodes that had colour 2 in the original solution that have not been painted. (Problem 13.2 asks you to justify this remark.) You will be able to paint all these with colour 2, and maybe some more nodes as well. (The presence of extra nodes of colour 1 cannot make it impossible to paint an unpainted node with colour 2.) Continuing in this way, when you finish colour 1 you will have painted at least as many nodes as had colour 1 in the original optimal solution; when you finish colour 2 you will have painted in all at least as many nodes as had colour 1 or colour 2 in the original solution; and so on, until when you finish colour k you will have painted at least as many nodes as had colours $1, 2, \dots, k$ in the original solution: in other words you will have painted all the nodes. Thus you have found a solution using just k colours, which is optimal.

On the negative side, there are graphs that make this heuristic as bad as you choose. More precisely, there are graphs that can be coloured with just k colours for which, if you are unlucky, the heuristic will find a solution using c colours where c/k is as large as you please. To see this, consider a graph with $2n$ nodes numbered from 1 to $2n$. When i is odd, node i is adjacent to all the even-numbered nodes except node $i + 1$; when i is even, node i is adjacent to all the odd-numbered nodes except node $i - 1$. Figure 13.2 shows such a graph for the case $n = 4$. This graph is _bipartite_: the nodes can be divided into two sets N_1 and N_2 (the odd and even-numbered nodes respectively, in this example) such that every edge joins a node in N_1 to a node in N_2. Such a graph can always be coloured with just two colours.

For example, we might paint the odd-numbered nodes red and the even-numbered nodes blue. The greedy heuristic will find this optimal solution if it tries to paint√ nodes in the order $1, 3, \ldots, 2n - 1, 2, 4, \ldots, 2n$, for example. On the other hand, if it √looks at nodes in the natural order $1, 2, \ldots, 2n - 1, 2n$, then it is easy to see that it finds a solution requiring n colours: nodes 1 and 2 can be painted with colour 1, then nodes 3 and 4 must be painted with a new colour 2, nodes 5 and 6 must be painted with a new colour 3, and so on. By choosing n sufficiently large, we can make this solution as bad as we please.

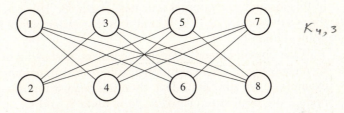

$K_{4,3}$

Figure 13.2. A bipartite graph

This procedure is definitely a heuristic and not an approximate algorithm: there is no way to establish bounds for the error in the solution it provides. You might try to protect yourself against major errors by running the heuristic several times on the same graph with different, randomly chosen orderings of the nodes. Even so, the absence of proper error bounds makes the procedure of little practical use. For a graph with n nodes, in the worst case (when the graph is complete) the heuristic might have to use n colours; for each colour it has to look at every one of the n nodes; and for every node that is not yet painted it might have to look at $n - 1$ neighbours. The running time is thus in $O(n^3)$.

13.1.2 The travelling salesperson

This problem was introduced in Section 12.5.2. We know the distances between a certain number of towns. The travelling salesperson wants to leave one of these towns, to visit each other town exactly once, and to arrive back at the starting point having travelled the shortest distance possible. We assume that the distance between two towns is never negative. Like the previous problem, the travelling salesperson problem is $\mathcal{NP}$–hard, and the known algorithms are impractical for large instances. (Of course this depends what you mean by "large". Using linear programming and cutting plane techniques of a kind not described in this book, problems involving a few hundred towns can now be solved routinely. At the time of writing, the largest real instance of the problem that had been solved involved 4461 towns; see Section 11.9.)

  The problem can be represented as a complete undirected graph with n nodes. (The graph can also be directed if the distance matrix is not symmetric. We shall not consider this possibility here.) We remind the reader that a cycle in the graph that √ passes through each node exactly once is called a *Hamiltonian cycle*. Our problem ✓ therefore requires us to find the shortest Hamiltonian cycle in a given graph.

For example, suppose our problem concerns six towns with the following distance matrix.

From To:	2	3	4	5	6
1	3	10	11	7	25
2		8	12	9	26
3			9	4	20
4				5	15
5					18

In this instance the optimal tour has length 58. This can be achieved with a tour that visits nodes 1, 2, 3, 6, 4, and 5 in that order before returning to the starting point at node 1.

One obvious greedy heuristic consists of starting at an arbitrary node, and then choosing at each step to visit the nearest remaining unvisited node. In the example, if we start at node 1, then the nearest unvisited node is node 2. From node 2 the nearest unvisited node is node 3, and so on. After visiting the last node we come back to the starting point. The tour constructed in this way visits nodes 1, 2, 3, 5, 4, 6 and 1, and has a total length of 60. Thus although the greedy algorithm does not find an optimal solution in this case, it is not far wrong. With other examples, however, it can be catastrophic; see Problem 13.4. Is it possible to find an approximate algorithm that is guaranteed to find a reasonably good solution? We are about to see that the answer is yes if we restrict the class of instances considered (Section 13.2.1), and probably no otherwise (Section 13.3.2).

13.2 Approximate algorithms

13.2.1 The metric travelling salesperson

As we shall see in Section 13.3.2, finding a good approximate algorithm for the travelling salesperson problem is impossible unless $P = \mathcal{NP}$. Here we describe an efficient approximate algorithm for a special case. A distance matrix is said to have the *metric* property if the triangle inequality holds: for any three towns i, j and k

$$distance(i, j) \leq distance(i, k) + distance(k, j).$$

In other words, the direct distance from i to j is never more than the distance from i to j via k. In particular, this property holds in *Euclidean* problems, where the towns are considered to lie in a plane and the distances are the straight-line distances between them. When by "distance" we actually mean a cost, the property may arise less naturally. In the example above the distance matrix does indeed have the metric property. For instance

$$10 = distance(1,3) \leq distance(1,2) + distance(2,3) = 3 + 8 = 11,$$

and a similar condition holds for every choice of three nodes.

Let G be a complete undirected graph with n nodes, and consider any Hamiltonian cycle in this graph. Suppose this cycle has length h. Clearly it consists of n edges. If we remove any one of these, the remaining $n - 1$ edges form a path that visits each node of G exactly once but does not return to its starting point: this is called a *Hamiltonian path*. Since the edge removed has a nonnegative length, the length of this Hamiltonian path is at most h. However, the Hamiltonian path is also a spanning tree for the graph G. If the length of a *minimum* spanning tree for G is $m(G)$, it follows that the Hamiltonian path must have length greater than or equal to $m(G)$. Thus for any Hamiltonian cycle in G, $h \geq m(G)$.

Now suppose the distance matrix of G has the metric property. We illustrate how the approximate algorithm works using the distance matrix given above. First find a minimum spanning tree for G using either Kruskal's or Prim's algorithm; see Sections 6.3.1 and 6.3.2. Figure 13.3 shows a minimum spanning tree for our example. It is drawn with node 1 at the root since we are interested in tours that start and finish at this node (but see Problem 13.8). The minimum spanning tree has length 34. Now imagine you are an ant crawling round the outside of this figure. You start at the root (node 1), crawl down the left-hand side of edge $\{1,2\}$ to node 2, round node 2, back up the right-hand side of edge $\{1,2\}$ to node 1, down the left-hand side of edge $\{1,5\}$ to node 5, past node 5 and down the left-hand side of edge $\{5,3\}$ to node 3, round node 3, and so on. Eventually you arrive back at the root after crawling up the right-hand sides of edges $\{4,6\}$, $\{4,5\}$ and $\{5,1\}$. The dotted line in the figure illustrates your complete track.

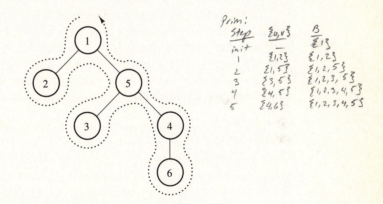

Figure 13.3. A minimum spanning tree

Since the tree spans the underlying graph, you are sure to visit each node at least once during your tour. In fact, as the example shows, you may visit some nodes more than once: the complete tour in the figure visits nodes 1, 2, 1, 5, 3, 5, 4, 6, 4, 5 and 1 in that order. Call this tour t_0. It is clear that during your tour you crawl along each edge in the spanning tree twice, once down the left-hand side and once up the right-hand side. If the length of the minimum spanning tree is $m(G)$, therefore, the length of your tour, $len(t_0)$ say, is $2m(G)$.

The approximate algorithm now proceeds by cutting out duplicate nodes from the tour. In the example, the first node revisited is node 1, which is revisited between nodes 2 and 5. We shorten the tour by omitting this second visit to node 1.

The new tour is 1, 2, 5, 3, 5, 4, 6, 4, 5, 1. If we call this tour t_1, then

$$len(t_0) - len(t_1) = distance(2, 1) + distance(1, 5) - distance(2, 5),$$

which must be greater than or equal to zero by the metric property of the distance matrix. Thus t_1 is no longer than t_0. In t_1 node 5 is revisited between nodes 3 and 4. As before, we can omit the second visit to node 5, obtaining a new tour t_2 that visits nodes 1, 2, 5, 3, 4, 6, 4, 5, 1. A similar argument to the previous case shows that $len(t_2) \le len(t_1)$. Proceeding thus, we omit successively from the tour any nodes that have been visited previously (except for the final return to node 1); each new tour obtained is no longer than its predecessor. In the example, the final tour obtained, that we shall call simply t, visits nodes 1, 2, 5, 3, 4, 6 and 1. Its length is 65. In general, since $len(t) \le len(t_0) = 2m(G)$, and the length h of any Hamiltonian cycle in G is at least $m(G)$, we have that

$$len(t) \le 2m(G) \le 2h. \checkmark$$

The length of the tour found by this approximate algorithm is therefore no more than twice the length of the optimal tour. In the example, the length of the optimal tour is at least 34 and at most 65.

Although the proof that the algorithm works required us to obtain t in a roundabout way, it is easy to see that in fact t is simply a list of the nodes in a minimum spanning tree of G in preorder; see Section 9.2. Implementing the algorithm is straightforward. For a graph with n nodes, finding a minimum spanning tree takes a time in $\Theta(n^2)$ using Prim's algorithm; see Section 6.3.2. Exploring this tree in preorder takes a time in $\Theta(n)$. The approximate algorithm therefore takes a time in $\Theta(n^2)$.

Using a more sophisticated approximate algorithm, we can guarantee to get within a factor $^3/_2$ of the optimal solution; see Problem 13.10. There are many variations on the theme of the travelling salesperson problem. For example, the graph may be directed, so that $distance(i, j)$ is not necessarily equal to $distance(j, i)$, or certain of its edges may be missing. We shall not study these variations here, beyond noting that for the case of a directed graph no heuristic with a guaranteed worst-case performance is known even in the metric case.

13.2.2 The knapsack problem (5)

We have encountered several variations on the theme of the knapsack problem in this book. Recall that we are given n objects and a knapsack. For each i, $1 \le i \le n$, object i has a positive integer weight w_i and a positive integer value v_i. The knapsack can carry a total weight not exceeding W. Our aim is to fill the knapsack in a way that maximizes the value of the included objects, while respecting the capacity constraint. In Section 6.5, we allowed objects to be split: we could carry one-third of object i, for instance, with benefit $v_i/3$ and cost $w_i/3$. In this case, we saw that a simple greedy algorithm finds the optimal solution in a time in $O(n \log n)$: it suffices to choose the objects in nonincreasing order of value per unit weight and to stuff the knapsack until it is full, splitting the last object considered if necessary.

In Section 8.4 we tackled the more challenging problem of finding an optimal solution when splitting objects is not allowed: we may take an object or leave it behind, but we may not take a fraction of an object. In this case, we saw that the greedy algorithm can be suboptimal, which is not surprising since this version of the problem is $\mathcal{NP}$–hard. Nevertheless, we saw a dynamic programming algorithm that finds an optimal solution in a time in $\Theta(nW)$, which may be prohibitive when W is large. Finally, we saw a third variation on the theme in Sections 9.6.1 and 9.7.2. This will not concern us here, but look at Problem 13.12.

Although suboptimal when splitting objects is not allowed, the greedy algorithm is so efficient in terms of computing time that it may be useful if its relative error is guaranteed to be within control. For definiteness, we state this algorithm explicitly.

function $greedy\text{-}knap(w[1..n], v[1..n], W)$
    Sort the instance so $v[i]/w[i] \geq v[j]/w[j]$ for all $1 \leq i \leq j \leq n$
    $weight, value \leftarrow 0$
    for $i = 1$ **to** n **do**
        if $weight + w[i] \leq W$ **then** $value \leftarrow value + v[i]$
                           $weight \leftarrow weight + w[i]$
    return $value$

Unfortunately, this algorithm can be arbitrarily bad. To see this, fix an integer $x > 2$ as large as you wish and consider the instance consisting of a knapsack of capacity $W = x$ and two objects whose weights and values are $w_1 = 1$, $v_1 = 2$, $w_2 = x$ and $v_2 = x$. The objects are in order of nonincreasing value per unit weight since $v_1/w_1 = 2$ is larger than $v_2/w_2 = 1$. The algorithm first places object 1 into the knapsack because $w_1 \leq W$; this reaps value 2. As a result, the second object no longer fits into the knapsack and the algorithm returns 2 as its approximate solution. Of course, the optimal solution in this case is to leave out object 1 and pack object 2 instead, for a yield of x. Thus the greedy algorithm returns a value that is within a factor $x/2$ of optimality, which can be made as bad as desired.

Fortunately, it is easy to fix this. Consider the following slight modification of the greedy algorithm, which assumes for simplicity that no object weighs more than the knapsack's capacity.

function $approx\text{-}knap(w[1..n], v[1..n], W)$
    $biggest \leftarrow \max\{v[i] \mid 1 \leq i \leq n\}$
    return $\max(biggest, greedy\text{-}knap(w, v, W))$

We now prove that the solution returned by $approx\text{-}knap$ is always within a factor 2 of the optimal. Consider an arbitrary instance. Assume the knapsack is too small to contain all the objects at once, since otherwise the greedy algorithm returns the trivial optimal solution that includes all the objects. Assume too that the objects are already sorted in order of nonincreasing value per unit weight. Let opt and $\widehat{opt}$ be the optimal solution and the solution returned by $approx\text{-}knap$, respectively. Let ℓ be the smallest integer such that $\sum_{i=1}^{\ell} w_i \gneq W$. Such an ℓ exists by assumption. Consider a modified instance of the knapsack problem that uses the same objects but for which the capacity of the knapsack is increased to $W' = \sum_{i=1}^{\ell} w_i$. The proof of Theorem 6.5.1 applies *mutatis mutandis* to show that for the modified instance it is optimal to pack the first ℓ objects. The solution of this instance is therefore $opt' = \sum_{i=1}^{\ell} v_i$. But the optimal solution of the original instance cannot be larger than that of the modified instance since more value cannot be packed into a smaller knapsack when the same objects are available: $opt \le opt'$. It remains to note that $greedy\text{-}knap(w, v, W) \ge \sum_{i=1}^{\ell-1} v_i$ because the greedy algorithm will put the first $\ell - 1$ objects into the knapsack before failing to add the ℓ–th. (It may put in a few more as well.) Moreover, $biggest \ge v_\ell$, where $biggest$ is the largest v_i as calculated in *approx-knap*. Putting it all together, and using the fact that $\max(x, y) \ge (x + y)/2$, we finally obtain

$$\widetilde{opt} = \max(biggest, greedy\text{-}knap(w, v, W))$$
$$\ge (biggest + greedy\text{-}knap(w, v, W))/2$$
$$\ge \left(v_\ell + \sum_{i=1}^{\ell-1} v_i \right) /2 = \sum_{i=1}^{\ell} v_i/2 = opt'/2$$
$$\ge opt/2,$$

which proves that the approximate solution is within a factor 2 of the optimum, as desired. In Section 13.5, we shall see that still better approximations can be obtained efficiently for the knapsack problem.

13.2.3 Bin packing

Rather as in the knapsack problem, we are given n objects. Object i has weight w_i, $1 \le i \le n$. We are also given a number of identical storage bins, each of which can hold any number of objects provided their total weight does not exceed the bin capacity W. Objects may not be split between bins. Two related problems arise. Given k bins, what is the greatest number of objects we can store? Alternatively, what is the least number of bins needed to store all the n objects? The second problem is usually called the *bin-packing problem*. Both problems are $\mathcal{NP}$–hard.

We begin by looking at the first problem. Suppose without loss of generality that the objects to be stored are numbered in order of nondecreasing weight, so $w_i \le w_j$ when $i \le j$. For the simple case when $k = 1$ it is obviously optimal to load objects into the single bin in numerical order. Now consider the following straightforward greedy algorithm for the case when $k = 2$. Take each object in turn in numerical order. Put as many as possible into bin 1; when bin 1 is full put as many of the remaining objects as possible into bin 2; then stop.

A simple example suffices to show that this algorithm does not always give the optimal solution to our problem. For instance, if $n = 4$, the weights of the four objects are 2, 3, 4 and 5 respectively, and the capacity of each bin is 7, the greedy algorithm puts objects 1 and 2 into bin 1 and object 3 into bin 2, then stops. Thus it has managed to store just 3 objects in the two bins. The optimal solution is obviously to put objects 1 and 4 into bin 1, and objects 2 and 3 into bin 2, for a total of 4 objects. However the greedy algorithm is never in error by more than 1 object, as we shall now show.

Let the optimal solution to the instance with two bins be s, that is, we can load s objects into the two bins. Suppose first, however, that instead of two bins with capacity W each, we have just one bin with capacity $2W$. Construct the optimal solution to this new instance by putting objects into the bin in numerical order. Suppose t objects can be loaded in this way. Clearly $s \le t$ since splitting one large bin into two can never allow us to include more objects than before. In the optimal solution for the instance with one large bin, let j be the smallest index such that $\sum_{i=1}^{j} w_i > W$. The index j is well defined unless $\sum_{i=1}^{n} w_i \le W$, in which case the trivial optimal solution is to put all n objects in the first bin. Using this, and the fact that $\sum_{i=1}^{t} w_i \le 2W$, we obtain $\sum_{i=j+1}^{t} w_i < W$. The situation is illustrated in Figure 13.4.

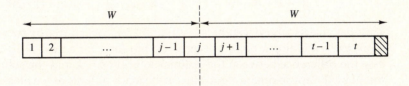

√**Figure 13.4. Packing one large bin of capacity** $2W$

Returning to the instance with two bins, it is therefore possible to load objects 1 to $j - 1$ into the first bin and objects $j + 1$ to t into the second bin. However because the objects are numbered in order of nondecreasing weight, we have

$$\sum_{i=j}^{t-1} w_i \le \sum_{i=j+1}^{t} w_i,$$

so the greedy approximate algorithm will put objects 1 to $j - 1$ into the first bin, and objects j to $t - 1$ into the second. Object t may possibly fit into the second bin, too. The solution found by the greedy algorithm is therefore at least $t - 1$. Since $s \le t$, this solution is in error by at most one object.

If the n objects are not initially sorted then a time in $\Theta(n \log n)$ is required to sort them. Thereafter the greedy approximate algorithm takes a time in $\Theta(n)$.✓ The approximate algorithm can be extended in the obvious way to the case where k bins are available. In this case the solution it finds is never in error by more than $k - 1$ items. This can be proved by an easy extension of the argument above.

The second of the two related problems asks, given n objects, how many bins are needed to store them all. It is tempting to try the obvious variant of the approximate algorithm described above: take the objects in order of nondecreasing weight, put as many of them as possible into the first bin, then into the second bin, and so on, and count how many bins are necessary to store all the n objects.

Let b be the optimal number of bins required, and let s be the solution found by this approximate algorithm. This time it is not true that the absolute error $s - b$ is bounded by a constant; however it *is* true that s is less than a constant multiple of b. In other words, s/b is bounded. To illustrate the impossibility of obtaining a constant additive error bound with this approximate algorithm, consider the following family of instances.

We are given $n = 2k$ objects and a supply of bins of capacity $2W$. It is convenient to suppose that k is even. The exact value of W is immaterial provided it is larger than $3(k-1)$. The n objects have weights $W - k$, $W - (k-1)$, ..., $W - 1$, $W + 1$, ..., $W + (k-1)$, $W + k$. Clearly these n objects can be packed into k bins by taking the √optima lightest with the heaviest, the next lightest with the next heaviest, and so on. The greedy algorithm on the other hand first puts the object whose weight is $W - k$ in a bin with the object whose weight is $W - (k-1)$. The third object cannot go in the same bin because

$$W - k + W - (k-1) + W - (k-2) = 3W - 3(k-1) > 2W.$$

Thus the objects whose weight is less than W are packed two by two into $k/2$ bins, while the remaining k objects occupy one bin each, for a total of $3k/2$ bins. In this case the difference between the optimal solution $b = k$ and the solution $s = 3k/2$ found by the approximate algorithm can be made as large as we please by choosing k large enough. On the other hand, for this family of instances the ratio $s/b = 3/2$ is constant.

In general it can be shown that for this approximate greedy algorithm

$$\checkmark s \le 2 + \frac{17}{10}b.$$

√A better approximate algorithm is obtained if objects are considered in order of non*increasing* weight. Now we take each object in turn and try to add it to bin 1; if it will not fit, we try to add it to bin 2, and so on; if it will not fit in any of the bins used so far, we start a new bin with the next highest number. Observe that for the instance discussed in the previous paragraph, this algorithm finds the optimal packing. In general for this approximate greedy algorithm $s \le 4 + \frac{11}{9}b$. The proofs of the bounds given in this paragraph are not simple.

13.3 $\mathcal{NP}$–hard approximation problems

Chapter 12 may have left you with the impression that there is no significant difference in the difficulty of solving one $\mathcal{NP}$–complete problem or another. Nothing could be farther from the truth when it comes to finding approximate solutions. We saw for example in Section 13.2.3 that even though it is $\mathcal{NP}$–hard to determine the greatest number of objects we can store in two bins, a simple greedy algorithm quickly finds a solution that never falls short of optimality by more than one item. In contrast, other optimization problems remain $\mathcal{NP}$–hard even if we are satisfied with keeping the *relative* error within control. For instance, given any $\alpha > 1$, it is $\mathcal{NP}$–hard to find a tour for the travelling salesperson problem whose length is guaranteed to be within a factor α of the optimum; see Section 13.3.2. Other problems fall in between: the *metric* travelling salesperson problem can be solved efficiently within a factor 2 of the optimum with the algorithm seen in Section 13.1.2—and better approximate algorithms exist (see Problem 13.10)—yet no efficient approximate algorithm can guarantee a fixed upper bound on the absolute error of its solutions unless $\mathcal{P} = \mathcal{NP}$; see Section 13.3.1. A spectacular example of how the same optimization problem may give rise to two quite different approximation problems is presented in Section 13.4.

Consider an optimization problem and let $opt(X)$ denote the value of an optimal solution to instance X. For example, if we consider the graph colouring problem of Section 13.1.1 and if G is a graph, $opt(G)$ denotes the chromatic number of G: the smallest number of colours sufficient to colour the vertices of G so that no two adjacent vertices are assigned the same colour. On instance X, an approximate algorithm will find some value $\widetilde{opt}(X)$ that may be suboptimal but is required to be *feasible*. For example, if graph G can be coloured with five colours but no less, then $opt(G) = 5$ and an algorithm that returns $\widetilde{opt}(G) = 7$ is suboptimal yet acceptable, because it *is* possible to colour G with seven colours provided there are at least this many vertices. An algorithm that returned $\widetilde{opt}(G) = 4$, on the other hand, would be incorrect because G cannot be coloured with four colours. In most cases, requiring feasibility corresponds to requiring $\widetilde{opt}(X) \geq opt(X)$ for minimization problems and $\widetilde{opt}(X) \leq opt(X)$ for maximization problems. In practice, we may want the optimal or approximate solution itself rather than merely its value or cost: we may want an actual assignment of colours to the nodes of G using no more than $\widetilde{opt}(G)$ colours. However, these problems are often equivalent by virtue of decision-reducibility: see Problem 12.43.

Let c and ε be positive constants. To each optimization problem P, there correspond absolute and relative approximation problems. Assume for simplicity that all feasible solutions to instances of problem P are strictly positive. The *c-absolute approximation* problem, denoted c–abs–P, is the problem of finding, for any instance X, a feasible solution $\widetilde{opt}(X)$ whose absolute error compared to the optimal solution $opt(X)$ is at most c:

$$opt(X) \leq \widetilde{opt}(X) \leq opt(X) + c \quad \text{or}$$
$$opt(X) - c \leq \widetilde{opt}(X) \leq opt(X),$$

for minimization and maximization problems, respectively. The *ε-relative approximation* problem, denoted ε–rel–P, is the problem of finding, for any instance X, a feasible solution whose relative error compared to the optimal solution is at most ε:

$$opt(X) \leq \widetilde{opt}(X) \leq (1 + \varepsilon)\, opt(X) \quad \text{or}$$
$$(1 - \varepsilon)\, opt(X) \leq \widetilde{opt}(X) \leq opt(X),$$

for minimization and maximization problems, respectively. Note that $\varepsilon \geq 1$ is interesting only for minimization problems, unless it is a challenge to find a feasible solution even without optimality constraints.

For example, we saw efficient algorithms for the 1-absolute approximation problem corresponding to determining the greatest number of objects we can store in two bins and for the 1-relative approximate metric travelling salesperson problem. We shall now see that the latter problem is harder to approximate than the former, in the sense that the c-absolute approximate metric travelling salesperson problem is just as hard as the exact problem no matter how large we are willing to choose c. The unconstrained travelling salesperson problem is harder still to approximate: even the ε-relative approximate travelling salesperson problem is as hard as the exact problem no matter how large we choose ε. To prove these results, we use the notion of polynomial reductions seen in Section 12.5.2 to show how the exact problem could be solved efficiently if only we knew how to solve the corresponding approximation problem efficiently.

13.3.1 Hard absolute approximation problems

Denote the metric travelling salesperson problem by MTSP. Assume for simplicity that the distances between towns are integers. We saw in Section 13.1.2 an efficient algorithm for 1–rel–MTSP. We shall now prove that MTSP $\leq_T^p$ c–abs–MTSP for any positive constant c. For this, assume that an arbitrary algorithm to solve the c-absolute approximate metric travelling salesperson problem is available. We are to find an algorithm for the exact metric travelling salesperson problem that is efficient provided we do not take account of the time spent using the approximate algorithm. Therefore, any efficient algorithm for the approximation problem will translate into an efficient algorithm for the exact problem. Assuming the exact metric travelling salesperson problem is genuinely hard (which is more than likely since it is $\mathcal{NP}$–hard—a fact rather hard to prove), we conclude that no efficient algorithm can exist to find c-absolute approximations to the metric travelling salesperson problem.

Theorem 13.3.1   MTSP $\leq_T^p$ c–abs–MTSP *for any positive constant c.*

Proof   Let c be a positive constant and consider an arbitrary algorithm to solve c–abs–MTSP, the c-absolute approximate metric travelling salesperson problem. Consider an instance of MTSP represented by a symmetric $n \times n$ integer matrix M that respects the triangle inequality. Let $opt(M)$ be the length of an optimal tour on this instance. Construct a new instance M' by multiplying each entry of M by $\lfloor c \rfloor + 1$. It is clear that M' also satisfies the triangle inequality and that it is symmetric; hence it defines a legitimate instance of MTSP. It is equally clear that any optimal tour of the cities according to distance matrix M is also optimal according to M', and vice versa, except that the length of the tour is $\lfloor c \rfloor + 1$ times greater according to M'. Therefore, $opt(M') = (\lfloor c \rfloor + 1)opt(M)$. Consider now the result $\widetilde{opt}(M')$ of running our assumed c-absolute approximate algorithm on M'. By definition,

$$(\lfloor c \rfloor + 1)opt(M) = opt(M') \leq \widetilde{opt}(M') \leq opt(M') + c$$
$$= (\lfloor c \rfloor + 1)opt(M) + c < (\lfloor c \rfloor + 1)(opt(M) + 1).$$

Dividing by $\lfloor c \rfloor + 1$, we obtain

$$opt(M) \leq \frac{\widetilde{opt}(M')}{\lfloor c \rfloor + 1} < opt(M) + 1.$$

We conclude that $opt(M) = \lfloor \widetilde{opt}(M')/(\lfloor c \rfloor + 1) \rfloor$ because $opt(M)$ is an integer. Thus the exact solution to MTSP instance M is easily obtained from any c-absolute approximate solution to MTSP instance M', which completes the reduction.   ∎

There are many other problems for which it is $\mathcal{NP}$–hard to find c-absolute approximate solutions, no matter how large c is allowed to be. Among these are the knapsack problem and the maximum clique problem; see Problems 13.15 and 13.16. This is the case for all problems that allow "scaling up": if any instance can be transformed efficiently into another whose optimal solution is $\lfloor c \rfloor + 1$ times larger, and if the optimal solution is a positive integer, then it is just as hard to find c-absolute approximate solutions as to find optimal solutions. .

13.3.2 Hard relative approximation problems

Denote the unconstrained—as opposed to metric—travelling salesperson problem by TSP. (We used TSP in Section 12.5.2 to denote the problem of finding an optimal tour rather than determining its length; this is admissible because both versions of the problem are easily seen to be polynomially equivalent.) Not only are absolute approximations to this problem as hard to find as exact solutions, but this is also true for relative approximations. In symbols, $\text{TSP} \leq_T^p \varepsilon\text{–rel–TSP}$ for any positive constant ε. Rather than prove this directly, however, we shall show how ε-relative approximations to TSP can serve to solve the Hamiltonian cycle decision problem HAMD encountered in Section 12.5.2. The technique is similar to that used in Theorem 12.5.9 to prove that the *exact* solution to TSP can be used to solve HAMD. The desired conclusion follows as Corollary 13.3.3 because the Hamiltonian cycle problem is $\mathcal{NP}$–complete.

Theorem 13.3.2 $\text{HAMD} \leq_T^p \varepsilon\text{–rel–TSP}$ *for any positive constant ε.*

Proof   Let ε be a positive constant and consider an arbitrary algorithm to solve ε–rel–TSP, the ε-relative approximate travelling salesperson problem. Consider an instance of the Hamiltonian decision problem HAMD given by a graph $G = \langle N, A \rangle$. Let the number of nodes in G be n and assume without loss of generality that $N = \{1, 2, \ldots, n\}$. Construct an instance M of the travelling salesperson problem as follows.

$$M_{ij} = \begin{cases} 1 & \text{if } \{i, j\} \in A \\ 2 + \lfloor n\varepsilon \rfloor & \text{otherwise} \end{cases}$$

Let $opt(M)$ denote an optimal solution to the travelling salesperson problem M and let $\widetilde{opt}(M)$ denote the approximation returned by our assumed ε-relative approximate algorithm. By definition,

$$opt(M) \leq \widetilde{opt}(M) \leq (1 + \varepsilon)\, opt(M).$$

There are two cases.

⋄ If there is a Hamiltonian cycle in G, this cycle defines a tour for the travelling salesperson problem that uses only edges of length 1. Hence there is a solution of length n, which is clearly optimal. In this case,

$$\widetilde{opt}(M) \le (1 + \varepsilon)\, opt(M) = (1 + \varepsilon)\, n.$$

⋄ If there are no Hamiltonian cycles in G, any tour for the travelling salesperson must use at least one edge of length $2 + \lfloor n\varepsilon \rfloor$ in addition to $n - 1$ edges of length at least 1 each, for a total length of at least $2 + \lfloor n\varepsilon \rfloor + (n - 1) > (1 + \varepsilon)\, n$. Therefore,

$$\widetilde{opt}(M) \ge opt(M) > (1 + \varepsilon)\, n.$$

Thus we can decide whether or not there is a Hamiltonian cycle in G by looking at the answer returned by the approximate algorithm for the travelling salesperson problem: there is a Hamiltonian cycle if and only if $\widetilde{opt}(M) \le (1 + \varepsilon)\, n$. This completes the reduction. ∎

Note that the instance of the travelling salesperson problem constructed in the above proof is *not* metric. If there is an edge in G between vertices i and k and between vertices k and j but not between vertices i and j, and if $n \ge 1/\varepsilon$,

$$distance(i, j) = 2 + \lfloor n\varepsilon \rfloor > 2 = distance(i, k) + distance(k, j).$$

This was inevitable given that 1–rel–MTSP can be solved efficiently.

Corollary 13.3.3   TSP $\le^p_T \varepsilon$–rel–TSP *for any positive constant* ε.

Proof   Recall from just before Theorem 12.5.9 that TSPD denotes the travelling salesperson *decision* problem. We know from Problem 12.47 that the travelling salesperson problem is decision-reducible in the sense that TSP $\equiv^p_T$ TSPD. On the other hand, we know from Problem 12.50 that the Hamiltonian cycle problem is $\mathcal{NP}$–complete. By definition of $\mathcal{NP}$–completeness and from the obvious fact that TSPD belongs to $\mathcal{NP}$, it follows that TSPD $\le^p_T$ HAMD. We have just shown that HAMD $\le^p_T \varepsilon$–rel–TSP. We reach the desired conclusion by transitivity of polynomial reductions. ∎

There are many other problems for which it is $\mathcal{NP}$–hard to find ε-relative approximate solutions, no matter how large ε is allowed to be (subject to $\varepsilon < 1$ in the case of maximization problems). Among these are the minimum cluster problem (see Section 13.4 below), the maximum clique problem and the problem of finding the chromatic number of a graph. In fact the latter two problems are known to be even harder than this to approximate: assuming $\mathcal{P} \ne \mathcal{NP}$, no polynomial-time algorithm can find a clique in an n-node graph that is guaranteed to be within a factor $\sqrt[\delta]{n}$ of the optimal for $\delta > 6$, and the same holds for optimal graph colouring with $\delta > 14$. On the other hand, there are optimization problems such as the metric

travelling salesperson problem for which it is easy to find ε-relative approximations
for large enough ε, yet the approximation problem becomes $\mathcal{NP}$–hard when ε is
too small; see Section 13.5 for additional examples.

13.4 The same, only different

Let $G = \langle N, A \rangle$ be an undirected graph and let $c : A \to \mathbb{R}^+$ be a cost function. Consider a partition of N into three subsets N_1, N_2 and N_3, henceforth called *clusters*,
such that each node in N belongs to exactly one of the clusters. For each node u,
let $set(u)$ denote the unique i such that $u \in N_i$. This partitions the edges of G
between those that link two nodes in the same cluster, called *internal* edges, and
those that link nodes from different clusters, called *cross* edges. Our optimization
problem is to select N_1, N_2 and N_3 so the total cost of the cross edges is maximized or, equivalently, the total cost of the internal edges is minimized. This problem is $\mathcal{NP}$–hard—an immediate consequence of the proof of Theorem 13.4.2 below. Figure 13.5 shows an example where the optimal solution is to form clusters
$N_1 = \{a, b\}$, $N_2 = \{c, d\}$ and $N_3 = \{e\}$ so the total cost of the internal edges is 4 and
that of the cross edges is 31.

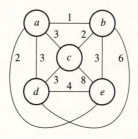

Figure 13.5. The MIN–CLUSTER/MAX–CUT problems

Although it is equivalent to maximize the total cost of the cross edges or to minimize the total cost of the internal edges, consider the following two optimization
problems.

⋄ **MAX–CUT** is the problem of maximizing the total cost of the cross edges over
all partitions of N.

⋄ **MIN–CLUSTER** is the problem of minimizing the total cost of the internal edges
over all partitions of N.

Surprisingly, these two identical optimization problems become entirely different
when seen as approximation problems: the ε–rel–MAX–CUT problem can be solved
efficiently for $\varepsilon \geq {}^1\!/_3$ whereas the ε–rel–MIN–CLUSTER problem remains $\mathcal{NP}$–hard
for all positive values of ε.

> Theorem 13.4.1 $^1/_3$-*relative approximations to the* **MAX–CUT** *problem can be calculated efficiently.*

Proof   Let $G = \langle N, A \rangle$ be a graph and $c : A \to \mathbb{R}^+$ be a cost function. Consider the following greedy approximate algorithm. Initially, N_1, N_2 and N_3 are empty; they will form a partition of N by the time the algorithm terminates. Consider each node of G in turn. Add it to the cluster that causes the smallest increase in the cost of the internal edges, and thus the largest increase in the cost of the cross edges. On the graph in Figure 13.5, the algorithm first puts nodes a, b and c into N_1, N_2 and N_3, respectively. It then considers node d. Adding it to cluster N_1, N_2 or N_3 would increase the cost of internal edges by 3, 2 or 3, respectively: thus the algorithm adds it to cluster N_2, which becomes $\{b, d\}$. Finally, adding node e to cluster N_1, N_2 or N_3 would increase the cost of internal edges by 6, 7 or 8, respectively: thus the algorithm adds it to cluster N_1, which becomes $\{a, e\}$. The solution returned by the algorithm is $N_1 = \{a, e\}$, $N_2 = \{b, d\}$ and $N_3 = \{c\}$, whose cost in terms of cross edges is 27, better than 87% of the optimal solution 31.

Before we prove that the cost of cross edges returned by this algorithm is never less than two-thirds of the optimum, it is useful to give explicit code for this approximate algorithm. Here, *sum* accumulates the total cost of all edges in G and *clstr* accumulates the cost of all internal edges in the approximate solution that is chosen. The desired cost of all cross edges is given by the difference between *sum* and *clstr*, which is computed at the end of the algorithm.

```
function MAX-CUT-approx(G = ⟨N, A⟩, c : A → ℝ⁺)
    N₁, N₂, N₃ ← ∅
    clstr, sum ← 0
    for each u ∈ N do
        mincost ← ∞
        for i ← 1 to 3 do
            cost ← 0
            for each v ∈ Nᵢ do
                if {u, v} ∈ A then cost ← cost + c({u, v})
            sum ← sum + cost
            if cost < mincost then mincost ← cost
                                  k ← i
        Nₖ ← Nₖ ∪ {u}
        clstr ← clstr + mincost
    return sum − clstr
```

For each node u, let z_1, z_2 and z_3 be the values accumulated in *cost* when $i = 1$, 2 and 3, respectively; this is the increase in the total cost of the internal edges that would be incurred by adding u to the corresponding cluster. The algorithm adds u to the cluster N_k that minimizes z_i and adds that value of z_k to *clstr*. All three z's are added to *sum*. Therefore, each time round the outer loop, the value of *sum* is increased by at least three times the increase in *clstr*. Since both *sum* and *clstr* are initialized to zero, it follows that $sum \geq 3 \times clstr$ at the end of the algorithm. The total cost of the cross edges in the solution discovered by the algorithm is thus

$$\widetilde{opt}(G, c) = sum - clstr \geq \tfrac{2}{3} \, sum.$$

But the total cost $opt(G, c)$ of the cross edges in an optimal solution cannot be smaller than the cost of the cross edges in the approximate solution found by the algorithm, and it cannot be greater than the total cost *sum* of all the edges in the graph. It follows that

$$(1 - {}^1/_3)opt(G, c) \leq \tfrac{2}{3} \, sum \leq \widetilde{opt}(G, c) \leq opt(G, c).$$

By definition, this says that our algorithm supplies a $^1/_3$-relative approximation to the MAX–CUT problem. ∎

Even though the algorithm presented in this proof is guaranteed to perform well on the MAX–CUT problem, it can be arbitrarily bad on the otherwise identical MIN–CLUSTER problem. On the graph of Figure 13.5, for example, it finds 27 as the approximate cost of a maximum cut, which is not bad compared to 31, the real maximum. At the same time, it finds 8 as the approximate cost of the minimum cluster, which is twice the true minimum. Problem 13.23 asks you to show that this algorithm can be arbitrarily bad at finding approximations to the MIN–CLUSTER problem, even on four-node graphs. Now we prove that this is not the fault of this particular algorithm: no efficient algorithm is guaranteed to find a good ε-relative approximation to the MIN–CLUSTER problem unless $\mathcal{P} = \mathcal{NP}$.

Theorem 13.4.2   MIN–CLUSTER $\leq_T^p$ ε-rel–MIN–CLUSTER *for any positive constant ε.*

Proof   We shall in fact prove that 3COL $\leq_T^p$ ε-rel–MIN–CLUSTER, where 3COL is the problem encountered in Section 12.5.4 of deciding if a given graph can be painted with three colours. The desired result follows along the lines of Corollary 13.3.3 from the fact that 3COL is $\mathcal{NP}$–complete (Theorem 12.5.19) and MIN–CLUSTER is decision-reducible. We leave the details to the reader.

To prove that 3COL $\leq_T^p$ ε-rel–MIN–CLUSTER, let ε be a positive constant and consider an arbitrary algorithm to solve ε-rel–MIN–CLUSTER. Let $G = \langle N, A \rangle$ be a graph; we would like to know if it can be coloured with three colours. Consider the complete graph K on node set N; in this graph there is an edge between u and v for each distinct u and v in N. Define the following cost function on the edges of K.

$$c(\{u, v\}) = \begin{cases} 1 & \text{if } \{u, v\} \notin A \\ \lceil (1 + \varepsilon) \, n^2 \rceil & \text{if } \{u, v\} \in A \end{cases}$$

Let $opt(K,c)$ denote an optimal solution to the minimum cluster problem on graph K with cost function c, and let $\widetilde{opt}(K,c)$ denote the approximation returned by our assumed ε-relative approximate algorithm. By definition,

$$opt(K,c) \le \widetilde{opt}(K,c) \le (1+\varepsilon)\,opt(K,c).$$

There are two cases.

⋄ If graph G is three-colourable, consider an arbitrary colouring of it in green, blue and red. Form clusters N_1, N_2 and N_3 as the sets of green, blue and red nodes, respectively. By definition of a three-colouring, there are no edges of G between two nodes in the same cluster. By definition of the cost function on K, the internal edges defined by N_1, N_2 and N_3 all have cost 1. Clearly, there are less than n^2 edges in K, and thus less than n^2 internal edges as well. Therefore, the total cost of the internal edges is less than n^2. We conclude that the optimal solution to the minimum cluster problem is less than n^2, and thus:

$$\widetilde{opt}(K,c) \le (1+\varepsilon)\,opt(K,c) < (1+\varepsilon)\,n^2.$$

⋄ If graph G is not three-colourable, any partition of N into three clusters necessarily contains at least one internal edge belonging to A. By definition of the cost function on K, the cost of that edge is $\lceil (1+\varepsilon)\,n^2 \rceil$, so the optimal solution to the minimum cluster problem cannot be less than that:

$$\widetilde{opt}(K,c) \ge opt(K,c) \ge \lceil (1+\varepsilon)\,n^2 \rceil \ge (1+\varepsilon)\,n^2.$$

Thus we can decide whether or not graph G is three-colourable by looking at the answer returned by the approximate algorithm for the minimum cluster problem: the graph is three-colourable if and only if $\widetilde{opt}(K,c) < (1+\varepsilon)\,n^2$. This completes the reduction. ∎

13.5 Approximation schemes

Until now, the ε-relative approximate algorithms we have seen work for a specific value of ε. For example, we saw in Section 13.4 an efficient $1/3$-relative approximate algorithm for the maximum cut problem, but there is no obvious way to improve this algorithm to guarantee a better approximation. Similarly, we saw in Section 13.1.2 an efficient 1-relative approximate algorithm for the metric travelling salesperson problem. Although Problem 13.10 asks you to find a better algorithm for the same problem that is $1/2$-relative approximate, the new algorithm is entirely different from the one we saw. Moreover, it is $\mathcal{NP}$–hard to find ε-relative approximations to the metric travelling salesperson problem when ε is sufficiently small. Another example is provided by Problem 13.19 according to which it is easy to find a $1/3$-relative approximate algorithm for the problem of painting a planar graph with the minimum number of colours, yet any improvement in the approximation would be as hard to compute in the worst case as the optimal solution.

In contrast, there are problems for which arbitrarily good ε-relative approximations can be obtained. An *approximation scheme* is an algorithm that takes as input, in addition to the instance itself, an upper bound ε on the acceptable relative error. Even though it is natural to expect the algorithm to work harder when ε is smaller, it is best if the tolerance can be reduced at a reasonable cost in computing time. We say that the approximation scheme is *fully polynomial* if a time in $O(p(n, {}^1/_\varepsilon))$ is sufficient in the worst case to find ε-relative approximations for instances of size n, where p is some fixed polynomial in two variables.

There are many $\mathcal{NP}$–hard problems for which fully polynomial approximation schemes cannot exist unless $\mathcal{P} = \mathcal{NP}$ and there are others for which they are known to exist. Here we give one example of each situation.

13.5.1 Bin packing revisited

We saw in Section 13.2.3 that there is an efficient approximate greedy algorithm for the bin packing problem that guarantees a solution using no more than $4 + \frac{11}{9}opt$ bins to store the objects, where opt is the optimal number of bins required. However, a fully polynomial approximation scheme cannot exist for this $\mathcal{NP}$–hard problem if $\mathcal{P} \neq \mathcal{NP}$ because it would be easy to obtain an optimal solution in polynomial time from such a scheme. To see this, assume the existence of an algorithm $BPapprox(w[1..n], W, \varepsilon)$ that runs in a time in $O(p(n, {}^1/_\varepsilon))$ for some polynomial p and is guaranteed to find an ε-relative approximation to the problem of storing n objects of weight $w[1..n]$ in as few bins of capacity W as possible. Assume for the problem to make sense that $w[i] \leq W$ for each i. Consider the following algorithm.

> **function** $BP(w[1..n], W)$
>   **return** $\lfloor BPapprox(w, W, 1/(n+1)) \rfloor$

Clearly, algorithm BP runs in a time polynomial in the size of the instance since $1/\varepsilon = n + 1$ in this case. By definition of ε-relative approximations, the solution $\widetilde{opt}$ returned by $BPapprox(w, W, 1/(n+1))$ must be such that

$$opt \leq \widetilde{opt} \leq (1 + 1/(n+1))\, opt = opt + opt/(n+1).$$

But $opt/(n+1) < 1$ since it is surely possible to store the objects in n separate bins. Therefore,

$$opt \leq \widetilde{opt} < opt + 1,$$

and so $opt = \lfloor \widetilde{opt} \rfloor$ since opt is an integer. This completes the proof that BP finds an exact solution in polynomial time in the worst case. This is impossible if $\mathcal{P} \neq \mathcal{NP}$ since the bin packing problem is $\mathcal{NP}$–hard.

13.5.2 The knapsack problem (6)

We pay one final visit to the knapsack problem to show that it admits a fully polynomial approximation scheme. Continuing from Section 13.2.2, we use the version of the problem introduced in Section 8.4. Recall that in Section 13.2.2 we saw an approximate algorithm that finds a solution guaranteed to be within a factor 2 of the optimum in a time in $O(n \log n)$: this is a $^1/_2$-relative approximate algorithm. We also saw in Section 8.4 a dynamic programming algorithm that finds the optimal solution in a time in $O(nW)$, where n is the number of objects and W is the size of the knapsack. We now use these two algorithms together, except that first we modify slightly the dynamic programming algorithm.

Recall from Section 8.4 that the heart of the dynamic programming algorithm is a table $V[1..n, 0..W]$, with one row for each available object and one column for each weight from 0 to W. In the table, $V[i, j]$ gives the maximum value of the objects we can transport if the weight limit is j and if we only take objects among the first i. The table is built one entry at a time using the rule

$$V[i, j] = \max(V[i - 1, j], V[i - 1, j - w_i] + v_i)$$

and the solution is then found in $V[n, W]$. (Return to Section 8.4 for details.)

A similar approach uses a table $U[1..n, 0..M]$, where M is an upper bound on the optimal value that we can carry in the knapsack, again with one row for each object available, but now with one column for each possible total value that can fit inside the knapsack. We can obtain the bound M by running our $^1/_2$-relative approximate algorithm and multiplying its answer by 2. (The value *opt'* defined in Section 13.2.2 when we proved that our approximate algorithm returns a value that is at least half the optimum is slightly better and easier to compute.) This time, $U[i, j]$ gives the minimum *weight* of the objects we can transport to reap exactly value j if we only take objects among the first i. This table is built one entry at a time using the rule

$$U[i, j] = \min(U[i - 1, j], U[i - 1, j - v_i] + w_i).$$

Out-of-bound values are taken to be $+\infty$ (or any value larger than W) with the exception of $U[0, 0]$, which is taken to be 0. Intuitively, this rule says that to reap value j with the first i objects, we may either not use object i at all, in which case the load weighs at least $U[i - 1, j]$, or we may add object i to a collection of objects among the first $i - 1$ whose total value was $j - v_i$ and thus whose total weight was at least $U[i - 1, j - v_i]$ before the addition of object i. Once the table is constructed, the solution is given by the largest j such that $U[n, j] \leq W$. This approach takes a time in $O(n \log n + nM)$ since a time in $O(n \log n)$ is needed to calculate the upper bound M, each of the nM entries of U takes constant time to fill in, and a time in $O(M)$ is spent at the end to scan the n-th row of U. Table U can also be used to determine not only the value of the optimal load, but also its composition, much as in Section 8.4.

You may wonder why anyone would use this approach, which is slightly more complicated and perhaps less natural than the dynamic programming algorithm of Section 8.4. The point is that this new algorithm is preferable when the values are smaller than the weights, since the time it requires depends on the total value of the optimal solution rather than the total weight capacity of the knapsack. As we shall see, we can force the values—but not the weights—to be small provided we are satisfied with an approximate solution.

Consider an instance of the knapsack problem consisting of a knapsack of capacity W and n objects. Object i has a positive integer weight w_i and a positive integer value v_i. Let ε be the relative error we are willing to tolerate, $0 < \varepsilon < 1$. Let opt be the (unknown) optimal solution to this instance. Let k be an integer constant to be determined later. From the original instance, we create a new instance using the same knapsack and the same number of objects, where each object weighs the same as before, but the value of object i is reduced to $v_i' = v_i \div k$. (This may create objects of value zero, which is not allowed in the definition of the knapsack problem. However this is of no consequence because the $^1/_2$-relative approximate and the dynamic programming algorithms still work in this case.) We say that $X \subseteq \{1, 2, \ldots, n\}$ is *feasible* if we can fit the corresponding objects into the knapsack: $\sum_{i \in X} w_i \leq W$. This notion of feasibility does not depend whether we are talking about the original or the modified instance since we modified neither the weights of the objects nor the capacity of the knapsack. Let $X^\star$ be a collection of objects we can put into the knapsack that is optimal for the original instance: $X^\star$ is feasible and $\sum_{i \in X^\star} v_i = opt$. Let X' be a collection of objects we can put into the knapsack that is optimal for the modified instance. Finally, let $\widetilde{opt} = \sum_{i \in X'} v_i$.

Because X' is optimal for the modified instance and $X^\star$ is feasible, it follows that

$$\sum_{i \in X'} v_i' \geq \sum_{i \in X^\star} v_i'.$$

Similarly,

$$opt = \sum_{i \in X^\star} v_i \geq \sum_{i \in X'} v_i = \widetilde{opt} \tag{13.1}$$

since $X^\star$ is optimal for the original instance and X' is feasible. By definition of v_i' we have $v_i \geq k v_i' > v_i - k$. Putting it all together,

$$\widetilde{opt} = \sum_{i \in X'} v_i \geq k \sum_{i \in X'} v_i'$$

$$\geq k \sum_{i \in X^\star} v_i' \geq \sum_{i \in X^\star} (v_i - k)$$

$$= \sum_{i \in X^\star} v_i - \sum_{i \in X^\star} k$$

$$\geq opt - kn.$$

It suffices to choose $k \leq \varepsilon\, opt / n$ to obtain

$$\widetilde{opt} \geq opt - \varepsilon\, n\, opt / n = (1 - \varepsilon)\, opt. \tag{13.2}$$

Equations 13.1 and 13.2 say that $\widetilde{opt}$ is an ε-relative approximation to opt.

It may seem at first that a proper choice of k cannot be made until we know the value of the optimal solution, but this is not the case thanks to our $^1/_2$-relative approximate algorithm *approx-knap*. To summarize, the approximation scheme proceeds as follows:

1. Compute $A = approx\text{-}knap(w, v, W)$. If $\varepsilon < 2n/A$, run the modified dynamic programming algorithm on the original instance to find an exact optimal solution, using $M = 2A$ as an upper bound on the optimal solution. Otherwise, set $k = \lfloor \varepsilon A/n \rfloor \geq 2$, which is indeed no larger than $\varepsilon\, opt/n$ as required, and proceed with the following steps.

2. Form the modified instance in which $v_i' = v_i \div k$.

3. Use the modified dynamic programming algorithm to find a choice $X' \subseteq \{1, 2, \ldots, n\}$ of objects that maximizes $\sum_{i \in X'} v_i'$ subject to $\sum_{i \in X'} w_i \leq W$. As first step of this algorithm, use $M' = \lfloor 2A/k \rfloor$ as an upper bound on the optimal solution of the modified instance. This is a valid upper bound because the optimal solution of the original instance is bounded from below by k times the optimal solution of the modified instance and bounded from above by $2A$.

4. Return $\widetilde{opt} = \sum_{i \in X'} v_i$ as an ε-relative approximation to the optimal solution of the original problem.

It remains to see how long it takes to compute this approximation. The first step takes a time in $O(n \log n)$ to compute the $1/2$-relative approximation. If $\varepsilon < 2n/A$, it takes a time in $O(nM)$ to obtain the exact solution by dynamic programming. This is in $O(n^2/\varepsilon)$ since $nM = 2nA < 4n^2/\varepsilon$. If $\varepsilon \geq 2n/A$, the time taken by the other steps is analysed as follows. The second step is negligible. The third step takes a time in $O(nM')$, where $M' = \lfloor 2A/k \rfloor$ is the upper bound on the optimal solution of the modified instance used by the dynamic programming algorithm. This is also in $O(n^2/\varepsilon)$ since $k > \frac{\varepsilon A}{n} - 1 \geq \varepsilon A/2n$. The last step is negligible. In conclusion, this approximation scheme takes a time in $O(n^2/\varepsilon)$, which is indeed fully polynomial. Another scheme is known that can find an ε-relative approximate solution to the knapsack problem in a time in $O(n \log n + n/\varepsilon^2)$; yet another takes a time in $O(n \log 1/\varepsilon + 1/\varepsilon^4)$.

13.6 Problems

Problem 13.1.   Give an efficient algorithm to determine whether a graph can be painted with just two colours, and if so how to do it.

Problem 13.2.   In Section 13.1.1, while proving that the greedy heuristic can always find an optimal solution, we remarked that "When you apply colour 2, some nodes that had this colour in the original solution may already have been painted with colour 1. However there are sure to be one or more nodes that had colour 2 in the original solution that have not been painted." Justify this remark.

Problem 13.3.   Show that any *planar* graph (one that you can draw on a sheet of paper in such a way that none of the edges cross) can be painted using at most four colours.

Problem 13.4.   Show that the greedy heuristic from Section 13.1.2 can be arbitrarily bad: as a function of parameter $\alpha > 1$, construct an explicit instance of the travelling salesperson problem on which the heuristic finds a tour at least α times longer than the optimum.

Problem 13.5.   Devise and implement an algorithm to determine whether an $n \times n$ distance matrix has the metric property or not. How much time does your algorithm take?

Problem 13.6.   Consider the complete undirected graph with 8 nodes and the following distance matrix.

From	To:	2	3	4	5	6	7	8
1		41	19	99	83	108	120	140
2			35	88	96	121	137	151
3				80	70	95	108	127
4					53	66	87	86
5						26	42	57
6							22	34
7								27

This distance matrix has the metric property. Use the algorithm of Section 13.1.2 to obtain an approximate solution to the travelling salesperson problem for this graph. You can do this without a computer. If you do have a machine available, use an exhaustive search to obtain the exact solution.

Problem 13.7.   The approximate algorithm of Section 13.1.2 begins by finding a minimum spanning tree of the graph. Is there a good reason for preferring either Kruskal's algorithm or Prim's algorithm in this context?

Problem 13.8.   To illustrate the approximate algorithm of Section 13.1.2, after finding a minimum spanning tree of the graph we arbitrarily chose node 1 as the root of the tree. However any other node would serve as well. Using the example of Section 13.1.2, explore what happens if you choose another node as the root. Does the left-to-right order of the branches make a difference to the approximation found?

Problem 13.9.   In some instances it is possible to find a shorter optimal tour for the travelling salesperson if he is allowed to pass through the same town more than once. Give an explicit example illustrating this. On the other hand, show that if the distance matrix has the metric property then it is never advantageous to pass through the same town more than once.

Problem 13.10.   We saw in Section 13.1.2 an efficient approximate algorithm for the metric travelling salesperson problem that is guaranteed to find a solution within a factor 2 of the optimum. Give another efficient algorithm that is guaranteed to find a solution within a factor $^3/_2$ of the optimum.

Problem 13.11.   We saw in Section 13.2.2 an approximate algorithm *approx-knap* for the knapsack problem that returns an answer guaranteed to be at least half the optimal load. The first step of this algorithm is to sort the n objects by order of value per weight. For this reason, the algorithm takes a time in $\Omega(n \log n)$ in the worst case. Find a way to compute the same approximation in a time in $O(n)$ by use of the linear-time median-finding algorithm of Section 7.5.

Problem 13.12.   We saw in Section 13.2.2 that the greedy algorithm of Section 8.4 can be arbitrarily bad at solving the knapsack problem. Show that this is not the case when we consider the variation on the knapsack theme studied in Sections 9.6.1 and 9.7.2: the greedy algorithm is guaranteed to return a solution within a factor 2 of the optimum if we can use as many copies as we wish of each available object.

Problem 13.13.   You are given 9 objects whose weights are respectively 2, 2, 2, 3, 3, 4, 5, 6 and 9, and a number of bins of capacity 12. Use the approximate algorithms of Section 13.2.3 to estimate (a) what is the most objects you can pack into 2 bins, and (b) how many bins are needed to pack all 9 objects. Find the optimal solutions and compare these to your approximate answers.

Problem 13.14.   Is it meaningful to consider ε-relative approximations to maximization problems when $\varepsilon \geq 1$?

Problem 13.15.   For every constant c, prove that it is just as hard to find a c-absolute approximate solution to the knapsack problem as to find an exact solution.

Problem 13.16.   Prove that finding a c-absolute approximate solution to the maximum clique problem is $\mathcal{NP}$–hard for every positive constant c. For this, prove that CLKO $\leq_T^p c$–abs–CLKO for all c, where CLKO was defined in Problem 12.45. You may use the results of Problems 12.45 and 12.55.

Problem 13.17.   Continuing Problem 13.16, prove that finding an ε-relative approximate solution to the maximum clique problem is $\mathcal{NP}$–hard for every positive constant ε smaller than 1. Be warned that this is very difficult.

Problem 13.18.   Failing Problem 13.17, prove that for any positive constants ε and δ smaller than 1, finding an ε-relative approximation to the maximum clique problem is polynomially equivalent to finding a δ-relative approximation. In symbols, prove that ε–rel–CLKO $\equiv_T^p \delta$–rel–CLKO.

Problem 13.19.   Following Problem 13.3, prove that it is easy to compute 1-absolute as well as $^1/_3$-relative approximations to the problem of painting a planar graph with the minimum number of colours. On the other hand, prove that better approximations would be as hard to compute as the optimal solution.

Problem 13.20.   Prove that finding an ε-relative approximate solution to the bin packing problem of Section 13.2.3 is $\mathcal{NP}$–hard for any $\varepsilon < {}^1/_2$. You may use without proof the fact that PARTITION is $\mathcal{NP}$–complete; see Problem 12.56.

Problem 13.21.   Prove that it is as hard to find a 1-relative approximation to the chromatic number of general graphs as it is to find the exact solution.

Problem 13.22.   Continuing Problem 13.21, prove that it is as hard to find an ε-relative approximation to the chromatic number of general graphs as it is to find the exact solution for all $\varepsilon > 0$.

Problem 13.23.   Prove that algorithm *MAX-CUT-approx* from the proof of Theorem 13.4.1, which is guaranteed to find a $^1/_3$-relative approximation to the MAX–CUT problem, can yield arbitrarily bad relative approximations to the MIN–CLUSTER problem. For this, show how to assign positive integer costs to the edges of the complete graph on four nodes as functions of an arbitrary $\alpha > 1$ so that the approximate solution found by the algorithm for the MIN–CLUSTER problem is at least α times greater than the optimum.

Problem 13.24.   The maximum cut and minimum cluster problems can be generalized in the obvious way to the case where we wish to create k clusters for any constant $k \geq 2$. This gives rise to the problems k–MAX–CUT and k–MIN–CLUSTER. Although we introduced these problems with $k = 3$ to make the proof of Theorem 13.4.2 easier, it is more usual to define MAX–CUT and MIN–CLUSTER with $k = 2$.

(a) Give an efficient $^1/_k$-relative approximate algorithm for k–MAX–CUT for all $k \geq 2$.

(b) For all $k \geq 3$ and $\varepsilon > 0$, prove that finding an ε-relative approximate solution to k–MIN–CLUSTER is as hard as finding an exact solution.

Problem 13.25.   We continue Problem 13.24 with the special case $k = 2$.

(a) Prove that 2–MAX–CUT (and therefore 2–MIN–CLUSTER) is $\mathcal{NP}$–hard. *Hint*: Use the fact that PARTITION is $\mathcal{NP}$– complete; see Problem 12.56.

(b) We know from Problem 13.24 that there exists an efficient $^1/_2$-relative approximate algorithm for 2–MAX–CUT; find a better approximate algorithm. At the time of writing, the best efficient algorithm known is 0.12144-relative approximate.

(c) On the other hand, prove the existence of a positive ε such that it is $\mathcal{NP}$–hard to find an ε-relative approximate solution to 2–MAX–CUT.

(d) Prove that it is $\mathcal{NP}$–hard to find an ε-relative approximate solution to 2–MIN–CLUSTER for all positive ε. (The proof of Theorem 13.4.1 fails in the case of two clusters because it is easy to decide if a graph can be painted with two colours.)

Problem 13.26.   Give an elementary proof that there cannot exist a fully polynomial approximation scheme for the maximum clique problem, unless $\mathcal{P} = \mathcal{NP}$. This is obvious in the light of Problem 13.17, but no elementary proofs are known even for the existence of a positive $\varepsilon < 1$ for which finding an ε-relative approximate solution to the maximum clique problem is $\mathcal{NP}$–hard. You may use the fact that the maximum clique problem is $\mathcal{NP}$–hard.

Problem 13.27.   Consider the following instance of the knapsack problem. There are four objects whose weights are respectively 2, 5, 6 and 7 units, and whose values are 1, 3, 4 and 5. We can carry a maximum load of 11 units of weight.

(a) Apply the $^1/_2$-relative approximate greedy algorithm from Section 13.2.2 to this instance. Deduce an upper bound on the value of the optimal solution. (There are two ways to obtain this upper bound: one is obvious and one is clever.)

(b) Now that you have an upper bound on the value of the optimal solution, use it to apply the dynamic programming algorithm given in Section 13.5.2 to find an optimal solution. Give a table resembling that of Figure 8.4. Determine not only the optimal value that can be carried, but also the list of objects that should be packed.

Problem 13.28. In Section 8.4, we studied a dynamic programming algorithm for the exact solution of the knapsack problem, and applied it to an instance consisting of five objects, whose weights are respectively $1, 2, 5, 6$ and 7 units, and whose values are $1, 6, 18, 22$ and 28. We can carry a maximum load of 11 units of weight. Apply the fully polynomial approximation scheme of Section 13.5.2 to the same instance with $\varepsilon = 0.75$. You are probably on the wrong track if the solution to Problem 13.27 does not seem relevant. (In practice it would be silly to apply this algorithm with $\varepsilon = 0.75$ since the much simpler greedy algorithm from Section 13.2.2 is $1/2$-relative approximate, which is better than $3/4$-relative approximate. Unfortunately, the fully polynomial approximation scheme becomes useful only on instances that are too large to solve by hand.)

13.7 References and further reading

Good early references on approximation algorithms are Garey and Johnson (1976) and Sahni and Horowitz (1978). Approximate algorithms for the metric travelling salesperson problem are given by Christofides (1976), which includes the solution to Problem 13.10. Laporte (1992) surveys both exact and approximate algorithms for the general problem. Early approximate algorithms for the knapsack problems are given by Sahni (1975). Johnson (1973) proves the bounds for the approximate bin packing algorithms described in Section 13.2.3. Strong non-approximability results for the maximum clique problem and the problem of finding the chromatic number of a graph are from Bellare and Sudan (1994). They built on the earlier work of Arora, Lund, Motwani, Sudan and Szegedy (1992), which gives a solution to Problem 13.17. The approximation scheme we described for the knapsack problem is from Ibarra and Kim (1975). Other approximation schemes for the knapsack problem are given by Lawler (1979), where the solution to Problem 13.11 can be found. Problem 13.21 is from Johnson (1974). Problem 13.25(b) is from Goemans and Williamson (1994).

References

ABRAMSON, Bruce and Mordechai M. YUNG (1989), "Construction through decomposition: A divide-and-conquer algorithm for the *N*-queens problem", *Journal of Parallel and Distributed Computing*, vol. 6, no. 3, pp. 649–662.

ACKERMANN, Wilhelm (1928), "Zum Hilbertschen Aufbau der reellen Zahlen", *Mathematische Annalen*, vol. 99, pp. 118–133.

ADEL'SON–VEL'SKIĬ, Georgiĭ M. and Evgeniĭ M. LANDIS (1962), "An algorithm for the organization of information" (in Russian), *Doklady Akademii Nauk SSSR*, v ol. 146, pp. 263–266.

ADLEMAN, Leonard M. and Ming–Deh A. HUANG (1992), *Primality Testing and Abelian Varieties Over Finite Fields*, Lecture Notes in Mathematics, vol. 1512, Springer-Verlag.

ADLEMAN, Leonard M. and Kenneth MANDERS (1977), "Reducibility, randomness, and intractability", *Proceedings of the 9th Annual ACM Symposium on Theory of Computing*, pp. 151–163.

ADLEMAN, Leonard M., Carl POMERANCE and Robert S. RUMELY (1983), "On distinguishing prime numbers from composite numbers", *Annals of Mathematics*, vol. 117, pp. 173–206.

AHMES (1700bc), *Directions for Obtaining the Knowledge of All Dark Things*, Egyptian "Rhind" papyrus kept at the British Museum.

AHO, Alfred V., John E. HOPCROFT and Jeffrey D. ULLMAN (1974), *The Design and Analysis of Computer Algorithms*, Addison-Wesley.

AHO, Alfred V., John E. HOPCROFT and Jeffrey D. ULLMAN (1976), "On finding lowest common ancestors in trees", *SIAM Journal on Computing*, vol. 5, no. 1, pp. 115–132.

AHO, Alfred V., John E. HOPCROFT and Jeffrey D. ULLMAN (1983), *Data Structures and Algorithms*, Addison-Wesley.

AKL, Selim G. (1985), *Parallel Sorting Algorithms*, Academic Press.

AKL, Selim G. (1989), *The Design and Analysis of Parallel Algorithms*, Prentice-Hall.

ALFORD, W. R., A. GRANVILLE and Carl POMERANCE (1994), "There are infinitely many Carmichael numbers", *Annals of Mathematics*, vol. 139, pp. 703–722.

ALLISON, L., C. N. YEE and M. MCGAUGHEY (1989), "Three-dimensional queens problems", Technical Report no. 89/130, Department of Computer Science, Monash University, Australia.

ARLAZAROV, V. L., E. A. DINIC, M. A. KRONROD and I. A. FARADŽEV (1970), "On economical construction of the transitive closure of a directed graph" (in Russian), *Doklady Akademii Nauk SSSR*, vol. 194, pp. 487–488.

ARORA, Sanjeev, Carsten LUND, Rajeev MOTWANI, Madhu SUDAN and Mario SZEGEDY (1992), "Proof verification and hardness of approximation problems", *Proceedings of the 33rd Annual Symposium on Foundations of Computer Science*, pp. 14–23.

BAASE, Sara (1978), *Computer Algorithms: Introduction to Design and Analysis*, Addison-Wesley; 2nd edition, 1987.

BABAI, László (1979), "Monte Carlo algorithms in graph isomorphism techniques", Research Report no. 79–10, Département de mathématiques et de statistique, Université de Montréal.

BABAI, László and Shlomo MORAN (1988), "Arthur – Merlin games: A randomized proof system, and a hierarchy of complexity classes", *Journal of Computer and System Sciences*, vol. 36, pp. 254–276.

BACH, Eric, Gary MILLER and Jeffrey SHALLIT (1986), "Sums of divisors, perfect numbers and factoring", *SIAM Journal on Computing*, vol. 15, no. 4, pp. 1143–1154.

BACHMANN, Paul G. H. (1894), *Zahlentheorie; Volume 2: Die Analytische Zahlentheorie*, B. G. Teubner.

BALL, Walter W. R. (1967), *Mathematical Recreations and Essays*, 11th edition, Macmillan & Co.

BATCHER, Kenneth E. (1968), "Sorting networks and their applications", *AFIPS Conference Proceedings*, vol. 32, Spring Joint Computer Conference 1968, pp. 307–314.

BEAUCHEMIN, Pierre, Gilles BRASSARD, Claude CRÉPEAU, Claude GOUTIER and Carl POMERANCE (1988), "The generation of random numbers that are probably prime", *Journal of Cryptology*, vol. 1, no. 1, pp. 53–64.

BELLARE, Mihir and Shafi GOLDWASSER (1994), "The complexity of decision versus search", *SIAM Journal on Computing*, vol. 23, no. 1, pp. 97–119.

BELLARE, Mihir and Madhu SUDAN (1994), "Improved non-approximability results", *Proceedings of the 26th Annual ACM Symposium on Theory of Computing*, pp. 184–193.

BELLMAN, Richard E. (1957), *Dynamic Programming*, Princeton University Press.

BELLMAN, Richard E. and Stuart E. DREYFUS (1962), *Applied Dynamic Programming*, Princeton University Press.

BELLMORE M. and George NEMHAUSER (1968), "The traveling salesman problem: A survey", *Operations Research*, vol. 16, no. 3, pp. 538–558.

BENIOFF, Paul (1982), "Quantum Hamiltonian models of Turing machines", *Journal of Statistical Physics*, vol. 29, pp. 515–546.

BENNETT, Charles H., Gilles BRASSARD and Artur K. EKERT (1992), "Quantum Cryptography", *Scientific American*, vol. 267, no. 4, pp. 50–57.

BENTLEY, Jon L. (1980), "Multidimensional divide-and-conquer", *Communications of the ACM*, vol. 23, pp. 214–229.

BENTLEY, Jon L. (1984), "Programming pearls: Algorithm design techniques", *Communications of the ACM*, vol. 27, no. 9, pp. 865–871.

BENTLEY, Jon L., Dorothea HAKEN and James B. SAXE (1980), "A general method for solving divide-and-conquer recurrences", *ACM Sigact News*, vol. 12, no. 3, pp. 36–44.

BENTLEY, Jon L., Donald F. STANAT and J. Michael STEELE (1981), "Analysis of a randomized data structure for representing ordered sets", *Proceedings of the 19th Annual Allerton Conference on Communication, Control, and Computing*, pp. 364–372.

BERGE, Claude (1958), *Théorie des graphes et ses applications*, Dunod; 2nd edition, 1967. Translated as *The Theory of Graphs and Its Applications*, Methuen, 1962.

BERGE, Claude (1970), *Graphes et hypergraphes*, Dunod. Translated as *Graphs and Hypergraphs*, North Holland, 1973.

BERLEKAMP, Elwyn R., John H. CONWAY and Richard K. GUY (1982), *W inning Ways for Your Mathematical Plays; Volume 1: Games in General*, Academic Press.

BERLINER, Hans J. (1980), "Backgammon computer program beats world champion", *Artificial Intelligence*, vol. 14, pp. 205–220.

BERNSTEIN, Ethan and Umesh V. VAZIRANI (1993), "Quantum complexity theory", *Proceedings of the 25th Annual ACM Symposium on Theory of Computing*, pp. 11–20.

BERTHIAUME, André and Gilles BRASSARD (1995), "Oracle quantum computing", *Journal of Modern Optics*, vol. 41, no. 12, pp. 2521–2535.

BISHOP, Errett (1972), "Aspects of constructivism", *10th Holiday Mathematics Symposium*, New Mexico State University, Las Cruces.

BITTON, Dina, David J. DEWITT, David K. HSIAO and Jaishankar MENON (1984), "A taxonomy of parallel sorting", *Computing Surveys*, vol. 16, no. 3, pp. 287–318.

BLUM, Leonore, Manuel BLUM and Mike SHUB (1986), "A simple unpredictable pseudo-random number generator", *SIAM Journal on Computing*, vol. 15, no. 2, pp. 364–383.

BLUM, Manuel (1967), "A machine independent theory of the complexity of recursive functions", *Journal of the ACM*, vol. 14, no. 2, pp. 322–336.

BLUM, Manuel, Robert W. FLOYD, Vaughan R. PRATT, Ronald L. RIVEST and Robert E. TARJAN (1972), "Time bounds for selection", *Journal of Computer and System Sciences*, vol. 7, no. 4, pp. 448–461.

BLUM, Manuel and Silvio MICALI (1984), "How to generate cryptographically strong sequences of pseudo-random bits", *SIAM Journal on Computing*, vol. 13, no. 4, pp. 850–864.

BORODIN, Allan B. and J. Ian MUNRO (1975), *The Computational Complexity of Algebraic and Numeric Problems*, American Elsevier.

BORŮVKA, Otokar (1926), "O jistém problému minimálnim", *Práce Moravské Přírodověd Spolecnosti*, vol. 3, pp. 37–58.

BRASSARD, Gilles (1979), "A note on the complexity of cryptography", *IEEE Transactions on Information Theory*, vol. IT–25, no. 2, pp. 232–233.

BRASSARD, Gilles (1985), "Crusade for a better notation", *ACM Sigact News*, vol. 17, no. 1, pp. 60–64.

BRASSARD, Gilles (1988), *Modern Cryptology: A Tutorial*, Lecture Notes in Computer Science, vol. 325, Springer-Verlag.

BRASSARD, Gilles (1994), "Cryptology column — Quantum computing: The end of classical cryptography?", *ACM Sigact News*, vol. 25, no. 4, pp. 15–21.

BRASSARD, Gilles and Paul BRATLEY (1988), *Algorithmics: Theory and Practice*, Prentice-Hall.

BRASSARD, Gilles, Sophie MONET and Daniel ZUFFELLATO (1986), "L'arithmétique des très grands entiers", *TSI: Technique et Science Informatiques*, vol. 5, no. 2, pp. 89–102.

BRATLEY, Paul, Bennett L. FOX and Linus E. SCHRAGE (1983), *A Guide to Simulation*, Springer-Verlag; 2nd edition, 1987.

BRENT, Richard P. (1974), "The parallel evaluation of general arithmetic expressions", *Journal of the ACM*, vol. 21, no. 2, pp. 201–206.

BRESSOUD, David M. (1989), *Factorization and Primality Testing*, Springer-Verlag.

BRIGHAM, E. Oran (1974), *The Fast Fourier Transform*, Prentice-Hall.

BROWN, Mark R. (1978), "Implementation and analysis of binomial queue algorithms", *SIAM Journal on Computing*, vol. 7, no. 3, pp. 298–319.

BUNCH, James R. and John E. HOPCROFT (1974), "Triangular factorization and inversion by fast matrix multiplication", *Mathematics of Computation*, vol. 28, no. 125, pp. 231–236.

BUNEMAN, Peter and Leon LEVY (1980), "The Towers of Hanoi problem", *Information Processing Letters*, vol. 10, nos. 4–5, pp. 243–244.

CALINGER, Ronald (ed.) (1982), *Classics of Mathematics*, Moore Publishing Co.

CARASSO, Claude (1971), *Analyse numérique*, Lidec.

CARLSSON, Svante (1986), *Heaps*, doctoral dissertation, Department of Computer Science, Lund University, Sweden.

CARLSSON, Svante (1987a), "Average case results on heapsort", *BIT*, vol. 27, pp. 2–17.

CARLSSON, Svante (1987b), "The deap—A double-ended heap to implement double-ended priority queues", *Information Processing Letters*, vol. 26, no. 1, pp. 33–36.

CARTER, J. Larry and Mark N. WEGMAN (1979), "Universal classes of hash functions", *Journal of Computer and System Sciences*, vol. 18, no. 2, pp. 143–154.

CELIS, Pedro, Per–Åke LARSON and J. Ian MUNRO (1985), "Robin Hood hashing", *Proceedings of the 26th Annual Symposium on Foundations of Computer Science*, pp. 281–288.

CHANG, Lena and James F. KORSH (1976), "Canonical coin changing and greedy solutions", *Journal of the ACM*, vol. 23, no. 3, pp. 418–422.

CHERITON, David and Robert E. TARJAN (1976), "Finding minimum spanning trees", *SIAM Journal on Computing*, vol. 5, no. 4, pp. 724–742.

CHIN, Francis Y., John LAM and I–Ngo CHEN (1982), "Efficient parallel algorithms for some graph problems", *Communications of the ACM*, vol. 25, no. 9, pp. 659–665.

CHRISTOFIDES, Nicos (1975), *Graph Theory: An Algorithmic Approach*, Academic Press.

CHRISTOFIDES, Nicos (1976), "Worst-case analysis of a new heuristic for the traveling salesman problem", Research Report no. 388, Management Sciences, Carnegie-Mellon University, Pittsburgh, PA.

COBHAM, Alan (1964), "The intrinsic computational difficulty of functions", *Proceedings of the 1964 Congress on Logic, Mathematics and the Methodology of Science*, North-Holland, pp. 24–30.

COHEN, Henri and Arjen K. LENSTRA (1987), "Implementation of a new primality test", *Mathematics of Computation*, vol. 48, no. 177, pp. 103–121.

COLE, Richard (1988), "Parallel merge sort", *SIAM Journal on Computing*, vol. 17, no. 4, pp. 770–785.

COOK, Steven A. (1971), "The complexity of theorem-proving procedures", *Proceedings of the 3rd Annual ACM Symposium on Theory of Computing*, pp. 151–158.

COOK, Steven A. and Staal O. AANDERAA (1969), "On the minimum complexity of functions", *Transactions of the American Mathematical Society*, vol. 142, pp. 291–314.

COOLEY, James W., Peter A. W. LEWIS and Peter D. WELCH (1967), "History of the fast Fourier transform", *Proceedings of the IEEE*, vol. 55, pp. 1675–1679.

COOLEY, James W. and John W. TUKEY (1965), "An algorithm for the machine calculation of complex Fourier series", *Mathematics of Computation*, vol. 19, no. 90, pp. 297–301.

COPPERSMITH, Don and Shmuel WINOGRAD (1990), "Matrix multiplication via arithmetic progressions", *Journal of Symbolic Computation*, vol. 9, pp. 251–280.

CORMEN, Thomas H., Charles E. LEISERSON, and Ronald L. RIVEST (1990), *Introduction to Algorithms*, MIT Press and McGraw-Hill.

COUVREUR, Chantal and Jean–Jacques QUISQUATER (1982), "An introduction to fast generation of large prime numbers", *Philips Journal of Research*, vol. 37, pp. 231–264; errata (1983),
ibid., vol. 38, p. 77.

CURTISS, John H. (1956), "A theoretical comparison of the efficiencies of two classical methods
and a Monte Carlo method for computing one component of the solution of a set of linear
algebraic equations", in *Symposium on Monte Carlo Methods*, H. A. Meyer (ed.), Wiley,
pp. 191–233.

DAMGÅRD, Ivan B., Peter LANDROCK and Carl POMERANCE (1993), "Average case error estimates for the strong probable prime test", *Mathematics of Computatio n*, vol. 61, no. 203,
pp. 177–194.

DANIELSON, G. C. and C. LANCZOS (1942), "Some improvements in practical Fourier analysis
and their application to X-ray scattering from liquids", *Journal of the Franklin Institute*,
vol. 233, pp. 365–380, 435–452.

DE BRUIJN, Nicolaas G. (1961), *Asymptotic Methods in Analysis*, North-Holland.

DENNING, Dorothy E. R. (1983), *Cryptography and Data Security*, Addison-Wesley.

DEUTSCH, David (1985), "Quantum theory, the Church–Turing principle and the universal
quantum computer", *Proceedings of the Royal Society*, London, vol. A400, pp. 97–117.

DEUTSCH, David and Richard JOZSA (1992), "Rapid solution of problems by quantum computation", *Proceedings of the Royal Society*, London, vol. A439, pp. 553–558.

DEVROYE, Luc (1986), *Non-Uniform Random Variate Generation*, Springer-Verlag.

DEWDNEY, Alexander K. (1984), "Computer recreations — Yin and yang: Recursion and
iteration, the Tower of Hanoi and the Chinese rings", *Scientific American*, vol. 251, no. 5,
pp. 19–28.

DEYONG, Lewis (1977), *Playboy's Book of Backgammon*, Playboy Press.

DIFFIE, Whitfield and Martin E. HELLMAN (1976), "New directions in cryptography", *IEEE
Transactions on Information Theory*, vol. IT–22, no. 6, pp. 644–654.

DIJKSTRA, Edsger W. (1959), "A note on two problems in connexion with graphs", *Numerische
Mathematik*, vol. 1, pp. 269–271.

DIXON, John D. (1981), "Asymptotically fast factorization of integers", *Mathematics of Computation*, vol. 36, no. 153, pp. 255–260.

DROMEY, R. G. (1982), *How to Solve It by Computer*, Prentice-Hall.

DUNCAN, Ralph (1990), "A survey of parallel computer architectures", *Computer*, vol. 23,
no. 2, pp. 5–16.

EDMONDS, Jack (1965), "Paths, trees, and flowers", *Canadian Journal of Mathematics*, vol. 17,
no. 3, pp. 449–467.

EDMONDS, Jack (1971), "Matroids and the greedy algorithm", *Mathematical Programming*,
vol. 1, pp. 127–136.

ELKIES, Noam D. (1988), "On $A^4 + B^4 + C^4 = D^4$ ", *Mathematics of Computation*, vol. 51, no. 184,
pp. 825–835.

ERDŐS, Paul and Carl POMERANCE (1986), "On the number of false witnesses for a composite
number", *Mathematics of Computation*, vol. 46, no. 173, pp. 259–279.

EVEN, Shimon (1980), *Graph Algorithms*, Computer Science Press.

EVES, Howard (1983), *An Introduction to the History of Mathematics*, 5th edition, Saunders
College Publishing.

FEYNMAN, Richard (1982), "Simulating physics with computers", *International Journal of
Theoretical Physics*, vol. 21, nos. 6/7, pp. 467–488.

FEYNMAN, Richard (1986), "Quantum mechanical computers", *Foundations of Physics*, vol. 16, no. 6, pp. 507–531; originally appeared in *Optics News*, February 1985.

FISCHER, Michael J. and Albert R. MEYER (1971), "Boolean matrix multiplication and transitive closure", *Proceedings of the 12th Annual IEEE Symposium on Switching and Automata Theory*, pp. 129–131.

FLAJOLET, Philippe (1985), "Approximate counting: A detailed analysis", *BIT*, vol. 25, pp. 113–134.

FLAJOLET, Philippe and G. Nigel MARTIN (1985), "Probabilistic counting algorithms for data base applications", *Journal of Computer and System Sciences*, vol. 31, no. 2, pp. 182–209.

FLOYD, Robert W. (1962), "Algorithm 97: Shortest path", *Communications of the ACM*, vol. 5, no. 6, p. 345.

FOX, Bennett L. (1986), "Algorithm 647: Implementation and relative efficiency of quasirandom sequence generators", *ACM Transactions on Mathematical Software*, vol. 12, no. 4, pp. 362–376.

FREDMAN, Michael L. (1976), "New bounds on the complexity of the shortest path problem", *SIAM Journal on Computing*, vol. 5, no. 1, pp. 83–89.

FREDMAN, Michael L. and Robert E. TARJAN (1987), "Fibonacci heaps and their use in improved network optimization algorithms", *Journal of the ACM*, vol. 34, no. 3, pp. 596–615.

FREDMAN, Michael L. and Dan E. WILLARD (1990), "BLASTING through the information theoretic barrier with FUSION TREES", *Proceedings of the 22nd Annual ACM Symposium on Theory of Computing*, pp. 1–7.

FREIVALDS, Rūsiņš (1977), "Probabilistic machines can use less running time", *Proceedings of Information Processing '77*, pp. 839–842.

FREIVALDS, Rūsiņš (1979), "Fast probabilistic algorithms", *Proceedings of the 8th Symposium on the Mathematical Foundations of Computer Science*, Lecture Notes in Computer Science, vol. 74, Springer-Verlag.

FURMAN, M. E. (1970), "Application of a method of fast multiplication of matrices in the problem of finding the transitive closure of a graph" (in Russian), *Doklady Akademii Nauk SSSR*, vol. 194, p. 524.

GALIL, Zvi and Giuseppe F. ITALIANO (1991), "Data structures and algorithms for disjoint set union problems", *Computing Surveys*, vol. 23, no. 3, pp. 319–344.

GARDNER, Martin (1959), *The Scientific American Book of Mathematical Puzzles and Diversions*, Simon and Schuster.

GARDNER, Martin (1977), "Mathematical games: A new kind of cipher that would take millions of years to break", *Scientific American*, vol. 237, no. 2, pp. 120–124.

GARDNER, Martin and Charles H. BENNETT (1979), "Mathematical games: The random number omega bids fair to hold the mysteries of the universe", *Scientific American*, vol. 241, no. 5, pp. 20–34.

GAREY, Michael R., Ronald L. GRAHAM and David S. JOHNSON (1977), "The complexity of computing Steiner minimal trees", *SIAM Journal on Applied Mathematics*, vol. 32, pp. 835–859.

GAREY, Michael R. and David S. JOHNSON (1976), "Approximation algorithms for combinatorial problems: An annotated bibliography", in *Algorithms and Complexity: Recent Results and New Directions*, J. F. Traub (ed.), Academic Press, pp. 41–52.

GAREY, Michael R. and David S. JOHNSON (1979), *Computers and Intractability: A Guide to the Theory of NP-Completeness*, W. H. Freeman.

GIBBONS, Alan and Wojciech RYTTER (1988), *Efficient Parallel Algorithms*, Cambridge University Press.

GILBERT, Edgard N. and Edward F. MOORE (1959), "Variable length encodings", *Bell System Technical Journal*, vol. 38, no. 4, pp. 933–968.

GILL, John (1977), "Computational complexity of probabilistic Turing machines", *SIAM Journal on Computing*, vol. 6, pp. 675–695.

GODBOLE, Sadashiva S. (1973), "On efficient computation of matrix chain products", *IEEE Transactions on Computers*, vol. C–22, no. 9, pp. 864–866.

GOEMANS, Michel X. and David P. WILLIAMSON (1994), ".878-Approximation algorithms for MAX CUT and MAX 2SAT", *Proceedings of the 26th Annual ACM Symposium on Theory of Computing*, pp. 422–431.

GOLDREICH, Oded, Silvio MICALI and Avi WIGDERSON (1991), "Proofs that yield nothing but their validity, or all languages in NP have zero-knowledge proof systems", *Journal of the ACM*, vol. 38, pp. 691–729.

GOLDWASSER, Shafi and Joe KILIAN (1986), "Almost all primes can be quickly certified", *Proceedings of the 18th Annual ACM Symposium on Theory of Computing*, pp. 316–329.

GOLDWASSER, Shafi, Silvio MICALI and Charles RACKOFF (1989), "The knowledge complexity of interactive proof-systems", *SIAM Journal on Computing*, vol. 18, pp. 186–208.

GOLOMB, Solomon W. and Leonard D. BAUMERT (1965), "Backtrack programming", *Journal of the ACM*, vol. 12, no. 4, pp. 516–524.

GONDRAN, Michel and Michel MINOUX (1979), *Graphes et algorithmes*, Eyrolles. Translated as *Graphs and Algorithms*, Wiley, 1984.

GONNET, Gaston H. and Ricardo BAEZA-YATES (1984), *Handbook of Algorithms and Data Structures*, Addison-Wesley; 2nd edition, 1991.

GONNET, Gaston H. and J. Ian MUNRO (1986), "Heaps on heaps", *SIAM Journal on Computing*, vol. 15, no. 4, pp. 964–971.

GOOD, Irving J. (1968), "A five-year plan for automatic chess", in *Machine Intelligence 2*, E. Dale and D. Michie (eds), American Elsevier.

GRAHAM, Ronald L. and Pavol HELL (1985), "On the history of the minimum spanning tree problem", *Annals of the History of Computing*, vol. 7, no. 1, pp. 43–57.

GREENE, Daniel H. and Donald E. KNUTH (1981), *Mathematics for the Analysis of Algorithms*, Birkhauser.

GRIES, David (1981), *The Science of Programming*, Springer-Verlag.

GRIES, David and Gary LEVIN (1980), "Computing Fibonacci numbers (and similarly defined functions) in log time", *Information Processing Letters*, vol. 11, no. 2, pp. 68–69.

GUIBAS, Leonidas J. and Robert SEDGEWICK (1978), "A dichromatic framework for balanced trees", *Proceedings of the 19th Annual Symposium on Foundations of Computer Science*, pp. 8–21.

GUY, Richard K. (1981), *Unsolved Problems in Number Theory*, Springer-Verlag.

HALL, A. (1873), "On an experimental determination of π", *Messenger of Mathematics*, vol. 2, pp. 113–114.

HAMMERSLEY, John M. and David C. HANDSCOMB (1965), *Monte Carlo Methods*; reprinted by Chapman and Hall, 1979.

HARDY, Godfrey H. and Edward M. WRIGHT (1938), *An Introduction to the Theory of Numbers*, Oxford University Press; 5th edition, 1979.

HAREL, David (1987), *Algorithmics: The Spirit of Computing*, Addison-Wesley; 2nd edition, 1992.

HEATH, Sir Thomas L. (1926), *The Thirteen Books of Euclid's Elements*, 3 volumes, 2nd edition, Cambridge University Press; reprinted by Dover Publications, 1956.

HELD, M. and Richard KARP (1962), "A dynamic programming approach to sequencing problems", *SIAM Journal on Applied Mathematics*, vol. 10, no. 1, pp. 196–210.

HELLMAN, Martin E. (1980), "The mathematics of public-key cryptography", *Scientific American*, vol. 241, no. 2, pp. 146–157.

HILLIER, Frederick S. and Gerald J. LIEBERMAN (1967), *Introduction to Operations Research*, Holden-Day.

HIRSCHBERG, D. S., Ashok K. CHANDRA and D. V. SARWATE (1979), "Computing connected components on parallel computers", *Communications of the ACM*, vol. 22, no. 8, pp. 461–464.

HOARE, Charles A. R. (1962), "Quicksort", *Computer Journal*, vol. 5, no. 1, pp. 10–15.

HOPCROFT, John E. and Richard KARP (1971), "An algorithm for testing the equivalence of finite automata", Technical Report TR–71–114, Department of Computer Science, Cornell University, Ithaca, NY.

HOPCROFT, John E. and Leslie R. KERR (1971), "On minimizing the number of multiplications necessary for matrix multiplication", *SIAM Journal on Applied Mathematics*, vol. 20, no. 1, pp. 30–36.

HOPCROFT, John E. and Robert E. TARJAN (1973), "Efficient algorithms for graph manipulation", *Communications of the ACM*, vol. 16, no. 6, pp. 372–378.

HOPCROFT, John E. and Robert E. TARJAN (1974), "Efficient planarity testing", *Journal of the ACM*, vol. 21, no. 4, pp. 549–568.

HOPCROFT, John E. and Jeffrey D. ULLMAN (1973), "Set merging algorithms", *SIAM Journal on Computing*, vol. 2, no. 4, pp. 294–303.

HOPCROFT, John E. and Jeffrey D. ULLMAN (1979), *Introduction to Automata Theory, Languages, and Computation*, Addison-Wesley.

HOROWITZ, Ellis and Sartaj SAHNI (1976), *Fundamentals of Data Structures*, Computer Science Press.

HOROWITZ, Ellis and Sartaj SAHNI (1978), *Fundamentals of Computer Algorithms*, Computer Science Press.

HU, Te Chiang (1981), *Combinatorial Algorithms*, Addison-Wesley.

HU, Te Chiang and M. T. SHING (1982), "Computations of matrix chain products", Part I, *SIAM Journal on Computing*, vol. 11, no. 2, pp. 362–373.

HU, Te Chiang and M. T. SHING (1984), "Computations of matrix chain products", Part II, *SIAM Journal on Computing*, vol. 13, no. 2, pp. 228–251.

IBARRA, Oscar H. and Chul E. KIM (1975), "Fast approximation algorithms for the knapsack and sum of subset problems", *Journal of the ACM*, vol. 22, no. 4, pp. 463–468.

IRVING, Robert W. (1984), "Permutation backtracking in lexicographic order", *The Computer Journal*, vol. 27, no. 4, pp. 373–375.

JA'JA', Joseph (1992), *An Introduction to Parallel Algorithms*, Addison-Wesley.

JANKO, Wolfgang (1976), "A list insertion sort for keys with arbitrary key distribution", *ACM Transactions on Mathematical Software*, vol. 2, no. 2, pp. 143–153.

JARNÍK, V. (1930), "O jistém problému minimálnim", *Práce Moravské Přírodověd Spolecnosti*, vol. 6, pp. 57–63.

JENSEN, Kathleen and Niklaus WIRTH (1985), *Pascal User Manual and Report*, 3rd edition revised by Andrew B. Mickel and James F. Miner, Springer-Verlag.

JOHNSON, David S. (1973), *Near-Optimal Bin-Packing Algorithms*, doctoral dissertation, Massachusetts Institute of Technology, MIT Report MAC TR–109.

JOHNSON, David S. (1974), "Approximation algorithms for combinatorial problems", *Journal of Computer and System Sciences*, vol. 9, pp. 256–289.

JOHNSON, David S. (1990), "A catalog of complexity classes", in van Leeuwen (1990), pp. 67–161.

JOHNSON, Donald B. (1975), "Priority queues with update and finding minimum spanning trees", *Information Processing Letters*, vol. 4, no. 3, pp. 53–57.

JOHNSON, Donald B. (1977), "Efficient algorithms for shortest paths in sparse networks", *Journal of the ACM*, vol. 24, no. 1, pp. 1–13.

KAHN, David (1966), "Modern cryptology", *Scientific American*, vol. 215, no. 1, pp. 38–46.

KAHN, David (1967), *The Codebreakers: The Story of Secret Writing*, Macmillan.

KALISKI, Burt S., Ronald L. RIVEST and Alan T. SHERMAN (1988), "Is the Data Encryption Standard a group? (Results of cycling experiments on DES)", *Journal of Cryptology*, vol. 1, no. 1, pp. 3–36.

KARATSUBA, Anatoliĭ A. and Y. OFMAN (1962), "Multiplication of multidigit numbers on automata" (in Russian), *Doklady Akademii Nauk SSSR*, vol. 145, pp. 293–294.

KARP, Richard (1972), "Reducibility among combinatorial problems", in *Complexity of Computer Computations*, R. E. Miller and J. W. Thatcher (eds), Plenum Press, pp. 85–104.

KASIMI, T. (1965), "An efficient recognition and syntax algorithm for context-free languages", Scientific Report AFCRL–65–758, Air Force Cambridge Research Laboratory, Bedford, MA.

KIM, Su Hee and Carl POMERANCE (1989), "The probability that a random probable prime is composite", *Mathematics of Computation*, vol. 53, no. 188, pp. 721–741.

KINGSTON, Jeffrey H. (1990), *Algorithms and Data Structures: Design, Correctness, Analysis*, Addison-Wesley.

KIRKERUD, Bjørn (1989), *Object-Oriented Programming with Simula*, Addison-Wesley.

KLEENE, Stephen C. (1956), "Representation of events in nerve nets and finite automata", in *Automata Studies*, C. E. Shannon and J. McCarthy (eds), Princeton University Press, pp. 3–40.

KLINE, Morris (1972), *Mathematical Thoughts from Ancient to Modern Times*, Oxford University Press.

KNUTH, Donald E. (1968), *The Art of Computer Programming; Volume 1: Fundamental Algorithms*, Addison-Wesley; 2nd edition, 1973.

KNUTH, Donald E. (1969), *The Art of Computer Programming; Volume 2: Seminumerical Algorithms*, Addison-Wesley; 2nd edition, 1981.

KNUTH, Donald E. (1971), "Optimal binary search trees", *Acta Informatica*, vol. 1, pp. 14–25.

KNUTH, Donald E. (1973), *The Art of Computer Programming; Volume 3: Sorting and Searching*, Addison-Wesley.

KNUTH, Donald E. (1975), "Estimating the efficiency of backtrack programs", *Mathematics of Computation*, vol. 29, pp. 121–136.

KNUTH, Donald E. (1976), "Big omicron and big omega and big theta", *ACM Sigact News*, vol. 8, no. 2, pp. 18–24.

KNUTH, Donald E. (1977), "Algorithms", *Scientific American*, vol. 236, no. 4, pp. 63–80.

KOBLITZ, Neal (1987), *A Course in Number Theory and Cryptography*, Springer-Verlag.

KOZEN, Dexter C. (1992), *The Design and Analysis of Algorithms*, Springer-Verlag.

KRAITCHIK, Maurice B. (1926), *Théorie des nombres*, Tome II, Gauthier-Villars.

KRANAKIS, Evangelos (1986), *Primality and Cryptography*, Wiley-Teubner Series in Computer Science.

KRUSKAL, Joseph B., Jr. (1956), "On the shortest spanning subtree of a graph and the traveling salesman problem", *Proceedings of the American Mathematical Society*, vol. 7, no. 1, pp. 48–50.

KUČERA, Luděk. (1982), "Parallel computation and conflicts in memory access", *Information Processing Letters*, vol. 14, no. 2, pp. 93–96.

LAKSHMIVARAHAN, S. and Sudarshan K. DHALL (1990), *Analysis and Design of Parallel Algorithms: Arithmetic and Matrix Problems*, McGraw-Hill.

LAPORTE, Gilbert (1992), "The traveling salesman problem: An overview of exact and approximate algorithms", *European Journal of Operational Research*, vol. 59, pp. 231–247.

LAROUSSE (1968), *Grand Larousse Encyclopédique*, Librairie Larousse, article on "Pâque".

LAURIÈRE, Jean–Louis (1979), *Eléments de programmation dynamique*, Bordas.

LAWLER, Eugene L. (1976), *Combinatorial Optimization: Networks and Matroids*, Holt, Rinehart and Winston.

LAWLER, Eugene L. (1979), "Fast approximation algorithms for knapsack problems", *Mathematics of Operations Research*, vol. 4, pp. 339–356.

LAWLER, Eugene L. and D. W. WOOD (1966), "Branch-and-bound methods: A survey", *Operations Research*, vol. 14, no. 4, pp. 699–719.

LECARME, Olivier and Jean–Louis NEBUT (1985), *Pascal pour programmeurs*, McGraw-Hill.

LECLERC, Georges L., Comte de BUFFON (1977), *Essai d'arithmétique morale*.

L'ÉCUYER, Pierre (1988), "Efficient and portable combined random number generators", *Communications of the ACM*, vol. 31, no. 6, pp. 742–749 and 774.

L'ÉCUYER, Pierre (1990), "Random numbers for simulation", *Communications of the ACM*, vol. 33, no. 10, pp. 85–97.

LEIGHTON, F. Thomson (1992), *Introduction to Parallel Algorithms and Architectures: Arrays ∘ Trees ∘ Hypercubes*, Morgan Kaufmann.

LENSTRA, Arjen K., Hendrik W. LENSTRA Jr., Mark S. MANASSE and John M. POLLARD (1993), "The number field sieve", in *The Development of the Number Field Sieve*, A. K. Lenstra and H. W. Lenstra Jr. (eds), Lecture Notes in Mathematics, vol. 1554, Springer-Verlag, pp. 11–42.

LENSTRA, Arjen K. and Mark S. MANASSE (1990), "Factoring by electronic mail", in *Advances in Cryptology — Eurocrypt '89 Proceedings*, Lecture Notes in Computer Science, vol. 434, Springer-Verlag, pp. 355–371.

LENSTRA, Arjen K. and Mark S. MANASSE (1991), "Factoring with two large primes", in *Advances in Cryptology – Eurocrypt '90 Proceedings*, Lecture Notes in Computer Science, vol. 473, Springer-Verlag, pp. 72–82.

LENSTRA, Hendrik W., Jr. (1982), "Primality testing", in Lenstra and Tijdeman (1982), pp. 55–97.

LENSTRA, Hendrik W., Jr. (1987), "Factoring integers with elliptic curves", *Annals of Mathematics*, vol. 126, no. 3, pp. 649–673.

LENSTRA, Hendrik W., Jr. and R. TIJDEMAN (eds) (1982), *Computational Methods in Number Theory*, Part I, Mathematical Centre Tracts 154, Mathematisch Centrum, Amsterdam.

LEVIN, Leonid (1973), "Universal search problems" (in Russian), *Problemy Peredaci Informacii*, vol. 9, pp. 115–116.

LEWIS, Harry R. and Larry DENENBERG (1991), *Data Structures & Their Algorithms*, Harper Collins Publishers.

LEWIS, Harry R. and Christos H. PAPADIMITRIOU (1978), "The efficiency of algorithms", *Scientific American*, vol. 238, no. 1, pp. 96–109.

LLOYD, Seth (1993), "A potentially realizable quantum computer", *Science*, vol. 261, 17 September, pp. 1569–1571.

LUEKER, George S. (1980), "Some techniques for solving recurrences", *Computing Surveys*, vol. 12, no. 4, pp. 419–436.

MANBER, Udi (1989), *Introduction to Algorithms: A Creative Approach*, Addison-Wesley.

MARSH, D. (1970), "Memo functions, the graph traverser, and a simple control situation", in *Machine Intelligence 5*, B. Meltzer and D. Michie (eds), American Elsevier and Edinburgh University Press, pp. 281–300.

MAURER, Ueli M. (1995), "Fast generation of prime numbers and secure public-key cryptographic parameters", *Journal of Cryptology*, vol. 8, no. 3.

McCARTY, Carl P. (1978), "Queen squares", *The American Mathematical Monthly*, vol. 85, no. 7, pp. 578–580.

McDIARMID, Colin J. H. and Bruce A. REED (1989), "Building heaps fast", *Journal of Algorithms*, vol. 10, no. 3, pp. 352–365.

MELHORN, Kurt (1984a), *Data Structures and Algorithms 1: Sorting and Searching*, Springer-Verlag.

MELHORN, Kurt (1984b), *Data Structures and Algorithms 2: Graph Algorithms and NP-Completeness*, Springer-Verlag.

MELHORN, Kurt (1984c), *Data Structures and Algorithms 3: Multi-Dimensional Searching and Computational Geometry*, Springer-Verlag.

MERKLE, Ralph C. (1978), "Secure communications over insecure channels", *Communications of the ACM*, vol. 21, pp. 294–299.

METROPOLIS, I. Nicholas and Stanislaw ULAM (1949), "The Monte Carlo method", *Journal of the American Statistical Association*, vol. 44, no. 247, pp. 335–341.

MICHIE, Donald (1968), "'Memo' functions and machine learning", *Nature*, vol. 218, pp. 19–22.

MILLER, Gary L. (1976), "Riemann's hypothesis and tests for primality", *Journal of Computer and System Sciences*, vol. 13, no. 3, pp. 300–317.

MONIER, Louis (1980), "Evaluation and comparison of two efficient probabilistic primality testing algorithms", *Theoretical Computer Science*, vol. 12, pp. 97–108.

MORET, Bernard M. E. and Henry D. SHAPIRO (1991), *Algorithms from P to NP; Volume I: Design & Efficiency*, Benjamin/Cummings.

MORRIS, Robert (1978), "Counting large numbers of events in small registers", *Communications of the ACM*, vol. 21, no. 10, pp. 840–842.

NAIK, Ashish V., Mitsunori OGIWARA and Alan L. SELMAN (1993), "P-selective sets, and reducing search to decision vs. self-reducibility", *Proceedings of the 8th Annual IEEE Conference on Structure in Complexity Theory*, pp. 52–64.

NELSON, C. Greg and Derek C. OPPEN (1980), "Fast decision procedures based on congruence closure", *Journal of the ACM*, vol. 27, pp. 356–364.

NEMHAUSER, George (1966), *Introduction to Dynamic Programming*, Wiley.

NIEVERGELT, Jurg and Klaus HINRICHS (1993), *Algorithms and Data Structures with Applications to Graphics and Geometry*, Prentice-Hall.

NILSSON, Nils J. (1971) *Problem Solving Methods in Artificial Intelligence*, McGraw-Hill.

PAGEAU, Marie (1993), *Applications du probabilisme à l'algorithmique*, masters dissertation, Département d'informatique et de R.O., Université de Montréal.

PAN, Viktor Y. (1980), "New fast algorithms for matrix operations", *SIAM Journal on Computing*, vol. 9, pp. 321–342.

PAPADIMITRIOU, Christos H. (1994), *Computational Complexity*, Addison-Wesley.

PAPADIMITRIOU, Christos H. and Kenneth STEIGLITZ (1982), *Combinatorial Optimization: Algorithms and Complexity*, Prentice-Hall.

PERALTA, René C. (1986), "A simple and fast probabilistic algorithm for computing square roots modulo a prime number", *IEEE Transactions on Information Theory*, vol. IT–32, no. 6, pp. 846–847.

PIPPENGER, Nicholas (1978), "Complexity theory", *Scientific American*, vol. 238, no. 6, pp. 114–124.

PIPPENGER, Nicholas (1979), "On simultaneous resource bounds", *Proceedings of the 20th Annual Symposium on Foundations of Computer Science*, pp. 307–311.

POLLARD, John M. (1971), "The fast Fourier transform in a finite field", *Mathematics of Computation*, vol. 25, no. 114, pp. 365–374.

POLLARD, John M. (1975), "A Monte Carlo method of factorization", *BIT*, vol. 15, pp. 331–334.

PÓLYA, György (1945), *How to Solve It: A New Aspect of Mathematical Method*, Princeton University Press.

PÓLYA, György (1954), *Induction and Analogy in Mathematics*, Princeton University Press.

POMERANCE, Carl (1982), "Analysis and comparison of some integer factoring algorithms", in Lenstra and Tijdeman (1982), pp. 89–139.

POMERANCE, Carl (1984), "The quadratic sieve algorithm", in *Advances in Cryptology: Proceedings of Eurocrypt 84*, Lecture Notes in Computer Science, vol. 209, Springer-Verlag, pp. 169–182.

POMERANCE, Carl (1987), "Very short primality proofs", *Mathematics of Computation*, vol. 48, no. 177, pp. 315–322.

PRATT, Vaughan R. (1975), "Every prime has a succinct certificate", *SIAM Journal on Computing*, vol. 4, no. 3, pp. 214–220.

PRIM, Robert C. (1957), "Shortest connection networks and some generalizations", *Bell System Technical Journal*, vol. 36, pp. 1389–1401.

PURDOM, Paul W., Jr. and Cynthia A. BROWN (1985), *The Analysis of Algorithms*, Holt, Rinehart and Winston.

QUINN, Michael J. and Narsingh DEO (1984), "Parallel Graph Algorithms", *Computing Surveys*, vol. 16, no. 3, pp. 319–348.

RABIN, Michael O. (1976), "Probabilistic Algorithms", in *Algorithms and Complexity: Recent Results and New Directions*, J. F. Traub (ed.), Academic Press, pp. 21–39.

RABIN, Michael O. (1980a), "Probabilistic algorithms in finite fields", *SIAM Journal on Computing*, vol. 9, no. 2, pp. 273–280.

RABIN, Michael O. (1980b), "Probabilistic algorithm for primality testing", *Journal of Number Theory*. vol. 12, pp. 128–138.

RAWLINS, Gregory J. E. (1992), *Compared to What? An Introduction to the Analysis of Algorithms*, Computer Science Press.

REIF, John H. (1993), *Synthesis of Parallel Algorithms*, Morgan Kaufman.

REINGOLD, Edward M., Jurg NIEVERGELT and Narsingh DEO (1977), *Combinatorial Algorithms: Theory and Practice*, Prentice-Hall.

RICE, John A. (1988), *Mathematical Statistics and Data Analysis*, Duxbury Press; 2nd edition, 1995.

RIVEST, Ronald L. and Robert W. FLOYD (1973), "Bounds on the expected time for median computations", in *Combinatorial Algorithms*, R. Rustin (ed.), Algorithmics Press, pp. 69–76.

RIVEST, Ronald L., Adi SHAMIR and Leonard M. ADLEMAN (1978), "A method for obtaining digital signatures and public-key cryptosystems", *Communications of the ACM*, vol. 21, no. 2, pp. 120–126.

ROBSON, John M. (1973), "An improved algorithm for traversing binary trees without auxiliary stack", *Information Processing Letters*, vol. 2, no. 1, pp. 12–14.

ROSEN, Kenneth H. (1991), *Discrete Mathematics and Its Applications*, 2nd edition, McGraw-Hill.

ROSENTHAL, Arnie and Anita GOLDNER (1977), "Smallest augmentation to biconnect a graph", *SIAM Journal on Computing*, vol. 6, no. 1, pp. 55–66.

RUNGE, Carl D. T. and Hermann KÖNIG (1924), "Vorlesungen über numerisches Rechnen", *Die Grundlehren der Mathematischen Wissenschaften*, vol. 11, Springer-Verlag, Berlin, pp. 211–237.

SAHNI, Sartaj (1975), "Approximate algorithms for the 0/1 knapsack problem", *Journal of the ACM*, vol. 22, no. 1, pp. 115–124.

SAHNI, Sartaj and Ellis HOROWITZ (1978), "Combinatorial problems: Reducibility and approximation", *Operations Research*, vol. 26, no. 4, pp. 718–759.

SAVITCH, Walter J. (1970), "Relationship between nondeterministic and deterministic tape classes", *Journal of Computer and System Sciences*, vol. 4, pp. 177–192.

SCHAFFER, Russel and Robert SEDGEWICK (1993), "The analysis of heapsort", *Journal of Algorithms*, vol. 15, no. 1, pp. 76–100.

SCHARLAU, Winfried and Hans OPOLKA (1985), *From Fermat to Minkowski: Lectures on the Theory of Numbers and Its Historical Development*, Springer-Verlag.

SCHNEIER, Bruce (1994), *Applied Cryptography: Protocols, Algorithms, and Source Code in C*, Wiley.

SCHÖNHAGE, Arnold and Volker STRASSEN (1971), "Schnelle Multiplikation grosser Zahlen", *Computing*, vol. 7, pp. 281–292.

SCHWARTZ, Eugene S. (1964), "An optimal encoding with minimum longest code and total number of digits", *Information and Control*, vol. 7, no. 1, pp. 37–44.

SCHWARTZ, J. (1978), "Probabilistic algorithms for verification of polynomial identities", Technical Report no. 604, Computer Science Department, Courant Institute, New York University.

SEDGEWICK, Robert (1983), *Algorithms*, Addison-Wesley; 2nd edition, 1988.

SHALLIT, Jeffrey (1992), "Randomized algorithms in 'primitive' cultures, or what is the oracle complexity of a dead chicken", *ACM Sigact News*, vol. 23, no. 4, pp. 77–80; see also *ibid.* (1993), vol. 24, no. 1, pp. 1–2.

SHAMIR, Adi (1979), "Factoring numbers in $O(\log n)$ arithmetic steps", *Information Processing Letters*, vol. 8, no. 1, pp. 28–31.

SHOR, Peter W. (1994), "Algorithms for quantum computation: Discrete logarithms and factoring", *Proceedings of the 35th Annual Symposium on Foundations of Computer Science*, pp. 124–134.

SIMMONS, Gustavus J. (ed.) (1992), *Contemporary Cryptology: The Science of Information Integrity*, IEEE Press.

SIMON, Daniel R. (1994), "On the power of quantum computation", *Proceedings of the 35th Annual Symposium on Foundations of Computer Science*, pp. 116–123.

SLEATOR, Daniel D. and Robert E. TARJAN (1985), "Self-adjusting binary search trees", *Journal of the ACM*, vol. 32, pp. 652–686.

SLOANE, Neil J. A. (1973), *A Handbook of Integer Sequences*, Academic Press.

SOBOL', Il'ia M. (1974), *The Monte Carlo Method*, 2nd edition, University of Chicago Press.

SOLOMON, Herbert (1978), *Geometric Probability*, SIAM.

SOLOVAY, Robert and Volker STRASSEN (1977), "A fast Monte-Carlo test for primality", *SIAM Journal on Computing*, vol. 6, no. 1, pp. 84–85; erratum (1978), *ibid.*, vol. 7, no. 1, p. 118.

STANDISH, Thomas A. (1980), *Data Structure Techniques*, Addison-Wesley.

STINSON, Douglas R. (1985), *An Introduction to the Design and Analysis of Algorithms*, The Charles Babbage Research Centre, St. Pierre, Manitoba; 2nd edition, 1987.

STINSON, Douglas R. (1995), *Cryptography: Theory and Practice*, CRC Press, Inc.

STOCKMEYER, Larry J. (1973), "Planar 3-colorability is polynomial complete", *ACM Sigact News*, vol. 5, no. 3, pp. 19–25.

STOCKMEYER, Larry J. and Ashok K. CHANDRA (1979), "Intrinsically difficult problems", *Scientific American*, vol. 240, no. 5, pp. 140–159.

STONE, Harold S. (1972), *Introduction to Computer Organization and Data Structures*, McGraw-Hill.

STRASSEN, Volker (1969), "Gaussian elimination is not optimal", *Numerische Mathematik*, vol. 13, pp. 354–356.

TARJAN, Robert E. (1972), "Depth-first search and linear graph algorithms", *SIAM Journal on Computing*, vol. 1, no. 2, pp. 146–160.

TARJAN, Robert E. (1975), "On the efficiency of a good but not linear set merging algorithm", *Journal of the ACM*, vol. 28, no. 3, pp. 577–593.

TARJAN, Robert E. (1981), "A unified approach to path problems", *Journal of the ACM*, vol. 28, no. 3, pp. 577–593.

TARJAN, Robert E. (1983), *Data Structures and Network Algorithms*, SIAM.

TARJAN, Robert E. (1985), "Amortized computational complexity", *SIAM Journal on Algebraic and Discrete Methods*, vol. 6, no. 2, pp. 306–318.

TUCKER, Lewis W. and George G. ROBERTSON (1988), "Architecture and applications of the connection machine", *Computer*, vol. 21, no. 8, pp. 26–38.

TURING, Alan M. (1936), "On computable numbers with an application to the Entscheidungsproblem", *Proceedings of the London Mathematical Society*, vol. 2, no. 42, pp. 230–265.

TURK, J. W. M. (1982), "Fast arithmetic operations on numbers and polynomials", in Lenstra and Tijdeman (1982), pp. 43–54.

URBANEK, Friedrich J. (1980), "An $O(\log n)$ algorithm for computing the nth element of the solution of a difference equation", *Information Processing Letters*, vol. 11, no. 2, pp. 66–67.

VAN LEEUWEN, Jan (ed.) (1990), *Handbook of Theoretical Computer Science; Volume A: Algorithms and Complexity*, Elsevier and MIT Press.

VAZIRANI, Umesh V. (1986), *Randomness, Adversaries, and Computation*, doctoral dissertation, Computer Science, University of California, Berkeley, CA.

VAZIRANI, Umesh V. (1987), "Efficiency considerations in using semi-random sources", *Proceedings of the 19th Annual ACM Symposium on Theory of Computing*, pp. 160–168.

VERMA, Rakesh M. (1994), "A general method and a master theorem for divide-and-conquer recurrences with applications", *Journal of Algorithms*, vol. 16, pp. 67–79.

VICKERY, C. W. (1956), "Experimental determination of eigenvalues and dynamic influence coefficients for complex structures such as airplanes", in *Symposium on Monte Carlo Methods*, H. A. Meyer (ed.), Wiley, pp. 145–146.

VON NEUMANN, John (1951), "Various techniques used in connection with random digits", *Journal of Research of the National Bureau of Standards, Applied Mathematics Series*, vol. 3, pp. 36–38.

VUILLEMIN, Jean (1978), "A data structure for manipulating priority queues", *Communications of the ACM*, vol. 21, no. 4, pp. 309–315.

WAGNER, Robert A. and Michael J. FISCHER (1974), "The string-to-string correction problem", *Journal of the ACM*, vol. 21, no. 1, pp. 168–173.

WARSHALL, Stephen (1962), "A theorem on Boolean matrices", *Journal of the ACM*, vol. 9, no. 1, pp. 11–12.

WARUSFEL, André (1961), *Les nombres et leurs mystères*, Editions du Seuil.

WEGMAN, Mark N. and J. Larry CARTER (1981), "New hash functions and their use in authentication and set equality", *Journal of Computer and System Sciences*, vol. 22, no. 3, pp. 265–279.

WILLIAMS, Hugh (1978), "Primality testing on a computer", *Ars Combinatoria*, vol. 5, pp. 127–185.

WILLIAMS, John W. J. (1964), "Algorithm 232: Heapsort", *Communications of the ACM*, vol. 7, no. 6, pp. 347–348.

WINOGRAD, Shmuel (1980), *Arithmetic Complexity of Computations*, SIAM.

WINTER, Pavel (1987), "Steiner problem in networks: A survey", *Networks*, vol. 17, no. 2, pp. 129–167.

WOOD, Derick (1993), *Data Structures, Algorithms, and Performance*, Addison-Wesley.

WRIGHT, J. W. (1975), "The change-making problem", *Journal of the ACM*, vol. 22, no. 1, pp. 125–128.

YAO, Andrew C.-C. (1975), "An $O(|E| \log \log |V|)$ algorithm for finding minimum spanning trees", *Information Processing Letters*, vol. 4, no. 1, pp. 21–23.

YAO, Andrew C.-C. (1982), "Theory and applications of trapdoor functions", *Proceedings of the 23rd Annual Symposium on Foundations of Computer Science*, pp. 80–91.

YAO, Frances F. (1980), "Efficient dynamic programming using quadrangle inequalities", *Proceedings of the 12th Annual ACM Symposium on Theory of Computing*, pp. 429–435.

YOUNGER, Daniel H. (1967), "Recognition of context-free languages in time n^3 ", *Information and Control*, vol. 10, no. 2, pp. 189–208.

ZIPPEL, Richard E. (1979), *Probabilistic Algorithms for Sparse Polynomials*, doctoral dissertation, Massachusetts Institute of Technology, Cambridge, MA.

Index

÷, 13
2–3 tree, 159
2-edge-connected, 296

A

Aanderaa, S.O., 472
Abramson, B., 327
Absolute approximation
    problem, 486
Accepting computation, 459
Accounting trick, 116, 174
Ackermann, W., 186
Ackermann's function, 180,
    185–186, 283
Acyclic graph, 300
Adder, 257
Adel'son-Vel'skiĭ, G.M., 186
Adjacency matrix, 153
Adleman, L.M., 248, 258, 374,
    472
Advantage, 350
Adversary arguments, 423–427
Ahmes, 55
Aho, A.V., 55, 186, 327, 472, 473
Akl, S.G., 55, 412
al-Khowârizmî, 1
Alford, W.R., 374
Algorithm, 1–6
  approximate, 2, 474
  biased, 350
  efficiency, 59
  efficient, 441
  enciphering, 248
  greedy, characteristics of,
    188
  heuristic, 2, 474
  Las Vegas, 353–365
  Monte Carlo, 341–352
  nondeterministic, 458

parallel, optimal, 384
polynomial-time, 442
probabilistic, 2
  characteristics, 329
  numerical, 333–340
  smooth, 431
Algorithmics, defined, 3
Alice, 248
Allison, L., 327
Alpha-beta pruning, 319
Amortized analysis, 112–116
Amplification, 350–352
Analysis, amortized, 112–116
  of control structures, 98–104
  of divide-and-conquer
    algorithms, 224
  on the average, 63, 111
  quicksort, 232
  worst case, 62
Ancestor, 154, 293
Ancestry, 293
Approximate algorithm, 474
Approximation problem,
  absolute, 485
  relative, 485
Approximation scheme, 492
Arlazarov, V.L., 472
Arora, S., 500
Array, 147
Articulation points, 296–298
Assignment problem, 312–315
Associative table, 159
Asymptotic notation, 61, 79–92
  conditional, 88
  exact order, 87
  Omega, 85
    alternative, 94
  operations on, 91
  order, 79
  Theta, 87

with several parameters,
  91
At least quadratic, 431
Average, 46
Average case analysis, 63, 111
Average height of a tree, 416
Average time, 331
AVL tree, 159
Axiom of the least integer,
  19, 52

B

Baase, S., 55
Babai, L., 373, 472
Bach, E., 375
Bachmann, P.G.H., 97
Backtracking, 305–311
  general template, 311
Baeza-Yates, R., 55, 186
Ball, W.W.R., 327
Barometer, 104
Basic subalgorithm, 223
Batcher, K.E., 402, 412
Baumert, L., 327
Beauchemin, P., 374
Bellare, M., 472, 500
Bellman, R.E., 283
Bellmore, M., 327
Benioff, P., 472
Bennett, C.H., 258, 473
Bentley, J.L., 78, 146, 258, 375
Berge, C., 186, 326
Berlekamp, E.R., 327
Berliner, H.J., 327
Bernstein, E., 472
Berthiaume, A., 472
Bezzel, 327
Biased algorithm, 350
Bicoherent, 296

Biconnected, 296
Bin packing problem, 482–484,
    493
Binary counter, 113, 115–116
Binary search, 102, 226–228
Binary tree, 157, 416
    computing with, 379
Binomial coefficient, 40, 140, 260
Binomial heap, 170–175
    lazy, 174
Binomial tree, 170
Bipartite graph, 476
Bishop, E., 55
Bitton, D., 412
Blum, L., 373
Blum, M., 258, 373, 375, 472
Bob, 248
Book of Common Prayer, 2, 78
Borůvka, O., 217
Borodin, A.B., 55, 258, 473
Bottom-up, 259, 274
Branch-and-bound, 312–316
    general considerations, 316
Brassard, G., 55, 78, 97, 257, 258,
    327, 373–375, 472
Bratley, P., 55, 78, 258, 327, 374,
    375, 472
Breadth-first search, 302–305
Brent, R.P., 385, 412
Brent's theorem, 385
Bressoud, D.M., 374, 375
Brigham, E.O., 55
Brown, C.A., 146, 284
Brown, M.R., 186
Buffon's needle, 333–336
Bunch, J., 77, 472
Buneman, P., 146

C

Calinger, R., 56
Carasso, C., 374
Cardinality, 8
Carlsson, S., 186, 471
Carter, J.L., 375
Cartesian product, 8
Catalan number, 272, 280
Ceiling, 13
Celis, P., 375
Central Limit Theorem, 48, 335,
    352
Certificate, 443
Chained matrix multiplication,
    271–274
Chandra, A.K., 412, 473

Chang, L., 217, 283
Change of variable, 130
Characteristic equation, 118
Characteristic polynomial,
    120
Chen, I-N., 412
Cheriton, D., 218
Child, 155
Chin, F.Y., 412
Choosing a threshold:
    empirically, 225
    the hybrid approach, 226
Christofides, N., 55, 326, 500
Chromatic number, 455, 488
Chvátal, V., 412
Ciphertext, 248
Clause, 452
Clique, 469
Cluster, 489
co-$\mathcal{NP}$, defined, 462
Cobham, A., 472
Cohen, H., 374
Cole, R., 402, 412
Cole's parallel merge sort,
    402
Collatz's problem, 327
Collision, 160
Colouring, 455
Combination, 39
Common Prayer, Book of,
    2, 78
Comparator, 397
Complexity, 87
    of sorting, 418–421
Complexity classes, 460–464
    parallel, 463
    probabilistic, 462
Concurrent-read, exclusive-write
    model, 378
Conditional probability, 43
Confidence interval, 330, 336
Conjunctive normal form   452
Connected components, 387–392
Connectivity of a graph, testing,
    425
Constructive induction, 27–30,
    234, 241, 276, 292
Conway, J.H., 327
Cook, S.A., 451, 472
Cooley, J.M., 73, 78
Coppersmith, D., 243, 258
Cormen, T.H., 55
Counting, probabilistic, 338–340
Couvreur, C., 374
CRCW p-ram, 407

Crépeau, C., 374
CREW model, 378
Cryptography, an introduction,
    247–250
    public-key, 248
    RSA system, 248
Curtiss, J.H., 374
Cut, 395

D

Damgård, I.B., 374
Danielson, G.C., 74, 78
de Bruijn, N.G., 97
de l'Hôpital's rule, 33
de Moivre, 28, 66, 72, 121
Deap, 175
Decimal war, 243
Decision problem, 442
Decision-reducible, 448
Decision tree, 414
    valid, 418
Denenberg, L., 55, 186
Denning, D.E.R., 258
Deo, N., 55, 326, 412
Depth, 159
Depth-first search, 294–302
Depth of a network, 398
Dequeue, 148
Descendant, 155
Determinants, 110
Deterministic game, 289
Deutsch, D., 472
Devroye, L., 373
Dewdney, A.K., 146
DeWitt, D.J., 412
Deyong, L., 327
Dhall, S.K., 55, 412
Diffie, W., 248, 258
Dijkstra, E.W., 217
Dijkstra's algorithm, 198–202,
    217, 270
Dinic, E.A., 472
Disjoint set structure, 175–180,
    195, 212, 382, 387
Distributed computing, 408
Divide-and-conquer, 400, 402
Dixon, J.D., 375
Dot notation, 150
Double-ended heap, 175
Dreyfus, S.E., 283
Dromey, R.G., 55
Duality rule, 86
Duncan, R., 412

E

Easter, date of, 48, 74, 78
Edge, 153
Edmonds, J., 217, 472
Efficiency of parallel algorithms, 383–386
Efficient algorithm, 441
Eight queens problem, 308–311, 355–358
Einstein, 17
Ekert, A.K., 258
Elementary operation, 64
Elkies, N.D., 16, 55
Elliptic curve, 365
Enciphering algorithm, 248
Enqueue, 148
Erdős, P., 374
EREW p-ram, 407
Essentially complete, 162
Euclid, 14, 18
Euclid's algorithm, 2, 71, 77, 108, 255, 365
Euler, 16, 55, 56, 344
Euler path, 324
Euler's constant, 38
Evaluation function, 317
Even, S., 55, 326
Event, 42
Eventually nondecreasing 89
Eves, H., 55, 56
Exact order, 87
Expectation, 46
Expected time, 331
Exponentiation, 243–247
Expressions, parallel evaluation, 392–396

F

Factorizing large integers, 362–366, 409
False witness, 345
    strong, 346
Faradžev, I.A., 472
Fast Fourier transform, 73
Fermat, 16, 344
Fermat's little theorem, 344
Feynman, R., 472
Fibonacci, 28, 56
Fibonacci heap, 175, 216
Fibonacci sequence, 28, 72, 120
Fibonacci tree, 175, 184
Field, 150

Fischer, M.J., 284, 472
Flajolet, Ph., 374
Floor, 12
Floyd, R.W., 258, 284, 375
Floyd's algorithm, 269, 439
For loops, 99
Fox, B.L., 374
Fredman, M.L., 186, 217, 285, 471, 472
Freivalds, R., 374
Frye, 16
Full adder, 257
Function, 9
Functions see Programs
Fundamental theorem of arithmetic, 24
Furman, M.E., 472

G

Galil, Z., 186
Game, deterministic, 289
    symmetric, 289
Games and graphs, 285–291
Gardner, M., 146, 258, 473
Garey, M.R., 218, 472, 500
Gauss, 74, 78
Gauss-Jordan elimination, 68, 364
Generalized mathematical induction, 24
Gibbons, A., 412
Gilbert, E.N., 284
Gill, J., 472
Godbole, S., 284
Goemans, M.X., 500
Golden ratio, 28, 66
Goldner, A., 327
Goldreich, O., 473
Goldwasser, S., 374, 472
Golomb, S., 327
Gondran, M., 55, 326
Gonnet, G.H., 55, 186, 471
Good, I.J., 327
Goutier, C., 374
Graham, R.L., 218
Granville, A., 374
Graph, 152
    acyclic, 300
    bipartite, 477
    connected, 153
    planar, 322, 496
    strongly connected, 153, 323
Graph colouring problem, 441, 455, 475–477

Graphs and games, 285–291
Greatest common divisor 71
Greene, D.H., 146
Gries, D., 77, 258
Grundy's game, 327
Guibas, L.J., 186
Guy, R.K., 327

H

Haken, D., 146
Half-move, 286
Hall, A., 374
Halley, 17
Hamiltonian cycle, 479, 487
Hamiltonian cycle problem, 441, 446, 459
Hamiltonian path, 324, 479
Hammersley, J.M., 374
Handscomb, D.C., 374
Hanoi, Towers of, 109, 126
Hardy, G.H., 374
Harel, D., 55
Hash coding see Hashing
Hash function, 160
Hashing, 160
    universal, 360
Heap, 162–175
    binomial, 170–175
        lazy, 174
    double-ended, 174
    Fibonacci, 175, 216
    inverted, 170
    k-ary, 183, 216
Heap property, 163
heapsort, 68
Heath, T.L., 78
Height, 159
Held, M., 284
Hell, P., 217
Hellman, M.E., 248, 258
Heuristic, 2, 474
Hidden constant, 61
Hillier, F.S., 327
Hinrichs, K., 55
Hirschberg, D.S., 412
Hoare, C.A.R., 68, 231
Hopcroft, J.E., 55, 78, 186, 243, 258, 284, 327, 472, 473
Horowitz, E., 55, 186, 218, 500
Hsiao, D.K., 412
Hu, T.C., 283, 327
Huang, M.-D.A., 374
Huffman codes, 218

I

Ibarra, O.H., 500
Implicit graph, 306
Induction, constructive, 27–30,
      234, 241, 276, 292
   mathematical, 16–30
      generalized, 24
Information-theoretic arguments,
      414–423
Inorder, 291
Insertion sorting, 62, 107
Insertion sorting network 398
Instance, 58
   size of, 59
Integration, numerical, 336–338
Internal node, 155
Interval, 8
Invariance, principle of, 60
Inverted heap, 170
Irving, R.W., 327
Isthmus-free, 296
Italiano, G.F., 186

J

Ja'Ja', J., 55
Janko, W., 375
Jarník, V., 217
Jensen, K., 55
Johnson, D.B., 186, 217
Johnson, D.S., 218, 472, 500
Jozsa, R., 472

K

k-ary heap, 183, 216
k-smooth, 363
Kahn, D., 258
Kaliski, B.S., 374
Karatsuba, A., 55, 78, 257
Karp, R., 186, 284, 472
Kasimi, T., 284
Kasparov, G., 327
Kerr, L.R., 243, 258
Key, 248
Kilian, J., 374
Kim, C.E., 500
Kim, S.H., 374
Kingston, J.H., 55, 186
Kirkerud, B., 78
Kleene, S.C., 284
Kline, M., 55
Knapsack problem, 202–204,
      266–268, 306–308, 315,
      441, 480–482, 493–496

Knuth, D.E., 55, 78, 97, 146, 186,
      258, 284, 327, 373, 375,
      412
Koblitz, N., 258, 374, 375
König, H., 74, 78
Korsh, J., 217, 283
Kozen, D.C., 55, 186
Kraitchik, M., 375
Kranakis, E., 258, 374
Kronrod, M.A., 258, 472
Kruskal, J.B. Jr., 217
Kruskal's algorithm, 193–195, 217
Kučera, L., 412

L

L'Écuyer, P., 374
Lakshmivarahan, S., 55, 412
Lam, J., 412
Lanczos, C., 74, 78
Landis, E.M., 186
Landrock, P., 374
Laporte, G., 500
Larson, P.-A., 375
Las Vegas algorithm, 353–366
Laurière, J.-L., 283
Lawler, E.L., 55, 326, 327, 500
Lazy binomial heap, 174
Leaf, 155
Lecarme, O., 55
Leclerc, G.-L., 333, 374
Leighton, F.T., 55, 412
Leiserson, C.E., 55
Lenstra, A.K., 374, 375, 409, 412
Lenstra, H.W. Jr, 374, 375
Level, 159
Levin, G., 78, 258
Levin, L., 451, 472
Levy, L., 146
Lewis, H.R., 55, 186
Lewis, P.A., 78
lg, defined, 12
Lieberman, G.J., 327
Limit rule, 84, 87
Limits, 31
Linear reduction, 427–440
Linearly equivalent, 430
Linearly reducible, 430
List, 151, 380
Literal, 452
Lloyd, S., 472
Load factor, 161
Logarithm, 12
   iterated, 185
$\mathcal{LOGSPACE}$, defined, 462

Lucas, É, 146
Lueker, G.S., 146
Lund, C., 500

M

Making change, 187, 263–265
Manasse, M.S., 375, 409, 412
Manber, U., 55
Manders, K., 472
Marienbad game, 285
Marsh, D., 284
Martin, G.N., 374
Matrix multiplication, 242
   chained, 271–274
   verifying, 341–343
Maurer, U., 374
Maximum clique, 488
Maximum cut problem, 489
Maximum of an array, 424
Maximum rule, 81, 87
McCarty, C.P., 327
McDiarmid, C.J.H., 186
McGaughey, M., 327
Mean, 46
Median, approximation, 239
   complexity of finding, 426
   defined, 237
   finding, 237–242
Melhorn, K., 55, 326
Memory function, 276, 288
Mendeleev, 17
Menon, J., 412
mergesort, 68, 258
Merging networks, 400–401
Merging with help, 404
Merkle, R.C., 248, 258
Metric property, 478
Metropolis, I.N., 373
Meyer, A.R., 472
Micali, S., 374, 472
Michie, D., 284
Miller, G.L., 347, 374, 375
MIMD model, 408
Minimax principle, 317–319
Minimum cluster problem,
      489
Minimum spanning tree,
      190–198, 479
Minoux, M., 55, 326
Misère, 289
Modular arithmetic, 247
Monet, S., 77, 257
Monier, L., 374
Monte Carlo algorithm, 341–352

Montreal, 265
Moore, E.F., 284
Moran, S., 472
Moret, B.M.E., 55
Morris, R., 374
Motwani,R., 500
Move, 286
Multiple-instruction multiple
  data-stream model, 408
Multiple integral, 338
Multiplication, 3–6
  à la russe, 4, 26, 55
  Arabic, 49, 55
  classic, 3
  divide-and-conquer, 219
  of large integers, 70, 219–223
  of matrices, 242
Munro, J.I., 55, 186, 258, 375,
  471, 473

N

Naik, A.V., 472
Natural numbers, 8
Nebut, J.-L., 55
Nelson, G., 186
Nemhauser, G., 283, 327
Network, depth, 398
  size, 398
Newton, 40
Nievergelt, J., 55, 326
Nilsson, N., 55, 327
Nim, 285, 327
Node, 151
  depth, 159
  height, 159
  internal, 155
  level, 159
Nondeterministic algorithm,
  458
$\mathcal{NP}$, defined, 444
$\mathcal{NP}$-completeness, 441–460
$\mathcal{NP}$-complete, defined, 450
$\mathcal{NP}$-complete problems,
  450–456
$\mathcal{NP}$-hard approximation
  problems, 484–489
$\mathcal{NP}$-hard, defined, 457
Number field sieve, 365
Numerical probabilistic
  algorithm, 333–340

O

Odd-even networks, 402
Ofman, Y., 55, 77, 257
Ogiwara, M., 472
Omar Khayyam, 40
Operation, elementary, 64
Opolka, H., 56
Oppen, D.C., 186
Optimal parallel algorithm,
  384
Optimal speed-up, 384
Optimality, principle of, 265
Oracle, 446
Order, 61
Ordered pair, 8

P

$\mathcal{P}$, defined, 443
p-correct, 341
p-ram, 376–378
Pageau, M., 375
Pan, V., 243, 258
Papadimitriou, C.H., 55, 326,
  471, 472
Parallel complexity classes,
  463
Parallel evaluation of expres-
  sions, 392–397
Parallel random-access machine,
  376–378
Parallel sorting, 402–406
Parent, 155
Partition problem, 470
Pascal's triangle, 260
Path compression, 178
Peralta, R.C., 375
Percolate, 164
Perfect shuffle, 400
Permutation, 39
Permutations, generating, 309
Pigeonhole sorting, 69
Pippenger, N., 471, 472
Pisano, Leonardo see Fibonacci
Pivot, 231
Planar graph, 322, 496
Pointer, 150
Pointer doubling, 380–383, 390
Pollard, J.M., 257, 375
Pólya, G., 18, 55
Polylogarithmic time, 384
Polynomial reduction, 445–450
Polynomial-time algorithm,
  442
Pomerance, C., 374–375, 472

Pop, 148
Postorder, 291
Potential functions, 114
Pratt, V.R., 258, 472
Preconditioning, 292
Predicate, 9
Preorder, 291
Prim, R.C., 217
Prim's algorithm, 196–198, 217
Primality testing, 343–347
Prime Number Theorem, 44, 369
Principle of invariance, 60
Principle of optimality, 265
Probabilistic complexity classes,
  462
Probabilistic counting, 338–340
Probability measure, 42
Problem, 58
  smooth, 431
Procedures see Programs
Programs:
  adhocsort3, 419
  alter-heap, 165
  approx-knap, 481
  backpack, 308
  backtrack, 311
  badmergesort, 230
  bfs, 302
  Binary_Search, 103
  biniter, 228
  binrec, 227
  binsearch, 227
  Black, 318
  BP, 493
  Btest, 346
  C, 140, 260
  card, 368
  coinflip, 332
  coins, 264
  concomps, 391
  count, 113, 340
  DC, 140, 223
  DecideX, 449
  delete-max, 166
  DETint, 338
  dfs, 294
  dfs2, 302
  dfsearch, 294
  Dijkstra, 199
  draw, 371
  DumpEuclid, 14
  dynwin, 288
  Euclid, 71, 108
  expoDC, 245
  expoiter, 247

Programs (continued)
  expomod, 248
  exposeq, 244
  Fermat, 344
  Fibiter, 73, 100
  Fibonacci, 29, 65
  Fibrec, 72, 101
  find-max, 166, 407
  find-root, 407
  find1, 175
  find2, 176
  find3, 179
  flatten, 382
  Floyd, 269
  fm, 275
  fm-mem, 277
  Freivalds, 342
  Freivaldsepsilon, 343
  gcd, 71
  greedy-knap, 481
  Ham, 446
  HamD, 446
  HamND, 459
  Hanoi, 110
  heapsort, 169
  init, 340
  insert, 62, 107
  insert-node, 166
  knapsack, 203
  Kruskal, 195
  make-change, 188
  make-heap, 167
  MAX-CUT-approx, 490
  maxindex, 424
  MC3, 350
  MCint, 337
  merge, 229
  merge1, 175
  merge2, 176
  merge3, 178
  mergesort, 229
  MillRab, 347
  mult, 429
  Newprime, 14
  nim, 289
  P, 261
  pardist, 380
  paroper, 382
  parpaths, 387
  parsum, 379
  percolate, 166
  perm, 309
  peval, 396
  pigeonhole, 69
  pivot, 231

  pivotbis, 236
  Prim, 196, 197
  pseudomed, 239
  queens, 311
  queens1, 309
  queens2, 309
  queensLV, 356
  quicksort, 232
  quicksortLV, 360
  randomprime, 349
  recwin, 287
  RepeatFreivalds, 343
  RepeatLV, 354
  RepeatMC, 351
  RepeatMillRab, 347
  russe, 7
  search, 158, 303
  select, 62, 106
  selection, 238
  selectionLV, 359
  sequence, 210
  sequence2, 214
  sequential, 226
  series, 262
  sift-down, 165
  slow-make-heap, 166
  sq, 18
  square, 429
  stupid, 350
  Sum, 65
  tick, 340
  trialdiv, 362
  uniform, 332
  waste, 141
  White, 318
  Wilson, 64
  XND, 460
Programs, notation, 6
  parallel, notation, 378
Proof, by contradiction, 13–15
  by mathematical induction,
     16–30
  indirect, 13
  nonconstructive, 15
Proof space, 443
Proof system, 443
Property, 9
Propositional calculus, notation,
     7
Pseudoprime, 346
Pseudorandom generator, 332
$\mathcal{PSPACE}$, defined, 462
Public-key cryptography, 248

Purdom, P.W. Jr, 146, 284
Push, 148
Pythagoras, 15

Q

Quadratic sieve, 366
Quantifier, 10
Quantum computer, 249, 464
Quasi Monte Carlo integration,
     338
Queue, 148, 181
quicksort, 69, 231–237, 258
Quinn, M.J., 412
Quisquater, J.-J., 374
Quotient, 13

R

Rabin, M.O., 347, 374, 375
Rackoff, C., 472
Random number generator,
     331
Random variable, 46
Range transformations, 136
Rawlins, G.J.E., 146
Record, 150
Recurrences, asymptotic, 137
  change of variable, 130
  characteristic equation, 118
  characteristic polynomial,
     120
  linear, homogeneous, 119
     inhomogeneous, 123
  range transformations, 136
  solving, 116–139
Recursive calls, 101
Red-black tree, 159
Reduction, defined, 428
  linear, 427–440
  polynomial, 445–450
Reductions, among matrix
     problems, 433–438
  among shortest path problems,
     438–440
Reed, B.A., 186
Rehashing, 161
Reif, J.H., 412
Reingold, E.M., 55, 326
Relation, 9
Relative approximation problem,
     485
Repeat loops, 102
Rice, J.A., 374
Rivest, R.L., 55, 248, 258, 374,
     375

Robertson, G.G., 412
Robin Hood effect, 353
Robson, J.M., 327
Root, 154
Rosen, K.H., 55
Rosenthal, A., 327
RSA cryptographic system, 248
Rumely, R.S., 374
Runge, C., 74, 78
Rytter, W., 412

S

Sahni, S., 55, 186, 218, 500
Sample space, 41
Sarwate, D.V., 412
Satisfiability problem, 451
Satisfiable, 451
Savitch, W.J., 473
Saxe, J.B., 146
Schaffer, R, 186
Scharlau, W., 56
Scheduling, 205–214
  with deadlines, 207
Schneier, B., 258
Schönhage, A., 78, 257
Schrage, L.E., 374
Schwartz, E.S., 218
Schwartz, J., 375
Search tree, 157, 282
  optimal, 282–283
Sedgewick, R., 55, 186
Seed, 332
Selection, probabilistic, 358
Selection problem, 237
Selection sorting, 62, 106
Selection sorting network, 398
Selman, A.L., 472
Sentinel, 229
Sequential search, 227
Series, arithmetic, 34
  geometric, 35
  harmonic, 37
Set theory, notation, 8
Shallit, J., 373, 375
Shamir, A., 78, 248, 258
Shapiro, H.D., 55
Sherman, A.T., 374
Shing, M.T., 284
Shor, P.W., 258, 472
Shortest paths, 198–202, 268–270, 386, 438–440
Shub, M., 374

Sibling, 155
Sift down, 165
Sift up, 164
SIMD model, 377
Simmons, G.J., 258
Simon, D.R., 472
Simple path, 266, 270
Simplification, 223
Simulation, 333
Single-instruction, multiple data-stream model, 377
Sink, 323
Size of a network, 398
Sleator, D.D., 186
Sloane, N.J.A., 284
Smooth algorithm, 431
Smooth function, 89
Smooth problem, 431
Smoothness rule, 90
Sobol', I.M., 374
Solomon, H., 374
Solovay, R., 374
Sorting, 228
  by insertion, 62, 107
  by merging, 68, 228–231
  by selection, 62, 106
  comparison-based, 418
  complexity of, 418–421
  heapsort, 68, 169
  parallel, 402–406
  pigeonhole, 69
  probabilistic, 358
  quicksort, 68, 231–237
  topological, 300
Sorting networks, 397–402
Spanning tree, minimum, 191
Speed-up, optimal, 384
Splay tree, 159
Stack, 148, 152
Stanat, D.F., 375
Standard deviation, 47
Standish, T.A., 186
Steele, J.M., 375
Steiglitz, K., 55, 326
Steiner trees, 218
Stinson, D.R., 55, 258
Stirling's formula, 13
Stockmeyer, L.J., 473
Stone, H.S., 186
Strassen, V., 68, 78, 242, 257, 258, 374
Strassen's algorithm, 440
Strong false witness, 346
Strong pseudoprime, 346
Strongly connected graph 323

Strongly quadratic, 431
Student's *t* distribution, 336
Sudan, M., 500
Sum, conditional, 11
Switch circuit, 257
Symbol table, 160
Symmetric game, 289
Szegedy, M., 500

T

Table, associative, 159
Tally, 257
Tarjan, R.E., 55, 146, 180, 186, 217, 258, 284, 326, 327
Terminal position, 289
Threshold, 80–81
  for divide-and-conquer, 224
Threshold rule, 81, 87
Tictactoe, three-dimensional, 326
Tiling problem, 20
Top-down, 259, 274
Topological sorting, 300
Tournament, 256
Towers of Hanoi, 109, 126
Transitive closure, 439
Travelling salesperson problem, 409, 441, 449, 477, 487
  Euclidean, 478
  metric, 478–480, 486
Tree, 154–159
  2–3, 159
  AVL, 159
  binary, 157, 416
    essentially complete, 162
  binomial, 170
  Fibonacci, 175, 184
  free, 154
  height, 159
    average, 416
  k-ary, 157
  red-black, 159
  rooted, 154
  search, 157
  splay, 159
Tucker, L.W., 412
Tukey, J.W., 73, 78
Turing, A.M., 473
Turk, J.W.M., 258
Twenty questions, 414
Type:
  adjgraph, 153
  binary-node, 157

Type (continued)
  k-ary-node, 157
  lisgraph, 154
  tablelist, 160
  treenode1, 155
  treenode2, 156

U

Ulam, S., 373
Ullman, J.D., 55, 186, 284, 327, 472, 473
Unarticulated, 296
Universal$_2$ class of functions, 361
Universal hashing, 360
Urbanek, F.J., 78, 258

V

van Leeuwen, J., 55
Variance, 47
Vazirani, U.V., 374, 472
Verdict, 415
Verifying matrix multiplication, 341–343
Verma, R.M., 146

Vickery, C.W., 374
Virtual initialization, 106, 149, 277, 289
von Neumann, J., 373, 376
von Neumann machine, 376
Vuillemin, J, 186

W

Wagner. R.A., 284
Warshall, S., 284
Warshall's algorithm, 279, 439–440
Warusfel, A., 55
Wegman,M.N., 375
Weighing coins, 421
Welch, P.D., 78
While loops, 102
Wigderson, A., 473
Willard, D.E., 471
Williams, H., 374
Williams, J.W.J., 68, 169, 186
Williamson, D.P., 500
Wilson's theorem, 64, 76
Winograd, S., 243, 258, 473
Winter, P., 218
Wirth, N., 55

Witness, false, 345
  false, strong, 346
Wood, D., 186
Wood, D.W., 327
Work, 383–386
Work-efficient, 384
World Series, 261
Worst case analysis, 63
Wright, E.M., 374
Wright, J.W., 217, 283
Write-only memory, 367

Y

Yao, A.C., 374
Yao, F.F., 284
Yee, C.N., 327
Yeo, A.C., 217
Younger, D.H., 284
Yung, M.M., 327

Z

Zero-one principle, 399
Zippel, R.E., 375
Zuffellato, D., 78, 257